ITALIA
1940

dine
•Gorizia
VENEZIA
•Trieste
GIULIA
Fiume

•Pola

MARE ADRIATICO

erato

•Teramo
•Pescara
•Chieti
AGRUZZ
Abr. E

MOLISE

•Frosinone
oria   •Campobasso
        •Foggia
CAMPA   •Benevento   •Bari
Napoli •Avellino
    •Salerno •Matera •Brindisi
    •Potenza   •Lecce
•Capri   LUCANIA   •Taranto

•Cosenza

CALABRIA •Catanzaro

Isole Lipari

MAR
IONIO

•Palermo

        •Messina •Reggio
                  Calab.

CI
    •Enna •Catania
•Caltanissetta
•Agrigento
    •Ragusa •Siracusa

EAK

1. Daily Papers.
   5 or less A
   10 or less B
   15 or less C
   20 or less D
   20 or less F

In the study of a language
absolute profection is one's
goal.

2. assignments are due on designated
day, or no grade.

3.

PRESENT DAY

Italian

Present Day

ITALIAN

By JOSEPH LOUIS RUSSO, PH.D.

University of Wisconsin

18 85

D. C. HEATH AND COMPANY   BOSTON

Preface

THE principal aim of this book is to present clearly and concisely the fundamental principles of Italian grammar in such a manner that the student may acquire, with a reasonable amount of effort, facility in understanding, speaking, reading, and writing the language.

Purposely, a too detailed presentation of theory has been avoided. Whatever seemed non-essential has been relegated to the footnotes, which are to be used for reference only. Purposely, too, the larger part of the book is devoted to exercises.

No particular method of learning has been advocated. In fact, the author — believing that, in language study also, *tutte le strade menano a Roma* — has striven to endow this work with as much "elasticity" of approach as possible.

The book can thus be used profitably no matter what method is adopted. The teacher is left sole judge as to the choice of material to be taken up. He may have a class of brilliant students, and he may want to take a short cut and concentrate on grammar; in that case the sentences at the end of each lesson are of paramount importance. He may feel, in most cases, that a mixed method should be followed which will develop in the students' minds a balanced knowledge of the language; if so, he should try to use a little of each type of exercise. Finally, he may want to follow, for a time at least, the exclusively oral-aural method so much in vogue in recent years. In this case he will base his teaching on the *Dialoghi pratici* placed toward the end of the book, just before the *Appendix*, and supplement this work with the *Letture* and *Conversazioni* that form an essential part of each lesson. Ample material has been furnished for all needs and tastes.

The number of lessons has been limited to twenty-one for each semester, thus allowing sufficient time to do the work thoroughly and without haste.

The following remarks on specific points will help in using the book to the greatest advantage:

PRONUNCIATION. The rules given in the Introduction should be used exclusively for reference. Pronunciation, according to the latest methods, should be taught step by step, using the exercises presented at the beginning of the first thirteen lessons. Each particular sound has been treated independently, beginning with the vowels and those consonants that are pronounced almost identically in both languages. Special stress has been given to drills on the double consonants, one of the stumbling-blocks for English-speaking students. A new method of learning how to pronounce these double consonants, already introduced in the author's high-school text, *First Year Italian*, has been presented here too.

LESSONS. Each lesson contains the same elements, pronunciation drills excepted: *Note grammaticali, Lettura* (followed by an appropriate proverb), *Studio di parole, Conversazione, Esercizi.*

NOTE GRAMMATICALI. Grammar is taught inductively. Experience has shown that by placing the rules after the examples, and not before, the principles of the language are more likely to leave a lasting impression upon the student. The study of the verbs begins with the very first lesson, and each subject is taken up subsequently according to its importance in facilitating conversation.

LETTURA. The reading exercises are written in simple prose based exclusively on that part of the grammar and vocabulary with which the student is familiar, plus the new elements in grammar and vocabulary introduced in that particular lesson. Nothing has been taken for granted, and any average student can read and understand what he reads in a few minutes.

STUDIO DI PAROLE. Only a reasonable number of new words and idiomatic expressions — thirty at the most — has been included in each vocabulary, and the choice of words has been based on several published lists. The author, convinced that *repetita juvant*, has kept an accurate check on each expression used and has seen to it that the words studied recur at least five times in Italian and as many times in English in the subsequent lessons. This principle has complicated his task, but the results will justify his efforts. Only in the last three or four lessons this principle could not, for obvious reasons, be followed.

CONVERSAZIONE. After the *Lettura* and the *Studio di parole,* the student is ready for conversation. From fifteen to twenty-four questions have been included in each of the exercises. It is suggested that, in classroom work, one student should be asked to read each question aloud, while the others keep their books closed, and that the answers be given not by volunteers, but by students called on to do so by the instructor. Thus, timid students will be encouraged, and this very important exercise will not be reduced to a performance by the most gifted members of the class.

ESERCIZI. Each lesson includes a comprehensive set of exercises. They should be used only in part, unless time permits a longer drill, and may be worked out orally or in writing. There are two sets of sentences for translation into Italian, each forming a connected story and thereby affording a most useful drill on intelligent application of grammar rules. Only one set should be assigned in any given academic year, and the other should be reserved for the following year or for special tests. In this way, the teacher will find a relieving variety in his or her task, and the student will not be tempted to use copies of sentences corrected the preceding year.

Supplementary exercises are offered as follows: frequent review lessons as well as true-false and achievement tests on the basis of 100%. There is no need to state here that such achievement tests should not be used for grading students; a good teacher will prepare his own tests. The author's only purpose in including them in the book was to induce the student to try them out in preparation for the real tests, and there is no doubt that he will derive great benefit from the exercise.

Finally, a few words concerning the *Dialoghi pratici,* the Appendix, and the Index.

There are as many dialogues as there are lessons, twenty-one for each semester. They deal with practical aspects of life, refer to Italian customs and ways, and can be used entirely or in part for memory work, a most important means for acquiring facility in speaking. It will be noticed that each of them is accompanied by an English translation and that the translation appears on the reverse side of each page so as to induce the reader to make an effort to understand without the help offered. The last two assignments, instead of being devoted to dialogues, include specimens of private and business letters.

It is hoped that the teacher will use part of this material for dictation, a most useful exercise in that it develops knowledge of words, spelling ability, aural drill, and a speedy application of known grammar rules.

The Appendix contains, beside the complete conjugation of the regular verbs and auxiliaries, an exhaustive list of irregular verbs, handy for reference, and a complete table of the personal pronouns.

Particular care has been taken to make the analytical index complete in each detail, and reference has been given not only to pages but to sections as well.

In closing, the author wishes to thank his beloved wife, his colleague and very dear friend, Dr. Karl G. Bottke, and his gifted assistant, Mr. George W. Hefke, who devoted much of their time to help in reading the proofs of the book.

J.L.R.

University of Wisconsin

Contents

The Alphabet. Pronunciation. Stress and Accent. Syllabication. Elision and Apocopation. Capitals. Punctuation.

FIRST SEMESTER

PART I: *A SCUOLA*

Lesson

A. Conjugations. B. First and Second Conjugations: Present Indicative. C. Subject Pronouns. D. Question Form.

A. Indefinite Article. B. Gender of Nouns. C. Third Conjugation: Present Indicative. D. Negative Verbs.

A. Definite Article. B. Plural of Nouns. C. Adjectives in –o. D. Present Indicative of the Auxiliary Verbs.

A. Nouns and Adjectives in –e. B. **Lo** and **la** as Object Pronouns. C. Possession.

A. Contractions of Prepositions and Definite Article. B. Object Pronouns **li** and **le**. C. Some Cardinal Numerals.

A. Past Participles. B. Present Perfect. C. Use of the Auxiliary Verbs. D. Agreement of Past Participle.

PART II: *A CASA*

A. Some Relative Pronouns.   B. Imperative.   C. Partitive Construction.

A. Possessives.   B. Use of the Possessives.   C. Definite Article before Titles.   D. Apocopation of Titles Ending in **–ore.**

A. Possessives with Nouns Denoting Relationship.   B. Some Diminutives.   C. Present Indicative of the Irregular Verbs of the First Conjugation.

A. Position of Adjectives.   B. Reflexive Verbs.   C. **Non . . . che.**

A. Future.   B. Use of the Future.   C. Nouns and Adjectives in **–io.**

A. Masculine Nouns in **–a.**   B. Nouns in **–a** of Both Genders. C. Present Indicative of Some Irregular Verbs.

A. *Some* or *Any*.   B. Expressions of Weather.   C. Days of the Week.   D. Further Cardinal Numerals.

PART III: *IN CITTÀ*

SECOND SEMESTER

PART IV: *IN CAMPAGNA*

PART V: *IN VIAGGIO*

DIALOGHI PRATICI E LETTERE

FIRST SEMESTER

SECOND SEMESTER

I. Auxiliary Verbs. II. Regular Verbs. III. Irregular Verbs. IV. Personal Pronouns.

$\mathcal{L}$ist of $\mathcal{I}$llustrations

PRESENT DAY

Italian

Introduction

THE ALPHABET

1. The Italian alphabet consists of the following twenty-one letters:

LETTER	NAME	LETTER	NAME	LETTER	NAME
a	a	h	acca	q	cu
b	bi	i	i	r	ɛrre
c	ci	l	ɛlle	s	ɛsse
d	di	m	ɛmme	t	ti
e	ɛ	n	ɛnne	u	u
f	ɛffe	o	o	v	vu
g	gi	p	pi	z	zɛta

The letter **j** (*i lungo*) is rarely used in modern Italian, **i** having taken its place; **x** (*iccase*) is found only in such expressions as **ex deputato, ex ministro,** etc.; the letters **k** (*cappa*), **w** (*doppio vu*) and **y** (*ipsilon*) are used exclusively for the spelling of foreign words.

PRONUNCIATION

2. Stress Marks. When a word has two or more vowels, one vowel is stressed more than the other or others. Usually only a word stressed on the last vowel is marked in Italian with an accent; no sign marks the stress when it is on any other vowel. For the convenience of the student, however, certain symbols have been adopted in this book to mark the stress: printing in italic type, in the special type ɛ (called "open *e*"), and in the special type ɔ (called "open *o*").

camera   mɛdico   mɔbile

If none of the vowels is specially printed, the stress is on the next-to-the-last vowel.

veranda   cantare   locomotiva

3. Vowels. 1. The five vowel signs represent seven different sounds, and are pronounced as follows [1]:

a	as *a* in *father*	carta	sala	stalla
e (*close*)	as *a* in *late* [2]	mele	vedere	temere
e (*open*)	as *e* in *let*	sella	tɛma	tenda
i	as *i* in *machine*	siti	vini	finiti
o (*close*)	as *o* in *rope* [3]	sole	coda	colore
o (*open*)	as *o* in *soft*	porta	tɔro	vɔlta
u	as *oo* in *moon*	fumo	luna	tutto

Close and *open* vowels are not differentiated in spelling, but their pronunciation follows somewhat definite rules (*see* § 9).

2. In pronouncing Italian vowels an effort should be made to avoid nasal resonance entirely, and to carry the voice well forward in the mouth. The mouth should be well opened in pronouncing **a, e** *open* and **o** *open*, and almost closed with the lips drawn back when making the sound **i**. The student should note also that, while in English long vowels tend to become diphthongal (like *a* in *late* and *o* in *rope*), this tendency does not appear in Italian: Italian vowels are uniform throughout their utterance.

3. A marked difference in pronunciation between Italian and English is that in Italian the unstressed vowels keep their pure sound, while in English unstressed vowels are often slurred. This is due to the fact that Italian is not, like English, an explosive language, but rather a singing (chromatic) language. Accents are not strong stresses which mutilate preceding and following vowels, but rather soft stresses that are shown in the lengthening of the vowel sounds.

4. It may be useful to call the beginner's attention to the following cases in which Italian vowels are frequently mispronounced by English-speaking students:

[1] For practical purposes, the pronunciation will be explained by comparison with English sounds. It must never be forgotten, however, that the sounds of any two languages seldom correspond exactly. As for the vowels, note that those which occur in unstressed position at the end of a word are uttered slightly more rapidly than the others. [2] Without the *i* glide. [3] Without the *u* glide.

(*a*) Initial or final unstressed **a**, which should not be slurred:

amica   arɔma   arɛna

(*b*) The vowels **e, i, u**, when followed by **r**, should not be incorrectly pronounced like the *i* in *girl:*

Verdi   Curci   permesso   firma

(*c*) Initial, unstressed **o** should not be mispronounced like the *o* in *office:*

occupare   ostacolare   osservare

(*d*) The vowel **u**, followed by **l** or **n**, should not be pronounced like the *u* in *full:*

ultimo   punto

The beginner should strive to overcome such tendencies from the start, bearing in mind that the sound of the Italian vowels should be kept pure and distinct without regard to their position.

4. Semivowels. Unstressed **i** and **u**, placed before another vowel, are pronounced respectively like *y* in *yet* and *w* in *well*. They are often called semivowels.[1]

iɛri   aiuto   uɔmo   nuɔvo

5. Diphthongs. A combination of two vowels, uttered as one syllable, constitutes a diphthong. The vowels **a, e,** and **o** may combine with **i** or **u**, in which case the stress falls on the **a, e,** or **o;** or the diphthong may be **iu** or **ui**, in which case it is the second vowel which is stressed.

piɛno   biada   mai   rauco   pɔi   guida   suɔno

6. Consonants. The following consonants are pronounced approximately as in English: **b, d, f, l, m, n, p, q, t,** and **v.** In pronouncing **d, l, n,** and **t,** however, the tip of the tongue should touch the upper teeth, and **p** should be made with an effort to avoid the explosive aspiration which accompanies the same sound in English. It should also be noted that the letter **n,** when standing before a **c** which has the sound of *c* in *cap,* a **g** which has the sound of *g* in *go,* or a **q,** has the sound of *ng* in *bang.*

bianco   lungo   dovunque

---

[1] Semivowel i is written j by a few writers (*e.g.* **ajuto**), but this usage is rapidly growing obsolete.

c and **g** have either a *palatal* sound or a *guttural* sound. Before **e** or **i,** they take the palatal sound, that is, they are pronounced toward the front of the mouth: **c** like *ch* in *chill,* and **g** like *g* in *general.*[1] In all other cases the guttural sound occurs, that is, they are pronounced toward the rear of the mouth, and **c** corresponds to the English *k,* **g** to the *g* in *go.*

PALATAL	aceto	vicino	gentile	regina
GUTTURAL	sicuro	credo	gallo	grande

h   is always silent. It appears in a few short words.

ha	hai	ahi	ho

r   is trilled, that is, pronounced with a vibration of the tongue against the alveolar ridge, i.e. the inner ridge of the gum at the base of the upper front teeth.

caro	sera	mare	marito

s   has two different sounds: unvoiced **s,** like *s* in *sand,* and voiced **s,** like *s* in *rose.*

UNVOICED	spillo	sabbia	destino	frusta
VOICED	sleale	smemorato	prɔsa	esame

z   also is pronounced in two different ways: like a vigorous *ts* (unvoiced **z**), or like a prolonged *dz* (voiced **z**).

UNVOICED	marzo	azione	zio	tɛrzo
VOICED	romanzo	bronzo	zɛro	manzo

For rules concerning the sounds of **s** and **z,** see § **10.**

Each Italian consonant, except those forming digraphs (*see* § 8), has a distinct and separate sound value, and should be clearly pronounced.

The letters **l, m, n,** and **r,** when preceded by a stressed vowel and followed by another consonant, are uttered longer than usual.

palma	ambo	pianta	parte

7. Double Consonants.   In Italian the double consonant is always more prolonged and emphatic than the single, except in the case of **zz,** which is pronounced almost like **z.** A similar doubling occurs in English only when two words, the first of which

---

[1] In Tuscany and in some other parts of Italy, **c** and **g** between two vowels, the second of which is **e** or **i,** are pronounced respectively like the *sh* in *ship* and the *s* in *pleasure.*

ends and the second of which begins with the same consonant sound, are pronounced without a pause between, as *good day*, *pen-knife*, etc.

Note carefully also:

1. The stressed vowel is long before a single consonant (not final) and short before a double consonant.

2. Double consonants always represent a single, energetic, and prolonged sound. This is true also of double c and double g, which never are pronounced separately, as two distinct sounds, as in the English words *accept*, *suggest*, etc., but together, with more intensity and length than if they were single. Their palatal or guttural nature is determined by their being followed or not by e or i.

atto	vacca	accento	aggettivo	palla

8. Combined Letters. The following combinations, or digraphs, which really represent single sounds, are to be noted:

ch and **gh** (used only before e or i), the first representing the sound of a *k*, the second that of *g* in *go*.

chiave	laghi	schiavo

ci and **gi,** pronounced respectively like *ch* in *chill* and *g* in *general*, when followed by **a, o, u.** In the resulting groups (**cia, cio, ciu; gia, gio, giu**) the **i,** unless stressed, merely indicates that the **c** or **g** has the palatal sound before **a, o,** or **u.**

provincia	ciottolo	fanciullo
giallo	ragione	giusto

gli which is pronounced somewhat like *lli* in *billiards* and *million*, but with the tip of the tongue against the gum ridge above the upper teeth. When no vowel follows **gli,** the **i** is pronounced.

figlio	figli	egli	paglia	gigli

In the following words, however, **gl** sounds as in the English word *angle:* **A**nglia, poetic name of England; **anglicano,** *Anglican;* **anglicismo,** *Anglicism;* **glicerina,** *glycerine;* **geroglifico,** *hieroglyphic;* **negligere,** *to neglect;* the derivatives of **negligere,** and a few other uncommon words.

gn   which has a sound similar to that of *ni* in *onion*, but with the tip of the tongue against the lower teeth.

  bagno   ogni   guadagno   ognuno

qu   pronounced always like *kw*.

  quattro   quanto   questo

sc   pronounced like *sh* before **e** or **i**, like *sk* in any other case.

  scɛna   scimmia   oscuro   escluso

  In the groups **scia, scio, sciu**, the vowel **i**, unless stressed, is not sounded, serving only to indicate that **sc** must be pronounced *sh*.

  sciabola   lascia   sciupare

9. The Vowels *e* and *o*. The vowels **e** and **o** are always *close* in unstressed syllables.

  fame   delirio   domandare

In *stressed syllables*, **e** and **o** are *open* in the following cases:

ɛ: (*a*) In the ending –**ero** of words of more than two syllables.

  impɛro   ministɛro   sevɛro

(*b*) In the diphthong **ie**, or when **e** stands for **ie**.

  piɛno   altiɛro *or* altɛro   liɛto

(*c*) When followed by another vowel.

  idɛa   rɛo   nɛo   dɛa

(*d*) In many words in which **e** is followed by two or more consonants. [1]

  tɛrra   vɛspa   fɛbbre   pɛtto

(*e*) When **e** appears in the third-from-the-last syllable and is stressed. [2]

  sɛcolo   mɛdico   pɛttine   ventɛsimo

ɔ: (*a*) In the diphthong **uo**, or when **o** stands for **uo**.

  uɔmo   buɔno   uɔvo *or* ɔvo   cuɔre

---

[1] But in the endings –**egno**, –**emmo**, –**enna**, –**esco**, –**etto**, –**ezza**, –**mente**, **e** is *close*.   [2] Except in the ending –**evole**, in which **e** is *close*.

(*b*) When followed by another vowel.[1]

poi   noia   gioia   stoia

(*c*) If followed by double consonants.

fossa   gobbo   donna   lotta

(*d*) When o appears in the third-from-the-last syllable and is stressed.

monaco   povero   ottimo   ottico

(*e*) If at the end of a monosyllable or of a word stressed on the last syllable.

fo   andò   so   parlò

(*f*) When one or more consonants and a diphthong follow the o.

gloria   proprio   odio   fandonia

10. The Consonants s and z

s: The letter s is pronounced as a voiceless sibilant, like *s* in *sand:*

(*a*) When initial before a vowel.

sabato   seta   silenzio   santo

(*b*) When doubled (but here it is prolonged).

tassa   basso   assai   lusso

(*c*) If followed by the voiceless consonant c, f, p, q, or t.

scudo   sforzo   basta   aspettare

s: In the following cases s is pronounced as a voiced sibilant, like *s* in *rose:*

(*a*) When followed by the voiced consonant b, d, g, l, m, n, r, or v.

sbaglio   slitta   smalto   snello

(*b*) Between vowels.

vaso   tesoro   esame   uso

This latter rule has, however, some important exceptions. Though between vowels, s has the unvoiced sound:

(*a*) After a prefix, provided that the s is the first letter of the original word.

presentimento   risalutare   *But:* disonore

---

[1] But the o of noi and voi is *close.*

(b) In the adjective endings **–ese,**[1] **–oso,** and in words derived from such adjectives.

     inglese   curioso   curiosità

(c) In the past absolute and past participle of certain irregular verbs and their derivatives.

     difesi   raso   rasoio

(d) In the following words and their derivatives:

annusare	*to smell*	fuso	*spindle*	posa	*pose*
asino	*donkey*	mese	*month*	raso	*satin*
casa	*house*	naso	*nose*	riposo	*rest*
cosa	*thing*	peso	*weight*	riso	*rice, laughter*
così	*thus*	Pisa	*(Ital. city)*	susina	*plum*
desiderio	*desire*	pisello	*pea*	susurro	*whisper*

z: The letter **z** has the unvoiced sound (*ts*):

(a) When followed by **ia, ie,** or **io.**

     amicizia   grazie   vizio

(b) In all cases not mentioned in the following paragraph.

z: The letter **z** has the voiced sound (*dz*):

(a) In all verbs ending in **–izzare** which have more than four syllables in the infinitive.

     analizzare   scandalizzare   fertilizzare

(b) In words derived from Greek, Hebrew, or Arabic.

     protozoi   azzurro   zenit

(c) When initial, except in the following words, their derivatives, and others of minor importance:

zampa	*paw*	zitella	*spinster*
zampillo	*spurt*	zitto	*hush*
zampogna	*bagpipe*	zoccolo	*wooden shoe*
zanna	*tusk*	zolfo	*sulphur*
zappa	*hoe*	zoppo	*lame*
zattera	*raft*	zucca	*pumpkin*
zecca	*mint*	zucchero	*sugar*
zeppa	*wedge*	zuffa	*fray*
zingaro	*gypsy*	zuppa	*soup*
zio	*uncle*		

[1] But **cortese,** *courteous,* **francese,** *French,* and **palese,** *evident,* are pronounced with a voiced **s.**

11. Special Doubling of Consonant Sounds. When, in a
natural word group, a monosyllable ending with a vowel or a word
stressed on the final vowel precedes a word beginning with a consonant, this consonant is generally pronounced as if it were double.
There is, however, no such doubling after **di,** *of.*

a Roma (arroma)	chi sa (chissà)
lunedì sera (lunedissera)	più caro (piuccaro)

STRESS AND ACCENT

12. In an Italian word the stress falls nearly always on the same
syllable on which it falls in the corresponding Latin word. We
may find it on one of the following syllables:

on the last	fabbricò
on the next-to-the-last	fabbricare
on the third-from-the-last	fabbrico
on the fourth-from-the-last	fabbricano

Words having the stress on the final vowel are marked with a
grave accent (ˋ). No written accent is used on other words, except occasionally in order to avoid ambiguity, but it may be a help
for the student to remember: (*a*) that most Italian words are
stressed on the next-to-the-last syllable, fewer on the third-from-
the-last, and only a very limited number on the fourth-from-the-
last; (*b*) that *e open* (ɛ) and *o open* (ɔ) are always stressed.

13. Besides being used on words stressed on the last syllable,
as stated above, the grave accent is used also on the words **già,
giù, più, può,** and on the following monosyllables which otherwise might be confused with others of the same spelling but of
different meaning:

chè	*because*	che	*that*
dà	*gives*	da	*by, from*
dì	*day*	di	*of*
è	*is*	e	*and*
là, lì	*there*	la, li	(*articles*)
nè	*nor*	ne	*of it, of them*
sè	*himself*	se	*if*
sì	*yes*	si	*himself*
tè	*tea*	te	*thee, you*

SYLLABICATION

14. Italian words are divided into syllables according to these rules:

1. A single consonant between vowels belongs to the syllable which follows.

ma-ri-to ru-mo-re re-gi-na

2. Double consonants are separated.

sab-bia at-to vac-ca

3. Two consonants, the first of which is **l, m, n,** or **r,** are also separated.

al-to an-ti-co cor-dia-le

4. Two consonants in any other combination belong to the syllable which follows.

giu-sto fi-glio u-scio

5. Of three consonants, the first one belongs to the preceding syllable, provided it is not an **s.**

com-pro al-tro com-plε-to

But: a-stro ma-sche-ra co-stru-zio-ne

6. Vowels forming a diphthong are never separated.

glɔ-ria uɔ-mo piε-no

ELISION AND APOCOPATION

15. Elision is the dropping of the final vowel of a word, before another word beginning with a vowel. It is indicated by the apostrophe.

l'amico (= lo amico)
un'ɔpera d'arte (= una ɔpera di arte)
un onεst'uɔmo (= un onεsto uɔmo)
dovrεbb'εssere (= dovrεbbe εssere)

While optional otherwise, the elision is generally required in the following cases: (*a*) articles; (*b*) the conjunctive personal pronouns **mi, ti, si, ci, vi, lo,** and **la;** (c) demonstrative adjectives; (d) the adjectives **bɛllo, buɔno, grande,** and **santo;** (e) the preposition **di.**

16. Apocopation (called in Italian **troncamento**) is the dropping of the final vowel or of the entire final syllable of one word before another word, no matter how the latter begins. No apostrophe is required when the apocopation affects only the last vowel; when the entire final syllable is dropped, the apostrophe is used in certain instances, while in others it is omitted.

The apocopation is in most cases a matter of choice, being based on euphony and current usage. As a rule, it takes place with words of more than one syllable which end with an **e** or an **o** preceded by **l, m, n,** or **r.**

fatal(e) destino *fatal destiny*	son(o) andati *they have gone*
siam(o) perduti *we are lost*	lasciar(e) tutto *to leave all*

CAPITALS

17. Capital letters are used in Italian as they are in English, except that small letters are used:

(a) With proper adjectives, unless used as plural nouns.

una grammatica italiana	*an Italian grammar*
un francese	*a Frenchman*
But: gl'Italiani	*the Italians*

(b) With names of months and days.

ogni giovedì di marzo   *every Thursday in March*

(c) With titles, when followed by a proper name.

il principe Colonna	*Prince Colonna*
il signor Guidi	*Mr. Guidi*

(d) In contemporary poetry, for the first word of each line unless a capital letter should be required by the rules of prose.

(e) With the pronoun **io,** *I.*

s'io fossi in Italia   *if I were in Italy*

On the other hand, the personal pronouns **Ella**, **Lɛi**, **Loro**, *you* (singular and plural), used in formal address, are generally capitalized.

verrɔ con Lɛi   *I shall come with you*

PUNCTUATION

18. The same punctuation marks exist in Italian as in English. Their Italian names are:

. punto	— lineetta
, virgola	... punti sospensivi
; punto e virgola	« » virgolette
: due punti	( ) parentesi
? punto interrogativo	[ ] parentesi quadra
! punto esclamativo	⌢ grappa
- stanghetta	* asterisco

They are used as in English, except that the **punti sospensivi** are often employed in place of the English dash, while the latter (**lineetta**) commonly serves to denote a change of speaker in a conversation.

8. **Combined Letters.** Giugno luglio sciocco boschi negligente vecchia fichi liscio freschi meglio ogni figlio facchino unghia quasi quaglia pigliare camicia discesa sciupare perchè slitta lasciare.

II

1. Europa Italia Roma Milano Napoli Torino Genova Palermo Firenze Bologna Venezia Trieste Brescia Ferrara Ravenna Cagliari Chieti Aiaccio Perugia Reggio Foggia Lecce.

2. Flavio Gioia, Marco Polo, Vivaldi, Cristoforo Colombo, Amerigo Vespucci, Giovanni e Sebastiano Caboto, Giovanni da Verrazzano, Pessagno, Usodimare, Beltrami, Bianchi, Bottego.

3. Pietro d'Abano, Pomponaccio, Bernardino Telesio, Giordano Bruno, Fra Paolo Sarpi, Campanella, Giambattista Vico, Antonio Genovesi, Cesare Beccaria, Filangieri, Romagnosi, Galluppi, Rosmini, Gioberti, Mazzini, Pareto, Croce, Gentile.

4. Panfilo Castaldi, Leonardo da Vinci, Achillini, Tartaglia, Cardano, Andrea Cesalpino, Aldovrandi, Luigi Ferrari, Fallopio, Giambattista della Porta, Eustachio, Botallo, Galileo Galilei, Bonaventura Cavalieri, Giovanni Branca, Torricelli, Viviani, Redi, Malpighi, Morgagni, Spallanzani, Galvani, Volta, Aldini, Avogadro, Canestrini, Palmieri, Piatti, Schiaparelli, Secchi, Caselli, Giovanni Cavalieri, Brioschi, Luigi Cremona, Meucci, Pacinotti, Cantoni, Angelo Mosso, Guglielmo Marconi, Enrico Fermi.

5. Cimabue, Niccolò Pisano, Giotto, l'Orcagna, Iacopo della Quercia, Brunelleschi, Ghiberti, Donatello, il Beato Angelico, il Masaccio, Luca della Robbia, Alberti, Filippo Lippi, Giovanni Bellini, Mantegna, il Verrocchio, Bramante, Botticelli, il Ghirlandaio, il Perugino, Leonardo da Vinci, il Pinturicchio, Michelangelo Buonarroti, Tiziano, il Giorgione, Raffaello Sanzio, Andrea del Sarto, Giulio Romano, il Sansovino, Cellini, il Tintoretto, Palladio, Guido Reni, il Domenichino, Bernini, Salvator Rosa, Carlo Dolci, Luca Giordano, Tiepolo, Vanvitelli, Canova, Bartolini, Palizzi, Morelli, Segantini, Michetti, Sacconi.

6. Guido d'Arezzo, Palestrina, Caccini, Iacopo Peri, Claudio Monteverdi, Frescobaldi, Cavalli, Carissimi, Lulli, Alessandro e

Exercises in Pronunciation

Note: *The following exercises should be carefully read under the supervision of the instructor, and used as material for dictation and syllabication.*

I

1. Consonants and the Vowels *a, i, u*. Luna gala durata vita unità finiti cara partita animali guida italiana minuti gai vini vicini caricatura libri naviganti cicala mai via marina unica natura banditi punti radunati prima puliti tardi muri crudi mulini carta civiltà diamanti gridi tristi valigia panini grigi bauli cantata cura luci giganti manuali.

2. Double Consonants. Tutti annata frutta mulatta nulla palazzi ricci panna affitti mamma babbi ricca arrivi assai lussi raggi mucca addii palla.

3. Close *e*. Cena vele veduta pene fedele cera catene temere vegetale pere vendette cadere bere rete tele tenere prevedere te candele vere generale energia elementare rene.

4. Open *e*. Affetti ɛrba fɛrri gɛnti iɛri bɛlla ciɛli parɛnti diɛci grɛci tɛrra cappɛlli pɛrla lɛtti attɛnta vɛnti cɛntri mɛdici trɛni anɛlli lɛi pɛssima bɛne ɛcco sevɛra.

5. Close *o*. Voce dottore bocca ora onda pronto amore rumori borgo colore dove conto pollo proporre profondo secondo contro rotondo come locomotiva modista professore rosso.

6. Open ɔ. Fɔrte cuɔre ɔlio hɔ pɔrta ɔtto gɔtico mɔnaco mɔda sɔlito dɔ nɔtte tɔrto fuɔco ɔttimo nuɔva dɔnna uɔvo trɔppo uɔmini pɔvero stɔmaco pɔco sɔ ɔffro nɔnna ɔrto.

7. Voiced *s* and *z*. Uso viso zɛro vaso mɛzzo entusiasmo caso esatto sbarco visita sguardo utilizzare dɔse manzo rɔsa slitta misɛria pranzo zanzara svago musica azzurro.

Domenico Scarlatti, Torelli, Corelli, Vivaldi, Marcello, Stradella, Pergolese, Iommelli, Piccinni, Sacchini, Paisiello, Boccherini, Cimarosa, Viotti, Cherubini, Spontini, Paganini, Mercadante, Rossini, Donizetti, Vincenzo Bellini, Giuseppe Verdi, Ponchielli, Boito, Smareglia, Catalani, Martucci, Giacomo Puccini, Leoncavallo, Franchetti, Mascagni, Cilea, Ferruccio Busoni, Umberto Giordano, Montemezzi, Wolf-Ferrari, Ottorino Respighi, Pizzetti, Malipiero, Zandonai.

7. Dante Alighieri, Francesco Petrarca, Giovanni Boccaccio, Pontano, Boiardo, Pulci, Lorenzo de' Medici, Masuccio Salernitano, Sannazaro, Poliziano, Niccolò Machiavelli, Bembo, Ludovico Ariosto, Ruccellai, Buonarroti, Bandello, Guicciardini, Alamanni, Berni, Cellini, Grazzini, Caro, Tansillo, Vasari, Vittoria Colonna, Gaspara Stampa, Guarini, Torquato Tasso, Chiabrera, Tassoni, Marino, Basile, Testi, Filicaia, Metastasio, Goldoni, Gaspare Gozzi, Parini, Alfieri, Monti, Foscolo, Manzoni, Leopardi, Giusti, Aleardi, De Sanctis, Carducci, Verga, Fogazzaro, Pascoli, Gabriele D'Annunzio, Giacosa, Panzini, Luigi Pirandello, Novaro, Ada Negri, Ojetti, Beltramelli, Pastonchi, Grazia Deledda, Papini, Bacchelli.

CLASSROOM EXPRESSIONS

Buon giorno!	Good morning! Good day!
Buona sera!	Good evening!
Sì signore.	Yes, sir.
No, signore.	No, sir.
Signore. Signor Brown.	Sir. Mr. Brown.
Signora. Signora Smith.	Madam. Mrs. Smith.
Signorina. Signorina Jones.	Madam. Miss Jones.
Per favore! or Per piacere!	Please!
Grazie!	Thanks!
Prego! or Niente! or Non c'è di che!	Don't mention it!
Bene!	Good!
Benissimo! or Molto bene!	Very good!
Con piacere.	Gladly. With pleasure.
Arrivederci!	Good-bye! Till we meet again!

SINGULAR (*Lεi* form)	PLURAL (*Loro* form)	SING. AND PL. (*voi* form)	
S'alzi.	S'*a*lzino.	Alz*a*tevi.	Stand up.
Si sεgga.	Si sεggano.	Sed*e*tevi.	Be seated.
Vεnga.	Vεngano.	Venite.	Come.
Vada.	V*a*dano.	Andate.	Go.
Scriva.	Scrivano.	Scrivete.	Write.
Lεgga.	Lεggano.	Leggete.	Read.
Ascolti.	Asc*o*ltino.	Ascoltate.	Listen.
Ripεta.	Ripεtano.	Ripetete.	Repeat.
Risponda.	Risp*o*ndano.	Rispondete.	Answer.
Traduca.	Trad*u*cano.	Traducete.	Translate.
Corrεgga.	Corrεggano.	Correggete.	Correct.
Cancεlli.	Cancεllino.	Cancellate.	Erase.
Cominci.	Com*i*ncino.	Cominciate.	Begin.
Apra.	*A*prano.	Aprite.	Open.
Chiuda.	Chi*u*dano.	Chiudete.	Close.
Prεnda.	Prεndano.	Prendete.	Take.
Mi dia.	Mi d*i*ano.	Datemi.	Give me.
Mi sc*u*si.	Mi sc*u*sino.	Scus*a*temi.	Excuse me.

Come si chiama Lεi? *or* **Come vi chiamate?**	What is your name?
Mi chiamo Maria Nelson.	My name is Mary Nelson.
Come si chiama questo in italiano?	What is this called in Italian?
Che cɔsa ὲ questo?	What is this?
Questo ὲ un libro.	This is a book.
Chi ὲ questo giovanɔtto?	Who is this young man?
Chi sono questi giovanɔtti?	Who are these young men?
Chi ὲ questa signorina?	Who is this young lady?
Attenzione!	Attention!
Che c'ὲ?	What is there? *or* What is the matter?
Che c'ὲ sulla scrivania?	What is there on the desk?
C'ὲ un calamaio.	There is an inkwell.
Ci sono dei libri.	There are some books.
Ad alta voce!	Aloud!
In silεnzio!	Silently!

A che pagina?	On what page?
A pagina sɛtte.	On page seven.
A che riga?	In what line?
A riga dodici.	In line twelve.
Al principio.	At the beginning.
Alla fine.	At the end.
Alla lavagna!	To the blackboard!
Sulla lavagna.	On the blackboard.
A posto!	To your seat! To your seats!
Silɛnzio!	Silence!
Bravo!	Fine!
Dettato.	Dictation.
Virgola.	Comma.
Punto e virgola.	Semicolon.
Due punti.	Colon.
Punto e continuando.	Period, same paragraph.
Punto e da capo.	Period, new paragraph.
Punto e basta.	Period (the end).
Leggerò da capo.	I shall read again.

Parte Prima

A SCUOLA

❧ *Lezione Prima* ❧

I. ESERCIZIO DI PRONUNZIA

a: ga-la	sa-la	da-ta	can-ta
la-na	pa-la	ba-sta	man-ca
na-ta	pa-ga	pa-pa	san-ta
la-va	na-na	gam-ba	ban-ca
e: ve-le	se-te	be-ve	te-me-te
ne-ve	me-le	fe-de	ve-de-te
pe-pe	ve-de	spe-se	te-ne-te
me-se	pe-ne	mon-te	spen-de-te

Note:

1. The mouth should be well opened in pronouncing **a.**

2. A marked difference in pronunciation between Italian and English is that in Italian the unstressed vowels keep their pure sound, while in English unstressed vowels are often slurred.

3. While the English long vowels tend to become diphthongal (like *a* in *late* or *o* in *rope*), this tendency does not appear in Italian. Italian vowels are uniform throughout their utterance.

II. NOTE GRAMMATICALI

19. Conjugations

I	II	III
✗**comprare,** *to buy*	**vendere,** *to sell*	**finire,** *to finish, end*
cantare, *to sing*	**vedere,** *to see*	**partire,** *to depart*
suonare, *to play*	**correre,** *to run*	**servire,** *to serve* (*A*) (*servo*)

1. Italian verbs are divided, according to their infinitive endings −**are**, −**ere**, −**ire**, into three conjugations.

2. The stem of any regular verb (found by dropping the infinitive ending) is unchanged throughout the conjugation. To it are added the endings indicating mood, tense, person, and number.

20. Present Indicative of *comprare* and *vendere*

Stems: **compr–**		Endings: **–are**		
vend–		**–ere**		

SINGULAR

PERSONS	STEM + ENDING	MEANING	STEM + ENDING	MEANING
1.	compr **o**	I buy	vend **o**	I sell
2.	compr **i**	you buy	vend **i**	you sell
3.	compr **a**	he, she, it buys	vend **e**	he, she, it sells

PLURAL

PERSONS	STEM + ENDING	MEANING	STEM + ENDING	MEANING
1.	compr **iamo**	we buy	vend **iamo**	we sell
2.	compr **ate**	you buy	vend **ete**	you sell
3.	compr **ano**	they buy	vend **ono**	they sell

Note carefully that the Italian present renders not only the English simple present but also the emphatic and, very often, the progressive present tenses: **compro** = *I buy* or *I do buy* or *I am buying.*

An Italian progressive present exists, however, and will be studied in a later lesson.

21.   Subject Pronouns

	SINGULAR		PLURAL	
1st person	**io**	I	**noi**	we
2nd person	**tu**	thou, you	**voi**	you
3rd person	**egli**	he		
	ella	she		
	esso	he *or* it	**essi**	they (*m.*)
	essa	she *or* it	**esse**	they (*f.*)
	Ella *or* **Lɛi**	you	**Loro**	you

1. As the endings of the Italian tenses ordinarily indicate person and number, the subject pronouns are seldom necessary for clearness and, unless emphasis is desired, may be omitted: **compriamo,** *we buy.* Because of the ending **–iamo,** we understand that the subject is *we.*

Note, however, that the subject cannot be omitted if it is used with an adverb, such as **anche,** *also.* Note also that two subjects in contrast must be expressed: **egli parla e io ascolto,** *he speaks and I listen.*

2. The pronouns **egli** and **ella** refer to persons only, while **esso** and **essa, essi** and **esse** may refer to persons, animals, or things.

3. ADDRESSING ONE PERSON   ADDRESSING TWO OR MORE PERSONS

(a) **Tu ascolti.**	**Voi ascoltate.**
(b) **Voi ascoltate.**	**Voi ascoltate.** } You listen.
(c) **Ella** (*or* **Lɛi**) **ascolta.**	**Loro ascoltano.**

There are three forms of address in Italian:

(a) *Intimate:* **Tu** (*pl.* **voi**) is used in addressing a close relative, an intimate friend, or a child.

(b) *Familiar:* **Voi** is commonly used, in addressing one or more persons, as an intermediate form between the intimate **tu** and the formal **Ella** or **Lɛi.**

(c) *Formal:* **Ella** or, more colloquially, **Lɛi** with the verb in the 3rd person singular and **Loro** with the verb in the 3rd person plural are used in formal address. The student should use these forms in translating the English *you* unless instructed otherwise, or unless **tu** or **voi** is obviously required.

4. Ella e io impariamo.	*She and I are learning.*
Voi e Paolo imparate.	*You and Paul are learning.*

A verb with two or more subjects is plural.

The subjects may differ in person. In that case, if one of them is in the 1st person (**io** or **noi**), the verb is in the 1st person plural, as shown in the first example; otherwise the verb is in the 2nd person plural, as shown in the second example.

22.   **Question Form**

Maria parla italiano e inglese?	
Parla Maria italiano e inglese?	*Does Mary speak Italian and English?*
Parla italiano e inglese Maria?	

1. A sentence can be made interrogative merely by the inflection of the voice and the use of the question mark.

2. The subject may follow the verb (yet less frequently than in English) or be placed at the very end of the sentence.

3. The verb *to do,* used in English questions, is not expressed in Italian.

III. LETTURA

Parliamo italiano

— Caterina parla italiano e inglese. Parla italiano anche Lei, signorina De Chiara?

— Sì, signore (signora, signorina), — risponde Maria De Chiara, — anch'io parlo italiano e inglese. Ora parlo italiano.

5 Essa parla e voi ascoltate per imparare a parlare. Poi io domando:

— Riccardo e Paolo, ascoltano anche Loro?

— Sì, signore, — Paolo risponde, — anche noi ascoltiamo.

Caterina ascolta attentamente e poi scrive.

10 — Perchè scrive Caterina?

— Essa scrive per imparare.

Ora parla Riccardo. Noi ascoltiamo Riccardo e impariamo perchè ascoltiamo attentamente.

PROVERBIO

Chi ama il suo lavoro lo fa bene.   *He who loves his work does it well.*

IV. STUDIO DI PAROLE [1]

Caterina Catherine	**inglese** English [2]
Maria Mary	**italiano** Italian
Paolo Paul	
Riccardo Richard	**ascoltare** to listen, listen to
	domandare to ask
signora lady, madam, Mrs.	**imparare (a)** to learn [3]
signore *m.* gentleman, sir, Mr.	**parlare** to speak, talk
signorina young lady, Miss	**rispondere** to answer, reply

[1] Note that the words in the vocabularies of each lesson are always arranged as follows: names, nouns, pronouns, adjectives, verbs, all the rest. [2] Adjectives of nationality are written with small letters in Italian. [3] When, in the vocabulary, a verb is followed by a preposition in parentheses, that preposition must be used in case the verb is followed by an infinitive, as **imparo a parlare.**

scrivere to write (I R R U)

anche also, too [1]
attentamente attentively
e and
ora now

per conj. (followed by the infinitive) in order to
perchè? why? **perchè** because
poi then, afterward
sì yes

V. CONVERSAZIONE

1. Parla italiano Caterina? 2. Parlo italiano io ora? 3. Ascolta Lei? 4. Ascoltano Riccardo e Paolo? 5. Parla inglese Lei? 6. Perchè scrive Caterina? 7. Impara Lei? 8. Ascolta attentamente Maria? 9. Ascolta anche Lei? 10. Perchè ascolta attentamente?

VI. ESERCIZI

A. Sostituire la lineetta con un soggetto (*Substitute a subject for the dash*):

1. _____ vendete. 2. _____ parli. 3. _____ rispondono. 4. _____ domando. 5. _____ ascolta. 6. _____ scriviamo. 7. _____ imparate. 8. _____ vende. 9. _____ comprano. 10. _____ rispondo. 11. _____ parlo. 12. _____ impara. 13. _____ scrivono. 14. _____ domandiamo. 15. _____ vendi.

B. Completare (*Complete*):

1. Essi compr—. 2. Io rispond—. 3. Esse impar—. 4. Paolo e io parl— inglese. 5. Maria scriv—. 6. Io vend—. 7. Noi parl— italiano. 8. Tu compr—. 9. Voi ascolt— Riccardo. 10. Anche tu ascolt—. 11. Lei rispond—. 12. Caterina e Maria impar—. 13. Esse ascolt— attentamente. 14. Tu e Riccardo parl— italiano. 15. Voi scriv—.

C. Formare domande (*Form questions*):

1. Egli parla inglese. 2. Paolo scrive attentamente. 3. Essi parlano inglese e italiano. 4. Noi rispondiamo. 5. Ora Maria e Caterina imparano.

D. Tradurre in italiano (*Translate into Italian*):

I

1. Do you speak Italian, Miss Maglioni? 2. Yes, sir, I speak Italian. 3. Now they speak and I listen. 4. I am listening attentively in order

---

[1] **Anche** generally precedes the word to which it refers, and becomes **anch'** if followed by a word beginning with **e** or **i**.

to learn.   5. Catherine is listening too.   6. She also is learning to talk Italian.   7. Are you writing, Mary?   8. Yes, Mrs. Brown, I am writing. 9. Paul and I are learning because we are listening.   10. They are listening attentively.

II

1. I speak and Mary writes.   2. Afterward Catherine speaks and you listen.   3. We too listen attentively to Catherine.   4. Are you listening, Richard?   5. "Yes, sir," he answers.   6. He is listening attentively in order to learn.   7. Paul and I are writing now.   8. We are learning to write Italian.   9. Do you speak Italian, Mary?   10. Yes, Mrs. Parini I speak Italian, and English too.

❧ *Lezione Seconda* ☙

I. ESERCIZIO DI PRONUNZIA

ɛ:	mɛ-ta	lɛn-ta	stɛn-da	ca-dɛn-te
	tɛn-da	dɛn-te	spɛn-da	pa-tɛn-te
i:	vi-ta	mi-ti	fi-ni-ti	li-mi-ti
	vi-ni	ti-pi	ban-di-ti	vi-mi-ni

Note:

1. The mouth should be well opened in pronouncing ɛ.
2. The mouth should be almost closed with the lips drawn back, when making the sound i.

II. NOTE GRAMMATICALI
23.   **Indefinite Article**

1.

MASCULINE		FEMININE	
un uno		una (un') } a *or* an	
un fratello	*a brother* [1]	una sorella	*a sister*
un alunno	*a pupil* (m.)	un'alunna	*a pupil* (f.)
uno specchietto	*a little mirror*	una matita	*a pencil*
uno zio	*an uncle*	una zia	*an aunt*

[1] Always learn the new words that occur in the examples.

Before a masculine word the usual form of the indefinite article is **un**. **Uno** is used only before a masculine word beginning with **s** impure (that is, **s** followed by another consonant) or with **z**.

Una is the feminine form of the indefinite article; it becomes **un'** before a feminine word beginning with a vowel.

2. un fratello e una sorella   *a brother and sister*

The indefinite article must be repeated before each noun to which it refers.

24.   Gender of Nouns

There are no neuter nouns in Italian. There are only two genders, masculine and feminine.

Nouns ending in –**o** are all masculine, except **la mano**, *the hand*, and **la radio**, *the radio*.[1] The word **eco**, *echo*, is feminine in the singular (**la bella eco**) and masculine in the plural (**gli echi**).

Nouns ending in –**a** are usually feminine.

25.   Third Conjugation: Present Indicative

finire, *to finish*		partire, *to depart*	
Stem: **fin**– Ending: –**ire**		Stem: **part**– Ending: –**ire**	
fin **isc** o	I finish	part **o**	I depart
fin **isc** i	you finish	part **i**	you depart
fin **isc** e	he, she, it finishes	part **e**	he, she, it departs
fin **iamo**	we finish	part **iamo**	we depart
fin **ite**	you finish	part **ite**	you depart
fin **isc** ono	they finish	part **ono**	they depart

1. The larger part of the verbs of the third conjugation, like **finire**, add –**isc** to their stem in all the persons of the singular and in the third person plural of the present indicative (present subjunctive and imperative).

2. Other verbs are conjugated like **partire** in the tenses just mentioned; that is, they do not add –**isc** to their stem.

3. Note that the personal endings are exactly the same for all verbs of this conjugation.

[1] Also **la dinamo**, *the dynamo*.

4. In all other tenses, all verbs of the third conjugation are inflected alike.

26.   **Negative Verb**

Ella non parla inglese.	*She does not speak English.*
Maria non ha carta.	*Mary has no paper.*
Riccardo non ascolta.	*Richard is not listening.*

1. A verb is made negative by placing **non** before it.
2. The verb *to do*, used as an auxiliary, is not expressed in Italian.

III. LETTURA

Scriviamo

Scriviamo con una penna, una penna stilografica, o una matita.
Un'alunna scrive con un pezzo di gesso.
Paolo non scrive.   Non scrive perchè non ha carta.
— Ecco carta e matita, Paolo.
5 Anch'io scrivo; scrivo con penna e inchiostro.
Riccardo dà una gomma a Paolo, e Paolo cancella uno sbaglio.
Poi parliamo italiano.
— Mi mostri una carta sugante.
— Ecco una carta sugante.
10 — Apra un libro.
Io capisco e apro un libro.
— Chi ha uno specchietto?
— Maria ha uno specchietto.
— Chi è Maria?
15 — Maria è un'alunna.
Caterina domanda:
— Ha Riccardo uno zio?
Maria capisce e risponde:
— Sì, Caterina, Riccardo ha uno zio e anche una zia.

PROVERBIO

Diligenza passa scienza.	*Diligence surpasses learning.*

IV. STUDIO DI PAROLE

carta paper
carta sugante blotter
gesso chalk
gomma (rubber) eraser
inchiostro ink
libro book
penna pen
penna stilografica fountain pen
pezzo piece
sbaglio mistake

che? *or* che cosa [1]? what?
chi? who? whom?

matita – pencil.

aprire [apro] to open; apra open
cancellare [cancello] to erase
capire [capisco] to understand
dà gives
è is
ha has
mostrare to show; mi mostri
  show me

a to, at
con with
di of
ecco here is, here are [2]
o or

specchietto – little mirror

V. CONVERSAZIONE

1. Con che cosa scriviamo? 2. Con che cosa scrive Lei?
3. Perchè Paolo non scrive? 4. Che cosa dà a Paolo un alunno?
5. Mi mostri una penna stilografica. 6. Mi mostri una matita.
7. Mi mostri un pezzo di gesso. 8. Mi mostri una carta sugante.
9. Apra un libro. 10. Con che cosa cancelliamo uno sbaglio?
11. Mi mostri una gomma. 12. Chi ha uno specchietto? 13. Ha
Riccardo uno zio? 14. Capisce Lei?

VI. ESERCIZI

A. Completare con l'articolo indefinito [3] (*Complete with the indefinite article*):

1. Ecco _una_ signorina. 2. Paolo ha _un_ pezzo di carta. 3. Caterina
ha _uno_ specchietto. 4. Riccardo ha _una_ carta sugante. 5. Ecco
_un_ fratello e _una_ sorella. 6. Mi mostri _una_ alunna. 7. Chi ha
una radio? 8. Maria ha _uno_ zio. 9. Caterina ha _una_ penna.
10. Ecco _uno_ alunno. 11. Egli cancella _uno_ sbaglio. 12. Io scrivo
con _un_ pezzo di gesso.

[1] The word cosa means *thing*.   [2] Also *there is, there are, lo! behold!*
[3] Called *articolo indeterminativo* by Italian grammarians.

B. Coniugare nel presente dell'indicativo (*Conjugate in the present indicative*):

1. Vendere un libro.
2. Partire con Paolo.
3. Cancellare uno sbaglio.

4. Non capire Maria.
5. Comprare una gomma.
6. Non finire un libro.

C. Completare:

1. Voi part⸺. 2. Egli cap⸺. 3. Maria e Caterina fin⸺. 4. Anch'io fin⸺. 5. Tu apr⸺ un libro. 6. Anch'ella apr⸺ un libro. 7. Noi non part⸺. 8. Loro part⸺. 9. Io non cap⸺. 10. Lei cap⸺. 11. Voi e io fin⸺. 12. Esse part⸺.

D. Tradurre in italiano:

I

1. We are writing now. 2. Paul writes with a piece of chalk. 3. Catherine writes with pen and ink. 4. Mary writes with a fountain pen and I am writing with a pencil. 5. Who has an eraser? 6. Here is a mistake. 7. A pupil (*f.*) understands and gives an eraser to Richard. 8. Richard erases and then writes. 9. He is not speaking now; he is writing attentively. 10. Then a pupil speaks Italian and we understand.

II

1. Who has a fountain pen? 2. Catherine hasn't a fountain pen; she has a pencil. 3. She has an eraser too. 4. Show me a piece of paper. 5. I understand. Here is a piece of paper. 6. Now I am not writing; I am talking Italian. 7. Paul and you are talking Italian too. 8. A pupil (*f.*) asks: "Who has a blotter and a little mirror?" 9. Mary understands and answers: "Here are a blotter and a little mirror." 10. Paul and I are not speaking; we are listening attentively in order to learn.

I. ESERCIZIO DI PRONUNZIA

o:	so-lo	fon-do	mol-to	se-con-do
	col-mo	gol-fo	mon-do	co-no-sco
ɔ:	mɔ-do	gɔ-do	sɔl-do	cɔ-mo-do
	pɔ-co	pɔ-sta	pɔ-po-lo	stɔ-ma-co
u:	u-na	lu-na	al-cu-no	bu-sta
	du-ca	pun-to	la-gu-na	su-bi-to

Note:

The mouth should be well opened in pronouncing ɔ.

II. NOTE GRAMMATICALI

27. **Definite Article**

		MASCULINE	FEMININE	
Singular	il	lo (l')	la (l')	} the
Plural	i	gli (gl')	le (l')	

1. il ragazzo, i ragazzi — *the boy, the boys*
   il libro, i libri — *the book, the books*
   lo stesso libro, gli stessi libri — *the same book, the same books*
   lo zio, gli zii — *the uncle, the uncles*
   l'altro zio, gli altri zii — *the other uncle, the other uncles*
   l'italiano, gl'Italiani — *the Italian, the Italians*

Il and its plural, i, are the usual masculine forms of the definite article. Lo and gli are used before masculine words beginning with s impure, z, or a vowel. Before a vowel, however, lo becomes l', while gli becomes gl' only before i.

2. la ragazza, le ragazze — *the girl, the girls*
   la penna, le penne — *the pen, the pens*
   l'altra penna, le altre penne — *the other pen, the other pens*
   l'entrata, l'entrate — *the entrance, the entrances*

La and its plural, le, are the feminine forms of the definite article. La becomes l' before any of the vowels, le becomes l' only before e.

3. la penna e l'inchiostro   *the pen and ink*

The definite article must be repeated before each noun to which it refers.

28.   Plural of Nouns

From the examples given above it can be seen that nouns ending in −o form their plural by changing that o to i, and that feminine nouns ending in −a form their plural by changing that a to e.

29.   Adjectives in −*o*

The examples above (altro, altri — altra, altre) show also that:
1. Italian adjectives vary in gender and number in agreement with their nouns.[1]
2. Adjectives ending in −o have four forms:

	MASCULINE	FEMININE
Singular	−o	−a
Plural	−i	−e

30.   Present Indicative of the Auxiliary Verbs

avere, *to have*		essere, *to be*	
hɔ	I have	sono	I am
hai	you have	sɛi	you are
ha	he, she, it has	ɛ̀	he, she, it is
abbiamo	we have	siamo	we are
avete	you have	siɛte	you are
hanno	they have	sono	they are

III. LETTURA

Chi capisce?

Paolo pulisce la lavagna e scrive. Mentre egli scrive, noi parliamo italiano.

Il maestro apre un libro e domanda: « Dove siamo noi ora, si-

[1] An adjective modifying two or more nouns of different genders is masculine plural.

gnorina Miller? » La ragazza risponde: « Siamo in un'aula di questa scuola. »

« Bene », dice il maestro. E poi domanda: « Quest'aula è al pian terreno? » La stessa ragazza capisce e risponde: « No, signore, quest'aula non è al pian terreno; è al piano superiore. » 5

Ora il maestro chiama un'altra alunna, Maria Jones, e dice: « Che cosa vede in quest'aula, signorina? » Maria non risponde: ella non capisce. Risponde Riccardo e dice: « Vedo una scrivania, un calamaio, una riga e molti libri. »

« E Lei », domanda il maestro a [1] Caterina, « che altro vede? » 10 Caterina risponde: « Vedo una carta geografica, molti banchi e molte lavagne. »

« Indichi la scrivania », dice il maestro, e Caterina indica la scrivania. « Prenda i libri », dice egli poi, e Caterina prende i libri. 15

La ragazza capisce e risponde bene perchè studia attentamente.

PROVERBIO

Chi è paziente è sapiente.   *He who is patient is wise.*

IV. STUDIO DI PAROLE

aula classroom
banco (*pl.* **banchi**) student's desk
calamaio inkwell
carta geografica map
lavagna blackboard
maestro, maestra teacher
piano floor; **al pian terreno** on the ground floor; **al piano superiore** on the upper floor
riga ruler
scrivania desk
scuola school

molto much, (*pl.*) many
questo this [2]

chiamare to call, call on
dice says
indicare [**indico**] to point at *or* to; **indichi** point at *or* to
prendere to take; **prenda** take
pulire [**pulisco**] to clean
studiare [**studio**] to study
vedere to see

bene well, good
dove where [3]
in in, into
mentre while
no no

[1] Note that *to ask of a person* is **domandare a una persona.**   [2] Before a word beginning with a vowel **questo** becomes **quest'.**   [3] **Dove** becomes **dov'** before a word beginning with e.

V. CONVERSAZIONE

1. Che cosa pulisce Paolo? 2. Chi apre il libro? 3. Che cosa domanda il maestro? 4. Che risponde la ragazza? 5. Chi è Maria Jones? 6. Perchè Maria non risponde? 7. Che cosa dice Riccardo? 8. Che cosa vede Lei in quest'aula? 9. Indichi la scrivania. 10. Indichi i banchi. 11. Prenda un libro. 12. Prenda un pezzo di gesso.

VI. ESERCIZI

A. Coniugare nel presente dell'indicativo:

1. Avere una penna stilografica.   4. Essere in una scuola.
2. Essere in quest'aula.   5. Avere molti libri.
3. Avere una carta geografica.   6. Essere al pian terreno.

B. 1. Mettere l'articolo definito [1] davanti alle seguenti parole (*Place the definite article before the following words*):

1. signorina. 2. alunna. 3. inchiostro. 4. zia. 5. specchietto. 6. alunno. 7. fratello. 8. zio. 9. entrata. 10. ragazzo. 11. scuola. 12. sorella. 13. maestro. 14. stesso libro. 15. altra mano.

2. Dare il plurale delle stesse parole con gli articoli definiti (*Give the plural of the above words with the definite articles*).

C. Sostituire la lineetta con un soggetto (*Substitute a subject for the dash*):

1. _____ ha l'altro calamaio. 2. _____ siete in quest'aula. 3. _____ hanno fratelli e sorelle. 4. _____ siamo al piano superiore. 5. _____ hai la stessa scrivania. 6. _____ sono inglesi. 7. _____ non avete una carta geografica? 8. _____ non sei italiano. 9. _____ non ho altre zie. 10. _____ è con le ragazze. 11. _____ hai uno specchietto. 12. _____ siete un alunno.

D. Tradurre in italiano:

I

1. We clean the blackboards and then we write. 2. The other pupils write also. 3. They write with pens and pencils. 4. Then the teacher (*f.*) asks: "Where are the entrances to (di) this classroom?" 5. Paul does not understand; he does not study. 6. The teacher calls on Catherine Venturini and the girl answers well. 7. Catherine is Italian

---

[1] Called *articolo determinativo* by Italian grammarians.

and has many sisters. 8. Do the girls speak Italian? 9. No, madam; they speak English. 10. They are learning to (a) speak Italian in this school.

II

1. Show me the other mistake. 2. Here is the mistake. 3. Who has an eraser? 4. Mary gives the eraser to Richard. 5. The boy erases the mistake. 6. The teacher (*m.*) now asks: "Where are you, Paul?" 7. I understand and answer: "I am on the ground floor of this school, sir." 8. While we talk, many pupils are listening attentively. 9. Then the teacher calls on Catherine. 10. The girl does not answer well; she does not understand.

❧ Lezione Quarta ❧

I. ESERCIZIO DI PRONUNZIA

ca	che	chi	co	cu
c: ca-sa	an-che	chi-no	co-me	cu-na
ca-ne	a-mi-che	po-chi	con-to	a-cu-to
bu-ca	stan-che	fi-chi	co-mi-co	al-cu-no

cia	ce	ci	cio	ciu
a-*c*a-cia	ce-na	ci-ma	ciò	ciu-co
ci*a*n-cia	cɛn-to	ci-bo	ba-cio	ciur-ma
ca-m*i*-cia	cɛ-le-bre	*a*-ci-do	gan-cio	ta-ciu-to

II. NOTE GRAMMATICALI

31.   **Nouns and Adjectives in −*e***

1. il padre, i padri	*the father, the fathers*
la madre, le madri	*the mother, the mothers*
la lezione, le lezioni	*the lesson, the lessons*

Italian nouns may end in −**e,** in which case the ending gives no clue as to gender.[1] Nouns in −**e,** whether masculine or feminine, form their plural in −**i.**

[1] Remember that all nouns ending in −**one** (*but not* −**ione**) or −**ore** are masculine, and that abstract or collective nouns ending in −**ione** (such as **azione,** *action;* **discussione,** *discussion;* **nazione,** *nation,* etc.) are feminine.

2. Il libro è verde.　　　　*The book is green.*
   La matita è verde.　　　　*The pencil is green.*
   I libri sono verdi.　　　　*The books are green.*
   Le matite sono verdi.　　*The pencils are green.*

Adjectives ending in –e have the same form for both masculine and feminine; their plural is in –i.

32.　　　　*Lo* and *la* as **Object Pronouns**

Lo capisco.　　　*I understand him* (or *it*).
La capisco.　　　*I understand her* (or *it*).
L'indico.　　　　*I point at him* (or *her,* or *it*).

The forms **lo** and **la** are also used as direct object pronouns. **Lo** means *him* or *it;* **la** means *her* or *it;* and both normally precede the verb. Like the definite article, **lo** and **la** become **l'** before a word beginning with a vowel.

33.　　　　　　　**Possession**

Il libro di Caterina.　　　*Catherine's book.*
Lo zio d'Antonio.　　　　*Anthony's uncle.*
Lo zio di Maria e di Paolo.　*Mary's and Paul's uncle.*

Possession is denoted by the preposition **di,** which becomes **d'** before a vowel. This preposition must be repeated before each noun that it modifies.

III. LETTURA

Una lezione

La lezione comincia. Il professore chiama i nomi d'ogni studente e d'ogni studentessa per vedere se sono presenti. Ogni alunno risponde « Presente ». Anch'io rispondo; ma quando il professore chiama Laura, un'altra ragazza dice: « Assente ».
5 Laura non è in classe oggi.

　　— Ora — dice il professore — noi apriamo i libri e cominciamo la lettura.

　　Egli chiama Paolo, e Paolo legge una frase. La legge attentamente, e il professore dice: « Lei pronunzia bene. »

Poi egli chiama Riccardo. Riccardo legge un'altra frase. Non la legge bene e non capisce le nuove parole.

Io capisco ogni parola. La lettura d'oggi non è difficile; è facile. Capisco perchè studio bene e ascolto sempre attentamente in classe. 5

Quando la lettura finisce, il professore comincia la conversazione e dice a una studentessa:

— Indichi la lavagna.

Essa l'indica.

— Mi mostri una penna stilografica. 10

E la ragazza la prende e dice:

— Ecco una penna stilografica.

PROVERBIO

L'esercizio fa maestro. *Practice makes perfect.*

IV. STUDIO DI PAROLE

classe *f.* class
conversazione *f.* conversation
frase *f.* sentence
lettura reading
nome *m.* name, noun
parola word
professore *m.* professor
studente *m.* (boy) student
studentessa (girl) student

assente absent
difficile difficult, hard
facile easy
nuovo new

ogni every [1]
presente present

cominciare (a) [**comincio**] to begin, start
leggere to read
pronunziare [**pronunzio**] to pronounce

ma but
oggi today
quando when
se if, whether
sempre always, ever

V. CONVERSAZIONE

1. Perchè il professore chiama i nomi d'ogni studente? 2. Laura è presente? 3. Chi risponde « Assente »? 4. Chi comincia la lettura? 5. Che cosa legge Paolo? 6. Che cosa dice il professore a Paolo? 7. Chi legge poi? 8. Che cosa non capisce Riccardo?

[1] The adjective **ogni** is invariable; that is, it has the same form for both the masculine and feminine, and is always singular.

9. Lei capisce la parola « difficile »? 10. È difficile la lezione d'oggi? 11. Chi comincia la conversazione? 12. Che cosa indica una studentessa? 13. Che cosa mostra essa poi? 14. Dove siamo noi ora?

VI. ESERCIZI

A. Mettere l'articolo definito davanti alle seguenti parole:

1. lezione. 2. studente. 3. mano. 4. professore. 5. stesso nome. 6. padre. 7. classe. 8. frase. 9. madre. 10. radio. 11. altra conversazione. 12. studentessa.

B. Dare il plurale di:

(*a*) 1. questa lezione. 2. lo stesso padre. 3. la stessa frase. 4. il nuovo professore. 5. questo studente.

(*b*) 1. La studentessa è assente. 2. Lo studente è presente. 3. Il professore è italiano. 4. Questo ragazzo è inglese. 5. La lettura è facile. 6. Questa lezione non è difficile. 7. Questa frase non è italiana. 8. La penna è verde. 9. La frase è nuova. 10. Questa è la lezione.

C. Sostituire a ciascun complemento oggetto il corretto pronome oggettivo (*Substitute for each direct object the proper object pronouns*), e.g. **prendo la carta = la prendo:**

1. Finiscono la lezione. 2. Chiamo Paolo. 3. Ascoltiamo il professore. 4. Scrivo una frase. 5. Indica la carta geografica. 6. Indica un banco. 7. Capisco la parola. 8. Essa pulisce la lavagna. 9. Impariamo la lezione. 10. Scriviamo un nome.

D. Tradurre in italiano:

I

1. Mary is present, but Laura is absent. 2. The professor calls the names and the students answer. 3. Paul's sister doesn't answer; she is absent today. 4. We open the books and the reading begins. 5. Richard's book is green; don't you see it? 6. I read a sentence and then I write it. 7. Paul and Richard read the new words and the professor says: "You pronounce well, boys." 8. Today's reading is easy. 9. I understand every sentence. 10. Every student understands.

II

1. When the professor calls Laura's name, I answer: "She is not present." 2. Many students are absent today. 3. If they are absent,

they don't learn.   4. Catherine's brother and I are always present.
5. Now the class listens attentively while the professor speaks Italian.
6. He writes a new word and I understand it.   7. The new words are
easy.   8. While we talk, Richard's sister writes a sentence with a piece
of chalk.   9. Then the teacher points out [1] a mistake.   10. Every student sees it.

❧ Lezione Quinta ❧

I. ESERCIZIO DI PRONUNZIA

sc:	sca	sche	schi	sco	scu
	sca-la	ta-sche	schi-fo	sco-po	scu-do
	pe-sca	mo-sche	bo-schi	ca-pi-sco	scul-tu-ra
	sca-to-la	sche-da	di-schi	pa-sco-lo	o-scu-ri-tà

	scia	sce	sci	scio	sciu
	la-scia	sce-na	u-sci	li-scio	a-sciu-go
	li-scia	scel-to	fa-sci	scial-to	sciu-pa-re
	sciar-pa	scen-do	fa-sci-no	scio-pe-ro	pa-sciu-to

II. NOTE GRAMMATICALI

34. Contractions of Prepositions and Definite Article

When the prepositions **a** (*to, at*), **da** (*by, from*), **di** (*of*), **in** (*in,
into*), **su** (*on, upon*), **con** (*with*), and **per** (*for, through*) precede the
definite article, preposition and article are combined in one word,
as shown in the following table:

	il	i	lo	gli	la	le	l'
a	**al**	**ai**	**allo**	**agli**	**alla**	**alle**	**all'**
da	**dal**	**dai**	**dallo**	**dagli**	**dalla**	**dalle**	**dall'**
di	**del**	**dei**	**dello**	**degli**	**della**	**delle**	**dell'**
in	**nel**	**nei**	**nello**	**negli**	**nella**	**nelle**	**nell'**
su	**sul**	**sui**	**sullo**	**sugli**	**sulla**	**sulle**	**sull'**
con	**col**	**coi**	(collo)	(cogli)	(colla)	(colle)	(coll')
per	**pel**	**pei**	(pello)	(pegli)	(pella)	(pelle)	(pell')

[1] Same as *points at.*

1. The prepositions **con** and **per** usually combine only with the articles **il** and **i**. The forms printed in parentheses are obsolete.

2. Sometimes in poetry, and in a few rarer cases in prose also, other prepositions are used separately from the article.

35.   **Object Pronouns *li* and *le***

Li capisco.	*I understand them.*
Egli li indica.	*He points at them.*
Voi le ascoltate.	*You listen to them.*

Li and **le** are respectively the plural forms of the direct object pronouns **lo** and **la,** already studied. Observe that these plural forms are not elided before a verb beginning with a vowel.

36.   **Some Cardinal Numerals**

1 **uno, –a**	5 **cinque**	9 **nɔve**
2 **due**	6 **sɛi**	10 **diɛci**
3 **tre**	7 **sɛtte**	11 **undici**
4 **quattro**	8 **ɔtto**	12 **dodici**

Uno has a feminine, **una,** and when used adjectively has the forms of the indefinite article (*see* § 23, p. 28). Examples:

	un pɛzzo	*one piece*
	un'alunna	*one pupil*
But:	uno dei pɛzzi	*one of the pieces*
	una delle alunne	*one of the pupils*

All other numbers are invariable.

III. LETTURA

Leggiamo e parliamo

Il professore è in piɛdi, diɛtro alla scrivania. Sulla scrivania ci sono tre libri: una grammatica, un libro di lettura e un dizionario. Anche noi abbiamo un libro di lettura, e ora leggiamo.

Maria lɛgge ad alta voce; lɛgge bɛne e pronunzia chiaramente 5 ogni parɔla. Noi leggiamo in silɛnzio le stesse parɔle, e le capiamo. La lezione d'ɔggi non è diffʲcile.

Dopo Maria, altri alunni lɛggono. Il professore li corrɛgge.

Quando la lettura finisce, comincia la conversazione.

— Sono vicino alla pɔrta o a una delle finɛstre? — domanda il professore a Ɛlena.

Ɛlena non risponde, e il professore è scontɛnto. Risponde Lorɛnzo:

— Nɔ, signore, Lɛi non è vicino alla pɔrta, e non è vicino alla 5 finɛstra; Lɛi è davanti alla classe.

E indica la classe col dito.

— Bɛne, Lorɛnzo. E quanti ragazzi e quante ragazze ci sono in questa classe? — domanda di nuɔvo il professore.

— Ci sono nɔve ragazzi e undici ragazze. 10

— Che cɔsa c'è sul banco, davanti a Lɛi? — il professore domanda a Riccardo.

— C'è un libro, un quadɛrno, una penna stilografica e una matita.

— Il quadɛrno è sul libro?

— Nɔ, signore; il libro è sul quadɛrno. 15

Riccardo risponde bɛne, e il professore è contɛnto.

PROVƐRBIO

Scopa nuɔva scopa bɛne.　　*A new broom sweeps clean.*

IV. STUDIO DI PARƆLE

Ɛlena Helen
Lorɛnzo Lawrence

dito finger
dizionario dictionary
finɛstra window
grammatica grammar
libro di lettura reader
pɔrta door
quadɛrno notebook
silɛnzio silence; in silɛnzio silently
voce *f.* voice; ad alta voce [1] aloud

contɛnto glad, satisfied

quanto how much; (*pl.*) how many
scontɛnto dissatisfied

c'è there is *or* is there [2]?
ci sono there are *or* are there [2]?
corrɛggere to correct

chiaramente clearly
davanti a before, in front of
diɛtro a behind
di nuɔvo again, anew
dopo after
ed and [3]
in piɛdi standing
vicino a near

---

[1] Note that the preposition **a** becomes **ad** before a word beginning with **a**.
[2] While ɛcco is used in pointing at somebody or something, c'è and ci sono are used in simple statements without the idea of pointing. [3] Generally used only before a word beginning with **e**.

V. CONVERSAZIONE

1. Dov'è il professore? 2. Che c'è sulla scrivania? 3. Che cosa abbiamo noi? 4. Chi legge ad alta voce? 5. Leggiamo anche noi ad alta voce? 6. Chi legge ad alta voce dopo Maria? 7. Quando la lettura finisce, che cosa comincia? 8. Il professore è vicino alla finestra? 9. Chi è davanti a Lei? 10. Chi è dietro a Lei? 11. Quante signorine ci sono in questa classe? 12. Quanti studenti sono assenti oggi? 13. Quante finestre ha quest'aula? 14. Mi mostri una porta e una finestra.

VI. ESERCIZI

A. 1. Dare la corretta forma italiana corrispondente alle parole in parentesi (*Supply the proper Italian form for the words in parentheses*):

(*with the*) ragazzo	(*of the*) zio	(*from the*) mano
(*from the*) classe	(*on the*) nome	(*upon the*) banco
(*of the*) entrata	(*in the*) aula	(*in the*) scuola
(*with the*) gesso	(*to the*) madre	(*of the*) specchietto
(*for the*) padre	(*for the*) studente	(*by the*) stesso ragazzo

2. Dare il plurale dell'espressioni già completate (*Give the plural of the completed expressions*).

B. Leggere ad alta voce:

2, 5, 11, 9, 6, 1, 8, 4, 3, 7, 12, 10

C. Sostituire a ciascun complemento oggetto il corretto pronome oggettivo (*Substitute for each direct object the proper object pronoun*), e.g. **leggo i libri = li leggo:**

1. Prendiamo le matite. 2. Indico le studentesse. 3. Vediamo i banchi. 4. Ascolta le parole. 5. Egli impara le lezioni. 6. I ragazzi aprono i libri. 7. Abbiamo il quaderno. 8. Abbiamo i quaderni. 9. Ascolto la ragazza. 10. Ascolto le ragazze.

D. Tradurre in italiano:

I

1. The readers are on the students' desks. 2. The students open them and read. 3. Lawrence reads aloud and the other pupils read silently.

4. I am behind Helen's brother. 5. Paul does not pronounce a new word well [1] and the professor is dissatisfied. 6. He corrects him and speaks to the students. 7. We listen to the professor's words. 8. Many other students read and I listen to them. 9. There are twelve young ladies and seven boys in the class. 10. Mary and Helen are not listening, and the professor calls them to the blackboard.

II

1. The boys and the girls are silently listening [2] to the teacher. 2. He is not behind his [3] desk now. 3. He is standing before the class with the grammar in [his] [4] hand. 4. He pronounces eight words and Helen writes them on the blackboard. 5. She writes them with [5] chalk. 6. When she finishes, the teacher says: "There is a mistake on the board." 7. Lawrence and four other [6] students see it. 8. Lawrence points to it with his [3] finger and says: "Here is the mistake." 9. The teacher calls on him and he erases the words. 10. Then he writes them again.

❧ Lezione Sesta ❧

I. ESERCIZIO DI PRONUNZIA

g:	ga	ghe	ghi	go	gu
	ga-la	se-ghe	a-ghi	go-la	gu-sto
	gam-ba	pa-ghe	la-ghi	go-de-te	la-gu-na
	pa-ga-te	stan-ghe	lun-ghi	te-go-lo	an-gu-sto

	gia	ge	gi	gio	giu
	gia-ce	gen-te	gi-ta	a-gio	giu-sto
	gri-gia	ge-ne-si	a-gi-te	gio-co	giun-to
	giar-di-no	gen-ti-le	pa-gi-na	ca-gio-ne	con-giun-to

[1] An adverb usually follows the verb it modifies.   [2] Translate: *are listening silently*.   [3] Replace the possessive *his* with the definite article.   [4] Do not translate the words in brackets.   [5] Use the definite article.   [6] The word altro normally precedes a numeral.

II. NOTE GRAMMATICALI

37. Past Participles

	INFINITIVE	PAST PART.	MEANING
1st conjugation	**comprare**	compr **ato**	bought
2nd conjugation	**vendere**	vend **uto**	sold
3rd conjugation	**finire**	fin **ito**	finished
Auxiliary verbs {	**avere**	**avuto**	had
	εssere	**stato**	been

The past participle of regular as well as many irregular verbs is formed by adding **–ato** to the stem of verbs in **–are, –uto** to the stem of verbs in **–ere, –ito** to the stem of verbs in **–ire.**

Besides serving as an adjective (for example: **la parɔla cancellata,** *the erased word*), the past participle is used — in conjunction with the auxiliary **avere** or **εssere** — in forming the perfect tenses.

38. Present Perfect

comprare, *to buy*	**partire,** *to depart*
I bought or *have bought, etc.*	*I departed* or *have departed, etc.*
hɔ comprato	**sono partito, –a**
hai comprato	**sεi partito, –a**
ha comprato	**ὲ partito, –a**
abbiamo comprato	**siamo partiti, –e**
avete comprato	**siεte partiti, –e**
hanno comprato	**sono partiti, –e**

The present perfect is formed by the present of **avere** or **εssere** followed by the past participle.

39. Use of Auxiliary Verbs

1. Hɔ veduto Beatrice.   *I saw* (or *have seen*) *Beatrice.*
    Abbiamo studiato.   *We studied* (or *have studied*).
    Ella ha viaggiato.   *She traveled* (or *has traveled*).

Avere is used in conjugating all transitive and many intransitive verbs.[1]

[1] Transitive verbs are those that may take a direct object, such as *to see;* intransitive verbs are those that are used without an object, such as *to go.*

THE ADORATION OF THE SHEPHERDS *By Giorgione*

BUST OF THE HOLY CHILD
By Desiderio da Settignano

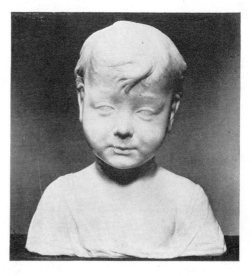

A VIEW OF THE DUCAL PALACE, VENICE *By Canaletto*

MONUMENT TO VICTOR EMMANUEL II AND THE TRAJAN COLUMN, ROME

2. Siamo stati in Italia.   *We were* (or *have been*) *in Italy.*
    Ella è partita.   *She departed* (or *has departed*).
    Sono diventati poveri.   *They became* (or *have become*) *poor.*

Contrary to English usage, essere is used in conjugating:

(*a*) the verb essere itself;

(*b*) most, but not all, intransitive verbs denoting motion, rest, or change of condition.[1]

3.   Ho cominciato il lavoro.   *I started my work.*
    But: Il lavoro è cominciato.   *The work has started.*

    Egli ha finito la lezione.   *He finished his lesson.*
    But: La lezione è finita.   *The lesson has ended.*

Many verbs that usually are transitive and are therefore conjugated with **avere,** take essere when used intransitively.

4.   Margherita è salita.   *Margaret came up.*
    But: Essa ha salito la scala.   *She climbed the stairs.*

On the other hand, a few intransitive verbs of motion (marked °
in the list in the footnote below) are sometimes used transitively,
in which case they take the auxiliary **avere.**

---

[1] For future reference, here is a list of the most frequently used intransitive verbs that take the auxiliary essere:

andare to go	**restare** to remain
arrivare to arrive	**rimanere** (*p.p.* **rimasto**) to remain
cadere to fall	° **ritornare** to return
° **correre** (*p.p.* **corso**) to run	° **salire** to go up, come up, climb
diventare to become	° **saltare** to jump, hop, jump over
durare to last	° **sbarcare** to land
entrare to enter	° **scendere** (*p.p.* **sceso**) to go down,
° **giungere** (*p.p.* **giunto**) to arrive,	come down
join	**stare** to stay, be, stand
morire (*p.p.* **morto**) to die	**uscire** to go out, come out
nascere (*p.p.* **nato**) to be born	**venire** (*p.p.* **venuto**) to come
partire to depart, leave	° **vivere** (*p.p.* **vissuto**) to live

The auxiliary essere is used also in conjugating: (*a*) reflexive verbs (*see*
§ **54,** p. 76); (*b*) impersonal verbs (*see* § **65,** p. 92 and § **125,** p. 205); (*c*) the
passive voice (*see* § **117,** p. 181); (*d*) the verbs **sembrare** and **parere,** *to
seem;* **piacere,** *to please, be pleasing,* and **dispiacere,** *to displease, be displeasing.* (*See also* § **173,** p. 315.)

40. **Agreement of Past Participle**

1. Maria è stata studiosa.	*Mary was studious.*
Esse sono partite.	*They have departed.*
Siamo ritornati.	*We have returned.*

A past participle used with **essere** agrees with its subject in gender and number.

2. Quanti studenti hai veduti?	*How many students have you seen?*
La casa che ha comprata.	*The house he bought.*
L'ha comprata.	*He bought it.*
But: Ha comprato due case.	*He bought two houses.*

A past participle used with **avere** agrees with its *direct object*, provided the direct object precedes the verb.[1] When the direct object follows the verb (which is usually the case), there is no agreement, as shown in the last example.

3. Tu sei arrivato.
Voi siete arrivato. } *You have arrived* (addressing a man).
Lei è arrivato.

Tu sei restata.
Voi siete restata. } *You have remained* (addressing a woman).
Lei è restata.

L'abbiamo chiamato. *We have called you* (addressing a man).
L'ho riconosciuta. *I recognized you* (addressing a woman).

The pronouns used in direct address are considered masculine or feminine according to the sex of the person addressed, and the past participle agrees accordingly.

III. LETTURA

In classe

Il sole entra per le finestre.

Il professore è andato alla lavagna, l'ha pulita, e ora prende un pezzo di gesso e scrive. Tutti gli alunni guardano attentamente

---

[1] Some prefer to have the past participle agree with the preceding direct object only if the latter is a personal pronoun (**l'ha comprata**); others go to the other extreme and have the past participle agree with the direct object even if the latter comes after the verb (**ha comprate due case**). The student is advised to follow the rule as given above.

la lavagna. Egli scrive una frase, l'esempio d'una nuova regola
di grammatica.

La regola è facile, e io la capisco subito. Anche gli altri alunni
la capiscono.

Ogni studente scrive in un quaderno un'altra frase dettata dal 5
professore: è un altro esempio. Molti alunni scrivono con la
matita, ma io scrivo con la penna stilografica perchè mi piace scrivere bene.

Il professore ha cancellato le parole dalla lavagna ed è ritornato
alla scrivania. Poi ha chiamato quattro studenti. Ognuno di 10
questi studenti comincia a scrivere cinque frasi sulla lavagna.
Mentr'essi scrivono, la conversazione in italiano comincia.

Lorenzo legge le domande dal libro, e noi rispondiamo uno alla
volta. Se un alunno sbaglia, il professore lo corregge.

— Signorina Pratt, — egli dice, — Lei pronunzia chiaramente. 15
La lezione finisce quando il campanello suona.

PROVERBIO

Roma non fu fatta in un giorno.   *Rome was not built in a day.*

IV. STUDIO DI PAROLE

campana bell; **campanello**
(small) bell
domanda question
esempio example
regola rule
sole *m.* sun, sunlight

ognuno, ognuna every one

elettrico electric
tutto all, whole; **tutto il libro**
the whole book; **tutti i libri** all
books

andare (a) to go [1]
dettare to dictate
entrare to enter [2]
guardare to look, look at
mi piace I like
ritornare (a) to return [1]
sbagliare [**sbaglio**] to make a mistake
suonare [**suono**] to sound, play
(*an instrument*), ring [3]

subito at once, immediately
uno alla volta one at a time

[1] Conjugated with essere.   [2] The verb **entrare** is always intransitive
(*I enter a classroom* = **Entro in un'aula**) and is conjugated with essere.
[3] Conjugated with essere when used intransitively.

V. CONVERSAZIONE

1. Per dove entra nell'aula il sole? 2. Dov'è andato il professore? 3. Perchè è andato alla lavagna? 4. Chi guarda attentamente la lavagna? 5. Con che cosa scrive il professore? 6. La nuova regola è difficile? 7. Su che cosa scrivono gli studenti? 8. Lei perchè scrive con una penna? 9. Che cosa ha cancellato il professore dalla lavagna? 10. Dov'è ritornato poi? 11. Mentre quattro studenti scrivono sulla lavagna, che cosa cominciamo noi? 12. Che cosa legge Lorenzo? 13. Chi risponde alle domande? 14. Quando finisce la lezione?

VI. ESERCIZI

A. Dare il participio passato (*Give the past participle*) di:

1. finire	2. vedere	3. avere	4. pulire
essere	partire	capire	vendere
comprare	guardare	chiamare	studiare

B. 1. Coniugare nel presente perfetto [1]:

1. Capire una frase.   4. Entrare nell'aula.
2. Non avere quaderni.   5. Vendere quattro libri.
3. Essere in una scuola.   6. Suonare il campanello.

2. Completare col presente perfetto del verbo in parentesi:

1. (*vedere*) Voi non ____ ____ il dizionario. 2. (*imparare*) Essi ____ ____ la lezione. 3. (*essere*) Elena e Maria ____ ____ assenti. 4. (*vendere*) Io non ____ ____ i libri. 5. (*partire*) Oggi le signore ____ da New York. 6. (*capire*) Riccardo li ____ ____. 7. (*cancellare*) Noi ____ ____ le frasi. 8. (*ritornare*) La zia di Paolo ____ ____ subito. 9. (*avere*) Io ____ ____ dodici matite. 10. (*chiamare*) Perchè tu non le ____ ____?

C. 1. Dare la corretta forma italiana corrispondente alle parole in parentesi:

(*by the*) studente	(*in the*) classi	(*at the*) entrata
(*with the*) penna	(*to the*) signorine	(*by the*) ragazzi
(*of the*) esempio	(*for the*) madre	(*to the*) sole
(*in the*) aule	(*at the*) lavagna	(*with the*) stessi nomi
(*on the*) specchietti	(*with the*) zii	(*of the*) entrate

---

[1] Called *passato prossimo* by Italian grammarians.

2. Leggere ad alta voce:

6, 4, 7, 11, 3, 9, 1, 12, 8, 2, 5, 10

D. Tradurre in italiano:

I

1. The whole class was present today.   2. The teacher dictated six Italian [1] sentences.   3. Then he called on Helen.   4. The girl went immediately to the blackboard.   5. She cleaned it in order to write the new words of today's lesson.   6. Every one understood them. 7. Today's lesson was easy.   8. I like Helen; she is Catherine's sister. 9. When she returned to her [2] desk, we began to (a) read.   10. But now the bell rings: the lesson is over.[3]

II

1. I have Catherine's fountain pen.   2. Catherine is Helen's sister; she was absent today.   3. Mary also was absent; I haven't seen her. 4. When the professor entered [4] the classroom, he dictated a new rule to the students.   5. Then he asked: "Did you understand it?" 6. "Yes, sir, we understood it immediately."   7. The professor then called all students, one at a time, to the blackboard.   8. I also went to the board to (a) write an example, and the professor looked at it. 9. "You are mistaken; this word is not Italian."   10. And he pointed at one of the words.

❧ *First Review Lesson* ❧

I. VOCABULARY DRILL

A. Translate into Italian, first in the singular, then in the plural, the following nouns with their articles:

1. The ruler	2. The father	3. The finger
the paper	the desk	the school
the uncle	the name	the mother
the ink	the lesson	the brother
the eraser	the hand	the entrance
the teacher	the classroom	the blackboard

---

[1] Place the adjective after the noun.   [2] Replace the possessive with the definite article; and what is the correct translation of *desk*, in this case, **scrivania** or **banco?**   [3] Translate, *has ended.*   [4] Attention !

B. Give the Italian singular forms, masculine and feminine, for each of the following adjectives:

1. Absent, easy, all, much, English, glad, other, this, new.
2. Dissatisfied, green, difficult, present, Italian, electric, same, every.

C. Give the Italian for the following verbs:

1. To be	2. To have	3. To ring
to ask	to take	to read
to open	to call	to clean
to erase	to write	to begin
to learn	to answer	to depart
to dictate	to correct	to pronounce

D. Give the Italian for the following expressions:

Silently, aloud, there is, standing, there are, again, on the upper floor, one at a time.

II. ARTICLES

1. When is the article **uno** used? Give two examples.
2. What is **s** impure?
3. When is the article **un'** used? Give an example.
4. Give the rules concerning the article **lo** and its plural, **gli,** and furnish four examples.

III. NOUNS

1. How many genders are there in Italian?
2. What is usually the gender of nouns ending in –**a**? Give two examples.
3. How do feminine nouns ending in –**a** form their plural? Give an example.
4. What is the gender of nouns ending in –**o**? Give three examples.
5. Are all nouns ending in –**o** masculine in gender? Mention two that are not.
6. How do nouns ending in –**o** form their plural? Give an example.
7. What gender are nouns ending in –**e**? Give three examples.
8. How do nouns ending in –**e** form their plural? Give an example.

IV. ADJECTIVES

1. How many forms has an adjective ending in –o? Give two examples.
2. How many forms has an adjective ending in –e? Give two examples.
3. Count from 1 to 12.
4. Count from 12 to 1.

V. PRONOUNS

1. Give a list of the subject pronouns.
2. Are subject pronouns always necessary?
3. When are they necessary? Give two examples.
4. Give the four object pronouns studied so far.
5. Do they precede or follow the verb?
6. Are they all elided before a verb beginning with a vowel?

VI. VERBS

1. How many conjugations are there in Italian?
2. How do we find the stem of a verb?
3. Give three possible meanings of **compro**.
4. Conjugate the present indicative of **dettare, correggere, partire,** and **pulire.**
5. What is a transitive verb? Give two examples in Italian.
6. How is a past participle formed? Give an example for each of the three conjugations.
7. What auxiliary is used in conjugating a transitive verb?
8. When do we use the auxiliary **essere** in forming a perfect tense?
9. Mention a few intransitive verbs of motion.
10. Conjugate the present perfect of **ritornare** and **capire.**

VII. PREPOSITIONS

1. Give the Italian for: *by, through, of, with, on, at, into, upon, to, from, in, for.*
2. Give the contractions resulting from the prepositions **di** and **in** with the articles **il, i, lo, gli, la, le, l'.**

LETTURA IN SILENZIO

Sì o no?

1. __ Un alunno è sulla scrivania.
2. __ Caterina è il fratello di Paolo.
3. __ Scriviamo sulla lavagna.
4. __ Pulisco la lavagna col gesso.
5. __ Quest'aula è al pian terreno.
6. __ L'inchiostro è nel campanello.
7. __ Il maestro vende carta.
8. __ Paolo è uno studente.
9. __ Anche Maria è uno studente.
10. __ Un dito ha cinque mani.
11. __ Rispondiamo a ogni domanda.
12. __ Scriviamo con una scrivania.
13. __ La madre d'Elena ha una radio.
14. __ Dall'esempio capiamo la regola.
15. __ La lavagna è dietro ai banchi.

ACHIEVEMENT TEST NO. 1

VOCABULARY

Give the Italian for the following words:

1. the ladies	_____	11. the hand	_____
2. English	_____	12. there is	_____
3. to erase	_____	13. to begin	_____
4. satisfied	_____	14. difficult	_____
5. aloud	_____	15. all boys	_____
6. to answer	_____	16. the uncles	_____
7. the sisters	_____	17. again	_____
8. to clean	_____	18. same	_____
9. at once	_____	19. the sun	_____
10. I like	_____	20. to go	_____

(Deduct 1 point for each mistake.)

GRAMMAR

A. *Replace the dash with the indefinite article:*

1. ____ piano. 2. ____ alunno. 3. ____ specchietto. 4. ____ conversazione. 5. ____ entrata.

B. Replace the dash with the definite article:

1. ____ inchiostri. 2. ____ banchi. 3. ____ stesso libro. 4. ____ quaderno. 5. ____ zio.

C. Complete the following sentences with a subject pronoun:

1. ____ partono. 2. ____ sei italiano. 3. ____ cancellate le parole. 4. ____ non rispondiamo. 5. ____ la guarda.

D. Supply the correct Italian forms for the words in parentheses:

1. Io (*study*) _____ attentamente. 2. Voi (*are not*) _____ contenti. 3. Egli (*is looking at*) _____ Riccardo. 4. Riccardo e io (*are*) _____ fratelli. 5. Essi (*are calling*) _____ le signore. 6. Tu (*understand*) _____ la regola. 7. Caterina (*is leaving*) _____ per Chicago. 8. Maria (*cleans*) _____ la finestra. 9. Voi (*are correcting*) _____ con una matita. 10. Noi (*have not*) _____ lo stesso maestro.

E. Substitute for each direct object the proper object pronoun (example: scrivo la frase = la scrivo):

      1. Abbiamo un dizionario.   _____
      2. Ascolto i ragazzi.   _____
      3. Non vedete lo sbaglio.   _____
      4. Egli detta le frasi.   _____
      5. Anch'io ho una radio.   _____

F. Supply the proper Italian form for the words in parentheses:

1. (*of the*) _____ libro   6. (*from the*) _____ banchi
2. (*with the*) _____ pezzi   7. (*to the*) _____ studenti
3. (*by the*) _____ madre   8. (*upon the*) _____ scrivania
4. (*in the*) _____ aula   9. (*into the*) _____ scuole
5. (*to the*) _____ zii   10. (*of the*) _____ esempio

G. Supply the correct form of the present perfect of the verb given in the infinitive:

1. (*essere*) Noi ____ a scuola. 2. (*pulire*) Essa ____ la penna. 3. (*vendere*) Voi non le ____. 4. (*finire*) Io ____ la lezione. 5. (*ritornare*) Maria ____ con le ragazze. 6. (*essere*) La sorella d'Elena ____ contenta. 7. (*cancellare*) Tu ____ tre parole. 8. (*sbagliare*) Anche voi ____. 9. (*partire*) Il padre e la zia di Paolo ____ oggi. 10. (*guardare*) Voi non li ____.

(Deduct 1 point for each mistake.)

READING

Translate the Italian passage that your instructor will write on the board or hand to you on a mimeographed sheet.

(This part counts 20 points.)

DICTATION

Your instructor will dictate twice a short Italian passage.

(This part counts 10 points.)

PERFECT SCORE: 100

Parte Seconda

A CASA

✦ *Lezione Settima* ✦

I. ESERCIZIO DI PRONUNZIA

d	l	n	t	p
da-do	la-go	na-no	tí-to-lo	pe-pe
do-ve-te	lí-vi-do	nɔ-no	tu-tɛ-la	pa-pa-le
do-di-ci	vo-la-te	ca-ni-no	ma-ti-ta	pɔ-po-lo
do-man-da	la-va-to	ve-nu-to	ta-lɛn-to	piom-bo

Note:

1. In pronouncing **d, l, n,** and **t,** the tip of the tongue should touch the upper front teeth.

2. The sound **p** should be made with an effort to avoid the explosive aspiration that accompanies the English *p*.

II. NOTE GRAMMATICALI

41.   **Some Relative Pronouns**

Il signore che suona.	*The gentleman who is playing.*
Il ragazzo che chiamo.	*The boy whom I call.*
Il libro che leggo.	*The book that I am reading.*
I quaderni che abbiamo.	*The notebooks we have.*
La penna con cui scrivo.	*The pen with which I write.*
La signora di cui parlo.	*The lady of whom I am speaking.*
L'aula in cui siamo.	*The classroom in which we are.*

The most important relative pronouns are **che** and **cui.**

Both are invariable, that is, do not change because of gender and number; and both may refer to either persons or things. They stand, according to the meaning, for the English *who, whom, that,* or *which.*

Che is used only as a subject or a direct object; **cui** is used chiefly as the object of prepositions.

As seen in the 4th example, the relative pronoun (direct object), often omitted in English, must always be expressed in Italian.

42. Imperative

	I		II	
2nd pers. sing.	compr a	buy	vend i	sell
(3rd pers. sing.	compr i	buy)	(vend a	sell)
1st pers. pl.	compr iamo	let us buy	vend iamo	let us sell
2nd pers. pl.	compr ate	buy	vend ete	sell
(3rd pers. pl.	compr ino	buy)	(vend ano	sell)

	III			
2nd pers. sing.	fin isc i	finish	part i	depart
(3rd pers. sing.	fin isc a	finish)	(part a	depart)
1st pers. pl.	fin iamo	let us finish	part iamo	let us depart
2nd pers. pl.	fin ite	finish	part ite	depart
(3rd pers. pl.	fin isc ano	finish)	(part ano	depart)

1. The Italian imperative has no 3rd person. The forms given in parentheses are borrowed from the present subjunctive, and are used in commands in the **Lɛi** or **Loro** forms of direct address (**compri** — or **comprino** — i fiori, *buy the flowers*) or in indirect commands to a third person (**finisca il lavoro**, *let him finish his work*).

2. Note that, except for the 2nd person singular of the first conjugation (**compra**), the imperative has the same forms as the present indicative.

3. Note also that the larger part of the verbs of the 3rd conjugation add –isc to their stem in the same persons as the present indicative (*see* § 25, 1, p. 29).

43. Imperative of the Auxiliary Verbs

	avere		ɛssere	
Sing.	abbi	have	sii	be
	(abbia	have)	(sia	be)
Pl.	abbiamo	let us have	siamo	let us be
	abbiate	have	siate	be
	(abbiano	have)	(siano	be)

44.   **Negative Imperative**

> **non comprare,** *do not buy, etc.*
> (**non compri**)
>
> **non compriamo**
> **non comprate**
> (**non comprino**)

A peculiarity of the imperative is that the negative form of the
2nd person singular is made by **non** and the infinitive. For the
other forms, just place **non** before the positive imperative.

45.   **Partitive Construction**

Vedo del gesso.	*I see some chalk.*
Cancello delle parole.	*I am erasing some words.*
Avete dei fratelli?	*Have you any brothers?*
Avete delle sorelle?	*Have you any sisters?*

The English *some* or *any* is frequently rendered in Italian by
the contraction of **di** and the definite article. This is called *partitive construction.*

III. LETTURA

La casa d'Elena

Elena abita in Via Cristoforo Colombo 11.[1]

La casa d'Elena non è grande, ma è molto bella e comoda.
Ha due piani e un piccolo giardino.

Nel giardino vediamo degli alberi e un prato. Ora gli alberi
non hanno foglie, ma il prato è verde.   5

Il pian terreno ha quattro stanze: il salotto, lo studio, la sala
da pranzo e la cucina. Al piano superiore ci sono tre camere e
una stanza da bagno.

— Entra in salotto,[2] — Elena dice.

— Con piacere.   10

---

[1] Notice the way an address is given in Italian.   [2] Note this idiomatic
expression (omission of the definite article), and try to remember similar
ones: **in casa, in sala da pranzo, in camera, in cucina,** etc.

Il salɔtto mi piace molto. È bɛllo e ha delle grandi finɛstre. Lo studio è piccolo, ma anch'esso mi piace perchè ha una bɛlla scrivania e dei grandi scaffali con molti libri.

La sala da pranzo non è grande e non è piccola; è diɛtro al 5 salɔtto e ha tre finɛstre.

— Non entriamo in cucina.

Non hɔ domandato perchè, e in cucina non siamo entrate. Ma siamo salite al piano superiore, che ha tre camere molto bɛlle, piɛne d'aria e di sole. Una è d'Ɛlena, una è del padre e della 10 madre d'Ɛlena, e l'altra è della zia.

Ɛlena è molto contɛnta d'avere una bɛlla casa.

PROVƐRBIO

A ogni uccɛllo suo nido è bɛllo.   *There is no place like home.* (*To every bird its nest is beautiful.*)

IV. STUDIO DI PARɔLE

Cristɔforo Colombo Christopher Columbus

albero tree
aria air
bagno bath
camera bedroom
casa house, home
cucina kitchen, cooking
fɔglia leaf
giardino garden
piacere *m.* pleasure; **per piacere** please [1]
pranzo dinner
prato lawn, meadow
sala room, hall; **sala da pranzo** dining room

salɔtto parlor, living room
scaffale *m.* bookshelf
stanza room [2]; **stanza da bagno** bathroom
studio study
via street

bɛllo beautiful, handsome, fine
cɔmodo comfortable
grande large, big, great
piccolo little, small
piɛno full

abitare [abito] to live, dwell
salire to go up, climb, get on [3]

molto *adv.* very, very much, a great deal

---

[1] Another way to say *please* is **per favore.**   [2] **Stanza** is any kind of room; **sala** is a rather large room or a room in a public building (school, library, railroad station, etc.).   [3] Conjugated with ɛssere when used intransitively.

V. CONVERSAZIONE

1. Dove abita Elena? 2. Dove abita Lei, signor . . .? 3. Dove abita Lei, signorina . . .? 4. La casa d'Elena è grande? 5. Quanti piani ha? 6. Che cosa vediamo nel giardino? 7. Che stanze ci sono al pian terreno? 8. Che stanze ci sono al piano superiore? 9. Che cosa c'è nello studio? 10. Dov'è la sala da pranzo? 11. La sala da pranzo è piccola? 12. Il salotto è dietro alla sala da pranzo? 13. Perchè sono belle le camere al piano superiore? 14. Di chi sono le camere? 15. Perchè Elena è contenta?

VI. ESERCIZI

A. Dare la corretta forma italiana delle parole in parentesi:

1. Il quaderno (*in which*) scrivo. 2. La grammatica (*that*) vedi. 3. La signora (*who*) ascolta. 4. L'alunna (*with whom*) studio. 5. I ragazzi (*whom*) noi guardiamo. 6. Il campanello (*that*) suona. 7. La carta (*of which*) parlate. 8. La conversazione (*that*) comincia. 9. La parola (*that*) Cristoforo non capisce. 10. Le sorelle (*to whom*) ho parlato.

B. 1. Completare con la seconda persona singolare dell'imperativo affermativo e negativo del verbo in parentesi:

1. (*pronunziare*) _____ questa frase. 2. (*essere*) _____ presente. 3. (*pulire*) _____ la lavagna. 4. (*correggere*) _____ questo sbaglio. 5. (*avere*) _____ molte cose. 6. (*finire*) _____ la lezione.

2. Completare con la prima e seconda persona plurale dell'imperativo affermativo del verbo in parentesi:

1. (*imparare*) _____ questa regola. 2. (*essere*) _____ contenti. 3. (*pronunziare*) _____ chiaramente. 4. (*aprire*) _____ i libri di lettura. 5. (*correggere*) _____ le frasi. 6. (*avere*) _____ tutti i libri.

3. Tradurre in italiano nelle forme Lei e **Loro:**

1. Show [me] a window. 2. Sell the bookshelf. 3. Don't be dissatisfied. 4. Have a rule. 5. Understand Laura. 6. Open the grammar.

C. Completare col partitivo:

1. Cancello _____ parole. 2. Ella compra _____ carta. 3. Mi mostri _____ gesso. 4. Ci sono _____ specchietti. 5. Ecco _____ inchiostro.

6. Avete _____ zii? 7. Vedo _____ quaderni. 8. Ecco _____ studentesse.
9. La stanza ha _____ scaffali. 10. Compro _____ carta sugante. 11. Ho
_____ campanelli. 12. Scrivo _____ nomi. 13. Ha _____ pezzi di carta.
14. Studiamo _____ regole. 15. Pronunziate _____ frasi.

D. Tradurre in italiano:

I

1. I like the house in which Lawrence lives very much.[1] 2. He lives
at (**in**) 12 Grant Street.[2] 3. In front of the house there is a garden
that is large and beautiful. 4. The house is new and the trees in (**di**)
the garden are small. 5. Enter, please. Look at the rooms. 6. Some
rooms are large, others are small. 7. Lawrence's bedroom is very
comfortable; it is on the ground floor, behind the study. 8. All other
bedrooms are on the upper floor. 9. Show me, please, where Lawrence's sister [3] is now. 10. She is in the living room with some other
girls.

II

1. We are in Helen's home. 2. She lives at (**in**) 9 Jackson Street.[2]
3. The house in which we are is not new, but it is large and comfortable. 4. Open [4] the dining room door, Laura, please. 5. It's a
fine room with large windows. 6. Look at Helen's brother; he is
standing before a window. 7. Don't speak aloud; he is reading some
papers. 8. Let's look at the garden from this window. 9. It's a small
garden, but it has a lawn and some large trees. 10. Where is Helen's
mother? — She is in the kitchen.

❧ *Lezione Ottava* ☙

I. ESERCIZIO DI PRONUNZIA

r:	tra-ma	tri-na	me-tro	so-pra	ve-ri-tà
	tre-no	tren-ta	dro-ga	ca-pre	ri-go-re
	dra-go	tre-di-ci	por-ta	ri-de-re	ri-di-re
	ora-rio	ri-tor-no	co-lo-re	ri-fa-re	ra-ri-tà

[1] An adverb usually follows the verb it modifies.   [2] Write out the number.   [3] Place *Lawrence's sister* at the end of the sentence.   [4] Use the **tu**
form of address in these sentences.

Note:

The Italian **r** is trilled, that is, pronounced with a vibration of the tongue against the alveolar ridge, i.e. the inner ridge of the gum at the base of the upper front teeth. The sound is more easily acquired by practicing first with words in which **r** comes immediately after **d** or **t**.

II. NOTE GRAMMATICALI

46.   **Possessives**

MASCULINE		FEMININE		MEANING
Sing.	*Pl.*	*Sing.*	*Pl.*	
il mio	i miei	la mia	le mie	my, mine
il tuo	i tuoi	la tua	le tue	thy, thine, your, yours
il suo	i suoi	la sua	le sue	his, her, hers, its, your, yours
il nostro	i nostri	la nostra	le nostre	our, ours
il vostro	i vostri	la vostra	le vostre	your, yours
il loro	i loro	la loro	le loro	their, theirs, your, yours

1. The possessives are usually preceded by the definite article.[1]

2. Note that the masculine plural forms of **mio, tuo,** and **suo** are irregular, that **loro** is invariable, but that otherwise possessives change their endings like adjectives in **–o.**

3. Note also that **il suo** is the possessive of **Ella** or **Lɛi; il loro,** of **Loro.**

47.   **Use of the Possessives**

1. la mia penna e la mia matita   *my pen and pencil*

The possessives are repeated before each noun to which they refer.

2. il loro vaso e il mio   *their vase and mine*

They may be used as adjectives or as pronouns.

3. il mio posto *or* il posto mio   *my place*

Usually both article and possessive precede the noun, but the article precedes and the possessive follows the noun if possession is emphasized.

---

[1] For important exceptions to this rule, see § **50,** p. 70.

4. il suo salotto *his* (or *her*, or *its*, or *your*) *parlor*

Possessive adjectives or pronouns agree in gender and number with the object possessed, not, as in English, with the person who possesses. **Suo** has thus four different meanings, but the context usually makes clear who the possessor is.

5.   Il mio amico prende il suo posto.   *My friend (m.) takes his place.*

    La mia amica prende il suo posto.   *My friend (f.) takes her place.*

But: Egli prende il posto di lei.   *He takes her place.*

Ella prende il posto di lui.   *She takes his place.*

When the possessor is not the subject of the sentence, ambiguity, if there be any, is avoided by the use of **di lui**, for *his;* **di lei**, for *her;* **di Lei** or **di Loro**, for *your:* and **di loro**, for *their.* These phrases usually follow the noun.

48.   **Definite Article before Titles**

Il signor Fantoni è in casa.   *Mr. Fantoni is at home.*

Scrivo alla contessa Bindi.   *I am writing to Countess Bindi.*

But: Buon giorno, signor professore.   *Good morning, Professor.*

A title followed by a proper name takes the definite article in Italian. The article is, however, omitted when the title is used in direct address, as in the last example.

49.   **Apocopation of Titles Ending in** *–ore*

Titles ending in **–ore** (all of masculine gender), such as **signore, professore,** etc., drop the final **e** when followed by a proper name or another title, as in the examples in the preceding section.

III. LETTURA

La tavola è apparecchiata

Abbiamo invitato a pranzo degli amici: il signore e la signora Corradini e la loro figlia Margherita.

Beatrice, che ora apparecchia la nostra tavola, è molto contenta perchè ama la sua piccola amica Margherita. Le due ragazze studiano alla stessa scuola.

La cameriera ha portato dalla cucina i piatti e i bicchieri, e ora li mette sulla credenza.

— Son ben puliti, Caterina? 5

— Sì, signorina, li ho lavati adesso.

Beatrice prende dalla credenza una nuova tovaglia, otto tovaglioli e l'argenteria. Poi stende la tovaglia sulla tavola e mette a ogni posto un piatto, un bicchiere, un cucchiaio, due forchette e due coltelli. Mette i tovaglioli a sinistra dei piatti. 10

— Dov'è il mio posto? — domando io.

— A destra della mia amica, — risponde Beatrice.

Ella sorride, e poi dice:

— E il mio è a sinistra del signor Corradini.

La tavola è apparecchiata, e Beatrice va in giardino a prendere 15 dei fiori. Poi ritorna, li mette in un vaso, e mette il vaso sulla tavola.

PROVERBIO

Trova un amico e troverai un tesoro.   *A good friend is a treasure.*

IV. STUDIO DI PAROLE

Margherita Margaret

argenteria silverware
bicchiere *m.* glass
cameriere *m.* butler, waiter, steward; **cameriera** maid
coltello knife
credenza buffet, sideboard
cucchiaio spoon
figlio son; **figlia** daughter
fiore *m.* flower
forchetta fork
piatto dish, plate
tavola table
tovaglia tablecloth
tovagliolo napkin
vaso vase

amare to love
apparecchiare [**apparecchio**] to prepare, set
invitare (**a**) to invite
lavare to wash
mettere to put, place
portare [**porto**] to bring, carry, wear (*clothes*)
sorridere to smile
stendere to spread, lay
va goes

adesso now
a destra at *or* to the right
a sinistra at *or* to the left
stamane *or* **stamani** this morning

V. CONVERSAZIONE

1. Chi abbiamo invitato a pranzo? 2. Perchè Beatrice è molto contenta? 3. Chi ha lavato i piatti? 4. La cameriera da dove ha portato i piatti e i bicchieri? 5. Dove li mette? 6. Che cosa prende Beatrice dalla credenza? 7. Che cosa stende sulla tavola? 8. Che cosa mette a ogni posto? 9. Dove mette i tovaglioli? 10. Che cosa domando io a Beatrice? 11. Che cosa risponde Beatrice? 12. Che dice ella poi? 13. Dove va Beatrice quando ha apparecchiato la tavola? 14. Perchè va in giardino? 15. Dove mette i fiori?

VI. ESERCIZI

A. Dare la corretta forma italiana delle parole in parentesi:

1. (*My*) finestre sono piccole. 2. (*Our*) alberi non hanno foglie. 3. (*Their*) prati sono verdi. 4. (*His*) calamaio è sul banco. 5. (*My*) camera è comoda. 6. La carta geografica è (*on his*) scaffale. 7. Ecco (*our*) stanza da bagno. 8. (*Her*) fratelli studiano. 9. Egli dà (*his*) penna stilografica a Cristoforo. 10. (*My*) zii non sono inglesi. 11. Pulisco (*their*) camera. 12. Ecco (*our*) sorelle. 13. (*Their*) lezioni sono difficili. 14. (*Its*) stanze sono molte. 15. (*My*) mano è piccola. 16. Ecco (*my*) riga. 17. (*Our*) grammatica è sulla scrivania. 18. Mi piace (*their*) salotto. 19. (*Its*) cucina è grande. 20. (*My*) coltelli sono nuovi.

B. 1. Tradurre in italiano:

1. My radio and his. 2. Their map and mine. 3. His finger and mine. 4. My notebooks and his. 5. Their teachers and hers. 6. Her classroom and ours.

2. Tradurre in tre modi usando il **tu,** il **voi** e il **Lei** (*Translate in three ways using the* **tu,** **voi,** *and* **Lei** *forms of address*):

1. Your house. 2. Your pencils. 3. Your ruler. 4. Your waiter. 5. Your ink. 6. Your hands. 7. Your questions. 8. Your maid.

C. Tradurre in italiano:

1. Professor Ruffino. 2. Mrs. Mancini. 3. Yes, sir. 4. Yes, Mr. Luciani. 5. Countess Narni is at home. 6. No, Professor. 7. No, Mr. Maruffi. 8. Mr. Maruffi is dissatisfied.

D. Tradurre in italiano:

I

1. I am in the kitchen [1] with Margaret.   2. We have washed our dishes and glasses.   3. We have cleaned the silverware.   4. Listen,[2] Mary, please! Carry everything into the dining room.   5. Then Margaret takes a tablecloth and some napkins from the buffet.   6. We lay the tablecloth on the table.   7. We set the table.   8. My place is to the right of Margaret; Beatrice's place is to the left of Paul.   9. At every place there is a knife, a fork, and a spoon.   10. Your flowers are in a vase on the table.

II

1. I have invited Mr. Thomas for (a) dinner.   2. I invited him this morning.   3. "Set [3] the table, please," Catherine says to our maid. 4. The maid has brought some flowers from our garden.   5. They are now in a vase on the buffet.   6. Mr. Thomas rings the bell, enters the house.[4]   7. While the maid sets the table, Catherine and I are with Mr. Thomas in the living room.   8. We are talking before one of the windows.   9. "I like your garden," he says. "The lawn is very green." 10. From the window we see the garden and our street.

❧ *Lezione Nona* ☙

I. ESERCIZIO DI PRONUNZIA

s	**s**	**z**	**z**
se-ta	u-so	zi-o	zɛ-lo
se-ra	va-so	tɛr-zo	zɛ-bra
ca-sa	rɔ-sa	stan-za	bron-zo
san-to	sbar-co	de-cɛn-za	zan-za-ra

English equivalents:

	s in *sand*	*s* in *rose*	*ts*	*dz*

[1] See footnote 2, p. 61.   [2] Use the **tu** form of address.   [3] Use the **voi** form of address.   [4] See footnote 2, p. 61, and remember that **entrare** is always intransitive.

II. NOTE GRAMMATICALI

50.   Possessives with Nouns Denoting Relationship

As a general rule (*see* § 46, 1, p. 65), the Italian possessives are preceded by the definite article. Note, however, the following:

mia sorella *or* la sorella mia	*my sister*
le mie sorelle	*my sisters*
la mia buona sorella	*my good sister*
la mia sorellina	*my little sister*
la loro sorella	*their sister*
la sua nonna	*his grandmother*

No article is used when the possessive precedes a noun denoting a degree of relationship, provided that:

(*a*) the noun is singular,
(*b*) not accompanied by another adjective,
(*c*) nor modified by a suffix.

The article is not omitted when the possessive follows the noun (emphatic position), when it is **loro,** or when the noun denoting a degree of relationship is one of the following:

babbo	*daddy*	nonno	*grandfather*
mamma	*mamma*	nonna	*grandmother*

Of the examples given above, only the first one (**mia sorella**) meets all the conditions implied in this rule.

51.   Some Diminutives

una ragazzina	*a little girl*	i fratellini	*the little brothers*
una cameretta	*a small bedroom*	delle cosette	*some little things*

The original meaning of a noun is often modified in Italian by means of a suffix. The suffixes −**ino** and −**etto,** both of which convey the idea of *little*, *small*, are by far the most common. A noun to which (after dropping its final vowel) one of these suffixes is added is called a *diminutive.*

The choice of the suffix depends on euphony and current usage.

52. Present Indicative of the Irregular Verbs of the First Conjugation

There are only four irregular verbs in the first conjugation: an-dare, *to go;* dare, *to give;* fare, *to do* or *make;* and stare, *to stay* or *be.*

andare	dare	fare	stare
I go, etc.	*I give, etc.*	*I do* or *make, etc.*	*I stay* or *am, etc.*
vado *or* vo	do	faccio *or* fo	sto
vai	dai	fai	stai
va	dà	fa	sta
andiamo	diamo	facciamo	stiamo
andate	date	fate	state
vanno	danno	fanno	stanno

1. Note that the 3rd person singular of dare is accented. The accent serves to distinguish this verbal form from the preposition da.

2. The verb stare implies a temporary condition, and is used in such phrases as: Come state? *How are you (now)?* Stiamo bene. *We are well.*

III. LETTURA

La famiglia di Roberto

— Buon giorno, signor Giannini! Come state?

— Sto bene, Riccardo, grazie. E tu come stai? Come stanno i tuoi genitori?

— Anch'io sto bene, grazie, e anche il mio babbo e la mia mamma stanno in buona salute. Andate a casa, signor Giannini?   5

— Sì. Arrivederci, Riccardo.

— Arrivederci, signor Giannini.

Il signor Giannini è il padre del mio amico Roberto, con cui faccio spesso le mie lezioni. La loro famiglia è di nove persone: Roberto, i suoi genitori, tre fratelli, una sorellina, il nonno e una   10 giovane zia.

Uno dei fratelli di Roberto è già quasi un uomo, e studia all'università; gli altri due sono piccoli e vanno alla scuola elementare; e la sorellina è una bella bambina che adesso comincia a parlare.

Il nonno è vecchio. Egli è il padre della madre di Roberto, e abita con la famiglia Giannini perchè sua moglie è morta.

5 La zia del mio amico è una sorella di suo padre. È una buona donna, giovane e bella, che mi piace perchè sorride spesso. Essa ama i suoi nipoti e tutta la famiglia.

Anch'io ho una zia, ma mia zia non abita in casa nostra. Essa ha una figlia, la mia bionda cugina Bianca, e un figlio, il mio cuginetto 10 Lorenzo. Suo marito è uno dei fratelli del mio babbo.

PROVERBIO

Chi cerca, trova.   *He who seeks, finds.*

IV. STUDIO DI PAROLE

Bianca Blanche
Roberto Robert

bambino, –a baby
cugino, –a cousin
donna woman
famiglia family [1]
genitore *m.* parent
giorno day; **buon giorno** good day, good morning
marito husband
moglie *f.* wife
nipote *m. or f.* nephew, niece, grandson, granddaughter
persona person [2]
salute *f.* health

università university
uomo man

biondo blond
buono good
elementare elementary
giovane young
morto dead
vecchio old

arrivederci good-bye, so long
come how, as
già already
grazie thanks
quasi almost
spesso often

V. CONVERSAZIONE

1. Con chi parla Riccardo? 2. Che cosa dice Riccardo al signor Giannini? 3. Che risponde il signor Giannini? 4. Dove va il

---

[1] The word *family* does not imply, of course, any specific degree of relationship. [2] Even though **persona** is feminine, it may refer to a man or a woman.

signor Giannini? 5. Chi è Roberto? 6. Quante persone ha la famiglia di Roberto? 7. Chi sono queste persone? 8. Dove studiano i fratelli di Roberto? 9. Chi è la sorellina di Roberto? 10. È giovane il suo nonno? 11. Perchè abita egli con la famiglia Giannini? 12. Chi è la zia di Roberto? 13. Dov'è il suo nonno, signor ...? 15. Ha dei cugini, signorina ...?

VI. ESERCIZI

A. Dare la corretta forma italiana delle parole in parentesi:

1. (*My*) fratello sorride. 2. (*Your*) babbo è giovane. 3. (*Our*) zio è inglese. 4. (*Their*) padre parte oggi. 5. (*His*) nipote è quasi un uomo. 6. (*His*) cuginetta è bionda. 7. Ella studia (*with her*) cugino. 8. (*My*) nonna è vecchia. 9. (*Their*) madre ascolta. 10. (*Your*) sorelle sono piccole. 11. Amo (*my*) fratelli. 12. (*Our*) cugina pronunzia chiaramente. 13. Egli va (*with his*) nonno. 14. Invito (*her*) cugina. 15. Correggo (*our*) piccolo fratello. 16. Maria parla (*of her*) zio. 17. Abito (*with my*) genitori. 18. Parliamo (*of their*) zii. 19. (*His*) cugina è bella. 20. Prendo i fiori (*of my*) madre.

B. Tradurre:

1. il mio fratellino. 2. una frasetta. 3. la sorellina. 4. due regolette. 5. i cuginetti. 6. dei ragazzini. 7. una casetta. 8. lo scaffalino. 9. il cucchiaino. 10. un dizionarietto.

C. 1. Coniugare nel presente dell'indicativo:

1. Non andare a casa.
2. Stare in salotto.
3. Fare un pranzo.
4. Fare uno sbaglio.
5. Dare un coltello.
6. Andare in cucina.

2. Completare col presente del verbo in parentesi:

1. (*andare*) Essi _____ in sala da pranzo. 2. (*fare*) Voi non _____ bene. 3. (*dare*) Io _____ una penna stilografica a Margherita. 4. (*stare*) I miei cugini _____ nello studio. 5. (*dare*) Tu _____ una gomma a Cristoforo. 6. (*andare*) Io _____ nella stanza da bagno. 7. (*fare*) Noi _____ tutto. 8. (*stare*) Voi _____ in buona salute. 9. (*dare*) Noi _____ un pranzo a molte persone. 10. (*andare*) Bianca _____ nel nostro giardino. 11. (*fare*) Io _____ come Roberto. 12. (*stare*) Tu _____ coi bambini. 13. (*dare*) Non tutti gli alberi _____ dei fiori. 14. (*stare*) Beatrice _____

davanti alla finestra. 15. (*andare*) Lei _____ con suo marito. 16. (*fare*) Esse _____ le loro lezioni. 17. (*stare*) Io _____ alla tua sinistra. 18. (*andare*) Noi non _____. 19. (*dare*) Loro _____ dei fiori. 20. (*fare*) Chi lo _____ ?

D. Tradurre in italiano:

I

1. The bell rings, and here is [1] Professor Minto. 2. He enters the living room and smiles at every one. 3. Good day, ladies and gentlemen! How are [2] you? 4. He is an old friend of my father, and Blanche, his niece, goes to school with my little sister. 5. The two girls are in [the] garden now. 6. But I see many other persons in this room. 7. There is Mrs. De Vitis, who is having [3] some conversation with my grandmother. 8. There is a gentleman with his wife and their baby. 9. If I am not mistaken, [4] the two boys with whom Mary is talking are her cousins. 10. I don't see them often in this house.

II

1. My dad's friend has a young niece, Blanche. 2. She is blond and is a good girl, goes to our school, but does not study a great deal. 3. Her parents are dead; that's (ecco) why she lives with her [5] uncle and aunt. 4. My little cousin Margaret loves her. 5. The two girls are not in the living room now. 6. Who is the gentleman who is saying good-bye to your husband? 7. He is an old friend of my family. 8. What does he do? — He studies at the university. 9. While we are having [3] this conversation, the bell rings. 10. Then some other friends enter the room, a gentleman with two ladies.

[1] Pointing is implied in this case.   [2] Use the **voi** form.   [3] Use the verb **fare.**   [4] See Vocabulary.   [5] See § 47, 1, p. 65.

✦ *Lezione Decima* ✦

I. ESERCIZIO DI PRONUNZIA

gn:	se-gno	o-gni	ba-gno	ca-gna	de-gno
	pu-gni	le-gno	vi-gna	ra-gno	sta-gno
gli:	e-gli	a-gli	gi-gli	fi-glia	va-glia
	mo-glie	pa-glia	me-glio	fɔ-glie	fa-mi-glia

Note:

1. Both **gn** and **gli** are uttered as single sounds.

2. Pronounce **gn** like *ni* in *onion*, but with the tip of the tongue against the lower teeth.

3. The sound **gli** is somewhat similar to that of *lli* in *billiards*, but with the tip of the tongue against the gum ridge above the upper teeth. When no vowel follows **gli,** the **i** is pronounced.

II. NOTE GRAMMATICALI

53.   **Position of Adjectives**

1. la lingua italiana — *the Italian language*
   una donna cattolica — *a Catholic woman*
   l'inchiostro rosso — *the red ink*
   la tavola rotonda — *the round table*
   la lezione seguente — *the following lesson*
   una ragazza bellina — *a pretty girl*
   una stanza molto grande — *a very large room*

The normal position of an attributive adjective [1] is after the noun. This is especially the case with those adjectives which ascribe to the noun a distinctive quality, such as nationality, religion, color, shape, etc., and with verbal adjectives, such as **seguente** (from **seguire,** *to follow*). All adjectives modified by a suffix or by an adverb (such as **molto**) regularly follow the noun.

2.   una bella cosa — *a beautiful thing*
         un giovane studente — *a young student*

[1] Other kinds of adjectives usually precede the noun. This is particularly true with numerals and such adjectives implying quantity as **molto, poco** (*little*), **parecchio** (*a lot;* pl. *several*), **assai** (*enough, much*), etc.

Some adjectives of very common use generally precede the noun, provided they are not modified by a suffix or an adverb. Such, among others, are:

bɛllo	beautiful	giovane	young
brutto	ugly	vɛcchio	old
buɔno	good	nuɔvo	new
cattivo	bad	antico	ancient
grande	big, large	lungo	long
piccolo	little, small	brɛve	brief, short

3. Ɛ̀ un ragazzo cattivo.   *He is a bad boy.*
Pɔrto l'abito nuɔvo.   *I am wearing the new suit.*

But even the adjectives just listed follow the noun
(*a*) if used emphatically;
(*b*) if used in order to distinguish one thing from others of the same kind.

4. un pɔvero ragazzo   *a poor boy* (= an *unfortunate* boy)
un ragazzo pɔvero   *a poor boy* (= a boy who is *not rich*)
la bianca neve   *the white snow*
le verdi colline   *the green hills*

On the other hand, an adjective that normally follows the noun may precede it
(*a*) if prompted by emotion or used in a sense that is not literal;
(*b*) if it is an adjective that designates a characteristic color.

54.   Reflexive Verbs

1. A verb the object of which is the same person as its subject is called a reflexive verb. Any transitive verb may be made reflexive by the use of one of the following pronouns:

mi	myself	ci	ourselves
ti	yourself	vi	yourself, yourselves
si	himself, herself, itself, oneself, yourself	si	themselves, yourselves

The pronoun **vi** may mean *yourself* or *yourselves*, depending on whether one or more persons are addressed in the **voi** form. The pronoun **si,** being of the 3rd person (singular or plural), is used with the meaning of *yourself* or *yourselves* in the **Lɛi** or **Loro** forms of direct address.

2. Io mi diverto.	*I amuse myself.*
Egli non si divɛrte.	*He is not having a good time.*
Divertirsi.	*To amuse oneself, have a good time.*

These pronouns (like the object pronouns **lo, la, li, le,** which we have already studied) are *conjunctive;* that is, they are used only in connection with the verb. Normally they immediately precede the verb of which they are the object (1st and 2nd examples), but when the verb is an infinitive (3rd example) they follow the verb and are written as one word with it. Note, however, that in this case the infinitive loses its final **e.** Note also, from the 2nd example, that if the verb is negative, **non** precedes the conjunctive pronoun.

3.	Io m'alzo.	*I get up.*
	Egli s'alza.	*He gets up.*
	Noi ci alziamo.	*We get up.*
	Noi c'invitiamo.	*We invite ourselves.*

Certain verbs, as **alzarsi,** *to get up,* are reflexive in Italian while not so in English. Note from the examples that the reflexive pronouns may drop the vowel and take an apostrophe before a verb beginning with a vowel; **ci,** however, elides only before **e** or **i.**

4. Egli s'ɛ divertito.	*He amused* (or *has amused*) *himself.*
Noi ci siamo divertiti.	*We amused* (or *have amused*) *ourselves.*

Reflexive verbs are conjugated in the perfect tenses with **ɛssere,** and the past participle agrees in gender and number with the subject.

55.   *Non . . . che*

Non abbiamo che due zii.	*We have only two uncles.*
Non vedo che un albero.	*I see only one tree.*

The English *only* is often rendered in Italian by placing **non** before the verb and **che** [1] after it.

---

[1] In this case **che** is a conjunction, the usual translation of which is *that* or *than.*

III. LETTURA

La mia cameretta

Il mio amico Lorenzo Miragli è venuto poco fa, insieme coi suoi genitori, a visitare la mia famiglia.

Mentre il signore e la signora Scrugli sono in salotto e parlano con mio padre e con mia madre, Lorenzo e io ci alziamo, ci scu-
5 siamo, e saliamo al piano superiore. Il mio amico desidera di vedere i nuovi mobili che i miei genitori hanno comprati per la mia cameretta.

— Di che legno sono? — domanda, mentr'io vado avanti per la scala.

10   — Di noce.

Apro la porta, entriamo.

La mia camera è piccola, ma è bella e allegra perchè il sole entra per due finestre che danno sul [1] giardino.

Mostro a Lorenzo ogni cosa: i mobili, i quadri alle pareti, il
15 tappeto grigio e rosso sul pavimento. A destra del letto ho un tavolino [2]; a sinistra, una poltrona verde. La scrivania è davanti a una delle finestre; l'armadio, che ha un grande specchio, è in un angolo. Poi c'è un cassettone, c'è uno scaffale, ci sono due sedie.

20   — Bello, eh?

— Sì, tutto è bello e comodo, — dice il mio amico.

Ci sediamo e parliamo di molte cose: dell'università e del professor Venturi, d'un libro inglese che leggiamo in classe, e anche d'una studentessa bionda che abita in via Lincoln e che pensa a
25 divertirsi, non a studiare.

La nostra conversazione non finisce che quando il signor Scrugli chiama suo figlio per andar via.

PROVERBIO

Giovane ozioso, vecchio bisognoso.   *Lazy youth makes needy old age.*

---

[1] The expression **dare su,** used only in connection with windows, means *to face:* try to remember it.   [2] Note this masculine diminutive of the feminine **tavola.**

CATHEDRAL AND LEANING TOWER, PISA

PALAZZO COMUNALE, PERUGIA

FAÇADE OF THE CAMPANILE OF SAN GIOVANNI EVANGELISTA, RAVENNA

IV. STUDIO DI PAROLE

angolo corner
armadio closet, wardrobe
cassettone *m.* chest of drawers
legno wood
lɛtto bed
mɔbile *m.* piece of furniture; i
mɔbili the furniture
noce *f.* walnut; *m.* walnut tree
parete *f.* wall (*of a room*)
pavimento floor [1]
poltrona armchair
quadro picture, painting
scala stairs
sɛdia chair
spɛcchio mirror
tappeto rug, carpet

allegro gay, jolly
grigio gray

rosso red

desiderare (di) [desidero] to desire, wish
pensare (a) [pɛnso] to think;
pɛnso a Ɛlena I am thinking of
Helen [2]
scusare to excuse
sedere to sit, be seated; sedersi
sit down
venire (a) to come [3]; *irr. past part.*
venuto
visitare [visito] to visit

avanti *or* prima (*adverbs*) before,
first; prima di (*prep.*) before [4]
fa ago; poco fa a short time ago
insiɛme together
via away

V. CONVERSAZIONE

1. Chi sono i genitori di Lorɛnzo? 2. In che stanza sono essi
seduti? 3. Dove vanno i giovani amici mentre i loro genitori
parlano in salɔtto? 4. Che cɔsa fanno essi prima d'andar via?
5. Che cɔsa vanno a vedere i due amici? 6. Chi va avanti per
la scala? 7. Perchè è bɛlla la cameretta dell'amico di Lorɛnzo?
8. Di che legno sono i mɔbili? 9. Che cɔsa c'è sul pavimento?
10. Che cɔsa c'è a dɛstra del lɛtto? 11. Che cɔsa c'è a sinistra
del lɛtto? 12. Che cɔsa c'è in un angolo della camera? 13. Che
altro c'è nella camera? 14. Di che cɔsa parlano i due amici?
15. Quando finisce la loro conversazione?

---

[1] Do not confuse this word with **piano,** which also means *floor,* but in
the sense of *story.* [2] Note carefully the use of **a** after the verb **pensare.**
[3] Conjugated with ɛssere. [4] **Avanti** and the already studied preposition
davanti a refer to *place;* the adverb **prima** and the preposition **prima di**
refer to *time.*

VI. ESERCIZI

A. Dare il contrario di (*Give the opposite of*):

1. buono	2. facile	3. nuovo
lungo	bello	cattivo
grande	breve	giovane
vecchio	assente	presente

B. Usare l'aggettivo in parentesi mettendolo, secondo le regole, davanti o dopo il nome, e cambiare l'articolo o il partitivo, se ciò è necessario (*Use the adjective in parentheses, placing it, according to rules, before or after the noun and changing the article or the partitive, if necessary*):

Example: (buono) Degli studenti. = Dei buoni studenti.

1. (contento) Delle ragazze.
2. (breve) Una lezione.
3. (inglese) Dei libri.
4. (piccolo) Dei pezzi.
5. (bello) Una signorina.
6. (cattivo) Un amico.
7. (rosso) Delle matite.
8. (comodo) Una poltrona.
9. (grande) Degli alberi.
10. (nuovo) Lo studente.
11. (difficile) Le regole.
12. (italiano) Una donna.
13. (grigio) Un tappeto.
14. (brutto) Dei quadri.

C. 1. Coniugare nel presente perfetto:

1. Alzarsi da tavola.
2. Divertirsi insieme.
3. Scusarsi con ognuno.
4. Sedersi alla scrivania.
5. Pulirsi molto bene.
6. Guardarsi nello specchio.

2. Usare gli stessi verbi in brevi frasi.

D. Tradurre in italiano:

I

1. We went [1] to the upper floor of my house. 2. Mr. Moretti, who came only a short time ago, wishes to see my little bedroom. 3. I go first [2] and open the door. 4. Mr. Moretti enters my bedroom. 5. My furniture is not beautiful, but it is good and comfortable. 6. My friend and I sit down; he sits in the green armchair, I, in the red [one].

---

[1] Use the verb **salire**. [2] An adverb of place.

7. As you see, Mr. Moretti, I have a bed, a chest of drawers, a desk, and some chairs.   8. At this desk your son and I do our lessons together.   9. On this little shelf I have my books.   10. This is my new English-Italian and Italian-English dictionary.

II

1. Mrs. Moretti is a young Italian friend of my mother's who visits her often.   2. The two women are now in my bedroom to [1] look at my new furniture.   3. I do my lessons at this desk, Mrs. Moretti.   4. "I like the rug [2] you have on the floor," she says.   5. Then she looks at the pictures on (a) the walls, at my little table, at the chest of drawers, at the large bookshelf.   6. On the desk I have many things: pen and ink, pencils, some paper, a ruler, and my Italian grammar.   7. In a gray vase there are only three red flowers.   8. "Here is a comfortable chair," says Mrs. Moretti.   9. Then she goes to the closet that is in a corner behind the armchair.   10. She is now looking at herself in the long mirror.

❖ Lezione Undicesima ❖

I. ESERCIZIO DI PRONUNZIA

	1	2	3	4	5
Consonanti	ε-be	ε-co	fa-ce	ca-di	tu-fo
doppie:	εb-be	εc-co	fac-ce	cad-di	tuf-fo
	Giu-ba	ba-co	ca-cio	ri-da	bu-fa
	giub-ba	Bac-co	cac-cio	rid-da	buf-fa

Read carefully the remarks on the pronunciation of the double consonants in the Introduction (§ 7, p. 6).

Your instructor will first read to you, column after column, the words listed: listen to him very attentively, and mark the difference in sound between the words having a single consonant and those having a double consonant. Particular care has been taken

[1] Learn to recognize when the English *to* stands for *in order to*.   [2] What word is missing here?

to offer examples in which the only difference in pronunciation between two words is the one on which you are expected to drill by contrast.

After reading the words alone, your instructor will ask the class to pronounce them after him; finally, you will be asked to pronounce them by yourself.

II. NOTE GRAMMATICALI

56.   **Future**

I	II	III
I shall buy, etc.	*I shall sell, etc.*	*I shall finish, etc.*
comprer ɔ	vender ɔ	finir ɔ
comprer **ai**	vender **ai**	finir **ai**
comprer **à**	vender **à**	finir **à**
comprer **emo**	vender **emo**	finir **emo**
comprer **ete**	vender **ete**	finir **ete**
comprer **anno**	vender **anno**	finir **anno**

1. The infinitive, minus the final vowel, is used as a stem in forming this tense; a peculiarity of the first conjugation is, however, that the **a** of the infinitive ending –**are** changes to **e**: **comprare** = **comprer–**.

2. The endings of the future are the same for all Italian verbs.

3.   Partiremo presto.   *We are going to leave soon.*
     But: Ora mi vesto.   *Now I am going to dress.*

Normally the Italian future renders also the English *to be going to;* if, however, the sentence is introduced by an adverb implying present time (**ora** or **adɛsso**), the present tense is preferred.

57.   **Future of the Auxiliary Verbs**

avere		ɛssere	
I shall have, etc.		*I shall be, etc.*	
avrɔ	avremo	sarɔ	saremo
avrai	avrete	sarai	sarete
avrà	avranno	sarà	saranno

58.   **Use of the Future**

1. Quando arriverò a casa, studierò.   *When I arrive home, I shall study.*

Se Clara leggerà questa lettera, che dirà?   *If Clara reads this letter, what will she say?*

Besides being used as in English, the future is also used in Italian in subordinate clauses referring to the future that are introduced either by a conjunction of time or by **se,** *if.*

2. Questo caffè sarà troppo dolce.   *This coffee is probably too sweet.*

The future is often used in Italian to express what is probable in the present (*Future of Probability*).[1]

59.   **Nouns and Adjectives in** *–io*

SINGULAR	PLURAL
il nostro studio, *our study*	i nostri studi
il vaso grigio, *the gray vase*	i vasi grigi
But: mio zio, *my uncle*	i miei zii

Nouns and adjectives ending in **–io** form their plural simply by dropping the final **o,** unless the preceding **i** is stressed (as in **zio**), in which case the plural ending is **–ii.**

III. LETTURA

Domani

Domani Roberto s'alzerà presto per studiare. Egli non ha ancora finito di leggere un libro per la lezione d'inglese.

Mentre sarà occupato a fare un bagno e a vestirsi, la sua mamma, che s'alza prima degli altri della famiglia, sarà in cucina a preparare la colazione.   5

La colazione di Roberto è molto semplice: della frutta, del pane tostato con burro e marmellata, e una buona tazza di caffè con latte. Egli prende il suo caffè con poco zucchero perchè lo desidera quasi amaro; sua sorella Margherita, invece, lo prende molto dolce.

---

[1] Probability in the future must be expressed with the adverb **probabilmente.** Probability in the past may be expressed with the future perfect, a tense that will be studied in a later lesson (§ **100,** p. 149).

Subìto dopo la colazione, Roberto studierà. Finirà le sue lezioni e, se il professore lo chiamerà, risponderà bene.

Dopo la scuola, egli ritornerà a casa. Domani suo padre sarà assente dal pranzo perchè sarà occupato in città.

5 Come in tutti i pomeriggi, anche nel pomeriggio di domani Roberto uscirà a fare una lunga passeggiata o a divertirsi con gli amici.

Ritornerà a casa a sera e, dopo cena, salirà in camera,[1] si sederà alla sua scrivania e si preparerà per le classi del giorno dopo.

PROVERBIO

L'ozio è il padre di tutti i vizi.   *Idleness is the root of all vices.*

IV. STUDIO DI PAROLE

burro butter

caffè *m.* coffee; café

cena supper

città city, town; **in città** in *or* to the city, downtown

colazione *f.* breakfast, lunch [2]; **fare colazione** to have (*or* eat) breakfast (*or* lunch)

frutta *or* **frutto** (*irr. pl.* **le frutta**) fruit

latte *m.* milk

marmellata marmalade, jam

pane *m.* bread; **pane tostato** toast

passeggiata walk, ride; **fare una passeggiata** to take a walk, take a ride

pomeriggio afternoon; **nel pomeriggio** in the afternoon

sera evening; **a sera** in the evening

tazza cup

zucchero sugar

amaro bitter

dolce sweet

poco *or* **po'** little, not much; (*pl.*) few

semplice simple

fare un bagno to take a bath

occupare [occupo] to occupy; **occupato** busy

preparare to prepare [3]

uscire to go out [4]

vestire [vesto] to dress; **vestirsi** dress (*oneself*)

ancora still, yet

domani tomorrow

invece instead, on the contrary

presto soon, early, quickly

---

[1] Note this idiomatic expression.   [2] Sometimes *breakfast* is called **prima colazione** to distinguish it from **colazione**, *lunch;* but when the meaning is obvious, it is better not to add that extra word.   [3] Use this word, not **apparecchiare**, in the general sense of *to prepare*.   [4] Conjugated with **essere**.

V. CONVERSAZIONE

1. Quando s'alzerà presto Roberto? 2. Perchè s'alzerà presto?
3. Come sarà egli occupato quando s'alzerà? 4. Quando s'alza
la sua mamma? 5. Dove sarà occupata la sua mamma mentre
Roberto si vestirà? 6. Che cosa prende Roberto per colazione?
7. Come prende il caffè? 8. Come lo prende, invece, sua sorella
Margherita? 9. Quando studierà Roberto? 10. Che cosa finirà
egli? 11. Dove ritornerà Roberto dopo scuola? 12. Chi sarà
assente dal pranzo? 13. Perchè sarà assente suo padre? 14. Perchè uscirà Roberto nel pomeriggio di domani? 15. Come sarà
egli occupato, a sera?

VI. ESERCIZI

A. Coniugare nel futuro:

1. Capire ogni cosa.	4. Divertirsi molto.
2. Sedersi a tavola.	5. Lavare i bicchieri.
3. Essere scontento.	6. Prendere i mobili.

B. Completare col futuro del verbo in parentesi:

1. (*ascoltare*) Io _____ la nonna. 2. (*essere*) Essi _____ presto a casa.
3. (*sorridere*) Chi non _____ a queste parole? 4. (*scusarsi*) Noi _____
_____ subito. 5. (*avere*) Voi _____ dell'argenteria. 6. (*stendere*) Tu _____
la tovaglia. 7. (*vestirsi*) Io _____ _____ prima di Cristoforo. 8. (*essere*)
Chi _____ a casa? 9. (*rispondere*) Voi _____ chiaramente. 10. (*entrare*)
Lei _____ insieme con gli altri. 11. (*sedersi*) Chi _____ _____ nella poltrona? 12. (*mettere*) Lei ed Elena _____ i libri su questo nuovo scaffale.
13. (*essere*) Esse non _____ presenti a scuola. 14. (*apparecchiare*) Tu
e io _____ la tavola per la colazione di domani. 15. (*aprire*) Lei, per
favore, non _____ la finestra.

C. Tradurre in italiano:

1. Some mistakes. 2. If he departs tomorrow. 3. Twenty spoons.
4. They are probably at home. 5. Their examples. 6. Some mirrors.
7. Tomorrow, when she rings the bell. 8. Three dictionaries. 9. He
is going to write soon. 10. Our old parents. 11. Now I am going to
call him. 12. These closets.

D. Tradurre in italiano:

I

1. Now I am going to take a bath; then I shall dress. 2. The maid is preparing our breakfast in the kitchen. 3. We shall sit at [the] table in the dining room. 4. I shall take some fruit (*pl.*), some toast with butter, and a cup of coffee. 5. You (**tu**) will put some marmalade on your toast and take some milk. 6. Then we shall get up from [the] table and get ready [1] to (**ad**) go to school. 7. Today's lessons are simple and easy. 8. We shall be busy the whole day. 9. We shall return home [2] in the evening. 10. After supper we are going to study.

II

1. Robert and his brother are having [their] breakfast. 2. "This coffee is bitter," says Robert. "I shall take another lump [3] of sugar." 3. What will you have [4]? — I shall have [4] some toast with butter and jam. 4. When the two boys finish their [5] breakfast they will get up from [the] table. 5. Robert is not satisfied this morning because he has not prepared his lessons. 6. He will not answer well if the professor calls on him. 7. His brother, on the contrary, is well prepared. 8. After school the boys will return home.[2] 9. In the afternoon, first they are going to study, then they will amuse themselves. 10. They will go out again in the evening to [6] take a walk.

❧ *Lezione Dodicesima* ☙

I. ESERCIZIO DI PRONUNZIA

	1	2	3	4	5
Consonanti doppie:	gra-vi	a-gio	be-la	fu-mo	pe-na
	ag-gra-vi	ag-gio	bɛl-la	fum-mo	pen-na
	gan-cio	rɛ-gia	pa-la	sa-re-mo	nɔ-no
	ag-gan-cio	reg-gia	pal-la	sa-rem-mo	nɔn-no

[1] Same as *prepare ourselves.* [2] *Home* in the sense of *in* or *to the house* is **a casa.** [3] Same as *piece.* [4] Use the verb **prɛndere.** [5] Replace the possessive with the definite article. [6] See footnote 1, p. 81.

6	7	8	9	10
pa-pa	a-ra	ca-sa	fa-to	a-vi
pap-pa	ar-ra	cas-sa	fat-to	hav-vi
ru-pe	ca-ro	ri-sa	bru-to	sta-vi
rup-pe	car-ro	ris-sa	brut-to	stav-vi

Follow the instructions given for the same type of exercise in the preceding lesson.

II. NOTE GRAMMATICALI

60. **Masculine Nouns in −*a***

SINGULAR	PLURAL
il programma, *the program*	i programmi
il profeta, *the prophet*	i profeti

Not all nouns ending in −a are of feminine gender. A certain number of them, ending in −**ca,** −**ga,** −**ma,** or −**ta,** and mostly of Greek origin, are masculine and form their plural in −**i.**

61. **Nouns in −*a* of Both Genders**

SINGULAR	PLURAL
il *or* la suicida, *the suicide*	i suicidi, le suicide
il *or* la pianista, *the pianist*	i pianisti, le pianiste

Nouns ending in −**cida** (of which there are very few) and nouns ending in −**ista** (which are very common and usually denote professions) are of both genders and have a masculine plural in −**i** and a feminine plural in −**e.**

62. **The Verbs *dovere, potere,* and *volere***

The verbs **dovere,** *to be obliged,* **potere,** *to be able,* and **volere,** *to want,* have the following irregular present indicative:

I must, am obliged, have to, etc.	*I can, may, am able, etc.*	*I want, etc.*
devo (*or* debbo)	posso	voglio
devi	puoi	vuoi
deve	può	vuole
dobbiamo	possiamo	vogliamo
dovete	potete	volete
devono (*or* debbono)	possono	vogliono

63.   **The Verbs *dire* and *uscire***

The verbs **dire**, *to say* (a contraction of the obsolete **dicere**), and **uscire** (also **escire**), *to go out*, are conjugated in the present indicative as follows:

I say, etc.		*I go out, etc.*	
dico	diciamo	ɛsco	usciamo
dici	dite	ɛsci	uscite
dice	dicono	ɛsce	ɛscono

III. LETTURA

Professioni

Tutti dobbiamo lavorare, dicono. Adɛsso che siamo studɛnti il nɔstro lavoro è lo studio; ma arriverà prɛsto il giorno in cui usciremo dall'università per cominciare una professione.

Il mio amico Farucci, che è figlio d'un farmacista, dice che vuɔl
5 prɛndere la professione di suo padre. Suo padre ha una bɛlla farmacia in via Pontano.

Cantɛlli vuɔl fare l'avvocato, e studia il latino perchè questa lingua è molto utile negli studi di legge. Tovɛllo sarà scrittore — egli dice — e forse anche poɛta; per questo, a scuɔla, noi lo
10 chiamiamo Dante Alighiɛri. Ogni giorno egli è presɛnte in classe, e studia molto, specialmente la lingua italiana.

Spesso io mi domando quale professione prenderɔ.

Mio padre fa il mɛdico, ma io non dɛvo diventare mɛdico per questo, anche perchè mio fratɛllo Paolo già studia medicina
15 all'università, e mio cugino Cristɔforo fa il dentista. Mio padre e mia madre dicono che ognuno dɛve prɛndere la professione che vuɔle.

Pɔsso fare l'artista, diventare pittore, o scultore, o musicista, ma mia madre dice che gli artisti sono quasi tutti pɔveri e che
20 dɛvono lavorar molto e avere molto talɛnto e molta fortuna se vɔgliono arrivare a farsi un nome.

La professione d'artista non è facile, lo capisco, ma è così bɛlla! E pɔi, dico io, quale professione è facile?

PROVERBIO

Non c'è rosa senza spine.   *There is no rose without thorns.*

IV. STUDIO DI PAROLE

artista *m. or f.* artist
avvocato lawyer
dentista *m. or f.* dentist
farmacia pharmacy, drugstore
farmacista *m. or f.* druggist
fortuna fortune, good luck
lavoro work
legge *f.* law
medicina medicine
medico physician
musicista *m. or f.* musician
pittore *m.* painter
poeta *m.* poet
professione *f.* profession
scrittore *m.* writer
scultore *m.* sculptor

talento talent

latino Latin; **il latino** *or* **la lingua latina** the Latin language [1]
quale which, what
utile useful

arrivare to arrive [2]
diventare (divento) to become [2]
fare l'avvocato, il medico, *etc.* to be a lawyer, a physician, etc.[3]
lavorare to work

così so, thus
forse perhaps
specialmente especially

V. CONVERSAZIONE

1. Che cosa dicono che dobbiamo fare? 2. Qual è adesso il nostro lavoro? 3. Quale giorno arriverà presto? 4. Perchè Farucci dice che vuol fare il farmacista? 5. Dov'è la farmacia di suo padre? 6. Che cosa vuol fare Cantelli? 7. Perchè Cantelli studia il latino? 8. Che cosa vuol fare Tovello? 9. Come lo chiamano a scuola? 10. Quale professione vuole prendere Lei? 11. Che cosa fa suo padre? 12. Chi di Loro ha un fratello che studia all'università? 13. Per quale professione si prepara egli? 14. Che cosa deve avere un artista per farsi un nome? 15. Che cosa deve fare?

[1] Likewise, **l'italiano** or **la lingua italiana**, **l'inglese** or **la lingua inglese**, etc. [2] Conjugated with **essere**. [3] This idiomatic phrase implies *practicing* a profession or a trade; **essere medico, avvocato,** etc., would merely indicate a *title to practice* a profession or a trade.

VI. ESERCIZI

A. Dare il plurale dei seguenti nomi:

1. il poeta, il programma, il profeta, il diagramma, il teorema, il pilota, il problema, l'idiota, il pianeta, il poema.
2. la violinista, il pianista, il socialista, l'artista (*m. and f.*), lo specialista, il musicista, il giornalista, il dentista.

B. Coniugare nel presente dell'indicativo:

> 1. Dover partire domani.   5. Uscire dalla cucina.
> 2. Non potere andar via.   6. Poter anche sbagliare.
> 3. Dire dov'egli sarà.   7. Voler vendere la radio.
> 4. Non volere scusarlo.   8. Dire che cosa egli pensa.

C. Completare col presente del verbo in parentesi:

1. (*volere*) Io _____ venire. 2. (*dovere*) Voi _____ apparecchiare la tavola. 3. (*dire*) Noi non _____ il suo nome. 4. (*potere*) Essi _____ occupare questi posti. 5. (*uscire*) I bambini _____ con la loro nonna. 6. (*volere*) Noi _____ stare allegri. 7. (*dovere*) Tu non _____ sbagliare. 8. (*dire*) Lei _____ così. 9. (*uscire*) Io _____ con mio marito. 10. (*potere*) Chi _____ correggere Roberto? 11. (*dovere*) Io _____ finire il mio lavoro. 12. (*dire*) È come voi _____. 13. (*volere*) Esse _____ divertirsi. 14. (*uscire*) Margherita non _____ oggi. 15. (*potere*) Tu _____ invitare suo figlio. 16. (*dovere*) Lei non _____ andar via. 17. (*potere*) Io _____ lavare i piatti. 18. (*volere*) Tu _____ scusarti. 19. (*dovere*) Loro _____ parlare chiaramente. 20. (*dire*) Tu _____ bene.

D. Tradurre in italiano:

I

1. What profession do you want to take [up], Miss Wells? — I want to be an artist. 2. My brother is a sculptor and I want to become a pianist. 3. Not all artists are poor, as we [1] often say. 4. But they must work a lot. 5. You must have talent and good luck if you want [2] to be a musician. 6. Many students go out of (**da**) this university to become lawyers. 7. I also want to be a lawyer, and I am studying Italian because my dad says that this language will be very useful in my profession. 8. Our students can study Dante's language if they want [to]. 9. My cousin wants to be a physician. 10. He must take [up] his father's profession.

---

[1] Omit the subject pronoun.   [2] *Now* is understood here; use the present

II

1. Not all poets are good. 2. Many call themselves poets, but a poet must have a great deal of [1] talent. 3. Perhaps I shall study medicine. 4. I must study a lot, they [2] say, but I have an uncle who is a physician, and I like his profession. 5. You don't have to be a druggist because your father has a drugstore. 6. We can take [up] the profession [3] we want [to], I say.[4] 7. Paul is preparing himself to (a) become a writer. 8. Lawrence, on the other hand,[5] wants to be a sculptor or a painter. 9. And I want to study law in this university. 10. As you see, every one is thinking of [6] the profession that he will take [up].

❧ *Lezione Tredicesima* ☙

I. ESERCIZIO DI PRONUNZIA

Dittonghi:	ia	iɛ	io	iɔ	íu
	pia-no	iɛ-ri	fio-re	chiɔ-do	più
	sia-mo	siɛ-te	bion-do	piɔp-po	fiu-me
	bian-co	piɛ-de	piom-bo	piɔg-gia	chiu-do
	ua	**ue**	**uɛ**	**ui**	**uɔ**
	lin-gua	ac-que	guɛl-fo	qui	uɔ-mo
	guan-to	que-sto	guɛr-ra	gui-da	cuɔ-re
	qua-dro	quel-lo	quɛr-cia	quin-to	buɔ-no
	ai	**ei–ɛi**	**oi–ɔi**	**au**	**ɛu**
	stai	dei	noi	cau-sa	fɛu-do
	lai-co	sɛi	voi	lau-ro	rɛu-ma
	trai-no	lɛi	poi	pau-sa	nɛu-tro

II. NOTE GRAMMATICALI

64.   *Some* or *Any*

Qualche studente scrive.	*Some students are writing.*
Avete qualche nipote?	*Have you any nephews?*

---

[1] See Vocabulary.   [2] Omit the subject pronoun.   [3] What word is missing here?   [4] Place the subject in emphatic position, after the verb.   [5] Same as *on the contrary*.   [6] See footnote 2, p. 79.

Diamo alcuni esempi.	*We give some examples.*
Voglio un po' di pane.	*I want some bread.*
Abbiamo libri utili.	*We have (some) useful books.*
Ecco coltelli, forchette e cucchiai.	*Here are knives, forks, and spoons.*

The partitive idea, which is frequently rendered by the preposition **di** and the definite article (*see* § **45, p.** 61), may also be expressed in Italian in one of the following ways:

1. By **qualche** or **alcuno,** whenever *some* or *any* stands for *a few*. Note, however, that **qualche** (together with its noun and its verb) is always singular, as shown in the 1st example, while **alcuno** agrees in gender and number with the noun to which it refers.

2. By **un po' di,** in case *some* or *any* has the meaning of *a little*.

3. By the noun alone, whenever such construction is correct in English. The latter way is to be preferred in case of enumeration (last example).

Note: For *any* with negative verbs, see § **98,** p. 144. For *some* or *any* used as pronouns (*some of it, some of them,* etc.) see § **92,** 5, p. 137.

65. Expressions of Weather

1. Many impersonal expressions are used in reference to natural phenomena. The most important of them are:

Che tempo fa?	What kind of weather is it?
Fa bel tempo.	It is fine weather.
Fa cattivo tempo.	It is bad weather.
Fa caldo.	It is warm.
Fa molto caldo.	It is hot.
Fa fresco.	It is cool.
Fa freddo.	It is cold.
Piove.	It is raining.
Nevica.	It is snowing.
Tira vento.	The wind blows. It's windy.
Tuona.	It is thundering.
Lampeggia.	It is lightning.

2. Note that the *it* used in English impersonal expressions is not translated into Italian. Note also that the verbs **piovere,**

nevicare, tuonare, and lampeggiare are usually conjugated with essere.

66. Days of the Week

Memorize: **I giorni della settimana sono: lunedì, martedì, mercoledì, giovedì, venerdì, sabato e domenica.**

Note that: 1. The week begins in Italy (and all over the continent of Europe) with Monday and ends with Sunday. 2. The names of the days are usually written with small letters. 3. They are all masculine, except **domenica,** *Sunday.*

Remember the idiomatic expressions: **il lunedì,** *on Mondays;* **il martedì,** *on Tuesdays;* **la domenica,** *on Sundays,* etc.

67. Further Cardinal Numerals

13	tredici	17	diciassette
14	quattordici	18	diciotto
15	quindici	19	diciannove
16	sedici	20	venti

III. LETTURA

Una domenica a casa

Quando vado all'università, il lunedì, il martedì, il mercoledì, il giovedì e il venerdì, m'alzo presto; ma oggi è domenica, e stamane mi sono alzato dopo tutti gli altri della mia famiglia.

— Saremo in ritardo per la messa, — ha osservato mia madre.

Allora io son saltato dal letto, mi son lavato e vestito in poco 5 tempo e, dopo una breve colazione, sono uscito coi miei genitori e con la mia sorellina per andare in chiesa.[1]

Quando la messa è finita, siamo andati nella nostra automobile a fare una passeggiata per la città, e poi siamo ritornati a casa.

A casa abbiamo trovato pronto il pranzo, ci siamo seduti subito 10 a tavola. Ora che abbiamo pranzato, stiamo tutti insieme in salotto.

Questo pomeriggio non usciremo perchè avremo alcune visite, e anche perchè fa cattivo tempo. Nevica e tira vento.

[1] Note this idiomatic expression, similar to those already studied (**in casa, in salotto, in città,** etc.).

Fuɔri, le vie, le case, gli alberi, ogni cɔsa è copɛrta di neve, e altra neve cade. Fa freddo, ma quí in salɔtto stiamo caldi e cɔmodi.

Mio padre, seduto nella sua poltrona, lɛgge i suɔi giornali e 5 qualche rivista; la mia mamma suɔna il pianofɔrte, e la mia sorellina giɔca con la sua bambola.

Io stɔ vicino a una delle finɛstre e guardo sulla via. Aspɛtto il mio amico Cantoni che dɛve arrivare da un momento all'altro.

Studieremo insiɛme. Dobbiamo lɛggere per domani quíndici o 10 sedici pagine d'un libro di letteratura inglese. Sarɔ contɛnto quand'egli sarà quí perchè, solo, non mi piace di studiare.

PROVɛRBIO

Nessuno è meno solo di chi è solo.   *Never less alone than when alone.*

IV. STUDIO DI PARɔLE

automɔbile *f.* automobile
bambola doll
chiɛsa church
giornale *m.* newspaper
letteratura literature
messa Mass
momento moment; **da un momento all'altro** any moment
neve *f.* snow
pagina page
pianofɔrte *m.* piano
rivista review, magazine
tɛmpo time, weather; tense
visita visit

copɛrto (di) covered (with)
pronto ready, prompt

solo alone, only [1]
vicino near, neighboring, near-by [2]

aspettare [aspɛtto] to wait, wait for
cadere to fall [3]
ɛssere in ritardo to be late
giocare [giɔco] to play (*a game*) [4]
osservare [ossɛrvo] to observe
pranzare to dine
saltare to jump, hop [3]
trovare [trɔvo] to find

allora then, at that time [5]
fuɔri out, outside
quí here

[1] **Solo** is also used as an adverb.   [2] We have met the preposition **vicino a** (Lesson V); **vicino** is also an adjective (**la casa vicina**), an adverb (**ɑbitano vicino**), and a noun (**i miɛi vicini,** *my neighbors*).   [3] Conjugated with **ɛssere.**   [4] Do not confuse this verb with **suonare**, the meaning of which is *to play an instrument or a piece of music.*   [5] **Allora** and **pɔi** both mean *then*, but **allora** is used in the sense of *at that time* or *in conclusion*, while **pɔi** means only *afterward.*

V. CONVERSAZIONE

1. In quali giorni della settimana andiamo a scuola? 2. In quali giorni non andiamo a scuola? 3. Che giorno è oggi? 4. Che giorno sarà domani? 5. Domenica s'è alzato presto lo studente della *Lettura?* 6. Che cosa ha osservato sua madre? 7. S'è alzato egli allora? 8. Dov'è andato coi suoi genitori e con la sua sorellina? 9. Dove sono andati tutti, quando la messa è finita? 10. Perchè non vanno fuori nel pomeriggio? 11. Che tempo fa oggi? 12. Che cosa fanno in salotto i genitori dello studente? 13. Che cosa fa la sua sorellina? 14. Quando arriverà l'amico Cantoni? 15. Che cosa leggeranno insieme i due studenti?

VI. ESERCIZI

A. Tradurre in italiano usando gli equivalenti di (*using the equivalents of*) *some* o *any* studiati in questa lezione:

1. We visit some churches. 2. Have you any chalk? 3. They want some paper. 4. I have returned with some gentlemen. 5. You will find some places. 6. Do you want any notebooks? 7. I must buy some butter. 8. I shall speak to some artists. 9. She bought some dishes, glasses, and cups. 10. Do you want some sugar in your coffee?

B. Completare col presente, col presente perfetto, o col futuro del verbo in parentesi, secondo il senso (*according to sense*):

1. (*piovere*) Forse domani ____. 2. (*far freddo*) Stamane ____ fuori. 3. (*lampeggiare*) Oggi non ____. 4. (*far cattivo tempo*) In questo momento non ____. 5. (*tirar vento*) Tutta la settimana ____. 6. (*far fresco*) Adesso ____. 7. (*piovere*) Quando ____ non esco. 8. (*far caldo*) Fuori nevica, ma qui ____. 9. (*piovere*) Tutto questo pomeriggio ____. 10. (*tuonare*) Poco fa ____.

C. 1. Tradurre in italiano:

Friday, Thursday, on Tuesdays, on Sundays, Wednesday, on Saturdays.

2. Leggere ad alta voce:

11, 16, 20, 17, 14, 12, 19, 13, 18, 15
19, 15, 11, 12, 16, 20, 13, 17, 14, 18

3. Continuare:

(a) Tre più (*plus*) uno, quattro; tre più due . . . ecc.[1]
(b) Due per (*times*) due, quattro; due per tre . . . ecc.

D. Tradurre in italiano usando gli equivalenti di *some* o *any* studiati in questa lezione:

I

1. Today is Sunday and we go to church.[2] 2. I got up early this morning, even [3] before my mother. 3. Immediately after breakfast I went out to buy some newspapers and a magazine. 4. My sister got up after all the rest [4] of our family. 5. "She will be late for Mass," [5] observed my aunt Clara. 6. But Margaret dresses quickly [6] and she will be ready any moment. 7. It is bad weather this morning and the streets are covered with snow. 8. We must take the automobile because our church is not near; we live at (**in**) 19 Hamilton Street.[7] 9. It's cold outside, but here in our house it's warm. 10. We shall return home early because we have some ladies for (**a**) dinner.

II

1. My cousin Helen is standing near the piano. 2. She is listening to my sister, who is playing. 3. Outside some snow is falling and it's cold, but here it's warm. 4. Seated [8] in my armchair, I am looking at some magazines. 5. I like to read on Sundays. 6. Tomorrow, Monday, I shall have [9] many things to (**da**) do at the University. 7. In the afternoon I must see some students who live at (**in**) 17 Lee Street.[7] 8. I must also buy a map, some paper, and the new Italian reader. 9. Now Beatrice is going upstairs to get her doll; she wants to play. 10. We are waiting for Uncle [5] Richard; he is late, but may arrive any moment.

[1] This abbreviation stands for **eccetera,** *etc.* [2] See footnote, p. 93. [3] *Even* is **anche.** [4] Translate, *all the others.* [5] Use the definite article. [6] Translate, *in little time.* [7] Write out the number and see footnote 1, p. 61. [8] This is a past participle used as an adjective. [9] Use the verb **avere.**

❧ *Second Review Lesson* ❧

I. VOCABULARY DRILL

A. Translate into Italian, first in the singular, then in the plural, the following nouns with their articles:

1. The fork	2. The rug	3. The baby
the dish	the glass	the knife
the sugar	the spoon	the buffet
the bread	the mirror	the napkin
the corner	the lawyer	the kitchen
the picture	the armchair	the grandson
the silverware	the newspaper	the magazine

B. Give the Italian singular forms, masculine and feminine, for each of the following adjectives:

1. Bitter, cold, ready, young, jolly, cool, dead, short.
2. Sweet, full, blond, bad, poor, ancient, useful, old.
3. Red, gray, ugly, simple, long, busy, comfortable, elementary.

C. Give the Italian for the following verbs:

1. To fall	2. To find	3. To give
to love	to smile	to snow
to come	to think	to wash
to dress	to jump	to dine
to excuse	to become	to go out
to go up	to be able	to observe
to wait for	to occupy	to be obliged

D. Give the Italian for the following expressions:

1. This morning, at that time, near, already, to the left, soon, together, to be late, to take a bath, any moment.
2. Often, to the right, before, almost, outside, even, a short time ago, to take a walk, to be a physician, it's windy.

II. NOUNS

1. Which are the most common diminutive endings? Give two examples.

2. Are there masculine nouns ending in −a? Mention some, and tell how their plural is formed.

3. Are there nouns in –a of both genders? Give a few examples.

4. How do you form the plural of a noun (or adjective) ending in –io?

III. ADJECTIVES

1. Give the masculine possessive adjectives, singular and plural.

2. Give the feminine possessive adjectives, singular and plural.

3. In how many ways can you render the English *your* in Italian?

4. Mention as many adjectives as you can that normally precede the noun.

5. Count from 1 to 20.

6. Count from 20 to 1.

IV. PRONOUNS

1. Give the complete list of the reflexive pronouns.

2. Reflexive pronouns, as well as the object pronouns **lo, la, li,** and **le,** are called conjunctive; why?

3. How are conjunctive pronouns used with an infinitive? Give an example.

4. How are they used with an inflected verb?

V. VERBS

1. Give the imperative of **dettare, stendere, pulire,** and **aprire.**

2. What persons of the imperative are borrowed from the subjunctive?

3. What is the use of these borrowed forms?

4. How do you form a negative imperative? Give the negative imperative of **essere.**

5. What stem is used in forming the future tense?

6. Conjugate the future of **dettare.**

7. Give three possible translations of **laverò.**

8. What does the *future of probability* express? Give an example.

9. In what other case is the Italian future used to render the English present tense?

10. Which auxiliary is used in conjugating a reflexive verb? Translate into Italian: *She excused herself.*

11. Give the 1st person plural of the present of **andare, dare, fare, stare, dovere, potere, volere, dire,** and **uscire.**

12. What expressions referring to natural phenomena do you remember?

LETTURA IN SILENZIO

Sì o no?

1. __ Il burro è grigio.
2. __ Il pianoforte è presto.
3. __ In salotto c'è un tavolino.
4. __ Saliamo in un piccolo quadro.
5. __ Studiamo nel pomeriggio.
6. __ La bambina ha una bambola.
7. __ Il giornale cade sul pavimento.
8. __ Ci sediamo sulla sera del salotto.
9. __ Quando tuona fa bel tempo.
10. __ La sala da pranzo ha un tappeto.
11. __ Il letto è nella stanza da bagno.
12. __ L'armadio è sulla sedia.
13. __ Il cassettone è una lingua antica.
14. __ La nostra grammatica è rossa.
15. __ Ogni domenica andiamo a messa.

ACHIEVEMENT TEST NO. 2

VOCABULARY

Give the Italian for the following words:

1. please	_____	11. busy	_____
2. the maid	_____	12. the knife	_____
3. perhaps	_____	13. jolly	_____
4. the husband	_____	14. any moment	_____
5. simple	_____	15. to be late	_____
6. the fork	_____	16. this morning	_____
7. to sit down	_____	17. good-bye	_____
8. comfortable	_____	18. the closet	_____
9. in the evening	_____	19. to be a lawyer	_____
10. instead	_____	20. a short time ago	_____

(Deduct 1 point for each mistake.)

GRAMMAR

A. Translate:

1. uno scaffalino _____
2. i tovagliolini _____

3. un pezzetto _____
4. un pranzetto _____

B. Give the 2nd person singular, affirmative and negative, of the imperative of the following verbs:

pensare	1. _____	2. _____
avere	3. _____	4. _____
essere	5. _____	6. _____

C. Write out in Italian the following numbers:

1. 17 _____
2. 13 _____

3. 15 _____
4. 19 _____

D. Translate into Italian:

1. their ink _____
2. my parents _____
3. our flowers _____
4. your father _____

5. our grandfather _____
6. her newspaper _____
7. his sister _____
8. your old uncle _____

E. Supply the Italian for the words in parentheses, rendering some *or* any *by* **qualche, alcuno,** *or* **un po' di:**

1. Vogliamo (*some sugar*). _____
2. Vedete (*any ladies*)? _____
3. Invito (*some friends*). _____
4. Detta (*some sentences*). _____

5. Avete (*any paper*)? _____
6. Vedo (*some mistakes*). _____
7. Comprerò (*some butter*). _____
8. Ha egli (*any cousins*)? _____

F. Translate into Italian:

1. To wash oneself. _____
2. You will get up. _____
3. She sees herself. _____

4. We amuse ourselves. _____
5. I prepare myself. _____
6. They are dressing. _____

G. In each case supply the correct form of the present perfect and future of the verb in parentheses:

Noi (*essere*) nello studio.	1. _____	2. _____
Bianca (*pulire*) la casa.	3. _____	4. _____
Roberto (*alzarsi*) ora.	5. _____	6. _____
I mobili ch'io (*comprare*).	7. _____	8. _____

H. *Complete each of the following sentences with a suitable adjective:*

1. Questa sedia non è _____   4. La lettura è _____
2. Oggi il tempo è _____   5. Quest'albero è _____
3. Il caffè non è _____   6. Degli alunni sono _____

(Deduct 1 point for each mistake.)

READING

Translate the Italian passage that your instructor will write on the board or hand to you on a mimeographed sheet.

(This part counts 20 points.)

DICTATION

Your instructor will dictate twice a short Italian passage.

(This part counts 10 points.)

PERFECT SCORE: 100

Parte Terza

IN CITTÀ

❧ *Lezione Quattordicεsima* ❧

I. NƆTE GRAMMATICALI

68. ### Past Descriptive

I	II	III
I bought, was buying, used to buy, etc.	*I sold, was selling, used to sell, etc.*	*I finished, was finishing, used to finish, etc.*
compr **avo**	vend **evo**	fin **ivo**
compr **avi**	vend **evi**	fin **ivi**
compr **ava**	vend **eva**	fin **iva**
compr **avamo**	vend **evamo**	fin **ivamo**
compr **avate**	vend **evate**	fin **ivate**
compr *avano*	vend *evano*	fin *ivano*

Note that, except for the fact that each conjugation retains its characteristic vowel (**a** in the first, **e** in the second, and **i** in the third), the endings of this tense are the same for all Italian verbs. The only exception to this general rule is the verb εssere, as will be seen in the next paragraph.

69. ### Past Descriptive of the Auxiliary Verbs

avere		εssere	
I had, was having, used to have, etc.		*I was, was being, used to be, etc.*	
avevo	avevamo	εro	eravamo
avevi	avevate	εri	eravate
aveva	avevano	εra	εrano

70. ### Use of the Past Descriptive

Ella sorrideva.	*She was smiling.*
Egli veniva a casa mia.	*He was coming to my house.*
Ogni giorno scrivevo una lεttera.	*Every day I wrote (or used to write) a letter.*
Leggevo quand'egli è entrato.	*I was reading when he entered.*
Parlavano mentre io scrivevo.	*They spoke (or were speaking) while I wrote (or was writing).*

1. As its name implies, this tense conveys a descriptive idea in the past (1st example).

2. It is used also:

(*a*) to express an incomplete or habitual action (2nd and 3rd examples);

(*b*) to state what was taking place when something else happened or was happening (4th and 5th examples).

It corresponds to such English past phrases as *I was doing* or *I used to do*, or to a simple past which usually stands for one of these phrases.

71. Nouns and Adjectives in −*ca* or −*ga*

SINGULAR	PLURAL
la barca, *the boat*	le barche
il monarca, *the monarch*	i monarchi
la lega, *the league*	le leghe
il collega, *the colleague*	i colleghi
bianca, lunga, *white, long*	bianche, lunghe

In forming the plural of nouns and adjectives ending in −**ca** or −**ga,** an **h** is inserted before the final **e** or **i.** This is done in order to keep the guttural sound of the **c** or **g.**

72. Nouns and Adjectives in −*cia* or −*gia*

SINGULAR	PLURAL
la faccia, *the face*	le facce
grigia, *gray*	grige
But: la farmacia, *the drugstore*	le farmacie
la bugia, *the lie*	le bugie

Nouns and adjectives ending in −**cia** or −**gia** usually drop the **i** before the ending −**e** of the plural, provided that the **i** is unstressed; they keep it if it is stressed, as shown in the last two examples.

II. LETTURA

Alla posta

Mia cugina Irene è venuta a passare dieci o dodici giorni a casa nostra. Essa non conosce questa città, e noi due usciamo spesso insieme, facciamo delle lunghe passeggiate.

Stamane siamo andate alla pɔsta; essa doveva mandare una lɛttera raccomandata, e io volevo comprare dei francobolli.

Mentre camminavamo, parlavamo di molte cɔse, e io hɔ spiegato a Irɛne perchè la nɔstra nuɔva pɔsta mɛrita una visita. Questa città non ha forse un altro edifizio così bɛllo e semplice al tɛmpo stesso.   5

Quando siamo arrivate nella larga piazza in cui esso si trɔva,[1] ci siamo fermate a guardarlo. Pɔi siamo entrate.

Molte persone stavano in fila davanti a gli sportɛlli, mentre gl'impiegati ricevevano e consegnavano lɛttere, vendevano franco-   10 bolli e cartoline, rispondevano a qualche domanda, davano in-formazioni. Un uɔmo, davanti a Irɛne, aveva in mano[2] molte lɛttere. Io stavo diɛtro a mia cugina.

Quando Irɛne ha raccomandato la sua lɛttera e io hɔ comprato i miɛi francobolli, siamo uscite.   15

Alla pɔrta dell'edifizio abbiamo incontrato le mie amiche Ɔlga e Laura, l'una vestita di bianco, l'altra di marrone, e ognuna por-tava un piccolo pacco. Allora le hɔ fermate e hɔ presentato Irɛne alle ragazze:

— Mia cugina Irɛne Fusco. Le signorine Minati e De Carolis.   20
— Piacere!
— Il piacere è tutto mio!

PROVɛRBIO

Dimmi con chi tu pratichi e ti dirɔ   *Birds of a feather flock together.*
chi sei.   *(Tell me with whom thou goest,*
                                                                 And I'll tell thee what thou doest.)

III. STUDIO DI PARɔLE

cartolina post card   **impiegato, –a** clerk
edifizio building   **informazione** *f.* information[3]
fila line, row   **lɛttera** letter; **lɛttera raccoman-**
francobollo stamp   **data** registered letter

[1] **Trovarsi,** *to be.* Remember this expression.   [2] Note that the possessive is missing, as is frequently the case in Italian when its meaning is obvious.
[3] This word is used in the plural when more than one item of information is implied.

pacco parcel, package
piazza square
posta post office, mail
sportello window (*of an office*)

bianco white; di bianco in white [1]
largo broad, wide
marrone brown [2]

camminare to walk [3]
conoscere to know
consegnare to hand
fermare, fermarsi to stop [4]
incontrare to meet

mandare (a) to send
meritare [merito] to merit, deserve
passare to pass, spend (*time*)
presentare [presento] to present,
introduce (*a person*)
raccomandare to recommend, register (*at the post office*)
ricevere to receive
spiegare [spiego] to explain, unfold

piacere! pleased to meet you!

IV. CONVERSAZIONE

1. Quanti giorni è venuta a passare Irene in casa di sua cugina? 2. Conosce ella questa città? 3. Che cosa fanno le due cugine? 4. Che cosa doveva mandare Irene? 5. Che cosa voleva comprare la cugina d'Irene? 6. Perchè la posta di questa città merita una visita? 7. Chi vediamo dietro a gli sportelli, alla posta? 8. Che cosa fanno gl'impiegati della posta? 9. Che aveva in mano l'uomo ch'era davanti a Irene? 10. Dov'erano le altre persone? 11. Chi hanno incontrato le due cugine alla porta dell'edifizio? 12. Com'erano vestite le due amiche? 13. Con quali parole la cugina d'Irene ha presentato Irene alle amiche? 14. Che cosa rispondono esse? 15. Che cosa dice Irene allora?

V. ESERCIZI

A. Coniugare nel passato descrittivo [5]:

1. Studiare legge.
2. Avere delle medicine.
3. Venire ogni mercoledì.
4. Stendere la tovaglia.
5. Essere in una sala.
6. Portare i fiori alla nonna.

---

[1] This idiom, used in connection with the verb **vestire** (or **vestirsi**), applies, of course, to any color. [2] **Marrone,** as an adjective, is invariable, i.e. has the same form for singular and plural; **marrone,** *m.* noun, means *chestnut,* and, as such, has a plural, **marroni.** [3] **Camminare,** though an intransitive verb of motion, is conjugated with **avere.** [4] **Fermare** is used transitively (*to stop somebody* or *something*); **fermarsi** translates the English intransitive *to stop* (*oneself*). [5] Called *imperfetto* by Italian grammarians.

B. Completare col passato descrittivo del verbo in parentesi:

1. (*avere*) Egli non _____ figli. 2. (*osservare*) Io l'_____ ogni giorno.
3. (*dovere*) Noi _____ occuparci. 4. (*essere*) Lei _____ coi bambini.
5. (*giocare*) Le ragazze _____ con alcune bambole. 6. (*capire*) Egli non
_____ questa frase. 7. (*aprire*) Tu _____ gli armadi. 8. (*piovere*) Quasi
ogni settimana _____. 9. (*diventare*) Suo marito _____ vecchio. 10. (*essere*) Voi non _____ con Margherita. 11. (*scrivere*) Esse _____ delle
cartoline. 12. (*prendere*) Io _____ pane tostato e marmellata. 13. (*venire*) Chi _____ spesso a casa tua? 14. (*vendere*) Lei _____ la sua casa
allora. 15. (*divertirsi*) Noi _____ la domenica.

C. Scrivere il plurale di:

la riga	l'amica	la domenica
poca medicina	la carta bianca	la poltrona grigia
la grammatica	la lunga visita	la piazza larga
la casuccia	il patriarca	lo stratega

D. Tradurre in italiano:

I

1. Robert received two long letters from his mother this morning.
2. Then he went to the post office to (**a**) register a letter and buy some
stamps. 3. He wanted to send some post cards. 4. Robert used to
know a young clerk at the post office. 5. His friend was often behind
the window for (**di** + *def. article*) registered letters. 6. But he is in
another city now. 7. While he was buying the stamps, a young lady
dressed in white came behind Robert. 8. She was carrying a little
parcel.[1] 9. Good morning, Miss Burke! How are you? — [Very]
well, Robert, thanks! And how are you?[2] 10. Then she introduced
Robert to another young lady dressed in brown. — Pleased to meet
you! — The pleasure is all mine![3]

II

1. Laura does not know this city, its long streets, its wide and beautiful
squares.[4] 2. This morning she went out with her friend Olga.
3. "What building is this?" asked Laura. 4. The two friends were
at the entrance of our new post office. 5. Then they entered because
Olga wished to send a parcel to her brothers. 6. Few persons were

[1] Don't use the diminutive; use the adjective **piccolo**. [2] Don't omit this
pronoun. [3] Omit the definite article before this possessive. [4] Leave the
adjectives before this noun.

in line in front of the window. 7. The clerk was giving some information to a woman who wanted to send a registered letter. 8. Then Olga handed [in] the parcel, in which there were [1] three books and two fountain pens.[2] 9. Laura bought some stamps in order to send post cards. 10. How many stamps do you wish? — Fifteen, please!

❧ *Lezione Quindicesima* ❧

I. NOTE GRAMMATICALI

73.   Some Uses of the Definite Article

1. I libri sono utili.   *Books are useful.*
   Mi piace il pane italiano.   *I like Italian bread.*
   L'oro è un metallo prezioso.   *Gold is a precious metal.*
   La gratitudine è rara.   *Gratitude is rare.*
   Gli Americani amano la libertà.   *Americans love liberty.*

The definite article is required before a noun used in a general sense or an abstract noun.

2. La Cantoni non c'era.   *Mrs. (or Miss) Cantoni wasn't there.*
   Il Bacci vende anche vino.   *Bacci sells wine too.*
   Le poesie del Leopardi.   *Leopardi's poems.*
But: Una poesia di Giacomo Leopardi.[3]   *A poem by Giacomo Leopardi.*
   Un quadro di Raffaello.   *A painting by Raphael.*

Usually the surname of a man, and always the surname of a woman, takes the definite article in Italian, provided that the surname is not preceded by a given name. (*Review also* § 48, p. 66).

---

[1] You know the expression **ci sono;** use it now in the past descriptive.
[2] The word **stilografico** is an adjective.   [3] Note the use of the preposition **di** to indicate authorship.

THE SMALL COWPER MADONNA *By Raffaello*

TEMPLE OF CERES, METAPONTO

74.   **Demonstrative Adjectives**

Questa regola è facile.	*This rule is easy.*
Leggete codesta lettera.	*Read that letter.*
Quelle piante e quegli alberi sono in fiore.	*Those plants and trees are in bloom.*
Quell'uomo e quei bambini non sono americani.	*That man and those children are not Americans.*

There are three demonstrative adjectives in Italian: **questo, codesto,** and **quello.**

1. **Questo,** *this,* refers to somebody or something near the person who speaks. **Codesto** (spelled also **cotesto**), *that,* refers to somebody or something near the person addressed. **Quello,** *that,* refers to somebody or something far from both the person speaking and the one addressed.

2. **Questo** and **codesto** drop the final vowel and take the apostrophe before a singular word beginning with a vowel; **quello** takes forms similar to those of the definite article, and **quel, quei, quello, quegli, quella, quelle, quell'** are used according to the rules given for **il, i, lo, gli, la, le, l'.**

3. With two or more nouns, the demonstrative adjective must be repeated before each of them.

75.   **Adverbs of Place**

Parallel to the demonstrative adjectives given above, the following adverbs of place should be noted:

> **qua** or **qui,** *here* — near the person who speaks
> **costà** or **costì,** *there* — near the person addressed
> **là** or **lì,** *there* — far from both

76. **Imperative of the Four Irregular Verbs of the First Conjugation**

Sing.	**va',** *go, etc.*	**da',** *give, etc.*	**fa',** *make or do, etc.*	**sta',** *stay or be, etc.*
	(vada)	**(dia)**	**(faccia)**	**(stia)**
Pl.	**andiamo**	**diamo**	**facciamo**	**stiamo**
	andate	**date**	**fate**	**state**
	(vadano)	**(diano)**	**(facciano)**	**(stiano)**

II. LETTURA

Al giardino zoologico

— Guardate! — dice il signor Liviani ai suoi figli Vittorio e Franco e al loro cugino Riccardo, mentre si fermano davanti a una delle gabbie dei leoni. — Guardate! L'aspetto del leone dice chiaramente ch'esso è il re degli animali!

5   — Codesta leonessa pare un enorme gatto, — osserva il piccolo Franco.

A queste parole, Vittorio e Riccardo sorridono.

— Sì, — dice il babbo, — hai ragione; pare un enorme gatto. E impara che il leone, la tigre, il leopardo e il gatto son della stessa 10 famiglia. Ma ora usciamo da questo posto in cui l'aria è cattiva; andiamo all'aperto a vedere gli altri animali.

Fuori tutto era così bello! I prati già verdi, gli alberi con le prime foglie, i fiori e il sole davano a quel giardino zoologico un aspetto allegro. C'erano molte signore e signorine, tra cui alcune 15 studentesse che Vittorio e Riccardo conoscevano: la Burini, la Coppola, la Minaro...

— Venite qua! — dice il signor Liviani, e gli altri lo seguono.

Poco dopo essi erano già davanti alle gabbie degli orsi.

Alcuni di quegli animali erano di color marrone, altri erano neri, 20 e uno, in una grande gabbia, era bianco

Franco guardava gli orsi e sorrideva. Erano buffi come camminavano su e giù.

— Andiamo là a veder quegli uccelli, babbo, — dice Franco qualche momento dopo.

25   La gabbia degli uccelli era enorme. Quanti e quanti uccelli, e di quanti colori! Grigi, rossi, gialli, neri... E cantavano, e saltavano, e volavano.

— Non far così! — dice un momento dopo il signor Liviani a Franco, che stuzzicava quegli animali con un ramoscello. Franco 30 aveva torto.

Ma già era tempo di ritornare a casa, dove la signora Liviani li aspettava per la cena. In un pomeriggio non potevano veder tutto.

PROVERBIO

Chi troppo abbraccia, nulla stringe.   *He that too much embraceth holds little.*

III. STUDIO DI PAROLE

Franco Frank
Vittorio Victor

animale *m.* animal
aspetto aspect, appearance
colore *m.* color
gabbia cage
gatto cat
leone *m.* lion
leonessa lioness
leopardo leopard
orso bear
ramoscello twig
re *m.* king
tigre *f.* tiger
uccello bird

buffo droll, funny

enorme enormous, huge
giallo yellow
nero black
primo first
zoologico zoological

aver ragione to be right
aver torto to be wrong
cantare to sing
parere to seem, look like [1]
seguire [**seguo**] to follow
stuzzicare [**stuzzico**] to tease
volare to fly

all'aperto in the open, outdoors
fra *or* **tra** between, among, within
giù down
poco dopo soon after

IV. CONVERSAZIONE

1. Con chi è il signor Liviani nel giardino zoologico? 2. Che cosa dice l'aspetto del leone? 3. Che cosa osserva il piccolo Franco? 4. Che cosa dice il signor Liviani? 5. Che cosa era bello, fuori? 6. Quali animali vedono i ragazzi dopo i leoni? 7. Di che colore sono gli orsi? 8. Perchè sorrideva Franco? 9. Era piccola la gabbia degli uccelli? 10. Di che colore sono gli uccelli? 11. Che cosa fanno gli uccelli? 12. Che cosa dice a Franco il signor Liviani? 13. Perchè il signor Liviani dice così? 14. Perchè era tempo di ritornare a casa? 15. Ha questa città un giardino zoologico?

---

[1] Conjugated with **essere**.

V. ESERCIZI

A. 1. Completare con l'articolo definito o col partitivo, secondo il senso:

1. Egli mostrava ____ oro. 2. ____ buoni alunni studiano le loro lezioni. 3. ____ dizionari sono ____ libri utili. 4. ____ ragazze sono allegre. 5. Abbiamo ____ buoni dentisti. 6. ____ Americani parlano inglese. 7. ____ bambini amano giocare. 8. ____ studentesse imparano subito. 9. ____ genitori sono scontenti. 10. ____ pavimenti sono di legno. 11. ____ programmi sono belli. 12. Abbiamo ____. buone amiche.

2. Leggere ad alta voce applicando (*applying*) la regola studiata al § 73, 2:

1. [Mrs.] Sacchini. 2. [Miss] Marucci. 3. Victor Lulli. 4. Lulli. 5. Dante. 6. D'Annunzio. 7. Carlo Saroni. 8. Saroni. 9. [Mrs.] Bindi. 10. Leonardo.

B. Mettere la forma corretta di **quello** davanti alle seguenti parole:

1. scala. 2. entrate. 3. oro. 4. bagni. 5. armadio. 6. cassettone. 7. scaffale. 8. cartoline. 9. sbagli. 10. zucchero. 11. neve. 12. mariti. 13. specchio. 14. credenza. 15. esempi. 16. talento. 17. favori. 18. riviste. 19. dito. 20. argenteria.

C. Coniugare nell'imperativo:

1. Andare alla posta.
2. Non stare in piedi.
3. Dare un po' di pane.
4. Fare un brutto sbaglio.
5. Non far colazione.
6. Non andare in città.
7. Stare con degli amici.
8. Dare delle informazioni.

D. Tradurre in italiano:

I

In translating these sentences, use the **tu** *form in direct address.* 1. Go there, to that zoological garden; it is very beautiful. 2. Look at the trees and the flowers, at the green [1] lawns. 3. See the animals, but don't tease them,[2] as [Miss] Rovetti [3] does. 4. The lions, the tigers, and the leopards are not in the open now. 5. It's still cold, especially if

---

[1] Leave the adjective before the noun.   [2] Place the pronoun before the verb.   [3] Place this name at the end of the sentence.

the wind blows. 6. See the bears; bears are funny animals. 7. Some [1]
are brown,[2] others are black, and one is white. 8. Look at those birds
in that huge cage. 9. They sing, they hop, they fly up and down.
10. Birds have many colors; they are red, black, yellow, green, and
gray.

II

Unless instructed otherwise, use the Lɛi *form in direct address.* 1. Go
to the zoological garden; you will find there three students whom
you know: [Miss] McCormick, [Miss] Salter, and [Mr.] Narni.
2. See those lions; aren't they beautiful? 3. The lion is the king of
all animals; its appearance shows it clearly. 4. The lioness looks like
a cat, Frank says. 5. This is because lions, tigers, leopards, and cats
are of the same family. 6. Victor was there, near the cage of the
birds, and teased them with a twig. 7. Be [3] good to (con) animals!
8. Go to (a) see the bears too, if you have time.[4] 9. Some [1] of those
animals are large, others are small, but they are all funny. 10. Their
cages are out in the open.

❧ *Lezione Sedicɛsima* ☙

I. NOTE GRAMMATICALI

77.   **Past Absolute**

I	II	III
I bought, etc.	*I sold, etc.*	*I finished, etc.*
compr **ai**	vend **ei** (**–ɛtti**)	fin **ii**
compr **asti**	vend **esti**	fin **isti**
compr **ɔ**	vend **è** (**–ɛtte**)	fin **ì**
compr **ammo**	vend **emmo**	fin **immo**
compr **aste**	vend **este**	fin **iste**
compr **arono**	vend **erono** (**–ɛttero**)	fin **irono**

[1] Use the word **alcuni.**   [2] See footnote 2, p. 108.   [3] Use the 2nd person
plural when addressing more than one person.   [4] Use no article with this noun.

1. Note that, with the exception of the 3rd person singular of the verbs in –are (comprɔ́), the characteristic vowel of each conjugation is retained in this tense. Note also that, except for this characteristic vowel, the endings are the same for all three conjugations.

2. The 1st person singular, the 3rd person singular, and the 3rd person plural of the past absolute of many, but not all, verbs of the second conjugation may also end respectively in –ɛtti (vendɛtti), –ɛtte (vendɛtte), –ɛttero (vendɛttero). This set of forms is less commonly used.

78.   Past Absolute of the Auxiliary Verbs

avere		ɛssere	
I had, etc.		*I was, etc.*	
ɛbbi	avemmo	fui	fummo
avesti	aveste	fosti	foste
ɛbbe	ɛbbero	fu	furono

79.   Use of the Past Absolute

Like the present perfect, already studied, this tense is used in stating what happened (not what *was happening*, nor what *used to happen*) at a certain time in the past. The two tenses differ, however, as far as their usage is concerned, as follows:

1. Stamane hɔ comprato un quadro.　*This morning I bought a picture.*
Questo mese non hɔ lavorato.　*This month I have not worked.*
Ella ha imparato a cantare.　*She has learned to sing.*

The present perfect is used in stating, *with reference to the present*, what took place in the past. The action may have occurred:

(*a*) this very day, as in the first example;

(*b*) in a period of time not yet completed, as in the second example;

(*c*) in a time not determined, but with effects still lasting, as in the third example.

2. Iɛri comprai un calamaio.　*Yesterday I bought an inkwell.*
Dante morì in esìlio.　*Dante died in exile.*

The past absolute is used in stating, *without reference to the present*, what happened in the past.

After such expressions of concluded periods of time as **ieri,** *yesterday;* **due giorni fa,** *two days ago;* **un mese fa,** *a month ago;* **l'anno scorso,** *last year,* etc.,[1] always use the past absolute rather than the present perfect, unless the connection with the present time is evident, as in the following example: **Ecco la lettera che ho ricevuta ieri.** *Here is the letter I received yesterday.*

80.   **Irregular Adjectives**

The adjectives **bello,** *beautiful, handsome, fine;* **buono,** *good;* **grande,** *large, big, great;* and **santo,** *saint, saintly, holy,* while perfectly regular when placed after a noun or a verb, are subject to the following changes whenever they precede a noun:

1.		
	un bel cielo	*a beautiful sky*
	i bei fiori	*the beautiful flowers*
	un bello specchio	*a fine mirror*
	i begli alberi	*the beautiful trees*
	un bell'uomo	*a handsome man*
	una bell'amica	*a beautiful friend*

Bello takes forms similar to those of the definite article,[2] and **bel, bei, bello, begli, bella, belle, bell'** are used according to the rules given for **il, i, lo, gli, la, le, l'.**

2.		
	un buon pane	*(a) good bread*
	un buon armadio	*a good closet*
	un buono stomaco	*a good stomach*
	una buona bambina	*a good baby*
	una buon'alunna	*a good pupil*

Buono has, in the singular, forms similar to those of the indefinite article, and **buon, buono, buona, buon'** are used the same way as **un, uno, una, un'.**

3.		
	un gran poeta	*a great poet*
	un grande scrittore	*a great writer*
	un grand'albero	*a large tree*

---

[1] Learn these expressions.   [2] The same changes occur, as we have seen (§ 74, p. 111), in the forms of the demonstrative adjective **quello.**

| San Carlo, Santo Stefano | *St. Charles, St. Stephen* |
| Sant'Andrea, Sant'Anna [1] | *St. Andrew, St. Ann* |

Grande and **santo** become **gran** and **san** before a masculine noun beginning with any of the consonants except **s** impure and **z,** and elide before a noun, whether masculine or feminine, beginning with a vowel.

II. LETTURA

Fra due amiche

— Buɔn giorno, Bianca.　Come stai ?

— Buɔn giorno, Anna.　Stɔ bɛne, grazie; e come stai tu ?　Dove vai così di buɔn'ora ?

— Vado in Piazza Santo Stɛfano.　Nel giornale di stamane c'è
5 l'annunzio d'una vendita speciale di cappɔtti e di pellicce: vɔglio vedere se pɔsso trovare una pelliccia di mio gusto per l'invɛrno venturo.

— Fai molto bɛne, Anna.　La primavɛra è una buɔna stagione per avere pellicce a buɔn mercato.　Hɔ comprato la mia in autunno,
10 e l'hɔ pagata parecchio.

— E tu dove vai, Bianca ?

— Vado anch'io a far delle spese.　Vɔglio comprare una vɛste d'estate, fresca e senza maniche, e forse anche delle calze.

— Bɛne!　Allora possiamo andare insiɛme: vuɔi ?

15 — Con piacere, mia cara; ma se non vogliamo pɛrder tɛmpo, andiamo in automɔbile.　Hɔ la mia qua vicino, all'angolo di Via San Carlo.

— Ma Piazza Santo Stɛfano non è lontana e, se camminiamo, possiamo guardare le vetrine dei negozi, la gɛnte che passa ...
20 — Non hai tɔrto.　Specialmente ɔggi che è sabato è una buɔn'idɛa guardare le vetrine.　Se trɔvo una vɛste che mi piace, vɔglio comprar anche delle scarpe bianche.

Le due giovani amiche s'avviarono.　Si fermarono davanti a qualche vetrina, e pɔi entrarono in un gran negɔzio.　Bianca com-
25 prɔ la vɛste che desiderava, un bɛl cappello, e anche le calze e le scarpe; Anna, invece, non ɛbbe molta fortuna perchè le pellicce che trovɔ ɛrano brutte o care.　Comprɔ dei bɛi guanti.

[1] Learn these names.

Le belle penne fanno il bell'uccello.   *Fine feathers make fine birds.*

III. STUDIO DI PAROLE

annunzio announcement, advertisement

calza stocking

cappello hat

cappotto overcoat

gente *f.* people

guanto glove

gusto taste; **di mio gusto** to my taste

idea idea

manica sleeve

negozio store, shop

pelliccia fur, fur coat

scarpa shoe

vendita sale

veste *f.* dress

vetrina show window

caro dear, expensive

lontano far, far away, distant

parecchio a lot, quite a lot; *pl.* several

speciale special

venturo next, coming

avviarsi to start on one's way

fare delle spese to shop

pagare to pay

perdere to lose, waste

a buon mercato cheap, cheaply

di buon'ora early

senza without

Le stagioni sono: **la primavera, l'estate** (*f.*), **l'autunno e l'inverno.**

I mesi dell'anno sono: **gennaio, febbraio, marzo, aprile, maggio, giugno, luglio, agosto, settembre, ottobre, novembre e dicembre.** *All the names of the months are masculine.*

IV. CONVERSAZIONE

1. Che dice Anna quando vede la sua amica? 2. Che cosa risponde Bianca? 3. Dove andava Anna? 4. Quale annunzio c'era nel giornale? 5. Che cosa voleva vedere Anna? 6. Quale stagione è buona per comprare delle pellicce a buon mercato? 7. Quali sono i mesi di primavera? 8. Quali sono i mesi delle altre stagioni? 9. Che cosa voleva comprare Bianca? 10. Che cosa voleva fare per non perder tempo? 11. Che cosa guardarono le due amiche mentre camminavano? 12. In quale negozio entrarono? 13. Che cosa comprò Bianca? 14. Perchè Anna non ebbe fortuna? 15. Che cosa comprò ella?

V. ESERCIZI

A. Coniugare nel passato assoluto [1]:

1. Essere povero.
2. Lavarsi le mani.
3. Ricevere una visita.
4. Aver molta fortuna.
5. Vestirsi per uscire.
6. Perdere qualche cosa.

B. 1. Sostituire la lineetta con un soggetto:

1. ____ presentò. 2. ____ fui. 3. ____ indicaste. 4. ____ ricevettero. 5. ____ ebbe. 6. ____ ti divertisti. 7. ____ potemmo. 8. ____ cominciarono. 9. ____ fosti. 10. ____ perdè. 11. ____ seguiste. 12. ____ incontrai.

2. Completare col passato assoluto del verbo in parentesi:

1. (*dettare*) La maestra ____ alcune frasi. 2. (*dovere*) Tu ____ partire. 3. (*prendere*) Voi ____ una tazza di latte. 4. (*avere*) Io ____ una lettera raccomandata. 5. (*pulire*) Le donne ____ l'argenteria. 6. (*essere*) Lei non ____ presente. 7. (*consegnare*) L'impiegato ____ il pacco. 8. (*avere*) Le bambine ____ delle bambole. 9. (*divertirsi*) Ieri sera io non ____. 10. (*essere*) Voi ____ molto contento. 11. (*aprire*) Chi ____ l'armadio? 12. (*passare*) Noi ____ il giovedì in città. 13. (*essere*) Anch'esse ____ a buon mercato. 14. (*capire*) Il tuo avvocato ____ subito. 15. (*potere*) Lei non ____ lavorare.

C. 1. Completare con la forma corretta di **bello**:

1. un ____ bagno. 2. una ____ credenza. 3. un ____ specchio. 4. dei ____ armadi. 5. due ____ poltrone. 6. alcuni ____ tavolini. 7. un ____ letto. 8. quei ____ posti. 9. un ____ vaso. 10. dei ____ uccelli.

2. Completare con la forma corretta di **buono**:

1. un ____ farmacista. 2. una ____ pianista. 3. un ____ re. 4. un ____ cameriere. 5. ____ avvocato. 6. una ____ impiegata. 7. un ____ poeta. 8. un ____ scultore. 9. il ____ vento. 10. il ____ scrittore.

3. Completare con la forma corretta di **grande**:

1. un ____ giornale. 2. una ____ farmacia. 3. un ____ artista. 4. un ____ momento. 5. un ____ uomo. 6. il ____ quadro. 7. il ____ vento. 8. un ____ programma. 9. i ____ musicisti. 10. il ____ talento.

---

[1] Called *passato remoto* by Italian grammarians.

4. Mettere la forma corretta di **santo** davanti ai seguenti nomi:

1. Margherita. 2. Olga. 3. Paolo. 4. Andrea. 5. Stefano. 6. Carlo. 7. Irene. 8. Vittorio. 9. Bianca. 10. Elena.

D. Tradurre in italiano:

I

1. Blanche and Helen often go downtown together to (a) shop. 2. The two friends were walking two days ago on (in) St. Charles Street. 3. They wanted [1] to visit the shops. 4. Helen wished to buy some [2] white shoes, a hat, and a dress with long [3] sleeves. 5. Blanche wanted to see if she could [4] find a fur coat to [suit] her taste for next winter.[5] 6. "Spring is a good season to (per) buy furs," Helen [6] observed. 7. They found several dresses in a large store not far from St. Paul's church. 8. But they were not cheap, and Helen had to [7] pay a lot for the dress she bought. 9. Blanche was lucky,[8] because she found a fur coat which was not expensive. 10. I bought a fine overcoat, instead.[9]

II

1. Last week Ann and I went downtown together [10] to (a) shop. 2. We visited several stores and bought many things. 3. There was a special sale in a shop in St. Lawrence Square. 4. We went out early and took our car. 5. I bought a fine overcoat, a red dress without sleeves, a large hat, and some [2] white shoes. 6. Ann bought a gray dress with long [3] sleeves, stockings, and gloves. 7. In another shop [they] were selling fur coats and fine hats cheap. 8. But I already [10] have a fur coat; I bought it this year. 9. In today's newspaper there is the announcement of a sale of summer dresses.[11] 10. Perhaps you can [12] find a dress to your taste at a low price.[13]

[1] This verb (and others that appear in the sentences that follow) expresses a lingering desire; it is the equivalent of *they were wanting.* [2] Use the partitive. [3] Place the adjective after the noun for emphasis. [4] A past descriptive. [5] Use the definite article. [6] Place the subject after the verb. [7] What is the Italian for *to have to?* [8] See Vocabulary. [9] Place this word right after the subject. [10] See footnote 1, p. 64. [11] Translate, *dresses of summer.* [12] *Now* is understood. [13] Same as *cheap.*

I. NOTE GRAMMATICALI

81. **Cardinal Numerals**

1	uno	17	diciassette	38	trentotto
2	due	18	diciotto	40	quaranta
3	tre	19	diciannove	50	cinquanta
4	quattro	20	venti	60	sessanta
5	cinque	21	ventuno	70	settanta
6	sei	22	ventidue	80	ottanta
7	sette	23	ventitrè	90	novanta
8	otto	24	ventiquattro	100	cento
9	nove	25	venticinque	101	cento uno
10	dieci	26	ventisei	180	cento ottanta
11	undici	27	ventisette	200	duecento
12	dodici	28	ventotto	1000	mille
13	tredici	29	ventinove	1300	mille trecento
14	quattordici	30	trenta	4000	quattro mila
15	quindici	31	trentuno	100,000	cento mila
16	sedici	35	trentacinque	1,000,000	un milione

Note that **venti, trenta, quaranta,** etc. drop the final vowel in combining with **uno** or **otto.**

82. **Use of the Cardinal Numerals**

1.
un dito	*one finger*	una mano	*one hand*
uno specchio	*one mirror*	un'entrata	*one entrance*

Uno has a feminine, **una,** and when used adjectively has the forms of the indefinite article.[1]

2.
quarantuna lira ⎫
lire quarantuna ⎭ *forty-one lire*

If the noun modified by **ventuno, trentuno,** etc. follows the numeral, it is preferable to put it in the singular.

[1] In the sentence **Ho perduto uno dei libri,** *I lost one of the books,* **uno** is used as a pronoun, not as an adjective.

3.   mille novecento   *nineteen hundred*

Eleven hundred, twelve hundred, etc. are translated *one thousand one hundred, one thousand two hundred*, etc.

4. Contrary to English usage, **uno** is omitted before **cento** and **mille**. **Mille** has a plural, **mila**.

5.   due milioni d'abitanti   *two million inhabitants*

Milione is the only number that is a noun; it has a plural, **milioni**, and it requires the preposition **di** before the noun to which it refers.

6. In compound numbers no conjunction is used.

7.   tutti e due i cugini   *both cousins*
                     tutte e due le donne   *both women*

Both is **tutti e due** (**tutte e due**); *all three*, **tutti e tre** (**tutte e tre**), etc. If a noun follows, it takes the definite article.

83.   **Hours of the Day**

          È l'una.   *It's one o'clock* (A.M.).
          Sono le tredici.   *It's one o'clock* (P.M.).

In Italy it is becoming more and more customary to count the hours from midnight to midnight, and therefore the hours after noon are counted from 12 to 24. The numeral indicating the time is preceded by the definite article, and both article and verb agree with **ora,** *hour*, or **ore,** *hours*, understood.

Study the following expressions:

Che ora è? *or* **Che ore sono?**	What time is it?
È mezzogiorno.	It's noon.
È mezzanotte.	It's midnight.
Sono le tre meno un quarto.	It's a quarter to three (A.M.).
Sono le venti e un quarto.	It's a quarter past eight (P.M.).
È l'una e quaranta.	It's forty minutes past one (A.M.).
Sono le diciassette meno dieci.	It's ten minutes to five (P.M.).
A che ora?	At what time?
Alle due e mezza (*or* **mezzo**).	At half past two (A.M.).

| Stamane (*or* stamani); stasera. | This morning; this evening. |
| Stanotte. | Last night (*until noon; after noon it means* tonight). |

84.   **Dates**

il primo febbraio	*on February first*
l'otto maggio 1548	*May eighth, 1548*
il 1948	*1948*
nel 1956	*in 1956*
nel luglio del 1960	*in July, 1960*

1. The cardinal numerals are used to express the days of the month, with the single exception of **primo,** *first.*

2. A date is generally preceded by the masculine definite article (**giorno, mese,** or **anno** being understood), and it is written in the following order: day, month, year. The English *on* is never translated.

85.   **Age**

Quanti anni avete? ⎫	
Che età avete? ⎭	*How old are you?*
Ho diciannove anni.	*I am nineteen years old.*
Il bimbo ha tre mesi.	*The baby is three months old.*

Age is expressed by means of the verb **avere** and the cardinal numbers.

II. LETTURA

Andiamo al cinematografo

— Che ora è? — domando a mio fratello Giacomo.

— Sono le quattordici meno un quarto.

— Bene. Andiamo insieme a un cinematografo. Ritorneremo a casa in tempo per la cena.

5   — Mi dispiace, ma ho un appuntamento con la signorina Guidetti. Devo andare a casa sua. Piuttosto, perchè non andiamo là insieme, tu e io? Essa ha una sorella, e tutti e quattro possiamo poi uscire per fare una passeggiata o per andare a un cinematografo, se esse vogliono.

— Come si chiama questa ragazza? — domando.

— La sorella della signorina Guidetti? Irene.

— E quanti anni ha?

— Avrà diciotto anni il 28 luglio. È una bella ragazza, bionda, di gusto tuo.   5

— Allora facciamo come dici, e telefona alla tua amica.

Giacomo sorride.

— Non ha telefono.

— Dove abita?

— In Via Mazzini. Non ricordo bene se il numero è 1658 o 10 1858; riconosco però la casa, se la vedo.

Questa volta rido io.

Poco dopo siamo già nella nostra automobile, che mio fratello guida.

Prendiamo Via Giusti, arriviamo in Piazza del Duomo, l'attra- 15 versiamo, andiamo per il Corso Cristoforo Colombo, e arriviamo in Via Mazzini.

Ora guardiamo i numeri delle case; leggiamo 26, poi 28, poi 30, poi 32, alla nostra destra. Siamo ancora lontani, e l'automobile corre.   20

Dopo quindici minuti siamo al numero 988. Giacomo guarda attentamente: 1116, 1196, 1250, 1324. Ancora un poco e arriveremo.

Adesso l'automobile va lentamente, e io leggo: 1632, 1640, 1654 ...   25

— Ah! — esclama Giacomo. — Ecco la casa! È al numero 1658.

E ferma l'automobile. Scendiamo, entriamo nella casa. Mio fratello sorride, felice.

Saliamo al primo piano,[1] suoniamo il campanello, e poco dopo 30 un giovanotto molto gentile apre la porta: è il fratello delle signorine, e dice che tutte e due le sorelle sono andate a fare una passeggiata con delle loro amiche.

Fu così che Giacomo e io andammo, sì, a un cinematografo, ma « taciti, soli e senza compagnia ».[2]   35

[1] What is called in Italy **primo piano** is our second floor; our first floor is the Italian **pian terreno**.   [2] Dante, *Inferno*, Canto XXIII.

PROVERBIO

Chi si contenta gode.   *The greatest wealth is contentment with little.*
(He who is satisfied is happy.)

III. STUDIO DI PAROLE

Giacomo James

appuntamento appointment
cinematografo cinema, movie
compagnia company
corso avenue, course
duomo cathedral
giovanotto young man
minuto minute
numero number
telefono telephone
volta time (turn)

felice happy
gentile kind, courteous, gentle
tacito silent

attraversare [attraverso] to cross

chiamarsi to be called; **mi chiamo** my name is
correre (a) to run, speed [1]
esclamare to exclaim
guidare to guide, drive
mi dispiace I am sorry
riconoscere to recognize
ricordare [ricordo] to remember, recall
ridere to laugh
scendere to descend, go (*or* get) down [1]
telefonare [telefono] to telephone

lentamente slowly
però however
piuttosto rather

IV. CONVERSAZIONE

1. Come si chiama Lei?   2. Quanti anni ha?   3. Quanti anni ha suo padre?   4. Dove vuole andare il fratello di Giacomo?   5. Che cosa dice Giacomo?   6. Che cosa vuol egli fare?   7. Come si chiama la sorella della signorina Guidetti?   8. Quanti anni ha?   9. Perchè Giacomo non telefona alla signorina Guidetti?   10. Dove abita questa signorina?   11. Chi guida l'automobile dei due giovanotti?   12. Che cosa fa il fratello di Giacomo mentre Giacomo guida?   13. Chi apre la porta della casa delle signorine?   14. Che cosa dice?   15. Andarono al cinematografo i due fratelli?   16. Che ora è adesso?

[1] Conjugated with **essere** when used intransitively.

V. ESERCIZI

A. 1. Leggere:

21, 27, 30, 35, 40, 48, 51, 57, 63, 84, 88, 99, 100, 191, 203, 333, 362, 765, 838, 917, 1000, 1265, 1321, 1492, 1884, 1958, 2814, 5511, 15,144, 276,666, 1,516,983, 16,376,915.

2. Continuare:

1. Due per due: quattro (i.e. $2 \times 2 = 4$), due per tre: ____, ecc. *as far as* due per venti. 2. Tre per due: sei; tre per tre: ____, ecc. *as far as* tre per dodici. 3. Quattro per due: otto; quattro per tre: ____, ecc. *as far as* quattro per dieci. 4. Cinque per due: dieci; cinque per tre: ____, ecc. *as far as* cinque per dieci.

B. Tradurre in italiano:

1. Probably he thinks so.[1] 2. It's 1:30 P.M. 3. It's midnight. 4. It's probably 11:15 A.M. 5. It's probably noon. 6. It was 7:35 A.M. 7. Our lesson begins at 10 A.M. 8. It ends at 10:50 A.M. 9. This evening we shall go out at 8 P.M. 10. It was 11 P.M.

C. 1. Dare le seguenti date in italiano:

1. La data d'oggi. 2. La data d'una settimana fa. 3. La data d'un mese fa. 4. La data in cui Cristoforo Colombo scoprì [2] l'America.

2. Rispondere alle seguenti domande:

1. Quanti anni ha Lei? 2. Quanti anni avrà questa signorina? 3. Che età avrà questo giovanotto? 4. Che età hanno i suoi zii? 5. Quanti anni ha suo fratello? 6. Che età ha sua sorella?

D. Tradurre in italiano:

I

1. I am sorry, but my brother James is not at home. 2. He went out at 2:30 [3] P.M. with a friend whose name is [4] Andrew. 3. That young man is twenty-two years old and has a beautiful car. 4. Both have gone out to (a) take a ride. 5. I called Beatrice on (a) the phone a short time ago. 6. I invited her to (ad) go to a movie this evening, at eight o'clock. 7. We have an appointment at a drugstore in Cathedral Square.[5] 8. Why don't you go to her house? — Because she lives far away, at (in) 2118 Jefferson Avenue. 9. At what time

---

[1] See § **58**, 2, p. 83.   [2] *discovered.*   [3] Write out all the numbers in this exercise.   [4] Same as *who is called.*   [5] Translate, *Square of the Cathedral.*

will you meet her? — At 7:45, if she is not late. 10. I shall not return home before midnight.

II

1. Will you recognize [1] Ann's house if you see it? 2. I don't remember what number it is, 673 [2] or 637. 3. She lives on (in) Adams Avenue, near the University. 4. The house in which she lives is not far from the movie where we wish to go. 5. I telephoned Ann [3] ten minutes ago and invited her. 6. I like Ann; she is a very kind girl and a good student. — How old is she? — She is nineteen years old. 7. How many sisters has she? — Two, Irene and Helen. Helen is a baby, however; she is only two years old. 8. While we are talking, Clara drives her car, and now we slowly cross the square. 9. Soon after, we are in front of Ann's house. 10. It's 7 P.M., the hour of our appointment, and the movie begins at 7:15.

❧ *Lezione Diciottesima* ❧

I. NOTE GRAMMATICALI

86.　　　　　　　　**Past Perfect**

I	II	III
I had bought, etc.	*I had sold, etc.*	*I had departed, etc.*
avevo avevi } comprato aveva	avevo avevi } venduto aveva	ɛro ɛri } partito, −a ɛra
avevamo avevate } comprato avevano	avevamo avevate } venduto avevano	eravamo eravate } partiti, −e ɛrano
AUXILIARY VERBS		
I had had, etc.	*I had been, etc.*	
avevo avuto, etc.	ɛro stato, −a, etc.	

[1] Don't use the future; use the present.　　[2] Write out all the numbers in this exercise.　　[3] Translate, *to Ann.*

87.   **Second Past Perfect**

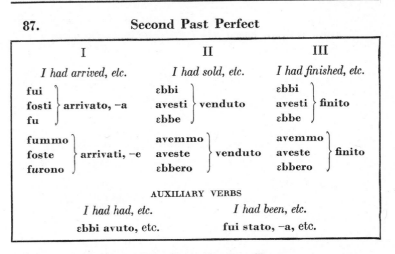

I	II	III
I had arrived, etc.	*I had sold, etc.*	*I had finished, etc.*
fui ⎫	ɛbbi ⎫	ɛbbi ⎫
fosti ⎬ arrivato, –a	avesti ⎬ venduto	avesti ⎬ finito
fu ⎭	ɛbbe ⎭	ɛbbe ⎭
fummo ⎫	avemmo ⎫	avemmo ⎫
foste ⎬ arrivati, –e	aveste ⎬ venduto	aveste ⎬ finito
furono ⎭	ɛbbero ⎭	ɛbbero ⎭

AUXILIARY VERBS

I had had, etc.	*I had been, etc.*
ɛbbi avuto, etc.	fui stato, –a, etc.

88.   **Use of the Past Perfect Tenses**

Both the past perfect and the second past perfect have the
same meaning; like the English past perfect, they denote *what
had happened.*

1. Avevo salutato quel signore.   *I had greeted that gentleman.*
   Ɛrano arrivati presto.   *They had arrived early.*

In a principal clause the past perfect is used.

2. Appena aveva finito di stu-   *As soon as he had finished studying,*
       diare, usciva.   *he used to go out.*
   Appena ɛbbe finito di stu-   *As soon as he had finished studying,*
       diare, uscì.   *he went out.*
   Quando aveva dormito bɛne,   *When he had slept well, he used to*
       lavorava con piacere.   *enjoy his work.*
   Quando ɛbbe dormito bɛne,   *When he had slept well, he enjoyed*
       lavorò con piacere.   *his work.*

In a secondary clause of *time* (introduced by **quando, appena,
dopo che,** etc.), a sequence of tenses must be followed. If in
the principal clause there is a past descriptive, the past perfect is
used, as shown in the 1st and 3rd examples; if the verb of the
principal clause is a past absolute — as in the 2nd and 4th examples — the second past perfect is required.

3. Sorrise (*or* sorrideva) perchè aveva ricevuto buone notizie.

He smiled (or *was smiling*) *because he had received good news.*

Parlò (*or* parlava) del libro che avevamo letto.

He spoke (or *was speaking*) *of the book we had read.*

In all other kinds of secondary clauses the past perfect is used.

89. **Nouns and Adjectives in *–co***

SINGULAR	PLURAL
il fuoco, *the fire*	i fuochi
il pacco, *the parcel*	i pacchi
bianco, *white*	bianchi
But: il monaco, *the monk*	i monaci

Nouns and adjectives ending in *–co* form their plural in *–chi* if the stress of the word is on the syllable before the last; if the stress falls on another syllable, the plural is in *–ci*.

This rule, however, has several exceptions, the most important of which are:

(*a*) **amico**, *friend*, **greco**, *Greek*, **nemico**, *enemy*, and **porco**, *pig*, which form their plural in *–ci*;

(*b*) **carico**, *load, loaded*, **incarico**, *task*, and **manico**, *handle*, the plural of which is in *–chi*.

90. **Nouns and Adjectives in *–go***

SINGULAR	PLURAL
il dialogo, *the dialogue*	i dialoghi
l'ago, *the needle*	gli aghi
vago, *vague*	vaghi

As a general rule, nouns and adjectives ending in *–go* form their plural in *–ghi*.

Note, however, that nouns ending in *–ologo* referring to scientists (**geologo**, *geologist*, **teologo**, *theologian*, **filologo**, *philologist*, etc.) have a plural in *–gi*. Also a few rare nouns ending in *–fago*, such as **antropofago**, *cannibal*, have a plural in *–gi*.

II. LETTURA

Al museo

Due giorni fa, Carlo era andato a visitare il museo insieme con suo cugino Andrea. Essi non erano usciti di casa che verso le quattordici, ma il museo è vicino, ed erano arrivati già alla porta di quell'edifizio pochi minuti dopo. Appena ebbero comprato i biglietti, entrarono.   5

In una delle sale al pian terreno ebbero la fortuna d'incontrare il professor Tognini, della nostra università. Lo salutarono e cominciarono a conversare. Un momento dopo, il professore, gentile come sempre, mostrava e spiegava ai due giovanotti le cose principali.   10

— La collezione di statue che qui ammiriamo è quasi tutta arte antica, arte greca e romana; i quadri, al piano superiore, sono antichi e moderni, italiani e stranieri: ci son quadri francesi, tedeschi, olandesi e spagnoli; ci son pure dei quadri di pittori americani.   15

Di tanto in tanto essi si fermavano a guardare, e il professore spiegava le cose che vedevano, dava informazioni artistiche e storiche.

Una mezz'ora dopo salirono per andare a vedere i quadri.

— I quadri moderni non son sempre di mio gusto, — continuò 20 il profesore, e indicò un brutto quadro. — Preferisco mille volte i nostri buoni artisti antichi!

— Visita spesso il museo? — domandò Andrea.

— Sì, è forse il mio svago preferito.

Il nostro museo è ricco di magnifici quadri.   25

Carlo aveva parlato poco; aveva camminato dietro a gli altri e guardato attentamente ogni cosa. Aveva ammirato specialmente un quadro che rappresentava un piccolo borgo di pescatori olandesi, vicino a un lago, all'ora del tramonto.

PROVERBIO

L'arte non ha maggior nemico dell'ignoranza.	*Art hath no greater enemy than ignorance.*

III. STUDIO DI PAROLE

arte *f.* art
biglietto ticket
borgo hamlet, village
collezione *f.* collection
lago lake
museo museum
pescatore *m.* fisherman
statua statue
svago amusement
tramonto sunset

americano American
artistico artistic
francese French
magnifico magnificent
moderno modern
olandese Dutch
principale principal, main
ricco rich

romano Roman
spagnolo Spanish
storico historic
straniero foreign
tedesco German

ammirare to admire
continuare (a) [continuo] to
    continue
conversare [converso] to talk,
    chat
preferire [preferisco] to prefer
rappresentare [rappresento] to
    represent
salutare to greet

appena as soon as, scarcely
di tanto in tanto once in a while
pure also
verso toward

IV. CONVERSAZIONE

1. Dov'era andato Carlo due giorni fa? 2. A che ora erano usciti di casa i due giovanotti? 3. Che cosa comprarono per entrare nel museo? 4. Chi incontrarono essi nel museo? 5. Dove l'incontrarono? 6. Che cosa mostrò e spiegò il professor Tognini? 7. Che cosa c'era al pian terreno del museo? 8. Dov'erano i quadri? 9. Erano tutti moderni i quadri al piano superiore? 10. Erano tutti italiani? 11. Che cosa osservò il professore mentre indicava un brutto quadro? 12. Quali artisti preferisce Lei? 13. Che cosa domandò Andrea al professore? 14. Perchè il professor Tognini visita spesso il museo? 15. Di che è ricco il museo? 16. Che cosa rappresentava il quadro che Carlo aveva ammirato?

V. ESERCIZI

A. Coniugare prima nel passato perfetto [1] e poi nel secondo passato perfetto [2]:

---

[1] Called *trapassato prossimo*, or *più che perfetto*, or *piuccheperfetto* by Italian grammarians. [2] Called *trapassato remoto* by Italian grammarians.

1. Preferire quegli svaghi.
2. Vedere dei bei laghi.
3. Andare in alcuni borghi.

4. Essere con degli amici tedeschi.
5. Conversare di tanto in tanto.
6. Avere dei libri magnifici.

B. Completare con la forma corretta del passato perfetto o del secondo passato perfetto del verbo in parentesi:

1. (*arrivare*) Quando mia cugina ___ ___ a casa, trovò una lettera.
2. (*occupare*) Noi ___ ___ due tavole. 3. (*sedersi*) Appena ella ___ ___, cominciò a conversare. 4. (*pulire*) Ogni sabato, dopo che ___ ___ la casa, mia sorella usciva. 5. (*pranzare*) Quand'essi ___ ___, andavano a prendere il caffè in salotto. 6. (*vendere*) Appena essi ___ ___ l'automobile, ritornarono a casa. 7. (*partire*) Quand'essi ___ ___, andai a letto. 8. (*raccomandare*) Guido ___ ___ la lettera. 9. (*vedere*) Appena io ___ ___ la tua nonna, la salutai. 10. (*comprare*) Dopo ch'io ___ ___ i biglietti, entrammo nel cinematografo. 11. (*essere*) Quando Anna ___ ___ un mese a casa, voleva partire. 12. (*divertirsi*) Quando Roberto ___ ___ ___, fu contento.

C. Scrivere il plurale di:

1. il nemico principale
   il medico nostro
   il piccolo lago
   il borgo vicino

2. il pane fresco
   il vostro pacco
   il lungo studio
   il teologo greco

3. lo studente ricco
   il magnifico edifizio
   il francobollo antico
   lo scrittore greco

4. l'edifizio bianco
   il geologo tedesco
   il gusto artistico
   il medico italiano

D. Tradurre in italiano:

I

1. Two days ago my friends (*m.*) and I visited the museum of this city. 2. In one of the rooms in which the statues [1] are, I met Professor Patti. 3. After [2] I had greeted him, I introduced my friends and we began to (a) chat. 4. I had been in one of his classes when I was studying at the university. 5. As soon as we had seen the statues,

[1] Place this noun after the verb.   [2] *After* + subject (if any) + verb is **dopo che.**

we went [1] upstairs to (a) look at the paintings. 6. Some [2] were old,[3] others were modern; [it] was a rich [4] collection. 7. I prefer Italian, Spanish, and German paintings to all others. 8. In one of the rooms the principal painting represented Saul and his enemies. 9. In another I admired some magnificent [4] American paintings. 10. One [of them] represented two neighboring villages on one of the Great Lakes at the hour of sunset.[5]

II

1. Italian museums are very rich. 2. My grandfather and I used to spend several hours in those rooms. 3. To go to a museum or to walk in the old streets were our preferred [6] amusements. 4. Our artistic tastes were the same. 5. I had bought some books on the old [7] Italian artists. 6. After [8] we had read [9] them, we found [out] that they were full of useful information.[10] 7. Once in a while we visited some historic places.[11] 8. We had become friends with several Italian and German artists. 9. They were very kind, especially Guidoni, a Roman painter. 10. One of his paintings represented two Greek hamlets toward the hour of sunset.[5]

✥ *Lezione Diciannovεsima* ✥

I. NOTE GRAMMATICALI

91. **Conjunctive Personal Pronouns**

The pronouns which are given in the table that follows are called *conjunctive* because they are used only in connection with a verb, serving as direct objects, indirect objects, or reflexive objects.

---

[1] Use the verb **salire.** [2] **Alcuni.** [3] Use the adjective **antico.** [4] Leave this adjective before the noun. [5] Use the definite article. [6] A past participle used as an adjective. [7] Use the adjective **antico.** [8] *After* + subject (if any) + verb is **dopo che.** [9] The verb lεggere has an irregular past participle: lεtto. [10] See footnote 3, p. 107. [11] Use the word luɔgo.

DIRECT OBJECTS	INDIRECT OBJECTS	REFLEXIVE OBJECTS
mi me	**mi** to me	**mi** myself
ti thee, you	**ti** to thee, to you	**ti** thyself, yourself
lo him, it ⎫	**gli** to him, to it ⎫	**si** himself, herself, itself, yourself
la her, it ⎬	**le** to her, to it ⎬	
La you ⎭	**Le** to you ⎭	
ci us	**ci** to us	**ci** ourselves
vi you	**vi** to you	**vi** yourself, yourselves
li them (m.) ⎫	**loro** to them ⎫	
le them (f.) ⎬	⎬	**si** themselves, yourselves
Li you (m.) ⎬	**Loro** to you ⎭	
Le you (f.) ⎭		

ne of it, of them, some, some of it, some of them, any, any of it, any of them

Note, from the table above, that:

1. In the 1st and 2nd persons, singular and plural, the same forms are used for the three different functions while only the 3rd person offers different forms.

2. The 3rd person renders the English *you* as follows:

Addressing one person:	**La** ⎫	**Le** ⎫		**si** yourself
Addressing more than one man,				
or men and women:	**Li** ⎬ you	**Loro** ⎬ to you	**si** yourselves
Addressing two or more				
women:	**Le** ⎭	**Loro** ⎭		**si** yourselves

92. Use of the Conjunctive Personal Pronouns

POSITION

1.	Egli mi conosce.	*He knows me.*
	Scriverò loro.	*I shall write to them.*
	L'ho usato.	*I have used it.*
	Non lo capii.	*I did not understand him.*

The conjunctive personal pronouns, except **loro**, immediately precede the verb. If the verb is a compound tense (3rd example), the pronoun precedes the auxiliary; if the verb is negative (4th example), **non** precedes the pronoun.

2.	Vɔglio conoscerla.	*I want to know her.*
	Imparandolo.	*In learning it.*
	Imparatolo.	*Having learned it.*
	Rispettiamoli.	*Let us respect them.*
	Dammi la minuta.	*Give me the bill of fare.*
	Dagli un libro.	*Give him a book.*
	Parlatene loro.	*Speak of it to them.*
	Scrivetelo.	*Write it.*
	Ɛccola.	*Here it is.*

But when the verb is an infinitive,[1] a present participle, a past participle used without auxiliary, or an affirmative imperative,[2] the pronoun follows the verb, and is written as one word with it.

Note that:

(*a*) In combining with a pronoun, the infinitive loses its final **e** (**conoscerla**).

(*b*) An imperative ending in a stressed vowel causes the doubling of the initial consonant of the pronoun which is attached to it (**dammi**). **Gli** is the only exception to this rule.

(*c*) **Loro** is never attached to the verb (**parlatene loro**).

(*d*) The stress of the verb remains unchanged, in spite of the addition of the pronoun (**scrivetelo**).

(*e*) The interjection ɛcco takes the pronouns appended just as if it were an imperative (**ɛccola**).

ELISION

3.	M'ha veduto.	*He has seen me.*
	L'hɔ usato.	*I have used it.*

Most of the conjunctive personal pronouns may drop the final vowel and take an apostrophe before a verb beginning with a vowel. The elision, however, occurs more frequently with **mi, ti, vi, si,** and nearly always with **lo, la. Ci** elides only before **e** or **i.**

---

[1] Not the infinitive used, with a negative, as imperative (*see* § 44, p. 61).
[2] Not the negative imperative, nor the subjunctive used as an imperative (*see* § 42, 1, p. 60).

RECIPROCAL MEANING

| 4. Ci rispettiamo. | *We respect ourselves. We respect one another.* |
| Ci rispettiamo l'un l'altro. | *We respect one another.* |

The plural reflexive pronouns are used also as reciprocal pronouns. The sense is usually clear, but ambiguity can be avoided by adding to the verb **l'un l'altro,** *one another*, which emphasizes the reciprocal meaning.

USE OF "NE"

5. Ne ho già parlato.	*I have already spoken of it.*
Ne avevo quattro.	*I had four (of them).*
Datene.	*Give some of them.*
Ne ho avuti molti.	*I have had many (of them).*
Non voglio comprarne.	*I don't want to buy any.*

The conjunctive pronoun **ne,** *of it, of them*, translates also *some* or *any*, whenever these words stand for *some of it, some of them, any of it, any of them*. It is never omitted when a numerical adjective or a similar word stands after the verb without the noun (2nd example).

When **ne** is used with a compound tense (4th example), the past participle agrees with it as if it were a direct object form (*see* § **40, 2**, p. 48).

Note: For the use of two conjunctive pronouns, see § **121**, p. 199.

93.   **Conjunctive Adverbs of Place**

Egli ci viene spesso.	*He comes here often.*
Ci andai ieri.	*I went there yesterday.*
Ritornateci.	*Return there.*
Vi ritornai.	*I returned there.*
Ne uscimmo.	*We went out of there.*
C'è un bel teatro in questa città.	*There is a fine theater in this city.*
Ci sono bicchieri?	*Are there any glasses?*

Here and *there*, when they denote a place already mentioned, and no particular stress is laid upon them, are rendered by **ci** or

vi. In the same manner, *thence, from there, of there* are rendered by **ne.**

These adverbs are used only in connection with a verb and precede or follow it according to the same rules given for the pronouns **ci, vi, ne** (*see* § 92, p. 135).

There is, there are, etc., are translated **c'è** or **v'è, ci sono** or **vi sono,** etc.

II. LETTURA

Al ristorante

Bianca e Olga sono uscite coi loro genitori per andare a pranzare in un ristorante in città. Oggi è il compleanno della mamma, e la piccola famiglia lo festeggia.

È già sera quand'essi lasciano la casa; ora le vie e le piazze,
5 le vetrine dei negozi sono illuminate. Siamo in primavera, non fa freddo, ed è bello camminare.

Saranno le diciannove quand'essi arrivano al Ristorante Gigli, in Corso Garibaldi. Il babbo apre la porta, la mamma entra prima, gli altri la seguono.

10 — Buona sera, avvocato! Buona sera, signora e signorine! — dice un vecchio cameriere, che li riconosce.

Il ristorante è pieno di gente, ma v'è ancora qualche tavola libera, ed essi occupano la prima che trovano apparecchiata per quattro.

15 — La minuta, Giovanni, — dice l'avvocato Favezzani appena s'è seduto.

— Ecco, signore. Che vino devo portare?

— Portateci del Capri bianco in ghiaccio, per favore.

Mentre il cameriere va via, il babbo passa la minuta alla mamma.

20 — Hai appetito, Anna? — le dice.

— Sì, grazie. Ho appetito e ho sete, — gli risponde la signora Favezzani. Poi guarda la minuta e dice: — Questi maccheroni alla siciliana devono esser buoni. Poi desidero un po' di pesce.

Ma già il cameriere ritorna col vino in un secchietto pieno di
25 ghiaccio, e il signor Favezzani gli dà l'ordine:

— Serviteci prima un po' d'antipasto; poi portateci dei macche-

roni alla siciliana, pesce fritto, pollo arrosto con patate e piselli,
insalata, frutta e torta.

— Devo portarvi il caffè quando servirò la torta? — gli domanda
Giovanni mentre passa dietro alle signore e versa loro del vino
nei bicchieri. 5

— Sì, quattro tazzine di caffè nero.

— Sta bene, avvocato!

Bianca e Olga vedono una studentessa che conoscono, seduta a
una delle tavole a sinistra. La salutano e le sorridono.

Qualche momento dopo cominciano a mangiare, e il pranzo dura 10
un'ora.

PROVERBIO

L'appetito vien mangiando.   *Appetite comes with eating.*

III. STUDIO DI PAROLE

Giovanni John

antipasto appetizers
appetito appetite; **aver appetito**
  to be hungry
compleanno birthday
ghiaccio ice
insalata salad
maccherone m. macaroni [1]
minuta bill of fare
ordine m. order
patata potato
pesce m. fish
pisello pea
pollo chicken; **pollo arrosto** roast
  chicken
ristorante m. restaurant
secchietto little pail

sete f. thirst; **aver sete** to be
  thirsty
torta cake
vino wine

fritto fried
libero free, empty

durare to last [2]
festeggiare [**festeggio**] to celebrate
illuminare [**illumino**] to light
lasciare [**lascio**] to leave [3]
mangiare [**mangio**] to eat
servire [**servo**] to serve
versare [**verso**] to pour

alla siciliana Sicilian style
sta bene! all right! very well!

[1] Used currently in the plural; **maccherone** is only one *string* of macaroni.
[2] Conjugated with **essere**.   [3] Used only transitively; the English intransitive *to leave* is **andar via** or **partire**.

IV. CONVERSAZIONE

1. Dove vanno Bianca e Ɔlga coi loro genitori? 2. Che cɔsa festeggia la famiglia Favezzani? 3. C'è ancora il sole quand'essi lasciano la casa? 4. Perchè camminano? 5. A che ora arrivano al ristorante? 6. Chi entra prima nel ristorante? 7. Che cɔsa dice il cameriɛre quando li vede? 8. Come si chiama il cameriɛre? 9. Sono libere molte tavole? 10. Che cɔsa domanda l'avvocato Favezzani al cameriɛre? 11. Che cɔsa dice la signora Favezzani quando lɛgge la minuta? 12. Che cɔsa pɔrta loro Giovanni prima di tutto? 13. Che ordine gli dà l'avvocato? 14. Bianca e Ɔlga chi vedono a una delle tavole? 15. Che cɔsa fanno allora? 16. Che cɔsa fanno tutti qualche momento dopo?

V. ESERCIZI

A. Tradurre in italiano:

1. We speak of it. 2. Let us visit her. 3. I buy twelve of them. 4. They answer us. 5. He tells her to (**di**) sit down. 6. Let's send her those flowers. 7. I am giving him everything. 8. How many of them have they? 9. Let us look at them (*two ways*). 10. Speak (*four ways* [1]) of it. 11. There they are (*two ways*). 12. Follow me (*four ways*).

B. Sostituire all'oggɛtto indiretto il pronome personale congiuntivo (e.g. egli dà la matita a Giovanni = egli gli dà la matita):

1. Giacomo parla ad Anna. 2. Io vendo un bigliɛtto a Vittɔrio. 3. Maria non rispondɛrà a Ɔlga. 4. Lɛi parla alle bambine. 5. Io dɔ un appuntamento a Paolo. 6. Chi dà qualche cɔsa ai pɔveri? 7. Diamo dei fiori alla mamma! 8. Scrivete una lunga lɛttera ai vɔstri genitori. 9. Parla a quelle signorine! 10. Egli dice una parɔla a sua mɔglie.

C. Sostituire (*Substitute*) **ci, vi** o **ne** ai complementi introdotti da (*for the prepositional phrases with*) **in, a, di** o **da** (e.g. essi ɛscono dalla scuɔla = essi ne ɛscono):

1. Saremo a casa alle diɛci. 2. Desideravo un pɔ' di latte. 3. Arrivano da Chicago. 4. Parlai di quegli annunzi. 5. Ɛlena ɛra in sala da pranzo. 6. Prendɛrɔ del ghiaccio. 7. Ritorna in salɔtto, Clara!

---

[1] **Tu, voi, Lɛi,** and **Loro** forms of direct address.

8. Non voglio parlare di quella cosa. 9. Ritornava dal giardino.
10. Andiamo alla posta. 11. Egli era in chiesa. 12. Uscì dalla cucina.

D. Tradurre in italiano:

I

1. Where is the bill of fare, waiter? — Here it is, madam. May I
bring you some wine? 2. Yes, bring me some white Capri [1]; I prefer
this wine to all others. 3. Then bring me some appetizers and butter;
I am hungry this evening. 4. My dinner will be macaroni, fish Sicilian
style, and roast chicken. 5. The waiter is listening to the lady; then
he says to her, "Very well, Madam," and goes away. 6. She unfolds
her [2] napkin and looks at the neighboring tables. 7. What a crowd! [3]
Few tables are still empty. 8. A girl student is entering the restaurant
now. 9. The lady knows her; she smiles at her [4] and greets her.
10. Soon after, both [5] women begin to (a) chat.

II

1. Some friends (*m.*) are celebrating John's birthday. 2. They occupy
a large table set [6] for twelve in a restaurant downtown. 3. There are
some red and yellow flowers on the table. 4. The restaurant is well
lighted [6] and full of people. 5. Some tables are still empty; they are
few, however. 6. Waiter, bring us some ice and some other glasses,
please; we are thirsty and want some wine. 7. The waiter goes to
(**in**) the kitchen and returns from there soon after with a little pail full
of ice. 8. The dinner begins: appetizers, macaroni Sicilian style, fried
chicken, salad, and cake. 9. With the chicken the twelve friends eat
potatoes and peas. 10. I call the waiter and ask him [7] to (**di**) serve
us another wine. "Very well, sir!" he answers me.

[1] The names of wines are considered masculine. [2] An obvious possessive;
translate it with the definite article. [3] Translate, *how many people*, using the
singular form. [4] Translate as if the English were *to her*. [5] Use the definite
article after *both*. [6] A past participle used as an adjective. [7] An indirect
object.

I. NOTE GRAMMATICALI

94. **Disjunctive Personal Pronouns**

While the conjunctive personal pronouns, studied in the preceding lesson, are used only in connection with a verb, the pronouns listed below — called *disjunctive* — are used independently of it. Their most common usage is as objects of prepositions.[1]

	SINGULAR			PLURAL	
1st person	me	me		noi	us
2nd person	te	thee, you		voi	you
3rd person	lui	him		loro	them (*m. or f.*)
	lɛi	her			
	esso	him, it		essi	them (*m.*)
	essa	her, it		esse	them (*f.*)
	Lɛi	you		Loro	you
	sè	himself, herself, itself, yourself		sè	themselves, yourselves

Volete venire con me ?	*Do you want to come with me?*
Lavorava per lɛi (*or* per essa).	*He was working for her.*
Scriviamo con essa.	*We write with it.*
Parla di loro (*or* d'essi).	*He is speaking of them.*
Lo troverete fra essi (*or* fra loro).	*You will find it among them.*

Note that **lui, lɛi,** and their plural, **loro,** are used only with reference to persons, while **esso, essa, essi,** and **esse** may refer to persons, animals, or things.

95. **Comparison**

A qualifying adjective may express three degrees of any given quality: the positive (the adjective itself), the comparative, and the superlative.

The comparative may be of equality or inequality; the superlative may be relative or absolute.

---

[1] For other uses of the disjunctive personal pronouns, see § 154, p. 267.

PALERMO'S NORMAN CATHEDRAL

CATHEDRAL, CAMPANILE, AND BAPTISTRY, PARMA

A VIEW OF GENOA BEFORE THE SECOND WORLD WAR

ESEDRA FOUNTAIN, ROME

96.   The Comparative of Equality

Egli è così biondo come Carlo. } Egli è biondo come Carlo. }	*He is as blond as Charles.*
Ella non è tanto alta quanto lui. } Ella non è alta quanto lui. }	*She is not so tall as he is.*
Egli è tanto buono quanto gentile.	*He is as good as he is kind.*

Equality is expressed by the correlative forms **così ... come,** or **tanto ... quanto,** which stand for the English *as ... as,* or *so ... as.*

Note that **così** and **tanto** may be omitted.

Note also, from the 3rd and 4th examples, that a personal pronoun used as a second term of comparison is rendered in Italian by its disjunctive form.

97.   The Comparative of Inequality

1. Luigi è più diligente.	*Louis is more diligent.*
Giorgio è meno diligente.	*George is less diligent.*

Inequality is expressed by **più,** *more,* or **meno,** *less.*

2. Lo studio è più grande del sa- lotto.	*The study is larger than the living room.*
Egli è più ricco di te.	*He is richer than you.*
Ho meno di venti lire.	*I have less than twenty lire.*

Than is **di** before nouns, pronouns, or numerals.

Note that when **di** is used before a noun preceded by the definite article, as in the 1st example, **di** contracts with the article.

Note also that if a personal pronoun follows **di,** the disjunctive form is used (2nd example).

3. La sala è più lunga che larga.	*The hall is longer than it is wide.*
Ama più dare che ricevere.	*He likes to give more than to receive*

In most other cases, **che** is used to express the English *than.*[1]

---

[1] For other ways of translating *than,* see § **136,** p. 225.

98. Negative Sentences

1. Egli non capisce.	*He does not understand.*

As we have already seen, a verb is made negative by placing **non** before it.

2. Non ho inchiostro.	*I haven't any ink.*
Ella non ha libri.	*She hasn't any books.*
Ella non ha nessun libro.	*She hasn't any book.*
Non parlo con nessuno.	*I speak to nobody.*

The English *any* is not translated whenever, in a negative sentence, it is followed by a singular noun that does not take a numerical modifier (1st example [1]), or by a plural noun (2nd example).

When, however, *any* is followed by a singular noun that may take a numerical modifier (as **libro**), it is usually rendered by **nessuno**, which takes the same endings as the indefinite article (**nessun, nessuno, nessuna, nessun'**). As **nessuno** means *not one*, or *not any*, or *nobody*, it will be seen that the *double negative* occurs rather frequently in Italian, conveying, however, only a single negative idea. In other words, contrary to English grammar, two negatives in Italian do not make the meaning affirmative.

3. Egli non ascolta mai.	*He never listens.*
Non voglio niente (*or* nulla).	*I don't want anything.*
Non parla nè tedesco nè spagnolo.	*He speaks neither German nor Spanish.*
Non ho nemmeno un dollaro.	*I don't even have a dollar.*

Other negative expressions used in connection with negative verbs are: **mai**, *never;* **niente** or **nulla**, *nothing;* **nè ... nè**, *neither ... nor;* **neanche**, or **nemmeno**, or **neppure**, all three meaning *not even*, etc.

4. Nessuno parte.	*Nobody leaves.*
Nulla è impossibile.	*Nothing is impossible.*
Egli mai capisce.	*He never understands.*

When one of the above-mentioned negative expressions precedes the verb, **non** is omitted.

---

[1] Other examples of nouns that do not take a numerical modifier are: **aria, ghiaccio, burro, latte, zucchero,** etc.

II. LETTURA

Irene fa delle spese

Irene è troppo buona con suo fratello Giovanni; non gli dice mai no quand'egli domanda dei favori, ed egli non la ringrazia nemmeno; non è gentile con lei.

Poco fa essa ha pulito e stirato l'abito marrone ch'egli porta all'università; prima la giacca, poi il panciotto, e poi i pantaloni. 5 Ma neanche così Giovanni è contento, e adesso domanda a sua sorella se ella ha stirato tutte le sue cravatte.

— No, Vanni, — Irene gli risponde, — non posso far niente altro per te ora perchè la mia amica Clara sta per arrivare, e devo ancora vestirmi. Qui nessuno m'aiuta, ed è tardi. 10

— Esci con lei? Dove vai?

— Andiamo a far delle spese. Oggi è sabato e le cose sono più a buon mercato che negli altri giorni. Clara vuol comprarsi una veste e un cappello, e io ho bisogno di guanti, d'un ombrello, e d'un paio di soprascarpe. 15

— Bene! E per me non ci sarà nulla?

— Di che hai bisogno tu?

— D'un po' di tutto: di qualche camicia, di calzini . . . e d'una cravatta più bella di questa, se ne trovi una.

— Ne hai anche troppe di cravatte, mi pare. 20

— Le cravatte non son mai troppe.

Qualche ora dopo, le due amiche vanno da un negozio della città all'altro per trovare le cose di cui hanno bisogno. È vero che ci sono delle vendite speciali, ma in alcuni negozi i prezzi sono così alti come negli altri giorni. 25

Irene è fortunata, e compra a prezzo basso le cose che vuole per sè e quelle che Giovanni desidera, fra cui un fazzoletto di seta e un'elegante cravatta gialla e azzurra. L'amica Clara ha meno fortuna di lei; compra la veste che vuole, ma non trova nessun cappello di suo gusto. 30

PROVERBIO

Buon mercato sfonda la borsa.   *A good bargain is a pickpocket.*
                                  (Cheap buying knocks out the bot-
                                  tom of the purse.)

III. STUDIO DI PAROLE

abito suit of clothes
calzino sock
camicia shirt
cravatta necktie
fazzoletto handkerchief
giacca coat, jacket
ombrello umbrella
paio pair, couple
panciotto vest
pantaloni *m. pl.* trousers
prezzo price
seta silk
soprascarpa overshoe, rubber

alto high, tall

azzurro blue
basso low
elegante elegant, stylish, smart
fortunato fortunate, lucky
troppo too much, (*pl.*) too many
vero true

aiutare (a) to help, aid
aver bisogno di to need
ringraziare [ringrazio] to thank
stare per to be about to
stirare to iron, press

tardi late [1]
troppo *adv.* too, too much

IV. CONVERSAZIONE

1. È cattiva Irene con suo fratello? 2. Come chiama ella suo fratello? 3. Che cosa dice Irene quando Giovanni le domanda dei favori? 4. La ringrazia Giovanni? 5. Che cosa ha ella pulito poco fa? 6. Che le dice Giovanni? 7. Che cosa gli risponde Irene? 8. Dove va Irene? 9. Che cosa vuol comprare Clara? 10. Di che ha bisogno Irene? 11. Di che cosa Giovanni dice che ha bisogno? 12. Perchè è bene far delle spese il sabato? 13. I prezzi sono bassi in tutti i negozi? 14. Quale delle due amiche è più fortunata? 15. Che cosa compra Irene? 16. Che cosa compra Clara?

V. ESERCIZI

A. Tradurre in italiano:

1. I go with him. 2. We shall return with her. 3. He works for them. 4. I shall clean the room with it (*m.*). 5. We don't need you (*four ways*). 6. She goes out with them. 7. He shops with me. 8. I washed myself in it (*f.*). 9. We ate with you (*four ways*). 10. She plays with them. 11. He got up for her. 12. I shall dine with him.

[1] This word expresses the idea of *late* in an absolute sense; *late* with reference to a specific time is **in ritardo**.

B. 1. Completare le seguenti frasi con **di** o con **che:**

1. Egli è più giovane _____ sua cugina. 2. Ho più _____ quarant'anni.
3. Ama più leggere _____ divertirsi. 4. Carlo è meno occupato _____
Lei. 5. C'erano più donne là _____ qua. 6. Codesta cosa è meno utile
_____ quella. 7. Ha più _____ sessant'anni. 8. Il Bacci è meno vecchio
_____ sua moglie. 9. Questa stanza da bagno è meno grande _____
quella. 10. Laura è più buona _____ bella. 11. Sono stato più gentile
_____ loro. 12. Gli alunni di questa classe sono più _____ venti.

2. Tradurre in italiano:

1. This building is as fine as that [one]. 2. I am as busy as you [are].
3. It's colder today than yesterday. 4. She is less jolly than Helen.
5. It's as warm as in July. 6. He is poorer than you. 7. My chair
is not so comfortable as yours. 8. She is less happy than before. 9. My
uncle is not so old as my aunt. 10. My car is less loaded than his.

C. 1. Dare la forma negativa delle seguenti frasi:

1. Ho un coltello. 2. Hanno forchette e cucchiai. 3. Ho telefonato
a un uomo. 4. Mangia qualche cosa. 5. Ella canta qualche volta
per noi. 6. Aveva nemici. 7. Aveva anche amici. 8. Sorride qualche
volta. 9. Ho padre e madre. 10. Ho pure uno zio. 11. Scrive una
lettera. 12. Abbiamo ricevuto qualche cosa.

2. Tradurre in due modi, con o senza **non:**

1. He never studies. 2. No one looked at him. 3. Not even a post
card has arrived. 4. Nobody greets them. 5. I can't do anything.

D. Tradurre in italiano:

I

1. Irene wishes to go shopping [1] with me this afternoon. 2. She says
that there is a special sale today, that things are cheaper than on (**in**)
other days. 3. Perhaps she is not wrong, because it [2] is Saturday, but
I don't need anything. 4. She wants to buy a top coat [3] and a pair of
rubbers. 5. Next week [4] is my dad's birthday, and I want to buy
something for him. 6. It's difficult, however, to find something to
[suit] his taste. 7. He needs [5] neither shirts, nor socks, nor handkerchiefs. 8. I shall be glad if I find a pretty silk tie [6] to (**da**) go with his

[1] See Vocabulary.   [2] See § **65,** 2, p. 92.   [3] Same as *overcoat.*   [4] Use
the definite article.   [5] Repeat **di** immediately before each noun.   [6] Translate *a necktie of silk.*

new gray suit. 9. Irene will help me; she is younger than I, but she has good taste. 10. I like to shop with her.

II

1. I like to wear [a] black [1] coat and vest and a pair of gray trousers. 2. Yesterday, however, I bought a brown suit. 3. The clerk who sold me that suit showed me other things, too. 4. I don't need [2] either shirts or socks, and I don't even need gloves. 5. So I bought a blue and yellow silk necktie.[3] 6. I was [4] downtown less than two hours, and John was [5] with me. 7. He bought himself an overcoat, an umbrella, and a pair of rubbers. 8. These things are more useful than beautiful. 9. I haven't any friend so dear [to me] as John. 10. He is taller than I, but this is perhaps because I am younger than he [is].

❧ *Lezione Ventunesima* ❧

I. NOTE GRAMMATICALI

99. **Future Perfect**

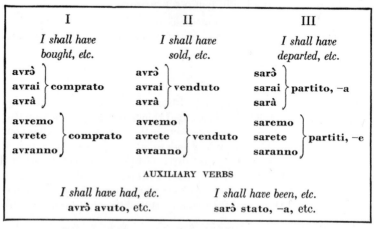

I	II	III
I shall have bought, etc.	*I shall have sold, etc.*	*I shall have departed, etc.*
avrò ⎫ avrai ⎬ comprato avrà ⎭	avrò ⎫ avrai ⎬ venduto avrà ⎭	sarò ⎫ sarai ⎬ partito, −a sarà ⎭
avremo ⎫ avrete ⎬ comprato avranno ⎭	avremo ⎫ avrete ⎬ venduto avranno ⎭	saremo ⎫ sarete ⎬ partiti, −e saranno ⎭

AUXILIARY VERBS

I shall have had, etc.	*I shall have been, etc.*
avrò avuto, etc.	sarò stato, −a, etc.

[1] See footnote 1, p. 51. [2] Repeat **di** immediately before each noun.
[3] Translate, *a necktie of silk.* [4] Past absolute. [5] Past descriptive.

100.   Use of the Future Perfect

Allora l'avremo meritato.	*Then we shall have deserved it.*
Se Margherita li avrà invitati, essi accetteranno.	*If Margaret has invited them, they will accept.*
Sarà stato povero, ma non pareva.	*Probably he was poor, but he did not seem so.*

The rules given for the use of the future (*see* § 58, p. 83), apply also to the future perfect.

Note that, while probability in the present is expressed by the future tense, probability in the past is expressed by the future perfect tense.

101.   The Relative Superlative

Egli è il più alto.	*He is the tallest* (or *the taller*).
Essa era la più famosa attrice d'Italia.	*She was the most famous actress in Italy.*
Carlo è il meno studioso della classe.	*Charles is the least studious in the class.*
Egli è l'alunno meno studioso.	*He is the least studious pupil.*

The relative superlative is formed by placing the definite article before a comparative of inequality.

If, however, as in the last example above, the superlative follows a noun that already has a definite article, no other article is required.

Note from the 1st example that there is no distinction between a comparative with the definite article and the relative superlative.

Note also very carefully (2nd and 3rd examples) that the English *in* after a superlative is rendered by **di**.

102.   The Absolute Superlative

una signora gentil*issima*	*a very kind lady*
una bell*issima* statua	*a very beautiful statue*
un uomo molto felice	*a very happy man*
un'amica assai cara	*a very dear friend*

The absolute superlative is usually formed in one of the following ways [1]:

(*a*) By adding –issimo to the adjective after its last vowel has been dropped. Note, however, that some adjectives, in adding this suffix, undergo orthographic changes like those we studied in the formation of the plural (*see* § **59**, p. 83, and §§ **89–90**, p. 130): **vecchio, vecchissimo; ricco, ricchissimo,** etc.

(*b*) By placing before the adjective some qualifying adverb, such as **molto** or **assai,** *very, quite;* **immensamente,** *immensely;* **estremamente,** *extremely,* etc.

II. LETTURA

La vostra città

La vostra città non ha che 160,000 abitanti, ma è ricca di bellezze naturali e artistiche, e offre quasi tutti i vantaggi d'un gran centro. Stamane l'ho veduta dal tetto d'uno dei più alti edifizi di Piazza del Duomo; Guido era con me e mi mostrava le cose
5 più interessanti. Saremo stati una mezz'ora lassù, e non ero stanco di guardare, tanto più che il tempo era bello e l'aria limpida.

— Qua sotto, — mi spiegava il mio amico, — abbiamo la piazza principale. Codesti due bei palazzi, a destra, sono il Municipio e la Posta; a sinistra, dietro a quegli alberi, c'è il nostro più gran
10 teatro, e vicino al teatro puoi vedere la mia banca.

— Che è quella via larga che mena a quel parco lontano? — ho domandato.

— È il Corso Washington. Esso è lunghissimo, come vedi, e ha bellissimi negozi e parecchi cinematografi. Quando avremo
15 finito di guardare e saremo in piazza, prenderemo un'automobile per ritornare a casa, e passeremo per quella via.

— Benissimo! E quali chiese sono quelle due a sinistra del Corso Washington?

— La più grande è la chiesa di San Paolo, l'altra è quella di
20 Sant'Antonio, una delle più antiche della città.

Potei riconoscere sulla verde collina, vicino al lago, l'università

---

[1] There are other ways, less frequently used, of forming an absolute superlative (*see* § **155,** p. 268).

coi suoi begli edifizi di stile Rinascimento, fra cui quelli di legge
e di medicina, e la biblioteca.

— Vicino alla ferrovia, — continuava Guido, — le vie sono
strette e brutte. È là che abitano le famiglie povere. Ma guarda
la piazza davanti alla stazione, con quella fontana al centro e 5
quelle due statue. Non è bella?

— Dove abita la gente ricca? — ho domandato.

— Costà a destra, in quelle case tra il verde degli alberi. È lì
che abitano i miei amici Vittorio e Carlo, i più allegri studenti
dell'università. Il loro nonno è un uomo ricchissimo; è il pro- 10
prietario d'uno dei più eleganti negozi della città.

PROVERBIO

Chi ha danaro ha ciò che vuole.   *Money is the ace of trumps.* (*He who
has money, has what he wants.*)

III. STUDIO DI PAROLE

Antonio Anthony
Rinascimento Renaissance

abitante *m.* inhabitant
banca bank
bellezza beauty
biblioteca library
centro center
collina hill
ferrovia railroad
fontana fountain
municipio city hall
palazzo palace, building
parco park
proprietario owner
stazione *f.* station
stile *m.* style

teatro theater
tetto roof
vantaggio advantage

interessante interesting
limpido limpid, clear
naturale natural
stanco tired
stretto narrow

menare to lead, take (*in the sense of*
to lead)
offrire [offro] to offer

lassù up there, over there
sotto under, below
tanto più che all the more because, all the better because

IV. CONVERSAZIONE

1. Quanti abitanti ha la città che Guido mostrava? 2. Di che
è ricca la città? 3. Da dove hanno veduto la città i due amici?

4. Perchè vedevano chiaramente ogni cosa? **5.** Quanto tempo saranno stati lassù? **6.** Quali edifizi i due amici vedevano in Piazza del Duomo? **7.** Che via era quella che dalla piazza menava al parco? **8.** Che cosa c'è in quel corso? **9.** Quali chiese erano quelle a sinistra del Corso Washington? **10.** È moderna la chiesa Sant'Antonio? **11.** Che cosa riconosceva l'amico di Guido? **12.** Di che stile erano gli edifizi dell'università? **13.** Chi abita vicino alla ferrovia? **14.** Dove abita la gente ricca? **15.** Chi è il nonno di Vittorio e di Carlo?

V. ESERCIZI

A. **1.** Coniugare nel futuro perfetto [1]:

1. Essere contentissimo.
2. Servire delle frutta.
3. Ricevere un pacchetto.
4. Ringraziare gli amici.
5. Vestirsi di nuovo.
6. Non pagare niente.

2. Completare con la forma corretta del futuro perfetto del verbo in parentesi:

1. (*arrivare*) Noi non ＿＿ ＿＿ ancora. **2.** (*essere*) I nipoti ＿＿ ＿＿ parecchi. **3.** (*aiutare*) Guido e Franco l'＿＿ ＿＿ con piacere. **4.** (*perdere*) Voi li ＿＿ ＿＿. **5.** (*festeggiare*) Esse ＿＿ ＿＿ il suo compleanno. **6.** (*avere*) Noi non ＿＿ ＿＿ bisogno di nulla. **7.** (*essere*) Lei non ＿＿ ＿＿ felice. **8.** (*lavare*) Chi ＿＿ ＿＿ i piatti? **9.** (*ricevere*) Tu ＿＿ ＿＿ la lettera raccomandata. **10.** (*servire*) La cameriera ＿＿ ＿＿ il caffè.

B. Usare queste parole in brevi frasi:

proprietario	gente	agosto	pianoforte
appuntamento	calza	bambino	marmellata
biblioteca	ghiaccio	ombrello	professione

C. **1.** Tradurre in italiano:

1. This is my youngest cousin (*f.*). **2.** Here is the most comfortable chair in the study. **3.** James is the tallest boy in the class. **4.** Ann is the most beautiful. **5.** John is the least fortunate. **6.** I am the least busy. **7.** This painting is the most artistic thing in the house. **8.** She was the least satisfied. **9.** Here is the largest room in the building. **10.** You are the least happy.

[1] Called *futuro anteriore* by Italian grammarians.

2. Dare due differenti superlativi assoluti per ciascuno (*each*) dei seguenti aggettivi:

caldo	buffo	ricco	stanco
bianco	fresco	felice	antico
povero	carico	libero	moderno

D. Tradurre in italiano:

I

1. Our city is very old,[1] but now it has only 156,000 [2] inhabitants. 2. It is very beautiful and it offers several advantages. 3. From the hill of the university or from the roof of the city hall you can see everything. 4. This morning I showed the most interesting places to my friend Victor. 5. We probably [3] spent three hours together and, in order not to waste time, we went in my car. 6. I took him from the station to the park and from the library to the cathedral. 7. In the large square in (a) the center of the city he admired the fountain and our most beautiful buildings. 8. From the roof of my bank we saw the whole beauty of our city, all the better because the air was clear. 9. Which church is that [one in] Renaissance style [4] there, on the hill? — St. Anthony's,[5] the largest in our city. 10. I like this city. When I have finished [3] my studies and have become a lawyer, I shall live [6] here.

II

1. "The natural and artistic beauties of this city are many," observed Frank. 2. It has a very fine zoological garden, two other [7] parks, a large theater, and some fountains. 3. When we have arrived [3] in Alfieri Square, I'll show you [8] some very fine buildings [in] Renaissance style.[4] 4. Then I'll take you to the cathedral, and we shall go up [9] on the roof. 5. From up there we saw,[10] a half hour later, the whole city, from the railroad to the most distant hills. 6. Frank showed me the most interesting places and pointed out the city hall, the library, some banks, and the church of St. Anthony. 7. We saw everything

---

[1] Use the adjective **antico**. [2] Write out the number. [3] Attention! [4] Translate, *of Renaissance style*. [5] *The Church of St. Anthony*. [6] Use the verb **abitare**. [7] The adjective **altro** usually precedes a numeral. [8] Two intimate friends are talking; use the **tu** form. [9] How do you say, in Italian, *to go up*? [10] Use the past absolute.

clearly, all the better because the air was clear.   8. Look at those [1] narrow streets here below; they are the oldest streets in our city. 9. My uncle is the owner of a restaurant in that very long avenue that leads to the center of the city.   10. After [2] we have seen everything, we shall dine there.

❧ *Third Review Lesson* ❧

I. VOCABULARY DRILL

A. Make a separate list of four nouns for each of the following subjects:

1. Animals.	5. Food.	9. Buildings.
2. Clothing.	6. House.	10. Post office.
3. Relations.	7. School.	11. Table articles.
4. Professions.	8. Furniture.	12. Divisions of time.

B. Give the Italian for the following adjectives:

1. Loaded, kind, wide, black, free, next, white, happy, dear, funny.
2. Sicilian, blue, yellow, true, tired, holy, fried, first, far, low.
3. Greek, magnificent, special, artistic, half, historic, huge, high, lucky, stylish.

C. Give the Italian for the following verbs:

1. To say	2. To fly	3. To stop
to lead	to know	to run
to eat	to seem	to lose
to last	to press	to serve
to sing	to help	to greet
to pour	to laugh	to tease
to offer	to thank	to follow
to remember	to represent	to go down

D. Give the Italian for the following expressions:

1. Sicilian style, both, soon after, to be right, please, cheap, to need, downtown, a month ago, to be about to.

---

[1] Use **codesto**.   [2] See footnote 2, p. 133, and be careful how you translate the verb that follows.

2. To shop, early, to my taste, last year, to be wrong, from time to time, all the more because, my name is Charles, to be hungry, what time is it?

II. DEFINITE ARTICLE

1. Mention two cases in which the definite article is used in Italian, and not in English.

2. Translate:

work, talent, beauty, order, amusement, birthday, advantage

III. NOUNS

1. How do you form the plural of nouns or adjectives ending in –ca or –ga? Give some examples.

2. How do you form the plural of nouns or adjectives ending in –cia or –gia? Give some examples.

3. Do all nouns or adjectives ending in –co form their plural in the same way? Give the rule, mention the exceptions, and furnish a few examples.

4. How do you form the plural of nouns or adjectives ending in –go? Give an example.

5. How about nouns ending in –ologo? Give an example.

IV. ADJECTIVES

1. What difference of meaning is there between codesto and quello?

2. What other demonstrative adjective, besides the two just mentioned, do you know?

3. How are quello and bello inflected before a noun? Give a few examples.

4. Give the rule regarding the use of buono before a noun, and furnish some examples.

5. When must we use the form san, rather than santo or sant', before a Christian name?

V. COMPARISON

1. How many degrees of a given quality may an adjective express?

2. How is a comparative of equality formed? Give two examples.

3. How is a comparative of inequality formed?

4. When is *than* rendered by **di**? Give three examples.

5. When is *than* rendered by **che**? Give an example.

6. Give an English example of a relative superlative.

7. How do we form a relative superlative in Italian?

8. How do we translate the English *in* after an Italian relative superlative? Give two examples.

9. Give an English example of an absolute superlative.

10. How is an absolute superlative formed in Italian? Give four possible absolute superlatives of **ricco**.

VI. CARDINAL NUMERALS

1. Count in Italian from 11 to 30.

2. Read in Italian:

40, 50, 60, 70, 80, 90, 100, 1100, 2300

3. Translate:

both women   twenty-one times   one million inhabitants

VII. TIME

1. Translate:

It's 8 A.M.; it's 10:30 A.M.; it's 11:55 A.M.; it's 4:15 P.M.; it's 7:45 P.M.; it's noon; it's midnight.

VIII. DATES

1. How is a date expressed in Italian?

2. Translate:

August 23rd, 1952.   On Tuesday, June 1st.   On October 13th, 1960

IX. AGE

1. What verb is used to express age?

2. Translate:

How old is your grandfather?   He is seventy-nine years old.

X. CONJUNCTIVE PERSONAL PRONOUNS

1. Why are these pronouns called *conjunctive?*

2. What is their normal position in a sentence? Give two examples.

3. How about **loro?** Give an example.

4. When are the conjunctive personal pronouns appended to the verb? Give two examples.

5. What happens to the final **e** of the infinitive when a pronoun is added to it? Show it with an example.

6. What takes place if an imperative ends in a stressed vowel? Give an example.

7. How are conjunctive personal pronouns used with εcco? Give an example.

XI. DISJUNCTIVE PERSONAL PRONOUNS

1. Are the disjunctive personal pronouns used in connection with a verb?

2. What is their most general use?

3. Give the disjunctive personal pronouns corresponding to the following subject forms: **io, noi, tu, Lεi, voi, essi, egli, Loro, esso, ella, esse, essa.**

4. Use **me, lεi,** and **sε** each in an original sentence.

XII. VERBS

1. What English phrases does the Italian past descriptive usually render?

2. Give the past descriptive of **guidare** and εssere.

3. Give the past absolute of **saltare, sedersi, servire, avere,** and εssere.

4. What is the difference in usage between the past absolute and the present perfect? Give two examples.

5. What is the difference in usage between the past absolute and the past descriptive? Give two examples.

6. Give the past perfect of **dettare** and **cadere.**

7. Give the second past perfect of **presentare** and **salire.**

8. When do we use the past perfect ?
9. When do we use the second past perfect ?
10. Give the future perfect of **ricordare, vendere,** and **partire.**
11. Translate:

Probably she was happy.   Probably we were wrong.

12. Give the 3rd person singular of the present indicative of **andare, dare, fare, stare, dire, uscire, dovere, potere,** and **volere.**

XIII. ADVERBS

1. Give a complete list of the adverbs of place.
2. What difference of meaning is there between **costà** and **là**? Give two examples.
3. Give the three conjunctive adverbs and their meanings.
4. Use **ci** in a sentence.
5. Use **ne** in a sentence.
6. Give the Italian for *never, nothing, not even.*

LETTURA IN SILENZIO

Sì o nɔ?

1. __ Il giardino zoologico stuzzica.
2. __ Il gatto fa collezione d'uccelli.
3. __ Non tutti amano gli svaghi.
4. __ L'antipasto è un grosso svago.
5. __ Apriamo la pɔrta con un secchietto.
6. __ L'orso è carico di frutta fresche.
7. __ Molti preferiscono il pesce fritto.
8. __ Altri preferiscono il ghiaccio fritto.
9. __ È bɛne per tutti mangiare tramonti.
10. __ Quando andiamo via, salutiamo gli amici.
11. __ Vi ringrazio della vɔstra salute.
12. __ Hɔ comprato una vɛste e dei guanti.
13. __ In alcuni mesi queste colline son bianche.
14. __ Diamo con piacere un incarico a quell'uɔmo.
15. __ Prendo pane tostato e burro per collezione.

ACHIEVEMENT TEST NO. 3

VOCABULARY

Give the Italian for the following words:

1. to walk _____
2. the amusement _____
3. expensive _____
4. a young man _____
5. outdoors _____
6. to be wrong _____
7. the stamp _____
8. to deserve _____
9. too much _____
10. broad _____

11. once in a while _____
12. to shop _____
13. the railroad _____
14. to be thirsty _____
15. the clerk _____
16. soon after _____
17. all right! _____
18. to need _____
19. the owner _____
20. to go down _____

(Deduct 1 point for each mistake.)

GRAMMAR

A. Write out in Italian:

1. It's noon. _____   2. It's 1:30 P.M. _____
   3. On May 16th, 1328. _____

B. Complete with the correct form of **bɛllo:**

1. un _____ palazzo.   2. dei _____ svaghi.   3. i _____ libri.

C. Complete with **buɔno** *or* **grande,** *according to sense:*

1. una _____ alunna.   2. un _____ cameriɛre.   3. un _____ parco.

D. Place the correct form of **Santo** *before the following names:*

1. _____ Giacomo.   2. _____ Ɛlena.   3. _____ Antɔnio.

E. In each case, supply the correct form of the past descriptive and of the past absolute of the verb in parentheses:

Noi (*avere*) parecchi biglietti.	1. _____	2. _____
Tu e io (*ɛssere*) occupati.	3. _____	4. _____
Lɛi (*consegnare*) il pacco.	5. _____	6. _____
Esse (*preferire*) giocare.	7. _____	8. _____
Voi non (*offrire*) niɛnte.	9. _____	10. _____

F. Give the plural of the following expressions:

1. Il giardino zoologico. _____   3. Il teologo tedesco. _____
2. L'artista greco.   _____   4. Il magnifico parco. _____

G. Supply the Italian for the words in parentheses:

1. Mi piace camminare (*with him*) _____.   2. Ho parlato (*for her*) _____.   3. Le due cugine (*looked at each other*) _____. 4. Il libro di lettura (*is not there*) _____.   5. Ecco delle cartoline; voglio (*to send them*) _____.   6. Esse sono meno povere (*than she*) _____.   7. Non voglio (*to speak of it*) _____.   8. I bambini usciranno (*with me*) _____.   9. Il medico (*spoke to him*) _____.   10. Quella città è bella, ma non possiamo (*to go there*) _____.   11. (*Give him*) _____ una penna stilografica. 12. Egli era (*very rich*) _____ 13. Anche noi (*are doing*) _____ così. 14. Ella (*was about to*) _____ versare del vino.

H. Complete with the past perfect or the second past perfect of the verb in parentheses, as the case may be:

1. (*salire*) Ella _____ in automobile.   2. (*lavorare*) Quand'egli _____ bene, era contento.   3. (*presentare*) Dopo ch'io li _____, camminammo insieme.   4. (*vedere*) Appena noi _____ che non c'era, andammo via.   5. (*partire*) Essi _____ di buon'ora.

I. Supply the Italian equivalent of than:

1. Era più nero ____ bianco.   2. Egli aveva più ____ trenta cravatte.
3. Ho meno appetito ____ lui.   4. Mi piace più conversare ____ giocare.
5. Fu meno gentile ____ Elena.

(Deduct 1 point for each mistake.)

READING

Translate the Italian passage that your instructor will write on the board or hand to you on a mimeographed sheet.

(This part counts 20 points.)

DICTATION

Your instructor will dictate twice a short Italian passage.

(This part counts 10 points.)

PERFECT SCORE: 100

Parte Quarta

IN CAMPAGNA

❧ *Lezione Ventiduɛsima* ❧

I. NOTE GRAMMATICALI

103. Orthographical Changes of Certain Verbs

1. **giocare,** *to play:* **giɔchi, giochiamo, giocherà,** *etc.*
pagare, *to pay:* **paghi, paghiamo, pagherete,** *etc.*

Verbs ending in **−care** or **−gare** insert **h** after the **c** or **g** whenever these letters precede **e** or **i.**

2. **lasciare,** *to leave:* **lasci, lasciamo, lasceremo,** *etc.*
viaggiare, *to travel:* **viaggi, viaggiamo, viaggerɔ,** *etc.*

Verbs ending in **−ciare** or **−giare** drop the **i** before **e** or **i.**

3. **studiare,** *to study:* **studi, studiamo,** *etc.*

Other verbs ending in **−iare** drop the **i** before another **i.**

4. **crescere,** *to grow:* **cresciuto,** *but* **cresco, crescono,** *etc.*

Verbs ending in **−cere** [1] insert **i** after the **c** only before the **u** of the past participle.

104. Past Absolute of *prɛndere*

presi, I took, etc.	prendemmo
prendesti	prendeste
prese	presero

The irregularity of this past absolute should be carefully noted. It affects three forms only: the 1st and 3rd singular, and the 3rd plural. These forms have in common an irregular stressed stem, and they have respectively the endings **−i, −e, −ero.** The three other forms are perfectly regular, both in stem and endings.

105. Irregular Past Absolute

What has been stated in the preceding paragraph applies not only to the verb **prɛndere,** but also to all irregular past absolutes in Italian, except three: those of the verbs **ɛssere, dare,** and **stare.**

---

[1] Verbs ending in **−gere** (all of which have an irregular past participle) undergo no orthographical changes: **piangere,** *to weep;* **piango, piangi,** *etc.*

Learn the following:

conoscere [1]	ridere [2]
conobbi, I knew, etc.	*risi, I laughed, etc.*
conoscesti	ridesti
conobbe	*rise*
conoscemmo	ridemmo
conosceste	rideste
conobbero	*risero*

dire [3]: dissi, dicesti, *etc.*
fare [4]: feci, facesti, *etc.*
rispondere: risposi, rispondesti, *etc.*
vedere [5]: vidi, vedesti, *etc.*

II. LETTURA

Una sorpresa allo zio Antonio

Ieri l'altro Guido e Stefano, insieme coi loro genitori, andarono a passare la giornata in campagna.

Era una magnifica domenica d'aprile; un bel sole di primavera splendeva nell'azzurro cielo, e tutta la natura pareva sorridere.

5　— Andiamo a fare una sorpresa allo zio Antonio! — aveva esclamato il signor Locatello dopo la messa, mentre usciva dalla chiesa con la moglie e i figli. — Mangeremo in campagna!

I due giovanotti mostrarono gran piacere a quelle parole, ma la mamma disse:

10　— Dobbiamo prima telefonare a Rosa per dirle che veniamo; non dimentichiamo ch'ella deve preparare un pranzo per noi!

Rosa è sua cognata, la moglie dello zio Antonio.

— E la sorpresa allora non ci sarà!

— Sì. Posso dire a Rosa di non parlarne ad Antonio.

15　La signora andò a telefonare in una farmacia vicina, e qualche minuto dopo tutti salivano in automobile.

Lo zio Antonio, fratello della signora Locatello, ha un grande e bel

---

[1] **Riconoscere,** *to recognize,* is conjugated like **conoscere.**　[2] **Sorridere,** *to smile,* is conjugated like **ridere.**　[3] **Dire** is a contraction of **dicere** (obsolete).　[4] **Fare** is a contraction of **facere** (obsolete).　[5] **Rivedere,** *to see again,* is conjugated like **vedere.**

podere a circa due ore di ferrovia dalla città; ma sull'ottima strada
che mena in quella direzione, l'automobile guidata dal signor
Locatello non prese che un'ora e tre quarti per portarli davanti
alla casa dello zio.

Al loro arrivo un grosso cane grigio li riconobbe e abbaiò.   5

— Zio Antonio, siamo qui! — gridò Guido.

Un momento dopo lo zio uscì dalla casa, sorrise, ed esclamò:

— Perbacco! Che magnifica sorpresa!

Poi disse al cane: « Passa là! » e andò a stringere la mano a
tutti e quattro, mentr'essi scendevano dall'automobile.   10

Intanto pure la zia, e Margherita, e la piccola Laura — cugine
di Guido e di Stefano — erano uscite in fretta dalla casa e stringe-
vano la mano a ognuno.

— E Andrea dov'è? — domandò il signor Locatello a suo cognato.   15

Andrea è il fratello delle due ragazze.

— Sarà andato a dar da mangiare ai polli e ai conigli, scommetto, — gli rispose lo zio Antonio. — Quel ragazzo non sta mai
senza far nulla.

PROVERBIO

La pigrizia è la chiave della povertà.   *Sloth is the key to poverty.*

III. STUDIO DI PAROLE

Rosa Rose

arrivo arrival

campagna country; **in campagna** in *or* to the country

cane *m.* dog

cielo sky, heaven

cognata sister-in-law

cognato brother-in-law

coniglio rabbit

direzione *f.* direction

fretta haste, hurry; **in fretta in
a hurry; aver fretta** to be in a
hurry

giornata day (*in its duration*) [1]

natura nature

podere *m.* farm

sorpresa surprise

strada road

[1] This word is also used with reference to weather (**una bella giornata**)
or work (**tre giornate a paga doppia**, *three days with double pay*). Other
words that are used in the same way, and that you should remember, are:
mattinata, *morning;* **serata,** *evening;* **nottata,** *night;* and **annata,** *year.*

grosso big
ottimo very good, excellent
abbaiare [abbaio] to bark
dare da mangiare to feed
dimenticare (di) [dimentico] to forget
gridare to cry
scommettere to bet

splendere to shine, sparkle
stringere to press, bind; **stringere la mano a** to shake hands with
circa about, nearly, almost
ieri l'altro day before yesterday
intanto meantime, meanwhile
perbacco! by Jove!

IV. CONVERSAZIONE

1. Dove andarono ieri l'altro Guido e Stefano? 2. Com'era il tempo? 3. Che cosa aveva esclamato il signor Locatello dopo la messa? 4. Che cosa disse la signora Locatello? 5. Chi è la signora Rosa? 6. Che cosa fecero allora? 7. Che cosa ha lo zio Antonio? 8. Quanto è lontano dalla città il suo podere? 9. Quanto tempo prese l'automobile per portare la famiglia Locatello al podere? 10. Che cosa fece il cane quando li vide? 11. Che cosa esclamò lo zio appena fu uscito dalla casa? 12. Che cosa diss'egli poi al cane? 13. Come si chiamavano le figlie dello zio Antonio? 14. Come si chiamava suo figlio? 15. Che cosa facciamo quando incontriamo degli amici? 16. Dov'era andato Andrea?

V. ESERCIZI

A. Scrivere sulla lavagna la traduzione (*translation*) italiana delle seguenti frasi:

1. She will play in the garden. 2. We pronounce clearly. 3. I have recognized her. 4. You (**tu**) forget. 5. They will begin their supper. 6. We are setting the table for fourteen. 7. You (**tu**) tease her too much. 8. We shall never forget. 9. They will not eat now. 10. The woman will explain everything. 11. I shall never pay. 12. We shall leave you here.

B. Dare il contrario di:

finire	salire	dare	ricordare
alzarsi	perdere	entrare	domandare
fermarsi	prendere	partire	ritornare

C. 1. Coniugare nel passato assoluto:

1. Non vedere nessun amico.
2. Riconoscere ogni persona.
3. Fare una buona colazione.
4. Prendere un po' di latte.

5. Ridere al cinematografo.
6. Rispondere alle domande.
7. Non dire mai brutte parole.
8. Sorridere di tanto in tanto.

2. Completare col passato assoluto del verbo in parentesi:

1. (*rivedere*) Chi li _____ più? 2. (*conoscere*) Io _____ molte signorine.
3. (*sorridere*) Il cognato _____ a quelle parole. 4. (*prendere*) Lei _____
del pollo arrosto. 5. (*fare*) Noi non _____ niente. 6. (*dire*) Voi non
_____ chi egli era. 7. (*vedere*) I vicini ci _____. 8. (*rispondere*) Io non
_____ a quella cartolina. 9. (*ridere*) Mia figlia _____ quando lo vide.
10. (*riconoscere*) Ella lo _____ subito. 11. (*fare*) Chi _____ colazione
con lui? 12. (*dire*) Essi non _____ come si chiamavano. 13. (*rivedere*)
Quand'io la _____, essa non era più giovane. 14. (*conoscere*) Essi lo
_____ l'anno scorso. 15. (*dire*) Anch'io _____ così.

D. Tradurre in italiano:

I

1. Day before yesterday I said to my friend Laura: "Let's spend a
day in the country; let's go to (a) visit my aunt." 2. She answered
me: "With pleasure, but let's not forget to (di) telephone to her first."
3. I did so,[1] and said that I was bringing a fine cake to her. 4. Yesterday Laura and I ate breakfast very early, and left home [2] at a
quarter past seven. 5. Laura has a fine car, and drives it well. 6. It
had rained, the air was cool, the roads were excellent, and we arrived
at my aunt's farm in about two hours. 7. Lord,[3] the big black dog,
recognized me at once, as soon as [it] saw me, and barked. 8. First
my cousins (*m.*) and then my aunt came out of [4] the old house. 9. Laura
and I shook hands with every one of the family. 10. "How is your [5]
mother, Mary?" asked my aunt. — "She is very well, thanks," I answered her,[6] "and how are you, Aunt Olga?"

II

1. Nature is beautiful in spring, and in April the country is all green.
2. My aunt's farm is large and has many fine trees. 3. "This is a

---

[1] Translate, *I did it.* [2] Translate, *departed from home.* [3] Do not translate the dog's name. [4] *To come out of,* **uscire da.** [5] An uncle or an aunt
always addresses a nephew or a niece in the intimate (**tu**) form; on the other
hand, a nephew or a niece normally uses the **voi** form in talking to an uncle
or aunt. [6] An indirect object.

surprise!" she said, and smiled. We entered [1] the house. 4. The house in which my aunt lives is neither large nor small; it is very comfortable. 5. As soon as we sat down [2] in the living room, we began to (a) chat. 6. Then Aunt [3] Olga got up and went to (in) the kitchen. 7. She made some excellent coffee for us, and I drank [4] it with pleasure, for I was thirsty. 8. "At what time shall we eat, Mother [5]?" asked my cousin James. — "At one," she answered him.[6] 9. When we had finished our coffee, Laura and I went outdoors with my cousins, and walked leisurely [7] in all directions for nearly two hours. 10. Laura saw everything: chickens, rabbits, and many other animals.

❧ *Lezione Ventitreεsima* ❧

I. NƆTE GRAMMATICALI

106.   **Present Participle**

I	II	III
buying	*selling*	*finishing*
compr *ando*	**vend *εndo***	**fin *εndo***

having	*being*
avεndo	**essεndo**

The present participle of a regular verb is formed by adding —**ando** to the stem for the first conjugation, —**εndo** for the second and third conjugations. Note that the present participle of the auxiliary verbs is regular.

107.   **Perfect Participle**

I	II	III
having bought	*having sold*	*having left*
avεndo comprato	**avεndo venduto**	**essεndo partito**

having had	*having been*
avεndo avuto	**essεndo stato**

[1] Attention!   [2] Translate, *we had sat down.*   [3] Use the definite article.   [4] Translate, *took.*   [5] Use the affectionate word **mamma.**   [6] An indirect object.   [7] Same as *without haste.*

108. **Use of the Present Participle**

1. The present participle is invariable in form; that is, it does not undergo any change on account of gender, number, or person.

2. It translates the English present participle whenever the latter has a verbal function.[1]

3. Sbagliando impariamo.	*We learn by making mistakes.*
Scrivendo, feci uno sbaglio.	*In writing, I made a mistake.*
Arrivando, ci salutò.	*On arriving, he greeted us.*

Besides rendering the English present participle used alone with a verbal force, the Italian present participle translates also the English present participle preceded by the prepositions *by, in, on, through,* or the conjunction *while.*

4. Parlando di lui, arrivammo a casa.	*While we were speaking of him, we arrived home.*
Essendo ricco, può viaggiare.	*Since he is rich, he can travel.*
Vendendo a tal prezzo, non guadagno nulla.	*If I sell at such a price, I don't gain anything.*

The present participle may replace a clause of time, cause, or condition.

5. PROGRESSIVE CONSTRUCTION

Sto ancora lavorando.	*I am still working.*
Essi stavano dormendo.	*They were sleeping.*
Andava imparando.	*He was learning.*

The present participle of a verb may be combined with a form of **stare** or **andare,** to form a progressive construction. **Stare** is by far more commonly used, but **andare** is preferred to convey an idea of motion or growth.

As has already been explained (*see* § 20, p. 24 and § 70, p. 105), the progressive idea can be expressed by both the simple present (**compro,** *I was buying*) and the past descriptive (**compravo,** *I was buying*). Because of this, the progressive construction is less frequently used in Italian than in English, and when used it implies more emphasis. **Sto pescando.** = *I am in the act of fishing.*

---

[1] For the translation of the English present participle used as a noun or an adjective, see respectively § 161, p. 289, and § 170, p. 308.

109.   **Adverbs of Manner**

1.   amaro, *bitter*   amaramente, *bitterly*
        cortese, *courteous*   cortesemente, *courteously*

Adverbs of manner are usually formed by adding –**mente** to
the feminine singular of the adjective.

2.   leale, *loyal*   lealmente, *loyally*,
        regolare, *regular*   regolarmente, *regularly*
  But: folle, *mad*   follemente, *madly*
        mediocre, *mediocre*   mediocremente, *moderately*

Adjectives which end in –**le** or –**re** drop the final vowel when
–**mente** is added, provided that no consonant precedes those
endings.

II. LETTURA

Animali domestici

Andrea ritornò a casa qualche minuto dopo e fu contentissimo
di trovare in sala da pranzo Guido, Stefano e i loro genitori, a
cui sua madre stava offrendo, proprio in quel momento, una tazza
di caffè.

5   — Che fanno i polli? — domandò Guido ridendo, mentre strin-
geva la mano al cugino.

— Mangiano molto, — rispose Andrea, — ma fanno poche uova.
Volete venire a vederli?

I due fratelli accettarono l'invito con piacere, principalmente
10 perchè desideravano di ritornare all'aperto. Appena ebbero finito
in fretta di bere il caffè:

— Con permesso! — dissero. — Scusateci!

E uscirono.

Com'era bello il verde degli alberi e dei campi! Com'era azzurro
15 il cielo!

— Vi meno prima a vedere i polli e i conigli, — disse Andrea
camminando, — e poi vi mostrerò gli altri animali.

Andando in direzione del pollaio, si fermarono due o tre volte a
guardare delle vacche e delle pecore che stavano pascolando.

Ma ɛccoli già al poll*a*io. Esso conteneva da sessanta a ottanta galline, alcuni galli e un tacchino.

— Vedo che avete anche un tacchino, — disse Stɛfano.

— Uno solo, e forse lo venderemo . . .

— Mostraci gli altri animali, — disse Guido dopo alcuni minuti. 5

Non lontano dal poll*a*io c'ɛrano delle *a*nitre, delle ɔche, e dei maiali grandi e p*i*ccoli, molto s*u*dici.

Stɛfano, guard*a*ndoli, rise allegramente.

— E dire, — esclamɔ̀, — che la loro carne è così bu*ɔ*na!

Pɔco dopo Andrɛa menɔ̀ i su*ɔ*i cugini alla stalla, in cui c'ɛrano 10 quattro robusti cavalli, tre muli e un *a*sino.

PROVƐRBIO

L'ɔcchio del padrone ingrassa il ca- vallo.	*The master's eye makes the horse fat.* *(i.e. Under the master's supervi- sion everything prospers.)*

III. STUDIO DI PARɔLE

*a*nitra duck
*a*sino ass, donkey
campo field
carne *f.* flesh, meat
cavallo horse
gallina hen
gallo rooster
invito invitation
maiale *m.* pig, swine, pork
mulo mule
ɔca goose
pɛcora sheep
permesso permission; con per-
    messo! with your permission!
poll*a*io poultry yard

stalla stable
tacchino turkey
u*ɔ*vo (*irr. pl.* le u*ɔ*va) egg
vacca cow

domɛstico domestic
robusto robust, sturdy
s*u*dicio dirty, filthy

accettare (di) [accɛtto] to accept
bere to drink
contenere to contain
pascolare [p*a*scolo] to graze, pas-
    ture

prɔprio just, really

IV. CONVERSAZIONE

1. Che cɔsa offrì la madre d'Andrɛa ai giovanɔtti e ai loro ge- nitori? 2. Che disse Guido ad Andrɛa? 3. Che cɔsa gli rispose Andrɛa? 4. Perchè Guido e Stɛfano accettarono con piacere l'in-

vito del loro cugino? 5. Che cosa dissero prima d'uscire? 6. Che cosa disse Andrea camminando con loro? 7. Perchè si fermarono due o tre volte andando al pollaio? 8. Che cosa conteneva il pollaio? 9. Che cosa disse Andrea quando Stefano osservò che c'era pure un tacchino? 10. Che cosa c'era non lontano dal pollaio? 11. Com'erano i maiali? 12. Che cosa fece Stefano guardando i maiali? 13. Che cosa esclamò? 14. Dove andarono poi i tre giovanotti? 15. Che c'era nella stalla? 16. Di che colore sono i cavalli, i maiali e le anitre?

V. ESERCIZI

A. 1. Dare il participio presente [1] dei seguenti verbi:

preferire	piovere	salire	vestirsi
correggere	gridare	stirare	nevicare
festeggiare	seguire	correre	scommettere

2. Dare il participio perfetto [2] di:

sedersi	pagare	uscire	rivedere
ringraziare	essere	scusare	attraversare

B. Tradurre in italiano usando la costruzione progressiva:

1. They were introducing their friends. 2. We are cleaning this dining room. 3. He was writing with my fountain pen. 4. She is eating some salad. 5. Ann was playing the piano. 6. They were learning French. 7. It's snowing. 8. We are serving some wine. 9. The young lady is not coming alone. 10. I was correcting that mistake.

C. 1. Formare avverbi di maniera coi seguenti aggettivi:

povero	facile	semplice	vero
amaro	naturale	difficile	enorme
gentile	artistico	elegante	libero

2. Usare gli stessi avverbi in brevi frasi originali.

D. Tradurre in italiano usando, sempre che sia possibile (*whenever it is possible*), la costruzione progressiva:

---

[1] Called *gerundio presente* by Italian grammarians. [2] Called *gerundio passato* by Italian grammarians.

I

1. Aunt [1] Olga was saying [2] that on (in) her farm she had many fine animals. 2. "May I see them?" asked Laura. — "Of course [3]! My niece will take [4] you to (a) see them." 3. We got up, excused ourselves, and went out. 4. Talking of several things, I led my friend to the stable. 5. In it there were five horses, a mule, and two pigs. 6. We stopped a little to (a) look at them, and Laura remarked that among all the domestic animals she preferred the horses. 7. Those horses were sturdy; two of them were white, the others brown.[5] 8. "Where are the cows?" asked my friend, smiling. "I wish to see them." 9. "They are probably in (a) the meadow," I answered her. "Follow [6] me, I shall guide you." 10. A moment after we were slowly walking toward the meadow, where thirty or forty cows and some sheep were grazing.

II

1. "Please lead [6] me to the poultry yard," said Laura to me. 2. I did it promptly, and soon after we were walking in that direction. 3. After [7] we had arrived, she looked smilingly [8] at the hens, the roosters, and the turkeys. 4. "Look! Another pig!" she exclaimed. — "Where is it?" — "There it is!" 5. And she showed me a large [9] pig that was running behind the poultry yard. 6. "I like that animal," she said laughing. "It is very funny." 7. "But it is very dirty, too!" I observed, laughing at the same time. 8. At (in) that moment Aunt [1] Olga called us from the house. 9. Our dinner was ready, and we were [10] very glad to (di) be able to eat. 10. While we were returning to the house, we saw ducks, geese, and rabbits.

[1] Use the definite article.   [2] Use the uncontracted stem of **dire**. See footnote 3, p. 164.   [3] Same as *naturally*.   [4] Use **menare**.   [5] See footnote 2, p. 108.   [6] Two intimate friends address each other in the **tu** form.   [7] See footnote 2, p. 133.   [8] Translate, *smiling*.   [9] Use a more appropriate adjective than **grande**.   [10] A past absolute.

I. NOTE GRAMMATICALI

110. **Present Subjunctive**

I	II	III	
I (may) buy, etc.	*I (may) sell, etc.*	*I (may) finish, etc.*	*I (may) depart, etc.*
compr i	vend a	fin isc a	part a
compr i	vend a	fin isc a	part a
compr i	vend a	fin isc a	part a
compr iamo	vend iamo	fin iamo	part iamo
compr iate	vend iate	fin iate	part iate
compr ino	vend ano	fin isc ano	part ano

Note that:

1. The three persons of the singular in this tense are identical with each other in all Italian verbs, no matter whether they are regular or irregular.

2. All verbs of the third conjugation that add –isc to their stem in forming the three persons of the singular and the 3rd person plural of the present indicative, as explained in § 25, 1 (p. 29), do so in the present subjunctive as well.

3. The 3rd person singular and the 3rd person plural of this tense are used, as has been seen in § 42, 1 (p. 60), to supply the missing forms of the imperative.

111. Present Subjunctive of the Auxiliary Verbs

avere		essere	
I (may) have, etc.		*I (may) be, etc.*	
abbia	abbiamo	sia	siamo
abbia	abbiate	sia	siate
abbia	abbiano	sia	siano

SAN GIMIGNANO, TUSCANY

CONVENT AND UPPER SAINT FRANCIS CHURCH, ASSISI

STREET SCENE IN THE VILLAGE OF ALBEROBELLO, SOUTHERN ITALY

LAKE LUGANO AND SAN SALVATORE MOUNTAIN
(Lake Lugano is partly Swiss and partly Italian)

112.   **Present Perfect Subjunctive**

I	II	III
I bought, or (*may*) have bought, etc.	*I sold*, or (*may*) have sold, etc.	*I departed*, or (*may*) have departed, etc.
abbia abbia abbia } comprato	abbia abbia abbia } venduto	sia sia sia } partito, –a
abbiamo abbiate abbiano } comprato	abbiamo abbiate abbiano } venduto	siamo siate siano } partiti, –e

AUXILIARY VERBS

I had, or (*may*) have had, etc.

I was, or (*may*) have been, etc.

abbia avuto, etc.   sia stato, –a, etc.

113.   **The Subjunctive in Noun Clauses** [1]

Desidero che tu parli con lui.	*I wish you to talk with him.*[2]
Evita ch'essi ti vedano.	*Avoid their seeing you.*
Egli ordina che tu sia pronto.	*He orders you to be ready.*
È meglio che voi restiate.	*It is better for you to stay.*
Non so se egli abbia ragione.	*I don't know whether he is right.*
Son contento ch'essa sia qui.	*I am glad she is here.*[3]
Credo ch'essi siano arrivati.	*I think (= presume) they have arrived.*

But: Credo che arriveranno. *I think they will arrive.*

1. The subjunctive is used after verbs expressing:
   (*a*) desire, will, preference;
   (*b*) command, prohibition;
   (*c*) expression of opinion;
   (*d*) doubt, ignorance;

[1] A clause that is the subject or the object of a verb is called a *noun clause.*
[2] Note that the Italian construction is, literally: *I wish that you talk with him.* The same remark applies to the next examples too (*Avoid that they . . . He orders that you . . .*). Keep this in mind when translating this type of sentence into Italian.   [3] Note again that the conjunction *that,* often omitted in English, is never omitted in Italian.

(*e*) emotion (joy, sorrow, wonder, fear, anger, shame, etc.);
(*f*) believing, thinking, hoping, suspecting, — provided that doubt is implied.

2. Note that in all the cases just mentioned the subjunctive is used only if the main clause and the noun clause have *different subjects*.

Note also that, in all cases except the first two, the verb in the noun clause must not express *a future idea*, for, if it does, not the subjunctive but the future is used, as shown in the last example.

Voglio che tu ti diverta domani.	*I want you to have a good time to-morrow.*
Ordino ch'egli parta il mese venturo.	*I order him to leave next month.*

Verbs mentioned under (*a*) and (*b*) take the present subjunctive to render a future idea in the noun clause.

3. The examples given show that the infinitive, the present participle, or a tense of the indicative may be found in English where the Italian syntax requires the subjunctive.

114. The Infinitive in Noun Clauses

Desidero di pagare.	*I wish to pay.*
Son contento d'esser venuto.	*I am glad I came.*

If the principal and the dependent verbs of a sentence have the same subjects, the infinitive must be used instead of the subjunctive.

II. LETTURA

Nell'orto

Mentre le donne di casa erano occupate in cucina a preparare il pranzo, e i giovanotti camminavano pei campi, i Locatello [1] eran restati soli in salotto a conversare con lo zio Antonio.

— Dov'è Laura? — domandò la signora Locatello.

5 — Credo che sia fuori. Forse sta giocando col cane.

— È diventata veramente una bella ragazza.

— Sì, ma è bene che tu non lo dica davanti a lei; è già vanitosa

[1] Note that surnames do not change in the plural.

abbastanza, — disse lo zio Antonio alzandosi. — Ma venite con me; andiamo anche noi all'aperto. Voglio che vediate il nostro orto.

Uscirono tutti e tre, passarono dietro alla casa.

— Non immaginate, — continuò lo zio Antonio, — che sia molto 5 grande; lo coltivo solamente pei bisogni della famiglia. Ma c'è un po' di tutto: ieri, per esempio, mangiammo i primi piselli.

— Così presto? — disse sua sorella. — In città non ne vendono ancora.

— E se ne vendono, dovete pagarli cari. Pure i carciofi son 10 maturi, e li mangeremo tra poco a tavola.

— Bravo! È la verdura che preferisco!

Adesso camminavano sul sentiero che divideva l'orto.

— Che piante son codeste? — domandò il signor Locatello indicando alcune file di piccole piante d'un colore verde chiaro. 15

— Cipolle, — rispose suo cognato. — Le altre tre file son cavoli; poi ci sono i fagioli, e là abbiamo i piselli, i carciofi e i pomodori.

— E costà, a sinistra?

— Queste son patate; poi vi sono spinaci, lattughe, sedani e ravanelli. Ebbi l'idea, il mese scorso, di piantare anche delle 20 melanzane, ma poi non lo feci perchè Rosa non ne mangia.

— Peccato che non siano di suo gusto! — disse la signora Locatello. — Sono deliziose, specialmente alla parmigiana . . .

Ma proprio allora Margherita chiamò dalla porta della cucina. Il pranzo era pronto. 25

PROVERBIO

Ognuno ha i suoi gusti.   *Every man to his taste.*

III. STUDIO DI PAROLE

carciofo artichoke
cavolo cabbage
cipolla onion
fagiolo bean; **fagiolino** string bean
lattuga lettuce
melanzana eggplant
orto vegetable garden

peccato sin; **peccato!** too bad!
pianta plant
pomodoro tomato
ravanello radish
sedano celery
sentiero path
spinaci *m. pl.* spinach
verdura vegetable

chiaro clear, light (*in color*)
delizioso delightful, delicious
maturo mature, ripe
vanitoso vain, conceited

coltivare to cultivate, grow
credere to believe, think
dividere to divide
immaginare (di) [immagino] to imagine

piantare to plant
restare [rɛsto] to remain, be left [1]

abbastanza enough
alla parmigiana Parmesan style; **alla romana** Roman style
bravo! fine!
tra poco soon, before long

IV. CONVERSAZIONE

1. Dov'ɛrano le dɔnne di casa mentre i Locatɛllo ɛrano in salɔtto? 2. Che cɔsa domandɔ la signora Locatɛllo? 3. Che le rispose suo fratɛllo? 4. Che cɔsa osservɔ allora la signora? 5. Che disse lo zio Antɔnio? 6. Che cɔsa fecero pɔi tutti e tre? 7. Perchè lo zio Antɔnio coltivava quell'ɔrto? 8. Che cɔsa avevano mangiato il giorno prima? 9. Che cɔsa mangeranno a tavola tra pɔco? 10. Dove camminavano lo zio Antɔnio e i Locatɛllo? 11. Che domanda fece il signor Locatɛllo? 12. Di che colore ɛrano le piante ch'egli indicava? 13. Quali piante ɛrano quelle? 14. Quali altre verdure c'ɛrano nell'ɔrto? 15. Che idɛa ɛbbe il mese prima lo zio Antɔnio? 16. Perchè pɔi non lo fece? 17. Che cɔsa disse allora la signora Locatɛllo?

V. ESERCIZI

A. Coniugare:

1. Il farmacista vuɔle ch'io ritorni tra pɔco, il farmacista vuɔle che tu . . ., ecc.
2. Ella non crede ch'io sia stato con mio cugino, ella non crede che tu . . ., ecc.
3. Egli pɛnsa ch'io abbia tɔrto, egli pɛnsa che tu . . ., ecc.
4. Mia madre desidera ch'io non pɛrda tɛmpo, mia madre desidera che tu . . ., ecc.
5. Clara pɛnsa ch'io preferisca restare, Clara pɛnsa che tu . . ., ecc.
6. È bɛne ch'io gli parli? È bɛne che tu . . ., ecc.

---

[1] Conjugated with ɛssere.

B. Completare col presente del congiuntivo, e poi col presente perfetto del congiuntivo,[1] del verbo in parentesi:

1. (*restare*) Son contento che mia sorella ____ a casa. 2. (*perdere*) Egli pensa ch'io ____ la lettera. 3. (*capire*) È bene ch'essi ci ____. 4. (*seguire*) Mi dispiace che voi ____ il suo esempio. 5. (*essere*) Non crediamo ch'essi ____ stanchi. 6. (*imparare*) Mi piace assai che Rosa ____ a suonare il pianoforte. 7. (*rivedere*) Siamo contenti che tu ____ i vecchi amici. 8. (*arrivare*) Mi dispiace che il cognato d'Anna ____ in ritardo. 9. (*pagare*) È bene che Lei ____. 10. (*essere*) Credo che voi ____ fortunato.

C. Tradurre in italiano:

1. I want you to erase that sentence. 2. She believes they are very tired. 3. We are glad you came. 4. She thinks you are thirsty. 5. We want them to be happy. 6. Do you believe that it will rain today? 7. I am sorry you lost your fountain pen. 8. He doesn't think she needs him. 9. They believe you loved her. 10. She doesn't want me to invite him.

D. Tradurre in italiano:

I

1. I think the dinner was simple enough [2] but good. 2. I did not eat much meat because I prefer eggs and vegetables. 3. The eggs, of course, were very fresh; the vegetables, very good: peas with onions, tomatoes, and potatoes. 4. "I am glad you girls came," said my aunt. "We never see anybody here." 5. "We shall return soon," I answered her,[3] "next summer at the latest." 6. "Then [4] we shall have other vegetables to (da) eat," she observed, "artichokes, spinach, eggplants." 7. I have always thought that eggplants [5] Parmesan style are delicious, and said so [6] to Aunt [5] Olga. 8. "Fine!" she said. "My boys too prefer them to cabbage [5] or beans.[5]" 9. My cousins smiled; they were not talking much, they were eating [7] with great appetite. 10. We were not in a hurry, and remained at [the] table for more than one hour.

---

[1] Called *passato del congiuntivo* by Italian grammarians. [2] Place *enough* before *simple*. [3] An indirect object. [4] Do not use **poi**; the meaning is not *afterward*, but *at that time*. [5] Use the definite article. [6] Same as *I said it*. [7] Use the progressive construction.

II

1. Aunt [1] Olga had spoken to us of her vegetable garden, and in the afternoon she said: "I want you to see it." 2. Laura and I went out with her and my cousins. 3. While we were walking [2] on the narrow path that divided the garden, I was talking with Lawrence. 4. "How old is your friend?" he asked me. — "I think she is twenty-two," I answered. 5. "Too bad [3] she is so young!" he said a moment later. Lawrence is nearly forty years old. 6. "What plants are those?" asked Laura, pointing at some little plants of a light green color. 7. "Eggplants," James answered, "I planted them this month." 8. The other rows were celery,[4] lettuce, and radishes; then, to the right, there were beans, cabbages, tomatoes, and onions. 9. "Last month,[5]" James continued, "I had [6] the idea of [7] planting some artichokes, but then I didn't do it." 10. "I can't imagine that there is a more delicious vegetable than artichokes, but my brother prefers spinach!"

❧ Lezione Venticinquɛsima ☙

I. NOTE GRAMMATICALI

115. **Impersonal Construction**

1. Si fa così.	*One does so, people do so, we do so, they do so, etc.*
Si dɛve lavorare.	*One (people, we, they, etc.) must work.*
Si è felici.	*One is happy.*
S'è stati felici.	*One was happy.*
Si parte contɛnti.	*One leaves in a good frame of mind.*
Si rɛsta soli.	*One remains alone.*
S'è diventati ricchi.	*One has become rich.*

The reflexive verb is used, in the 3rd person singular, to express a fact or action with an impersonal subject such as *one, people, we, they, a man, a person,* etc.

[1] Use the definite article. [2] Translate *while we were walking* with one word. [3] Add *that*, and pay attention: this is an expression of sorrow. [4] Use the plural with all these names of vegetables. [5] See Vocabulary. [6] Use the past absolute. [7] Translate, **di** + the infinitive.

As shown in the 3rd and 4th examples, the verb ɛssere, although used in the singular, takes the following adjective (and the past participle, if the verb is a perfect) in the plural. The intransitive verbs of motion, rest, or change of condition listed on page 47 (footnote 1) follow the same construction.

2. Si parla italiano.   *Italian is spoken.*
  Si parlano molte lingue.   *Many languages are spoken.*
  Si fa un'eccezione.   *An exception is made.*
  Si vedono molte persone.   *Many persons are seen.*
  S'aiutavano i poveri.   *The poor were aided.*

The impersonal construction is used also instead of the passive verb when no agent [1] is expressed. Note, however, that in this case the 3rd person plural is used whenever the subject (which usually follows the verb) is a plural noun.[2]

116. Another Use of the Reflexive Verb

  Egli si toccò il mento.   *He touched his chin.*
  Mi levai il cappello.   *I took off my hat.*

The reflexive verb is used in order to avoid the use of the possessive with parts of the body or clothing.

117. Passive Voice

  Essi sono coltivati da me.   *They are cultivated by me.*
  Egli fu lodato da lɛi.   *He was praised by her.*
  Le due signorine furono   *The two young ladies were*
    vedute da noi.   *seen by us.*

The passive voice is formed by means of the auxiliary ɛssere and the past participle of the verb conjugated, the participle agreeing in gender and number with the subject. This voice is less frequently used in Italian than in English because of the fact

---

[1] In the sentence *The poor are aided by them*, the agent is *by them*.   [2] When two or more singular subjects follow the verb, the verb can be in the 3rd person plural or (elliptically) in the 3rd person singular. It is equally correct to say **Si vedono un uɔmo, una dɔnna e un bambino**, or **Si vede un uɔmo, una dɔnna e un bambino.**

that, as explained in the preceding paragraph, the reflexive is preferred when no agent is expressed.

For the conjugation of the passive voice, see Appendix II.

II. LETTURA

Buon appetito

I giovanotti ritornarono dalla loro passeggiata pei campi proprio in tempo per il pranzo, e andarono subito a lavarsi le mani, mentre la zia Rosa già cominciava a servire degli ottimi spaghetti al pomodoro.

5 — Avete appetito, ragazzi? — domandò ella quando tutti si furono seduti a tavola.

— Come lupi usciti dal bosco, v'assicuro io, zia! — esclamò Guido.

Si rise, si dissero delle barzellette.

10 — Il buon appetito è dato dall'aria della campagna, — osservò il signor Locatello.

Si cominciò a mangiare. Tutti erano contenti d'essere insieme, e ognuno prendeva parte alla conversazione, anche Margherita, di solito un po' timida.

15 Erano serviti da una ragazza di diciotto o venti anni, figlia d'un contadino dello zio Antonio. Essa ora andava in giro versando dell'acqua nei bicchieri.

Dopo gli spaghetti si mangiò del maiale arrosto con carciofi fritti, fagiolini e patate; poi la ragazza servì insalata, formaggio 20 e frutta. Per frutta c'erano aranci, pere e noci.

— Se volete gustare delle buone frutta, — disse la zia Rosa, — dovete venire in estate. Spero che ritornerete allora, se non prima.

— Non dimenticheremo l'invito! — esclamò Stefano.

— Verso la fine di giugno, — continuò a dire la zia, — qui si 25 mangeranno delle deliziose albicocche, e ciliege, e pere. Allora i frutti [1] dei nostri alberi saranno maturi.

— Sta bene, — disse la signora Locatello, — ma desidero che veniate a visitarci in città prima d'allora.

---

[1] Note that, when the word **frutto** refers to a fruit on a tree, its plural is not **le frutta**, but **i frutti**.

— Volentieri, se non vi diamo disturbo . . .
— Mi fai ridere, Rosa! Tra noi non si fanno complimenti!
Lo zio Antonio rise, e poi disse:
— Fra poco vi mostrerò i nostri alberi. Ne ho un gran numero,
e son tutti belli: meli, peri, noci, albicocchi, ciliegi . . .   5

PROVERBIO

L'albero si conosce dal frutto.   *A tree is known by its fruit.*

III. STUDIO DI PAROLE

acqua water
albicocca apricot; albicocco apricot tree
arancio orange, orange tree
barzelletta joke
bosco woods
ciliegia cherry; ciliegio cherry tree
complimento compliment; far complimenti to stand on ceremony
contadino farm laborer
disturbo trouble, annoyance; dar disturbo a to trouble
fine *f.* end
formaggio cheese

lupo wolf
mela apple; melo apple tree
parte *f.* part, share
pera pear; pero pear tree
spaghetti *m. pl.* spaghetti

solito usual; di solito usually
timido bashful, timid

assicurare (di) to assure, insure
gustare to taste, relish, enjoy
sperare (di) [spero] to hope

al pomodoro with tomato sauce
in giro around
volentieri gladly

IV. CONVERSAZIONE

1. Da dove ritornarono i giovanotti? 2. Che cosa fecero appena furono arrivati a casa? 3. Che cosa cominciava a servire la zia Rosa? 4. Che cosa disse ai giovanotti la zia Rosa? 5. Che cosa le rispose Guido? 6. Che cosa dà buon appetito? 7. Chi prendeva parte alla conversazione? 8. Da chi erano serviti a tavola? 9. Che versava la ragazza? 10. Che si mangiò dopo gli spaghetti? 11. Quali frutta furono servite? 12. Che disse la zia Rosa circa le frutta? 13. Che esclamò Stefano? 14. Che disse allora la signora Locatello? 15. Che le rispose la zia Rosa? 15. E che disse allora la signora Locatello? 17. Quali alberi aveva lo zio Antonio?

V. ESERCIZI

A. Tradurre in italiano:

1. We help each other. 2. One remains young. 3. People were not satisfied. 4. They are washing their hands. 5. One answers thus. 6. I shall sell my fur coat. 7. One becomes old. 8. People are poor. 9. English was spoken. 10. They used to write to each other. 11. We do it so. 12. People go there to have a good time.

B. Dare il pronome riflessivo e il presente perfetto del verbo in parentesi:

1. (*mostrare*) Essi non ___ ___ ___. 2. (*capire*) Esse ___ ___ ___. 3. (*aiutare*) Noi ___ ___ ___. 4. (*perdere*) Lei ___ ___ ___. 5. (*vestire*) Anna ___ ___ ___. 6. (*raccomandare*) Tu ___ ___ ___ a loro. 7. (*servire*) I giovanotti ___ ___ ___. 8. (*presentare*) Voi ___ ___ ___. 9. (*divertire*) Noi ___ ___ ___. 10. (*conoscere*) Essi ___ ___ ___.

C. Tradurre in italiano queste frasi, di cui alcune hanno l'agente, altre non l'hanno:

1. That road was preferred by him. 2. That road was preferred. 3. Two languages were spoken. 4. The dog was seen by me. 5. A letter was received. 6. Ann was recognized by you. 7. Seventy plants were planted by them. 8. Everything was explained. 9. She was stopped by me. 10. The suit will be pressed.

D. Tradurre in italiano:

I

1. It seems that time passes more quickly when one is among good friends. 2. When we got up from [the] table, it was three o'clock. 3. "Let's not forget to (**di**) see Aunt Olga's trees this afternoon," I said. 4. "Yes," said my aunt, "I want you to see them now that they are in blossom." 5. Soon after, we were guided by James on a narrow path between two fields. 6. "It is good (**bene**) to take a walk after dinner," observed Laura. "So they say, and it is especially true in my case,[1] because I ate too much." 7. When one is in the country, one is always hungry. 8. My aunt's trees were on a hill; we arrived there, without hurry, in about forty minutes. 9. Many jokes [2] were

---

[1] Translate, *for me.*   [2] Attention to the position of the subject!

told while we were walking.[1]   10. The trees were beautiful, and almost all in blossom: apricot, cherry, pear, and apple trees.

II

1. Some [of the] trees were in blossom; others had small fruit [2] not yet ripe.   2. James said: "They will be ripe soon if it rains a little."   3. "Well," he continued, "you girls must return if you want to taste them."   4. "Our apricots and cherries are delicious, but we don't have many of them; only for the needs of our family and for our friends who visit us."   5. "Apples and pears are plentiful,[3] and [they] are sold."   6. I do not walk enough, they say, but that afternoon we went [4] around for more than two hours.   7. "I am sorry to trouble you," said Laura to James, when we returned to the house, "but I am thirsty; please give us a glass of water."   8. James, who is usually bashful, paid [5] her [6] a compliment, and went to (in) the kitchen.   9. A moment later he came back with the water, and offered us some oranges, too.   10. "I hope they are cold," he said; "here, in the country, we don't have any [7] ice."

❧ *Lezione Ventiseiεsima* ☙

I. NOTE GRAMMATICALI

118.   **Ordinal Numerals and Fractions**

1.

1st	**primo**	13th	**tredicεsimo**
2nd	**secondo**	14th	**quattordicεsimo**
3rd	**tεrzo**	15th	**quindicεsimo**
4th	**quarto**	20th	**ventεsimo**
5th	**quinto**	21st	**ventunεsimo**
6th	**sεsto**	22nd	**ventiduεsimo**
7th	**sεttimo**	23rd	**ventitreεsimo**
8th	**ottavo**	30th	**trentεsimo**
9th	**nɔno**	33rd	**trentatreεsimo**
10th	**dεcimo**	40th	**quarantεsimo**
11th	**undicεsimo**	100th	**centεsimo**
12th	**dodicεsimo**	1000th	**millεsimo**

[1] Use the progressive construction.   [2] See footnote, p. 182.   [3] Same as *many.*   [4] Past absolute.   [5] Use the verb **fare.**   [6] An indirect object.   [7] The word *ice* does not take a numerical modifier. See § 98, 2, p. 144.

Except for the first ten numbers, ordinal numerals are formed by dropping the last vowel of the corresponding cardinal numeral and adding –ɛsimo. Note, however, that the last vowel of **ventitrè, trentatrè,** etc., being accented, is kept: **ventitreɛsimo, trentatreɛsimo,** etc.

2.   i primi giorni   *the first days*
                    la nɔna fila   *the ninth row*

Ordinal numerals are adjectives in **–o,** and as such agree in gender and number with the noun they modify. Their normal position is before the noun, but if they are used emphatically or in titles of chapters, lessons, etc., they usually follow the noun: **lezione ventiseiɛsima.**

3.   FRACTIONS

With the exception of $\frac{1}{2}$, fractions are formed by using the ordinal numeral as the denominator.

$\frac{1}{2}$	{ **la metà** (*noun*) **mɛzzo** (*adjective*)	$\frac{1}{4}$	**un quarto**
		$\frac{3}{4}$	**tre quarti**
$\frac{1}{3}$	**un tɛrzo**	$\frac{1}{5}$	**un quinto**
$\frac{2}{3}$	**due tɛrzi**	$\frac{6}{10}$	**sɛi dɛcimi**

119.   Idiomatic Uses of *da*

1.   Vado dal dottor De Viti.   *I am going to Dr. De Viti's.*
       Ritornò da sua madre.   *He returned to his mother's home.*
       Vanno da lui.   *They are going to his place.*
       Venite da noi.   *Come to our house.*
But: Vado a casa mia.   *I am going to my house.* (**Vado da me** would mean *I am going by myself.*)

The preposition **da** is frequently used with the meaning of *at* or *to the house* (*home, shop, office, place,* etc.) *of,* when followed by a proper name or a noun referring to a person. This use is current also with **da** preceding a disjunctive personal pronoun (3rd and 4th examples), provided that the subject and the pronoun which is the object of **da** refer to different persons, for otherwise the meaning would be *by myself, by yourself,* etc.

2. il bimbo dai capelli ricci   *the baby with curly hair*
   la signora dalla veste nera   *the lady in the black dress*
   la casa dal tetto rosso   *the house with a red roof*

Da, followed by the definite article, is used in describing a personal, characteristic quality, in place of the English *with* or *in.*

3. Parlò da uomo d'onore.   *He spoke as a man of honor.*
   Cantò da vero artista.   *He sang as a real artist.*

Da is used also as the equivalent of the English *as, like,* when they stand for such phrases as *in the manner of, in the character of.* Note that, in this case, the indefinite article is omitted in Italian.

4. una veste da casa   *a house dress*
   una carta da visita   *a visiting card*
   una sala da fumare   *a smoking room*

Finally, **da** is used before a noun or a verb to imply purpose.

120.   Omission of the Indefinite Article

The indefinite article, though used in English, is omitted in Italian in the following cases:

1. Pisa, città di Toscana.   *Pisa, a city in Tuscany.*

Often, but not always, before a noun in apposition.

2.   Ella è americana.   *She is American.*
          Mio zio è medico.   *My uncle is a physician.*
   But: Mio zio è un buon me-   *My uncle is a good physician.*
           dico.

Before an unqualified predicate noun.

3. Che peccato!   *What a pity!*
   Quale magnifica idea!   *What a magnificent idea!*

After **che** or **quale** in exclamations.

4. Before **cento** and **mille** (*see* § 82, 4, p. 123).
5. After **da** in the sense of *in the manner of* (*see* § 119, 3, above).

II. LETTURA

Così finisce una bɛlla giornata

I due cognati e i giovanɔtti pass*arono* qu*el* pome*ri*ggio nei campi e non ritorn*arono* che dopo il tramonto.

Le dɔnne e le ragazze rest*arono* a casa perchè la signora Locatɛllo ɛra un pɔ' stanca. Vɛrso tardi però, anch'esse usc*irono* all'a-
5 pɛrto e and*arono* in giardino, attirate dal sole che ancora splendeva.

Il giardino ɛra situato fra la casa e un campo di grano in cui alcuni contadini ancora lavor*avano*. Un vɛcchio contadino dalla barba bianca si levò il cappɛllo quando le signore pass*arono*.

— Si chiama Bindi, — disse la zia Rɔsa, — ed è da molti e molti
10 anni che lavora per noi.

Nel giardino c'ɛrano molte piante, tutte in fila, in bɛll'*o*rdine.

— Le prime tre file, — cominciò a dire la zia Rɔsa, — son di violette; la quarta e la quinta son di garɔfani; pɔi nella sɛsta e sɛttima fila abbiamo dei giacinti; e nell'ottava, nɔna e dɛcima,
15 delle rɔse. Costà, alla tua dɛstra, ci son le piante di margherite.

— Che bɛi fiori! — esclamò la signora Locatɛllo.

— Sì, son bɛlli e guadagniamo abbastanza vendɛndoli ai fiorai, ma pure pei fiori dovete venire fra un mese o due. Adɛsso non ci sono ancora rɔse, come vedi, nè margherite, e i giacinti son pɔchi,
20 i primi di quɛst'anno. Ne vuɔi alcuni?

E Margherita già coglieva per la zia violette, giacinti e garɔfani, mentre la p*i*ccola Laura correva sull'ɛrba del prato diɛtro a una grande farfalla dalle ali gialle, nere e rosse.

— Quando vi decidere a pass*ar* qualche giorno da noi, in città?
25 — domandò a sua cognata la signora Locatɛllo.

— Forse prɛsto, tanto più che abbiamo parecchie cɔse da fare. Antɔnio dɛve andare da un mɛdico per alcuni dolori che ha al br*a*ccio sinistro, e io dɛvo and*ar* dalla sarta e dalla modista con le ragazze.

30 — Bɛne; v'aspetteremo.

Già cominciava ad annottare quando gli altri ritorn*arono* dalla loro passeggiata, ed ɛra tɛmpo d'and*ar* via. I Locatɛllo ringraz*i*arono cordialmente i loro parɛnti e sal*i*rono in automɔbile.

— Ritornate prɛsto!

— Sì! Sì! Ma voi dovete venir prima da noi!

In quella magnifica sera d'aprile il viaggio di ritorno fu delizioso. La luna e le stelle splendevano nel cielo, e la campagna odorava.

PROVERBIO

Tutto è bene quel che finisce bene.   *All's well that ends well.*

(Shakespeare)

III. STUDIO DI PAROLE

ala (*pl.* **le ali**) wing
barba beard
braccio (*pl.* **le braccia**) arm
dolore *m.* pain, ache, sorrow
ɛrba grass, herb
farfalla butterfly
fioraio florist
garofano carnation
giacinto hyacinth
grano wheat
luna moon
margherita daisy
modista milliner
parɛnte *m. or f.* relative
rosa rose

sarta dressmaker
stella star
viaggio trip, journey, voyage;
  viaggio di ritorno return trip
violetta violet

situato located

annottare [**annotta** [1]] to get dark
attirare to attract
cogliere to pick
decidersi (**a**) to decide
guadagnare to earn
levare [**lɛvo**] to take off, remove
odorare to smell, smell good

cordialmente cordially

IV. CONVERSAZIONE

1. Perchè le donne e le ragazze restarono a casa? 2. Che cosa fecero poi? 3. Dov'ɛra situato il giardino? 4. Chi salutò le signore? 5. Come si chiamava quel vecchio contadino? 6. Quali piante c'ɛrano nel giardino? 7. Che cosa esclamò la signora Locatello? 8. Che cosa disse allora la zia Rosa? 9. Quali fiori Margherita offrì a sua zia? 10. Dove correva la piccola Laura? 11. Perchè correva? 12. Che cosa domandò la signora Locatello a sua cognata? 13. Perchè lo zio Antonio doveva andare in città? 14. Perchè la zia Rosa doveva andare in città? 15. Quando ritornarono gli altri dalla loro passeggiata? 16. Che cosa risposero

---

[1] **Annottare**, being an impersonal verb, is used only in the 3rd person singular.

i Locatello alle parole « ritornate presto » ？   17. Perchè fu delizioso
il viaggio di ritorno ？

V. ESERCIZI

A. 1. Scrivere in italiano:

3rd, 5th, 1st, 7th, 10th, 2nd, 9th, 4th, 8th, 6th, 11th, 14th, 17th,
21st, 23rd, 54th, 83rd, 100th, 1000th.

2. Leggere ad alta voce le seguenti frazioni:

$$\tfrac{1}{2}, \tfrac{1}{3}, \tfrac{1}{5}, \tfrac{2}{7}, \tfrac{3}{4}, \tfrac{4}{9}, \tfrac{4}{10}, \tfrac{6}{15}, \tfrac{9}{22}, \tfrac{23}{100}.$$

B. Tradurre in italiano usando la preposizione **da** in ciascuna
frase:

1. I like that girl with the red hat. 2. I am talking to you as a friend.
3. We buy our shoes at De Palma's. 4. He is not going to her house.
5. I often see the man with the blond beard. 6. Margaret has come
to my place. 7. They want some writing paper. 8. He spoke as a
physician. 9. Do you want to come to my house ？ 10. I cannot go
to their place. 11. Please come to my office. 12. They live in the
house with the large windows.

C. Tradurre in italiano:

1. What a surprise for us! 2. He was [1] a musician. 3. What a fine
statue! 4. Bologna, a city of nearly 300,000 inhabitants, is very ancient. 5. His brother-in-law is [1] a poet. 6. He is a good poet. 7. What
an enormous building! 8. What an appetite! 9. His library has more
than a thousand books. 10. Mr. Righi was an excellent dentist.

D. Tradurre in italiano:

I

1. My aunt has five sons and three daughters. 2. Each one of her
daughters has [a] husband, and only two of her sons, Lawrence and
James, live with her. 3. Lawrence is her second child [2]; James, her
seventh. 4. Her first son, Victor, a man with a blond beard, is [1] a
druggist. 5. His brother Christopher lives at his house; he is my
aunt's eighth child. [2] 6. That afternoon James invited us to (ad) go
into the garden with him. 7. When Laura saw it, she exclaimed:
"What a beautiful garden!" 8. It was at the left of the house, near a
field of wheat in which some laborers were still working. 9. When
they saw us they took off their hats and we greeted them cordially.

---

[1] Do not use the idiom with **fare**. [2] Use the word **figlio.**

10. In the garden we saw carnations, daisies, hyacinths, and violets, and on a red rose I saw a large butterfly with black and white wings.

II

1. My cousins' names are Mary, Clara, and Helen. 2. Mary is the third of my aunt's children [1]; Clara and Helen are the fourth (*f.*) and sixth (*f.*). 3. They weren't at their mother's home [on] that day; what a pity! 4. I said so [2] to James, and he said: "They will be at our place on (a) mother's [3] birthday, August 13th.[4]" 5. Meantime he was picking violets, carnations, and hyacinths for us,[5] and we thanked him. 6. "Let's sit a little [while] on the grass," he said a moment later. 7. We did so [6] and continued to (a) chat. What a good young man he is! 8. It was getting dark, and the moon and the stars were beginning to (a) shine when we got up. 9. We cordially thanked my relatives for that beautiful day [7] we had spent with them. 10. I said: "When will you decide to come to our house, Aunt Olga?" — "When I need [8] to go to the dressmaker's," she answered.

❧ *Fourth Review Lesson* ❧

I. VOCABULARY DRILL

A. Give the Italian for the following nouns:

1. The egg
   the star
   the pear
   the field
   the plant
   the donkey

2. The bean
   the road
   the water
   the florist
   the relative
   the sister-in-law

3. The hen
   the trip
   the path
   the pain
   the horse
   the tomato

4. The meat
   the moon
   the onion
   the celery
   the carnation
   the apple tree

5. The cow
   the wolf
   the sheep
   the woods
   the turkey
   the violet

6. The wheat
   the arm
   the beard
   the lettuce
   the dressmaker
   the farm laborer

[1] Use **figlio** in the plural; it includes girls too. [2] Translate, *I said it.* [3] Use the word **mamma**. [4] Spell out. [5] Place *for us* after *was picking.* [6] Translate, *we did it.* [7] A day in its duration. [8] Future time is implied.

B. Give the Italian plural forms, masculine and feminine, for each of the following adjectives:

1. Clear, domestic, tired, lucky, ripe, sturdy, located, usual, big, delightful.
2. Excellent, bashful, vain, filthy, light, interesting, true, high, free, blue.

C. Give the Italian for the following verbs:

1. To pour	3. To pick	5. To cry
to hope	to bark	to bet
to shine	to plant	to thank
to smell	to graze	to drink
2. To serve	4. To decide	6. To forget
to earn	to remain	to taste
to assure	to divide	to contain
to cultivate	to take off	to believe

D. Give the Italian for the following expressions:

1. Day before yesterday, with tomato sauce, usually, to his house, nearly, enough, to be hungry, meanwhile, to stand on ceremony, too bad!
2. With your permission, to be in a hurry, to shake hands with, to be thirsty, Parmesan style, to my place, to feed, to trouble, by Jove! fine!

II. INDEFINITE ARTICLE

1. In what cases is the indefinite article, though used in English, omitted in Italian?

2. Translate:

He is an American.   My brother-in-law is a lawyer.   What an idea!

III. ORDINAL NUMERALS

1. Give the first ten ordinal numerals.
2. How are ordinal numerals from 11th on formed? Give two examples.
3. Are there cases in which the final vowel of the cardinal numeral is kept in forming the ordinal numerals? Give an example.
4. Give the ordinal numerals from 11th to 20th.

IV. VERBS

1. Mention the orthographical changes that take place in the conjugation of certain verbs.

2. Translate:

I shall forget.	She will begin.
I have known him.	You (tu) thank her.

3. How is an irregular past absolute formed? Give an example.

4. Give the 1st person singular of the past absolute of **conoscere, dire, fare, prendere, ridere, rispondere,** and **rivedere.**

5. Translate in different ways the word **coltivando.**

6. Tell how the progressive construction is formed in Italian, and explain why the progressive construction is less frequently used in Italian than in English.

7. Translate, using the progressive construction:

It is getting dark.   She is betting.   They are following.

8. Give the present subjunctive of **pagare, stendere, capire,** and **offrire.**

9. Give the present perfect subjunctive of **accettare** and **restare.**

10. What is a noun clause? Give two examples in English.

11. What verbs require, in Italian, the subjunctive in their noun clauses? Mention some of them.

12. If the noun clause has a future idea, what tense shall we use?

13. Why must we pay attention to the subject of a noun clause?

14. Translate:

I want to sing.	I think he understands.
I want her to sing.	I think he will understand.

15. Explain how the impersonal construction is formed in Italian, tell how it is usually translated, and give an example.

16. Translate:

People are kind.	He washed his hands.
Many things are done.	They love each other.

17. Justify the Italian translation of each of the preceding sentences.

18. How do you form the passive voice in Italian? Give an example.

V. IDIOMATIC USES OF **DA**

1. Mention the use of **da** to indicate a place, and give an example.

2. How is **da** used in descriptive phrases? Give an example.

3. What other uses of **da** do you remember? Give two examples.

VI. ADVERBS OF MANNER

1. How do we form an adverb of manner from a qualifying adjective?

2. Form adverbs from **caldo, amaro, elementare, speciale, elegante,** and **gentile.**

3. Use each of the adverbs just formed in an original sentence.

LETTURA IN SILENZIO

Sì o no:

1. __ La melanzana è un frutto.
2. __ Gli aranci sono alberi.
3. __ Facciamo il pane col grano.
4. __ Il cavallo è nella stella.
5. __ Sua cognata abbaia qualche volta.
6. __ Anche gli asini abbaiano spesso.
7. __ La lattuga è una verdura.
8. __ Se lavoriamo, abbiamo buon appetito.
9. __ Noi ci lavoriamo spesso le mani.
10. __ Il tacchino è sullo scaffale.
11. __ I carciofi hanno pecore e maiali.
12. __ Le albicocche sono gialle.
13. __ La vacca è un grosso animale.
14. __ Il contadino abita in campagna.
15. __ La sarta fa un'elegante veste di sete.

ACHIEVEMENT TEST NO. 4

VOCABULARY

Give the Italian for the following words:

1. the hen _____
2. nearly _____
3. to earn _____
4. bashful _____
5. sturdy _____
6. the dog _____
7. to feed _____
8. usually _____
9. to smell _____
10. to drink _____
11. the water _____
12. delightful _____
13. to forget _____
14. meanwhile _____
15. in the country _____
16. the tomato _____
17. the horse _____
18. interesting _____
19. to be hungry _____
20. to be in a hurry _____

(Deduct 1 point for each mistake.)

GRAMMAR

A. Write out in Italian:

12th _____ 8th _____ 23rd _____ 5th _____

B. Translate into Italian, using the progressive construction:

1. They are going up. _____
2. We are erasing. _____
3. You are writing. _____
4. He is dressing himself. _____

C. Give the 3rd person plural of the future of each of the following verbs:

1. pagare _____
2. indicare _____
3. lasciare _____
4. giocare _____

*D. Replace the words in parentheses with their Italian equivalents, using **da** whenever it is possible:*

1. Vado (*to her house*). _____
2. (*What a*) bella ragazza! _____
3. Parla (*as a teacher*). _____
4. Ritornerò (*to my house*). _____
5. Sono (*a farm laborer*). _____
6. Volete venire (*to our house*)? _____
7. Egli è (*a good musician*). _____
8. La signora (*in the blue dress*). _____

E. *Give the adverbs of manner corresponding to each of the following adjectives:*

1. semplice _____
2. naturale _____
3. lontano _____
4. elementare _____

F. *Translate into Italian, using the impersonal construction:*

1. People eat too much. _____
2. Many words were said. _____
3. We don't say so. _____
4. One remains poor. _____
5. We have been lucky. _____
6. Six languages are spoken. _____

G. *Ten of the following sentences require the subjunctive in Italian. List the numbers of those that do:*

1. He thinks I need a new hat.   2. I believe they haven't understood us.   3. I am glad she will arrive tomorrow.   4. She thinks he is here. 5. I want you to smile.   6. You don't believe he is right.   7. I hope he will forget.   8. She wants me to have a good time.   9. We hope he will leave.   10. It's a good thing that he is late.   11. I hope he is wrong. 12. You think that I don't know him.   13. I am glad I am here. 14. Olga wants you to clean the rooms.   15. We wish to remain.

(Deduct 1 point for each mistake.)

H. *Translate into Italian sentences 2, 6, 7, 12, and 14 in the preceding question.*

(Each sentence counts 2 points.)

READING

Translate the Italian passage that your instructor will write on the board or hand to you on a mimeographed sheet.

(This part counts 20 points.)

DICTATION

Your instructor will dictate twice a short Italian pasasge.

(This part counts 10 points.)

PERFECT SCORE: 100

Parte Quinta

IN VIAGGIO

I. NOTE GRAMMATICALI

121. Use of the Conjunctive Personal Pronouns

Me lo mostrerai?	*Will you show him* (or *it*) *to me?*
Parlatecene.	*Speak of it* (or *of him*, or *of her*, or *of them*) *to us.*
Non ce ne parlate.	*Don't speak of it* (*etc.*) *to us.*
Voglio dartelo.	*I want to give it to you.*
Dandomeli.	*In giving them to me.*
Lo diamo loro.	*We give it to them.*
Glieli mostriamo.	*We show them to him* (or *to her*, or *to you* [1]).

1. When two conjunctive personal pronouns are used with the same verb, the indirect object precedes the direct object (contrary to English usage), and both precede or follow the verb, as in the case of a single pronoun (*see* § 92, p. 135).

2. **Loro,** as always, follows the verb and is written as a separate word.

3. Before **lo, la, li, le,** and **ne:**

(*a*) **mi, ti, si, ci,** and **vi,**[2] change **i** to **e,** and become respectively **me, te, se, ce,** and **ve;**

(*b*) **gli** and **le** alike become **glie,** which is written as one word with the following pronoun, giving these forms:

> **glielo** ⎫ *it to him, or it to her, or it to you*
> **gliela** ⎭
>
> **glieli** ⎫ *them to him, or them to her, or them to you*
> **gliele** ⎭
>
> **gliene** *some to him, or some to her, or some to you*

122.   *Sapere* and *Conoscere*

1. Non so il suo nome.	*I don't know his name.*
Sapete chi parlerà?	*Do you know who will speak?*

[1] This refers, of course, to the **Lei** form of address.   [2] Also the adverbs **ci** and **vi** (see § 93, p. 137).

Ella non sa cantare.	*She does not know how to (she cannot) sing.*
Ho saputo ch'egli è qui.	*I learned (found out) that he is here.*

Sapere means *to know* a thing or a fact. It also renders the English *can* in the sense of *to know how*, and such expressions as *to learn, find out*

2. Conoscete la signora Nardi?   *Are you acquainted with (do you know) Mrs. Nardi?*

Conosco quel ristorante.   *I know that restaurant.*

Non conosco la lingua russa.   *I don't know the Russian language.*

Conoscere means *to be acquainted* with a person, or *to know* something that is more complex than a single thing or fact.

123. Study the complete conjugation of **sapere** (*Appendix III*).

II. LETTURA

Alla stazione

È una calda sera di giugno. Un'automobile si ferma non lontano dall'entrata principale della stazione di Syracuse, N.Y., e ne scendono un signore, una signora e una bionda signorina di poco più di vent'anni.

5   Sapete chi sono? Sono il signore e la signora Walker, e la loro figlia Lucia, che sta per partire per New York. I genitori son venuti ad accompagnarla, a darle un addio al treno.

Il signor Walker prende la valigia e la valigetta di sua figlia, e ora chiama un facchino e gliele dà.

10   — Devo portarle al diretto delle ventidue e un quarto?

— Sì. Carrozza a letti numero sette.

Appena i tre entrano nella stazione, gli occhi di Lucia vanno al grand'orologio; ora ella sa che il treno non partirà che fra trentotto minuti. E guarda intorno: cerca la sua amica Luisa Avery

15 con cui deve partire. Luisa non è ancora venuta all'appuntamento? Forse arriverà da un momento all'altro.

— È possibile, — dice la signora Walker, — che sia in sala d'aspetto.

E tutti e tre vanno là.

Sì, Luisa è in sala d'aspetto con suo zio e sua sorella, e sta conversando con loro. Appena le due amiche si vedono, corrono a stringersi la mano sorridendo.

Non c'è bisogno di presentazioni perchè le due famiglie si conoscono da molto tempo, e il viaggio delle signorine è stato concertato insieme. 5

Al loro arrivo, nella stazione di New York, le due ragazze incontreranno domani la signorina Fontana, insegnante d'italiano in una scuola di Chicago, e con lei partiranno poi per fare un lungo 10 viaggio in Italia. Ogni estate essa guida una comitiva di studenti e studentesse a visitare il suo paese nativo.

— Sa con che treno voi arriverete? — dice il signor Avery a sua nipote. — Sarà bene che tu le mandi un telegramma.

— Mandaglielo tu, zio. Non te ne dimenticherai? 15

— No, cara, non me ne dimenticherò.

— Appena il treno partirà, andate a dormire, — raccomanda la signora Walker, — e poi, quando sarete in Italia, scriveteci spesso.

Ma il treno dev'essere già arrivato, ed essi, seguendo i facchini con le valige, escono. 20

Prima di salire in treno, le due ragazze abbracciano e baciano i loro parenti.

— Arrivederci! Buon viaggio!

— Divertitevi e scriveteci spesso!

— Anche voi! Addio! 25

E il treno si muove, parte.

PROVERBIO

Ogni cosa ha il suo tempo. *Everything has its time.*

III. STUDIO DI PAROLE

Italia Italy
Lucia Lucy
Luisa Louise

addio farewell; dare un addio to say farewell

carrozza coach; carrozza a letti sleeping car
comitiva party
facchino porter
insegnante *m. or f.* instructor

ɔcchio eye
orolɔgio clock, watch
paese *m.* country
presentazione *f.* introduction
sala d'aspɛtto waiting room
telegramma *m.* telegram
trɛno train; trɛno dirɛtto express train
valigia valise, suitcase

nativo native
possibile possible

abbracciare [**abbraccio**] to embrace
accompagnare to accompany
baciare [**bacio**] to kiss
cercare to look for, seek, try
concertare [**concɛrto**] to arrange, devise
dormire [**dɔrmo**] to sleep
fare un viaggio to take a trip
muɔvere, muɔversi to move [1]

intorno around

IV. CONVERSAZIONE

1. Dove si ferma l'automɔbile ɔ 2. Chi ne scende ɔ 3. Perchè il signore e la signora Walker son venuti alla stazione ɔ 4. Che cɔsa prɛnde il signor Walker dall'automɔbile ɔ 5. A chi le dà ɔ 6. Che cɔsa domanda il facchino ɔ 7. Che gli risponde il signor Walker ɔ 8. Che cɔsa fa Lucia appena entra nella stazione ɔ 9. Chi è Luisa Avery ɔ 10. Che cɔsa dice la signora Walker a sua figlia ɔ 11. Che cɔsa fanno allora ɔ 12. Che cɔsa fanno le due amiche quando si vedono ɔ 13. Perchè non c'è bisogno di presentazioni ɔ 14. Chi incontreranno le due ragazze nella stazione di New York ɔ 15. Che cɔsa fa ogni estate la signorina Fontana ɔ 16. Che cɔsa dice il signor Avery a sua nipote ɔ 17. Che gli risponde Luisa ɔ 18. Che cɔsa raccomanda la signora Walker ɔ 19. Che cɔsa fanno le due ragazze prima di salire in trɛno ɔ 20. Come si saluta una persona cara che parte ɔ

V. ESERCIZI

A. Tradurre in due mɔdi (*in two ways*):

1. Dateglielo. 2. Gliela venderemo. 3. Non gliene parleranno ancora. 4. Gliene dɔ sɛi. 5. Margherita glieli offrì. 6. Tu non glieli hai spiegati. 7. Glielo dissi. 8. Scriviglielo. 9. Non gliela lɛggere. 10. Portagliene.

---

[1] **Muɔvere** is a transitive verb (*to move something*); **muɔversi** translates the English intransitive *to move.*

B. Tradurre in italiano:

1. I shall show it to him. 2. He will send them to her. 3. She will not bring her any. 4. They told (*p. abs.*) it to me. 5. You did not send them to us. 6. I shall introduce them (*f.*) to you (*four ways*). 7. We shall speak of it to them. 8. She gives me five of them. 9. He recommended her to us. 10. They will send it to me. 11. You didn't send it to them. 12. I shall speak of it to you (*four ways*). 13. Speak of it to her (*four ways*). 14. In showing them to me. 15. Don't send it to him (*four ways*).

C. 1. Coniugare:

1. Io non so parlare tedesco, tu . . ., ecc.
2. Io seppi ch'egli era in Italia, tu . . ., ecc.
3. Io saprò se ella ha sbagliato, tu . . ., ecc.
4. Maria non vuole ch'io lo sappia, Maria non vuole che tu . . ., ecc.
5. Io conobbi quelle signorine, tu . . ., ecc.

2. Completare con la forma corretta del presente dell'indicativo di **sapere** o di **conoscere,** secondo il senso:

1. Io ____ molte persone. 2. Egli non ____ a che ora il treno arriverà. 3. Tutti ____ che i giorni della settimana sono sette. 4. Essi ____ sua cognata. 5. Noi non ____ nè il francese nè il tedesco. 6. Tu non ____ che numero è. 7. ____ voi quello scrittore? 8. Lei mi ____. 9. Noi ____ che Laura canta bene. 10. Voi non ____ che cosa egli dirà. 11. Quell'uomo ____ molto l'arte. 12. Io ____ com'egli si chiama.

D. Tradurre in italiano:

I

1. "I want you to have a good time this summer," said Mr. Walker to his daughter. 2. He had bought for her [1] a ticket for New York, and now was handing it to her. 3. I can't [2] tell you how happy Lucy is.[3] 4. She will start [4] on (**per**) a long journey with her friend Louise. 5. I know that the two girls will take the 9:45 express [5] tomorrow evening, because they have spoken of it to me. 6. In the New York station [6] they will meet Miss Rose Fontana and her party. 7. Miss Fontana is Italian, knows her native country well,[7] and will show it to them. 8. "Take [8] only one suitcase and one bag with you," says

---

[1] Translate, *to her.*   [2] Same as *I don't know how.*   [3] Rearrange, *how Lucy is happy.*   [4] Use the verb **partire.**   [5] Translate, *the express of 9:45,* and write out the number.   [6] That is, *in the station of New York.*   [7] Attention! [8] Use the verb **portare.**

Mr. Walker, and I think he is right. 9. "I want you to sleep well when you are in your sleeping car," says Mrs. Walker. 10. We don't know whether she will prefer to chat with Louise.

II

1. If you don't know it, I'll tell it to you: that young lady in [1] the gray dress is Louise Avery. 2. The gentleman who is chatting with her is her uncle. 3. They [2] say he is an excellent lawyer, but I don't know him. 4. Just now Louise has looked at her watch. 5. She knows that Lucy must arrive any moment, for they must leave together. 6. But Lucy enters the waiting room, followed by a porter with her suitcase. Her parents are with her. 7. "I am glad she hasn't come too late," says Louise to her uncle. 8. And the two young friends embrace and kiss each other. 9. Louise wishes to send a telegram to Miss Fontana, speaks to her uncle, and tells him so. [3] 10. "I'll send it to her," he says, "but now let's go; I know the train is about to arrive."

❧ Lezione Ventottesima ❧

I. NOTE GRAMMATICALI

124.　　　　　　**Irregular Comparison**

1.

Questa torta è più buona. ⎫
Questa torta è migliore. ⎬ *This cake is better.*

È il ragazzo più cattivo. ⎫
È il ragazzo peggiore. ⎬ *He is the worst boy.*

The following adjectives are compared both regularly and ir-regularly. The irregular forms are:

POSITIVE	COMPARATIVE	RELATIVE SUPERLATIVE	ABSOLUTE SUPERLATIVE
buono, *good*	**migliore**	**il migliore**	**ottimo**
cattivo, *bad*	**peggiore**	**il peggiore**	**pessimo**
alto, *high*	**superiore**	**il superiore**	**supremo**
basso, *low*	**inferiore**	**l'inferiore**	**infimo**
grande, *big*	**maggiore**	**il maggiore**	**massimo**
piccolo, *little*	**minore**	**il minore**	**minimo**

[1] See § 119, 2, p. 187.　[2] Use the impersonal construction, and don't forget that this is an expression of doubt.　[3] Translate, *tells it to him.*

Maggiore and **minore** very often mean *older* and *younger*.
Superiore and **inferiore** are generally used in a figurative sense.

Note carefully that ɔttimo, pɛssimo, etc., being absolute superlatives, do not mean *best, worst*, etc., but *very good, very bad*, etc.

2. The following adverbs, except for the absolute superlative,
are compared only irregularly:

POSITIVE	COMPARA- TIVE	RELATIVE SUPERLATIVE	ABSOLUTE SUPERLATIVE
bɛne, *well*	mɛglio	il mɛglio	**ottimamente** *or* **benissimo**
male, *badly*	pɛggio	il pɛggio	**pessimamente** *or* **malissimo**
molto, *much*	più	il più	**moltissimo**
pɔco, *little*	meno	il meno	**pochissimo**

125.   Impersonal Verbs

Mi sembra che sia Carlo.[1]	*It seems to me that it is Charles.*
Mi pare che tu sia stanco.	*It seems to me that you are tired.*
Bisogna ch'egli parta.	*It is necessary for him to leave.*
È dubbio ch'ella ritorni.	*It is doubtful whether she will return.*
È possibile ch'io lo veda.	*I may possibly see him.*
Occorre vederlo.	*It is necessary to see him.*

1. A verb used in the 3rd person singular without a definite
subject is called impersonal. As with the expressions of weather
already studied (§ **65**, p. 92) — which are also impersonal — the
pronoun *it* that precedes an impersonal verb in English is not translated into Italian.

2. After an impersonal expression of doubt, necessity, possibility,
desire, or emotion, the subjunctive is used if the dependent clause
has a personal subject (all examples but the last). If there is no
personal subject (last example), the infinitive is used instead.

3. M'è sembrato che sia stata   *It seemed to me that it was that girl.*
    quella ragazza.

Impersonal verbs are conjugated with ɛssere.

[1] Learn the new verbs used as examples in this section: **sembrare** or
parere, *to seem;* **bisognare** or **occorrere**, *to be necessary*, but use only those
in –are for the time being, as those in –ere are irregular.

126. The Definite Article Before Names of Countries, etc.

1.
l'Europa, l'America, l'Africa [1]	*Europe, America, Africa*
la Francia, il Belgio, il Perù	*France, Belgium, Peru*
la California, il Wisconsin	*California, Wisconsin*
la Toscana, l'Umbria, il Lazio	*Tuscany Umbria, Latium*
la Sicilia, la Sardegna, la Corsica	*Sicily, Sardinia, Corsica*

But: small islands: **Capri, Ischia, Malta;** large islands: **Candia, Cuba, Borneo, Sumatra, Giava** (Java), etc.

Contrary to English usage, the names of continents, countries, states, regions, and of some large islands take the definite article in Italian.[2]

2.
Il cielo d'Italia.	*Italy's sky* or *the Italian sky.*
Saremo in Toscana.	*We shall be in Tuscany.*
But: Le foreste del Canadà.	*Canada's forests.*
La Germania è più popolosa dell'Inghilterra.	*Germany is more populous than England.*
Siamo nella bella Toscana.	*We are in beautiful Tuscany.*

After the prepositions **di** or **in,** however, no article is used, provided that the name of the continent, country, state, region, or large island is feminine, ends in –a, and is not accompanied by any qualifying adjective; and provided also, in the case of **di,** that preposition and noun are equivalent to an adjective of nationality, as shown in the first example.

II. LETTURA

Il viaggio comincia

Le due ragazze non avevano molto sonno, ma quando furono nella carrozza a letti e la trovarono al buio, già preparata per la notte, non restò loro altro da fare che coricarsi e cercar di dormire.

---

[1] Learn the geographical names contained in this section. [2] Of the Italian islands, besides those given in the examples, only one takes the definite article (and it is a relatively small island), **l'Elba.** Non-Italian islands that take the definite article are just a few: **il Madagascar, la Tasmania,** etc. **L'Irlanda** (Ireland) and **l'Islanda** (Iceland) should be classified, of course, among countries.

A VIEW OF THE ROMAN FORUM THROUGH THE ARCH
OF SEPTIMIUS SEVERUS

THE ISLAND OF NISIDA TAKEN FROM THE POSILLIPO IN NAPLES

MIRAMAR CASTLE, TRIESTE

Sia Lucia che Luisa erano studentesse, e fra le migliori, dell'Università di Syracuse. Luisa, bruna, dai capelli e dagli occhi neri, era maggiore di qualche anno della sua amica e, pochi giorni prima della partenza, aveva ottenuto il suo diploma. Tutt'e due s'erano specializzate in italiano, e già avevano una buona cultura gene- 5 rale.

Conoscevano la letteratura inglese e anche un po' l'italiana; avevano studiato storia antica e moderna, geografia, filosofia, fisica e chimica, e sapevano un po' di francese e di tedesco. Ora andavano insieme a visitare l'Italia, la terra dei loro sogni, a pas- 10 sarvi tutta l'estate sotto la competente guida della signorina Fontana.

Alcune altre studentesse della stessa università erano già partite con un'altra comitiva per andare in Inghilterra e nella Francia Settentrionale, e per visitare poi rapidamente anche il Belgio, 15 l'Olanda, la Germania e la Svizzera. Non veder l'Italia, fra tanti paesi, pareva a Lucia e a Luisa un pessimo sbaglio.

La mattina dopo, mentre si stava per arrivare, le ragazze s'alzarono e si vestirono in fretta per esser pronte a scendere. Avevano appena finito, quando il treno entrò nella stazione di New 20 York.

Luisa chiamò un facchino, e — quasi allo stesso tempo — Lucia, indicando una giovane signora dall'abito azzurro che agitava un fazzoletto, disse:

— Mi sembra che sia la signorina Fontana. 25

— Sì, sì! È la signorina!

E già andavano in fretta a stringerle la mano.

La signorina Fontana fece la presentazione d'alcune ragazze e d'alcuni giovanotti della comitiva ch'eran venuti alla stazione con lei, e poi disse: 30

— Andiamo a depositare le valige, e facciamo colazione. Dopo una nottata di viaggio l'appetito non mancherà, e bisogna che mangiate abbastanza perchè oggi non si pranzerà prima delle tredici.

PROVERBIO

La vita è un sogno.   *Life is a dream.*

III. STUDIO DI PAROLE

Olanda Holland
Svizzera Switzerland

capello hair [1]
chimica chemistry
cultura culture, education
diploma *m.* diploma, degree
filosofia philosophy
fisica physics
geografia geography
guida guide, guidance [2]
mattina morning
notte *f.* night
partenza departure
sogno dream
sonno sleep; aver sonno to be
  sleepy
storia history

terra land, earth

bruno brunet, dark
competente competent
generale general
settentrionale northern

agitare [agito] to wave, shake
coricarsi to lie down, go to bed
depositare [deposito] to deposit,
  check (*baggage, a parcel, etc.*)
mancare to be lacking, be missing,
  fail [3]
ottenere to obtain
specializzarsi to specialize, major

al buio in the dark
rapidamente rapidly
sia . . . che both . . . and

IV. CONVERSAZIONE

1. Era illuminata la carrozza a letti di Lucia e Luisa? 2. Che cosa restò loro da fare? 3. Chi erano Lucia e Luisa? 4. Quale delle due era minore d'età? 5. Era bionda Luisa? 6. Quando aveva ottenuto il suo diploma Luisa? 7. In che cosa s'erano specializzate le due ragazze? 8. Che cosa avevano studiato all'università? 9. Dove andavano adesso? 10. In quali paesi andavano altre studentesse della stessa università? 11. È una buon'idea andare in Europa senza visitare l'Italia? 12. Perchè Lucia e Luisa si vestirono in fretta la mattina dopo? 13. Quando avevano finito di vestirsi? 14. Luisa chi chiamò appena il treno si fu fermato? 15. Che cosa disse Lucia allo stesso tempo? 16. Chi era venuto alla stazione con la signorina Fontana? 17. Quale fu la prima cosa che la signorina Fontana fece? 18. Che

---

[1] Use the plural, i capelli, with adjective or verb likewise in the plural, when *hair* has the collective meaning.   [2] Like the word persona (see footnote 2, p. 72), the word guida is feminine even though it most often refers to a man, *a guide*.   [3] Conjugated with essere in the sense of *to lack, be lacking, be missing;* conjugated with avere in the sense of *to fail.*

cosa fecero delle loro valige le ragazze? 19. Perchè l'appetito non
mancava? 20. Perchè si doveva mangiare abbastanza a colazione?

V. ESERCIZI

A. Tradurre in italiano:

1. This is my younger brother. 2. That man is a very bad dentist.
3. I bought these shirts at a very low price. 4. They understood us
better. 5. I finished it very well. 6. She is the oldest daughter.
7. Their library is very good. 8. This movie is the worst in town.
9. He used to work very badly. 10. We had a higher advantage.
11. To go is bad, to remain here is worse. 12. I sang with the greatest
pleasure.

B. Completare le seguenti frasi:

1. Bisogna che voi . . .   5. Mi sembra che tu . . .
2. Mi dispiace che Lei . . .   6. Occorre che Guido . . .
3. Ci pare che tu . . .   7. Mi piace che tua cugina . . .
4. È meglio che noi . . .   8. Bisogna che i ragazzi . . .

C. Completare con la forma corretta delle parole in parentesi:

1. (*Sicily*) è molto bella. 2. Abitiamo (*in California*). 3. Siamo (*in
Ohio*). 4. (*Italy*) è la terra dei fiori. 5. Partiremo (*for Germany*).
6. Una delle sue cognate era (*in Belgium*). 7. (*In America*) si parla
inglese. 8. (*America*) è il nostro paese. 9. Essi sono adesso (*in
Northern France*). 10. (*In England*) piove sempre. 11. I vini (*of
Italy*) sono ottimi. 12. Mi piace (*Holland*) più (*than Belgium*).
13. Egli visiterà (*Sardinia*). 14. (*Switzerland*) è un paese piccolo ma
bellissimo. 15. (*Europe*) non è così grande come (*Africa*).

D. Tradurre in italiano:

I

1. You must [1] know something about two of the best students (*f.*) of
the University of Syracuse, my friends Lucy and Louise. 2. Lucy is
a blonde, and her eyes are blue; Louise is a brunette, and her eyes
and hair are black. 3. Lucy seems to be [2] a little taller [3] than Louise,

---

[1] Translate, *it is necessary that you* . . .   [2] Translate, *it seems that Lucy
is* . . .   [3] Use the regular comparative of **alto.**

and she is the younger of the two. 4. Both Lucy and Louise know the Italian language very well,[1] and can [2] speak French, too. 5. They know something about (**di**) the geography, history, and literature of Italy. 6. I know that they were very poor [3] students in chemistry and physics. 7. You must [4] excuse them, however, for one cannot be excellent in everything. 8. Now both Lucy and Louise are about to visit Italy under the guidance of Miss Fontana. 9. I don't know Miss Fontana, but I know that she is one of the best instructors (*f.*) in (**di**) Italian in a large Chicago school. 10. It seems that Italy is her native country.

II

1. The following morning, the two girls were chatting in their sleeping car. 2. I am still sleepy; have you [5] slept well, Lucy? — No, I spent a very bad night.[6] 3. I never sleep well on a train; but you must [4] get dressed in a hurry, dear, for we are about to arrive. 4. Doesn't it seem to you that this trip is like a dream? — Yes, and what a beautiful dream! 5. Too bad [7] our parents are not with us! — One cannot have everything! 6. Do you know that those four girls who came [8] on the train with us last night,[9] are going to (**in**) Europe also? 7. No; how do you know it? — I spoke with one of them, the oldest.[10] This is their second trip. 8. It seems that they know France, England, and Belgium very well. 9. This time they will visit Northern Italy, German Switzerland, part of Germany, and Holland. 10. One of them, the youngest,[10] can [2] speak French and German.

[1] Pay attention to the position of the abverb, and use the form studied in this lesson. [2] That is, *know how.* [3] Same as *very bad.* [4] Translate, *it is necessary that you . . .* [5] Remember that two intimate friends are talking. [6] *Night* in its duration. [7] An expression of sorrow, and a word missing. [8] Use the present perfect of **salire.** [9] See Vocabulary. [10] Add *in* (**di**) *age.*

I. NOTE GRAMMATICALI

127. **Past Subjunctive**

I	II	III
I bought, or might buy, etc.	*I sell, or might sell, etc.*	*I finished, or might finish, etc.*
compr **assi**	vend **essi**	fin **issi**
compr **assi**	vend **essi**	fin **issi**
compr **asse**	vend **esse**	fin **isse**
compr *assimo*	vend *essimo*	fin *issimo*
compr **aste**	vend **este**	fin **iste**
compr *assero*	vend **essero**	fin *issero*

Note that:

1. We have already met the forms **compraste, vendeste,** and **finiste** of the 2nd person plural when we studied the past absolute. They are identical in both that tense and in the past subjunctive.

2. Except for the characteristic vowel — **a** in the first conjugation, **e** in the second, and **i** in the third — the endings of this tense are the same for all Italian verbs, whether regular or irregular.

128. **Past Subjunctive of the Auxiliary Verbs**

avere		essere	
I had, or might have, etc.		*I was, or might be, etc.*	
avessi	avessimo	fossi	fossimo
avessi	aveste	fossi	foste
avesse	avessero	fosse	fossero

129.   Past Perfect Subjunctive

I	II	III
I had bought, or *might have bought, etc.*	*I had sold,* or *might have sold, etc.*	*I had departed,* or *might have departed, etc.*
avessi avessi } comprato avesse	avessi avessi } venduto avesse	fossi fossi } partito, −a fosse
avessimo aveste } comprato avessero	avessimo aveste } venduto avessero	fossimo foste } partiti, −e fossero

AUXILIARY VERBS

I had had, or *might have had, etc.*	*I had been,* or *might have been, etc.*
avessi avuto, etc.	**fossi stato, −a,** etc.

130.   Use of the Tenses of the Subjunctive

1. Desidero che tu dorma.   *I want you to sleep.*
   Non penserà che Maria si sia già avviata.   *He will not think that Mary has already started on her way.*
   Ditegli che scriva presto.   *Tell him to write soon.*

A principal verb in the present, future, or imperative is normally followed by the present or present perfect subjunctive.[1]

2. Temè ch'io fossi malato.   *He feared I might be ill.*
   Voleva ch'ella li guidasse.   *He wanted her to guide them.*
   Temevo che tu avessi sbagliato.   *I feared you had made a mistake.*
   Avevo pensato ch'essi fossero arrivati.   *I had thought that they had arrived.*
   Eviterebbe ch'ella fosse là.   *He would avoid her being there.*

[1] Sometimes the present in the principal clause is followed by the past subjunctive. This happens whenever the dependent clause, if it were independent, would have the verb in the past absolute or past descriptive. Examples: **Credo che Cicerone dicesse così.** (What I believe is: **Cicerone disse così.**) **Non so se Lincoln parlasse francese.** (What I don't know is: **Parlava francese Lincoln?**) — On the other hand: **Credo che tu abbia detto così.** (What I believe is: **Tu hai detto così.**)

A principal verb in a past tense or in the conditional [1] is followed by the past or past perfect subjunctive.

3. Ha detto che tu ritorni a casa.   *He said you should return home.*
   Ha voluto ch'io fossi presente.   *He wanted me to be present.*

A principal verb in the present perfect is followed by the present or the past subjunctive as the sense may require. In the 1st example the subjunctive expresses an uncompleted action; in the 2nd, a completed one.

131.   **Nouns in −*i* and in −*u***

SINGULAR	PLURAL
la crisi, *the crisis*	le crisi
la tesi, *the thesis*	le tesi
il brindisi, *the toast*	i brindisi
la virtù, *the virtue*	le virtù
la schiavitù, *slavery*	le schiavitù

Italian nouns may end in −i or in −u. In both cases, they are invariable.

Those ending in −i are feminine if of Greek origin,[2] masculine otherwise. Those ending in −u are all accented, and all feminine except a few of foreign origin, such as **il bambù,** *the bamboo;* **il caucciù,** *the rubber*, etc.

II. LETTURA

L'imbarco

Quando la colazione fu finita, alcuni della comitiva che non conoscevano New York s'affrettarono a uscire dalla stazione per fare un giro della metropoli. Altri, e tra questi Lucia e Luisa, restarono con la signorina Fontana per andare a visitare dei negozi e fare delle ultime spese.   5

Il piroscafo non partiva che a mezzogiorno e un quarto, e c'erano

---

[1] The conditional will be studied in a later lesson.   [2] Nouns of Greek origin are easily recognizable for, as a rule, they have quite a similar form in English: genesi, *genesis;* ipotesi, *hypothesis;* dieresi, *dieresis*, etc. Try to remember these words and all the examples given in § 131.

più di tre ore di tempo per l'imbarco. La signorina Fontana voleva solo che tutti fossero a bordo prima di mezzogiorno.

— Bisogna ch'io compri delle pellicole per la mia macchina fotografica, — disse uno dei giovanotti, Carlo Aldrich.

5 — Allora andiamo con te, e forse comprerò una macchinetta cinematografica, — disse un altro studente che si chiamava Guido Capponi.

— Noi, invece, prenderemo un tassì che ci porterà al Times Square, — disse alle ragazze la signorina Fontana.

10 Non le seguiremo nel lungo giro ch'esse fecero da un negozio all'altro comprando parecchie cose: calze di seta, diari, guanti, libretti per indirizzi, fazzoletti, cosmetici. Diremo solo, in parentesi, che pareva che avessero bisogno d'un po' di tutto.

Circa mezz'ora prima del tempo fissato, ognuno era sulla ban-
15 china, pronto all'imbarco, fra il viavai di facchini che portavano valige e bauli, e di passeggieri che parlavano, ridevano, si salutavano coi loro amici.

Bisognò che i membri della comitiva della signorina Fontana si mettessero in fila per mostrare i loro passaporti e i biglietti di
20 viaggio, e finalmente potettero salire a bordo.

Un cameriere molto gentile, che parlava inglese ottimamente, li guidò alle loro cabine, ma essi non vi restarono che pochi minuti, perchè tutti volevano vedere dalla coperta la partenza del piroscafo.

25 Una gru caricava valige e bauli, i camerieri andavano in fretta da un posto all'altro, alcuni passeggieri abbracciavano e baciavano parenti e amici ch'eran venuti a dar loro un ultimo addio.

Finalmente l'ora della partenza arrivò.

PROVERBIO

Chi guarda ogni nuvola non fa mai viaggio.	*He who is afraid of the weather never gets anywhere.*

III. STUDIO DI PAROLE

banchina pier	**cabina** stateroom, cabin
baule *m.* trunk	**coperta** cover, deck
bordo board; **a bordo** on board	**cosmetico** cosmetic

diario diary
giro tour; **fare un giro** to take a
  tour
gru *f.* crane
imbarco embarking
indirizzo address
macchina cinematografica
  movie camera
macchina fotografica camera
membro member
metropoli *f.* metropolis
parentesi *f.* parenthesis
passaporto passport

passeggiero, –a passenger
pellicola film
piroscafo steamer, liner
tassì *m.* taxicab
viavai *m.* going and coming

fissato fixed
ultimo last, final

affrettarsi (a) to hurry, hasten
caricare [carico] to load

finalmente finally, at last

IV. CONVERSAZIONE

1. Chi s'affrettò a uscire dalla stazione? 2. Perchè gli altri membri della comitiva restarono con la signorina Fontana? 3. Quando partiva il piroscafo? 4. Quanto tempo c'era ancora? 5. Che cosa voleva la signorina Fontana? 6. Come si chiamava il giovanotto che voleva comprare le pellicole? 7. Che cosa disse Guido Capponi? 8. Che cosa disse alle ragazze la signorina Fontana? 9. Che cosa fecero le ragazze? 10. Che cosa comprarono? 11. Di che cosa pareva che avessero bisogno? 12. A che ora erano tutti sulla banchina? 13. Che cosa portavano i facchini? 14. Che cosa fanno, di solito, i passeggieri poco prima della partenza? 15. Che cosa dovettero fare i membri della comitiva prima dell'imbarco? 16. Quand'ebbero mostrato passaporti e biglietti, che cosa fecero? 17. Chi li guidò alle loro cabine? 18. Perchè restarono pochi minuti nelle cabine? 19. Che cosa caricava una gru? 20. Che cosa arrivò finalmente?

V. ESERCIZI

A. 1. Coniugare:

1. Essa credeva ch'io avessi torto, essa credeva che tu . . ., ecc.
2. Egli pensava ch'io fossi ricco, egli pensava che tu . . ., ecc.
3. Anna credè ch'io l'accompagnassi, Anna credè che tu . . ., ecc.
4. Rosa sperava ch'io le scrivessi, Rosa sperava che tu . . ., ecc.
5. Egli sperava ch'io non partissi, egli sperava che tu . . ., ecc.

2. Completare, secondo le regole, col presente perfetto o col passato del congiuntivo [1] del verbo in parentesi:

1. (*essere*) Voleva ch'egli ____ felice. 2. (*partire*) Fui contento ch'essi ____. 3. (*cantare*) Non so se Beatrice ____. 4. (*avere*) Spero che voi ____ parecchi svaghi. 5. (*capire*) Volevo ch'esse mi ____ bene. 6. (*riconoscere*) Bisognava ch'ella ci ____. 7. (*essere*) Carlo desiderò che noi ____ occupati. 8. (*credere*) Preferisco che Lei ____ così. 9. (*uscire*) Non è possibile che tu ____ con lui. 10. (*dimenticare*) Le sembrava che noi la ____. 11. (*seguire*) Mi piace che tu ____ l'esempio di tuo cognato. 12. (*invitare*) È bene che voi le ____.

B. Tradurre in italiano:

1. She wanted me to be in the party. 2. He didn't know whether I was right. 3. We are glad that you needed us. 4. She didn't know whether they were happy. 5. He didn't want to be always alone. 6. I believe they were wrong. 7. She wanted us to walk with her. 8. You hoped that they were not in a hurry. 9. I was not thinking that she would come. 10. He had hoped that we might remain.

C. Riconoscere il significato (*the meaning*) delle seguenti parole d'origine greca, e usare ciascuna d'esse in una breve frase:

1. Diagnosi. 2. Enfasi. 3. Tubercolosi. 4. Tesi. 5. Paralisi. 6. Analisi. 7. Sintesi. 8. Metropoli. 9. Crisi. 10. Ipotesi.

D. Tradurre in italiano:

I

1. The girls had to [2] take two taxicabs. 2. Some minutes later, they were in front of one of the largest stores in New York. 3. "I didn't think [3] that it was nearly nine o'clock," said [Miss] Corelli looking at her watch. 4. She was only seventeen years old, and was the daughter of an Italian physician. 5. There was another Italian girl in the party; her name was Margaret Filpo. 6. Margaret could [4] speak French and German, played the piano, sang very well, and had many other accomplishments.[5] 7. The girls hastened to (a) enter the store among the going and coming of the people. 8. Some [6] of them bought silk stockings, cosmetics, gloves, or handkerchiefs; others bought diaries, films for their cameras, and other useful things. 9. Miss

---

[1] Called *imperfetto del congiuntivo* by Italian grammarians.   [2] Translate, using the past absolute, *it was necessary that* . . .   [3] Use the past descriptive.   [4] That is, *knew how*.   [5] Same as *virtues*.   [6] Use **alcuno.**

Fontana, who bought a movie camera, wanted them to see some other stores, too. 10. It was nearly eleven when they finally returned to the station to get their suitcases; the hour of embarking [1] was near.

II

1. The members of the party who had wished to take a tour of the metropolis arrived in two taxicabs. 2. They met the others on the pier at the appointed [2] time. [3] 3. They had amused themselves, and now they were ready to (a) go [4] on board. 4. First it was [5] necessary, however, that they get [6] in line to show their passports and tickets. 5. A young steward guided them afterward to their staterooms. 6. They had to [5] pass among the going and coming of the passengers and their relatives and friends. 7. All returned on deck immediately after. 8. Guido wanted the others to see the cranes that were loading trunks and suitcases. 9. The girls were looking at the people [7] who had come to say farewell to the passengers. 10. Finally, at twelve fifteen, the hour of departure [1] arrived.

❧ *Lezione Trentesima* ☙

I. NOTE GRAMMATICALI

132.   **Other Relative Pronouns**

Besides the relative pronouns already studied (**che** and **cui**, *see* § 41, p. 59), note the following:

1. L'avvocato Lucci, il quale parla così bene, darà una conferenza domani.	*Lawyer Lucci, who speaks so well, will give a lecture tomorrow.*
Il marito d'Olga, al quale sto scrivendo, è ora in Francia.	*Olga's husband, to whom I am writing, is in France now.*
Il giovanotto e la signorina con la quale studio son fratello e sorella.	*The young man and the young lady with whom I am studying are brother and sister.*
Ecco i mobili dei quali v'ho parlato.	*Here is the furniture of which I spoke to you.*

---

[1] Use the definite article.   [2] Same as *fixed*.   [3] Use the word **ora**.   [4] The meaning is *to go up*.   [5] Use the past absolute of **bisognare**.   [6] Translate, *they put themselves.*   [7] See Vocabulary.

Another relative pronoun is **il quale**, which is inflected (**la quale, i quali, le quali**) and agrees in gender and number with its antecedent. A preposition preceding it combines in one word with the article, as shown in the 2nd and 4th examples.

This pronoun is rather sparingly used instead of **che** or **cui;** it implies emphasis, or helps to avoid ambiguity, as shown in the 2nd and 3rd examples. As it may refer to persons or things, and may be used as subject, direct object, or object of a preposition, it stands for the English *who, whom, that,* or *which.*

2. Ecco uno scrittore il cui nome   *Here is a writer whose name is really*
  è veramente famoso.   *famous.*
Vedemmo una casa le cui fine-   *We saw a house the windows of which*
  stre eran tutte chiuse.   *were all closed.*

Another relative pronoun is **il cui** (**la cui, i cui, le cui**, according to the word that follows), which translates the English *whose* or *of which*, whenever the latter has the meaning of *whose*.

3. Chi va in Italia deve veder   *He who goes to Italy must see Venice.*
  Venezia.
Evito chi non è sincero.   *I avoid those (the persons, the people)*
    who are not sincere.
Perdonate a chi vi fa del male.   *Forgive him (the man, the person)*
    who does you wrong.

Chi (which we have met as an interrogative pronoun) is also used as a relative pronoun, and stands for an indefinite *he who* or *him who, one who* or *one whom, a person who* or *a person whom, those who* or *those whom*, etc. Sometimes, instead of **chi, colui che** and **coloro che** are used; the first is singular; the latter, plural.

4. Non possiamo far sempre quel   *We cannot always do what we want*
  che (*or* quello che, *or* ciò   *to.*
  che) vogliamo.

Finally, note the expression **quel che** (or **quello che**, or **ciò che**), which is used in translating the English relative pronoun *what* whenever the latter is equivalent to *that which*.

133.   Other Invariable Nouns

SINGULAR	PLURAL
il re,[1] *the king*	i re
la qualità, *the quality*	le qualità
la specie, *the kind*	le specie
il lapis, *the pencil*	i lapis
lo sport, *the sport*	gli sport

Besides the nouns ending in −i and in −u (*see* § 131, p. 213), the following nouns do not change in the plural:

(*a*) those of one syllable;

(*b*) those ending in an accented vowel;

(*c*) the ones ending in −ie (except **la moglie**, pl. **le mogli**);

(*d*) those, usually Latin or foreign, that end in a consonant;

(*e*) the words **la radio,** *the radio,* **il vaglia,** *the money order,* and a few others rarely used.

134.   Irregular Nouns

1.

SINGULAR	PLURAL
il calcagno, *the heel*	le calcagna

A certain number of nouns in −o have an irregular plural in −a, which is feminine. Besides **calcagno,** the most frequently used are:

braccio, *arm* [2]	grido, *cry* (human) [7]
centinaio, *about a hundred* [3]	labbro, *lip* [8]
ciglio, *eyelash* [4]	lenzuolo, *sheet*
dito, *finger* [5]	membro, *member* (of the body) [9]
frutto, *fruit* [6]	migliaio, *about a thousand* [3]
ginocchio, *knee*	miglio, *mile*

---

[1] Learn all the Italian words given in this section.   [2] But when *arm* is used figuratively (*the arms of a river, a lake, etc.*), the plural is **i bracci.**   [3] **Centinaia** and **migliaia** mean, respectively, *hundreds* and *thousands* in an indefinite way.   [4] **Ciglio,** used figuratively in the sense of *edge of a ditch, precipice, etc.*, has the plural **i cigli.**   [5] When specific fingers are meant, e.g. **i diti mignoli,** *the little fingers,* the plural is regular.   [6] *Fruit,* as a food, is either **il frutto** or **la frutta;** the plural, in each case, is **le frutta.**   The word **il frutto** is also used in the sense of *produce,* as a fruit on a tree, or, metaphorically, to mean a reward, a benefit, an income. In all these cases the plural is regular: **i frutti.**   [7] But: **i gridi degli animali.**   [8] **Labbro** is used also to indicate the *rim of a vase;* in that case, the plural is **i labbri.**   [9] But: **i membri della comitiva.**

muro, *wall* (of a city) [1]
ɔsso, *bone* [2]
paio, *pair*

riso, *laughter*
sopracciglio, *eyebrow*
uɔvo, *egg* (as a food) [3]

Note that most of these nouns refer to parts of the body.

2. The following nouns have an entirely irregular plural:

SINGULAR	PLURAL
l'ala, *the wing*	le ali
il bue, *the ox*	i buɔi
il dio, *the god*	gli dɛi
la moglie, *the wife*	le mogli
l'uɔmo, *the man*	gli uɔmini

Note that **dio** is irregular also in that it takes the article **gli** in the plural, contrary to the rules.

135. Study the complete conjugation of the four irregular verbs in –are: **andare, dare, fare,** and **stare** (*Appendix III*).

II. LETTURA

Sul *Colombo*

Il *Colombo*, la grande e bella nave sulla quale la nɔstra comitiva s'ɛra imbarcata, stava girando lentamente nelle acque dell'Hudson, mentre centinaia d'uɔmini, dɔnne e ragazzi, agitando le braccia, gridavano dalla banchina parɔle d'addio. Quasi tutti i
5 passeggiɛri ɛrano sulla prima copɛrta e rispondevano a quei saluti.

Chi non ha veduto New York dall'Hudson non sa immaginare quanto sia affascinante la vista della grande metrɔpoli e dei suɔi grattaciɛli.

— Sai che dobbiamo fare? — disse Guido Capponi a suo fra-
10 tɛllo Mario. — Passarvi una settimana dopo il nɔstro viaggio di ritorno dall'Eurɔpa.

Ma già i camerieri chiamavano coi loro gɔng. La colazione ɛra pronta, e bisognava che ognuno scendesse in sala da pranzo.

---

[1] *The walls* of a house, or those around a garden, are **i muri**.   [2] When *bones* do not refer to the whole skeleton, the regular plural is used: **gli ɔssi delle braccia**.   [3] *The eggs* of a bird or a reptile are **gli uɔvi**.

La grande sala, dai cui finestrini si poteva vedere un pò' di mare e la costa del New Jersey, era piena di gente già seduta o che cercava dei posti; per la nostra comitiva erano state riservate tre tavole.

Tutti avevano grand'appetito, e il cibo era delizioso.   5

Avevano appena cominciato a mangiare quando si vide dai finestrini la Statua della Libertà, così cara a ogni cuore americano, e molti s'alzarono da tavola per vederla meglio.

Dall'antipasto alle frutta, ogni cosa fu gustata: gli ottimi spaghetti al pomodoro, l'arrosto d'agnello con patate, piselli e me- 10 lanzane, l'insalata all'italiana con uova sode, il formaggio, e il vino. Poi quasi ognuno prese una tazzina di caffè nero, secondo l'uso d'Italia.

Dopo la colazione, alcuni passeggieri salirono su coperta a passeggiare; altri andarono in sala da fumare; altri, invece, si riti- 15 rarono nelle loro cabine per aprire le valige e mettere le loro cose in ordine. Questo è quello che fecero Luisa Avery e Lucia Walker.

Aprirono le loro valige per appendere gli abiti negli armadietti della cabina, ma ahimè! in che stato erano le loro vesti! Bisognò che chiamassero la cameriera e che gliele dessero a stirare.   20

— Quando saranno pronte? — le domandò una delle ragazze.

— Non posso promettergliele per prima di domani sera, signorina, perchè abbiamo molto da fare.

PROVERBIO

Meglio tardi che mai.   *Better late than never.*

III. STUDIO DI PAROLE

Mario Marius

agnello lamb
cibo food
costa coast, shore
cuore m. heart
finestrino small window
gong m. gong
grattacielo skyscraper
libertà liberty

mare m. sea
nave f. ship
sala da fumare smoking room
saluto greeting
stato state, condition
uso use, custom
vista view, sight

affascinante fascinating, charming

sodo solid, (*referring to eggs*) hard
boiled

appendere to hang, hang up
girare to turn, go (*or* move) around
imbarcarsi to embark
passeggiare [passeggio] to take
a walk

promettere to promise
riservare [riservo] to reserve
ritirarsi to retire, withdraw, re-
treat

ahimè! alas!
secondo according to

IV. CONVERSAZIONE

1. Su quale nave s'era imbarcata la comitiva? 2. Che cosa facevano uomini, donne e ragazzi, dalla banchina? 3. Dov'erano
quasi tutti i passeggieri? 4. Che cosa facevano? 5. Quale vista
è affascinante per chi parte per l'Europa? 6. Che cosa facevano i
camerieri poco dopo? 7. Dove andarono i passeggieri? 8. Che
cosa si vedeva dai finestrini della sala da pranzo? 9. Dove andò
a sedere la nostra comitiva? 10. Che cosa si vide un momento
dopo? 11. Che cosa gustarono a tavola i passeggieri? 12. Che
cosa presero dopo? 13. Che cosa fecero alcuni passeggieri dopo
la colazione? 14. Dove andarono altri? 15. Perchè alcuni si ri-
tirarono nelle loro cabine? 16. Che cosa fecero Luisa e Lucia?
17. Perchè le due ragazze aprirono le loro valige? 18. Che cosa
bisognò che facessero poi? 19. Che cosa domandò una delle ragazze alla cameriera? 20. Che le rispose la cameriera?

V. ESERCIZI

A. Tradurre in italiano usando in ciascuna frase uno dei pronomi relativi studiati in questa lezione:

1. He who studies learns. 2. She is the young lady of whom I spoke
to you this morning. 3. He is the young man whose parents you know.
4. She knows what we want. 5. This is the garden in which we met
them. 6. The man whose sister-in-law sings so well will visit us.
7. The person who says so is right. 8. In the store in which he works
they sell shoes also. 9. I like what they do. 10. The men to whom
I gave the books thanked me. 11. He is the painter whose sons go
to school with us. 12. Italy is a country the history of which I have
not studied.

B. Dare il plurale di:

1. Il dio greco. 2. Il mio lapis. 3. Il trust. 4. L'uovo sodo. 5. Il giovedì. 6. Il re d'Inghilterra. 7. Il bel labbro. 8. L'uomo robusto. 9. La fraternità. 10. Il vecchio paio. 11. Il bue bianco. 12. Il buon tè. 13. La moglie tedesca. 14. Il nuovo sport. 15. Un miglio di strada. 16. Il miglior caffè. 17. Il ciglio nero. 18. Il frutto maturo. 19. Il vaglia di mio zio. 20. Il sopracciglio biondo.

C. 1. Completare con la forma richiesta (*required*) del verbo **andare:**

Futuro: 1. Voi ____ su una bella nave. 2. Non sappiamo se egli ____ in Germania. 3. Essi ____ via volentieri. 4. Io non ____ solo. 5. Tu ____ al municipio.
Presente del congiuntivo: 1. Vuole che io ____ da lui. 2. Spero che voi ____ a lavorare. 3. Peccato che essi ____ via! 4. Immagino che Lei ____ dalla sarta ora. 5. Penso che tu ____ con piacere.

2. Completare con la forma richiesta del verbo **dare:**

Passato assoluto e presente perfetto: 1. Essi ci ____ una pianta di garofani. 2. Che cosa ____ voi a sua figlia? 3. Noi non ____ niente. 4. Chi vi ____ quest'informazione? 5. Io non gli ____ la mia età.
Presente del congiuntivo: 1. Desidero che tu mi ____ un paio di calzini. 2. Voglio che voi le ____ qualche cosa. 3. Spero che i miei genitori mi ____ un orologio. 4. Egli pensa che Lei non gli ____ nulla. 5. Che vuoi che io ti ____?
Passato del congiuntivo: 1. Volevo che voi gli ____ del vino. 2. Desiderava che noi le ____ delle frutta. 3. Bisognò che io ____ loro la valigia. 4. Non immaginavo ch'egli vi ____ quel quadro. 5. Era possibile che sua madre le ____ una lezione.

3. Completare con la forma richiesta del verbo **fare:**

Passato assoluto e presente perfetto: 1. Io non ____ niente di utile. 2. Che cosa ____ voi mentr'io dormivo? 3. C'erano molte cose da fare, e Maria le ____. 4. I lavori ch'essi ____ sono stati utili. 5. Lei non ____ nè una cosa nè l'altra.
Presente del congiuntivo: 1. Volete ch'io ____ così? 2. Penso che voi ____ male. 3. È meglio che esse lo ____. 4. Crede ch'io non ____ nulla. 5. Vuole che tu ____ tutto.
Passato del congiuntivo: 1. Desiderava che voi ____ qualche cosa. 2. Non sapevo se essi ____ colazione. 3. Voleva ch'egli ____ il medico. 4. Sembrava che noi ____ bene. 5. Sperò ch'io non lo ____.

4. Completare con la forma richiesta del verbo **stare:**

Passato assoluto e presente perfetto: 1. Noi ____ in piedi. 2. Io ____ a guardarlo. 3. Esse ____ con noi tutta la giornata. 4. Dove ____ voi? 5. Il bambino ____ a letto.

Presente del congiuntivo: 1. Pare che sua cognata ____ in Europa. 2. Credo che voi ____ volentieri. 3. Bisogna ch'essi non ____ sempre a casa. 4. Vuoi tu ch'io ____ al posto tuo? 5. Egli pensa che Lei ____ per imbarcarsi.

Passato del congiuntivo: 1. Bisognò ch'io ____ solo. 2. Fu un'ottima cosa che voi ____ con lui. 3. Pensava che noi ____ in Olanda. 4. Voleva che Guido ____ là. 5. Che cosa pensò egli ch'io ____ facendo?

D. Tradurre in italiano usando i pronomi relativi studiati in questa lezione:

I

1. The ship on which we had embarked was moving slowly. 2. The men on the pier were lifting their [1] arms, the women were waving their [1] handkerchiefs. 3. The boys and girls in whose party I [2] am, and hundreds of other passengers, were on deck with me. 4. Have you never seen New York and its skyscrapers from the Hudson,[3] and don't you think that that sight is fascinating? 5. Two men and their wives were standing near me. 6. "Do you know," I asked [4] of (a) one of the ladies, "How many miles there are from here to the Statue of Liberty?" 7. She told [5] me, then asked: "Where is your party going [6]?" — "Only to (in) Italy," I answered. 8. But just then the stewards began to (a) call with their gongs. 9. "I must [7] go to my cabin to (a) wash my hands,[8]" I said. "Excuse me!" 10. When I arrived at (in) the dining room, Miss Fontana wanted [9] me to sit next to her, and Margaret to be [10] at my right.

II

1. We were all hungry, and on the liner on which we were the food was delicious. 2. I was seated [11] near one of the small windows from which one could see the coast of New Jersey.[3] 3. On the table there

---

[1] Replace the possessive with the definite article.   [2] Do not omit this pronoun.   [3] A masculine noun.   [4] Use the past absolute.   [5] Add *it*.   [6] Use the future of **andare.**   [7] Use **bisognare.**   [8] Avoid the use of the possessive after reviewing § 116, p. 181.   [9] Past absolute of **desiderare.**   [10] Translate, *that Margaret should be;* use the verb **stare.**   [11] Use the verb **stare** and the past participle of **sedere.**

were two qualities of wine. 4. After the appetizers and the spaghetti Sicilian style, some members of the party ate roast lamb. 5. Others ate fried fish or turkey, but I took a dish made [up] of several vegetables and hard-boiled eggs. 6. The American coast was distant when, after lunch, we went up on deck. 7. Some men whose appearance showed [1] that they were neither Americans nor Italians were talking [2] German. 8. Some little children [3] were playing.[2] 9. Three girls were taking a walk and passed several times in front of us. 10. "Now we shall go to the smoking room," said Paul Horn to me; "I must [4] give something to that steward."

❧ *Lezione Trentunesima* ❧

I. NOTE GRAMMATICALI

136.   **Translation of "than"**

As we have already seen (*see* § 97, p. 143), *than* is expressed in Italian by **di** whenever the second term of comparison is a noun, a pronoun, or a numeral, and by **che** in most other cases.

Note, however, the following:

1. Ho dato più lavoro a Riccardo che a te.	*I gave more work to Richard than to you.*
È più acqua che vino.	*It's more water than wine.*
Voi siete più invidioso che vostro fratello.	*You are more envious than your brother.*

Than is expressed by **che**:

(*a*) if the noun, or the pronoun (as in the 1st example), that forms the second term of comparison is preceded by a preposition;

(*b*) if the comparison is between two nouns and is not based on any distinct quality, as shown in the second example;

(*c*) if by using **di** there is the possibility of **di** being interpreted *of*. Thus, in the third example, if *than* had been rendered by **di,** the sentence might have been taken to mean: *you are more envious of your brother.*

---

[1] A past descriptive.   [2] Use the progressive construction.   [3] Use the diminutive.   [4] Use **bisognare.**

2. Egli arrivò più presto che noi non pensassimo.

He arrived sooner than we thought.

Ho pagato meno di quel che m'aspettavo.

I paid less than I expected (to pay).

Essi amano più divertirsi che studiare.

They like to have a good time more than to study.

Before an inflected verb (that is, a verb that is not an infinitive), *than* is either **che** + subject (if any) + **non,** or **di quel che.** Note, however, that **che . . . non** takes the subjunctive, while **di quel che** takes the indicative.

Before a verb in the infinitive, *than* is **che.**

137. **Idiomatic** Use of *a*

I miei amici sono a Roma.

My friends are in Rome.

Abitavano a New York.

They used to live in New York.

But: Questi eventi ebbero luogo in Napoli.

These events took place in Naples.

Before names of cities, the English *in* is generally rendered by **a,** but it may be rendered by **in** if the meaning is *within.*

138. Study the complete conjugations of **dire** and **volere** (*Appendix III*).

II. LETTURA

Una settimana sul *Colombo*

Come la signorina Fontana aveva detto quand'erano a New York, la traversata dell'oceano durò poco più di cinque giorni e, dopo una settimana di viaggio, il *Colombo* arrivò a Genova.

Nei primi giorni il mare era stato meno calmo di quel che s'era
5 sperato, perchè tirava vento da nord-ovest, ma il tempo diventò migliore quando il piroscafo passò vicino alle *Isole Azzorre,* e si conservò ottimo fino al momento dello sbarco. Fortunatamente, nessuno della comitiva soffrì di mal di mare.

Durante il viaggio i giovanotti e le signorine vollero divertirsi,
10 e a bordo trovarono più svaghi ch'essi non avessero immaginato. Due volte al giorno, di mattina e nel pomeriggio, andavano a nuotare nella piscina; nelle altre ore leggevano dei libri della

biblioteca della nave, giocavano a carte o a scacchi, facevano lunghe passeggiate su coperta, o ascoltavano la musica dell'orchestrina di bordo. Passavano poi le serate vedendo il cinematografo o ballando fino a tardi.

Eppure, come furono contenti quando finalmente videro le prime 5 coste d'Europa: prima quella del Portogallo, poi — verso sud-est — quella di Spagna, e lo stretto di Gibilterra!

A Gibilterra la nave si fermò, poco dopo il tramonto, per lo sbarco e l'imbarco dei passeggieri, e ripartì ch'era già notte, sotto un cielo pieno di stelle.   10

Se il viaggio era stato bello fino allora, quello sul Mediterraneo sembrò alla comitiva d'una bellezza ancor maggiore. Le acque di quel mare, d'un azzurro mai veduto, erano così calme che pareva come se si navigasse su un lago.

S'arrivò a Genova nelle prime ore del pomeriggio del settimo 15 giorno, dopo esser passati per parecchie ore così vicino alla costa francese, e poi a quella italiana, da poter vedere, tra il verde dei campi e dei boschi, case, strade e anche delle automobili.

PROVERBIO

Ognuno sa navigare quando è buon   *In a calm sea, every man is a pilot.*
vento.

III. STUDIO DI PAROLE

Azzorre *f. pl.* Azores
Genova Genoa
Gibilterra Gibraltar
Mediterraneo Mediterranean
Portogallo Portugal
Spagna Spain

est *m.* east
isola island
mal di mare *m.* seasickness
musica music
nord *m.* north
oceano ocean
orchestra orchestra
ovest *m.* west

piscina swimming pool
sbarco landing
stretto strait
sud *m.* south
traversata crossing

calmo calm

ballare to dance
conservare [**conservo**] to keep;
   conservarsi to remain
giocare a carte to play cards
giocare a scacchi to play chess
navigare [**navigo**] to sail
nuotare [**nuoto**] to swim

ripartire to depart again [1]
soffrire [**soffro**] to suffer

durante during

eppure and yet
fino a until, up to, as far as; **fino allora** until then

IV. CONVERSAZIONE

1. Che cosa durò poco più di cínque giorni? 2. Quando arrivò a Genova il *Colombo*? 3. Era stato calmo il mare nei primi giorni? 4. Perchè non era stato calmo? 5. Quando diventò migliore il tempo? 6. Come si conservò poi il tempo? 7. Chi soffrì di mal di mare? 8. Che cosa vollero fare i giovanotti e le signorine durante il *viaggio*? 9. Trovarono molti svaghi a bordo? 10. Che cosa facevano due volte al giorno? 11. Che cosa facevano durante le altre ore? 12. Che cosa sa giocare Lei? 13. Come passavano le serate a bordo? 14. Quando furono contenti gli studenti della comitiva? 15. Quali coste d'Europa videro essi prima? 16. Dove si fermò il piroscafo? 17. Perchè si fermò a Gibilterra? 18. Com'erano le acque del Mediterraneo? 19. Quando s'arrivò a Genova? 20. Che cosa si poteva vedere dalla nave prima d'arrivare a Genova?

V. ESERCIZI

A. Completare con l'equivalente di *than:*

1. Ella ha meno ____ diciannove anni. 2. Il treno era in ritardo più ____ pensavo. 3. Ci sono più alunne ____ alunni. 4. Il Molinari era più vecchio ____ sua cognata. 5. Aveva più nemici ____ io ____ immaginassi. 6. Ho più ____ tre mila francobolli. 7. Siete meno stanchi ____ io sono. 8. Scrivono più lettere a voi ____ a me. 9. Franco è meno tímido ____ te. 10. Ci sono più mobili qua ____ là. 11. Mi piace più Pisa ____ Verona. 12. Mi piace più leggere un buon libro ____ andare al teatro. 13. Fu meno fortunato ____ noi ____ fossimo. 14. Bianca è meno vanitosa ____ sua cugina diceva. 15. Vado più con Carlo ____ con Giacomo.

B. 1. Completare con la forma richiesta del verbo **dire:**

Presente dell'indicativo: 1. Egli ____ che fa bel tempo. 2. Tu non ____ tutto. 3. Che cosa ne ____ voi? 4. Io non ____ nulla. 5. Noi ____ che è meglio così.

---

[1] Conjugated like **partire.**

Passato descrittivo: 1. Egli ____ che aveva sete. 2. Noi ____ che era peggio non far niente. 3. I contadini ____ sempre che la campagna aveva bisogno d'acqua. 4. Lei ____ ch'esse erano in ritardo. 5. Tu ____ ch'era troppo.

Passato assoluto e presente perfetto: 1. Che cosa ____ i loro parenti? 2. Io non ____ questo. 3. Voi ____ che volevate un programma. 4. Noi ____ che avevamo sonno. 5. Guido ____ che non ricordava.

Presente del congiuntivo: 1. È meglio che Lei lo ____. 2. Bisogna che voi glielo ____. 3. Spero ch'esse lo ____. 4. Voi non immaginate ch'io ____ così. 5. Preferisco che tu lo ____.

2. Completare con la forma richiesta del verbo **volere:**

Passato assoluto: 1. Essi ____ vendere i buoi. 2. Il mio babbo non ____. 3. Io ____ parlargliene. 4. Tu non ____ andar da lui. 5. Perchè ____ voi ch'io gli stringessi la mano.

Futuro: 1. Cristoforo ____ dormire. 2. Non so che cosa essi ____. 3. Sarò felice se tu ____ scusarle. 4. S'io ____ divertirmi, saprò dove andare. 5. Non so quando voi ____ venire.

Presente del congiuntivo: 1. Spero ch'egli ____ specializzarsi in chimica. 2. Non so se esse ____ ballare. 3. Credo che voi ____ stuzzicarlo. 4. Pare che tu ____ scendere adesso. 5. Pensate che Mario ____ finir quella tesi?

C. Usare le seguenti espressioni idiomatiche in brevi frasi:

1. Uno alla volta.	5. Fare il pittore.	9. Aver sete.
2. Far complimenti.	6. A buon mercato.	10. Aver fretta.
3. Vestir di bianco.	7. Tanto più che.	11. Di solito.
4. Essere in ritardo.	8. Dare un addio.	12. Al buio.

D. Tradurre in italiano:

I

1. The crossing of the ocean was [1] better than we had imagined. 2. In New York I had bought a medicine for seasickness.[2] 3. I didn't need it, however, for I have been well during the whole trip. 4. Margaret told me that the ocean is usually calm in the summer months. 5. Some members of our party spent a great deal of time in the smoking room, playing cards or chess. 6. I, instead, found the greatest pleasure in staying on the upper deck and swimming in the swimming pool. 7. We

---

[1] Use the present perfect as the basic tense in these sentences.   [2] Use the definite article.

passed [1] to the north of the Azores. 8. Those islands are more beautiful than I thought. 9. Who will want to forget the sight of those small hamlets among the hills? 10. The liner stopped at Gibraltar at the hour of sunset [2] on the fifth day, for the landing and embarking of some passengers.

II

1. Mary Corelli was seasick [3] [on] the first day of our trip. 2. The day after she felt [4] better than we thought, and now she tells jokes, laughs, and plays with us. 3. Miss Fontana wanted [5] to give her some medicine, but she [6] didn't want [7] to take any.[8] 4. On board there are more girls than boys, especially among Americans. 5. We have a good time; in the morning [9] we swim in the swimming pool; in the afternoon we play cards or take a walk on deck; and in the evening [9] we see the movie and dance. 6. The liner stopped at Gibraltar day before yesterday, and departed again that same night. 7. Now we are about to arrive in (in) Italy. 8. When I am [10] in Genoa, the first thing I want to see is Christopher Columbus' house. 9. The other members of the party will want to see it with me. 10. The blue Mediterranean is now as calm as a lake.

❧ Fifth Review Lesson ❧

I. VOCABULARY DRILL

A. Give the Italian for the following nouns:

1. The ox	2. The chess	3. The eye
the arm	the trunk	the lip
the ship	the heart	the lamb
the food	the liner	the watch
the camera	the eyelash	the custom
the smoking room	the skyscraper	the going and coming

---

[1] The verb **passare** is here used intransitively, and takes the auxiliary **essere**. [2] Use the definite article. [3] Translate as if it were *suffered of seasickness*, and use the past absolute as the basic tense in these sentences. [4] Use the verb **stare**. [5] A past descriptive. [6] Don't omit this pronoun. [7] Past absolute. [8] How will you translate *any* in the sense of *any of it*? [9] See Vocabulary. [10] Future time implied.

4. The bone	5. The sea	6. The deck
the land	the cry	the night
the beard	the sheet	the sight
the crane	the dream	the island
the country	the taxicab	the porter
the seasickness	the swimming pool	the movie camera

B. *Give the Italian for the following geographical names:*

1. Europe, Italy, France, Spain, Portugal, Switzerland, Belgium, Holland.
2. Germany, England, Gibraltar, Azores, Tuscany, Latium, Sicily, Genoa.

C. *Give the Italian for the following adjectives:*

1. Fixed, last, fascinating, native, possible, excellent, worse, calm, greater, very great.
2. Northern, French, German, Dutch, hard boiled, better, lower, very low, brunette, very bad.

D. *Give the Italian for the following verbs:*

1. To kiss	3. To load	5. To sleep
to keep	to swim	to turn
to wave	to move	to dance
to specialize	to reserve	to navigate

2. To smoke	4. To obtain	6. To promise
to retire	to embark	to look for
to hasten	to suffer	to embrace
to hang up	to go to bed	to know how

E. *Give the Italian for the following expressions:*

1. To say farewell, on board, according to him, and yet, until Monday, at last, to play cards, during, alas!
2. To be sleepy, to take a tour, to be in a hurry, until then, to check a suitcase, to play chess, both . . . and, around, in the dark, good-bye!

II. DEFINITE ARTICLES

1. What geographical names take the definite article in Italian?

2. Here are some geographical names; place the definite article before those that require it:

Capri	Spagna	Europa	Sicilia	Africa	New York
Belgio	America	Bermuda	Genova	Germania	Portogallo

3. Give the rule concerning the use or omission of the definite article, after **di** or **in**, with certain geographical names. Give two examples with **di**, and two with **in**.

III. NOUNS

1. Explain the following table, and give examples:

Genders	F. M. F.	M.F. M.F.	M.F.	M. M.F. M.	F.
Noun Endings { Sing.	−a −a −à	−e −è	−i	−o −o −ò	−ù
Pl.	−e −i −à	−i −è	−i	−i −a −ò	−ù

2. What Italian nouns do not change in the plural? Give four examples.

3. Of what gender are the nouns ending in −i?

4. Of what gender are the nouns ending in −ù?

5. Give as many nouns as you can remember that end in −o and have a feminine plural in −a.

6. What nouns have an entirely irregular plural?

IV. COMPARISON

1. What adjectives have an irregular comparison?

2. Give the comparative, the relative superlative, and the absolute superlative of each of them.

3. What usual meanings have **maggiore** and **minore**?

4. In what sense are **superiore** and **inferiore** often used?

5. What adverbs have an irregular comparison?

6. Give the comparative, the relative superlative, and the absolute superlative of each of them.

7. When is *than* expressed by **di**? Give two examples.

8. As a general rule, when is *than* expressed by **che**? Give two examples.

9. There are three cases in which *than* before a noun or a pronoun is expressed by **che**. Do you remember them? Give three examples.

10. When is *than* expressed by **che . . . non** or **di quel che?**

11. What do you do with the verb after **che . . . non?** Give an example.

12. What do you do with the verb after **di quel che?** Give an example.

V. CONJUNCTIVE PERSONAL PRONOUNS

1. If two conjunctive personal pronouns are to be used with the same verb, in what order should they be?

2. What happens with **mi, ti, si, ci,** and **vi** if they precede **lo, la, li, le,** or **ne?** Give two examples, using respectively the verbs **dare** and **fare.**

3. What happens with **gli** or **le** before **lo, la, li, le,** or **ne?** Give two examples, using respectively the verbs **mandare** and **assicurare.**

4. According to what rules do two conjunctive personal pronouns precede or follow the verb?

VI. RELATIVE PRONOUNS

1. Explain in what cases the relative pronoun **il quale** should be preferred to **che** or **cui.** Use it in two brief sentences.

2. What is the meaning of **il cui?** Give two examples.

3. Give several meanings of **chi** used as a relative pronoun, and furnish an example.

VII. VERBS

1. What is an impersonal verb? Give two examples.

2. When do we use the subjunctive after an impersonal expression of possibility, necessity, desire, emotion, or doubt? Give an example with **bisogna** and another with **mi sembra.**

3. When, after the same expressions, must we use the infinitive? Give two examples using **è possibile** and **mi pare meglio.**

4. Give the past subjunctive of **caricare, cogliere,** and **offrire.**

5. Give the past perfect subjunctive of **imbarcarsi** and **ottenere.**

6. What tenses of the subjunctive must we use in the dependent clause, in case the verb of the principal clause is a present, a future, or an imperative? Give an example.

7. What tenses of the subjunctive must we use in case the verb of the principal clause is a past or a conditional? Give an example.

8. If the verb of the principal clause is a present perfect, what tenses of the subjunctive are used in the dependent clause? Give two examples.

VIII. IRREGULAR VERBS

1. **Sapere.** Give: (*a*) The present indicative. (*b*) The past absolute. (*c*) The 1st person singular of the future. (*d*) The present subjunctive. (*e*) The imperative.

Explain the difference of meaning between **sapere** and **conoscere,** and give two examples.

2. **Andare.** Give: (*a*) The present indicative. (*b*) The 1st person singular of the future. (*c*) The present subjunctive.

3. **Dare.** Give: (*a*) The present indicative. (*b*) The past absolute. (*c*) The present subjunctive. (*d*) The past subjunctive.

4. **Fare.** Give: (*a*) The present indicative. (*b*) The past descriptive. (*c*) The past absolute. (*d*) The present subjunctive. (*e*) The present and past participles.

5. **Stare.** Give: (*a*) The present indicative. (*b*) The past absolute. (*c*) The present subjunctive. (*d*) The past subjunctive.

6. **Dire.** Give: (*a*) The present indicative. (*b*) The 1st person singular of the past descriptive. (*c*) The past absolute. (*d*) The 1st person singular of the present and past subjunctive. (*e*) The present and past participles.

7. **Volere.** Give: (*a*) The present indicative. (*b*) The past absolute. (*c*) The 1st person singular of the future. (*d*) The present subjunctive.

IX. THE PREPOSITION A

When has the preposition **a** the meaning of the English *in?* Give two examples.

LETTURA IN SILENZIO

Sì o nɔ?

1. __ Non abbiamo piscine in questa scuɔla.
2. __ Nuotiamo le parɔle nuɔve col lapis.
3. __ I miei cognati sono dei grandi scacchi.
4. __ Giocare è uno svago.
5. __ Scriviamo gl'indirizzi su un libretto.
6. __ I facchini portano delle grandi tesi.
7. __ La pellicola è una barzelletta.
8. __ Bisogna appendere i cappotti negli armadi.
9. __ I buɔi mangiano ɛrbe e miglia.
10. __ Chi fa una cɔsa è chiamato un facchino.
11. __ Gli agnɛlli americani amano l'oceano.
12. __ Nei cinematɔgrafi vediamo delle pellicole.
13. __ Gli uccɛlli hanno bisogno di cibo.
14. __ Compriamo le lenzuɔla in una farmacia.
15. __ Il ghiaccio fritto è delizioso.

ACHIEVEMENT TEST NO. 5

VOCABULARY

Give the Italian for the following words:

1. both . . . and	_____	11. the sea	_____
2. the ship	_____	12. to embark	_____
3. the express train	_____	13. the suitcase	_____
4. to take a trip	_____	14. the waiting room	_____
5. around	_____	15. to be sleepy	_____
6. chemistry	_____	16. in the dark	_____
7. the address	_____	17. the camera	_____
8. finally	_____	18. the smoking room	_____
9. the swimming pool	_____	19. until then	_____
10. to dance	_____	20. to play cards	_____

(Deduct 1 point for each mistake.)

GRAMMAR

A. Give the plural of the following nouns:

1. il bue _____   3. l'ɔsso _____   5. la specie _____
2. il re _____   4. l'uɔmo _____   6. il dito _____

B. Replace the words in parentheses with their correct Italian equivalents, using the relative pronoun il quale *whenever it is possible:*

1. La sarta (*of whom*) _____ parlavo. 2. Il musicista (*whose*) _____ figlia conosco. 3. Gl'impiegati (*of whom*) _____ ho bisogno. 4. (*He who*) _____ sa nuotare si diverte.

C. Supply the correct form of the past subjunctive of the verbs given in parentheses:

1. (*essere*) Non era possibile ch'essi _____ a Genova. 2. (*dare*) Credeva ch'io gli _____ quell'orologio. 3. (*scusare*) Non voleva ch'ella lo _____. 4. (*avere*) Pensò che noi _____ dei nemici. 5. (*capire*) Desiderava che voi lo _____.

D. Replace the dashes with the correct equivalent of "than":

1. Ci saranno meno ____ trenta persone. 2. Ho più cravatte ____ avevo pensato. 3. Mi piace più la Spagna ____ l'Inghilterra. 4. V'erano meno posti liberi ____ pensassimo. 5. Mi piace più stare con voi ____ con loro.

E. Using only the irregular comparatives or superlatives, supply the Italian equivalents for the words in parentheses:

1. Abbiamo (*very good*) _____ libri. 2. Egli pronunziava (*very badly*) _____. 3. Pioveva (*worse*) _____ che mai. 4. La (*younger*) sorella _____ di Giacomo è qui. 5. Saliamo sulla (*higher*) coperta _____.

F. Supply the required form of the verbs given in parentheses:

Present indicative: 1. (*dire*) Noi glielo _____. 2. (*sapere*) Anche noi _____ queste cose. 3. (*volere*) Che cosa _____ essi fare?
Past absolute: 4. (*volere*) Io non _____ depositare le valige. 5. (*dare*) Noi _____ dei fiori alla nonna. 6. (*fare*) Che cosa _____ voi ieri l'altro? 7. (*stare*) Lei non _____ bene.
Future: 8. (*sapere*) Presto noi _____ se c'è posta. 9. (*volere*) Ella non _____ venire. 10. (*andare*) Voi dove _____ la settimana ventura?
Present perfect: 11. (*fare*) Noi _____ colazione di buon'ora. 12. (*dire*) Chi _____ queste cose?
Present subjunctive: 13. (*dire*) Desidero che Beatrice _____ tutto. 14. (*sapere*) Come vuoi ch'io _____ questo?
Past subjunctive: (*dire*) Era meglio ch'egli _____ dov'era stato.

(Deduct 1 point for each mistake.)

G. Translate into Italian:

1. He didn't want to speak of it to us.   1. _____
2. His sister bought a new dress and showed it   2. _____
   to them.
3. Paul met a friend and introduced him to me.   3. _____
4. I told him: "Introduce him to me."   4. _____
5. She had some roses and offered them to her.   5. _____

(This part counts 10 points.)

READING

Translate the Italian passage that your instructor will write on the board or hand to you on a mimeographed sheet.

(This part counts 20 points.)

DICTATION

Your instructor will dictate twice a short Italian passage.

(This part counts 10 points.)

PERFECT SCORE: 100

Parte Sesta

IN ITALIA
Dalle Alpi a Roma

I. NOTE GRAMMATICALI

139. **Conditional**

I	II	III
I should or *would buy, etc.*	*I should* or *would sell, etc.*	*I should* or *would finish, etc.*
comprer ɛi	vender ɛi	finir ɛi
comprer esti	vender esti	finir esti
comprer ɛbbe	vender ɛbbe	finir ɛbbe
comprer emmo	vender emmo	finir emmo
comprer este	vender este	finir este
comprer ɛbbero	vender ɛbbero	finir ɛbbero

Note the following:

1. Like the future, this tense has for a stem the infinitive less the final −e.

2. Also like the future, the **a** of the infinitive ending of the first conjugation changes to **e**.

3. The endings of the conditional are the same for all three conjugations.

4. The 1st person plural of the conditional differs from the 1st person plural of the future by having a double **m**. Make sure that you master the difference in pronunciation, stressing it by contrast. Pronounce: **parleremo, parleremmo, crederemo. crederemmo.**

140. **Conditional of the Auxiliary Verbs**

avere		ɛssere	
I should or *would have, etc.*		*I should* or *would be, etc.*	
avrɛi	avremmo	sarɛi	saremmo
avresti	avreste	saresti	sareste
avrɛbbe	avrɛbbero	sarɛbbe	sarɛbbero

141. Conditional Perfect

I	II	III
I should or *would have bought, etc.*	*I should* or *would have sold, etc.*	*I should* or *would have departed, etc.*
avrɛi avresti avrɛbbe } comprato	avrɛi avresti avrɛbbe } venduto	sarɛi saresti sarɛbbe } partito, –a
avremmo avreste avrɛbbero } comprato	avremmo avreste avrɛbbero } venduto	saremmo sareste sarɛbbero } partiti, –e

AUXILIARY VERBS

I should or *would have had, etc.*

avrɛi avuto, etc.

I should or *would have been, etc.*

sarɛi stato, –a, etc.

142. Conditional Clauses

1. Se avessi quel libro, studierɛi. (*This implies:* Non hɔ quel libro.)

   If I had that book, I would study.

   Se ricevessi quella lɛttera, sarɛi felice. (*This implies:* Ɛ dubbio, *doubtful,* ch'io riceva quella lɛttera.)

   If I should receive that letter, I should be happy.

   Se Carlo arrivasse, noi ve lo presenteremmo. (*This implies:* Ɛ dubbio ch'egli arrivi.)

   If Charles were to arrive, we would introduce him to you.

The past subjunctive is used in a conditional clause (or *if*-clause) to imply that the statement is either contrary-to-fact in the present or doubtful in the future. In the conclusion of such a sentence the conditional is used.

2. Se avessi avuto quel libro, avrɛi studiato. (*This implies:* Non avevo quel libro.)

   If I had had that book, I would have studied.

When the conditional clause refers to past time, the past perfect subjunctive is used, and the conclusion is rendered in the conditional perfect.

143.   Further Uses of the Conditional

1. Non glielo mostrerebbe.   *He would not show it to him.*

The conditional is used to express what is uncertain or indefinite in the principal clause.

2. Avrei piacere di vederlo.   *I should like to see him.*
   Avresti un po' di carta?   *Have you, by chance, any paper?*

It is used also in a statement or request expressed with reserve or deference.

3. Secondo lui, avrei torto.   *According to him, I am wrong.*

It expresses what is reported by hearsay, or on the authority of somebody else.

4. Dicono che sarebbe meglio.   *They say it would be better.*
   Pensò che avrebbe guada-   *He thought he would earn lots of*
   gnato (*or* guadagnerebbe)   *money.*
   molto danaro.

After a verb of saying, thinking, believing, etc., the conditional expresses either a mental reserve (as in the 1st example), or a future time in relation to a past tense (as in the 2nd example).[1] Note that, in the latter case, the past tense in the principal clause requires (contrary to English usage) the conditional perfect in the dependent clause; the use of the simple conditional is tolerated, however.

II. LETTURA

A Genova e in Riviera

La comitiva s'era riunita sulla prima coperta del *Colombo* per meglio godere la magnifica vista di Genova, mentre la nave stava per entrare in porto.

---

[1] **Pensa che guadagnerà,** *etc.* expresses future time in relation to the present.

— Che cos'è quel grand'edifizio bianco con quella bandiera? — domandò Mario Capponi.

— È uno dei migliori alberghi della città, — gli rispose la signorina Fontana.

5　— Sarebbe bello se potessimo alloggiarvi, — osservò Lucia.

— Costerebbe un po' troppo, mia cara, e poi anche il nostro albergo è buono.

— E vi prenderemo tutti i pasti? — domandò Olga Lewis.

— Non sempre.　Non preferireste che di tanto in tanto faces-
10 simo colazione in qualche ristorante?　È uno dei modi migliori di conoscere gli usi d'un paese che si visita per la prima volta.

— Sì, sì, è un'ottima idea! — dissero parecchi.

Lo sbarco ebbe luogo poco dopo l'arrivo del piroscafo alla stazione marittima, e i facchini del porto portaron subito i bagagli
15 in dogana.

Quando, circa un'ora dopo, la comitiva arrivò all'albergo, tutti s'affrettarono a salire alle loro camere, ad aprire le valige, e a prepararsi a uscire.　Dovevano riunirsi al più presto nell'atrio perchè la signorina Fontana aveva detto che sarebbero andati a
20 fare un giro in tassì prima dell'ora del pranzo.

Genova, chiamata La Superba per l'imponente bellezza dei suoi palazzi, è situata in una delle più incantevoli regioni d'Italia. Sarebbe stato un peccato veder quei luoghi in fretta.

La comitiva vi restò quasi una settimana, durante la quale non
25 solo ci fu tempo d'ammirare ogni cosa di maggiore interesse, — la casa di Cristoforo Colombo e il suo monumento, il Duomo, l'Università, i musei e il gran Cimitero, — ma anche di fare due escursioni in Riviera.

La prima volta andarono a San Remo e a Bordighera, in Riviera
30 di Ponente; un altro giorno visitarono la Riviera di Levante, passando per Quarto, da dove Garibaldi partì coi suoi Mille, nel 1860, per completare l'unificazione d'Italia.

PROVERBIO

Chi va piano va sano e va lontano.　*Haste makes waste.　(He who goes
slowly goes safely and goes far.)*

III. STUDIO DI PAROLE

Riviεra di Levante Eastern Riviera
Riviεra di Ponεnte Western Riviera; in Riviεra on the Riviera

albεrgo hotel
atrio lobby, entrance hall
bagaglio baggage [1]
bandiεra flag
cimitεro cemetery
dogana customs, custom house
escursione f. excursion; fare un'e-
scursione to take an excursion
interεsse m. interest
luogo place; aver luogo to take
place
modo manner, way
monumento monument
pasto meal

porto port, harbor
regione f. region
unificazione f. unification

imponεnte imposing
incantevole enchanting, charming
marittimo maritime
supεrbo superb, proud, haughty

alloggiare [alloggio] to lodge,
stay
completare [complεto] to complete
costare [costo] to cost [2]
godere [godo] to enjoy
riunire [riunisco], riunirsi to
assemble [3]

al più prεsto as soon as possible

IV. CONVERSAZIONE

1. Perchè la comitiva s'εra riunita sulla prima copεrta?
2. Dove stava per entrare la nave? 3. Che cosa domandò Mario
Capponi? 4. Che cosa gli rispose la signorina Fontana? 5. Che
cosa osservò Lucia? 6. Perchè la comitiva non poteva alloggiare
in quell'albεrgo? 7. Che cosa domandò Olga Lewis? 8. Che cosa
disse allora la signorina Fontana? 9. Perchè è bεne mangiare
qualche volta in un ristorante? 10. Quando εbbe luogo lo sbarco?
11. Che cosa fecero i facchini del porto? 12. Che cosa fecero i
mεmbri della comitiva quando arrivarono al loro albεrgo?
13. Dove dovevano riunirsi? 14. Che cosa aveva detto la signorina Fontana? 15. Com'è chiamata Gεnova? 16. Perchè è
chiamata La Supεrba? 17. Che cosa vide la comitiva a Gεnova?

---

[1] Used in the plural when more than one piece of baggage is meant.
[2] Learn the expression **Quanto costa?** (or **Quanto costano?**) *What's the
price of . . .?* [3] **Riunire** is a transitive verb (*to assemble people or things*);
riunirsi translates the English intransitive *to assemble.*

18. Quali escursioni furono fatte? 19. Chi partì da Quarto nel 1860? 20. Perchè Garibaldi partì coi suoi Mille?

V. ESERCIZI

A. Coniugare nel condizionale, e poi nel condizionale perfetto [1]:

1. Coltivare un campo.
2. Avere buon appetito.
3. Perdere molto tempo.
4. Essere vanitoso.
5. Ripartire al più presto.
6. Imbarcarsi su una nave.

B. Dare il condizionale, e poi il condizionale perfetto, del verbo in parentesi:

1. (*gridare*) Voi ____ a quella vista. 2. (*preferire*) Essi ____ restare in Inghilterra. 3. (*essere*) Io ____ occupato. 4. (*raccomandare*) Mario ____ quella lettera. 5. (*aiutare*) Tu l'____ volentieri. 6. (*riconoscere*) Noi ____ subito quella donna. 7. (*arrivare*) I miei parenti ____ col treno delle undici. 8. (*dormire*) Lei ____ bene in questo letto. 9. (*entrare*) Io non ____ mai là. 10. (*perdere*) Le bambine non ____ nulla. 11. (*essere*) Pure voi ____ stanchi. 12. (*avere*) Noi non ____ sonno. 13. (*essere*) Chi di noi ____ libero? 14. (*avere*) Tu ____ ragione. 15. (*dire*) Egli non ____ così.

C. Applicando (*applying*) le regole studiate nel § 142, fornire per ciascun verbo in parentesi due forme corrette (e.g. se io potessi, comprerei un'automobile; se io avessi potuto, avrei comprato un'automobile):

1. Se voi (*lavorare*) ____, i vostri genitori non (*essere*) ____ scontenti. 2. Se tu (*essere*) ____ in Italia, quali città (*visitare*) ____? 3. Se io (*potere*) ____, (*partire*) ____ per la Francia. 4. Se Lei (*fare*) ____ questo, io (*dire*) ____: bravo! 5. Se noi (*dire*) ____ queste cose, (*fare*) ____ uno sbaglio. 6. Se oggi (*piovere*) ____, noi non (*uscire*) ____. 7. Se voi (*potere*) ____, non (*invitare*) ____ suo cognato? 8. Se Laura (*essere*) ____ qua, noi la (*presentare*) ____ alla vostra amica Anna. 9. Se io (*essere*) ____ libero, (*passare*) ____ volentieri la serata con loro. 10. Se essi (*arrivare*) ____, tu li (*incontrare*) ____ alla stazione.

---

[1] Called *condizionale passato* by Italian grammarians.

D. Tradurre in italiano:

I

1. "If you hadn't told me,[1] I should never have believed that Genoa's harbor was so large," said Olga to Miss Fontana. 2. They were on deck with the others, admiring the sight of the city that Italians call "The Proud." 3. We shall stay at (in) an excellent hotel, but once in a while we shall eat in a restaurant. 4. If we took all [of] our meals at the hotel, we wouldn't meet many Italians. 5. We want to learn their language and customs[2] as soon as possible. 6. Miss Fontana said[3] that this would be the best way. 7. My friends and I are very glad of it. 8. Soon the landing will take place; the liner has stopped[4] near one of the piers of the maritime station. 9. By Jove, how many people[5]! Some men are waving their[6] arms; some ladies, their[6] handkerchiefs. 10. On the custom house, where our baggage will soon be carried, I see a large Italian flag.

II

1. We assembled[7] in the lobby of our hotel soon after our arrival. 2. Miss Fontana said that we would take four taxicabs in order to see the city. 3. But our tour lasted only a little more than one hour, because, if we had not hastened to (a) return, we should have been late for dinner.[8] 4. In this country they[9] usually dine at 8 P.M.[10] 5. If it were possible, I should prefer to eat a little sooner. 6. [On] the following day we saw the house of Christopher Columbus, and visited the Cathedral, some other churches, and the magnificent[11] Cemetery. 7. During the week we took two excursions, one of which[12] was[13] on the Western Riviera, and the other on the Eastern Riviera. 8. Many people[5] visit those places[14] because they are so beautiful in all seasons of the year. 9. You would admire the beauty of that region, its green[11] hills, and its enchanting sea. 10. I didn't forget to (di) take my camera with me, and I was[13] glad of it.

---

[1] Translate as if it were *told it to me.* [2] Repeat the possessive. [3] Use the present perfect. [4] A reflexive idea. [5] Use the singular form. [6] Replace the possessive with the definite article. [7] Use the past absolute as the basic tense in these sentences; *assembled* has here a reflexive meaning. [8] Use the definite article. [9] Use the impersonal construction. [10] Write out the number. [11] Leave the adjective before the noun. [12] Use **il quale.** [13] A past absolute. [14] Use the word **luɔgo.**

❧ Lezione Trentatreesima ❧

I. NOTE GRAMMATICALI

144. The Irregular Verb *porre, to put, place*

INFINITIVE AND PARTICIPLES

porre	*ponɛndo*	posto

INDICATIVE

Present	Past Descriptive	Past Absolute	Future
pongo	*ponevo*	posi	porrò
poni	*ponevi*	ponesti	porrai
pone	*poneva*	pose	porrà
poniamo	*ponevamo*	*ponemmo*	porremo
ponete	*ponevate*	*poneste*	porrete
pongono	*ponevano*	posero	porranno

SUBJUNCTIVE		CONDITIONAL	IMPERATIVE
Present	Past		
ponga	*ponessi*	porrɛi	
ponga	*ponessi*	porresti	poni
ponga	*ponesse*	porrɛbbe	
poniamo	*ponessimo*	porremmo	poniamo
poniate	*poneste*	porreste	ponete
pongano	*ponessero*	porrɛbbero	

145. Other Verbs Conjugated like *porre*

The following verbs, listed here mainly in order to give an idea of the great variety of Italian prefixes, are conjugated like **porre** and are called its *compounds*.

Remember those marked with a star, for they are going to be part of your active vocabulary.

anteporre, *to place before*
apporre, *to affix*
*comporre, *to compose*
contrapporre, *to set against*

deporre, *to lay down*
*disporre, *to dispose, arrange*
esporre, *to expose*
frapporre, *to insert*

imporre, *to impose*
interporre, *to interpose*
opporre, *to oppose*
*posporre, *to postpone*
preporre, *to put before*
*proporre, *to propose*

riporre, *to replace*
scomporre, *to decompose*
soprapporre, *to place over*
sottoporre, *to submit*
*supporre, *to suppose*
trasporre, *to transpose*

146.   Formation of Irregular Verbs

Certain parts of all irregular verbs (except εssere) are always regular. They are: the present participle, the past descriptive, the past subjunctive, the 2nd person plural of the present indicative, and the 2nd person singular and 1st and 2nd persons plural of the past absolute. These forms are printed in boldface italics in the conjugation of **porre** given above.

As for the irregular forms, the following rules should be noted:

1.   **porre** (for **pοnere**)   **condurre** (for **conducere**)
   ponεndo   **conducεndo**
   ponete   **conducete**

Several verbs of the 2nd conjugation have a contracted infinitive. In all such verbs the regular stem appears in the present participle, and must be used in forming the regular parts of the verb.

2.   **pongo**   **ponga**
   pongono   **pongano**

From the 1st person singular of the present indicative are formed: (*a*) The 3rd person plural of that tense; (*b*) The whole present subjunctive, except the 1st and 2nd persons plural. These can be made from the 1st person plural of the present indicative.

3.   **poni**   **poni**
   poniamo   **poniamo**
   ponete   **ponete**

The three forms of the imperative are precisely like the corresponding forms of the present indicative.

4.   **porrɔ̀**   **andrɔ̀**
   porrεi   **andrεi**

The only irregularity in the future and conditional is that they are contracted in many verbs, even when the infinitive is not contracted. The commonest type of contraction is shown in the verb **andare;** it consists of the dropping of the **e** which precedes the **r** of the infinitive used as a stem.

5.   posi
               pose
               posero

From the 1st person singular of the past absolute, as we have already learned in § 104 and 105, p. 163, are formed the 3rd singular and plural of that tense.

Note: The verbs ɛssere, **avere, andare, dare, fare, stare, dire, sapere,** and **volere** are exceptions to the rules given above, and for that reason we studied them separately.

II. LETTURA

Torino

Gli studɛnti avevano supposto che in Italia i trɛni fossero come quelli degli Stati Uniti, ed è facile immaginare la sorpresa che ɛbbero quando vìdero che il trɛno che da Gɛnova doveva portarli a Torino ɛra composto di carrɔzze di differɛnti classi, e che ogni
5 carrɔzza conteneva parecchi scompartimenti. In Eurɔpa tutti i trɛni son fatti così.

Quel primo viaggio in ferrovia fu brɛve e interessante, e i giovanɔtti e le signorine stɛttero spesso in piɛdi, nel corridoio ch'ɛra a un lato della carrɔzza, per godɛr mɛglio la vista dei monti fra i
10 quali si passava, gli Appennini.

Ɛra mezzogiorno quando arrivarono, e fuɔri della stazione li aspettava l'autobus del loro albɛrgo.

— Bɛn arrivati! — disse sorridɛndo il giovane autista mentre li aiutava a salire in vettura. — Com'è stato il viaggio?
15 — Più bɛllo che non immaginassimo, — rispose Margherita Filpo.

All'albɛrgo non si restò che il tɛmpo di lavarsi un pɔco e pɔi far colazione. S'uscì subito dopo.

Alcuni mɛmbri della comitiva avevano pregato la signorina

Fontana di mostrar loro, prima di tutto, la fabbrica delle famose automobili *Fiat*,[1] una delle più grandi del mondo, ma siccome era sabato, la cosa fu posposta al lunedì.

Quel pomeriggio visitarono i luoghi più importanti della città, ammirandone i larghi viali, i bellissimi monumenti, i magnifici 5 palazzi. Ciò che gustarono più di tutto fu la passeggiata che fecero nei Giardini del Valentino, lungo il Po. Di lì si godeva una vista incantevole: il gran fiume coi suoi bei ponti, le verdi colline sull'altra riva, e, lontano, le Alpi coperte di neve.

Ritornando all'albergo, la signorina Fontana propose di fer- 10 marsi a un gran caffè all'aperto davanti al quale un'orchestrina stava suonando, ma quasi tutti i tavolini erano occupati, ed era inutile pensarci.

— Come sono eleganti le signore di questa città! — osservò una studentessa, Irene Williamson.   15

— Torino, — le disse la signorina, — è il centro della moda in Italia.

PROVERBIO

L'uomo propone e Dio dispone.   *Man proposes, God disposes.*

III. STUDIO DI PAROLE

Alpi *f. pl.* Alps
Appennini *m. pl.* Apennines
Stati Uniti *m. pl.* United States
Torino *f.* Turin [2]

autista *m.* chauffeur, driver
autobus *m.* autobus
corridoio corridor, passage
fabbrica factory
fiume *m.* river
lato side
moda fashion
mondo world
monte *m.* mountain
ponte *m.* bridge

riva bank (*of a river*), shore
scompartimento compartment
vettura car, carriage
viale *m.* boulevard, lane (*of a park*)

differente different
famoso famous
importante important
inutile useless

pregare (di) [**prego**] to pray, beg

ben arrivato! welcome!
lungo along
siccome since, as

[1] This word is formed with the initials of *Fabbrica Italiana Automobili, Torino.*   [2] Names of cities, irrespective of their endings, are usually feminine.

IV. CONVERSAZIONE

1. Che cosa avevano supposto gli studenti della comitiva?
2. Com'era composto il treno che doveva portarli a Torino?
3. Solo in Italia i treni son fatti così?   4. Come fu quel primo
viaggio in ferrovia?   5. Perchè gli studenti stettero spesso in piedi
nel corridoio?   6. Dov'era il corridoio?   7. A che ora arrivarono
a Torino?   8. Che cosa li aspettava alla stazione di Torino?
9. Che cosa disse l'autista?   10. Che cosa rispose Margherita
Filpo?   11. Quanto tempo si restò all'albergo?   12. Che cosa
volevano vedere alcuni membri della comitiva?   13. Andarono
quel giorno a vedere la fabbrica delle automobili *Fiat?*   14. Che
cosa ammirarono, di Torino, gli studenti?   15. Che cosa gustarono più di tutto?   16. Che cosa si vedeva dai Giardini del Valentino?   17. Che cosa propose poi la signorina Fontana?   18. Perchè era inutile pensarci?   19. Che cosa osservò Irene Williamson?
20. Che le rispose la signorina Fontana?

V. ESERCIZI

A. Coniugare nei tempi richiesti:

1. disporre (*future*)
2. porre (*present indicative*)
3. supporre (*past absolute*)
4. proporre (*past descriptive*)
5. supporre (*conditional*)
6. proporre (*future perfect*)
7. disporre (*past subjunctive*)
8. porre (*present subjunctive*)

B. Usare ciascuna delle seguenti espressioni in una frase originale:

1. A bordo.
2. Si chiama.
3. Aver sete.
4. Aver luogo.
5. Al più presto.
6. Dare un addio.
7. Dare da mangiare.
8. Di tanto in tanto.
9. Fare un'escursione.
10. Stringere la mano a.
11. Tra poco.
12. Di solito.
13. Stare per.
14. Aver sonno.
15. Aver fretta.
16. Fare un giro.
17. Far colazione.
18. Aver appetito.
19. Giocare a scacchi.
20. Fare una passeggiata.

C. 1. Completare col presente dell'indicativo, e poi col passato assoluto e col futuro del verbo in parentesi:

1. (*porre*) Io _____ i libri sullo scaffale. 2. (*proporre*) Esse _____ di giocare a carte. 3. (*comporre*) Che cosa _____ il vostro amico? 4. (*porre*) Tu _____ il vaso sulla credenza. 5. (*supporre*) Noi non _____ niente di tutto questo. 6. (*porre*) Voi _____ ogni cosa in ordine.

2. Completare col presente perfetto, e poi col passato descrittivo e col condizionale del verbo in parentesi:

1. (*disporre*) Noi _____ i mobili in un altro modo. 2. (*posporre*) Lei _____ sempre quella vendita. 3. (*porre*) Tu _____ il bicchiere sul tavolino. 4. (*supporre*) Io _____ cose buone. 5. (*porre*) I bambini _____ le mani su tutto. 6. (*proporre*) Voi _____ di fare un'escursione.

D. Tradurre in italiano:

I

1. Since the party was composed of Miss Fontana and [1] fourteen students, they occupied [2] two compartments. 2. In a compartment of an Italian train there are eight seats. 3. If you suppose [3] that the students didn't observe with interest many new [4] things in that train you are mistaken. 4. On (**da**) one side of the coach there was a corridor from which [5] one could enjoy interesting sights. 5. And the train was passing through the Apennines, the beautiful mountains north [6] of Genoa. 6. If the students had been on an American train they would not have been seated [7] that way.[8] 7. Now they could [2] talk, tell jokes, and laugh as they wished, because they were by themselves.[9] 8. The trip did not last long (**molto**), and it wasn't yet noon when they arrived in Turin. 9. From the station to the hotel they rode in an autobus. 10. Turin is a beautiful city on the banks of the Po, the longest river in Italy.

II

1. Today we saw Turin, one of the most important cities in Italy. 2. When I was in the United States you and I spoke sometimes of the *Fiat* cars.[10] 3. Well, I suppose it [11] will not be a surprise for you to

---

[1] Repeat the preposition. [2] Past descriptive. [3] **Supporre** takes the subjunctive. [4] Place this adjective after the noun. [5] Use **il quale.** [6] Translate *to north of.* [7] Use the past participle of **sedere** as an adjective. [8] Translate *in that way.* [9] *Themselves* is **loro** in this case. [10] Place the name *Fiat* after *cars.* [11] Omit *it*, but don't forget to insert *that.*

learn[1] that we visited that famous[2] factory.   4. Charles proposed it this morning to Miss Fontana.   5. While [we were] riding in our cars through the boulevards of Turin our driver told us some interesting things about the city.   6. We saw magnificent palaces, beautiful bridges, and monuments.   7. Toward sunset[3] we visited the Valentino Gardens,[4] on the right bank of the Po.   8. Walking on (per) a lane along the river, we admired the view of the far-away[2] Alps.   9. The girls admired also the stylish dresses of the ladies we saw.   10. You don't suppose,[5] I imagine, that Turin is the center of Italian fashion.

❧ Lezione Trentaquattresima ☙

I. NOTE GRAMMATICALI

147.   The Subjunctive in Adjective Clauses[6]

The subjunctive is used in adjective clauses (introduced by a relative pronoun) in the following cases:

1. È il migliore alunno che ci sia in questa classe.

   He is the best pupil there is in this class.

   È il solo libro ch'io abbia.

   It is the only book I have.

After a relative superlative, or the word *only*.

2. Chiunque sia, non voglio vederlo.

   Whoever he is, I don't want to see him.

   Checchè (*or* Qualunque cosa) io dica, avrò torto.

   Whatever I may say, I am probably wrong.

After indefinites, such as: **chiunque,** *whoever;* **qualunque,** *whichever;* **checchè** (or **qualunque cosa**), *whatever,* etc.

3. Non c'era nessuno che parlasse italiano.

   There was no one who spoke Italian.

After negative expressions.

---

[1] Translate *to learn* with **sapere.**   [2] Leave this adjective before the noun.
[3] Use the definite article.   [4] Translate *the Gardens of the Valentino.*
[5] **Supporre** takes the subjunctive.   [6] A clause that modifies a noun or pronoun is called an adjective clause.

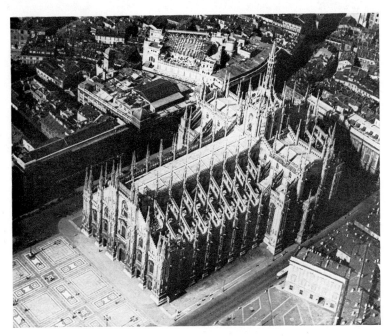

THE *DUOMO* SEEN FROM THE AIR, MILANO

NOLA ROAD, POMPEII

BASEMENT OF THE AMPHITHEATER, POZZUOLI

4. Cerco un ragazzo che sap-   *I am looking for a boy* (= *any boy*)
    pia suonare il violino.   *who can play the violin.*

But: Cerco il ragazzo che sa suo- *I am looking for the boy* (= *a def-*
    nare il violino.   *inite boy*) *who can play the violin.*

If the relative pronoun has an indefinite antecedent.

148.   *Piacere*

1. Quella ragazza piace a Enrico.   *Henry likes that girl.*   (Literally:
                                     That girl is pleasing to Henry.)

    Quella ragazza gli piace.   *He likes that girl.*   (*That girl is*
                                     pleasing to him.)

    Quelle ragazze gli piacciono.   *He likes those girls.*   (*Those girls are*
                                     pleasing to him.)

    Il libro le è piaciuto.   *She liked the book.*   (*The book was*
                                     pleasing to her.)

    I libri le sono piaciuti.   *She liked the books.*   (*The books were*
                                     pleasing to her.)

The verb **piacere,** the most common meaning of which is *to be pleasing,*[1] is currently used in rendering the English *to like.* Note carefully, however, that, in Italian, what is liked is the subject, and the person who likes is an indirect object. Naturally, when the English object of *to like* (Italian subject) is plural, the verb **piacere** must be plural.

The last two examples also show that **piacere** is conjugated with essere.

2. Mi piace molto nuotare. }
    Il nuotare mi piace molto. } *I like very much to swim.*

Piacere often has an infinitive as its subject. If the infinitive subject precedes **piacere,** the masculine definite article should be used with it.

3. Vi piace quell'edifizio ?   *Do you like that building?*
    No, non mi piace.   *No, I don't like it.*

The direct object pronoun of the English *to like* is usually

---

[1] *To please* is usually **contentare.**

omitted in the Italian translation because, being a subject, it may be understood.

4. Gli piace ch'ella si diverta.   *He likes her to have a good time.*
   A Beatrice non piaceva ch'egli   *Beatrice didn't like his going away.*
    andasse via.

When the verb **piacere** is followed by a noun clause the subject of which is a different person from the one to whom the indirect object refers, the noun clause must be in the subjunctive.

149.   *Dispiacere*

Il suo modo di fare gli dispiace.   *His way of acting displeases him (is displeasing to him).*
Questo le è dispiaciuto.   *This displeased her (was displeasing to her).*
Mi dispiace.   *I am sorry. (It is displeasing to me.)*
Gli dispiace non poter venire.   *He is sorry (It is displeasing to him) not to be able to come.*
Gli dispiace che voi siate solo.   *He is sorry (It is displeasing to him) that you are alone.*

The verb **dispiacere** means *to be displeasing* [1] and, therefore, takes the indirect object. In the 3rd person singular it is used in the meaning of the English *to be sorry*. Note, in this regard, that whatever has been said concerning **piacere** applies also to **dispiacere**.

150. Study the complete conjugations of **piacere** and **dispiacere** (*Appendix III*).

II. LETTURA

I Laghi e Milano

— Mi dispiace, ma domani mattina bisognerà alzarsi di buon'ora, perchè si partirà alle sette, — aveva detto la signorina Fontana l'ultima sera che la comitiva passò a Torino.

La mattina seguente, infatti, all'ora fissata, essi partirono in

[1] *To displease* is usually **scontentare**.

tre automobili. Invece d'andare a Milano per la via più breve, cioè in ferrovia, dovevan fare — secondo il programma del viaggio — un lungo giro che permettesse loro di vedere alcuni dei più bei laghi d'Italia: il Lago Maggiore, il Lago di Lugano e quello di Como. 5

Turisti d'ogni parte del mondo, in estate come in inverno, in primavera come in autunno, accorrono a visitare quei luoghi incantevoli, noti per il loro clima sempre mite e soprattutto perchè, essendo situati appiè delle Alpi, offrono all'occhio viste d'un incanto senza pari. 10

La sola cosa che dispiacesse a gli studenti quel giorno fu la breve durata del viaggio. Come sarebbe stato bello passar qualche settimana in alcune delle graziosissime cittadine che le automobili attraversavano: Stresa con le sue belle isolette, Locarno e Lugano in territorio svizzero, e Menaggio, e Bellagio, e Como! 15

Arrivarono a Milano poco dopo il tramonto, e andarono ad alloggiare in un albergo che piacque a ciascun di loro, e che è, infatti, uno dei migliori che ci siano in quella città.

Milano — che è il centro più importante dell'industria e del commercio d'Italia — col suo continuo viavai d'automobili, di 20 tranvai, d'autobus e di gente d'ogni specie, ricordava un po' a gli studenti le grandi metropoli americane. Ma quella bella città è anche uno dei maggiori centri della cultura europea, ed essi ebbero molte cose interessanti da vedere.

Passarono tutta una mattinata visitando il magnifico Duomo 25 che, tutto di marmo bianco, con le sue 135 guglie e le sue 2300 statue, è il capolavoro dell'arte gotica italiana. Ammirarono nella chiesa di Santa Maria delle Grazie L'Ultima Cena di Leonardo da Vinci, forse il più famoso affresco che il mondo conosca; visitaron poi il Museo e la Biblioteca di Brera, e il Castello Sforzesco, e 30 passarono una serata deliziosa sentendo l'Aida nel Teatro della Scala che, fortunatamente, quell'estate era aperto.

Non ci fu nessuno a cui Milano non piacesse immensamente.

PROVERBIO

Alla fortuna bisogna lasciare la porta aperta.

When fortune knocks, be sure to open the door.

III. STUDIO DI PAROLE

Castɛllo Sforzesco Sforza Castle
Milano *f.* Milan

affresco fresco
capolavoro masterpiece
cittadina small town
clima *m.* climate
còmmɛrcio commerce, trade
durata duration
grazia grace
guglia spire
incanto charm
industria industry
marmo marble
pari *m. or f.* equal
territɔrio territory
tranvai *m.* tramway, streetcar
turista *m. or f.* tourist

continuo continuous
europɛo European
gɔtico Gothic
grazioso graceful, pretty
mite mild
nɔto known
svizzero Swiss

ciascuno each, each one [1]

accorrere to run up, flock (together) [2]
permettere to permit, allow
sentire [sɛnto] to feel, hear

appiè di at the foot of
cioè that is (to say)
infatti in fact, indeed
soprattutto above all

IV. CONVERSAZIONE

1. Che cɔsa aveva detto la signorina Fontana l'ultima sera che la comitiva passɔ a Torino? 2. Partì in trɛno la comitiva la mattina seguɛnte? 3. Perchè non partì in trɛno? 4. Quali sono alcuni dei più bɛi laghi d'Italia? 5. In quali stagioni i turisti vanno a visitare quei luɔghi incantɛvoli? 6. Per che cɔsa sono nɔti quei luɔghi? 7. Che cɔsa dispiacque a gli studɛnti? 8. Dove sarɛbbe stato bɛllo passar qualche settimana? 9. Quando arrivarono a Milano? 10. Dove andarono ad alloggiare? 11. Di che cɔsa Milano è il cɛntro? 12. Perchè Milano ricordava un pɔ' a gli studɛnti le grandi metrɔpoli americane? 13. Come passɔ tutta una mattinata la comitiva? 14. Di che arte è il capolavoro il Duɔmo di Milano? 15. Che cɔsa ammirɔ la comitiva nella chiɛsa di Santa Maria delle Grazie? 16. Che cos'è *L'Ultima Cena* di Leonardo da Vinci? 17. Che altrò videro a Milano gli studɛnti?

---

[1] **Ciascuno** may be used as an adjective or as a pronoun; as an adjective, it takes the same endings as the indefinite article: **ciascun amico, ciascun'amica,** etc.   [2] Conjugated with **ɛssere.**

18. Dove passarono una serata deliziosa? 19. Quale opera senti-rono? 20. A chi non piacque Milano?

V. ESERCIZI

A. Completare con la forma corretta del verbo in parentesi:

1. (*sapere*) Non c'è nessuno che ____ suonare. 2. (*avere*) Questi sono i migliori coltelli ch'io ____. 3. (*essere*) Chiunque voi ____, egli non può vedervi. 4. (*dare*) Voglio un libro che mi ____ una buon'idea di Torino. 5. (*avere*) Era il peggior nemico ch'essi ____. 6. (*capire*) Qualunque cosa essa ____, sarà sempre lo stesso. 7. (*potere*) Non c'era niente che ____ farlo felice. 8. (*sapere*) Cerco un uomo che ____ parlar tedesco. 9. (*menare*) Mostratemi una via che ____ in Piazza del Duomo. 10. (*menare*) Ecco la via che ____ dove voi volete andare. 11. (*comprare*) Sto scrivendo al signore che ____ la mia casa. 12. (*proporre*) È la sola cosa ch'egli ____.

B. Coniugare:

1. Io piaccio a poche persone, tu . . ., ecc.
2. Io non piacqui alla signora Salvini, tu . . ., ecc.
3. Egli spera ch'io le piaccia, egli spera che tu . . ., ecc.
4. Io non dispiaccio a quell'uomo, tu . . ., ecc.
5. Io dispiacqui ai suoi parenti, tu . . ., ecc.
6. Non vuole ch'io gli dispiaccia, non vuole che tu . . ., ecc.

C. Tradurre in italiano:

1. I like Olga. 2. We like Paul. 3. I am sorry. 4. We are very sorry. 5. He likes those children. 6. They like eggs. 7. She didn't like to dance. 8. Are you sorry? 9. She was very sorry. 10. Do you like to stay at home? 11. I am sorry you don't want to go with them. 12. We don't like his being absent. 13. I liked it. 14. We didn't like them. 15. I am sorry you don't like her. 16. I have been very sorry. 17. He likes spaghetti. 18. She likes to do something. 19. I am sorry he proposed that. 20. There is no one who doesn't like Ann.

D. Tradurre in italiano:

I

1. "I am sorry, but you must go to bed early," said Miss Fontana, "because we shall leave at seven tomorrow morning." 2. I like to get

up at five or six during the summer months, and what she said did not displease me. 3. Whoever has seen the Italian lakes will understand me when I say that they are of an enchanting beauty. 4. Stresa is a pretty little town on Lake Maggiore.[1] 5. It is well [2] known for its mild climate and because it is in sight of the Alps. 6. Hundreds of American and European tourists flock there in each month of the year. 7. When we arrived on Swiss territory it was necessary for us to show our passports. 8. We went to (a) swim in Lake Lugano,[3] whose waters were very calm, and we enjoyed [4] the charm of another magnificent view. 9. Afterward we had lunch in one of the best hotels that there are in that town. 10. It was situated at the foot of a high hill.

II

1. We liked Milan, the great center of Italy's trade and industry. 2. The going and coming of automobiles, autobuses, and streetcars reminded us of our large cities in the United States. 3. But Milan is above all a center of culture and art.[5] 4. If you (**tu**) should see its Cathedral you would say that it has no equal in the world. 5. It has 135 [6] spires and 2300 statues, all of white marble. 6. From its roof we saw the whole metropolis and the far-away [7] Alps. 7. Perhaps the most famous work [8] of art that there is in Milan is the fresco by [9] Leonardo da Vinci called *The Last Supper;* it is in the church of Saint Mary of the Graces. 8. The party spent a whole morning visiting the Sforza Castle. 9. I was sorry that you (**tu**) weren't with us, because I know you would have liked it. 10. Today we visited the Brera Museum [10] and saw the house of Alessandro Manzoni, a great Italian poet and writer.

[1] Use the definite article. [2] **bɛn.** [3] Translate, *in the lake of . . .* [4] Use the verb **godere.** [5] Use no article with these two nouns. [6] Write out the numbers. [7] Leave this adjective before the noun. [8] Use the word **ɔpera,** the meaning of which is both *work* and *opera.* [9] See footnote 3, p. 110. [10] **la Pinacotɛca di Brɛra.**

❧ *Lezione Trentacinquesima* ❧

I. NOTE GRAMMATICALI

151. The Verb *fare* with a Dependent Infinitive

Fate aprire le porte.	*Have the doors opened.*
Mi farò fare un abito.	*I shall have a suit of clothes made (for myself).*
Si fece fare una veste.	*She had a dress made (for herself).*

The verb **fare** is used before an infinitive to express the idea that the action is to be done, was done, or will be done, by somebody else. It renders such English expressions as *to have something done, to get something done, etc.* If a reflexive pronoun is understood in English (as in the 2nd and 3rd examples), it must be expressed in Italian.

152. Conjunctive Pronouns with a Dependent Infinitive

1. Lo possiamo mandare. ⎫
   Possiamo mandarlo. ⎬ *We can send it.*

   Gliene devo parlare. ⎫
   Devo parlargliene. ⎬ *I must speak of it to him.*

Several verbs, among them **dovere, potere, volere, sapere,** and **osare** (*to dare*), have a sort of auxiliary function when followed by an infinitive. If the dependent infinitive has a pronoun object (or objects), the latter may either be appended to it or may precede the main verb.

2.
Lo fecero mandar via.	*They had him sent away.*
La vedo ammirare da tutti.	*I see her admired by all.*
Sento dire molte cose.	*I hear many things being said.*
Feci studiar la lezione a questo ragazzo.	*I made this boy study his lesson.*
Gliela feci studiare.	*I made him study it.*

On the other hand, certain verbs, like **fare, lasciare, sentire, udire** (*to hear*), and **vedere,** always take the object of the dependent infinitive. Note, however, that if the object of either verb is a noun (3rd example), it usually follows the verb; and that if the main verb also has an object (4th and 5th examples), that object becomes indirect.

153. Study the complete conjugations of **dovere, potere, salire,** and **scendere** (*Appendix III*).

II. LETTURA

Venezia e Bologna

Il programma del viaggio della nostra comitiva era stato fatto in modo da permettere di restar parecchi giorni nelle città principali e di visitar solo rapidamente — spesso fra un treno e l'altro — i centri minori.

5   Fra Milano e Venezia ci son due belle e antichissime città che meritano una visita: Verona e Padova. La comitiva si fermò per poche ore sia nell'una che nell'altra, e non arrivò a Venezia che verso sera.

Che strana impressione ebbero gli studenti quando, uscendo da
10 quella stazione, invece di trovare il solito autobus per portarli all'albergo, trovarono delle gondole! E poi, quando furono scesi in tre di esse e queste cominciarono a muoversi, che mistero in quei canali al buio, in quel silenzio interrotto solo dalla voce del gondoliere, quando si stava per passar vicino a un angolo! Che
15 Venezia fosse una città di mistero e romanzo l'avevano spesso sentito dire: ora lo vedevano.

— A Venezia si va in giro così, — disse la signorina Fontana.

— Chi ha fretta prende una barca a motore; gli altri o vanno in gondola, o a piedi.

20   — Come, a piedi? — domandò una delle ragazze, Caterina Miller. — A piedi nell'acqua?

Nella gondola tutti scoppiarono a ridere, ma la signorina fece capire a Caterina che le isolette sulle quali Venezia fu fondata sono unite fra loro da piccoli ponti, così che si può camminare da una
25 parte della città all'altra.

Nella settimana che passarono a Venezia, come si divertiron tutti, e quante cose incantevoli videro!

Qualche volta in gondola, qualche altra volta a piedi, la signorina Fontana li fece girare un po' dovunque. Naturalmente, ciò che ammirarono più di tutto furono i superbi edifizi sulla grande Piazza San Marco: la famosa Basilica, il Campanile, e il Palazzo dei Dogi. Ma passarono ore più interessanti che non avessero 5 immaginato visitando l'Accademia, il gran museo di Venezia, in cui una guida molto competente fece gustar loro la bellezza di molti quadri del Rinascimento.

Videro tanto, eppure ebbero abbastanza tempo libero per andare in giro dove volevano, per visitar negozi e comprare ricordi, 10 o per andare a nuotare al Lido, la più elegante spiaggia d'Europa.

Nessuno di loro potrà mai dimenticare l'incanto delle passeggiate in gondola sul Canal Grande, di sera, a luna piena!

Dopo Venezia, l'ultima città dell'Italia Settentrionale in cui la comitiva si fermò fu Bologna. 15

La signorina Fontana aveva parlato a gli studenti dell'università per cui quella città è famosa; università che, fondata nel 1088, è la più antica del mondo. Essi furon contenti di poterla visitare.

Nel pomeriggio che passarono a Bologna videro pure con grand'interesse le due torri pendenti menzionate da Dante nella 20 *Divina Commedia.*

PROVERBIO

Oggi a me, domani a te.   *Every dog has its day.* (*Today me, tomorrow thee.*)

III. STUDIO DI PAROLE

Doge *m.* Doge [1]
Marco Mark
Padova Padua
Venezia Venice

accademia academy
barca boat; **barca a motore** motorboat
basilica basilica
campanile *m.* bell tower

canale *m.* canal, channel
commedia comedy
gondola gondola
gondoliere *m.* gondolier
impressione *f.* impression
mistero mystery
piede *m.* foot; **a piedi** on foot
ricordo remembrance, souvenir
romanzo romance, novel
spiaggia beach

[1] The Doge was the chief magistrate of the ancient Republic of Venice.

torre *f.* tower

divino divine
pendente leaning
strano strange, odd

fondare to found
interrotto (*p. part. of* **interrom-**
pere) interrupted

menzionare to mention
scoppiare [**scoppio**] to burst [1];
scoppiare a ridere to burst out
laughing
unire [**unisco**] to unite, combine

dovunque everywhere
o . . . o either . . . or

IV. CONVERSAZIONE

1. Com'era stato fatto il programma del viaggio della comitiva?
2. Dove sono Verona e Padova? 3. Vi si fermò la comitiva?
4. A che ora gli studenti arrivarono a Venezia? 5. Quale strana
impressione ebbero uscendo da quella stazione? 6. Da che cosa
era interrotto il silenzio sui canali? 7. Che cosa avevano sentito
dire gli studenti? 8. Come si va in giro a Venezia? 9. Che cosa
domandò Caterina Miller? 10. Che cosa fecero tutti nella gondola? 11. Che cosa fece capire a Caterina la signorina Fontana?
12. Andarono sempre in gondola gli studenti nei giorni che passarono a Venezia? 13. Che cosa ammirarono più di tutto?
14. Quali sono i principali edifizi di Piazza San Marco? 15. Dove
passarono ore interessanti gli studenti? 16. Che cosa fecero nelle
ore libere? 17. Che cosa nessun di loro potrà mai dimenticare?
18. Dove andò la comitiva dopo aver visitato Venezia? 19. Dica
qualche cosa dell'Università di Bologna. 20. Che altro videro gli
studenti a Bologna?

V. ESERCIZI

A. Tradurre in italiano:

1. What made you do this? 2. Mary had a dress made for her little
sister. 3. I shall have a dress made. 4. Have the windows opened,
please. 5. We hear her playing the piano. 6. I bought a radio, and
now I shall let you see it. 7. I let her clean the gloves. 8. Have
your fur coat sent here. 9. We did not understand that word and
made him pronounce it again. 10. We had a boy sent to the post
office.

---

[1] Conjugated with essere.

B. Sostituire alle parole in parentesi il corretto equivalente, usando due forme se ciò è possibile:

1. Ho ricevuto questi libri; (*you can see them*) _____. 2. Non vi piace e (*you don't dare to say it*) _____. 3. Hai avuto una cartolina da lui e (*you don't want to show it to me*) _____. 4. Ho un pianoforte, ma (*I don't know how to play it*) _____. 5. Ecco i pacchi; (*we must send them*) _____ alla posta. 6. Aveva una rivista e (*he wanted to give it to her*) _____. 7. Entrai in quella sala e (*I heard those words being said*) _____. 8. Quella musica è bella e spesso (*we hear her playing it*) _____. 9. Son brutti sbagli e (*you must not make them*) _____. 10. Non ho che questa penna; mi dispiace, ma (*I cannot give it to you*) _____.

C. 1. Coniugare nel presente dell'indicativo, e poi nel presente del congiuntivo:

    1. Salire sul piroscafo.   2. Salire al terzo piano.

2. Coniugare nel passato assoluto, e poi nel presente perfetto:

    1. Scendere da cavallo.   2. Scendere al pian terreno.

3. Completare con la forma richiesta del verbo in parentesi:

Futuro: 1. (*dovere*) Noi _____ completare il lavoro. 2. (*potere*) Io lo _____ menzionare. 3. (*dovere*) Voi _____ unirvi. 4. (*potere*) Mario e tu _____ andar da lui. 5. (*dovere*) Lei non _____ bere caffè. 6. (*potere*) I gondolieri _____ aspettare.

Presente del congiuntivo: 1. (*salire*) Non sperate ch'egli _____ qui. 2. (*dovere*) Non so se voi _____ restare. 3. (*potere*) Spero che tu ti _____ imbarcare. 4. (*salire*) Voglio che voi _____ un po' da me. 5. (*dovere*) Chi pensa ch'essi _____ mancare? 6. (*potere*) È meglio che ognuno _____ servirsene. 7. (*salire*) Bisogna ch'io _____ con te. 8. (*dovere*) È possibile ch'egli _____ lavorar tanto? 9. (*salire*) Preferisco che tu _____ con lei. 10. (*potere*) Questa è la sola cosa che voi _____ fare.

Condizionale: 1. (*dovere*) Essi lo _____ dire. 2. (*potere*) Tu _____ soffrire. 3. (*dovere*) Io non _____ muovermi. 4. (*potere*) Lei _____ unirsi a loro. 5. (*dovere*) Voi non _____ scommettere. 6. (*potere*) Quegli uomini _____ aver fretta.

D. Tradurre in italiano:

I

1. Miss Fontana had us get [1] in three fine gondolas. 2. Our gondolier was a young man with [2] black eyes, who made us laugh with his jokes.

    [1] **scendere.**   [2] Attention!

3. He spoke [1] a little English, but oh! how funny his English was [2]!
4. "I am going up to my room," said Miss Fontana when we arrived at our hotel. She came down soon after, however. 5. We had [3] a good dinner and then went to (a) spend the evening at an outdoor café on (in) St. Mark's Square. 6. That is the most beautiful square in the world; I can [4] never forget it. 7. The following morning Miss Fontana wanted [5] us to visit St. Mark's Basilica and the Doges' Palace. 8. A competent guide showed them to us and had us see many interesting things. 9. That afternoon we took a motorboat on the Grand [6] Canal, and went to the Lido, the finest beach I have ever seen.[7] 10. We are going to spend a whole week in Venice; that's (ecco) what you (tu) ought [8] to do when you go to (in) Europe.

II

1. What an impression of mystery and romance the canals of Venice gave [9] me at (di) night! 2. What silence, interrupted only by the voice of the gondolier! 3. I shall never be able to forget it (m.), nor shall I forget the moon on the Grand [6] Canal. 4. One morning Miss Fontana had us go on foot to the Academy. 5. If you (tu) had been with us, you would have enjoyed the sight of many famous paintings of the Renaissance. 6. Everywhere one sees beautiful things here; I shall buy a little remembrance, and I shall have it sent to you by (per) mail. 7. Now the young men and the girls of our party are going up to their rooms; it's time to (di) go to bed. 8. Thursday we shall leave for Bologna to visit that famous university, founded in 1088.[10] 9. Dante mentions, in his *Divine Comedy*, the two leaning towers of that city; Miss Fontana will have us see them. 10. As you can see, our trip combines culture and amusement.[11]

[1] Past descriptive. [2] Place this verb right after *how*. [3] Use the verb **fare**. [4] Use the future. [5] Past absolute. [6] Place this adjective after the noun. [7] Attention! [8] Use the conditional of **dovere**. [9] Use the present perfect. [10] Write out the number. [11] Omit the article before these two nouns.

❧ *Lezione Trentaseiɛsima* ❧

I. NOTE GRAMMATICALI

154. Use of the Disjunctive Personal Pronouns

As stated in § 94 (p. 142), the most common use of the disjunctive personal pronouns is as objects of prepositions.[1]

This includes, of course, their use after **di**, meaning *than*, in comparatives of inequality.

Sɛi più alto di me.	*You are taller than I.*

Note, however, that the disjunctive personal pronouns are used also in the following cases:

1. Visiterò te ed essi.	*I shall visit you and them.*
Parlo a lui e a lɛi.	*I speak to him and to her.*

In place of the conjunctive pronouns, when the verb has two or more direct, or two or more indirect objects.

2. Seguirò voi.	*I shall follow <u>you</u>.* (The unemphatic form would be **Vi seguirò**.)
Amo te, non amo lui.	*I love you; I don't love him.*

In place of the conjunctive pronouns, for emphasis, clearness, or contrast.

3. Partirò io, non lui.	*I shall depart, not he.*
Lui l'ha scritto.	*He himself wrote it.*
Lui stesso l'ha detto.	*He himself said so.*
But: Io stesso l'ho detto.	*I myself said so.*

In place of the subject pronouns, for emphasis, but only if the pronoun is in the 3rd person, singular or plural. For greater emphasis, the adjective **stesso** may be added.

---

[1] Note that instead of **con me, con te,** and **con sè,** the forms **meco, teco,** and **seco** are sometimes used.

155. Remarks on the Superlatives

1. Il mare era calmo calmo. *The sea was very calm.*
   Son solo solo. *I am all alone.*
   Camminate piano piano. *Walk very slowly.*

An absolute superlative may be formed by repeating the adjective, though this is a rare usage. Note from the 3rd example that a repeated adjective may take the function of an adverb.

2.   acre, *sour*   acerrimo
    celebre, *celebrated*   celeberrimo
    integro, *righteous*   integerrimo
    misero, *wretched*   miserrimo
    salubre, *healthful*   saluberrimo

The adjectives listed above have an absolute superlative in −errimo.

3. chiaramente, *clearly*   chiarissimamente, *very clearly*
   gentilmente, *kindly*   gentilissimamente, *very kindly*

The suffix −**mente** is added to a superlative in −**issimo** (after the final **o** has been changed into an **a**) to form the absolute superlative of an adverb of manner.

156. The Verbs *nascere* and *vivere*

1. Quand'è nato questo ragazzo? *When was this child born?*
   Sono nato a Filadelfia. *I was born in Philadelphia.*
   Colombo nacque a Genova. *Columbus was born in Genoa.*
   Non ero nato ancora. *I wasn't born yet. (I hadn't yet been born.)*

Nascere means *to be born.* As to the correct translation of the English *was born*, note the following:

(*a*) If the person referred to is still alive, use the present perfect.

(*b*) If the person is dead, use the past absolute.

(*c*) If *was born* has the meaning of *had been born*, the translation should be in the past perfect, as shown in the last example.

2.   Egli ha vissuto in Europa. } *He lived in Europe.*
       Egli è vissuto in Europa.

The verb **vivere**, *to live*, is one of the few Italian verbs that are conjugated indifferently with **avere** or **essere**.[1]

Do not confuse **vivere** with **abitare**, which is used in the sense of *to dwell, reside*.

157. Study the complete conjugations of **aprire, chiudere,**[2] **nascere,** and **vivere** (Appendix III).

II. LETTURA

Firenze e Pisa

Il rapido sul quale la comitiva viaggiava era proprio allora uscito dalla galleria che, passando sotto gli Appennini, rende più breve la distanza tra Bologna e la Toscana.

— Com'era lunga! — esclamò Lucia.

— Quando arriveremo a Firenze? — domandò Mario quasi al   5 tempo stesso.

— Saremo a Firenze fra quaranta minuti, — rispose a lui la signorina Fontana. Poi, volgendosi a lei: — Lunga, sì; ma più lunga ancora è la galleria del Sempione, nelle Alpi, tra l'Italia e la Svizzera.   10

Firenze, patria d'uomini celeberrimi in ogni campo della cultura, Firenze, che è tutta un museo in cui sono accumulati tesori d'arte del Medio Evo e del Rinascimento, è una città che dovrebbe esser visitata pian piano, senza fretta. La bellezza della regione in cui è situata, i ricordi storici e artistici in essa contenuti, la 15 lingua che vi si parla così pura e dolce, la vita che vi si mena così comoda e piacevole, — tutto invita a restarvi lungo tempo. Ma, purtroppo, i giorni che la comitiva poteva passarvi eran pochi.

La prima cosa che gli studenti videro fu il Duomo, la cui facciata dai marmi di molti colori ognuno ammirò assai. Dirimpetto al 20 Duomo c'è l'antichissimo Battistero, e la comitiva vi si fermò parecchio tempo a osservarne le bellissime porte di bronzo, capolavoro del Ghiberti. Quello però che soprattutto piacque a ognuno fu l'elegante Campanile di Giotto, che è forse la più bella torre del mondo.   25

---

[1] Another of such verbs is **appartenere,** *to belong.*   [2] *to close.*

Molte ore furono passate nella Galleria degli Uffizi [1] e di Palazzo Pitti, e nel vicino Palazzo Vecchio, sede del governo dell'antica Repubblica di Firenze. Salirono pure in cima all'altissima torre di quell'edifizio, dalla quale si gode una vista incantevole della 5 città e di buona parte della valle dell'Arno.

In un'antica via, così stretta che una vettura vi poteva appena passare se ne incontrava un'altra, videro la casa in cui nacque Dante; ma era chiusa, e non vi potettero entrare. Dante, spiegò la signorina Fontana, nato del 1265, visse in esilio dal 1302 al 10 1321, anno in cui chiuse gli occhi per sempre nella città di Ravenna.

In quei giorni visitaron pure il Palazzo del Bargello, famoso pei suoi ricordi storici e per il suo museo. Andarono a vedere molte chiese importanti per l'arte e per la storia di Firenze: quella di Santa Maria Novella, che è una delle più belle e più antiche della 15 città; quella di San Lorenzo, famosa per le superbe tombe dei Medici, opere di Michelangelo; e quella di Santa Croce, dove son le tombe di molti grandi Italiani.

Fecero anche due escursioni: una alla vicina Fiesole, l'altra a Pisa, dove ammirarono tre capolavori dell'arte del Medio Evo: 20 il Duomo, il Battistero e la meravigliosa Torre Pendente.

PROVERBIO

Ogni trino è perfetto.   *All good things go by threes.*

III. STUDIO DI PAROLE

Firenze *f.* Florence
Medio Evo Middle Ages
Sempione *m.* Simplon

battistero baptistry
bronzo bronze
cima top; **in cima (a)** on *or* to the top (of)
distanza distance
esilio exile
facciata front (*of a building*)

galleria gallery, tunnel
governo government
opera work, opera
patria fatherland, native city
rapido flyer
repubblica republic
sede *f.* seat (*residence*)
tesoro treasure
tomba tomb
valle *f.* valley

[1] Do not translate the place names you are going to meet in the rest of this reading.

FOUNTAIN IN THE ROYAL PALACE, CASERTA

PITTI PALACE AND DUOMO, FLORENCE

PANORAMA OF ANCONA

GENERAL VIEW FROM PIAZZALE MICHELANGELO, FLORENCE

PANORAMA OF ISCHIA IN THE BAY OF NAPLES

VIEW OF BELLAGIO ON LAGO DI COMO

GARDEN OF THE VILLA D'ESTE, CERNOBBIO

CORSO IMPERATRICE, SAN REMO

vita life

meraviglioso marvelous, wonderful
piacevole pleasant, agreeable
piano slow, soft; *adv.* slowly,
softly
puro pure

accumulare [accumulo] to accumulate, gather
rendere to render, make
viaggiare [viaggio] to travel
volgersi to turn

dirimpetto (a) opposite
purtroppo unfortunately

IV. CONVERSAZIONE

1. Da quale galleria era uscito il rapido su cui la comitiva viaggiava? 2. Che cosa esclamò Lucia? 3. Che cosa domandò Mario?
4. Che cosa rispose loro la signorina Fontana? 5. Di chi è patria
Firenze? 6. Quali tesori d'arte sono accumulati in Firenze?
7. Com'è la lingua che vi si parla? 8. Potettero restarvi lungo
tempo i nostri studenti? 9. Che cosa videro prima? 10. Che
cosa c'è dirimpetto al Duomo di Firenze? 11. Che cosa piacque
soprattutto a ognuno? 12. Dove passò molte ore la comitiva?
13. Dove salirono gli studenti? 14. Dove videro la casa di Dante?
15. Quando nacque Dante? 16. In quali anni visse in esilio?
17. Perchè è importante la chiesa di Santa Maria Novella?
18. Perchè è importante la chiesa di San Lorenzo? 19. Perchè
è importante la chiesa di Santa Croce? 20. Che cosa ammirò
a Pisa la comitiva?

V. ESERCIZI

A. 1. Sostituire i nomi di persone con pronomi personali dis-
giuntivi:

1. Tu sei più timido d'Antonio. 2. Egli ha salutato Beatrice, non
Vittorio. 3. Incontreremo Giovanni e Clara. 4. Rispondo a Laura,
non a Franco. 5 Anna stessa l'ha detto.

2. Tradurre in italiano usando pronomi congiuntivi o disgiun-
tivi, secondo le regole studiate:

1. It seems that he sees you. 2. We thank him and her. 3. It is
necessary for them to understand you. 4. I offer my things to you,
not to him. 5. He himself said so. 6. I invite *you*, this time. 7. She
is rich; he is poor. 8. It seems that Olga works with you. 9. She
corrects him. 10. They spoke to us, not to them.

B. 1. Applicando le regole studiate in questa lezione, dare il superlativo assoluto di:

1. Poco. 2. Dolcemente. 3. Celebre. 4. Piano. 5. Salubre. 6. Utilmente. 7. Vicino. 8. Integro. 9. Scuro. 10. Nero. 11. Altamente. 12. Acre.

2. Usare i primi cinque superlativi in brevi frasi.

C. Completare con la forma richiesta del verbo in parentesi:

Passato assoluto: 1. (*aprire* [1]) Egli ____ le braccia quando lo vide. 2. (*vivere*) Dante ____ molti anni in esilio. 3. (*chiudere*) Io ____ il libro di lettura. 4. (*nascere*) Garibaldi ____ a Nizza. 5. (*aprire*) Gli alunni ____ i loro libri. 6. (*chiudere*) La cameriera ____ le finestre. 7. (*vivere*) Molti grandi poeti ____ poveri. 8. (*chiudere*) Essi ____ la cabina. 9. (*nascere*) Celeberrimi artisti ____ a Firenze. 10. (*vivere*) Goldoni ____ in Francia nei suoi ultimi anni.

Presente perfetto: 1. (*nascere*) Io ____ nel 1930. 2. (*aprire*) Chi ____ quando avete suonato il campanello? 3. (*vivere*) I miei cognati ____ in Europa. 4. (*chiudere*) L'impiegato ____ lo sportello. 5. (*aprire*) Io ____ quel pacco. 6. (*nascere*) Sua cognata ____ a Padova. 7. (*vivere*) Voi non ____ nel Belgio. 8. (*chiudere*) Tu non ____ la lettera. 9. (*vivere*) Egli ____ una vita molto utile alla Patria. 10. (*nascere*) Noi ____ negli Stati Uniti.

Condizionale: 1. (*vivere*) Se tu non fossi qui, noi ____ soli soli. 2. (*vivere*) Se potesse, ella non ____ in questa città. 3. (*vivere*) A Firenze, io ____ felice.

D. Tradurre in italiano:

I

1. I didn't believe [2] that that tunnel was so long. 2. The flyer on which we were traveling took thirteen minutes to (**per**) go through [3] it. 3. At last we arrived in Florence, the native city of hundreds of very famous [4] artists. 4. During the Middle Ages and the Renaissance it was the greatest [5] center of Italian arts. 5. We went first to (a) see the Cathedral, but, unfortunately, we found it closed. 6. We had to [6] return there the following morning. 7. I liked its front, I admired a great deal the bronze doors of the Baptistry, but I shall never forget

---

[1] Use only the irregular forms of the past absolute of **aprire.** [2] Past descriptive. [3] See Vocabulary. [4] Use **celebre.** [5] Use the irregular relative superlative. [6] Use **bisognare.**

the beauty of Giotto's tower. 8. Paul said that Giotto lived [1] at the time of Lawrence the Magnificent; Louise, that he was [2] more modern. 9. Both [3] he and she were [2] wrong; Giotto lived [1] in (a) Dante's time, for he was born in 1266,[4] one year after the great poet. 10. I opened [5] my guidebook and showed it to him and to her.

II

1. I thought [2] that Miss Fontana was born in Florence, and said so [6] to Lucy. 2. "No," she told me, "she [7] was born in Sicily, and her family is Roman; she has lived in America for (da) many years." 3. What artistic treasures are gathered [8] in Florence! 4. During these days we visited the Uffizi Gallery, that of the Pitti Palace, and other museums. 5. We climbed to the top of the tower of Palazzo Vecchio to enjoy a gorgeous view of the whole city and the valley of the Arno. 6. That building was once the seat of the government of the Republic of Florence. 7. I didn't know [2] it, but Miss Fontana told me.[9] 8. Life is so pleasant here! We went twice to the opera, and danced in a large hotel opposite ours. 9. I like the members of our party, Ann and Marius especially. She [7] is always ready to (a) say what she wants, and he,[7] who is very good,[10] does what she desires. 10. We are sorry to have to [11] tell you that, at this point, the girl who was writing these words closed her diary and went to bed.

❧ *Lezione Trentasettesima* ☙

I. NOTE GRAMMATICALI

158.   The Subjunctive in Adverbial Clauses [12]

Gli parlai prima ch'egli uscisse.	*I spoke to him before he went out.*
Lo mostrò perchè io lo comprassi.	*He showed it in order that I might buy it.*
Aspetterò purchè egli ritorni presto.	*I shall wait provided he returns soon.*

[1] Past absolute.   [2] Past descriptive.   [3] What is *both . . . and?*   [4] Write out the number.   [5] Present perfect.   [6] Translate, *I said it.*   [7] An emphatic pronoun.   [8] This is not a passive form; *gathered* has here the function of an adjective.   [9] Translate, *it to me.*   [10] Use an absolute superlative form studied in this lesson.   [11] Use the verb **dovere.**   [12] A clause that modifies a verb is called an adverbial clause.

Benchè fosse ricco, non εra gene- roso.	*Although he was rich, he was not generous.*
Uscì senza che lo vedessero.	*He went out without their seeing him.*

The subjunctive is used in adverbial clauses introduced by certain conjunctions, the most important of which are:

TIME: **prima che** or **avanti che,** *before;* **sεmpre che,** *whenever;* **finchè,** *until* (referring to the future)
PURPOSE: **perchè** or **affinchè,** *in order that*
CONDITION: **purchè,** *provided that;* **a meno che . . . non,** *unless*
CONCESSION: **benchè** or **quantunque** or **sebbεne,** *although;* **dato che,** *granted that;* **caso mai** or **se mai,** *in case*
NEGATION: **senza che,** *without*

159.   Remarks on the Possessives

1.

un mio parente	*a relative of mine*
questo mio libro	*this book of mine*
due suɔi amici	*two friends of his*
molte vɔstre lεttere	*many letters of yours*
delle nɔstre carte	*some papers of ours*

Note from the examples above that the possessive adjective is not always preceded by the definite article. Instead we sometimes may have an indefinite article, a demonstrative adjective, a numeral, an adjective indicating quantity, or the partitive. Thus the English *of* is not translated, and the examples above stand literally for *a my relative, this my book,* etc.

2. Mio caro amico, ascolta!   *My dear friend, listen!*

No article is used when the possessive modifies a vocative.

3. Questo baule è mio.   *This trunk is mine.*
   È il mio; non è il tuo.   *It's mine; it isn't yours.*

When the possessive stands alone in the predicate, the article is omitted if we merely wish to denote possession; it is not omitted if we wish to distinguish our possession from that of others.

4. Sacrificò la vita alla Patria.   *He sacrificed his life to his country.*

The possessive, when not necessary for clearness, is usually replaced by a definite article.

160. Study the complete conjugations of **cadere, correre, lɛggere,** and **scrivere** (*Appendix III*).

II. LETTURA

Siɛna, Perugia e Assisi

Affinchè la comitiva potesse pienamente godere la vista degl'incantevoli luɔghi, tra gli Appennini, che si trɔvano andando da
Firɛnze a Roma, ɛra stato disposto che il viaggio, anzichè in ferrovia, fosse fatto in tre grandi automɔbili.   E la prima fermata fu
a Siɛna.   5

Sotto molti aspɛtti, Siɛna è una città che ricɔrda il Mɛdio Ɛvo.
Bisognerɛbbe andarvi quando si fa la *Corsa del Palio*,[1] che è una
delle più caratterìstiche fɛste italiane e che ha luɔgo una vɔlta
l'anno nella grandìssima piazza al cɛntro della città.   Ɛ una corsa
di cavalli alla quale prɛndono parte numerosi fantini, vestiti in 10
abiti medioevali, che rappresɛntano i vari quartiɛri di Siɛna.
Tutto il pɔpolo segue la gara col màssimo entusiasmo, e migliaia
di forestiɛri vanno a vederla.

Purtrɔppo però, i nɔstri studɛnti non ɛbbero questa fortuna
perchè la fɛsta si fa il 16 agosto, ed essi arrivarono a Siɛna il 29 15
luglio per una vìsita d'un giorno solo.

Nel giro che fecero quɛl pomerìggio potɛttero ammirare molti
antichi palazzi e visitarono l'Accadɛmia di Bɛlle Arti, la Biblio-
tɛca e il magnìfico Duɔmo.   Il Palazzo Pùbblico con la sua ele-
gantìssima torre sembrɔ loro una meravìglia di bellezza.   20

Benchè fossero tutti un pɔ' stanchi, andarono a teatro quella
sera, a sentire una commɛdia del Pirandɛllo.   Quasi tutti ricordavano un'altra sua commɛdia, *Così è (se vi pare)*, che avevan lɛtta
a scuɔla, negli Stati Uniti.

La mattina seguɛnte la comitiva partì di buɔn'ora per Perugia, 25
lasciando la Toscana per entrare in una delle più bɛlle regioni
d'Itàlia, l'Umbria.   Tra i maggiori vantaggi che la natura le ha
dati, è quello d'avere un ɔttimo clima e un'aria salubɛrrima.   Sia
per questo, sia perchè essa ɔffre molte attrazioni dal punto di vista
stɔrico e artìstico, forestiɛri d'ogni paese la vìsitano in tutte le 30
stagioni dell'anno.

[1] Do not translate.

Perugia, la sua città principale, non ha che ottanta mila abitanti, ma, quantunque sia piccola, è, per varie ragioni, molto importante. Basta pensare che, durante il Rinascimento, essa fu un gran centro d'arte, e che in essa nacquero o vissero uomini famosi, fra i quali 5 il Perugino, celebre pittore e maestro di Raffaello; basta pensare ai suoi bellissimi edifizi e alla sua Università per gli Stranieri.

Assisi è a poche miglia da Perugia, e in un paio d'ore gli studenti potettero vedere quel che v'è di più importante. Tutti sanno che in quella cittadina fra i monti nacque e visse la maggior parte 10 della sua vita San Francesco, il gran santo che scrisse il *Cantico delle Creature*. La fermata ad Assisi era stata fatta soprattutto perchè gli studenti potessero visitare il suo Convento e la Basilica, in cui s'ammirano gli originalissimi affreschi di Giotto.

Con questo, il giro era finito, e la mattina del 31 luglio le tre 15 automobili corsero a grande velocità, lungo il Tevere, verso Roma.

PROVERBIO

Tutte le strade menano a Roma.   *All roads lead to Rome.*

III. STUDIO DI PAROLE

Francesco Francis
Raffaello Raphael
Roma Rome
Tevere *m.* Tiber

applauso applause, cheers
attrazione *f.* attraction
cantico canticle
convento convent, monastery
corsa race
creatura creature
entusiasmo enthusiasm
fantino jockey
fermata stop
festa feast, festival, party
foresti ero *or* **straniero** foreigner
gara contest, match

meraviglia marvel
popolo people, populace
punto point
quartiere *m.* ward, section (*of a city*)
velocità speed

caratteristico characteristic
medioevale medieval
numeroso numerous
originale original
pubblico public
vario various, different

bastare to be enough [1]

anzichè rather than

---

[1] Conjugated with essere.

IV. CONVERSAZIONE

1. Perchè era stato disposto che il viaggio da Firenze a Roma fosse fatto in automobile? 2. Che cosa ricorda Siena? 3. Quando bisognerebbe andarvi? 4. Che cos'è la Corsa del Palio? 5. Quando e dove ha luogo? 6. Come segue la gara il popolo? 7. Son tutti italiani quelli che vanno a vederla? 8. Perchè gli studenti non videro la Corsa del Palio? 9. Che cosa videro a Siena gli studenti? 10. Che cosa sembrò loro una meraviglia di bellezza? 11. Dove andarono quella sera? 12. Che cosa ricordavano quasi tutti gli studenti? 13. In quale regione sono Perugia e Assisi? 14. Che vantaggi ha dati la natura a quella regione? 15. Perchè è importante Perugia? 16. Di chi fu patria? 17. È Assisi lontana da Perugia? 18. Chi nacque ad Assisi? 19. Che cosa ammirarono ad Assisi gli studenti? 20. Dove corsero la mattina del 31 luglio le tre automobili?

V. ESERCIZI

A. 1. Riconoscere immediatamente il significato (*the meaning*) di queste parole:

1. Benchè. 2. Finchè. 3. Purchè. 4. Perchè. 5. Quantunque. 6. Se mai. 7. Dato che. 8. Prima che. 9. Sebbene. 10. A meno che . . . non. 11. Affinchè. 12. Senza che. 13. Avanti che. 14. Caso mai.

2. Completare con la forma corretta del verbo in parentesi:

1. (*porre*) La nonna disse così affinchè essi _____ ogni cosa in ordine. 2. (*soffrire*) Dategli questa medicina se mai egli _____. 3. (*parlare*) Lo capii senza ch'egli mi _____. 4. (*dire*) Dato che Carlo _____ questo, che volete ch'io faccia? 5. (*salire*) Ti parlerà volentieri purchè tu _____ da lui. 6. (*supporre*) Fa' come dico io, a meno che tu non _____ che sia troppo tardi. 7. (*vedere*) Andiamo via prima che Marco ci _____. 8. (*osare*) Sebbene io non _____ rispondergli, sapevo ch'egli aveva torto. 9. (*piacere*) Gli ho scritto queste cose perchè gli _____ venir da noi. 10. (*essere*) Benchè essi _____ ricchi, non davan niente ai poveri.

B. Tradurre in italiano:

1. A masterpiece of his. 2. Some of my friends. 3. Three of our plants. 4. Eleven of his comedies. 5. A magazine of hers. 6. That motor-

boat of mine. 7. Several of our small towns. 8. Many of your post cards. 9. Every handkerchief of mine. 10. Some of our banks.

C. 1. Coniugare nel presɛnte perfɛtto, e pɔi nel passato assoluto:

1. Cadere per la via.   3. Correre a casa.
2. Lɛggere ad alta voce.   4. Non scrivere in fretta.

2. Usare in due brɛvi frasi ciascuno dei seguɛnti vɛrbi, prima nel presɛnte perfɛtto e pɔi nel passato assoluto:

1. Cadere. 2. Chiudere. 3. Conoscere. 4. Correre. 5. Nascere. 6. Dire. 7. Lɛggere. 8. Posporre. 9. Sapere. 10. Vivere. 11. Scrivere. 12. Scɛndere.

D. Tradurre in italiano:

I

1. Although I am very busy, I often write to my relatives and friends in the United States. 2. This morning I wrote a letter to a cousin of mine and told her about (**di**) this trip of ours through (**attravɛrso**) Tuscany and Umbria. 3. We are now in Perugia, a small city that was an important center of arts during the Renaissance. 4. Here lived[1] Perugino,[2] that very celebrated painter who was Raphael's teacher. 5. I like Perugia, but I liked[3] even more Siena, where we were yesterday. 6. Before we arrived there Miss Fontana spoke to us of the *Corsa del Palio*, a festival that takes place in that city on August 16th. 7. Thousands of foreigners go to (**a**) see it, and the enthusiasm with which the populace follows that contest, with shouts, cheers,[4] and laughter,[4] is enormous. 8. Not only the jockeys, but also other men, wear medieval costumes. 9. "Unfortunately," said Miss Fontana, "we cannot see that race, unless the party stops[5] here for more than two weeks." 10. Every one liked[6] in Siena the lofty tower of the Public Building.[7]

II

1. I have read various books by[8] Pirandello, and I know that he was a very original writer. 2. This evening we shall go to a theater to hear one of his comedies. 3. Yesterday we spent some time at the University, where Guido met one of his American friends. 4. Although he knew that his friend was in Italy, imagine his surprise when the

[1] Past absolute of **vivere**.   [2] Use the definite article.   [3] Present perfect.
[4] Plural.   [5] See Vocabulary.   [6] Past absolute.   [7] Use the word **palazzo**.
[8] Attention!

young man ran to (**a**) shake hands with him! 5. He almost fell in running, and, although I knew that it wasn't a kind thing to do (**da farsi**), I burst out laughing. 6. Tomorrow we shall visit Assisi, that small town in (**fra**) the Apennines where St. Francis was born and lived.[1] 7. He wrote the *Canticle of the Creatures* that we have read in class this year. 8. In Assisi the main attractions are his Monastery and the Basilica. 9. We shall admire Giotto's frescoes, perhaps the best that that very celebrated painter ever made.[2] 10. Provided that everything goes according to schedule,[3] we shall be in Rome tomorrow evening.

❧ *Sixth Review Lesson* ❧

I. VOCABULARY DRILL

A. Give the Italian for the following nouns:

1. The meal
   the flag
   the tower
   the tunnel
   the baggage
   the remembrance
   the compartment

2. The stop
   the spire
   the marvel
   the factory
   the boulevard
   the baptistry
   the monastery

3. The life
   the river
   the valley
   the grace
   the harbor
   the streetcar
   the masterpiece

4. The tomb
   the charm
   the speed
   the bridge
   the fashion
   the lobby
   the government

5. The race
   the world
   the jockey
   the fresco
   the driver
   the custom house
   the native city

6. The side
   the beach
   the exile
   the hotel
   the bell tower
   the foreigner
   the festival

B. Give the Italian for the following adjectives:

1. Imposing, useless, mild, leaning, marvelous, medieval, graceful, proud, continuous, strange.
2. European, Gothic, Swiss, pleasant, slow, celebrated, various, sour, healthful, wretched.

---

[1] Past absolute of **vivere.**   [2] Place *ever* between the auxiliary and the past participle of the perfect tense needed here.   [3] Use the definite article.

C. Give the Italian for the following verbs:

1. To pray
   to found
   to enjoy
   to compose

2. To put
   to travel
   to mention
   to flock together

3. To feel
   to allow
   to lodge
   to postpone

4. To live
   to gather
   to combine
   to assemble

5. To turn
   to cost
   to assemble
   to propose

6. To burst
   to be born
   to suppose
   to be enough

D. Give the Italian for the following expressions:

1. To take place, since, at the foot of, above all, on foot, to the top of, rather than, although, provided that, either . . . or.

2. In order that, to burst out laughing, to take an excursion, as soon as possible, unless, along, that is to say, everywhere, opposite, unfortunately.

II. SUPERLATIVES

1. We have studied a new way, though rarely used, of forming an absolute superlative. Do you remember it? Give an example.

2. Mention the adjectives that have an absolute superlative in **–εrrimo.**

3. How is the absolute superlative of an adverb of manner formed? Give two examples.

III. POSSESSIVES

1. Instead of the definite article, what may we have before a possessive? Give a few examples.

2. What must we remember regarding the possessive in a vocative? Give an example.

3. When the possessive stands alone in the predicate, it is sometimes used with the article, other times without it. Explain, and give two examples.

4. When is the possessive omitted? Give an example.

IV. PRONOUNS

1. What is the most common usage of the disjunctive personal pronouns? Give two examples.

2. When is the disjunctive personal pronoun used instead of the conjunctive? Give two examples.

3. Can a disjunctive personal pronoun be used as a subject? If so, give a few examples.

V. VERBS

1. Give the conditional of **osare, rendere,** and **unire.**

2. Give the conditional perfect of **accumulare** and **ripartire.**

3. In an *if*-clause contrary-to-fact what tenses are used?

4. If the *if*-clause is contrary-to-fact, what tenses must we use in the conclusion?

5. Translate into Italian:

(*a*) If I knew him, I would speak to him.

(*b*) If she had arrived, we should have been happy.

6. Mention other cases in which the conditional is used, and give a few examples.

7. What is an adjective clause?

8. Mention the four cases in which the subjunctive is used in an Italian adjective clause. Give an example for each of them.

9. What is the most common meaning of **piacere**?

10. How would you translate *to please* into Italian?

11. What must we note in translating the verb *to like* into Italian?

12. Translate:

(*a*) Margaret likes the churches of Venice.

(*b*) He liked the enthusiasm of the populace.

(*c*) We don't like him to be dissatisfied.

13. What is the meaning of **dispiacere**?

14. How would you translate *to displease* into Italian?

15. In what meaning is the verb **dispiacere** used in the 3rd person singular? Give an example.

16. What meaning has the verb **fare** before an infinitive? Give two examples.

17. Some verbs may, or may not, take the pronoun object of the dependent infinitive. Can you list them? Give two examples.

18. Some other verbs always take the pronoun object of the dependent infinitive. Mention some of them, and give two examples.

19. What is an adverbial clause?

20. Mention as many conjunctions as you can that require the subjunctive, and give two examples.

VI. IRREGULAR VERBS

1. What parts of any of the verbs are always regular?

2. If the infinitive of a verb is contracted, like **porre**, where does the regular stem appear?

3. How is the present subjunctive of an irregular verb formed?

4. What must we remember about the formation of the imperative?

5. If the future is contracted, what other tense is contracted too?

6. Explain how an irregular past absolute is formed, and give the past absolute of **conoscere**.

7. **Porre.** Give: (a) The present indicative. (b) The 1st person of the past descriptive and future. (c) The past absolute. (d) The present subjunctive. (e) The present and past participles.

8. Mention some other verbs that are conjugated like **porre**.

9. **Piacere.** Give: (a) The present indicative. (b) The past absolute.

10. Mention a verb that is conjugated like **piacere**.

11. **Dovere** and **potere.** Give for each of them: (a) The 1st person of the future and conditional. (b) The present subjunctive.

12. **Salire.** Give the present indicative.

13. **Aprire, chiudere, correre, leggere, nascere, scendere,** and **scrivere.** Give for each of them: (a) The 1st and 2nd persons singular of the past absolute. (b) The past participle.

14. **Cadere.** Give: (a) The past absolute. (b) The 1st person of the future and conditional.

15. **Vivere.** Give: (a) The past absolute. (b) The 1st person of the future and conditional. (c) The past participle.

LETTURA IN SILENZIO

Sì o no?

1. __ Il quartiere è la quarta parte.
2. __ Il quartiere è una parte della città.
3. __ Il rapido è un treno che va a grande velocità.
4. __ Tutte le sarte bastano le vesti che fanno.
5. — Non son ricco, ma ho quel che mi basta.
6. __ Il vento muove le cime degli alberi.
7. __ La vettura è un mobile elegante da salotto.
8. __ Le antiche torri sono spesso sulle colline.
9. __ Il fantino è una delle carte con cui giochiamo.
10. __ Le guglie son qualche volta di marmo bianco.
11. __ Le nostre automobili andavano feste.
12. __ Il 4 luglio è un giorno di festa in America.
13. __ Molte case hanno una gara per le automobili.
14. __ Le gallerie son dei posti per galli e galline.
15. __ Le campane sono sui campanili.

ACHIEVEMENT TEST NO. 6

VOCABULARY

Give the Italian for the following words:

1. the factory	_____	11. the streetcar	_____
2. everywhere	_____	12. to enjoy	_____
3. celebrated	_____	13. the bell tower	_____
4. the flag	_____	14. above all	_____
5. graceful	_____	15. marvelous	_____
6. the bridge	_____	16. on foot	_____
7. the fashion	_____	17. the lobby	_____
8. unfortunately	_____	18. to travel	_____
9. the mountain	_____	19. the motor boat	_____
10. the baggage	_____	20. as soon as possible	_____

GRAMMAR

A. Supply the required forms of the verbs given in parentheses:

Present indicative: 1. (*piacere*) Noi gli _____. 2. (*salire*) I prezzi _____. 3. (*dispiacere*) Io non gli _____. 4. (*supporre*) Essi _____ che noi siamo là.

Past descriptive: 5. (*porre*) Dove _____ egli l'ombrello?
Past absolute: 6. (*chiudere*) Chi _____ il baule? 7. (*cadere*) Io
_____ dal letto. 8. (*leggere*) Laura _____ ad alta voce.
9. (*piacere*) Quel romanzo mi _____. 10. (*correre*) I nostri cavalli _____ bene. 11. (*scrivere*) Essi ci _____ una lettera.
12. (*nascere*) Il Boccaccio _____ nel 1313. 13. (*proporre*) Chi
_____ ciò?
Future: 14. (*vivere*) Essi _____ nel Belgio. 15. (*potere*) Voi
_____ accompagnarla.

B. Supply the Italian for the words in parentheses:

1. È la cosa più utile (*that there is*) _____. 2. Volevo una camera
(*that had*) _____ un buon armadio. 3. Ecco il giovanotto (*of whom
he spoke*) _____. 4. Io sono il solo (*who knows her*) _____.

C. Translate into Italian:

1. I liked his dog. _____   3. He will like her. _____
2. She was sorry. _____   4. Do you like those neckties? _____

D. Supply the required forms of the verbs given in parentheses:

Present subjunctive: 1. (*porre*) Voglio che tu _____ i fazzoletti
nel cassettone. 2. (*piacere*) Non so se questo gli _____.
Present perfect subjunctive: 3. (*chiudere*) È stato bene che Clara _____
le finestre. 4. (*aprire*) Credete ch'io li _____? 5. (*proporre*) È
stata la cosa peggiore ch'essi _____. 6. (*vivere*) Spero ch'essi
_____ felici. 7. (*scrivere*) Immagino che voi _____ a casa.
8. (*correre*) Benchè ella _____, non è giunta in tempo.
Past subjunctive: 9. (*posporre*) Vi piacerebbe ch'essi _____ la
festa?
Conditional: 10. (*dovere*) Io _____ ringraziarlo.

E. Supply the Italian for the words in parentheses:

1. Finii (*before*) _____ tu arrivassi. 2. Sua madre (*lets her go*)
_____ a teatro. 3. M'affretterò (*although*) _____ sia
stanco. 4. Per favore, (*have the coffee served*) _____. 5. La
festa (*takes place*) _____ il 27 settembre. 6. (*I shall make him
remember*) _____ le sue parole. 7. (*What's the price of*) _____
questa macchina fotografica?

F. *With special attention to the conjunctive personal pronouns, give two Italian translations of the words in parentheses:*

La cosa è importante e Riccardo   1. _____
(*must speak of it to him*).   2. _____

Queste parole sono difficili, e (*I*   1. _____
don't know how to pronounce   2. _____
them).

(Deduct 1 point for each mistake.)

G. *Translate into Italian:*

1. If he had this book, he would   1. _____
study.
2. If you had been in this city,   2. _____
you would have met him.
3. He would be happy if he could   3. _____
stay here.

(This part counts 6 points.)

READING

Translate the Italian passage that your instructor will write on the board or hand to you on a mimeographed sheet.

(This part counts 20 points.)

DICTATION

Your instructor will dictate twice a short Italian passage.

(This part counts 10 points.)

PERFECT SCORE: 100

Parte Settima

IN ITALIA
Roma, Napoli e La Sicilia

❧ Lezione Trentottesima ❧

I. NOTE GRAMMATICALI

161.   **Use of the Infinitive**

1. Il viaggiare è istruttivo.   *Traveling is instructive.*
   Preferisco il cavalcare.   *I prefer horseback riding.*
   Questo è vero soffrire.   *This is real suffering.*

An infinitive may be used as a verbal noun (subject, direct object, or predicate noun), in place of the English present participle (gerund).

When used as a subject or direct object it normally takes the masculine definite article.

2. Dal dire al fare, c'è di mezzo   *Between saying and doing lies the*
      il mare.   *depth of the sea.*
      S'è rovinata la salute per il   *He spoiled his health because of his*
      troppo fumare.   *smoking too much.*
      Fra il giocare a carte e il gio-   *Between playing cards and playing*
      care a scacchi, preferisco   *chess, I prefer the latter.*
      quest'ultimo.

But: Mi salutò prima d'uscire.   *He greeted me before going out.*
      Parlò senza esitare.   *He spoke without hesitating.*

The infinitive is used in Italian after a preposition where the English requires the present participle.[1] In this case also the masculine definite article usually precedes the infinitive, except when the infinitive follows **di**, *of;* **invece di**, *instead of;* **prima di**, *before;* **dopo** or **dopo di**, *after* [2]; **senza**, *without.*

3. Girare a sinistra.   *Turn to the left.*
   Agitare prima d'usare.   *Shake before using.*
   Aggiungere la cioccolata.   *Add the chocolate.*
   Tradurre in italiano.   *Translate into Italian.*

---

[1] But see § **108**, p. 169, for the Italian equivalent of the English present participle preceded by the prepositions *by, in, on, through,* or *while.*   [2] **Dopo** (or **dopo di**) takes the perfect infinitive: **dopo aver letto la lettera,** *after reading the letter.*

The infinitive is used exclusively in writing (in public signs, labels, recipes, textbooks, etc.) with the force of an imperative and the meaning of an impersonal command.

162.   **Certain Uses of the Numerals**

1.   Leone Decimo, *Leo the Tenth*

Benedetto Sedicesimo ⎫
Benedetto Decimo Sesto ⎬ *Benedict XVI*

Canto ventiduesimo ⎫
Canto ventesimo secondo ⎬ *Canto XXII*

Capitolo settimo, *Chapter seven*

Ordinal numerals are used, without the article, after names of rulers and the words **canto, capitolo, volume, lezione,** etc.

Note from the examples given that, from 11th on, the following forms are used also: 11th, **decimo primo;** 12th, **decimo secondo;** 85th, **ottantesimo quinto,** etc.

2.   il secolo quinto, *the fifth century*

il secolo quattordicesimo ⎫
il secolo decimo quarto ⎬ *the fourteenth century*
il Trecento ⎭

The number of a century is expressed by ordinals. Beginning, however, with the thirteenth century, it is more customary to use the following expressions:

il Duecento, *the 13th century*   il Seicento, *the 17th century*
il Trecento, *the 14th century*   il Settecento, *the 18th century*
il Quattrocento, *the 15th century*   l'Ottocento, *the 19th century*
il Cinquecento, *the 16th century*   il Novecento, *the 20th century*

Note that in this case also the forms **decimo primo, decimo secondo,** etc., may be used.

163. Study the complete conjugations of **condurre,**[1] **mettere,**[2] **togliere,**[3] **udire,** and **vedere**[4] (*Appendix III*).

[1] *To conduct, lead.*   [2] The verbs **permettere, promettere,** and **scommettere,** which we have already studied, are conjugated like **mettere.**
[3] *To take, take away, take off, carry off.*   [4] **Rivedere** is conjugated like **vedere.**

II. LETTURA

Nella Città Eterna

Un programma molto vario era stato preparato dalla signorina
Fontana pei giorni che la comitiva doveva passare a Roma. La
mattina andavano a visitare i più famosi monumenti della città
antica, o le chiese, i musei e le altre cose interessanti della Roma
dei Papi; il pomeriggio era riservato alla città moderna, alle sue 5
passeggiate, ai suoi parchi, ai suoi incantevoli dintorni; e la sera,
quando non s'era troppo stanchi, la signorina conduceva gli studenti a un teatro o a un ballo.

Fra il ballare e il nuotare sarebbe stato difficile dire quale fosse
lo svago preferito, e a Roma non mancava nè l'una cosa nè l'altra. 10
Si ballava spesso all'albergo in cui erano alloggiati, e s'andava
spesso alla bella spiaggia del Lido di Roma, a poche miglia di
distanza dalla città.

Un'ottima guida fu impegnata per condurre la comitiva ogni
mattina.   Egli conosceva molto bene la storia e i costumi della 15
sua città nativa, e l'udirlo parlare di tante cose interessanti era
un piacere per gli studenti.

Visitarono il Foro che, al tempo in cui la Città Eterna dominava
il mondo, era il centro della vita romana.

Dopo aver visto tutto quel che restava degli antichi edifizi, 20
andarono ad ammirare il magnifico Arco di Costantino e l'imponente Colosseo, simbolo della grandezza di Roma.

La guida parlò del martirio dei primi cristiani in quell'anfiteatro
e descrisse vividamente i grandi spettacoli che, per divertire il
popolo, in quel luogo si facevano.   25

— Com'è che parte dell'edifizio non c'è più ? — domandò Luisa.

Allora la guida spiegò che, durante il Medio Evo e il Rinascimento, i papi avevan permesso che si togliessero pietre dal Colosseo per costruire chiese e palazzi in Roma, e che a quest'abuso
non era stato posto fine che verso la metà del Settecento per ordine 30
di Papa Benedetto Decimo Quarto.

Un altro giorno la guida condusse la comitiva a visitare il Campidoglio e il suo famoso museo dedicato all'arte romana antica, e
spiegò che adesso il Campidoglio è la sede del municipio di Roma.

Durante la settimana andaron pure a vedere il Pantheon, antico tempio romano e ora chiesa cristiana, in cui sono la tomba del divino pittore Raffaello a quelle di Vittorio Emanuele II e d'Umberto I, primi re dell'Italia moderna. E passarono una serata
5 deliziosa alle Terme di Caracalla, dove udirono all'aperto, sotto un cielo pieno di stelle, l'opera *Mefistofele* del Boito.

Siccome faceva molto caldo — s'era alla fine del mese di luglio — e l'andare in giro nelle prime ore del pomeriggio non era piacevole, i membri della comitiva, nei giorni che stettero a Roma,
10 seguirono l'uso romano di schiacciare un sonnellino dalle tredici alle quindici.

PROVERBIO

Paese che vai, usanza che trovi.   *When in Rome, do as the Romans do*

III. STUDIO DI PAROLE

Benedetto Benedict
Campidoglio Capitol
Colosseo Colosseum
Costantino Constantine
Emanuele Emmanuel
Mefistofele Mephistopheles
Umberto Humbert

abuso abuse
anfiteatro amphitheater
arco arch
ballo ball, dance
costume *m.* custom
dintorni *m. pl.* surroundings
foro forum
grandezza greatness
martirio martyrdom
papa *m.* pope

pietra stone
simbolo symbol
spettacolo show
tempio temple
terme *f. pl.* thermae, thermal baths

cristiano Christian
eterno eternal

costruire [**costruisco**] to build
dedicare [**dedico**] to dedicate
descrivere to describe [1]
dominare [**domino**] to rule
impegnare to engage, hire
schiacciare [**schiaccio**] **un sonnellino** to take a nap

vividamente vividly

IV. CONVERSAZIONE

1. Che cosa era stato preparato dalla signorina Fontana?
2. Dove andavano gli studenti la mattina? 3. A che cosa era

---

[1] Conjugated like **scrivere.**

riservato il pomeriggio? 4. Che cosa si faceva la sera? 5. Qual
era lo svago preferito degli studenti? 6. Dove andavano a ballare?
7. Dove andavano a nuotare? 8. Chi conduceva la comitiva nelle
ore della mattina? 9. Che cos'era il Foro nei tempi antichi?
10. Dopo aver visto il Foro, dove andarono gli studenti? 11. Di
che cosa parlò la guida, nel Colosseo? 12. Che cosa descrisse vividamente? 13. Che cosa domandò Luisa? 14. Che cosa avevano permesso i papi? 15. Quand'era stato posto fine a quest'a-
buso? 16. Che cosa fece la guida un altro giorno? 17. A che
cosa è dedicato il Museo del Campidoglio? 18. Che cosa è adesso
il Campidoglio? 19. Che cos'è il Pantheon? 20. Dove passarono una deliziosa serata gli studenti? 21. Che uso seguirono a
Roma i membri della comitiva? 22. Perchè seguirono quest'uso?

V. ESERCIZI

A. Tradurre in italiano:

1. Studying was a pleasure for her. 2. I prefer reading to writing.
3. Telephoning is useless now. 4. By listening to him, you will learn
many things. 5. He departed without having spoken to us. 6. I do
not like staying alone. 7. It is studying that he does not like. 8. Instead of working, he was amusing himself. 9. She began by (**con**)
recognizing that she had been wrong. 10. He became rich by working hard (**molto**). 11. We like to take a nap after lunch. 12. We
shouldn't want to see the Eternal City without hiring a guide.

B. 1. Tradurre in italiano:

1. Paul III. 2. Francis IV. 3. James VI. 4. Victor Emmanuel II.
5. Benedict XV. 6. John XXII. 7. Charles VIII. 8. Charles XII.

2. Tradurre in italiano in due modi differenti:

1. The nineteenth century. 2. The fourteenth century. 3. The sixteenth century. 4. The twentieth century. 5. The fifteenth century.
6. The seventeenth century

C. 1. Coniugare nel presente dell'indicativo:

    1. Togliere qualche cosa.   2. Non udire chiaramente.

2. Coniugare nel passato assoluto:

    1. Condurre dei forestieri.   3. Togliere le tazze.
    2. Mettere tutto in ordine.   4. Vedere dei pescatori.

3. Completare con la forma richiesta del verbo in parentesi:

Passato assoluto e presente perfetto: 1. (*togliere*) Io ____ l'uccello dalla gabbia. 2. (*condurre*) Egli ci ____ all'anfiteatro. 3. (*mettere*) Essi ____ i mobili in una delle stanze. 4. (*vedere*) Lei non ci ____. 5. (*condurre*) Voi le ____ al giardino zoologico. 6. (*togliersi*) Egli ____ la giacca. 7. (*promettere*) Stefano ____ di studiare. 8. (*vedere*) Io ____ vostro marito. 9. (*scommettere*) Lei ____ cinquanta dollari. 10. (*condurre*) Voi li ____ troppo di buon'ora. 11. (*togliere*) Noi le ____ da quella scuola. 12. (*promettere*) Chi vi ____ di pagarvi?

Presente del congiuntivo: 1. (*condurre*) Vuole ch'io vi ____ a udire quell'opera. 2. (*udire*) Non è possibile ch'essi vi ____. 3. (*togliere*) Desidero ch'ella ____ queste carte. 4. (*udire*) Speriamo che nessuno ci ____. 5. (*condurre*) È meglio che voi le ____ a un buon ristorante. 6. (*togliere*) Occorre ch'io ____ la pellicola dalla macchina fotografica. 7. (*condurre*) Non sta bene ch'essi ti ____ in quel luogo. 8. (*udire*) Vuole ch'io ____ quella musica.

Condizionale: 1. (*vedere*) Essi ____ volentieri quello spettacolo. 2. (*udire*) Se non parlasse ad alta voce, nessuno l'____. 3. (*condurre*) Dove lo ____ voi? 4. (*vedere*) Tu non mi ____ mai più. 5. (*udire*) Io l'____ con piacere.

D. Tradurre in italiano:

I

1. Before starting our tour of Rome Miss Fontana wanted [1] us to assemble in the lobby of our hotel. 2. She introduced our guide to us, and then explained the program of the day. 3. "This morning," she said, "you will see the Forum and the Colosseum." 4. "We shall spend the afternoon at the Lido, and this evening we shall hear the opera *Mephistopheles* by [2] Boito." 5. "Where?" asked one of us girls. — "In the open, at the Thermae of Caracalla." 6. The guide conducted us well, and he told us interesting things about ancient Roman life. 7. After [3] seeing the Forum, we admired the Arch of Constantine, and then went to (a) see the near-by Colosseum. 8. Our guide knows [4] many things, but he doesn't hear well and we had to [5] speak loud in order to be understood. 9. He told us that during the fifteenth, sixteenth, and seventeenth centuries, many churches and [6] palaces of the Eternal City were built [7] with stones taken from the Colosseum.

---

[1] Past absolute.   [2] Attention!   [3] See footnote 2, p. 289.   [4] Use the verb **sapere**.   [5] Use the past absolute of **bisognare**.   [6] Repeat *many*.   [7] A passive past absolute.

10. In the eighteenth century Pope [1] Benedict XIV [2] put [an] end to this abuse.

II

1. The following morning the guide conducted us again to (a) see ancient [3] Rome. 2. I have a funny thing to (da) tell you: he doesn't hear well and talks loud to us as if *we* didn't hear [4] well. 3. But we like him because he is very kind and conducts us better than we dared to hope. 4. As [5] it was hot [on] that day, I took off my [6] coat to be (stare) more comfortable. 5. In the Capitol's museum the party saw many statues of the time in which the Eternal City ruled the world. 6. After [7] seeing the museum we learned [8] from the guide that the present [9] Capitol Square [10] was laid out [11] by Michelangelo in the first half of the sixteenth century. 7. "Provided you aren't tired," he said afterward, "we shall now see the Pantheon." 8. We didn't want [12] to return to the hotel without visiting that magnificent temple dedicated to all the gods. 9. In it we saw the tombs of Victor Emmanuel II [2] and Humbert I, first kings of Italy. 10. Victor Emmanuel II led [13] the Italians in the nineteenth century toward the unification of their fatherland.

❧ *Lezione Trentanovesima* ☙

I. NOTE GRAMMATICALI

164. **Demonstrative Pronouns**

1. Mi piacciono questi.   *I like these.*
   Questo cavallo è migliore di   *This horse is better than that one.*
   quello.

Demonstrative adjectives (see § 74, p. 111) are used also as pronouns. **Questo** often renders *this one;* **quello,** *the one, that one.*

---

[1] Do not use the article before this title.   [2] Write out the number.   [3] Place the adjective after the noun.   [4] Contrary-to-fact.   [5] = *since.*   [6] See § 116, p. 181.   [7] See footnote 2, p. 289.   [8] Use the verb **apprendere.**   [9] Leave the adjective before the noun.   [10] Translate, *Square of the Capitol.*   [11] Use the verb **disegnare.**   [12] Past descriptive.   [13] Use the verb **condurre.**

2. Ciò basta.   *This* (or *that*) *is enough.*
  Parleremo di ciò.   *We shall speak of this* (or *that*).

The pronoun **ciò** is often used instead of **questo** or **quello**.

3. Questi merita lode.   *This man deserves praise.*
  Il consiglio di costui è cattivo.   *This fellow's advice is bad.*

There are certain forms of demonstrative pronouns that are used exclusively with reference to persons. They are shown in the following table:

SINGULAR			PLURAL
Masc.		*Fem.*	*Masc. and Fem.*
questi / **costui** } this man		**costei** this woman	**costoro** { these men / these women
quegli / **colui** } that man		**colei** that woman	**coloro** { those men / those women

Questi and **quegli** are used only as subject pronouns. **Costui, costei,** and **costoro** generally convey an idea of disrespect.

4. Mazzini e Garibaldi nacquero in Liguria; questi a Nizza, e quegli a Genova.   *Mazzini and Garibaldi were born in Liguria; the former in Genoa, and the latter in Nice.*

  Anna e Luisa suonano bene; questa il violino, e quella il pianoforte.   *Ann and Louise play well; the former the piano, and the latter the violin.*

The English *former* and *latter* are rendered as follows: by **quegli** and **questi** (or **colui** and **costui**) respectively when referring to men; by **quella** and **questa** (or **colei** and **costei**) when referring to women; otherwise by **quello** and **questo,** which are inflected according to the meaning.

Note carefully that there is an inversion in translating from one language to the other, and that the idiom, as given in the examples above, is literally *the latter . . . the former.*

165. The Subjunctive in Independent Clauses

  Che Dio v'aiuti!   *May God help you!*
  Il Signore ti benedica!   *May the Lord bless you!*

Piovesse!	*Would that it might rain!*
Viva la libertà!	*Long live Liberty!*
Che sii maledetto!	*Be cursed!*

The subjunctive, preceded or not preceded by **che,** is used to express an omen, a wish, or an imprecation.

For other uses of the subjunctive in an independent clause (command in the **Lei** or **Loro** forms, indirect commands to a third person or persons), see § 42, 1, p. 60.

166. Study the complete conjugations of **chiedere, giungere, parere,**[1] **prendere,** and **venire** (*Appendix III*).

II. LETTURA

Roma dei Papi e Roma moderna

Appena erano giunti a Roma, i giovanotti e le signorine della comitiva avevano chiesto d'esser condotti a veder la Basilica di San Pietro. Come s'è visto però, essi passarono la prima mattinata visitando i maggiori monumenti dell'epoca romana, e la visita a San Pietro fu posposta al giorno dopo. 5

Una volta, per giungere al centro del mondo cattolico, bisognava attraversare un vecchio quartiere dalle vie strette e misere; ora non è più così, e i tassì che gli studenti presero passarono per uno dei più bei corsi della Roma moderna.

Chi potrebbe descrivere la meraviglia d'ognuno quando si 10 giunse sull'immensa piazza circondata dal superbo colonnato del Bernini, e si vide il gran tempio sormontato dalla cupola di Michelangelo? Nessuno degli studenti aveva immaginato tanta bellezza.

Parecchie ore furono passate nel visitare la basilica, e poi il 15 Vaticano con la sua Cappella Sistina, le Logge di Raffaello, il Museo e la Biblioteca, e fu una visita rapidissima perchè, a voler vedere tutto bene, anche parecchie giornate sarebbero parse poche. Eppure si trovò il tempo di salire, per mezzo d'un ascensore, in

---

[1] **Chiedere** means *to ask;* **giungere,** *to arrive;* **parere,** *to seem.* The last two are conjugated with **essere.** Use these three verbs from now on instead of **domandare, arrivare,** and **sembrare.**

cima alla cupola, dalla quale si gode una vista indimenticabile di
Roma e della campagna romana.

Numerose altre chiese furon visitate nei giorni seguenti, fra cui
quella di San Pietro in Vincoli,[1] dove s'ammira il *Mosè*, una delle
5 più caratteristiche statue di Michelangelo.

Le altre basiliche di Roma piacquero a gli studenti non meno
di quella di San Pietro, specialmente Santa Maria Maggiore [1] e
San Paolo; questa, situata fuori le mura; quella, al centro della
città.

10 L'ultima delle basiliche che videro fu quella di San Giovanni in
Laterano che, per la sua antichissima origine, è chiamata Chiesa
Madre; e siccome v'andarono di domenica, ebbero pure l'occa-
sione di sentirvi una messa.

Dirimpetto a quel famoso tempio c'è la Scala Santa, e da un
15 lato c'è il Palazzo Laterano in cui, nel 1929, fu firmato un trattato
fra la Chiesa e lo Stato Italiano, che creava, sotto la sovranità
del Papa, uno stato piccolissimo ma del tutto indipendente, chiamato Città del Vaticano.

Durante uno dei pomeriggi, la comitiva andò a visitare le Cata-
20 combe, cimiteri sotterranei dei primi cristiani.

— Tutti gli Americani che vengono a Roma, — disse la guida,
— vogliono vederle, e vi ci condurrò anch'io.

Tra le cose della Roma moderna, quelle che fecero la più pro-
fonda impressione sugli studenti furono il grandioso Monumento
25 a Vittorio Emanuele, tutto di marmo bianco; il Palazzo di Giustizia, lungo le rive del Tevere; le nuove vie, larghe e ricche
d'eleganti negozi, e — parrà strano — il nuovo centro degli sport,
costruito recentemente fuori città.

Roma è famosa per la bellezza delle sue fontane. In quella di
30 Trevi ciascuno degli studenti buttò un soldo perchè chi fa così,
dicono, è certo di rivedere la Città Eterna.

— Volesse il Cielo! — disse più d'uno, sorridendo.

PROVERBIO

Volere è potere.   *Where there is a will there is a way.*

[1] Do not translate.

III. STUDIO DI PAROLE

Cappella Sistina Sistine Chapel
Laterano Lateran
Mosè Moses
Piɛtro Peter
Vaticano Vatican

ascensore *m.* elevator, lift
catacomba catacomb
colonnato colonnade
cupola dome
ɛpoca epoch, time
giustizia justice
loggia loggia
occasione *f.* occasion, opportunity
origine *f.* origin
soldo penny
sovranità sovereignty
trattato treaty

cattolico Catholic
cɛrto certain, sure
grandioso grand, grandiose
indimenticabile unforgettable
indipendɛnte independent
profondo deep, profound
sotterraneo underground

buttare to throw, cast
circondare to surround
creare [crɛo] to create
firmare to sign
sormontare to surmount

da un lato on one side
del tutto entirely
per mɛzzo di by means of
recentemente recently

IV. CONVERSAZIONE

1. Che cosa avevano fatto gli studɛnti appena ɛrano giunti a
Roma? 2. Ɛrano andati subito a veder la Basilica di San Piɛtro?
3. Come si giungeva, una volta, in Piazza San Piɛtro? 4. Per
dove passarono i tassì che gli studɛnti presero? 5. Da che cosa
è circondata Piazza San Piɛtro? 6. Da che cosa è sormontata la
basilica? 7. Dove andarono gli studɛnti dopo aver visto la basilica? 8. Perchè fu una visita rapidissima? 9. Dove salirono
poi? 10. Che cosa s'ammira nella chiɛsa di San Piɛtro in Vincoli? 11. Quali altre basiliche piacquero specialmente alla comitiva? 12. Dove sono situate? 13. Perchè la Basilica di San
Giovanni in Laterano è chiamata Chiɛsa Madre? 14. Che cosa
c'è dirimpɛtto a quella basilica? 15. Che cosa creò il trattato
che fu firmato nel Palazzo Laterano? 16. Che cosa sono le Cata-
combe? 17. Quali cose della Roma modɛrna fecero la più pro-
fonda impressione sugli studɛnti? 18. Dov'è situato il Palazzo
di Giustizia? 19. Come sono le nuove vie di Roma? 20. Dov'è
il nuovo cɛntro degli sport? 21. Che cosa fecero gli studɛnti

quando andarono a vedere la Fontana di Trevi? 22. Perchè lo fecero?

V. ESERCIZI

A. Sostituire alle parole stampate in corsivo (*printed in italics*) un corretto pronome dimostrativo:

1. *Questa barca* è peggiore. 2. *Pietro* è un mio amico. 3. *Quest'uomo* non mi piace. 4. Le parole di *Giovanni e di Franco* furono ascoltate da ognuno. 5. Preferivo *questi scrittori*. 6. Non parlare con *questa donna*. 7. *Questo giovanotto* è mio cugino. 8. *Anna* desidera di venire con noi. 9. Non voglio che *Costantino* stia con te; la sua compagnia non è buona. 10. Ho parlato con *Raffaello*.

B. Tradurre in italiano:

1. Let them believe it! 2. May God help them! 3. Frank and Mark are my friends; the former is a lawyer [1] and the latter is a dentist. 4. Long live the Pope! 5. Let him tell it to us! 6. Lucy and Louise are in our party; the former is a blonde and the latter is a brunette. 7. Long live my friend Paul! 8. Let him put them there! 9. Emmanuel and Charles are two bad boys; the former does not want to study, and the latter always says ugly words. 10. Let them go out! 11. Let him hear my words! 12. The cow and the hen are useful animals; from the former we get [2] milk [3]; from the latter we get eggs.[3] 13. Let her come! 14. Let them postpone it!

C. 1. Coniugare nel presente dell'indicativo:

    1. Parere fortunato.   2. Venire in fretta.

2. Coniugare nel passato assoluto:

    1. Chiedere un favore.   3. Parere scontento.
    2. Giungere di buon'ora.   4. Venire volentieri.

3. Completare con la forma richiesta [4] del verbo in parentesi:

Passato assoluto e presente perfetto: 1. (*prendere*) Tu _____ la mia penna stilografica. 2. (*venire*) I forestieri non _____ con quel treno. 3. (*giungere*) Lei _____ in carrozza. 4. (*chiedere*) Io non _____ il suo nome. 5. (*parere*) Mario ——— assai felice. 6. (*prendere*) Ella _____ delle melanzane. 7. (*venire*) Io _____ senza far complimenti. 8. (*giungere*) Essi _____ a bordo del piroscafo. 9. (*chiedere*) Chi _____ di me? 10. (*pa-*

---

[1] Use the idiom with **fare.**   [2] Use the verb **avere.**   [3] Use the definite article.   [4] **Richiesto** is the past participle of **richiedere,** *to require,* conjugated like **chiedere.**

rere) Margherita ed Elena ____ stanche. 11. (*giungere*) Io non ____ in tempo. 12. (*parere*) Lo spettacolo ____ interessante.

Futuro e condizionale: 1. (*venire*) Pietro quando ____? 2. (*parere*) Le tue parole ____ molto strane. 3. (*venire*) I contadini non ____ a lavorare. 4. (*parere*) Noi ____ vanitosi. 5. (*venire*) Tu perchè non ____ a quel ballo? 6. (*parere*) Io ____ più ricco di quel che sono.

Presente del congiuntivo: 1. (*venire*) Non dirò niente questa volta purchè esse ____. 2. (*parere*) Volete ch'egli ____ peggiore che non sia? 3. (*venire*) Quel pittore è il solo amico che ____ di tanto in tanto. 4. (*parere*) Mettiamoli così affinchè non ____ pochi. 5. (*venire*) Sarà meglio ch'io ____ solo. 6. (*parere*) Credete che quel prezzo gli ____ troppo alto?

D. Tradurre in italiano:

I

1. When they arrived in Rome the students asked which[1] of the basilicas were the most important. 2. "Those of St. Peter's and St. John's in Lateran," answered Miss Fontana. "The former is the grandest temple that the Christians have ever built; the latter is the Mother Church of the Catholic world." 3. And yet,[2] that of St. Paul's seemed[3] to me much more beautiful. 4. It is very ancient too, having been founded by Constantine in the fourth century. 5. Buildings[4] of a very ancient time are so plentiful[5] here that those of the seventeenth and eighteenth centuries would seem modern to you.[6] 6. Before taking the elevator to go to the top of St. Peter's dome, I asked our guide[7] whether it would carry[8] us all the way.[9] 7. "[I wish it] were so[10]!" he said. "No, my dear lady, you will have to climb many stairs." 8. When we arrived there, I enjoyed an unforgettable view. 9. Beneath there was the huge square surrounded by Bernini's colonnade; on one side, the Vatican; on the other, a high hill surmounted by Garibaldi's[11] statue. 10. We had seen that statue the day before, and it had seemed to us much finer than the one of Victor Emmanuel.

II

1. Yesterday we went to (a) visit Humbert I Park. Won't it seem strange to you[6] if I tell you that that afternoon was[12] the best [one]

---

[1] Interrogative. An indirect question. [2] See Vocabulary. [3] Past absolute. [4] In general. [5] Same as *so many*. [6] Use the **tu** form. [7] An indirect object. [8] See § 143, 4, p. 243. [9] *All the way* is, in this case, **fin su**. [10] Place *it were* after so. [11] Use no article before this family name. [12] Use the present perfect.

I spent in Rome? 2. The reason is that I like animals, and in that park there is a fine zoological garden. 3. Lions, tigers, leopards, and wolves were not in cages, but outdoors, and at first sight they seemed to me [to be] free. 4. Not far from (di) there, there is the Borghese Museum, which Miss Fontana had us visit. 5. When our party arrived there, we found a guide who was talking [1] so loud that we couldn't [2] hear what we were saying. 6. "Bless his heart [3]!" said Olga. "This fellow [4] ought [5] to be in (a) Coney Island, not here!" And we [6] burst out laughing. 7. We admired many masterpieces, and especially the paintings by Guido Reni and Bernini's statues. 8. Both Reni and Bernini lived [7] in the seventeenth century, but the former was only [8] a painter, while the latter was great in several arts. 9. Today we saw the Lateran Palace in which a treaty [9] was signed that created an entirely independent state for the Church. 10. Although Rome is so rich in (di) ancient buildings, it is a very modern city, as all those who come to (a) visit it can see.

❧ *Lezione Quarantesima* ❧

I. NOTE GRAMMATICALI

167. **Idiomatic Present**

Aspetto da due ore. ⎫
Sono due ore che aspetto. ⎭   *I have been waiting two hours.*

Vivo in Italia da un anno. ⎰ *I have been living in Italy one year*
È un anno che vivo in Italia. ⎱ (and I am still there, *hence,* the present tense).

But: Siamo stati in Italia un anno. ⎰ *We were in Italy one year* (and we are not there now, *hence,* the present perfect).

To express an act or a state that continues from the past into the present, the present tense is used in Italian, while in English the present perfect is used.

---

[1] Use the progressive construction.   [2] Past descriptive.   [3] Translate, *God bless him!* and use the verb **benedire,** *to bless,* which is conjugated like **dire.**   [4] That expression shows dislike.   [5] Use the verb **dovere.**   [6] Do not omit this pronoun.   [7] Past absolute.   [8] Translate *only* with **solamente.**   [9] Place *a treaty* after *signed.*

FAÇADE OF THE HOUSE WITH THE WOODEN WALL, HERCULANEUM

THE BIG THERMAE OF THE HADRIAN VILLA, TIVOLI

PORTRAIT OF A LADY (GIULIA DI GONZAGA-COLONNA?) *By Titian*

DANTE MONUMENT, TRENTO

168.   **Absolute Construction**

Finito il lavoro, partirono.	*Having finished their work, they left.*
Rimasta sola, cominciò a scrivere.	*Having remained alone, she began to write.*
Visti quei quadri, egli volle comprarli.	*Having seen those paintings, he wanted to buy them.*

Very frequently a past participle is used alone, in Italian, in place of a perfect participle. If the verb is transitive, the participle agrees in gender and number with its object; otherwise, with its subject. This is called *absolute construction*.

169. Study the complete conjugations of **bere, offrire, rimanere,**[1] **scegliere,**[2] and **tenere**[3] (*Appendix III*).

II. LETTURA

A Napoli

Il sole era vicino al tramonto quando la comitiva giunse a Napoli.

Alla stazione c'erano ad aspettare alcuni parenti della signorina Fontana, ai quali ella aveva scritto giorni prima dando l'ora del loro arrivo.   5

La signorina era appena scesa dal treno che una sua nipotina, la piccola Amalia, corse a lei gridando « zia Rosetta, zia Rosetta! » e l'abbracciò e baciò. Un momento dopo anche gli altri, la mamma, il fratello Peppino a la cognata Cunegonda, facevano lo stesso.

Fatte le presentazioni e scambiate alcune parole, Peppino Fontana volle occuparsi dei bagagli della comitiva e chiese a sua sorella dove doveva farli portare dai facchini.   10

— L'albergo che ho scelto, — gli rispose lei, — è il Santa Lucia[4]; fuori ci dev'essere l'autobus ad aspettarci.

— Quanto tempo rimarrete a Napoli?   15

— Tutta una settimana, tra Napoli e dintorni.

— Odi, Rosetta, — le disse la mamma prendendola per un brac-

---

[1] *To remain;* conjugated with essere. Use it from now on instead of **restare.**   [2] *To choose, select.*   [3] *To hold, have, keep, take.*   [4] Notice that **Santa Lucia,** being in this case the name of a hotel, is considered masculine.

cio, — ora noi andiamo a casa in tassì, ma ci rivedremo fra poco perchè stasera terremo una piccola festa [1] per te e per la comitiva. Abbiamo invitato i Fiorentino,[2] i Del Giudice, i Lombardi e i Narni perchè godano anch'essi della tua compagnia e facciano 5 la conoscenza degli studenti americani.

— Oh, brava!

— Di' a tutti che, se non son troppo stanchi, li aspettiamo. Ma venite appena avrete finito di pranzare. Faremo un po' di musica, si ballerà, e berremo un bicchiere d'Asti spumante [3] per 10 festeggiar questa data. Son tre anni che non ti vedo, figlia mia!

La signorina ne parlò subito ai membri della comitiva, ed essi accettarono con espressioni di gioia l'invito così gentilmente offerto.

L'Albergo Santa Lucia è situato in uno dei più incantevoli posti 15 di Napoli, davanti al mare, e dalle sue finestre gli studenti potettero vedere buona parte del golfo, dal maestoso Vesuvio al Capo di Posillipo, dove già cominciavano ad apparire le prime luci della sera.

— È laggiù che la mia famiglia abita da molti anni, — disse la 20 signorina.

— Vicino al mare?

— Sì. S'esce dal giardino, e a pochi passi c'è il mare.

Inutile dirlo, gli studenti, finito il pranzo, presero subito dei tassì e, in meno d'una mezz'ora, giunsero a Posillipo.

25 Fu una serata assai piacevole. Si suonò, si ballò, si gustarono i rinfreschi, e s'andò pure a far due passi in giardino per godere l'affascinante vista del golfo sotto i raggi della luna.

La mattina dopo la comitiva fu guidata dalla signora Lombardi, una zia della signorina Fontana che s'era gentilmente offerta a 30 far ciò perchè la nipote potesse rimanere a casa con la sua mamma.

Visitarono il Museo di San Martino e il Museo Nazionale; questo, il più importante d'Europa nel campo dell'arte greco-romana; quello, artisticamente meno importante, ma dai cui balconi si gode una vista meravigliosa che tenne affascinati tutti gli 35 studenti.

---

[1] *party.*   [2] Note again that family names remain unchanged in the plural.
[3] Do not translate; it is the name of a famous Italian sparkling wine.

Fra le cose più interessanti viste negli altri giorni furono il Duomo, le chiese del Gesù e di San Lorenzo Maggiore, il superbo Castello Angioino, la Galleria, il Teatro di San Carlo e l'Università. Andarono pure in un negozio di gioielleria a comprare dei ricordi, e scelsero anelli, spille e collane di coralli che il gioielliere, 5 lontano parente della signora Lombardi, offerse loro a buon mercato.

PROVERBIO

Vedi Napoli e poi muori.   *See Naples and die.*

III. STUDIO DI PAROLE

Amalia Amelia	passo step; **fare due passi** to take a little stroll
Gesù Jesus	
Napoli *f.* Naples	raggio ray
Peppino Joe	rinfresco refreshment
Vesuvio Mt. Vesuvius	spilla pin
anello ring	angioino Angevin
balcone *m.* balcony	maestoso majestic
capo head, cape	nazionale national
collana necklace	
conoscenza acquaintance	affascinare [affascino] to fascinate
corallo coral	
espressione *f.* expression	apparire [apparisco *or* appaio] to appear [1]
gioia joy	
gioielleria jewelry	fare un po' di musica to play (*or* have) a little music
gioielliere *m.* jeweler	
golfo gulf, bay	scambiare [scambio] to exchange
luce *f.* light	
	laggiù down there

IV. CONVERSAZIONE

1. Chi c'era alla stazione di Napoli all'arrivo della comitiva? 2. Che cosa fece la piccola Amalia quando vide sua zia? 3. Quali altri parenti erano venuti alla stazione? 4. Che cosa volle fare Peppino Fontana? 5. Che cosa disse a sua sorella? 6. Che gli rispose lei? 7. Quanto tempo sarebbe rimasta a Napoli la co-

---

[1] Conjugated with essere.

mitiva? 8. Che cosa disse la mamma della signorina Fontana? 9. Perchè aveva ella invitato parenti e amici? 10. Che cosa potettero vedere gli studenti dalle finestre del loro albergo? 11. Dove abitava la famiglia Fontana? 12. Quando vi andò la comitiva? 13. Che cosa fecero gli studenti alla piccola festa? 14. Chi era la signora Lombardi? 15. Perchè s'era essa offerta a guidare gli studenti? 16. Che cosa andarono a vedere prima di tutto? 17. Perchè è famoso il Museo Nazionale di Napoli? 18. Perchè è famoso il Museo di San Martino? 19. Quali altre cose interessanti videro gli studenti in quei giorni? 20. In che negozio andarono? 21. Che cosa scelsero? 22. Chi era il gioielliere?

V. ESERCIZI

A. Tradurre in italiano:

1. I have been playing cards for one hour; now I am not playing so well. 2. I met him in New York, and he told me that he spent two years in France. 3. We have been studying Italian for almost a year. 4. It has been raining for the past three days. 5. He has been here for the past five months. 6. They have been talking more than one hour. 7. I have been away (**lontano**) from home six months, but I shall soon return there. 8. Laura has been playing the piano for the past two hours. 9. I have been working here for many years. 10. We have been walking one hour.

B. Sostituire in ciascuna delle seguenti frasi la costruzione assoluta al participio perfetto:

1. Essendo andato in campagna, volli divertirmi. 2. Avendo comprato i romanzi, desiderai di leggerli. 3. Avendo cominciato quelle cose, dovei finirle. 4. Avendo preso la medicina, andò a coricarsi. 5. Avendo condotto i forestieri all'albergo, li presentai al proprietario. 6. Essendo giunte in quel negozio, esse incontrarono il loro avvocato. 7. Avendo incontrato la sarta, le parlai di voi. 8. Avendo visto la tua amica, le dissi che tu eri qui.

C. 1. Coniugare nel presente dell'indicativo, e poi nel passato assoluto e nel presente perfetto:

1. Bere una tazza di latte.	3. Scegliere dei romanzi.
2. Rimanere al buio.	4. Tenere l'ombrello.

2. Coniugare nel futuro:

1. Bere dell'ottimo vino.   3. Tenere il cappello.
2. Rimanere in Europa.   4. Rimanere solo solo.

3. Completare con la forma richiesta del verbo in parentesi:

Passato assoluto e presente perfetto: 1. (*bere*) Io ____ alla vostra salute.
2. (*offrire*) Essi ____ delle rose. 3. (*rimanere*) Umberto e Marco ____
in sala da fumare. 4. (*scegliere*) Io ____ una collana di coralli. 5. (*tenere*) Ella ____ la sua parola. 6. (*bere*) Lucia ____ un bicchiere d'acqua.
7. (*offrire*) Io glieli ____. 8. (*rimanere*) Francesco ____ scontento.
9. (*scegliere*) Chi ____ quei garofani? 10. (*tenere*) Gli amici ____ una
cena.
Futuro e condizionale: 1. (*tenere*) Noi ____ un appuntamento. 2. (*rimanere*) Lei non ____ contento. 3. (*bere*) Voi ____ quel caffè. 4. (*tenere*) Chi li ____? 5. (*rimanere*) Tu ____ senza amici. 6. (*bere*) Giacomo ____ la medicina.
Presente del congiuntivo: 1. (*bere*) T'ho invitato affinchè tu ____ con
me un bicchiere d'Asti spumante. 2. (*rimanere*) Spero che quei suoi
parenti ____ negli Stati Uniti. 3. (*scegliere*) Vuole che tu stesso ____.
4. (*tenere*) Glieli darò purchè li ____ cari. 5. (*bere*) Sarà molto meglio
ch'essi ____ latte invece di vino. 6. (*rimanere*) Non faremo nulla a
meno che tu non ____ qui. 7. (*scegliere*) Glieli mostro affinchè Lei
____ quello che vuole. 8. (*tenere*) Non vuole ch'io ____ il cane in casa.

D. Tradurre in italiano:

I

1. Having arrived in Naples, the students met Miss Fontana's relatives. 2. "God be thanked!" said Mrs. Fontana embracing her
daughter. "I am so happy that you [1] have returned!" 3. "I ran to
(a) kiss you before the others, Aunt Rosie!" said her little niece,
Amelia. 4. Joe took his sister by (**per**) the arm and started to (**a**)
walk behind the porters. 5. They were carrying the baggage to the
autobus of the hotel chosen by Miss Fontana. 6. "How do you like
Naples?" asked the latter of (**a**) her brother. — "We have been here
two years," he answered, "and we like it more than I can tell you."
7. That evening the Fontanas gave (*tr.* held) a little party [2] and offered
refreshments to the students. 8. They had a little music, drank some

_____

[1] Don't forget that close relatives address one another with **tu.**   [2] Not
comitiva, of course; if you don't remember the right word, see Vocabulary.

Asti spumante, and Paul gave a toast [1] to the health of all.   9. They remained there until midnight, and danced too, because a cousin (*m.*) of Mrs. Fontana offered [2] to (a) play the piano for them.   10. Having taken a little stroll in the garden to see the distant [3] lights of the city and to admire the beautiful sky full of stars, they returned to their hotel.

II

1. Having visited the National Museum, Lucy asked me which [4] painting I thought was the best among the many we had seen.   2. I chose one [5] by Salvator Rosa, [a] very celebrated painter of the seventeenth century.   3. I bet you [6] would have chosen the same [one], for I know [7] your taste.   4. We have been in Naples almost a week, and I can tell you what [8] my impressions are.   5. The streets, churches, and monuments of this city are less beautiful than many that I have seen in other Italian cities.   6. Nothing in (a) the world, however, is so charming as its bay.   7. I have been [9] fascinated by its various aspects, by the sights I have enjoyed from Posillipo, from the balconies of the museum of San Martino, and from Mt. Vesuvius.   8. Nature is so beautiful here, and life is easy and comfortable; the food and the wines are delicious.   Do you know [7] a wine called Capri Bianco? I drank it yesterday.   9. Today we went shopping in a jewelry store [10] in which they were selling necklaces, pins, and rings with corals.   10. The jeweler offered them to us cheap, and I chose a ring and said: "I'll take this one, although it is the most expensive."

❧ *Lezione Quarantunesima* ❧

I. NOTE GRAMMATICALI

170.   **Verbal Adjectives**

1.   la lezione seguente   *the following lesson*
        una macchina parlante   *a talking machine*
        gl'insegnanti   *the teachers*

[1] See Vocabulary.   [2] Translate, *offered himself* and use the irregular past absolute.   [3] Leave the adjective before the noun.   [4] An indirect question. [5] Translate, *one of them.*   [6] Use the **voi** form.   [7] Use the verb **conoscere.** [8] Use **quale** and place *my impressions* at the end of the sentence.   [9] Translate the verb *to be,* in this case, with **rimanere.**   [10] *a store of jewelry.*

When in English the present participle is used as an adjective, it is rendered in Italian, not by the form that we have called the participle, but by a verbal adjective, which can be formed from almost any Italian verb by adding to the verbal stem the endings –ante for the first conjugation, and –ɛnte for the other two. Like all other adjectives, the verbal adjectives are inflected and may be used as nouns.

2.   un uccello che canta   *a singing bird*

Another way of rendering the English present participle used as an adjective is that of changing the participle into a relative clause. With many verbs this form is preferable.

171. Use of the Prepositions before the Infinitive

The infinitive may depend upon a noun, an adjective, or a verb.

1.   sala da fumare   *smoking room*
        acqua da bere   *drinking water*
        il bisogno di studiare   *the need of studying*

If the infinitive depends upon a noun, the preposition **da** is used whenever purpose is implied; in all other cases **di** is generally used.

2. (*a*) Sono contɛnto di rivederlo.   *I am glad to see him again.*
          È pesante a portare.   *It is heavy to carry.*

An infinitive depending upon an adjective is usually preceded by **di** or **a**; very seldom by **da**.

   (*b*) È inutile dire.   *It's useless to say.*

With adjectives like **utile, inutile, facile, difficile, possibile, impossibile, importante, giusto,** etc., no preposition is used.

3. (*a*) Desidero d'uscire.   *I wish to go out.*
          Offrì di pagare.   *He offered to pay.*

Most Italian verbs take **di** before the following infinitive.

   (*b*) Andò a comprare un paio   *He went to buy a pair of gloves.*
             di guanti.
          Stetti ad aspettare.   *I stood waiting.*
          Imparò a ballare.   *He learned to dance.*

An infinitive depending upon a verb of motion or rest, or upon a verb meaning the beginning, progress, or continuance of an action, or upon the verbs **imparare** and **insegnare,** *to teach,*[1] is regularly preceded by the preposition **a.**

(c) Devo lavorare.   *I must work.*
     So nuotare.   *I know how to swim.*

A certain number of verbs, very frequently used, take the infinitive without any preposition. The most important of them are:

ardire[2]	fare	potere	sentire
bastare	lasciare	preferire	udire
bisognare	osare	sapere	vedere
dovere	parere	sembrare	volere

172. Study the complete conjugations of **dirigere,**[3] **morire,**[4] **seppellire,**[5] **sorgere,**[6] and **tendere**[7] (*Appendix III*).

II. LETTURA

Nei dintorni di Napoli

— Quanti luoghi interessanti ci sarebbero da vedere nei dintorni di Napoli, se ce ne fosse il tempo! — disse a gli studenti la signora Lombardi mentre s'attendevano le automobili che dovevano portarli a Pompei.

5 — Quali? — chiese più d'uno.

— Pesto, per esempio, dove potreste ammirare il Tempio di Nettuno e altri ruderi dell'antichissima civiltà greca; Benevento, famosa per il suo Arco di Traiano, uno dei più belli e meglio conservati dell'epoca romana; Caserta, il cui Palazzo Reale, col suo

10 gran parco e con le sue fontane, ricorda la vita elegante del Settecento.

— Peccato che il nostro tempo sia così limitato! — disse Olga.

— Ma verremo un'altra volta in Italia, — aggiunse Guido, — e allora vedremo tutto senza fretta.

---

[1] Learn this verb.   [2] *to dare.*   [3] *To direct.*   [4] *To die;* conjugated with **essere.**   [5] *To bury.*   [6] *To arise;* conjugated with **essere.**   [7] *To tend, stretch out.*   Many verbs are conjugated like **tendere;** learn the following: **attendere,** *to wait, wait for;* **intendere,** *to intend, hear, understand;* **pretendere,** *to pretend.*

Poco dopo già partivano.

Gli studenti sapevano che un'eruzione del Vesuvio, nell'anno 79, aveva sepolto sotto una pioggia di ceneri Pompei e altre città vicine. Giunti là, una guida che parlava inglese con l'accento di Brooklyn (egli aveva vissuto alcuni anni in America) condusse la 5 comitiva per le strette vie della città morta. Visitarono prima il piccolo Museo degli Scavi, e lì la guida spiegò che gli oggetti più importanti trovati a Pompei son conservati nel Museo Nazionale di Napoli; poi videro il Foro, i due teatri, delle terme e alcune case, fra le quali quella dei Vettii che dette loro un'idea della vita 10 intima dei Romani.

Da Pompei le automobili si diressero verso Amalfi.

Chi non ha visto la strada d'Amalfi non può immaginarne l'incanto. Essa segue la costa meridionale della penisoletta di Sorrento e ha da un lato alti monti, dall'altro precipizi profondi che 15 scendono su un mare d'un azzurro meraviglioso. A ogni momento vi son viste nuove fra gli olivi e gli aranci di cui è ricca quella regione, e che aggiungono colore e bellezza a ciò che si vede.

Ad Amalfi gli studenti alloggiarono all'Albergo Santa Caterina. Vi giunsero in tempo per la colazione, che fu fatta su una veranda 20 dalla quale si godeva la vista di tutto il golfo di Salerno.

In quel pomeriggio la signora Lombardi condusse la comitiva alla vicina Ravello, sui monti, e fu un'escursione incantevole.

Se Amalfi è bella, non meno bella è Sorrento, dall'altro lato della penisola. Gli studenti v'andarono il giorno dopo col sole 25 nascente, e che giornata deliziosa fu quella per loro! Fra le altre cose, all'albergo in cui andarono ad alloggiare ci fu una piccola festa quella sera, e un gruppo d'artisti, vestiti in costumi del luogo, cantò delle canzoni napoletane e ballò la tarantella.[1]

A Capri, alla deliziosa isoletta che attira tanti turisti da tutto 30 il mondo, fu dedicato il terzo giorno. Vi giunsero col vaporetto che fa il giro del golfo, e andarono prima di tutto a visitare la Grotta Azzurra, in cui entrarono in piccole barche. Fecero colazione in uno dei migliori alberghi, e poi passarono il pomeriggio girando qua e là e comprando dei ricordi.   35

Ritornarono a Napoli di sera, mentre annottava. La luna piena

[1] A lively Neapolitan dance.

sorgeva da dietro al fumante Vesuvio, e le luci della metropoli si riflettevano nel mare.

PROVERBIO

Non lodar il bel giorno innanzi sera.   *Praise a fair day at night.*

III. STUDIO DI PAROLE

Nettuno Neptune
Pesto *f.* Paestum
Pompei *f.* Pompeii
Traiano Trajan

accento accent
canzone *f.* song
cenere *f.* ash
civiltà civilization
eruzione *f.* eruption
grotta grotto
gruppo group
oggetto object
olivo olive tree
penisola peninsula

pioggia rain
precipizio precipice
ruderi *m. pl.* ruins
scavo excavation
vaporetto small steamboat
veranda veranda

intimo intimate, familiar
meridionale southern
napoletano Neapolitan
reale royal, real

aggiungere to add [1]
limitare [**limito**] to limit
riflettere to reflect

IV. CONVERSAZIONE

1. Che cosa disse la signora Lombardi? 2. Che cosa attendevano gli studenti? 3. Che cosa si può ammirare a Pesto? 4. Per che cosa è famosa Benevento? 5. Che cosa ricorda il Palazzo Reale di Caserta? 6. Che cosa disse Olga? 7. Che aggiunse Guido? 8. Che cosa aveva fatto, nell'anno 79, un'eruzione del Vesuvio? 9. Chi condusse la comitiva quando si giunse a Pompei? 10. Perchè la guida parlava con l'accento di Brooklyn? 11. Che cosa disse la guida quando visitarono il Museo degli Scavi? 12. Che altro videro gli studenti a Pompei? 13. La strada d'Amalfi quale costa segue? 14. Che cosa si vede dalla strada d'Amalfi? 15. Dove fu fatta la colazione? 16. Che cosa fecero gli studenti nel pomeriggio? 17. Dove andò la comitiva il giorno seguente? 18. Dov'è situata Sorrento? 19. Che cosa ci fu quella

---

[1] Conjugated like **giungere.**

sera all'albergo in cui alloggiavano? 20. Che cos'è Capri?
21. Come vi giunse la comitiva? 22. Come s'entra nella Grotta
Azzurra? 23. Che cosa fecero gli studenti in quel pomeriggio?
24. Che cosa videro dal vaporetto, ritornando a Napoli quella
sera?

V. ESERCIZI

A. Tradurre in italiano rendendo il participio presente inglese
prima con l'aggettivo verbale e poi con una proposizione relativa:

1. The preceding[1] conversation. 2. The following sentences. 3. The
departing men. 4. The dying day. 5. Her smiling lips. 6. Some
amusing comedies. 7. The sparkling sun. 8. A pleasing maid. 9. The
falling leaves. 10. Fascinating music.

B. Quindici delle seguenti frasi richiedono una preposizione davanti all'infinito; sceglierle e completarle:

1. Non bisogna ____ occuparsi di ciò. 2. Impariamo ____ conservarci
calmi. 3. Anna mostrava ____ intendere. 4. Scrivetegli ____ affrettarsi. 5. Desideriamo ____ non far complimenti. 6. Domani non
potrebbero ____ imbarcarsi. 7. La sento ____ cantare. 8. Adesso
vado ____ fare una passeggiata. 9. Egli non vuole ____ giocare a
scacchi. 10. Cominciava ____ piovere. 11. Staremo ____ osservarli.
12. Ella m'insegnò ____ ballare. 13. Io non osai ____ dirglielo.
14. Essi hanno dimenticato ____ ringraziarci. 15. M'affrettai ____
contentarlo. 16. Speravo ____ stringerle la mano. 17. Prometto ____
venir di buon'ora. 18. Vi preghiamo ____ scriverci spesso. 19. Ba-
stava ____ farmelo sapere. 20. Propose ____ fare un viaggio. 21. Continuo ____ imparare. 22. Lo lasciai ____ parlare.

C. 1. Coniugare nel presente dell'indicativo, e poi nel futuro:

    1. Morire in esilio.   2. Morire di sete.

2. Coniugare nel passato assoluto e poi nel presente perfetto:

    1. Dirigere dei turisti.   4. Attendere il suo arrivo.
    2. Intendere ogni cosa.   5. Sorgere subito.
    3. Seppellire un tesoro.   6. Pretendere molto.

3. Completare con la forma richiesta del verbo in parentesi:
Passato assoluto e presente perfetto: 1. (*attendere*) Egli non m'____.
2. (*morire*) Quell'uomo ____ povero. 3. (*sorgere*) Il sole ____ alle

_____
[1] *To precede* is **precedere**.

cinque. 4. (*dirigersi*) Noi ____ verso casa. 5. (*pretɛndere*) Essi ____ trɔppe cɔse. 6. (*seppellire*) Carlo ____ il cane nel giardino. 7. (*dirigere*) Lɛi ____ bɛne quel lavoro. 8. (*intɛndere*) Io non ____ quella frase.

Presɛnte del congiuntivo: 1. (*morire*) È un peccato ch'ella ____ senza riveder suo figlio. 2. (*morire*) Vuɔi ch'essi ____ di freddo?

D. Tradurre in italiano:

I

1. We saw[1] the most enchanting surroundings of Naples in a tour that lasted three days. 2. First we went to see Pompeii, the dead city through whose streets a young guide directed us. 3. Already we knew that Pompeii had been buried under a rain of ashes in an eruption from (**di**) Mt. Vesuvius. 4. From what I saw and what I heard[2] from the guide, I had[3] a good idea of the family[4] life of the ancient Romans. 5. "I am dying[5] of thirst," said Lucy when, having visited[6] the excavations, she went[7] with the others toward our cars. 6. Fortunately, we found excellent drinking water in a near-by restaurant where we ordered some[8] coffee. 7. Afterward we went to Amalfi, a small town on the bay of Salerno, famous for its medieval history and for its beautiful cathedral. 8. The winding[9] road that leads there is one of the most wonderful I ever saw.[10] 9. It passes between mountains and precipices along the sea that is of an enchanting blue. 10. "And now," said Mrs. Lombardi with smiling eyes, when we finally arrived, "now we shall have lunch on a veranda from which we shall see the whole bay of Salerno."

II

1. I had heard[2] [people] say that near Amalfi there are interesting places to[11] see. 2. That afternoon we went up to Ravello, a delightful small town on the mountains. 3. Sorrento, where we went the following morning, is on the other side of the peninsula. 4. If Mrs. Lombardi had not told me,[12] I should not have known that the very celebrated poet Tasso was born in that city. 5. That evening we

---

[1] Use the past absolute as the basic tense in these sentences.   [2] Use the verb **intɛndere**.   [3] Past absolute.   [4] Same as *familiar*.   [5] Do not use the progressive construction.   [6] Use the absolute construction (§ **168**, p. 303).   [7] Use the verb **dirigersi**.   [8] Use the partitive construction.   [9] *To wind* is, in this meaning, **serpeggiare**.   [10] Attention!   [11] Purpose is implied.   [12] Translate, *said it to me.*

heard [1] some lovely Neapolitan songs in the garden of our hotel. 6. There were ten or twelve singers [2]; they were dressed in costumes, and afterward danced the tarantella.   7. A young man spoke to me; I understood [3] that he wanted to know how long I had been [4] in Italy. 8. "I have been here a little over [5] two months," I answered him,[6] "and I like Italy [7] more than I can tell you."   9. We had a good time in (a) Capri also, where we went [on] the third day, and we shall never forget the charm of the Blue Grotto.   10. While we were returning [8] to Naples on the small steamboat, the full moon rose from behind smoking [9] Mt. Vesuvius.

❧ *Lezione Quarantaduesima* ❧

I. NOTE GRAMMATICALI

173.   **Special Use of the Auxiliary Verbs**

1.	Avrei potuto, ma non ho voluto.	*I could have, but I didn't want to.*

The verbs **dovere, potere,** and **volere,** when used alone, are conjugated with **avere.**

2.	Ho dovuto studiare.	*I have been obliged to study.*
	Essa ha potuto mangiare.	*She was able to eat.*
	Avevamo voluto cantare.	*We had wanted to sing.*
But:	Son dovuto andar via.	*I have been obliged to go away.*
	Essa è potuta venire.	*She was able to come.*
	Eravamo voluti uscire.	*We had wanted to go out.*
	I ragazzi si son voluti divertire.	*The boys wanted to have a good time.*

When used with a dependent infinitive (which is most often the case), **dovere, potere,** and **volere** take **avere** or **essere,** accord-

---

[1] Use the verb **sentire.**   [2] Form a verbal noun from **cantare.**   [3] Use the verb **intendere.**   [4] Translate, *from how much time I was.*   [5] *Over* is, in this case, **più di.**   [6] An indirect object.   [7] Place *Italy* right after *and.*   [8] Translate *while* with **mentre** and use the progressive construction.   [9] Leave this adjective before the noun.

ing to which of the two auxiliaries the dependent infinitive requires.[1]

174. Compound Nouns and Adjectives

1.

SINGULAR	PLURAL
il lavamano, *the lavatory*	i lavamani
il capolavoro, *the masterpiece*	i capolavori
il gentiluomo, *the gentleman*	i gentiluomini
But: il capostazione, *the station master*	i capistazione
il capomastro, *the foreman*	i capimastri
il lustrascarpe, *the bootblack*	i lustrascarpe

Most compound nouns form their plural as though they were simple nouns.

Some of them, however, are inflected in the first member, others are inflected in both members, while a certain number of them have the same forms for the singular and the plural. The student is advised, in case of doubt, to consult a good dictionary.

2.

la guerra franco-tedesca	*the Franco-German war*
i giornali *i*talo-americani	*the Italo-American newspapers*

Compound adjectives, usually united by a hyphen, are inflected only in the second member.

175. Augmentatives and Diminutives

1. The meaning of an Italian noun, adjective, or adverb may be modified by a suffix. Usually the noun thus modified keeps its gender, but occasionally a suffix of masculine ending, added to a feminine noun, makes it masculine. In adding a suffix, the final vowel of the word must be dropped, and if the final vowel is preceded by **c** or **g**, the original sound of these letters must be kept. **Stanza + –ino = stanzina** or **stanzino, barca + –etta = barchetta, semplice + –one = semplicione.**

---

[1] This rule is often disregarded, and **avere** is used as the auxiliary no matter what the dependent infinitive is, particularly when **dovere, potere,** and **volere** are emphasized. It is frequently said, for instance, **ho dovuto andar via,** instead of **son dovuto andar via** (*4th example*); **i ragazzi hanno voluto divertirsi,** instead of **i ragazzi si son voluti divertire** (*last example*).

2. un amico, un amicone   *a friend, a great friend*
    una dɔnna, un donnone   *a woman, an enormous woman*
    una bottiglia, un bottiglione   *a bottle, a big bottle*
    una ragazza, una ragazzona   *a girl, a big girl*

The suffix denoting bigness is **–one**. It is masculine, but it has a feminine form, **–ona**, which is used only with nouns or adjectives having both a masculine and a feminine form (see last example). In other cases, that is, when no confusion might occur, a feminine noun takes the ending **–one** and becomes masculine.

3. una dɔnna, una donnetta   *a woman, a little woman*
    la campana, il campanello   *the bell, the little bell*
    la commedia, la commediola   *the play, the little play*
    Maria, Marietta   *Mary, little Mary*
    una casa, una casina   *a house, a pretty little house*
    bɛllo, bellino   *beautiful, pretty*
    caro, carino   *dear, darling*
    bɛne, benino   *well, rather well*
    Maria, Mariuccia   *Mary, dear little Mary*
    una dɔnna, una donnuccia   *a woman, a silly little woman*
    una contadina, una contadi-   *a peasant woman, a sturdy peasant*
      nɔtta   *girl*

The most important suffixes denoting smallness are:
–etto, –a; –ɛllo, –a; –ɔlo, –a, implying mere smallness;
–ino, –a, denoting smallness and endearment;
–uccio, –a, expressing affection if modifying a proper noun;
    pity or contempt if attached to a common noun;
–ɔtto, –a, denoting smallness combined with strength.

4. tɛmpo, tempaccio   *weather, nasty weather*
    parɔla, parolaccia   *word, nasty word*
    poeta, poetastro   *poet, poetaster*

The suffixes **–accio, –a** and **–astro, –a** convey an idea of contempt.

5. fratɛllo, *brother*   scalino, *step* (of a stair)
    sorɛlla, *sister*   signorina, *miss*
    libretto, *libretto*   loggione, *upper gallery*

Quite often the augmentative and diminutive endings lose their independent character and become inseparable parts of certain words.

6. These endings must be chosen according to precedent and euphony. The ear is a sufficient guide in this matter to a native Italian only; the student is, therefore, advised to use great discretion and to avoid employing forms he has not already met.

176. Study the complete conjugations of **dividere, muovere, perdere, piangere,**[1] and **spendere** [2] (*Appendix III*).

II. LETTURA

In Sicilia

La partenza da Napoli fu triste. I parenti della signorina Fontana erano venuti ad accompagnarla alla nave che doveva portare la comitiva a Palermo, e fra loro c'era qualcuno che piangeva.

Forse era ciò, forse era l'ora tarda della notte, fors'anche era
5 il rimpianto di dover partire da Napoli, dove s'eran tanto divertiti: il fatto è che anche gli studenti avevan perso la loro solita allegria.

A mezzanotte finalmente la nave si mosse, e ognuno si ritirò nella sua cabina per andare a dormire.

Quando, la mattina dopo, gli studenti salirono su coperta, s'era
10 già nel porto di Palermo, e il sole che splendeva sulla bella città, e il grandioso panorama che s'offriva alla vista, fecero allietare ogni cuore.

— Come si chiama quel monte che sembra la rocca di Gibilterra? — chiese Margherita alla signorina Fontana.
15 — Si chiama Monte Pellegrino.

— Bello!

Ma già i camerieri portavan su i bagagli, ed era tempo di sbarcare.

C'erano sei giorni da passare in Sicilia, e furono divisi così:
20 un giorno per vedere Palermo, tre giorni per fare un lungo giro che includeva Catania, Taormina e Agrigento, il quinto giorno riservato per una gita a Monreale, e l'ultimo giorno libero fino alle

---

[1] *To weep, cry.*   [2] *To spend.*

diciassette, ora dell'imbarco sul piroscafo *Vespucci* che doveva riportare la comitiva in America.

A tutti piacque la Sicilia, l'incantevole isola alla quale Natura
ha prodigato tante bellezze e che la storia di tre mila anni ha fatto
il crogiolo di tutte le razze e civiltà del Mediterraneo. Piacque 5
specialmente Taormina, che è senza dubbio il posto più affascinante di tutti. Situata presso il mare, appiè dell'Etna, — il maestoso vulcano la cui cima è coperta di neve buona parte dell'anno,
— essa è al centro d'una fertilissima regione che è tutta un giardino di vigne, palme, olivi, aranci e limoni.   10

Chi, andando in Sicilia, può fare a meno di visitare Monreale?
Se la sua cattedrale è una delle più belle che l'arte normanna ci
abbia lasciate, non meno attraente è la vista che di lì si gode,   .
non solo di Palermo e del mare, ma di tutta quella vasta e ricca
pianura chiamata Conca d'Oro, centro della coltivazione degli 15
aranci.

Giunse finalmente l'ultimo giorno, e ognuno volle spendere quel
po' di danaro italiano che ancora aveva, nel comprar dei ricordi
di Palermo.

Il magnifico viaggio che gli studenti avevan fatto per tutta 20
l'Italia era finito; ora si partiva per New York.

— Arrivederci, Italia!

Sul *Vespucci* tutti erano allegri, meno forse alcuni Italo-Ameri-
cani che lasciavano parenti in Sicilia. Fra i membri della nostra
comitiva non c'era nessuno che non pensasse di rivedere un giorno 25
il dolce paese del sole, dell'arte e dei canti.

PROVERBIO

La fine corona l'opera.   *The end crowns the work.*

III. STUDIO DI PAROLE

l'Etna *m.* Mt. Etna

allegria cheerfulness
canto song
cattedrale *f.* cathedral
coltivazione *f.* cultivation

conca shell
crogiolo melting pot
danaro money
dubbio doubt
fatto fact
gita trip

limone *m.* lemon, lemon tree
palma palm, palm tree
panorama *m.* panorama
pellegrino pilgrim
pianura plain
razza race
rimpianto regret
rɔcca rock
vigna vineyard
vulcano volcano

qualcuno somebody, someone

attraɛnte attractive

fɛrtile fertile
normanno Norman
tardo late
triste sad
vasto vast

allietare [alliɛto] to rejoice
fare a meno di to do without
includere to include
prodigare [prɔdigo] to lavish
riportare [ripɔrto] to bring back
sbarcare to land [1]

prɛsso near, by

IV. CONVERSAZIONE

1. Come fu la partenza da Napoli? 2. Perchè fu triste? 3. A che ora la nave finalmente si mɔsse? 4. Dove andarono allora gli studɛnti? 5. Che cɔsa allietò ogni cuɔre la mattina dopo? 6. Che cɔsa chiɛse Margherita alla signorina Fontana? 7. Che le rispose la signorina? 8. Che cɔsa facevano già i camerieri? 9. Quanti giorni c'erano da passare in Sicilia? 10. Dove avrɛbbero passato il primo giorno gli studɛnti? 11. Quali città avrɛbbero visitate nel secondo, tɛrzo e quarto giorno? 12. A che cɔsa ɛra riservato il quinto giorno? 13. Che cɔs'ɛra il *Vespucci?* 14. Che cɔsa ha dato la Natura alla Sicilia? 15. Che cɔsa ha fatto della Sicilia la stɔria? 16. Dov'è situata Taormina? 17. Che cɔsa è l'Ɛtna? 18. Quali coltivazioni ci sono nella regione in cui è Taormina? 19. Di che cɔsa non si può fare a meno, andando in Sicilia? 20. Perchè è famosa la cattedrale di Monreale? 21. Quale meravigliosa vista si gɔde da Monreale? 22. Che cɔsa fecero i mɛmbri della comitiva prima d'imbarcarsi sul pirɔscafo *Vespucci?* 23. Chi non ɛra allegro fra i passeggiɛri del *Vespucci?* 24. Che cɔsa pensavano i nɔstri studɛnti nel partire?

[1] Conjugated with ɛssere when used intransitively.

V. ESERCIZI

A. Dare la prima persona plurale del presente perfetto di:

1. Dover comprare dei guanti.   2. Poter giungere in tempo.   3. Voler ritornare.   4. Dover lavorare.   5. Poter lavarsi.   6. Voler fare una passeggiata.   7. Dover alzarsi di buon'ora.   8. Poter uscire.   9. Voler partire.   10. Dover dormire.

B. Tradurre in italiano usando in ogni caso uno dei suffissi studiati in questa lezione:

1. A bad book.   2. A poor little house.   3. A little train.   4. That awful boy.   5. A poor little theater.   6. A pretty little theater.   7. Dear little Helen.   8. A nasty novel.   9. Some little rooms.   10. A little dinner.   11. Rather good.   12. Extremely well.   13. Some little stores.   14. A great lord.   15. A bad lawyer.   16. A huge palace.   17. Little Ann.   18. A little garden.   19. Dear little Richard.   20. A big boy.

C. 1. Coniugare nel passato assoluto e poi nel presente perfetto:

1. Muovere dei mobili.	4. Dividere il lavoro.
2. Spendere molto danaro.	5. Non piangere mai.
3. Non perdere niente.	6. Muoversi da casa.

2. Completare col passato assoluto, e poi col presente perfetto del verbo in parentesi:

1. (*muoversi*) I ragazzi non ____.   2. (*piangere*) Io ____ vedendolo partire.   3. (*spendere*) Clara ____ poco.   4. (*muovere*) I facchini ____ i mobili.   5. (*dividere*) La nonna ____ la torta.   6. (*perdere*) Chi ____ una penna stilografica?   7. (*piangere*) Lucia ____ dalla gioia.   8. (*spendere*) Noi ____ quel che potevamo.   9. (*muoversi*) Il piroscafo ____. 10. (*dividere*) Lei non ____ bene il suo tempo.   11. (*perdere*) Essi ____ i loro migliori amici.   12. (*piangere*) Tu non ____ allora.   13. (*spendere*) Gli studenti non ____ quel danaro.   14. (*perdere*) Io li ____ con dispiacere.   15. (*muoversi*) Io ____ in fretta.

D. Tradurre in italiano:

I

1. Sicily was [1] the only [2] large Italian island that our party visited. 2. It was [1] a pity [3] that it wasn't possible to see the others too.   3. Yesterday we saw the most interesting things in Palermo, and took a

---

[1] Present perfect.   [2] See § 147, 1, p. 254.   [3] An expression of sorrow.

ride along the sea. 4. In the afternoon we visited some shops, and I spent my last Italian money buying some beautiful little things.[1] 5. We are now in Taormina, for Miss Fontana has divided our time so well as (da) to allow us to see several towns of the island. 6. Guido is not with us now; he wanted [2] to remain in Palermo in order to spend a day or two [3] with some relatives of his. 7. The finest [4] panorama that I admired in Italy, after that of the bay of Naples, is the one [5] I saw a moment ago. 8. Mt. Etna was before us, Taormina's ancient Greek theater on one side, and the blue [6] sea on the other. 9. How fertile this land is [7]! We saw vineyards and palms, and also many olive, orange, and lemon trees. 10. Tomorrow we shall visit Catania, Bellini's native city.

II

1. This morning we had to get up early in order to go to Monreale. 2. Monreale is a small town, but it has one of the finest cathedrals in the world, a masterpiece of Norman art. 3. What I have enjoyed above all in Monreale, however, is the panorama of the Golden Shell, that vast plain in which the Sicilian metropolis is located. 4. After our return to Palermo, several students went shopping. 5. I spent my last Italian money, and so did the others. 6. Finally, toward sunset,[8] we started [9] from our hotel and embarked on the liner *Vespucci*. 7. Now we are sailing toward America, and everybody in (di) the party is happy. 8. Many passengers among the Italo-Americans on board wept [2] when the ship moved.[2] 9. I am happy to know that I shall be with my family again a week from now.[10] 10. But I love Italy, I am leaving it with regret, and I hope to return there soon.

[1] Use a diminutive.   [2] Present perfect.   [3] Same as *a couple of days*.   [4] See § 147, 1, p. 254.   [5] See § 164, 1, p. 295.   [6] Leave the adjective before the noun.   [7] Place the verb after *how*.   [8] Use the definite article.   [9] Present perfect of **muoversi**.   [10] Same as *within a week*.

❧ Seventh Review Lesson ❧

I. VOCABULARY DRILL

A. *Give the Italian for the following nouns:*

1. The arch
   the ash
   the stone
   the temple
   the object
   the eruption
   the palm tree

2. The dome
   the song
   the race
   the treaty
   the justice
   the elevator
   the surroundings

3. The pope
   the ray
   the light
   the dance
   the jewelry
   the peninsula
   the expression

4. The ring
   the pin
   the plain
   the ruins
   the necklace
   the colonnade
   the acquaintance

5. The show
   the rain
   the penny
   the doubt
   the greatness
   the vineyard
   the refreshment

6. The joy
   the bay
   the fact
   the regret
   the balcony
   the martyrdom
   the small steamboat

B. *Give the Italian for the following adjectives:*

1. Christian, southern, royal, late, attractive, eternal, certain, grand, majestic.
2. Catholic, Neapolitan, Norman, sad, vast, unforgettable, national, independent, intimate.

C. *Give the Italian for the following verbs:*

1. To hire
   to add
   to build
   to surround

2. To rule
   to throw
   to describe
   to surmount

3. To sign
   to create
   to dedicate
   to fascinate

D. *Give the Italian for the following expressions:*

1. To take a nap, entirely, down there, to take a little stroll, on one side.
2. To play a little music, near, vividly, by means of, recently.

II. NOUNS

1. Which Italian suffix implies bigness?
2. Mention a few suffixes denoting smallness.

3. What Italian suffixes convey an idea of contempt?

4. Use the suffixes just mentioned in translating:

a little house	a big boat
the bad boy	the nice little woman
a huge palace	a contemptible lawyer
a small theater	a big table
little Lucy	dear little Helen

5. How do most compound nouns form their plural?

III. ADJECTIVES

1. What must you remember in using a numeral after the name of a ruler? Give two examples.

2. Translate: *Lesson XX, Canto XXXII.*

3. Is there another way to say *eleventh* in Italian, besides **undicesimo?**

4. Count in two different ways from 18th to 24th.

5. What is the usual way to say *the fourteenth century* in Italian?

6. Translate: *the 16th century, the 13th century, the 19th century.*

7. How are compound adjectives inflected? Give an example.

IV. PRONOUNS

1. What is the meaning of **ciò** ? Give an example.

2. Give the masculine demonstrative pronouns used exclusively with reference to persons.

3. Which of them convey an idea of contempt?

4. Give the feminine demonstrative pronouns used exclusively with reference to persons.

5. Which of them convey an idea of contempt?

6. What must we remember in translating the *former ... the latter?*

7. Translate: *Here are Paul and Charles; the former is a student, the latter is an artist.*

V. VERBS

1. How do we translate into Italian an English present participle used as a noun? Translate: *Studying is a pleasure.*

2. As a general rule, how do we translate into Italian an English present participle preceded by a preposition? Translate: *Instead of working.*

3. How do we translate *in speaking* or *by speaking?*

4. With what force is the infinitive used in Italian in public signs, labels, recipes, textbooks, etc.? Give a few examples.

5. In what cases is the subjunctive used in an independent clause? Give two examples.

6. Explain the Italian idiomatic present, and give an example.

7. What can we use in place of a perfect participle?

8. What is this construction called?

9. Translate each of these sentences in two ways:

   a. Having seen the house, he wanted to buy it.
   b. Having arrived in Rome, we went to our hotel.

10. How is a verbal adjective formed? Give two examples.

11. What can we use instead of a verbal adjective? Illustrate with an example.

12. Translate in two ways: *an amusing book.*

13. What auxiliary verb shall we use with **dovere, potere,** or **volere** whenever one of these verbs is followed by an infinitive?

14. Translate:

   a. I have been obliged to stay at home.
   b. We have been able to take a good train.
   c. She has been able to return with him.

VI. IRREGULAR VERBS

1. Give the 1st and 2nd persons singular of the present indicative of:

a. bere	*b.* rimanere	*c.* togliere
condurre	scegliere	udire
morire	tenere	venire
parere		

2. Give the 1st and 2nd persons singular of the past absolute of:

a. bere	b. offrire	c. sorgere
chiedere	parere	spendere
condurre	perdere	tendere
dirigere	piangere	tenere
dividere	prendere	togliere
giungere	prendere	vedere
mettere	rimanere	venire
muovere	scegliere	

3. Give the 3rd person singular of the conditional of:

a. bere	b. parere	c. udire
condurre	rimanere	vedere
morire	tenere	venire

4. Give the present participle of:

a. bere b. condurre

5. Give the past participle of:

a. bere	b. muovere	c. scegliere
chiedere	offrire	seppellire
condurre	parere	sorgere
dirigere	perdere	spendere
dividere	piangere	tendere
giungere	prendere	togliere
mettere	rimanere	vedere
morire		venire

VII. PREPOSITIONS

1. What prepositions usually precede an infinitive depending upon an adjective?

2. Mention some adjectives that take the following infinitive without any preposition.

3. What preposition is generally used before an infinitive depending upon a verb?

4. When is the preposition **a** used before an infinitive depending upon a verb?

5. How many verbs can you mention that take no preposition before a dependent infinitive?

6. Translate:

a. I am glad to be here.
b. She dared to say so.
c. Helen knows how to dance.
d. I have learned to speak Italian.
e. Everybody wants to go away.
f. It's easy to do as he says.

LETTURA IN SILƐNZIO

Sì o nɔ?

1. __ Mi piace giocare al ballo.
2. __ Guido preferisce giocare golfo.
3. __ Palazzo Pitti è un palazzo reale.
4. __ Il tƐmpo è danaro, si dice.
5. __ Domani si farà una razza di cavalli.
6. __ Aggiungeremo a un'ora tarda.
7. __ Bisogna riflƐttere e pɔi parlare.
8. __ L'Ɛtna è utile per fare il caffè.
9. __ Dopo colazione è bƐne far due passi.
10. __ Ɛcco un anƐllo; è il campanƐllo.
11. __ New York ha ferrovie sotterranee.
12. __ Alcuni oggƐtti son sɔldi a buɔn mercato.
13. __ Tutti gli alberghi hanno ascensori.
14. __ Un balcone dà molta luce a una stanza.
15. __ La cameriera spilla l'acqua qualche vɔlta.

ACHIEVEMENT TEST NO. 7

VOCABULARY

Give the Italian for the following words:

1. the bay _____
2. the pin _____
3. to sign _____
4. a penny _____
5. down there _____
6. the group _____
7. to weep _____
8. the race _____
9. the stone _____
10. sad _____

11. Neapolitan _____
12. the elevator _____
13. on one side _____
14. to fascinate _____
15. to reflect _____
16. the regret _____
17. the money _____
18. to do without _____
19. the necklace _____
20. unforgettable _____

GRAMMAR

A. Supply the Italian for the words in parentheses:

1. Egli parlò (*without looking at him*) _____. 2. Era papa, allora, Benedetto (*the Sixteenth*) _____. 3. Il Tasso visse (*in the sixteenth century*) _____. 4. Se vuol venire, per favore (*let him come*) _____. 5. (*This man*) _____ è el signor Balbi. 6. (*Studying*) _____ è un piacere per lui. 7. (*This fellow*) _____ non è gentile. 8. (*Having seen*) _____ la mia radio, volle comprarla.

B. Supply the required forms of the verbs given in parentheses:

Present indicative: 1. La nave (*moves*) _____. 2. Quell'uomo (*doesn't hear*) _____. 3. Essi (*seem*) _____ contentissimi. 4. Gl'Inglesi (*drink*) _____ molto.
Past absolute: 5. (*Did they spend*) _____ assai? 6. Caterina (*selected*) _____ un anello. 7. Io (*took*) _____ l'ombrello. 8. Quella ragazza (*directed*) _____ i turisti da noi. 9. Essi avevano sete e (*drank*) _____ con piacere. 10. Mio zio (*remained*) _____ solo.
Future: 11. Con chi (*will you remain*) _____? 12. A che ora tuo cugino (*will come*) _____?

C. Translate in the present perfect:

1. She wanted to go away. _____
2. We were not able to come. _____
3. They had to move. _____

D. Give two different translations of the words in parentheses:

Dirò tutto (*in the following letter*). 1. _____
 2. _____
(*Having remained alone*), ella lesse il 1. _____
telegramma. 2. _____
Vedo (*a sleeping baby*). 1. _____
 2. _____

E. Supply the required forms of the verbs given in parentheses:

Present subjunctive: 1. (*rimanere*) Benchè io _____ spesso a casa, son contento. 2. (*togliere*) Non vuole ch'egli _____ nulla. 3. (*udire*) Preferisco ch'essi non ci _____. 4. (*venire*) È bene

che Luisa _____. 5. (*condurre*) Spero ch'egli le _____
qui. 6. (*parere*) Voglio ch'ella _____ felice.
Present perfect subjunctive: 7. (*dirigere*) Non so dov'egli _____ il
suo amico. 8. (*intendere*) Credete che Anna _____ ciò? 9. (*togliere*) Sebbene voi m'_____ quel piacere, non dirò niente. 10. (*dividere*) Chi potrà dire che voi l'_____ male? 11. (*muovere*)
Margherita ha pulito la stanza senza ch'io _____ i mobili.
12. (*piangere*) Non penso ch'ella _____ per questo.
Past subjunctive: 13. (*condurre*) Se voi li _____ qui, io sarei felice.
Conditional: 14. (*morire*) Senz'acqua, questi fiori _____. 15. (*venire*) Non credo ch'io _____.

(Deduct 1 point for each mistake.)

F. Translate into Italian:

1. I like Florence and Naples; the former because   _____
   of (**per**) its arts, and the latter because of its   _____
   natural beauty.   _____
2. Richard and Paul are my friends; the former   _____
   is a writer, and the latter is a lawyer.   _____

(This part counts 6 points.)

READING

*Translate the Italian passage that your instructor will write on
the board or hand to you on a mimeographed sheet.*

(This part counts 20 points.)

DICTATION

Your instructor will dictate twice a short Italian passage.

(This part counts 10 points.)

PERFECT SCORE: 100

Dialoghi Pratici
e
Lettere

Dialoghi pratici e lettere

1. SALUTI [1]

La signora Mancini e la signorina Viani

SIGNORA MANCINI. Buon giorno, signorina Viani.

SIGNORINA VIANI. Oh, buon giorno, signora Mancini! Come sta?

SIGNORA MANCINI. Bene, grazie. E Lei? E la sua famiglia?

SIGNORINA VIANI. Stanno tutti bene, grazie, * meno il nonno.

SIGNORA MANCINI. Che ha?

SIGNORINA VIANI. I soliti dolori reumatici.

SIGNORA MANCINI. Mi dispiace molto!

SIGNORINA VIANI. Anche a me. Arrivederci, signora.

SIGNORA MANCINI. Arrivederci, signorina.

2. VADO A SCUOLA

La signora Morelli e la signorina Curci

SIGNORINA CURCI. Che bella giornata, non è vero?

SIGNORA MORELLI. Bella davvero!

SIGNORINA CURCI. Dove va, signora?

SIGNORA MORELLI. Vado a fare una passeggiata nel parco e poi a visitare una mia amica. E Lei?

SIGNORINA CURCI. Vado a scuola, signora; vado all'università.*

SIGNORA MORELLI. Che cosa studia?

SIGNORINA CURCI. Un po' di tutto: inglese, storia antica, zoologia, lingua italiana . . .

SIGNORA MORELLI. Le piace l'italiano?

SIGNORINA CURCI. Immensamente, anche perchè è facile.

SIGNORA MORELLI. È una lingua facile, bella e molto utile.

---

[1] If the instructor wishes to use parts of these dialogues as memory passages he may ask the students to memorize them as far as the asterisks.

Practical Conversations and Letters

1. GREETINGS

Signora Mancini and Signorina Viani

SIGNORA MANCINI. Good morning, Miss Viani.

SIGNORINA VIANI. Oh, hello, Mrs. Mancini! How are you?

SIGNORA MANCINI. I'm well, thanks. And you? And your family?

SIGNORINA VIANI. They are all well, thank you, * except for my grandfather.

SIGNORA MANCINI. What is the matter with him?

SIGNORINA VIANI. His usual rheumatic pains.

SIGNORA MANCINI. I'm very sorry!

SIGNORINA VIANI. I am, too. I'll be seeing you, Mrs. Mancini.

SIGNORA MANCINI. Good-bye, Miss Viani.

2. I AM GOING TO SCHOOL

Signora Morelli and Signorina Curci

SIGNORINA CURCI. What a beautiful day, isn't it?

SIGNORA MORELLI. Beautiful indeed!

SIGNORINA CURCI. Where are you going, Mrs. Morelli?

SIGNORA MORELLI. I'm going to take a walk in the park, and then I am going to visit a friend of mine. And you?

SIGNORINA CURCI. I'm going to school, Mrs. Morelli. I'm going to the University.*

SIGNORA MORELLI. What are you studying?

SIGNORINA CURCI. A little of everything: English, Ancient History, Zoology, Italian.

SIGNORA MORELLI. Do you like Italian?

SIGNORINA CURCI. Immensely. Also because it's easy.

SIGNORA MORELLI. It's an easy, beautiful, and very useful language.

COLUMNS OF SAN LORENZO, MILAN

ARCH OF AUGUSTUS, RIMINI

3. VENGA A TROVARCI

La signora Nuti e il signor Marulli

SIGNORA NUTI. Venga a trovarci qualche volta, signor Marulli.
MARULLI. Volentieri, signora. Di sera?
SIGNORA NUTI. Sì. Di sera siamo quasi sempre in casa.
MARULLI. Allora verrò una di queste sere, e Le telefonerò prima.
SIGNORA NUTI. Sarà meglio; così sarà sicuro di trovarci.*
MARULLI. Non mancherò, signora.
SIGNORA NUTI. Al piacere di rivederla, allora.
MARULLI. Il piacere sarà tutto mio. Tanti saluti a suo marito.
SIGNORA NUTI. Grazie. Arrivederci!

4. UNA TELEFONATA

Il signor Marulli e l'avvocato Nuti

MARULLI. Pronto?
NUTI. Pronto.
MARULLI. Parla Marulli. Buona sera, avvocato.
NUTI. Buona sera, signor Marulli. Come sta?
MARULLI. Non c'è male, grazie. La signora Nuti e Lei stanno in
casa stasera?
NUTI. Sì. Perchè?
MARULLI. Desidero di far Loro una visita.*
NUTI. Bravo! Venga!
MARULLI. Posso condurre un mio caro amico che vorrebbe fare
la loro conoscenza?
NUTI. Certamente! Vengano subito. Li aspettiamo.
MARULLI. Arrivederci, allora!

5. PRESENTAZIONE

Il signor Marulli, il dottor Badini e l'avvocato Nuti

MARULLI. Buona sera, avvocato!
NUTI. Buona sera, signor Marulli!

3. COME TO SEE US

Signora Nuti and Signor Marulli

SIGNORA NUTI. Come to see us sometime, Mr. Marulli.

MARULLI. Gladly, Mrs. Nuti. In the evening?

SIGNORA NUTI. Yes. In the evening we are nearly always at home.

MARULLI. Then I shall come one of these evenings, and I'll telephone you beforehand.

SIGNORA NUTI. That will be better. That way you'll be sure to find us at home.*

MARULLI. I won't fail to do it, Mrs. Nuti.

SIGNORA NUTI. Then, until I have the pleasure of seeing you again.

MARULLI. The pleasure will be all mine. My best greetings to your husband.

SIGNORA NUTI. Thank you. Good-bye!

4. A TELEPHONE CALL

Signor Marulli and Lawyer Nuti

MARULLI. Hello?

NUTI. Hello.

MARULLI. Marulli speaking. Good evening, Mr. Nuti.

NUTI. Good evening, Mr. Marulli. How are you?

MARULLI. Quite well, thanks. Are Mrs. Nuti and you at home tonight?

NUTI. Yes. Why?

MARULLI. I'd like to visit you.*

NUTI. Fine! Come over!

MARULLI. May I bring along a dear friend of mine who would like to meet you?

NUTI. Certainly! Come right away. We will expect you.

MARULLI. Good-bye, then!

5. AN INTRODUCTION

Signor Marulli, Dr. Badini, and Lawyer Nuti

MARULLI. Good evening, Mr. Nuti!

NUTI. Good evening, Mr. Marulli!

MARULLI. Ho il piacere di presentarle il mio amico, dottor Badini. L'avvocato Nuti.

NUTI. Piacere di fare la sua conoscenza, dottore.

BADINI. Il piacere è mio, avvocato.*

NUTI. Si vogliono accomodare?

MARULLI. La signora Nuti non è in casa?

NUTI. Sì. Verrà fra un momento. Sta mettendo a letto la bambina.

BADINI. Hanno una bambina?

MARULLI. Un amore di bimba.

NUTI. Sì, abbiamo una bambina di tre anni.

BADINI. Come si chiama?

NUTI. Beatrice. Posso offrirle una sigaretta?

BADINI. Grazie, avvocato. Non fumo.

NUTI. E Lei, signor Marulli?

MARULLI. Io, se permette, fumerò un sigaro.

NUTI. Bene. Mi dispiace solo ch'io non abbia sigari da offrirle. Ecco dei fiammiferi e una ceneriera.

MARULLI. Grazie infinite.

6. DOV'È LA CHIESA?

Un turista e un signore

TURISTA. Scusi, signore. Posso farle una domanda?

SIGNORE. Dica pure.

TURISTA. Dov'è la chiesa di San Lorenzo?

SIGNORE. In via Palestrina, a quattro o cinque isolati da qui.

TURISTA. In questa direzione?

SIGNORE. Sì. Vada sempre diritto. Non può sbagliare.*

TURISTA. E un'altra domanda, se permette: sa a che ora c'è messa?

SIGNORE. Alle sette, alle otto, e alle nove. La domenica poi c'è messa a ogni ora della mattina.

TURISTA. E l'ultima messa della domenica a che ora è?

SIGNORE. Credo a mezzogiorno, ma non ne son sicuro. Domandi al sagrestano quando sarà là.

MARULLI. I have the pleasure of presenting my friend Dr. Badini to you. This is Mr. Nuti.

NUTI. It's a pleasure to meet you, doctor.

BADINI. The pleasure is mine, sir.*

NUTI. Won't you make yourselves comfortable?

MARULLI. Mrs. Nuti isn't at home?

NUTI. Yes, she is. She will be here in a minute. She is putting the baby to bed.

BADINI. Do you have a baby?

MARULLI. An adorable baby.

NUTI. Yes, we have a three-year-old girl.

BADINI. What's her name?

NUTI. Beatrice. May I offer you a cigarette?

BADINI. Thank you, sir. I do not smoke.

NUTI. And you, Mr. Marulli?

MARULLI. If you allow me, I'll smoke a cigar.

NUTI. Fine. I am only sorry that I have no cigars to offer you. Here are some matches and an ash tray.

MARULLI. Thank you very much.

6. WHERE IS THE CHURCH?

A Tourist and a Gentleman

TOURIST. Excuse me, sir. May I ask you a question?

GENTLEMAN. Please do.

TOURIST. Where is St. Lawrence Church?

GENTLEMAN. It is on Palestrina Street, four or five blocks from here.

TOURIST. In this direction?

GENTLEMAN. Yes. Keep going straight ahead. You can't miss it.*

TOURIST. And another question, if I may (if you allow me): do you know at what time they have Mass?

GENTLEMAN. At seven, eight, and nine. Then, on Sunday, there is Mass every hour of the morning.

TOURIST. And what time is the last Mass on Sunday?

GENTLEMAN. At noon, I believe, but I am not sure. Ask the sexton when you are there.

Turista. Lo farò. Tante grazie.
Signore. Non c'è di che.

7. PIOVE?

Ida e la zia

Ida. Piove?
Zia. Non ancora, ma può piovere da un momento all'altro.
Ida. E io che devo uscire!
Zia. Portati l'ombrello e non dimenticare di metterti le sopra-scarpe.
Ida. Il mio ombrello è rotto.
Zia. Prendi il mio.
Ida. No, grazie, zia. Devo comprarne uno nuovo; lo comprerò stamane.*
Zia. Fa' come ti piace, ma non ti bagnare. Con questo brutto tempo è facile pigliare un raffreddore.
Ida. Non temere. Per farti contenta, mi metterò l'impermeabile.
Zia. Bene. Quello ti proteggerà anche meglio dell'ombrello.
Ida. Ma è vecchio, e quel colore mi sta male.
Zia. Pensi al colore? Pensa alla tua salute prima di tutto!
Ida. Sì, sì, cara zietta mia!

8. QUANTO COSTA?

Ida e l'ombrellaio

Ida. Per piacere, mi faccia vedere un buon ombrello.
Ombrellaio. Un ombrello di seta?
Ida. Sì, di seta, se non è troppo caro.
Ombrellaio. Ecco, signorina. Tutti gli ombrelli che sono in questa vetrina sono di pura seta. Alcuni son neri, altri marrone, altri di colori più gai.
Ida. Quanto costa questo?
Ombrellaio. Duecento lire.*
Ida. Duecento?!
Ombrellaio. Le pare troppo?

TOURIST. I'll do that. Many thanks.
GENTLEMAN. Don't mention it.

7. IS IT RAINING?

Ida and Her Aunt

IDA. Is it raining?
AUNT. Not yet, but it may rain any moment.
IDA. And I have to go out!
AUNT. Take your umbrella and don't forget to put on your rubbers.
IDA. My umbrella is broken.
AUNT. Take mine.
IDA. No, thank you, Aunt. I must buy a new one; I'll buy it this morning.*
AUNT. Do as you please, but don't get wet. With this bad weather, it is easy to catch a cold.
IDA. Don't worry. To make you happy, I'll put my raincoat on.
AUNT. Good. That will protect you even better than the umbrella.
IDA. But it's old, and that color isn't good on me.
AUNT. And you are thinking about the color! Think of your health first of all!
IDA. Yes, yes, my dear little aunt!

8. HOW MUCH DOES IT COST?

Ida and the Umbrella Seller

IDA. Please, let me see a good umbrella.
UMBRELLA SELLER. A silk umbrella?
IDA. Yes, a silk one, if it isn't too expensive.
UMBRELLA SELLER. Here, Miss. All the umbrellas that are in this showcase are of pure silk. Some are black, others are brown, others are in gayer colors.
IDA. How much does this one cost?
UMBRELLA SELLER. Two hundred lire.*
IDA. Two hundred?!
UMBRELLA SELLER. Does that seem too much to you?

IDA.   Certo che mi pare troppo! Pensavo di spendere al massimo un centinaio di lire.

OMBRELLAIO.   Impossibile, signorina. E poi, veda, quest'ombrello che Le piace ha un manico d'argento ch'è veramente bello.

IDA.   È vero argento?

OMBRELLAIO.   Garantito.

IDA.   Non può farmi una piccola riduzione sul prezzo?

OMBRELLAIO.   Mi dispiace, ma assolutamente non posso.

IDA.   Va bene;. lo prendo.

9. DAL FIORAIO

Il signor Canatti e il fioraio

CANATTI.   Quanto costa questo vaso?

FIORAIO.   Sessanta lire, signore.

CANATTI.   E quest'altro?

FIORAIO.   Cinquantadue.

CANATTI.   Ha rose fresche?

FIORAIO.   Certamente, signore. Freschissime.

CANATTI.   Vorrei vederle.

FIORAIO.   Favorisca qui. Ecco.

CANATTI.   Come le vende?

FIORAIO.   A diciotto lire la dozzina.

CANATTI.   Quali altri fiori ha?

FIORAIO.   Violette, garofani, mughetti, giacinti ... *

CANATTI.   Mandi questo vaso con una dozzina e mezza di rose all'indirizzo che Le darò.

FIORAIO.   Benissimo. Di che colore preferisce le rose?

CANATTI.   Mandi dodici rose rosse e sei gialle.

FIORAIO.   Adesso, se vuole scrivere l'indirizzo su uno di questi biglietti ...

CANATTI.   Grazie. Preferisco usare un mio biglietto da visita.

FIORAIO.   A suo piacere.

10. LA COLAZIONE

Una signorina e una cameriera

SIGNORINA.   Che frutta ci sono?

CAMERIERA.   Ciliege, fragole, pere, albicocche, susine ...

IDA. Of course I think it's too much! I was thinking of spending about one hundred lire at the most.

UMBRELLA SELLER. Impossible, Miss. And besides, you see, this umbrella that you like has a silver handle which is really beautiful.

IDA. Is it real silver?

UMBRELLA SELLER. Guaranteed.

IDA. Couldn't you make a small reduction in the price for me?

UMBRELLA SELLER. I'm sorry, but I absolutely cannot [do it].

IDA. All right. I'll take it.

9. AT THE FLOWER SHOP

Signor Canatti and the Florist

CANATTI. How much is this vase?

FLORIST. Sixty lire, sir.

CANATTI. And this other one?

FLORIST. Fifty-two.

CANATTI. Do you have any fresh roses?

FLORIST. Certainly, sir. Very fresh ones.

CANATTI. I'd like to see them.

FLORIST. Please come this way. Here they are.

CANATTI. How do you sell them?

FLORIST. Eighteen lire a dozen.

CANATTI. What other flowers do you have?

FLORIST. Violets, carnations, lilies of the valley, hyacinths . . . *

CANATTI. Send this vase with a dozen and a half roses to the address I'll give you.

FLORIST. Very well. What color of roses do you prefer?

CANATTI. Send twelve red roses and six yellow ones.

FLORIST. Now if you will write the address on one of these cards . . .

CANATTI. Thanks. I prefer to use one of my visiting cards.

FLORIST. As you please.

10. THE BREAKFAST

A Young Lady and a Waitress

YOUNG LADY. What kind of fruit do you have?

WAITRESS. Cherries, strawberries, pears, apricots, plums . . .

SIGNORINA. Non hanno fichi?

CAMERIERA. Nɔ, signorina, è un pɔ' trɔppo presto pei fichi.

SIGNORINA. Prenderɔ̀ allora delle fragole.

CAMERIERA. Con la panna?

SIGNORINA. Sì, con la panna. Le preferisco col limone, ma forse a stɔmaco digiuno è meglio prenderle con la panna.*

CAMERIERA. E pɔi che altro?

SIGNORINA. Due uɔva fritte.

CAMERIERA. Con panini?

SIGNORINA. Nɔ, con pane tostato.

CAMERIERA. Benissimo. Niente altro?

SIGNORINA. Sì: del burro, della marmellata e una tazza di caffè con panna. Ma mi serva presto, per favore, perchè hɔ fretta.

CAMERIERA. Immediatamente.

11. ALL'ALBERGO

Una signora e un impiegato

IMPIEGATO. In che cɔsa pɔsso servirla, signora?

SIGNORA. Hanno una buɔna camera a due letti per questa signorina e per me?

IMPIEGATO. Sì, signora. Con bagno o senza?

SIGNORA. Con bagno.

IMPIEGATO. Ne abbiamo una con un balcone che dà sul parco.

SIGNORA. A che piano?

IMPIEGATO. All'ultimo piano, ma c'è l'ascensore, signora.*

SIGNORA. È esposta a mezzogiorno?

IMPIEGATO. Sì, signora.

SIGNORA. Non sarà trɔppo calda in questa stagione dell'anno?

IMPIEGATO. Nɔ, signora. Se c'è un pɔ' di brezza, arriva certo lassù.

SIGNORA. Bene, ma sarà meglio vederla prima di prenderla. Mi dica del prezzo, per favore.

IMPIEGATO. Prenderanno i pasti in albergo?

SIGNORA. Non sɔ. Prenderemo certo la prima colazione.

IMPIEGATO. La camera è ottanta lire al giorno; la pensione completa è cento cinque a persona.

Young Lady. Haven't you any figs?

Waitress. No, Miss. It's a little too early for figs.

Young Lady. I shall have some strawberries then.

Waitress. With cream?

Young Lady. Yes, with cream. I prefer them with lemon, but on an empty stomach it's perhaps better to take them with cream.

Waitress. And then what else?

Young Lady. Two fried eggs.

Waitress. With rolls?

Young Lady. No, with toast.

Waitress. Very well. Nothing else?

Young Lady. Yes: some butter, some marmalade, and a cup of coffee with cream. But please serve me soon, because I am in a hurry.

Waitress. Immediately.

11. AT THE HOTEL

A Lady and a Clerk

Clerk. What can I do for you, Madam?

Lady. Do you have a good room with two beds for this young lady and myself?

Clerk. Yes, Madam. With or without bath?

Lady. With a bath.

Clerk. We have one with a balcony which overlooks the park.

Lady. On what floor?

Clerk. On the top floor. But there is an elevator, Madam.*

Lady. Does it have southern exposure?

Clerk. Yes, Madam.

Lady. Won't it be too hot this time of the year?

Clerk. No, Madam. If there is a little breeze, it certainly gets up there.

Lady. Fine. But it will be better to see it before taking it. Please tell me the price.

Clerk. Will you eat your meals at the hotel?

Lady. I don't know. We'll eat breakfast here for sure.

Clerk. The room is eighty lire a day. The room with meals is one hundred five lire per person.

12. UN APPUNTAMENTO

La signorina Franchetti e Miss Wood

SIGNORINA FRANCHETTI. Ha qualche cosa da fare stasera, Miss Wood ?

MISS WOOD. No, niente di speciale. Perchè mi domanda ?

SIGNORINA FRANCHETTI. Vuole andare con me a un cinematografo ?

MISS WOOD. Con molto piacere. A che ora vuole andare ?

SIGNORINA FRANCHETTI. Dopo cena.

MISS WOOD. Io finisco di mangiare verso le venti, e Lei ?

SIGNORINA FRANCHETTI. Anche noi ceniamo su per giù alla stessa ora.*

MISS WOOD. Benissimo!

SIGNORINA FRANCHETTI. Allora potremmo incontrarci alle venti e mezza.

MISS WOOD. Dove ? A casa sua ?

SIGNORINA FRANCHETTI. Forse sarebbe troppo disturbo per Lei.

MISS WOOD. Niente disturbo. E poi, se non sbaglio, la sua casa non è lontana da qui.

SIGNORINA FRANCHETTI. No, non è lontana: via Mazzini 16, secondo piano. Venga allora, e così avrò il piacere di presentarla alla mia mamma. Le ho spesso parlato di Lei.

MISS WOOD. Va bene, faremo così. Verrò a casa sua, e grazie infinite.

13. DOV'È LA POSTA ?

Mr. Cox e un signore

MR. COX. Mi dispiace disturbarla, signore. Sa dirmi dov'è la posta ?

SIGNORE. Niente disturbo. Vuole andare alla posta più vicina o alla posta centrale ?

MR. COX. Alla centrale.

SIGNORE. È piuttosto lontana da qui. Vada diritto in questa direzione e, dopo una ventina d'isolati, giri a destra. Poco dopo

12. AN APPOINTMENT

Signorina Franchetti and Miss Wood

SIGNORINA FRANCHETTI. Do you have anything planned for this evening, Miss Wood?

MISS WOOD. No, nothing special. Why do you ask?

SIGNORINA FRANCHETTI. Would you like to go to a movie with me?

MISS WOOD. Very gladly. What time do you want to go?

SIGNORINA FRANCHETTI. After supper.

MISS WOOD. I finish eating at about eight o'clock. And you?

SIGNORINA FRANCHETTI. We eat our supper at about the same hour, too.*

MISS WOOD. Excellent.

SIGNORINA FRANCHETTI. Then we could meet at half past eight.

MISS WOOD. Where? At your house?

SIGNORINA FRANCHETTI. Perhaps that would be too much trouble for you.

MISS WOOD. Not at all. And, besides, if I am not wrong, your house is not far from here.

SIGNORINA FRANCHETTI. No, it isn't far, — 16 Mazzini Street, third floor. Come then, and that way I'll have the pleasure of introducing you to my mother. I have often spoken to her about you.

MISS WOOD. O.K. We shall do so. I'll come to your house, and many thanks.

13. WHERE IS THE POST OFFICE?

Mr. Cox and a Gentleman

MR. COX. I hate to bother you, sir. Can you tell me where the post office is?

GENTLEMAN. No bother at all. Do you want to go to the nearest post office or to the main post office?

MR. COX. To the main post office.

GENTLEMAN. It's rather far from here. Go straight ahead in this direction and, after about twenty blocks, turn to your right.

troverà una grande piazza con una statua nel mezzo: è lì che si trova la posta centrale. Non può sbagliare.*

Mr. Cox. Sono un buon camminatore, ma una ventina d'isolati sono un po' troppi anche per me.

Signore. È quello che pensavo. Perchè non prende un tranvai?

Mr. Cox. Sì, ma quale?

Signore. Aspetti qui all'angolo il numero cinque e poi dica al conduttore dove vuole andare. Egli Le dirà quando deve scendere.

Mr. Cox. Farò quel che mi consiglia, signore. Le son molto grato.

Signore. Di nulla. Buon giorno, signore.

Mr. Cox. Buon giorno.

14. NEL RISTORANTE

Bill, George e un cameriere

Cameriere. Che vino devo servire, signori? Bianco o rosso?

Bill. Grazie. Non prendiamo vino. Metta piuttosto un po' di ghiaccio nei nostri bicchieri.

George. E ci dia la minuta, per favore.

Cameriere. Ecco, signore. Vado subito a prendere il ghiaccio.

Bill. Che c'è sulla minuta?

George. Vuoi antipasto?

Bill. Sì. E poi?

George. Io prenderò degli spaghetti al pomodoro, e tu?

Bill. No, preferisco un minestrone.

Cameriere. Ecco il ghiaccio, signori.*

George. Cameriere, ci porti dell'antipasto, degli spaghetti al pomodoro per me, e un minestrone per il mio amico.

Cameriere. Benissimo. Che posso servire poi?

Bill. Che pesce c'è?

Cameriere. Anguille alla livornese, tonno arrostito sulla gratella, fritto misto . . .

Bill. Prenderò il tonno.

George. A me, invece, porti delle costolette di vitello con patate e peperoni.

Soon you'll find a large square with a statue in the middle. That's where the main post office is. You can't miss it.*

MR. COX. I am a good walker, but twenty some blocks are a little too many even for me.

GENTLEMAN. That's what I thought. Why don't you take a streetcar?

MR. COX. Yes, but which one?

GENTLEMAN. Wait for streetcar number five here on the corner, and then tell the conductor where you want to go. He'll tell you when you have to get off.

MR. COX. I'll do what you advise, sir. I'm very grateful to you.

GENTLEMAN. Don't mention it. Good day, sir.

MR. COX. Good day.

14. IN THE RESTAURANT

Bill, George, and a Waiter

WAITER. What wine should I serve you, gentlemen? White or red?

BILL. Thanks. We won't take wine. Put a little ice in our glasses, instead.

GEORGE. And give us the menu, please.

WAITER. Here it is, sir. I'll go right away to get the ice.

BILL. What's on the menu?

GEORGE. Do you want appetizers?

BILL. Yes. And then?

GEORGE. I'll take spaghetti with tomato sauce, and you?

BILL. No, I prefer a vegetable soup.

WAITER. Here is the ice, gentlemen.*

GEORGE. Waiter, bring us some appetizers, spaghetti with tomato sauce for me, and vegetable soup for my friend.

WAITER. Very well. What may I serve you afterward?

BILL. What kind of fish do you have?

WAITER. Eels Leghorn style, broiled tuna, fried fish of many kinds.

BILL. I'll take the tuna.

GEORGE. Bring me, instead, veal cutlets with potatoes and peppers.

CAMERIERE. Posso servire qualche cosa da bere?

BILL. Del latte. E poi, col dolce, ci porterà due tazze di caffè con panna.

GEORGE. Ho dimenticato di dirle che, con la carne, vorrei pure dell'insalata.

CAMERIERE. Che specie d'insalata devo servire?

GEORGE. Che insalate hanno?

CAMERIERE. Lattuga, indivia, pomodori ...

GEORGE. Indivia.

BILL. Ne prenderò anch'io.

CAMERIERE. Va benissimo, signori.

15. BUON NATALE!

Miss Sullivan e la signorina Pini

MISS SULLIVAN. Oh, signorina Pini!

SIGNORINA PINI. Buon Natale, Miss Sullivan!

MISS SULLIVAN. Grazie! Altrettanto a Lei e alla sua famiglia.

SIGNORINA PINI. Resta qui per queste feste?

MISS SULLIVAN. No, vado a Roma dai miei genitori.

SIGNORINA PINI. Quando partirà?

MISS SULLIVAN. Col treno delle sette, domattina.*

SIGNORINA PINI. Son certa che a Roma si divertirà molto più che qui.

MISS SULLIVAN. Lo spero, ma in un albergo il Natale non sembrerà così bello come a casa nostra, negli Stati Uniti.

SIGNORINA PINI. È bello laggiù, non è vero?

MISS SULLIVAN. Sì. C'è tanta neve, c'è un gran fuoco nel camino, e poi c'è l'albero di Natale, ci sono i doni, c'è il gran pranzo di famiglia.

SIGNORINA PINI. Mi fa venir la voglia d'andare in America.

MISS SULLIVAN. Chi può sapere? Forse ci andrà un giorno.

SIGNORINA PINI. Son sogni, Miss Sullivan! Si diverta, faccia un buon Natale, e che l'anno nuovo Le porti molta felicità!

MISS SULLIVAN. Lo stesso a Lei, mia cara.

WAITER. Can I serve you something to drink?

BILL. Milk. And then, with the dessert, you'll bring us two cups of coffee with cream.

GEORGE. I forgot to tell you that, with the meat, I'd like to have some salad also.

WAITER. What kind of salad may I serve?

GEORGE. What kind do you have?

WAITER. Lettuce, endive, tomato . . .

GEORGE. Endive.

BILL. I'll have some, too.

WAITER. That's fine, gentlemen.

15. MERRY CHRISTMAS!

Miss Sullivan and Signorina Pini

MISS SULLIVAN. Oh, Miss Pini!

SIGNORINA PINI. Merry Christmas, Miss Sullivan!

MISS SULLIVAN. Thank you! The same to you and to your family.

SIGNORINA PINI. Are you going to stay here for the holidays?

MISS SULLIVAN. No, I'm going to Rome to my parents.

SIGNORINA PINI. When will you leave?

MISS SULLIVAN. On the seven o'clock train tomorrow morning.*

SIGNORINA PINI. I'm sure that you will have a much better time in Rome than here.

MISS SULLIVAN. I hope so, but in a hotel Christmas won't seem so lovely as it does in our home in the United States.

SIGNORINA PINI. It's beautiful over there, isn't it?

MISS SULLIVAN. Yes. There is so much snow, there is a grand fire in the fireplace, and then there is a Christmas tree, there are gifts, there is the big family dinner.

SIGNORINA PINI. You make me want to go to America.

MISS SULLIVAN. Who knows? Perhaps some day you'll go there.

SIGNORINA PINI. Those are dreams, Miss Sullivan. Enjoy yourself, have a merry Christmas, and may the New Year bring you lots of happiness!

MISS SULLIVAN. The same to you, my dear.

16. ANDIAMO ALL'ɔPERA

Mr. Springer e Mr. Ford

SPRINGER. Che cɔsa facciamo stasera?

FORD. Andiamo all'ɔpera!

SPRINGER. Perchè nɔ? Che ɔpera danno al San Carlo?

FORD. Non sɔ. Dov'è il giornale?

SPRINGER. Costà, sul tavolino.

FORD. Si darà la *Tosca*. È una della pɔche ɔpere che hɔ sentite al Metropolitan di New York.

SPRINGER. E la sentiresti di nuɔvo?

FORD. Altro che! È un'ɔpera magni*fi*ca, dramm*a*tica, appassionata, e la m*u*sica è molto b*e*lla.*

SPRINGER. Per me è nuɔva; ma se vuɔi andare, andiamo pure.

FORD. Ti spiegherɔ l'intreccio e, se vuɔi, possiamo anche comprare il libretto.

SPRINGER. Sarà m*e*glio. Quali posti prenderemo?

FORD. I migliori posti son quelli di poltrona. Naturalmente, sono anche i più cari.

SPRINGER. Che impɔrta? Non andiamo cɛrto tutte le sere all'ɔpera.

FORD. I posti distinti son più a buɔn mercato, e possiamo anche andare in giacca.

SPRINGER. Nɔ, facciamo le cɔse in r*e*gola! Prendiamo le poltrone.

FORD. Se ne troveremo.

SPRINGER. Che ora è?

FORD. Sono le tr*e*dici e venti.

SPRINGER. Allora non perdiamo t*e*mpo! Andiamo s*u*bito a comprare i biglietti!

17. ALLA PɔSTA

Miss Nyle e due impiegati

MISS NYLE. Per favore venti francobolli da settantaci*n*que cent*e*simi e s*e*i da una lira e ventici*n*que.

IMPIEGATO. Ɛcco. Sono in tutto qui*n*dici lire.

MISS NYLE. Ɔh, dimenticavo! Mi dia anche di*e*ci cartoline.

IMPIEGATO. Tre lire.

16. LET'S GO TO THE OPERA

Mr. Springer and Mr. Ford

SPRINGER. What shall we do tonight?

FORD. Let's go to the opera.

SPRINGER. Why not? What opera are they giving at the San Carlo?

FORD. I don't know. Where's the newspaper?

SPRINGER. There, on the little table.

FORD. *Tosca* will be given. It's one of the few operas I've heard at the Metropolitan in New York.

SPRINGER. And you would hear it again?

FORD. I should say so! It is a magnificent, dramatic, fiery opera, and the music is very beautiful.*

SPRINGER. It's new to me; but if you want to go, let's go.

FORD. I'll explain the plot to you and, if you want to, we can also buy the libretto.

SPRINGER. That will be better. What seats shall we get?

FORD. The *poltrone* are the best. They are also the most expensive, of course.

SPRINGER. What's the difference? We certainly don't go to the opera every night.

FORD. The *posti distinti* are cheaper, and we can also go in street clothes.

SPRINGER. No. Let's do things right. Let's get the *poltrone*.

FORD. If we find some.

SPRINGER. What time is it?

FORD. It's 1:20.

SPRINGER. Then let's not lose any time. Let's go right away to buy the tickets.

17. AT THE POST OFFICE

Miss Nyle and Two Clerks

NISS NYLE. Twenty 75 *centésimi* stamps, and six 1.25's, please.

CLERK. Here. That's fifteen lire in all.

MISS NYLE. Oh, I forgot! Give me ten post cards, too.

CLERK. Three lire.

Miss Nyle. E dove posso avere informazioni per mandare un pacco assicurato in America?

Impiegato. Al prossimo sportello, signora.

Miss Nyle. Grazie.*

* * *

Miss Nyle. Vorrei avere delle informazioni.

Impiegato. Dica.

Miss Nyle. Voglio mandare dei ricordi di Napoli a una mia amica negli Stati Uniti. Vuole dirmi come dev'essere fatto il pacco?

Impiegato. Dipende da quello che manda. È roba fragile?

Miss Nyle. Sì. Alcune cosette son fragili.

Impiegato. Allora ci vuole una cassetta di legno, e la parola « fragile » dev'essere scritta a grandi caratteri all'esterno. Il pacco sarà assicurato?

Miss Nyle. Sì, preferirei assicurarlo.

Impiegato. Allora dovrà essere sigillato.

Miss Nyle. Non ho nè sigillo nè ceralacca. Sa dirmi dov'è un cartolaio in queste vicinanze?

Impiegato. Proprio dirimpetto a quest'ufficio, signora.

Miss Nyle. Le sono immensamente obbligata.

Impiegato. Non c'è di che.

18. DAL PROFUMIERE

Mr. Wells, Mrs. Wells e il profumiere

Profumiere. In che posso servire i signori?

Mrs. Wells. Mi mostri, per piacere, del sapone d'ottima qualità.

Profumiere. Ne abbiamo di diverse specie. Quale profumo preferisce la signora?

Mrs. Wells. Violetta.

Profumiere. Ecco, signora. Abbiamo questo, questo, e questo; tutti di primissima qualità, specialmente quest'ultimo.

Mr. Wells. Vedo che vende anche spazzolini pei denti, saponi e pennelli per la barba. In America noi generalmente compriamo queste cose nelle farmacie.

Profumiere. Nelle farmacie? Qui in Italia le farmacie non vendono che medicine.*

MISS NYLE. And where can I obtain information about mailing an insured package to America?

CLERK. At the next window, ma'am.

MISS NYLE. Thanks.*

*   *   *

MISS NYLE. I'd like some information.

CLERK. Yes?

MISS NYLE. I want to send some souvenirs from Naples to a friend of mine in the United States. Will you tell me how the package should be wrapped?

CLERK. It depends on what you send. Is it breakable?

MISS NYLE. Yes. Some little things are breakable.

CLERK. Then you need a wooden box, and the word "fragile" should be written on the outside in large letters. Will the package be insured?

MISS NYLE. Yes. I'd prefer to have it insured.

CLERK. Then it will have to be sealed.

MISS NYLE. I have neither a seal nor sealing wax. Can you tell me where there is a stationery shop in this vicinity?

CLERK. Right opposite this building, Madam.

MISS NYLE. I am very much obliged to you.

CLERK. You are welcome.

18. AT THE PERFUME SHOP

Mr. Wells, Mrs. Wells, and the Owner of the Shop

OWNER. What can I do for you?

MRS. WELLS. Please show me some soap of the best quality.

OWNER. We have several kinds. What scent does Madam prefer?

MRS. WELLS. Violet.

OWNER. Here, Madam. We have this, this, and this; all of the very best quality, particularly this last one.

MR. WELLS. I see that you sell toothbrushes too, and shaving soap, and shaving brushes. In America we usually buy these things in drugstores.

OWNER. In drugstores? Here in Italy drugstores sell only medicine.*

Mrs. Wells. Come lo vende questo sapone?

Profumiere. Quaranta lire la scatola, signora.

Mrs. Wells. Ne prendo una scatola. Mi faccia vedere adesso una buona lozione tonica pei capelli, e delle forcine di tartaruga.

Profumiere. Subito. — Ecco, signora.

Mr. Wells. A mi faccia vedere delle forbicette per le unghie.

Profumiere. Guardi in questa vetrina, signore. Ne abbiamo di diverse qualità e grandezze. Può scegliere.

Mr. Wells. Ne voglio di grandezza media, come queste. Son buone?

Profumiere. Del migliore acciaio, signore.

Mrs. Wells. Prenderò una dozzina di queste forcine e anche una bottiglia di questa lozione.

Profumiere. E il signore prende le forbicette?

Mr. Wells. Quanto costano?

Profumiere. Ventisette lire.

Mr. Wells. Va bene; faccia un pacco di tutto.

19. PAESE CHE VAI, USANZA CHE TROVI

Mr. Dale e un signore

Mr. Dale. Per favore, dove posso comprare dei francobolli per mandare queste cartoline?

Signore. Vada laggiù. C'è un tabaccaio.

Mr. Dale. I tabaccai vendono francobolli?

Signore. Sì, signore. Vendono tutto ciò ch'è monopolio dello stato: tabacco, sigari, sigarette, francobolli, sale . . .

Mr. Dale. Non lo sapevo. Da noi, in America, non è così.*

Signore. E chi li vende i francobolli in America?

Mr. Dale. L'ufficio postale.

Signore. Naturalmente. Anche qui in Italia.

Mr. Dale. E le farmacie.

Signore. Le farmacie? Questa è bella! E che hanno a che fare i francobolli con le medicine?

Mr. Dale. Vero. Ma che hanno a che fare i francobolli col tabacco?

Signore. Ha ragione. Paese che vai, usanza che trovi.

MRS. WELLS. How do you sell this soap ♪

OWNER. Forty lire a box, Madam.

MRS. WELLS. I'll take a box. Now let me see a good hair tonic and some tortoise-shell hairpins.

OWNER. Right away. — Here they are, Madam.

MR. WELLS. Let me see some manicure scissors.

OWNER. Look at this showcase, sir. We have them in various qualities and sizes. You may choose.

MR. WELLS. I'd like them of medium size, like this one. Are they good ♪

OWNER. Of the best steel, sir.

MRS. WELLS. I'll take a dozen of these hairpins and also a bottle of this hair tonic.

OWNER. And the gentleman will also take the scissors ♪

MR. WELLS. How much are they ♪

OWNER. Twenty-seven lire.

MR. WELLS. Very well. Put them all in one package.

19. WHEN IN ROME, DO AS THE ROMANS DO

Mr. Dale and a Gentleman

MR. DALE. Please, where can I buy some stamps to send these post cards ♪

GENTLEMAN. Go over there. There is a tobacco shop.

MR. DALE. Do tobacco shops sell stamps ♪

GENTLEMAN. Yes, sir. They sell everything that is a state monopoly: tobacco, cigars, cigarettes, stamps, salt . . .

MR. DALE. I didn't know that. It's not that way in America.*

GENTLEMAN. And who sells stamps in America ♪

MR. DALE. The post office.

GENTLEMAN. Naturally. Here in Italy too!

MR. DALE. And the drugstores.

GENTLEMAN. The drugstores ♪ That's a good one! But what do stamps have to do with medicine ♪

MR. DALE. True. But what do stamps have to do with tobacco ♪

GENTLEMAN. You are right. When in Rome, do as the Romans do.

Mr. Dale. Un'altra domanda, signore: sa dirmi dove posso trovare una buca per le lettere?

Signore. A due isolati da qui, in questa direzione, proprio all'angolo di Piazza Garibaldi.

Mr. Dale. Grazie infinite.

Signore. Di niente. Arrivederci, signore.

Mr. Dale. Addio.

20. IN UN NEGOZIO D'ARTICOLI FOTOGRAFICI

Mr. Terry e un impiegato

Mr. Terry. Per piacere, sviluppi questa pellicola e faccia due copie di ciascuna negativa buona.

Impiegato. Benissimo, signore. Vuole le copie su carta lucida o su carta matta?

Mr. Terry. Le preferirei su carta semilucida.

Impiegato. Come questa fotografia?

Mr. Terry. Per l'appunto.

Impiegato. Ha bisogno di nuove pellicole?

Mr. Terry. Sì. Me ne dia una.*

Impiegato. Di trentasei o di diciotto prese?

Mr. Terry. Di diciotto. Non faccio molte fotografie, e le pellicole di trentasei restano troppo a lungo nella macchina fotografica.

Impiegato. In questo caso ha ragione. Le negative si guastano se si fa passare troppo tempo prima di farle sviluppare. Ecco, signore.

Mr. Terry. Quanto costa?

Impiegato. Dodici lire.

Mr. Terry. Quando devo ritornare per prendere le fotografie che ho ordinate?

Impiegato. Domani sera, dopo le diciotto.

Mr. Terry. Fino a che ora sta aperto il negozio?

Impiegato. Fino alle venti.

Mr. Terry. Grazie. Buona sera.

Impiegato. Buona sera, signore.

MR. DALE. Another question, sir. Can you tell me where I can find a letter box ⁇

GENTLEMAN. Two blocks from here, in this direction, right on the corner of Garibaldi Square.

MR. DALE. Many thanks.

GENTLEMAN. Don't mention it. Good-bye, sir.

MR. DALE. Good-bye.

20. IN A PHOTOGRAPH STORE

Mr. Terry and a Clerk

MR. TERRY. Please develop this film and make two copies of each good negative.

CLERK. Very well, sir. Do you want the copies on glossy or on dull paper ⁇

MR. TERRY. I'd prefer them on semi-glossy paper.

CLERK. Like this photograph ⁇

MR. TERRY. Exactly.

CLERK. Do you need new films, sir ⁇

MR. TERRY. Yes. Give me one.*

CLERK. Thirty-six or eighteen exposures ⁇

MR. TERRY. Eighteen. I don't take many pictures, and the thirty-six-exposure films stay too long in my camera.

CLERK. In that case, you are right. The negatives spoil if they stay too long before being developed. Here, sir.

MR. TERRY. How much is it ⁇

CLERK. Twelve lire.

MR. TERRY. When shall I return to call for the pictures I have ordered ⁇

CLERK. Tomorrow evening after six.

MR. TERRY. Until what time does the store stay open ⁇

CLERK. Until eight.

MR. TERRY. Thank you. Good evening.

CLERK. Good evening, sir.

21. INGRANDIMENTI

Mr. Terry e l'impiegato

MR. TERRY. Buona sera. Son pronte le mie fotografie?

IMPIEGATO. Buona sera, signore. Vuol darmi la ricevuta, per piacere?

MR. TERRY. Eccola.

IMPIEGATO. Son arrivate proprio in questo momento dal laboratorio.

MR. TERRY. Bene, bene. Alcune son riuscite ottimamente... e meritano d'essere ingrandite.

IMPIEGATO. Specialmente questa.

MR. TERRY. Sì, e queste altre due.

IMPIEGATO. Senza dubbio.

MR. TERRY. Allora faccia due ingrandimenti per ciascuna di queste negative, per piacere.*

IMPIEGATO. In che formato le vuole ingrandite?

MR. TERRY. Dodici per diciotto.

IMPIEGATO. Anche su carta semilucida?

MR. TERRY. Sì. E questa come verrebbe, ingrandita?

IMPIEGATO. Non troppo bene, signore. È fuori fuoco.

MR. TERRY. Sì, un poco. Ma vorrei che Lei provasse, perchè quest'istantanea mi piace assai.

IMPIEGATO. Proveremo.

MR. TERRY. Quando devo ritornare?

IMPIEGATO. Dopodomani, alla stessa ora.

MR. TERRY. Devo pagare a Lei?

IMPIEGATO. No, signore. Alla cassa, prego.

MR. TERRY. A dopodomani, allora.

IMPIEGATO. Arrivederla.

22. DAL BARBIERE

Mr. Shaw e il barbiere

MR. SHAW. Buon giorno.

BARBIERE. Buon giorno, signore.

MR. SHAW. Dovrò aspettare molto?

BARBIERE. Pochi minuti, signore.

21. ENLARGEMENTS

Mr. Terry and the Clerk

MR. TERRY. Good evening. Are my photographs ready ?

CLERK. Good evening, sir. Will you please give me your receipt ?

MR. TERRY. Here it is.

CLERK. They just arrived this moment from the laboratory.

MR. TERRY. Fine! Fine! Some have turned out very well . . . and are good enough to be enlarged.

CLERK. Especially this one.

MR. TERRY. Yes, and these other two.

CLERK. Without doubt.

MR. TERRY. Then make two enlargements from each of these negatives, please.*

CLERK. To what size do you want them enlarged ?

MR. TERRY. Twelve by eighteen.

CLERK. Also on semi-glossy paper ?

MR. TERRY. Yes. And this one, how would it look enlarged ?

CLERK. Not too good, sir. It's out of focus.

MR. TERRY. Yes, a little. But I'd like you to try because I like this snapshot very much.

CLERK. We'll try.

MR. TERRY. When should I come back ?

CLERK. Day after tomorrow, at the same time.

MR. TERRY. Should I pay you ?

CLERK. No, sir. At the cashier's, please.

MR. TERRY. Until the day after tomorrow, then.

CLERK. Good-bye.

22. AT THE BARBER SHOP

Mr. Shaw and the Barber

MR. SHAW. Good morning.

BARBER. Good morning, sir.

MR. SHAW. Will I have to wait long ?

BARBER. A few minutes, sir.

* * *

BARBIERE. Pronto. Si vuole accomodare?

MR. SHAW. Eccomi.

BARBIERE. Barba e capelli?

MR. SHAW. Sì. Mi faccia la barba e mi tagli i capelli. Poi mi farà un massaggio.

BARBIERE. Vuole che li tagli corti i capelli?

MR. SHAW. Non troppo corti.*

BARBIERE. Posso usare la macchinetta ai lati?

MR. SHAW. Ai lati e sulla nuca.

BARBIERE. Benissimo. Il signore è americano?

MR. SHAW. Sì. Come lo sapete?

BARBIERE. L'ho supposto dall'accento, dall'aspetto . . .

MR. SHAW. Ha indovinato.

BARBIERE. Bel paese l'America. Io ho un cugino che fa il barbiere a Newark.

MR. SHAW. Sì?

BARBIERE. È lontana da New York, Newark?

MR. SHAW. No, è vicinissima.

BARBIERE. Anch'io dovevo andare in America, ma poi cambiai idea.

MR. SHAW. Perchè?

BARBIERE. Perchè m'ammogliai, signore. Se fossi partito con mio cugino, com'era stato progettato, a quest'ora sarei in ben altre condizioni. Mio cugino è diventato ricco. Ha scritto che ha una bella casa e un'automobile.

MR. SHAW. In America quasi tutti hanno l'automobile.

BARBIERE. Davvero? Che paese! Che paese!

23. DAL GIOIELLIERE

Mrs. Hartman e il gioielliere

MRS. HARTMAN. Vorrei comprare un piccolo ricordo da offrire a una signorina.

GIOIELLIERE. Abbiamo anelli, spille, braccialetti, collane . . .

MRS. HARTMAN. Mi faccia vedere qualche cosa di grazioso.

GIOIELLIERE. Ecco dei begli anelli, signora.

MRS. HARTMAN. È oro questo?

* * *

BARBER. Ready. Will you please be seated ♪

MR. SHAW. Here I am.

BARBER. Shave and haircut ♪

MR. SHAW. Yes. Shave me and cut my hair. Then give me a massage.

BARBER. Do you want me to cut your hair short ♪

MR. SHAW. Not too short.*

BARBER. May I use the clippers on the sides ♪

MR. SHAW. All around. (On the sides and on the neck.)

BARBER. Fine. Are you American, sir ♪

MR. SHAW. Yes. How do you know that ♪

BARBER. I assumed it from your accent and your appearance.

MR. SHAW. You guessed right.

BARBER. A beautiful country, America. I have a cousin who is a barber in Newark.

MR. SHAW. Yes ♪

BARBER. Is Newark far from New York ♪

MR. SHAW. No. Very close.

BARBER. I was going to America too, but then I changed my mind.

MR. SHAW. Why ♪

BARBER. Because I got married, sir. If I had left with my cousin, as it had been planned, I'd be in a far better situation now. My cousin has become rich. He wrote that he has a beautiful house and a car.

MR. SHAW. In America nearly everybody has a car.

BARBER. Is that so ♪ What a country! What a country!

23. IN A JEWELRY SHOP

Mrs. Hartman and the Jeweler

MRS. HARTMAN. I would like to buy a small souvenir as a gift for a young lady.

JEWELER. We have rings, pins, bracelets, necklaces . . .

MRS. HARTMAN. Let me see something pretty.

JEWELER. Here are some beautiful rings, Madam.

MRS. HARTMAN. Is this gold ♪

GIOIELLIERE. Oro di quattordici carati.

MRS. HARTMAN. E che pietre son queste?

GIOIELLIERE. Coralli, lapislazzuli, turchesi ... *

MRS. HARTMAN. Questo è bellino. Quanto costa?

GIOIELLIERE. Trecento quaranta lire.

MRS. HARTMAN. Un po' caro, ma lo metta da parte, per piacere. E ora mi faccia vedere qualche cosa per un giovanotto.

GIOIELLIERE. Anche un anello?

MRS. HARTMAN. No. Piuttosto una spilla da cravatta.

GIOIELLIERE. Abbiamo anche dei bei bottoni da polsini.

MRS. HARTMAN. Mi mostri le une e gli altri, prego.

GIOIELLIERE. Spero che questi bottoni Le piaceranno.

MRS. HARTMAN. Anche questo è oro?

GIOIELLIERE. Garantito. Quattordici carati, come l'anello che ha scelto, signora.

MRS. HARTMAN. Qual è il prezzo di questi bottoni?

GIOIELLIERE. Duecento settanta lire.

MRS. HARTMAN. Li prendo.

24. GIOCATTOLI

Clara, Silvia, e poi un'impiegata

CLARA. Desidero di comprare dei giocattoli pei miei nipotini. Vediamo che cos'ha questo negozio.

SILVIA. Guardate quella bambola olandese. Non è carina?

CLARA. Scommetto che Maria sarebbe felice d'averla, specialmente se apre e chiude gli occhi.

SILVIA. E se dice papà e mammà.

CLARA. Ma che cosa posso comprare per Ricardo?

SILVIA. Entriamo, vediamo che c'è.*

* * *

CLARA. Ci faccia vedere, per favore, una bambola olandese come quella ch'è in vetrina.

IMPIEGATA. Ecco, signorina. Apre e chiude gli occhi; premendola qui, dice papà; premendola qui, dice mammà, ed è elegantemente vestita di lino e seta. Vede com'è bella!

SILVIA. Non è troppo delicata?

JEWELER. Fourteen carat gold.

MRS. HARTMAN. And what stones are these ?

JEWELER. Corals, lapis lazuli, turquoise . . . *

MRS. HARTMAN. This one is pretty. How much is it ?

JEWELER. Three hundred forty lire.

MRS. HARTMAN. A little expensive, but put it aside, please. And now let me see something for a young man.

JEWELER. Also a ring ?

MRS. HARTMAN. No. Rather a tie pin.

JEWELER. We also have some beautiful cuff links.

MRS. HARTMAN. Show me both, please.

JEWELER. I hope you'll like these links.

MRS. HARTMAN. Is this gold, too ?

JEWELER. Guaranteed. Fourteen carats, like the ring you have selected, Madam.

MRS. HARTMAN. What is the price of these links ?

JEWELER. Two hundred seventy lire.

MRS. HARTMAN. I'll take them.

24. TOYS

Clara, Sylvia, and then a Clerk

CLARA. I wish to buy some toys for my little nephew and niece. Let's see what this store has.

SYLVIA. Look at that beautiful Dutch doll. Isn't it cute ?

CLARA. I bet Mary would be happy to have it, especially if it opens and closes its eyes.

SYLVIA. And if it says *papa* and *mamma*.

CLARA. But what can I buy for Richard ?

SYLVIA. Let's go in and see what there is.*

* * *

CLARA. Let us see a Dutch doll, please, like that one that is in the show window.

CLERK. Here, Madam. It opens and closes its eyes; if you press it here, it says *papa;* if you press it here, it says *mamma,* and it is elegantly dressed in linen and silk. Look how beautiful it is!

SYLVIA. Isn't it too delicate ?

Impiegata. Certo, è una cosa delicata, ma è un giocattolo che durerà se s'userà con un po' di riguardo.

Clara. Quanto costa?

Impiegata. Novantacinque lire, signorina.

Clara. E che posso comprare per un maschietto?

Impiegata. Quanti anni ha?

Clara. Ha dieci anni.

Impiegata. Dei soldatini di piombo, un teatrino di marionette, un bel treno... Abbiamo dei treni elettrici che sono una meraviglia.

Clara. Ci faccia vedere uno di questi treni.

25. DALL'OROLOGIAIO

Mrs. Mason e l'orologiaio

Mrs. Mason. Quest'orologio non va. Vuol dirmi che guasto c'è?

Orologiaio. Signora, la molla è rotta, e l'orologio ha pure bisogno d'una pulitura.

Mrs. Mason. Quanto costerà in tutto?

Orologiaio. Ottantacinque lire.

Mrs. Mason. E può dirmi quando sarà pronto?

Orologiaio. Fra un mese.

Mrs. Mason. Non prima? Io devo imbarcarmi per l'America il 18 di questo mese.*

Orologiaio. Fra sei giorni? Allora è impossibile, signora. Mi dispiace molto.

Mrs. Mason. Come faccio senza orologio? Mi vedo perduta.

Orologiaio. Perchè la signora non compra un bell'orologio nuovo?

Mrs. Mason. Ne ha di buona marca?

Orologiaio. Delle migliori marche svizzere.

Mrs. Mason. Me ne faccia vedere qualcuno.

Orologiaio. Un orologetto da polso?

Mrs. Mason. No, preferisco un orologio da portare alla catena.

Orologiaio. Allora guardi questi, signora. Son tutti di primissima qualità, garantiti, in oro bianco di diciotto carati.

Mrs. Mason. Son cari, immagino.

Orologiaio. Non per quello che valgono, signora. Questa è una

CLERK. It's certainly a delicate thing, but it's a toy that will last if it is well taken care of.

CLARA. How much does it cost?

CLERK. Ninety-five lire, Madam.

CLARA. And what can I buy for a young fellow?

CLERK. How old is he?

CLARA. Ten.

CLERK. Little lead soldiers, a puppet show, a fine train ... We have electric trains that are marvelous.

CLARA. Let us see one of those trains.

25. AT THE WATCHMAKER'S

Mrs. Mason and the Watchmaker

MRS. MASON. This watch isn't running. Will you please tell me what's wrong with it?

WATCHMAKER. Madam, the spring is broken, and the watch needs cleaning, too.

MRS. MASON. How much will it cost in all?

WATCHMAKER. Eighty-five lire.

MRS. MASON. And can you tell me when it will be ready?

WATCHMAKER. In a month.

MRS. MASON. Not before? I have to sail for America the 18th of this month.*

WATCHMAKER. In six days? Then it's impossible, Madam. I am very sorry.

MRS. MASON. How can I get along without a watch? I am lost.

WATCHMAKER. Why don't you buy a beautiful new watch?

MRS. MASON. Do you have some of good makes?

WATCHMAKER. Of the best Swiss makes.

MRS. MASON. Let me see some of them.

WATCHMAKER. A wrist watch?

MRS. MASON. No, I prefer a watch to wear on a chain.

WATCHMAKER. Then look at these, Madam. They are all of the finest quality, guaranteed, in white gold of eighteen carats.

MRS. MASON. They are expensive, I imagine.

WATCHMAKER. Not for what they are worth, Madam. This is

spesa che si fa una vɔlta tanto. È meglio badare alla qualità soprattutto.

MRS. MASON. Ha ragione.

26. IN UNA FARMACIA

Mr. Swanson e il farmacista

SWANSON. Vuɔl darmi, per favore, delle compresse sonnifere?

FARMACISTA. Mi dispiace, signore, ma senza una ricetta del medico non pɔsso dargliele.

SWANSON. L'avevo immaginato. Ma come devo fare? Io non dɔrmo la nɔtte.

FARMACISTA. Ha provato a prendere dell'aspirina prima d'andare a letto?

SWANSON. Sì, ma non mi giova.

FARMACISTA. Allora senta il mio consiglio: consulti un medico.*

SWANSON. Son forestiero e, purtrɔppo, non conosco nessun medico in questa città.

FARMACISTA. Se vuɔle, pɔsso darle io l'indirizzo d'un buɔn medico.

SWANSON. Mi farebbe un favore.

FARMACISTA. Ecco. Dottor Carlo Marzetti, Via De Mura 6.

SWANSON. Parla inglese?

FARMACISTA. Credo di sì, ma Lei non ne ha bisogno. Lei parla italiano molto correttamente.

SWANSON. Ma sarɔ più contento se potrɔ parlare inglese con lui.

FARMACISTA. Tenti. Tentar non nuɔce, come si dice da noi.

SWANSON. Ecco: questo io non lo capisco.

FARMACISTA. Significa che non c'è nulla di male a tentare.

27. BUɔNA PASQUA!

Miss Hough e il signor Martinelli

MISS HOUGH. Buɔn giorno, Martinelli.

MARTINELLI. Ɔh! Buɔna Pasqua, signorina!

MISS HOUGH. Buɔna Pasqua anche a voi e alla vɔstra famiglia!

MARTINELLI. Grazie. Avete avuto notizie da casa?

MISS HOUGH. Sì, e ɔttime notizie. Pɔco fa hɔ ricevuto un marconigramma all'albergo.

an expense that one incurs once in a great while. It's wiser to pay attention to quality above all.

MRS. MASON. You are right.

26. IN A DRUGSTORE

Mr. Swanson and the Druggist

SWANSON. Will you give me some sleeping tablets, please?

DRUGGIST. I'm sorry, sir, but I can't give them to you without a doctor's prescription.

SWANSON. I had imagined that. But what can I do? I don't sleep nights.

DRUGGIST. Have you tried taking some aspirin before going to bed?

SWANSON. Yes, but it doesn't help me.

DRUGGIST. Then take my advice. Consult a doctor.*

SWANSON. I am a foreigner, and unfortunately I don't know any doctor in this city.

DRUGGIST. If you wish, I can give you the address of a good doctor.

SWANSON. You'd be doing me a favor.

DRUGGIST. Here it is. Doctor Carlo Marzetti, 6 De Mura Street.

SWANSON. Does he speak English?

DRUGGIST. I think so, but you don't need that. You speak Italian very correctly.

SWANSON. But I'll be happier if I can speak English with him.

DRUGGIST. Try it. It doesn't hurt to try, as we say here.

SWANSON. There you are! I don't understand that.

DRUGGIST. It means that there is nothing wrong in trying.

27. HAPPY EASTER!

Miss Hough and Signor Martinelli

MISS HOUGH. Good day, Martinelli.

MARTINELLI. Oh! Happy Easter, Miss Hough!

MISS HOUGH. Happy Easter to you and your family, too!

MARTINELLI. Thanks. Have you had any news from home?

MISS HOUGH. Yes, and the very best of news. A little while ago I received a radiogram at the hotel.

MARTINELLI. Con gli auguri ♪

MISS HOUGH. Con gli auguri e con una notizia che per me è stata una grande sorpresa.* Indovinate ♪

MARTINELLI. Come posso indovinare ♪

MISS HOUGH. Mio fratello è partito dagli Stati Uniti per raggiungermi qui.

MARTINELLI. Congratulazioni!

MISS HOUGH. Grazie.

MARTINELLI. E su che nave è partito ♪

MISS HOUGH. È partito sul *Washington*, una nave americana, e sbarcherà sabato a Cherbourg.

MARTINELLI. Ah! Allora non verrà qui direttamente.

MISS HOUGH. No. Vuol vedere prima Parigi.

MARTINELLI. Fa bene. Volete farmi sapere quando giungerà qui ♪ Vorrei fare la sua conoscenza.

MISS HOUGH. Appena saprò la data precisa, vi chiamerò al telefono.

MARTINELLI. Brava! Ci conto.

28. DALLA MODISTA

Mrs. Reeve e la modista

MRS. REEVE. Per favore, quanto costa il cappello rosso ch'è esposto in vetrina ♪

MODISTA. Cento ventinove lire, signora. Vuole provarlo ♪

MRS. REEVE. Sì, ma vorrei vederne anche degli altri.

MODISTA. Di che tipo ♪ Da mattina o da pomeriggio ♪

MRS. REEVE. Un feltro semplice da mattina.

MODISTA. Benissimo, signora. Favorisca qui, davanti allo specchio.*

MRS. REEVE. Vediamo. Oh, ma è troppo piccolo questo cappello per me! Non ne ha uno più grande dello stesso modello ♪

MODISTA. Mi dispiace, ma è il solo che abbiamo. Vuole provare quest'altro ♪ È così carino, e Le starà bene.

MRS. REEVE. M'ero innamorata di quel cappello rosso. Ma proviamo questo.

MARTINELLI. With the season's greetings?

MISS HOUGH. With the season's greetings and a bit of news that was a great surprise to me.* Can you guess?

MARTINELLI. How can I guess?

MISS HOUGH. My brother has left the United States to join me here.

MARTINELLI. Congratulations!

MISS HOUGH. Thank you.

MARTINELLI. And what ship did he sail on?

MISS HOUGH. He sailed on the *Washington*, an American ship, and he will land at Cherbourg next Saturday.

MARTINELLI. Oh! So he won't come here directly.

MISS HOUGH. No. He wants to see Paris first.

MARTINELLI. He is wise. Will you let me know when he arrives here? I would like to get acquainted with him.

MISS HOUGH. As soon as I know the exact date, I'll call you on the phone.

MARTINELLI. Excellent! I am counting on that.

28. AT THE MILLINER'S

Mrs. Reeve and the Milliner

MRS. REEVE. Please, what's the price of that red hat which is on display in the window?

MILLINER. One hundred twenty-nine lire, Madam. Do you want to try it on?

MRS. REEVE. Yes, but I'd like to see some of the others, too.

MILLINER. What kind? A street hat or a dressy one?

MRS. REEVE. A simple felt for street wear.

MILLINER. Very well, Madam. Please come over here, in front of the mirror.*

MRS. REEVE. Let's see. Oh, but this hat is too small for me! Don't you have a larger one of the same model?

MILLINER. I am sorry, but it's the only one we have. Do you want to try this other one? It's so pretty, and it will look well on you.

MRS. REEVE. I had fallen in love with that red hat. But let's try this one.

Modista. Lo metta un pochino più indietro e di lato, così.

Mrs. Reeve. Non è troppo giovanile per me?

Modista. Oh, no, signora! Le assicuro che pare fatto proprio per Lei.

Mrs. Reeve. Mi piace. Quanto costa questo cappello?

Modista. Lo stesso dell'altro, signora.

Mrs. Reeve. Può mandarmelo all'albergo?

Modista. Certo. Questo pomeriggio.

Mrs. Reeve. Bene. Lo prendo. Vorrei pure una veletta.

Modista. Ne abbiamo dell'ultima moda. Vuol favorire al banco?

29. AL CAFFÈ

Mr. Stanley, Mrs. Stanley e il cameriere

Mr. Stanley. Cameriere!

Cameriere. Pronto, signore!

Mr. Stanley, *alla moglie*. Tu che prendi?

Mrs. Stanley. Cameriere, che specie di gelati hanno?

Cameriere. Crema, crema e cioccolata, fragole, pesche, albicocche . . .

Mrs. Stanley. Mi porti un gelato di fragole, dei dolcini e una tazza di tè.

Cameriere. Con panna o limone?

Mrs. Stanley. Con panna.*

Cameriere. Benissimo, signora. E il signore?

Mr. Stanley. Io vorrei un bicchierino di marsala della migliore qualità . . .

Cameriere. Florio.

Mr. Stanley. . . . e mi porti l'occorrente per scrivere.

Cameriere. Subito, signore.

Mrs. Stanley. A chi vuoi scrivere?

Mr. Stanley. Al nostro albergo in Roma. Nella fretta della partenza, ho dimenticato il mio rasoio di sicurezza sul lavabo della nostra stanza da bagno. Me lo voglio far mandare.

Mrs. Stanley. E come ti sei fatta la barba stamane?

Mr. Stanley. Son andato dal barbiere.

MILLINER. Put it a little farther back and to the side, like this.

MRS. REEVE. Isn't it too youthful for me?

MILLINER. Oh, no, Madam! I assure you that it looks as though it were made for you.

MRS. REEVE. I like it. How much does this hat cost?

MILLINER. The same as the other, Madam.

MRS. REEVE. Can you send it to me at the hotel?

MILLINER. Certainly. This afternoon.

MRS. REEVE. Fine. I'll take it. I'd like a veil, too.

MILLINER. We have some of the latest style. Will you please come over to the counter?

29. AT THE COFFEE SHOP

Mr. Stanley, Mrs. Stanley, and a Waiter

MR. STANLEY. Waiter!

WAITER. Yes, sir!

MR. STANLEY, *to his wife.* What will you have?

MRS. STANLEY. Waiter, what kind of ices do you have?

WAITER. Vanilla, vanilla and chocolate, strawberry, peach, apricot . . .

MRS. STANLEY. Bring me a strawberry ice, some French pastry, and a cup of tea.

WAITER. With cream or lemon?

MRS. STANLEY. With cream.*

WAITER. Very well, Madam. And the gentleman?

MR. STANLEY. I'd like a small glass of the best quality of Marsala . . .

WAITER. Florio.

MR. STANLEY. . . . and bring me some stationery, pen and ink.

WAITER. Right away, sir.

MRS. STANLEY. To whom do you want to write?

MR. STANLEY. To our hotel in Rome. In the rush of our departure, I left my safety razor on the washbasin in our bathroom. I want to have it sent to me.

MRS. STANLEY. And how did you shave this morning?

MR. STANLEY. I went to the barber.

MRS. STANLEY. Si sta bene, al fresco, qua fuori, e si vede tanta
gente.

MR. STANLEY. I caffè sono una parte essenziale della vita italiana. Qui s'incontrano gli amici, si discutono gli affari e s'am-
mazza il tempo.

30. DAL PROFESSORE D'ITALIANO

Miss Chapman e il professor Minto

MISS CHAPMAN. Il professor Minto?

PROF. MINTO. Sì. In che cosa posso esserle utile?

MISS CHAPMAN. Mi ha mandata qui il maestro Donadio, da cui
prendo lezioni di canto. Mi chiamo Janet Chapman.

PROF. MINTO. Piacere. Prego, s'accomodi.

MISS CHAPMAN. Egli dice che la mia pronunzia italiana è di-
fettosa, e m'ha consigliato di venire da Lei per vedere se è disposto a darmi delle lezioni.

PROF. MINTO. Di pronunzia?

MISS CHAPMAN. Per l'appunto.*

PROF. MINTO. Lo farei con piacere ma, francamente, son troppo
occupato. Potrei però raccomandarle una mia ottima alunna che
ha una pronunzia perfetta perchè è sienese di nascita.

MISS CHAPMAN. La crede competente?

PROF. MINTO. Se non lo fosse, non la raccomanderei.

MISS CHAPMAN. È proprio fuori questione che Lei possa dedi-
carmi un po' del suo tempo?

PROF. MINTO. Purtroppo.

MISS CHAPMAN. Allora Le sarò grata se mi darà l'indirizzo di
questa sua alunna.

PROF. MINTO. Subito. — Ecco.

MISS CHAPMAN. Grazie.

PROF. MINTO. Da quanto tempo è in Italia?

MISS CHAPMAN. Da circa due mesi.

PROF. MINTO. E Le piace star qui?

MISS CHAPMAN. Immensamente.

MRS. STANLEY. One feels good in the cool air out here, and one sees so many people.

MR. STANLEY. The coffee shops are an essential part of Italian life. One meets friends here, discusses business, and kills time.

30. AT THE HOME OF THE ITALIAN PROFESSOR

Miss Chapman and Professor Minto

MISS CHAPMAN. Professor Minto?

PROF. MINTO. Yes. What can I do for you?

MISS CHAPMAN. Maestro Donadio, from whom I take singing lessons, sent me here. My name is Janet Chapman.

PROF. MINTO. It is a pleasure. Please be seated.

MISS CHAPMAN. He says that my Italian pronunciation is faulty, and he advised me to come to you to see if you are willing to give me lessons.

PROF. MINTO. In pronunciation?

MISS CHAPMAN. Precisely.*

PROF. MINTO. I would do it with pleasure, but frankly I am too busy. However, I could recommend to you a very good student of mine who has a perfect pronunciation because she is a native of Siena.

MISS CHAPMAN. You believe she is competent?

PROF. MINTO. If she weren't, I wouldn't recommend her.

MISS CHAPMAN. Is it absolutely out of the question for you to be able to give me a little of your time?

PROF. MINTO. Unfortunately, yes.

MISS CHAPMAN. Then I'll be grateful to you if you will give me the address of this student of yours.

PROF. MINTO. Immediately. — Here it is.

MISS CHAPMAN. Thank you.

PROF. MINTO. How long have you been in Italy?

MISS CHAPMAN. For about two months.

PROF. MINTO. And you like it here?

MISS CHAPMAN. Immensely.

31. MUSICA

Miss Chapman e il professor Minto

PROF. MINTO. Ha studiato musica in America?

MISS CHAPMAN. Sì, all'Università del Wisconsin.

PROF. MINTO. Bene, bene. E ha studiato anche canto?

MISS CHAPMAN. Sì. Son venuta in Italia a perfezionarmi.

PROF. MINTO. Ha voce di contralto?

MISS CHAPMAN. No, di mezzo soprano.

PROF. MINTO. E che cosa pensa di fare quando si sarà perfezionata?

MISS CHAPMAN. Chi lo sa? Cantare in concerti e, se avrò fortuna, fors'anche nell'opera.*

PROF. MINTO. Speriamo che abbia tutta la fortuna che desidera.

MISS CHAPMAN. Grazie.

PROF. MINTO. Quali opere Le piacciono?

MISS CHAPMAN. Molte, molte. Quelle di Verdi sono, naturalmente, le più famose, e non so che darei se potessi cantar la parte d'Amneris nell'*Aida*.

PROF. MINTO. Verdi non ha pari.

MISS CHAPMAN. Ora sto studiando col maestro Donadio la parte di Suzuki nella *Madama Butterfly*.

PROF. MINTO. Bella parte, specialmente nell'ultimo atto. Le piace la musica del Puccini?

MISS CHAPMAN. Moltissimo. Ma non voglio abusare più oltre della sua cortesia, professore. Grazie infinite e arrivederci.

PROF. MINTO. Arrivederci, Miss Chapman. Buona fortuna!

MISS CHAPMAN. Grazie.

32. DAL CARTOLAIO

Miss Conti e il cartolaio

MISS CONTI. Ho bisogno di parecchie cose.

CARTOLAIO. La servirò con piacere.

MISS CONTI. Ha della carta da scrivere di buona qualità?

CARTOLAIO. Foglietti e buste per lettere?

31. MUSIC

Miss Chapman and Professor Minto

PROF. MINTO. Did you study music in America?

MISS CHAPMAN. Yes, at the University of Wisconsin.

PROF. MINTO. Fine, fine. Did you study singing too?

MISS CHAPMAN. Yes. I came to Italy to perfect myself.

PROF. MINTO. Do you have a contralto voice?

MISS CHAPMAN. No, mezzo-soprano.

PROF. MINTO. And what do you intend to do when you are trained?

MISS CHAPMAN. Who knows? Sing in concerts, and if I am lucky, perhaps even in opera.*

PROF. MINTO. Let's hope that you have all the good luck you wish.

MISS CHAPMAN. Thank you.

PROF. MINTO. What operas do you like?

MISS CHAPMAN. Many of them. Verdi's are naturally the most famous, and I don't know what I'd give if I could sing the rôle of Amneris in *Aïda*.

PROF. MINTO. Verdi has no equal.

MISS CHAPMAN. Now I am studying the rôle of Suzuki in *Madama Butterfly* with Maestro Donadio.

PROF. MINTO. A beautiful rôle, especially in the last act. Do you like Puccini's music?

MISS CHAPMAN. Very much. But I don't want to take advantage of your kindness any longer, Professor. Many thanks and good-bye.

PROF. MINTO. Good-bye, Miss Chapman. Good luck!

MISS CHAPMAN. Thank you.

32. IN A STATIONERY STORE

Miss Conti and the Stationer

MISS CONTI. I need several things.

STATIONER. I'll be glad to help you.

MISS CONTI. Do you have good quality writing paper?

STATIONER. Sheets and envelopes for letters?

Miss Conti. Sì.

Cartolaio. Le mostrerò qualche cosa di veramente elegante. Ecco i due migliori tipi che abbiamo in negozio.

Miss Conti. Quanti foglietti e quante buste ci sono in ciascuna scatola?

Cartolaio. Cinquanta, signorina.*

Miss Conti. E che prezzo fanno queste scatole?

Cartolaio. Tutt'e due lo stesso prezzo: trentacinque lire la scatola.

Miss Conti. Caretto. Non ha nulla di più a buon mercato?

Cartolaio. Sicuramente. Ho mostrato quel che abbiamo di meglio. Ecco della carta meno di lusso.

Miss Conti. Oh, no! Non mi piace. Prenderò questa scatola.

Cartolaio. Che altro?

Miss Conti. Vorrei pure dell'inchiostro nero, un libretto per indirizzi e della ceralacca.

Cartolaio. Ceralacca per pacchi o per lettere?

Miss Conti. Per lettere. Preferibilmente azzurra o verde.

Cartolaio. Abbiamo delle scatolette con cinque cannelli di cinque colori differenti.

Miss Conti. Bravo! È proprio ciò che voglio.

33. ALLA BANCA

Mr. Hayes e un impiegato

Mr. Hayes. Vorrei aprire un conto corrente.

Impiegato. Con piacere. Posso chiederle quali referenze può fornire?

Mr. Hayes. Il console generale degli Stati Uniti.

Impiegato. Ottimamente. Quanto vuole depositare oggi?

Mr. Hayes. Venti mila lire. Le darò un assegno che ho ricevuto dall'America. Naturalmente, è in dollari.

Impiegato. Conteggeremo al cambio del giorno.

Mr. Hayes. Qual è il cambio d'oggi?

Impiegato. Diciannove e trenta.*

Mr. Hayes. Va bene.

Impiegato. Ora bisognerà riempire questo modulo. Nome?

Mr. Hayes. Graydon B. Hayes.

MISS CONTI. Yes.

STATIONER. I'll show you something really elegant. Here are the two best kinds we have in the store.

MISS CONTI. How many sheets and envelopes are there in each box?

STATIONER. Fifty.*

MISS CONTI. And how much do these boxes cost?

STATIONER. Both the same price. Thirty-five lire a box.

MISS CONTI. Rather expensive. Don't you have anything cheaper?

STATIONER. Surely. I have shown you the best we have. Here is some less fancy paper.

MISS CONTI. Oh, no! I don't like it. I'll take this box.

STATIONER. Anything else?

MISS CONTI. I'd also like some black ink, an address book, and some sealing wax.

STATIONER. Sealing wax for packages or for letters?

MISS CONTI. For letters. Preferably blue or green.

STATIONER. We have some little boxes with five sticks of five different colors.

MISS CONTI. Fine! That's just what I want.

33. AT THE BANK

Mr. Hayes and a Clerk

MR. HAYES. I'd like to open a checking account.

CLERK. Gladly. May I ask you what references you can furnish?

MR. HAYES. The consul general of the United States.

CLERK. Excellent. How much do you wish to deposit today?

MR. HAYES. Twenty thousand lire. I'll give you a check I have received from America. It's in dollars, of course.

CLERK. We shall figure it at today's exchange rate.

MR. HAYES. What's today's exchange rate?

CLERK. 19.30.*

MR. HAYES. Good.

CLERK. Now we shall have to fill out this blank. Name?

MR. HAYES. Graydon B. Hayes.

IMPIEGATO. Come si scrive?

MR. HAYES. Ecco; Le darò una mia carta da visita.

IMPIEGATO. Paternità?

MR. HAYES. Che vuol dire?

IMPIEGATO. Nome del padre.

MR. HAYES. Charles.

IMPIEGATO. Carlo. Nome di signorina di vostra madre.

MR. HAYES. Ida Fermo.

IMPIEGATO. Questo è più facile a scriversi.

MR. HAYES. Sì, mia madre è d'origine italiana.

IMPIEGATO. Dove e quando è nato?

MR. HAYES. A Boston, il 24 settembre 1931.

IMPIEGATO. Indirizzo di Roma?

MR. HAYES. Albergo Flora. Il mio indirizzo d'America è sulla mia carta da visita.

IMPIEGATO. L'ho visto, grazie. E ora voglia firmare qui.

34. VOLETE FARE UNA PASSEGGIATA?

La signorina Pucci e Mr. Hayes

SIGNORINA PUCCI. Che bella mattinata di maggio, non è vero?

MR. HAYES. Stupenda! Volete fare una passeggiata con me questo pomeriggio?

SIGNORINA PUCCI. Noi signorine non usciamo sole coi giovanotti.

MR. HAYES. Già, dimenticavo. Negli Stati Uniti non è così. Le signorine, da noi, hanno maggiore libertà.

SIGNORINA PUCCI. Siamo in Italia, Mr. Hayes, non in America.*

MR. HAYES. È giusto. Ma se vostra sorella venisse con noi, la cosa sarebbe possibile?

SIGNORINA PUCCI. Sì, e se la mamma dirà di sì.

MR. HAYES. Come lo potrò sapere?

SIGNORINA PUCCI. Telefonatemi.

MR. HAYES. Verso che ora?

SIGNORINA PUCCI. Un po' dopo mezzogiorno.

MR. HAYES. Non mancherò di farlo. Ma qual è il vostro numero di telefono?

SIGNORINA PUCCI. 3–7–1–2.

CLERK. How do you spell it?

MR. HAYES. Here. I'll give you one of my calling cards.

CLERK. Paternity?

MR. HAYES. What do you mean?

CLERK. The name of your father.

MR. HAYES. Charles.

CLERK. Carlo. Your mother's maiden name?

MR. HAYES. Ida Fermo.

CLERK. That is easier to write.

MR. HAYES. Yes, my mother is of Italian extraction.

CLERK. Where and when were you born?

MR. HAYES. In Boston, September 24th, 1931.

CLERK. Your Rome address?

MR. HAYES. Flora Hotel. My American address is on my calling card.

CLERK. I saw it, thank you. Now, please sign here.

34. DO YOU WANT TO TAKE A WALK?

Signorina Pucci and Mr. Hayes

SIGNORINA PUCCI. What a beautiful May morning, isn't it?

MR. HAYES. Stupendous! Do you want to take a walk with me this afternoon?

SIGNORINA PUCCI. We young ladies do not go out alone with young men.

MR. HAYES. Of course. I forgot. It isn't like that in the United States. Young ladies in our country have greater freedom.

SIGNORINA PUCCI. We are in Italy, Mr. Hayes, not in America.*

MR. HAYES. That's right. But if your sister were to come with us, would it be possible?

SIGNORINA PUCCI. Yes, and if Mother permits it.

MR. HAYES. How shall I [be able to] know?

SIGNORINA PUCCI. Call me up.

MR. HAYES. Around what time?

SIGNORINA PUCCI. A little after twelve.

MR. HAYES. I won't fail to do it. But what is your telephone number?

SIGNORINA PUCCI. 3712.

Mr. Hayes. Grazie.

Signorina Pucci. E dove andremmo?

Mr. Hayes. Dove voi volete, e poi . . .

Signorina Pucci. Poi?

Mr. Hayes. Poi potremo anche andare a un cinematografo.

Signorina Pucci. Purchè non si faccia troppo tardi.

Mr. Hayes. No. Vi prometto che vi condurrò a casa prima di notte.

35. DAL TABACCAIO

Mr. Guff e il tabaccaio

Tabaccaio. Che cosa desidera, signore?

Mr. Guff. Ha delle sigarette americane?

Tabaccaio. No, signore, ma ho le *Stelle d'Oro*, che sono molto simili alle sigarette americane.

Mr. Guff. Le proverò. Me ne dia un pacchetto.

Tabaccaio. Altro?

Mr. Guff. Una scatola di sigari buoni, del tabacco da pipa, e dei cerini.*

Tabaccaio. Ecco i migliori sigari che abbiamo, i *Trabucos*, ed ecco le due migliori qualità di tabacco da pipa. Questo è dolcissimo; questo è un po' più forte.

Mr. Guff. Quanto costa questo?

Tabaccaio. Otto lire il pacchetto.

Mr. Guff. E l'altro?

Tabaccaio. Lo stesso prezzo.

Mr. Guff. Prenderò un pacchetto di ciascuno per provare.

Tabaccaio. Una scatola di cerini?

Mr. Guff. No, due. Come le vende queste cartoline illustrate?

Tabaccaio. Ottanta centesimi l'una: nove lire la dozzina.

Mr. Guff. Ne sceglierò qualcuna.

Tabaccaio. Faccia pure.

36. DAL DENTISTA

Il signor De Palma e il dentista

De Palma. Buon giorno, dottore.

Dentista. Buon giorno, signor De Palma.

MR. HAYES. Thanks.

SIGNORINA PUCCI. And where would we go?

MR. HAYES. Wherever you want to, and then . . .

SIGNORINA PUCCI. Then?

MR. HAYES. Then we can go to a movie, too.

SIGNORINA PUCCI. Provided it won't get too late.

MR. HAYES. No. I promise I'll take you home before nightfall.

35. AT THE TOBACCO SHOP

Mr. Guff and the Tobacco Dealer

DEALER. What do you wish, sir?

MR. GUFF. Do you have any American cigarettes?

DEALER. No, sir, but I have *Stelle d'Oro*, which are very similar to American cigarettes.

MR. GUFF. I'll try them. Give me a package.

DEALER. Anything else?

MR. GUFF. A box of good cigars, some pipe tobacco, and some wax matches.*

DEALER. Here are the best cigars we have, *Trabucos*, and here are the two best qualities of pipe tobacco. This is very sweet; this is a little stronger.

MR. GUFF. How much does this cost?

DEALER. Eight lire a package.

MR. GUFF. And the other?

DEALER. The same price.

MR. GUFF. I'll take a package of each to try them.

DEALER. One box of matches?

MR. GUFF. No, two. How do you sell these picture post cards?

DEALER. Eighty *centésimi* apiece; nine lire a dozen.

MR. GUFF. I'll select some.

DEALER. Go right ahead.

36. AT THE DENTIST'S

Signor De Palma and the Dentist

DE PALMA. Good morning, doctor.

DENTIST. Good morning, Mr. De Palma.

De Palma. Dottore, ho una cavità in questo molare. Vorrei che me l'impiombasse, e vorrei pure che guardasse in che stato sono gli altri denti.

Dentista. Prego, s'accomodi e apra la bocca. Vediamo. Oh, sì! Il molare è cariato. Le fa male?

De Palma. Qualche volta. M'ha tenuto desto stanotte.*

Dentista. Ha fatto bene a venire. E meglio sarebbe stato se fosse venuto un po' prima. Il premolare vicino al dente guasto s'è anche cariato.

De Palma. Davvero?

Dentista. Sì, ma è una piccola cavità.

De Palma. In che stato son gli altri denti?

Dentista. Vediamo. Gl'incisivi e i canini sono in ottimo stato ... e pure gli altri molari.

De Palma. Meno male!

Dentista. Posso fare queste impiombature in oro. Poi avrebbe bisogno d'un ponte per riempire questo spazio vuoto e masticar bene

De Palma. Quanto costerebbe questo ponte?

Dentista. Da quattrocento a cinquecento lire.

De Palma. E in quanto tempo lo potrebbe mettere?

Dentista. Ciò dipende da quel che devo fare per le impiombature. Ma direi da venti giorni a un mese.

37. IN UN'AUTORIMESSA

Mr. Schulz e il meccanico

Meccanico. Benzina?

Mr. Schulz. Sì, anche benzina. Mi s'è sgonfiata una gomma. Può ripararla subito?

Meccanico. Certamente, signore.

Mr. Schulz. Bene. Allora scendo. Quanto tempo ci vorrà?

Meccanico. Una mezz'ora, su per giù. Quanta benzina devo mettere nel serbatoio?

Mr. Schulz. Lo riempisca.*

Meccanico. Quando s'è forata la gomma?

Mr. Schulz. Non lo so. Non me ne sono accorto che poco fa.

Meccanico. Il motore ha pure bisogno d'olio, signore.

DE PALMA. Doctor, I have a cavity in this molar. I'd like you to fill it for me, and I also would like you to see in what condition my other teeth are.

DENTIST. Please be seated and open your mouth. Let's see. Oh, yes! The molar is decayed. Does it hurt you?

DE PALMA. Sometimes. Last night it kept me awake.*

DENTIST. You did the right thing in coming. And it would have been better if you had come a little sooner. The premolar next to the bad tooth is also decayed.

DE PALMA. Really?

DENTIST. Yes, but it's a small cavity.

DE PALMA. In what condition are my other teeth?

DENTIST. Let's see. The incisors and the canines are in excellent condition . . . and so are the other molars.

DE PALMA. Thank Heaven!

DENTIST. I can make these two gold fillings. Then you would need a bridge to fill up this empty space and to chew well.

DE PALMA. How much would this bridge cost?

DENTIST. From 400 to 500 lire.

DE PALMA. And how soon could you put it in?

DENTIST. That depends on what I have to do for the fillings. But I would say from twenty days to a month from now.

37. IN A GARAGE

Mr. Schulz and the Garage Attendant

ATTENDANT. Gas?

MR. SCHULZ. Yes, gas, too. I have a flat tire. Can you repair it right away?

ATTENDANT. Certainly, sir.

MR. SCHULZ. Fine. Then I'll get out. How long will it take?

ATTENDANT. About a half hour. How much gas should I put in the tank?

MR. SCHULZ. Fill it up.*

ATTENDANT. When was the tire punctured?

MR. SCHULZ. I don't know. I noticed it only a little while ago.

ATTENDANT. The motor needs oil too, sir.

MR. SCHULZ. Ah, sì? Ce lo metta, allora. Io intanto andrò al caffè qui all'angolo.

MECCANICO. Ritorni fra una mezz'ora o quaranta minuti, e tutto sarà fatto.

MR. SCHULZ. Ci conto. E non dimentichi, per favore, di dare una pulitura al parabrezza. Ne ha bisogno.

MECCANICO. Non mancherò. Ha una bell'automobile, signore.

MR. SCHULZ. È una macchina americana.

MECCANICO. Me ne sono accorto.

MR. SCHULZ. Arrivederci, allora.

MECCANICO. Arrivederci, signore.

38. IN UN NEGOZIO DI DISCHI FONOGRAFICI
Miss Dodge e un'impiegata

MISS DODGE. Vorrei qualche disco di canzoni napoletane.

IMPIEGATA. Ecco il catalogo, signorina.

MISS DODGE. Dal catalogo non saprei scegliere perchè conosco pochissime canzoni napoletane. Non potrebbe consigliarmi Lei?

IMPIEGATA. Con piacere. Preferisce canzoni antiche o moderne?

MISS DODGE. M'è indifferente, purchè siano belle e ben cantate.*

IMPIEGATA. *La luna nova, Carmela, Mamma mia che vo' sapè*, cantata dal Villani, *Marechiare*, parole del Di Giacomo e musica del Tosti ...

MISS DODGE. Vorrei sentirle.

IMPIEGATA. Vuol favorire nella prima cabina? C'è lì un buon grammofono, e stamane v'ho messo un ago nuovo.

MISS DODGE. Volentieri. La musica italiana mi piace molto.

IMPIEGATA. Si suona molto in America?

MISS DODGE. Meno di quel che si dovrebbe. Adesso c'è una mania per la musica russa.

IMPIEGATA. Molta musica russa è bella, quella del Ciaicovski specialmente. In America piace anche la musica dello Stravinski?

MISS DODGE. Sì, purtroppo.

IMPIEGATA. Recentemente abbiamo ricevuto un magnifico concerto del Paganini. Vuol sentirlo? Son certa che Le piacerebbe.

Mr. Schulz. Oh, yes? Put it in, then. Meanwhile I'll go to the café there on the corner.

Attendant. Come back in half an hour or forty minutes, and everything will be done.

Mr. Schulz. I'll count on that. And please don't forget to clean the windshield. It needs it.

Attendant. I won't fail to do it. You have a fine car, sir.

Mr. Schulz. It's an American machine.

Attendant. I have noticed that.

Mr. Schulz. I'll be seeing you, then.

Attendant. Good-bye, sir.

38. IN A RECORD SHOP

Miss Dodge and a Clerk

Miss Dodge. I'd like some records of Neapolitan songs.

Clerk. Here is the catalogue, Madam.

Miss Dodge. I couldn't choose from the catalogue because I know very few Neapolitan songs. Couldn't you advise me?

Clerk. With pleasure. Do you prefer old or modern songs?

Miss Dodge. It makes no difference to me as long as they are beautiful and well sung.*

Clerk. *La luna nova, Carmela, Mamma mia che vo' sapè*, sung by Villani, *Marechiare*, words by Di Giacomo and music by Tosti . . .

Miss Dodge. I'd like to hear them.

Clerk. Will you please go into the first booth? There is a good phonograph there, and this morning I put in a new needle.

Miss Dodge. Gladly. I like Italian music very much.

Clerk. Is it played much in America?

Miss Dodge. Less than it ought to be. Now there is a craze for Russian music.

Clerk. Much of the Russian music is beautiful, especially that of Tchaikovsky. Is Stravinsky's music liked in America, too?

Miss Dodge. Unfortunately, yes.

Clerk. Recently we received a magnificent Paganini concerto. Would you like to hear it? I am certain you would like it.

Miss Dodge. Non ne dubito, ma non potrei portare molti dischi in una valigia al mio ritorno in America.

Impiegata. È vero.

Miss Dodge. E poi la musica del Paganini si può ottenere anche là.

Impiegata. Anche questo è vero. Ecco le canzoni, signorina. Favorisca qui.

39. DAL CALZOLAIO

Miss Kelly e un impiegato

Miss Kelly. Vorrei comprare un paio di scarpe.

Impiegato. Vuole accomodarsi, signorina? Che specie di scarpe desidera?

Miss Kelly. Delle scarpe comode, con tacchi piuttosto bassi, per camminare. No, no, non guardi queste che ho al piede perchè sono un po' strette.

Impiegato. Prenderò la misura del piede. Ha alcuna preferenza circa il colore?

Miss Kelly. Vorrei un marrone scuro.*

Impiegato. La servirò subito. — Ecco, signorina. Quest'è un bel paio di scarpe: solide, comode.

Miss Kelly. Me le faccia vedere. Oh, ma queste son troppo pesanti! Mi stancherebbero i piedi.

Impiegato. Ne ho di più leggere, ma d'un colore un po' più chiaro.

Miss Kelly. Allacciate, come queste?

Impiegato. Sì. Identiche a queste. — Ecco. Vuole provarle?

Miss Kelly. Proviamole.

Impiegato. Vanno benissimo. Vuol camminare un poco?

Miss Kelly. Quanto costano?

Impiegato. Cento cinquanta lire.

Miss Kelly. Le prendo. Può mandarmele all'albergo Metropoli, qui vicino?

Impiegato. Certo. Le piacerebbe vedere anche delle splendide calze di seta arrivate or ora da Milano?

Miss Kelly. Volentieri, se son di seta pura.

Impiegato. Favorisca al banco.

Miss Dodge. I don't doubt it, but I couldn't carry many records in a suitcase on my return to America.

Clerk. That's true.

Miss Dodge. Besides, Paganini's music can be obtained over there, too.

Clerk. That is also true. Here are the songs, Madam. Please come this way.

39. AT THE SHOE SHOP

Miss Kelly and a Clerk

Miss Kelly. I'd like to buy a pair of shoes.

Clerk. Will you please be seated, Madam ? What kind of shoes would you like ?

Miss Kelly. Comfortable shoes with rather low heels, for walking. No! No! Don't look at the ones I am wearing because they are a little tight.

Clerk. I'll take your foot measurement. Do you have any color preference ?

Miss Kelly. I would like a dark brown.*

Clerk. I'll take care of you immediately. — Here, Madam. This is a fine pair of shoes, solid, comfortable.

Miss Kelly. Let me see them. Oh, these are too heavy! They would tire my feet.

Clerk. I have some lighter ones, but of a little brighter color.

Miss Kelly. Laced, like these ?

Clerk. Yes, the same as these. Here. Would you like to try them on ?

Miss Kelly. Let's try them.

Clerk. They fit very well. Would you like to walk a little ?

Miss Kelly. How much are they ?

Clerk. One hundred fifty lire.

Miss Kelly. I'll take them. Can you send them to the Metropolis Hotel near by ?

Clerk. Certainly. Would you like to see some splendid silk hose, too, just arrived from Milan ?

Miss Kelly. Gladly, if they are of pure silk.

Clerk. Please come over to the counter.

40. IN UNO STABILIMENTO DI BAGNI

Jack e il cassiere

JACK. Una cabina per tre persone, per piacere.

CASSIERE. Diciotto lire.

JACK. Questo mio amico non ha costume da bagno. Sa dirmi dove potrà affittarne uno?

CASSIERE. Glielo darà il bagnaiolo a cui consegnerà questo biglietto.

JACK. E dove possiamo depositare i nostri portafogli e gli oggetti di valore?

CASSIERE. Allo sportello dirimpetto.

JACK. Tante grazie.

CASSIERE. Di nulla.*

Jack e l'impiegato

JACK. Abbiamo dei valori da depositare.

IMPIEGATO. Tutti e tre?

JACK. Sì, ciascun di noi.

IMPIEGATO. Firmino su questo registro. Scrivano affianco il loro indirizzo. Mettano poi i valori in queste tre buste, le chiudano, e firmino un'altra volta qui, di traverso sulla chiusura.

JACK. Ecco fatto.

IMPIEGATO. Cinquanta centesimi ciascuno. Grazie. Conservino queste targhette.

Jack e il bagnaiolo

BAGNAIOLO. Biglietto, prego.

JACK. Questo signore ha bisogno d'un costume da bagno.

BAGNAIOLO. Mi dispiace, ma costumi non ne abbiamo. Abbiamo mutandine.

JACK. Fa lo stesso.

BAGNAIOLO. Subito, signore.

JACK. E vuol dirmi dov'è la doccia?

BAGNAIOLO. Costà, a sinistra.

40. IN A BATHHOUSE

Jack and the Cashier

JACK. A cabin for three persons, please.

CASHIER. Eighteen lire.

JACK. This friend of mine has no bathing suit. Can you tell me where he can rent one?

CASHIER. The bath attendant, to whom you will give this ticket, will give him one.

JACK. And where can we check our wallets and valuables?

CASHIER. At the opposite window.

JACK. Many thanks.

CASHIER. You are welcome.*

Jack and the Clerk

JACK. We have some valuables to check.

CLERK. All three of you?

JACK. Yes, each of us.

CLERK. Sign on this register. Write your address on the side. Then put the valuables in these three envelopes, close them, and sign again here, across the flap.

JACK. Done.

CLERK. Fifty *centésimi* each. Thank you. Keep these tags.

Jack and the Bath Attendant

ATTENDANT. Ticket, please.

JACK. This gentleman needs a bathing suit.

ATTENDANT. I'm sorry, but we don't have any suits. We have trunks.

JACK. That will do just as well.

ATTENDANT. Right away, sir.

JACK. And can you tell me where the shower is?

ATTENDANT. There, to the left.

41. LETTERE PRIVATE

Signora Luisa De Chiara
Piazza Tasso 21
Sorrento
(Prov. di Napoli)

Dott. Carlo Martinelli
presso Fazio
Via Cernaia 14
Firenze

1. Raccomandazione

Gentilissima Signora,

Latrice della presente è Miss Mary Burke, ch'io conosco da diversi anni, e ch'è stata recentemente diplomata dall'Università di Boston.

È cattolica; ha maniere distinte, è dolce e modesta, ma energica al tempo stesso; parla diverse lingue moderne e suona bene il pianoforte.

Gliela raccomando perciò quale istitutrice per la signorina Sua figlia.

Coi più cordiali saluti, e sperando di rivederLa presto,

La Sua devotissima

PATRICIA KELLY

2. Un invito a pranzo

Egregio Dott. Martinelli,

Mia sorella e io vogliamo festeggiare, giovedì sera, il compleanno di mio marito, e abbiamo pensato di fargli una sorpresa invitando a pranzo, senza dir nulla a lui, alcuni dei suoi più cari amici.

Si pranzerà, come al solito, alle venti.   Potete venire?

So bene che avrei dovuto farvelo sapere un po' prima, ma la cosa è stata decisa solo mezz'ora fa.

Volete affidare la risposta, che speriamo affermativa, al latore della presente?

Salutandovi distintamente,

EMILIA TRAVENTINI

41. PERSONAL LETTERS

Mrs. Louise De Chiara
21 Tasso Square
Sorrento
(Province of Naples)

Dr. Charles Martinelli
c/o Fazio
14 Cernaia St.
Florence

1. *Recommendation*

My dear Madam,

The bearer of this letter is Miss Mary Burke, whom I have known for several years, and who recently graduated from Boston University.

She is a Catholic; she has fine manners, is sweet and modest, but at the same time energetic; she speaks several modern languages and plays the piano well.

I, therefore, recommend her to you as a governess for your daughter.

With best regards, and hoping to see you soon,

Sincerely yours,

PATRICIA KELLY

2. *A Dinner Invitation*

My dear Dr. Martinelli,

My sister and I wish to celebrate my husband's birthday on Thursday evening, and we thought of giving him a surprise party, inviting some of his dearest friends to dinner, without saying anything about it to him.

Dinner will be served, as usual, at eight. Can you come?

I know, of course, that I should have let you know a little earlier, but this was decided only a half hour ago.

Will you please give the answer, which we hope will be affirmative, to the bearer of this letter?

With sincere wishes,

EMILIA TRAVENTINI

3. Auguri a un'amica

Mia carissima Silvia,

Come vorrei trovarmi con te mercoledì, nel giorno del tuo onomastico, per farti a voce i miei più sinceri e affettuosi auguri!

Purtroppo, questo è impossibile, e perciò t'invio questi righi per
dirti che ti sarò vicina in pensiero e pregherò Dio che ti conceda
tutta la felicità che desideri, e salute, e fortuna in ogni cosa.

T'abbraccia e ti bacia

la tua amica

FLORA

42. LETTERE COMMERCIALI

1. A una casa editrice

Spett. Casa Editrice
Gius. Laterza & Figli
Bari

Avendo l'intenzione di formarmi una piccola biblioteca privata,
mi rivolgo a Voi per chiedere se sareste disposti ad accordarmi
uno sconto sul prezzo degli acquisti che farei presso di Voi.

M'interessa specialmente la vostra serie *Scrittori d'Italia*, e vorrei ordinare anche diversi libri del Croce.

Con distinti saluti,

GIULIO FIORENTINO
Via Vittorio Veneto 155, Roma

3. *Best Wishes to a Friend*

My dearest Sylvia,

How I would like to be with you on Wednesday, your Saint's day, to give you my most sincere and affectionate wishes in person!

Unfortunately that's impossible, and therefore I am sending you these lines to tell you that I'll be near you in thought, and I'll pray God that He may grant you all the happiness you wish, and health, and the best of luck in everything.

With much love,

Your friend

FLORA

42. BUSINESS LETTERS

1. *To a Publishing House*

Gius. Laterza & Sons
Publishers

Bari

Gentlemen:

Since I am planning to start a small private library, I take the liberty of writing to you to inquire whether you would be willing to grant me a discount on the price of the purchases I might make from you.

I am particularly interested in your series *Italian Writers*, and I should like to order also several of Croce's books.

Sincerely yours,

GIULIO FIORENTINO

155 Vittorio Veneto St., Rome

2. Dalla casa editrice

Sig. Giulio Fiorentino
Via Vittorio Veneto 155
Roma

In risposta alla pregiata v/ del 5 corr., siamo lieti d'informarVi che, nel v/ caso, siamo disposti ad accordarVi il 5% di sconto su gli acquisti che farete direttamente da noi, purchè questi siano d'un ammontare non inferiore alle lire mille.

Sotto fascia Vi spediamo il recentissimo catalogo delle n/ pubblicazioni, e intanto ci permettiamo di chiamare la v/ attenzione sull'altra n/ serie: *Biblioteca di Cultura Moderna.*

In attesa di v/ ordini, Vi salutiamo.

GIUS. LATERZA & FIGLI

3. Domanda d'impiego

Spett. Ditta Fratelli Falconi
Importazioni — Esportazioni
Genova

Gradirei sapere se codesta Ditta ha bisogno d'un provetto corrispondente per l'estero.

Ho perfetta conoscenza del francese, dello spagnolo e dell'inglese, e so esprimermi abbastanza bene in tedesco. Ho 29 anni, ho un diploma in scienze commerciali, e per gli ultimi sei anni sono stato occupato presso una ditta di New York.

Le migliori raccomandazioni e ogni altro schiarimento saranno forniti dietro richiesta.

Con rispettosi ossequi,

Devotissimo

WILLIAM GATES

2. *From the Publishing House*

Mr. Giulio Fiorentino
155 Vittorio Veneto St.
　　　　Rome

Dear Sir:

In reply to your favor of the 5th inst., we are glad to inform you that, in your case, we are willing to grant you a 5% discount on the purchases you make directly from us, provided that they amount to 1000 lire or more.

Under separate cover we are sending you the most recent catalogue of our publications, and, meanwhile, may we call your attention to our other series, *Library of Modern Culture?*

Trusting to hear from you soon,

　　　　　　　　Yours truly,

　　　　　　　　Gius. Laterza & Sons

3. *Application for a Job*

Falconi Brothers
Importers — Exporters
　　　　Genoa

Dear Sirs:

I would like to know whether your firm needs the services of a competent foreign correspondent.

I have a perfect knowledge of French, Spanish, and English, and can express myself sufficiently well in German. I am 29 years old, have a diploma in commercial science, and for the past six years have been employed by a New York firm.

The best references and any other information will be furnished to you upon request.

　　　　　　　　Respectfully yours,

　　　　　　　　William Gates

Appendix

I. AUXILIARY VERBS

avere

INFINITIVE	PERFECT INFINITIVE
avere, *to have*	avere avuto, *to have had*
PRESENT PARTICIPLE	PERFECT PARTICIPLE
avɛndo, *having*	avɛndo avuto, *having had*
PAST PARTICIPLE	
avuto, *had*	

INDICATIVE MOOD

PRESENT		PRESENT PERFECT		
I have, etc.		*I had or have had, etc.*		
hɔ	abbiamo	hɔ		abbiamo
hai	avete	hai } avuto		avete } avuto
ha	hanno	ha		hanno

PAST DESCRIPTIVE		PAST PERFECT		
I was having, used to have, etc.		*I had had, etc.*		
avevo	avevamo	avevo		avevamo
avevi	avevate	avevi } avuto		avevate } avuto
aveva	avevano	aveva		avevano

PAST ABSOLUTE		SECOND PAST PERFECT		
I had, etc.		*I had had, etc.*		
ɛbbi	avemmo	ɛbbi		avemmo
avesti	aveste	avesti } avuto		aveste } avuto
ɛbbe	ɛbbero	ɛbbe		ɛbbero

FUTURE		FUTURE PERFECT		
I shall have, am going to have, etc.		*I shall have had, etc.*		
avrɔ	avremo	avrɔ		avremo
avrai	avrete	avrai } avuto		avrete } avuto
avrà	avranno	avrà		avranno

SUBJUNCTIVE MOOD

PRESENT

I (may) have, etc.

abbia	abbiamo
abbia	abbiate
abbia	abbiano

PRESENT PERFECT

I (may) have had, etc.

abbia		abbiamo	
abbia	avuto	abbiate	avuto
abbia		abbiano	

PAST

I had or *might have, etc.*

avessi	avessimo
avessi	aveste
avesse	avessero

PAST PERFECT

I had had or *might have had, etc.*

avessi		avessimo	
avessi	avuto	aveste	avuto
avesse		avessero	

CONDITIONAL MOOD

PRESENT

I should have, etc.

avrɛi	avremmo
avresti	avreste
avrɛbbe	avrɛbbero

PERFECT

I should have had, etc.

avrɛi		avremmo	
avresti	avuto	avreste	avuto
avrɛbbe		avrɛbbero	

IMPERATIVE

Have, etc.

	abbiamo
abbi	abbiate

ɛssere

INFINITIVE	PERFECT INFINITIVE
ɛssere *to be*	ɛssere stato (–a) *to have been*
PRESENT PARTICIPLE	**PERFECT PARTICIPLE**
essɛndo *being*	essɛndo stato (–a) *having been*
PAST PARTICIPLE	
stato (–a) *been*	

INDICATIVE MOOD

PRESENT

I am, etc.

sono	siamo
sɛi	siɛte
ὲ	sono

PRESENT PERFECT

I was or have been, etc.

sono		siamo
sɛi	stato (–a)	siɛte	stati (–e)
ὲ		sono

PAST DESCRIPTIVE

I was being, used to be, etc.

ɛro	eravamo
ɛri	eravate
ɛra	ɛrano

PAST PERFECT

I had been, etc.

ɛro		eravamo
ɛri	stato (–a)	eravate	stati (–e)
ɛra		ɛrano

PAST ABSOLUTE

I was, etc.

fui	fummo
fosti	foste
fu	furono

SECOND PAST PERFECT

I had been, etc.

fui		fummo
fosti	stato (–a)	foste	stati (–e)
fu		furono

FUTURE

*I shall be, am going
to be, etc.*

sarɔ̀	saremo
sarai	sarete
sarà	saranno

FUTURE PERFECT

I shall have been, etc.

sarɔ̀		saremo
sarai	stato (–a)	sarete	stati (–e)
sarà		saranno

SUBJUNCTIVE MOOD

PRESENT

I (may) be, etc.

sia	siamo
sia	siate
sia	siano

PRESENT PERFECT

I (may) have been, etc.

sia		siamo
sia	stato (–a)	siate	stati (–e)
sia		siano

PAST

I was or might be, etc.

fossi	fossimo
fossi	foste
fosse	fossero

PAST PERFECT

I had been or might have been, etc.

fossi		fossimo
fossi	stato (–a)	foste	stati (–e)
fosse		fossero

CONDITIONAL MOOD

PRESENT		PERFECT	
I should be, etc.		*I should have been, etc.*	
sarɛi	saremmo	sarɛi	saremmo
saresti	sareste	saresti } stato (–a)	sareste } stati (–e)
sarɛbbe	sarɛbbero	sarɛbbe	sarɛbbero

IMPERATIVE

Be, etc.

	siamo
sii	siate

II. REGULAR VERBS

SIMPLE TENSES

1	II	III
	INFINITIVE	
compr–are, *to buy*	vend–ere, *to sell*	fin–ire, *to finish*
	PRESENT PARTICIPLE	
compr–ando, *buying*	vend–ɛndo, *selling*	fin–ɛndo, *finishing*
	PAST PARTICIPLE	
compr–ato, *bought*	vend–uto, *sold*	fin–ito, *finished*
	INDICATIVE MOOD	
	PRESENT	
I buy, do buy, am buying, etc.	*I sell, do sell, am selling, etc.*	*I finish, do finish, am finishing, etc.*
compr–o	vend–o	fin–isc–o [1]
compr–i	vend–i	fin–isc–i
compr–a	vend–e	fin–isc–e
compr–iamo	vend–iamo	fin–iamo
compr–ate	vend–ete	fin–ite
compr–ano	vend–ono	fin–isc–ono

[1] Certain verbs of the 3rd conjugation do not take –isc– in the present indicative, present subjunctive, and imperative.

Past Descriptive

I was buying, used to buy, etc.	*I was selling, used to sell, etc.*	*I was finishing, used to finish, etc.*
compr–**avo**	vend–**evo**	fin–**ivo**
compr–**avi**	vend–**evi**	fin–**ivi**
compr–**ava**	vend–**eva**	fin–**iva**
compr–**avamo**	vend–**evamo**	fin–**ivamo**
compr–**avate**	vend–**evate**	fin–**ivate**
compr–**avano**	vend–**evano**	fin–**ivano**

Past Absolute

I bought, etc.	*I sold, etc.*	*I finished, etc.*
compr–**ai**	vend–**ei** (–ɛtti)	fin–**ii**
compr–**asti**	vend–**esti**	fin–**isti**
compr–**ɔ̀**	vend–**ὲ** (–ɛtte)	fin–**ì**
compr–**ammo**	vend–**emmo**	fin–**immo**
compr–**aste**	vend–**este**	fin–**iste**
compr–**arono**	vend–**erono** (–ɛttero)	fin–**irono**

Future

I shall buy, am going to buy, etc.	*I shall sell, am going to sell, etc.*	*I shall finish, am going to finish, etc.*
comprer–**ɔ̀**	vender–**ɔ̀**	finir–**ɔ̀**
comprer–**ai**	vender–**ai**	finir–**ai**
comprer–**à**	vender–**à**	finir–**à**
comprer–**emo**	vender–**emo**	finir–**emo**
comprer–**ete**	vender–**ete**	finir–**ete**
comprer–**anno**	vender–**anno**	finir–**anno**

SUBJUNCTIVE MOOD

Present

I (may) buy, etc.	*I (may) sell, etc.*	*I (may) finish, etc.*
compr–**i**	vend–**a**	fin–**isc–a**
compr–**i**	vend–**a**	fin–**isc–a**
compr–**i**	vend–**a**	fin–**isc–a**
compr–**iamo**	vend–**iamo**	fin–**iamo**
compr–**iate**	vend–**iate**	fin–**iate**
compr–**ino**	vend–**ano**	fin–**isc–ano**

PAST

I bought or might buy, etc.	*I sold or might sell, etc.*	*I finished or might finish, etc.*
compr–**assi**	vend–**essi**	fin–**issi**
compr–**assi**	vend–**essi**	fin–**issi**
compr–**asse**	vend–**esse**	fin–**isse**
compr–**assimo**	vend–**essimo**	fin–**issimo**
compr–**aste**	vend–**este**	fin–**iste**
compr–**assero**	vend–**essero**	fin–**issero**

CONDITIONAL MOOD

PRESENT

I should buy, etc.	*I should sell, etc.*	*I should finish, etc.*
comprer–**εi**	vender–**εi**	finir–**εi**
comprer–**esti**	vender–**esti**	finir–**esti**
comprer–**εbbe**	vender–**εbbe**	finir–**εbbe**
comprer–**emmo**	vender–**emmo**	finir–**emmo**
comprer–**este**	vender–**este**	finir–**este**
comprer–**εbbero**	vender–**εbbero**	finir–**εbbero**

IMPERATIVE

Buy, etc.	*Sell, etc.*	*Finish, etc.*
compr–**a**	vend–**i**	fin–**isc-i**
compr–**iamo**	vend–**iamo**	fin–**iamo**
compr–**ate**	vend–**ete**	fin–**ite**

PERFECT TENSES

parlare, *to speak*　　　　　　**partire,** *to depart*

PERFECT INFINITIVE

avere parlato, *to have spoken*　　**εssere partito** (–a), *to have departed*

PERFECT PARTICIPLE

avεndo parlato, *having spoken*　　**εssendo partito** (–a), *having departed*

INDICATIVE MOOD

PRESENT PERFECT

I spoke or *have spoken, etc.*

ho ⎫
hai ⎬ parlato
ha ⎭

abbiamo ⎫
avete ⎬ parlato
hanno ⎭

I departed or *have departed, etc.*

sono ⎫
sɛi ⎬ partito (–a)
ὲ ⎭

siamo ⎫
siɛte ⎬ partiti (–e)
sono ⎭

PAST PERFECT

I had spoken, etc.

avevo ⎫
avevi ⎬ parlato
aveva ⎭

avevamo ⎫
avevate ⎬ parlato
avevano ⎭

I had departed, etc.

ɛro ⎫
ɛri ⎬ partito (–a)
ɛra ⎭

eravamo ⎫
eravate ⎬ partiti (–e)
ɛrano ⎭

SECOND PAST PERFECT

I had spoken, etc.

ɛbbi ⎫
avesti ⎬ parlato
ɛbbe ⎭

avemmo ⎫
aveste ⎬ parlato
ɛbbero ⎭

I had departed, etc.

fui ⎫
fosti ⎬ partito (–a)
fu ⎭

fummo ⎫
foste ⎬ partiti (–e)
furono ⎭

FUTURE PERFECT

I shall have spoken, etc.

avrɔ̀ ⎫
avrai ⎬ parlato
avrà ⎭

avremo ⎫
avrete ⎬ parlato
avranno ⎭

I shall have departed, etc.

sarɔ̀ ⎫
sarai ⎬ partito (–a)
sarà ⎭

saremo ⎫
sarete ⎬ partiti (–e)
saranno ⎭

SUBJUNCTIVE MOOD

PRESENT PERFECT

I (may) have spoken, etc.

$$\left.\begin{array}{l} abbia \\ abbia \\ abbia \end{array}\right\} parlato$$

$$\left.\begin{array}{l} abbiamo \\ abbiate \\ abbiano \end{array}\right\} parlato$$

I (may) have departed, etc.

$$\left.\begin{array}{l} sia \\ sia \\ sia \end{array}\right\} partito \ (-a)$$

$$\left.\begin{array}{l} siamo \\ siate \\ siano \end{array}\right\} partiti \ (-e)$$

PAST PERFECT

I had spoken or *might have spoken, etc.*

$$\left.\begin{array}{l} avessi \\ avessi \\ avesse \end{array}\right\} parlato$$

$$\left.\begin{array}{l} avessimo \\ aveste \\ avessero \end{array}\right\} parlato$$

I had departed or *might have departed, etc.*

$$\left.\begin{array}{l} fossi \\ fossi \\ fosse \end{array}\right\} partito \ (-a)$$

$$\left.\begin{array}{l} fossimo \\ foste \\ fossero \end{array}\right\} partiti \ (-e)$$

CONDITIONAL MOOD

PERFECT

I should have spoken, etc.

$$\left.\begin{array}{l} avrɛi \\ avresti \\ avrɛbbe \end{array}\right\} parlato$$

$$\left.\begin{array}{l} avremmo \\ avreste \\ avrɛbbero \end{array}\right\} parlato$$

I should have departed, etc.

$$\left.\begin{array}{l} sarɛi \\ saresti \\ sarɛbbe \end{array}\right\} partito \ (-a)$$

$$\left.\begin{array}{l} saremmo \\ sareste \\ sarɛbbero \end{array}\right\} partiti \ (-e)$$

PASSIVE VOICE

chiamare, *to call*

INFINITIVE	PERFECT INFINITIVE
to be called	*to have been called*
εssere chiamato (–a)	εssere stato (–a) chiamato (–a)

PARTICIPLE	PERFECT PARTICIPLE
being called	*having been called*
essendo chiamato (–a)	essendo stato (–a) chiamato (–a)

INDICATIVE MOOD

PRESENT	PRESENT PERFECT
I am called, etc.	*I was called or have been called, etc.*
sono chiamato (–a), *etc.*	sono stato (–a) chiamato (–a), *etc.*

PAST DESCRIPTIVE	PAST PERFECT
I was being called or used to be called, etc.	*I had been called, etc.*
εro chiamato (–a), *etc.*	εro stato (–a) chiamato (–a), *etc.*

PAST ABSOLUTE	SECOND PAST PERFECT
I was called, etc.	*I had been called, etc.*
fui chiamato (–a), *etc.*	fui stato (–a) chiamato (–a), *etc.*

FUTURE	FUTURE PERFECT
I shall be called, etc.	*I shall have been called, etc.*
sarɔ̀ chiamato (–a), *etc.*	sarɔ̀ stato (–a) chiamato (–a), *etc.*

SUBJUNCTIVE MOOD

PRESENT	PRESENT PERFECT
I (may) be called, etc.	*I (may) have been called, etc.*
sia chiamato (–a), *etc.*	sia stato (–a) chiamato (–a), *etc.*

PAST	PAST PERFECT
I was called or might be called, etc.	*I had been called or might have been called, etc.*
fossi chiamato (–a), *etc.*	fossi stato (–a) chiamato (–a), *etc.*

CONDITIONAL MOOD

<table>
<tr><td>PRESENT</td><td>PERFECT</td></tr>
<tr><td>I should be called, etc.</td><td>I should have been called, etc.</td></tr>
<tr><td>sarei chiamato (–a), etc.</td><td>sarei stato (–a) chiamato (–a), etc.</td></tr>
</table>

IMPERATIVE

Be called, etc.

sii chiamato (–a), *etc.*

III. IRREGULAR VERBS

All forms not listed below are regular. For the conjugation of the irregular past absolute, see § 104, p. 163; for the tense formation, see § 146, p. 249; for **avere** and **ɛssere**, see *Appendix I*.

Abbreviations used: *fut.* future; *impve.* imperative; *p. abs.* past absolute; *p. des.* past descriptive; *p. part.* past participle; *pres. ind.* present indicative; *pres. subj.* present subjunctive.

Verbs preceded by † are conjugated with **ɛssere**.

Verbs preceded by ° sometimes take **ɛssere**; sometimes, **avere**.

†1. **accadere** to happen (*impersonal*); *see* **cadere**

2. **accɛndere** to light

    P. Abs.   accesi, accendesti, *etc.*
    P. Part.   acceso

†3. **accingersi** to get ready; *see* **cingere**

4. **accludere** to enclose

    P. Abs.   acclusi, accludesti, *etc.*
    P. Part.   accluso

5. **accɔgliere** to receive; *see* **cɔgliere**

†6. **accɔrgersi** to be aware of; *see* **scɔrgere**

†7. **accorrere** to run up; *see* **correre**

8. **accrescere** to increase; *see* **crescere**

†9. **addirsi** (*contracted from* **addicersi**) to suit; *see* **dire**

10. **addurre** (*contracted from* **adducere**) to convey

Pres. Ind.	adduco, *etc.*
P. Des.	adducevo, *etc.*
P. Abs.	addussi, adducesti, *etc.*
Fut.	addurrò, *etc.*
P. Part.	addotto

11. **affiggere** to stick, fasten

P. Abs.	affissi, affiggesti, *etc.*
P. Part.	affisso

12. **affliggere** to afflict

P. Abs.	afflissi, affliggesti, *etc.*
P. Part.	afflitto

13. **aggiungere** to add; *see* **giungere**
14. **alludere** to allude; *see* **accludere**
15. **ammettere** to admit; *see* **mettere**
†16. **andare** to go

Pres. Ind.	vado *or* vɔ, vai, va, andiamo, andate, vanno
Fut.	andrò, *etc.*
Pres. Subj.	vada, andiamo, andiate, vadano
Impve.	va', andiamo, andate

17. **annettere** to annex

P. Abs.	annessi *or* annettei, annettesti, *etc.*
P. Part.	annesso

†18. **apparire** to appear

Pres. Ind.	appaio *or* apparisco, appari *or* apparisci, appare *or* apparisce, appariamo, apparite, appaiono *or* appariscono
P. Abs.	apparsi *or* apparvi *or* apparii, apparisti, *etc.*
Pres. Subj.	appaia *or* apparisca, appariamo, appariate, appaiano *or* appariscano
Impve.	appari *or* apparisci, appariamo, apparite
P. Part.	apparso *or* apparito

†19. **appartenere** to belong; *see* **tenere**
20. **appendere** to hang

P. Abs.	appesi, appendesti, *etc.*
P. Part.	appeso

21. **apporre** (*contracted from* **apponere**) to affix; *see* **porre**
22. **apprɛndere** to learn; *see* **prɛndere**
23. **aprire** to open

P. Abs.	apersi *or* aprii, apristi, *etc.*
P. Part.	apɛrto

24. **ardere** to burn

P. Abs.	arsi, ardesti, *etc.*
P. Part.	arso

†25. **arrɛndersi** to surrender; *see* **rɛndere**
°26. **ascendere** to ascend; *see* **scendere**
27. **assalire** to assail, assault; *see* **salire**
28. **assistere** to assist, be present

P. Part.	assistito

29. **assɔlvere** to absolve

P. Abs.	assɔlsi *or* assolvei *or* assolvɛtti, assolvesti, *etc.*
P. Part.	assɔlto *or* assoluto

30. **assumere** to assume

P. Abs.	assunsi, assumesti, *etc.*
P. Part.	assunto

†31. **astenersi** to abstain; *see* **tenere**
32. **attɛndere** to attend, wait; *see* **tɛndere**
33. **attingere** to draw up; *see* **tingere**
34. **attɔrcere** to twist, wring; *see* **tɔrcere**
†35. **avvedersi** to perceive; *see* **vedere**
†36. **avvenire** to happen (*impersonal*); *see* **venire**
37. **avvɔlgere** to wrap; *see* **vɔlgere**
38. **benedire** to bless; *see* **dire**
39. **bere** (*contracted from* **bevere**) to drink

Pres. Ind.	bevo, *etc.*
P. Des.	bevevo, *etc.*
P. Abs.	bevvi, bevesti, *etc.*
Fut.	berrɔ *or* beverɔ, *etc.*
P. Part.	bevuto

†40. **cadere** to fall

P. Abs.	caddi, cadesti, *etc.*
Fut.	cadrɔ, *etc.*

41. **chiεdere** to ask

> *Pres. Ind.* chiεdo *or* chiεggo, chiεdi, chiεde, chiediamo, chiedete, chiεdono *or* chiεggono
> *P. Abs.* chiεsi, chiedesti, *etc*
> *P. Part.* chiεsto

42. **chiudere** to close

> *P. Abs.* chiusi, chiudesti, *etc.*
> *P. Part.* chiuso

43. **cingere** to gird, embrace

> *P. Abs.* cinsi, cingesti, *etc.*
> *P. Part.* cinto

44. **cɔgliere** to gather

> *Pres. Ind.* cɔlgo, cɔgli, cɔglie, cogliamo, cogliete, cɔlgono
> *P. Abs.* cɔlsi, cogliesti, *etc.*
> *P. Part.* cɔlto

45. **commettere** to commit; *see* **mettere**
46. **commuɔvere** to move, affect; *see* **muɔvere**
†47. **comparire** to appear; *see* **apparire**
48. **compiacere** to please; *see* **piacere**
49. **compiangere** to pity; *see* **piangere**
50. **comporre** (*contracted from* **componere**) to compose; *see* **porre**
51. **comprεndere** to comprehend; *see* **prεndere**
52. **comprimere** to compress

> *P. Abs.* compressi, comprimesti, *etc.*
> *P. Part.* compresso

53. **concεdere** to concede, grant

> *P. Abs.* concεssi *or* concedei *or* concedεtti, concedesti, *etc.*
> *P. Part.* concεsso *or* conceduto

54. **conchiudere** *or* **concludere** to conclude; *see respectively* **chiudere** *and* **accludere**
55. **concɔrrere** to concur; *see* **cɔrrere**
†56. **condolersi** to condole with, complain; *see* **dolere**
57. **condurre** (*contracted from* **conducere**) to conduct; *see* **addurre**
58. **configgere** to drive in; *see* **figgere**
59. **confondere** to confuse, confound; *see* **fondere**
60. **congiungere** to join, connect; *see* **giungere**

61. **connɛttere** to connect; *see* **annɛttere**
62. **conoscere** to know

     P. Abs.   conobbi, conoscesti, *etc.*

†63. **consistere** to consist; *see* **assistere**
64. **contɛndere** to contend; *see* **tɛndere**
65. **contenere** to contain; *see* **tenere**
66. **contradire** to contradict; *see* **dire**
67. **contrarre** (*contracted from* **contraere**) to contract; *see* **trarre**
°68. **convenire** to agree, assemble; *see* **venire**
69. **convincere** to convince; *see* **vincere**
70. **convivere** to live together; *see* **vivere**
71. **coprire** to cover; *see* **aprire**
72. **corrɛggere** to correct; *see* **rɛggere**
°73. **correre** to run

     P. Abs.   corsi, corresti, *etc.*
     P. Part.   corso

74. **corrispondere** to correspond; *see* **rispondere**
75. **corrompere** to corrupt; *see* **rompere**
76. **costringere** to force; *see* **stringere**
77. **costruire** to construct, build

     P. Abs.   costrussi *or* costruii, costruisti, *etc.*
     P. Part.   costrutto *or* costruito

°78. **crescere** to grow

     P. Abs.   crebbi, crescesti, *etc.*

79. **cuɔcere** to cook

     Pres. Ind.   cuɔcio, cuɔci, cuɔce, cociamo, cocete, cuɔciono
     P. Abs.   cɔssi, cocesti, *etc.*
     P. Part.   cɔtto

80. **dare** to give

     Pres. Ind.   dɔ, dai, dà, diamo, date, danno
     P. Abs.   dɛtti *or* diɛdi, desti, *etc.*
     Fut.   darɔ, *etc.*
     Pres. Subj.   dia, diamo, diate, diano
     Past Subj.   dessi, *etc.*
     Impve.   da', diamo, date
     P. Part.   dato

81. **deci*d*ere** to decide

    P. Abs.   decisi, decidesti, *etc.*
    P. Part.   deci*s*o

†82. **decre*s*cere** to decrease; *see* **cre*s*cere**
83. **dedurre** (*contracted from* **dedu*c*ere**) to deduce, deduct; *see* **addurre**
84. **delu*d*ere** to delude, beguile; *see* **acclu*d*ere**
85. **deporre** (*contracted from* **deponere**) to depose, bear witness; *see* porre
86. **depr*i*mere** to depress; *see* **comprimere**
87. **der*i*dere** to deride; *see* **r*i*dere**
88. **descr*i*vere** to describe; *see* **scr*i*vere**
89. **dif*e*ndere** to defend

    P. Abs.   difesi, difendesti, *etc.*
    P. Part.   difeso

90. **diffondere** to diffuse; *see* **fondere**
†91. **dip*e*ndere** to depend; *see* **app*e*ndere**
92. **dip*i*ngere** to paint; *see* **p*i*ngere**
93. **dire** (*contracted from* **di*c*ere**) to say, tell

    Pres. Ind.   dico, dici, dice, diciamo, dite, d*i*cono
    P. Des.   dicevo, *etc.*
    P. Abs.   dissi, dicesti, *etc.*
    Fut.   dirò, *etc.*
    Pres. Subj. dica, diciamo, diciate, d*i*cano
    Impve.   di', diciamo, dite
    P. Part.   detto

94. **dir*i*gere** to direct

    P. Abs.   dir*e*ssi, dirigesti, *etc.*
    P. Part.   dir*e*tto

†95. **discendere** to descend; *see* **scendere**
96. **dischi*u*dere** to disclose, open; *see* **chi*u*dere**
97. **disci*o*gliere** to untie; *see* **sci*o*gliere**
98. **disc*o*rrere** to talk; *see* **c*o*rrere**
99. **discu*t*ere** to discuss

    P. Abs.   discussi, discutesti, *etc.*
    P. Part.   discusso

100. **disfare** (*contracted from* **disfacere**) to undo; *see* **fare**
101. **disgi*u*ngere** to disjoin, separate; *see* **gi*u*ngere**

102. **disilludere** to disappoint; *see* **accludere**
103. **disperdere** to disperse; *see* **perdere**
†104. **dispiacere** to be displeasing; *see* **piacere**
105. **disporre** (*contracted from* **disponere**) to dispose; *see* **porre**
106. **dissuadere** to dissuade; *see* **persuadere**
107. **distendere** to spread; *see* **tendere**
108. **distinguere** to distinguish

P. Abs.	distinsi, distinguesti, *etc.*
P. Part.	distinto

109. **distogliere** *or* **distorre** to dissuade, divert from; *see* **togliere**
110. **distrarre** (*contracted from* **distraere**) to distract, divert; *see* **trarre**
111. **distruggere** to destroy; *see* **struggere**
†112. **divenire** to become; *see* **venire**
113. **dividere** to divide

P. Abs.	divisi, dividesti, *etc.*
P. Part.	diviso

†114. **dolere** to ache, pain

Pres. Ind.	dɔlgo, duɔli, duɔle, doliamo, dolete, dɔlgono
P. Abs.	dɔlsi, dolesti, *etc.*
Fut.	dorrɔ̀, *etc.*
Pres. Subj.	dɔlga, doliamo, doliate, dɔlgano

°115. **dovere** to have to, be obliged, must

Pres. Ind.	dɛvo *or* dɛbbo, dɛvi, dɛve, dobbiamo, dovete, dɛvono *or* dɛbbono
Fut.	dovrɔ̀, *etc.*
Pres. Subj.	dɛva *or* dɛbba, dobbiamo, doviate *or* dobbiate, dɛvano *or* dɛbbano

116. **eleggere** to elect; *see* **leggere**
117. **elidere** to elide

P. Abs.	elisi, elidesti, *etc.*
P. Part.	eliso

118. **eludere** to elude; *see* **accludere**
†119. **emergere** to emerge

P. Abs.	emɛrsi, emergesti, *etc.*
P. Part.	emɛrso

120. **emettere** to emit; *see* **mettere**
121. **εrgere** to erect, raise

      P. Abs.   εrsi, ergesti, *etc.*
      P. Part.   εrto

122. **erigere** to erect, raise; *see* **dirigere**
123. **escludere** to exclude; *see* **accludere**
124. **esigere** to exact, collect

      P. Part.   esatto

†125. **esistere** to exist

      P. Part.   esistito

126. **espandere** to expand; *see* **spandere**
127. **espεllere** to expel

      P. Abs.   espulsi, espellesti, *etc.*
      P. Part.   espulso

128. **esplɔdere** to explode

      P. Abs.   esplɔsi, esplodesti, *etc.*
      P. Part.   esplɔso

129. **esporre** (*contracted from* **esponere**) to expose; *see* **porre**
130. **esprimere** to express; *see* **comprimere**
131. **estεndere** to extend; *see* **tεndere**
132. **estinguere** to extinguish; *see* **distinguere**
133. **estrarre** (*contracted from* **estraere**) to extract; *see* **trarre**
†134. **evadere** to evade.

      P. Abs.   evasi, evadesti, *etc.*
      P. Part.   evaso

135. **fare** (*contracted from* **facere**) to do, make

      Pres. Ind.   faccio *or* fɔ, fai, fa, facciamo, fate, fanno
      P. Des.   facevo, *etc.*
      P. Abs.   feci, facesti, *etc.*
      Fut.   farɔ, *etc.*
      Pres. Subj. faccia, facciamo, facciate, facciano
      Impve.   fa', facciamo, fate
      P. Part.   fatto

136. **fεndere** to split
      P. Part.   fesso

137. **figgere** to fix

P. Abs.	fissi, figgesti, *etc.*
P. Part.	fitto

138. **fingere** to feign, pretend; *see* **cingere**
139. **fondere** to melt

P. Abs.	fusi, fondesti, *etc.*
P. Part.	fuso

140. **frangere** to break

P. Abs.	fransi, frangesti, *etc.*
P. Part.	franto

141. **frapporre** (*contracted from* **frapponere**) to interpose, insert; *see* **porre**
142. **friggere** to fry

P. Abs.	frissi, friggesti, *etc.*
P. Part.	fritto

†143. **giacere** to lie

Pres. Ind.	giaccio, giaci, giace, giaciamo, giacete, giacciono
P. Abs.	giacqui, giacesti, *etc.*

°144. **giungere** to arrive, join (*the hands*)

P. Abs.	giunsi, giungesti, *etc.*
P. Part.	giunto

145. **godere** to enjoy

Fut.	godrò, *etc.*

146. **illudere** to delude, beguile; *see* **accludere**
147. **immergere** to immerse, plunge; *see* **emergere**
148. **imporre** (*contracted from* **imponere**) to impose; *see* **porre**
149. **imprimere** to imprint, impress; *see* **comprimere**
150. **incidere** to cut; *see* **decidere**
151. **includere** to include; *see* **accludere**
†152. **incorrere** to incur; *see* **correre**
†153. **increscere** to cause sorrow; *see* **crescere**
154. **incutere** to command, inspire; *see* **discutere**
155. **indurre** (*contracted from* **inducere**) to induce; *see* **addurre**
156. **inferire** to infer

P. Abs.	infersi *or* inferii, inferisti, *etc.*
P. Part.	inferto *or* inferito

157. **infliggere** to inflict; *see* **affliggere**
158. **infrangere** to break; *see* **frangere**
159. **insistere** to insist; *see* **assistere**
160. **intɛndere** to intend, understand; *see* **tɛndere**
161. **interporre** (*contracted from* **interponere**) to interpose; *see* **porre**
162. **interrompere** to interrupt; *see* **rompere**
†163. **intervenire** to intervene; *see* **venire**
164. **intraprɛndere** to undertake; *see* **prɛndere**
165. **intridere** to soak, temper

> P. *Abs.*   intrisi, intridesti, *etc.*
> P. *Part.*   intriso

166. **introdurre** (*contracted from* **introducere**) to introduce; *see* **addurre**
†167. **intrudersi** to intrude

> P. *Abs.*   m'intrusi, t'intrudesti, *etc.*
> P. *Part.*   intruso

168. **invadere** to invade; *see* **evadere**
169. **invɔlgere** to wrap; *see* **vɔlgere**
†170. **irrompere** to rush upon; *see* **rompere**
171. **iscrivere** to inscribe; *see* **scrivere**
172. **istruire** to instruct; *see* **costruire**
173. **lɛdere** to hurt, offend

> P. *Abs.*   lesi, ledesti, *etc.*
> P. *Part.*   leso

174. **lɛggere** to read

> P. *Abs.*   lɛssi, leggesti, *etc.*
> P. *Part.*   lɛtto

175. **maledire** (*contracted from* **maledicere**) to curse; *see* **dire**
176. **mantenere** to maintain; *see* **tenere**
177. **mettere** to put

> P. *Abs.*   misi, mettesti, *etc.*
> P. *Part.*   messo

178. **mɔrdere** to bite

> P. *Abs.*   mɔrsi, mordesti, *etc.*
> P. *Part.*   mɔrso

†179. **morire** to die

Pres. Ind.	muɔio, muɔri, muɔre, moriamo, morite, muɔiono
Fut.	morrɔ *or* morirɔ, *etc.*
P. Part.	mɔrto

180. **mungere** to milk

P. Abs.	munsi, mungesti, *etc.*
P. Part.	munto

181. **muɔvere** *or* **mɔvere** to move

Pres. Ind.	muɔvo *or* mɔvo, muɔvi *or* mɔvi, muɔve *or* mɔve, moviamo, movete, muɔvono *or* mɔvono
P. Abs.	mɔssi, movesti, *etc.*
P. Part.	mɔsso

†182. **nascere** to be born

P. Abs.	nacqui, nascesti, *etc.*
P. Part.	nato

183. **nascondere** to hide, conceal

P. Abs.	nascosi, nascondesti, *etc.*
P. Part.	nascosto

184. **nuɔcere** *or* **nɔcere** to hurt, harm

Pres. Ind.	nɔccio, nuɔci, nuɔce, nociamo, nocete, nɔcciono
P. Abs.	nɔcqui, nocesti, *etc.*

†185. **occorrere** to be necessary (*impersonal*); *see* **correre**
186. **offɛndere** to offend; *see* **difɛndere**
187. **offrire** to offer

P. Abs.	offɛrsi *or* offrii, offristi, *etc.*
P. Part.	offɛrto

188. **omettere** to omit; *see* **mettere**
189. **opporre** (*contracted from* **opponere**) to oppose; *see* **porre**
190. **opprimere** to oppress; *see* **comprimere**
191. **ottenere** to obtain; *see* **tenere**
†192. **parere** to seem, appear

Pres. Ind.	paio, pari, pare, paiamo *or* pariamo, parete, paiono
P. Abs.	parvi *or* parsi, paresti, *etc.*
Fut.	parrɔ, *etc.*
P. Part.	parso

193. **percorrere** to run over; *see* **correre**
194. **percuotere** to strike; *see* **scuotere**
195. **perdere** to lose

P. Abs.	pɛrsi *or* perdei *or* perdɛtti, perdesti, *etc.*
P. Part.	pɛrso *or* perduto

196. **permettere** to permit; *see* **mettere**
197. **persuadere** to persuade

P. Abs.	persuasi, persuadesti, *etc.*
P. Part.	persuaso

†198. **pervenire** to attain, arrive; *see* **venire**
†199. **piacere** to be pleasing

Pres. Ind.	piaccio, piaci, piace, piacciamo, piacete, piacciono
P. Abs.	piacqui, piacesti, *etc.*
Pres. Subj.	piaccia, piacciamo, piacciate, piacciano

200. **piangere** to cry, weep

P. Abs.	piansi, piangesti, *etc.*
P. Part.	pianto

201. **pingere** to paint

P. Abs.	pinsi, pingesti, *etc.*
P. Part.	pinto

†202. **piovere** to rain (*impersonal*)

P. Abs.	piɔvve

203. **porgere** to present, offer

P. Abs.	pɔrsi, porgesti, *etc.*
P. Part.	pɔrto

204. **porre** (*contracted from* **ponere**) to put, place

Pres. Ind.	pongo, poni, pone, poniamo, ponete, pongono
P. Abs.	posi, ponesti, *etc.*
Fut.	porrɔ̀, *etc.*
P. Part.	posto

205. **posporre** (*contracted from* **posponere**) to postpone; *see* **porre**
206. **possedere** to possess, own; *see* **sedere**

°207. **potere** to be able, may, can

Pres. Ind.	pɔsso, puɔi, puɔ̀, possiamo, potete, pɔssono
Fut.	potrɔ̀, *etc.*
Pres. Subj.	pɔssa, possiamo, possiate, pɔssano

208. **prediligere** to prefer

P. Abs.	predilɛssi, prediligesti, *etc.*
P. Part.	predilɛtto

209. **predire** (*contracted from* **predicere**) to predict; *see* **dire**

†210. **prefiggersi** to take into one's head; *see* **affiggere**

211. **premettere** to put before; *see* **mettere**

212. **prɛndere** to take

P. Abs.	presi, prendesti, *etc.*
P. Part.	preso

213. **preporre** (*contracted from* **preponere**) to prefer, place before; *see* **porre**

214. **prescegliere** to choose; *see* **scegliere**

215. **prescrivere** to prescribe; *see* **scrivere**

216. **presumere** to presume; *see* **assumere**

217. **pretɛndere** to pretend; *see* **tɛndere**

218. **prevedere** to foresee; *see* **vedere**

219. **prevenire** to anticipate, prevent, forewarn; *see* **venire**

220. **produrre** (*contracted from* **producere**) to produce; *see* **addurre**

221. **profferire** to utter; *see* **inferire**

222. **profondere** to pour out; *see* **fondere**

223. **promettere** to promise; *see* **mettere**

224. **promuɔvere** *or* **promɔvere** to promote; *see* **muɔvere**

225. **proporre** (*contracted from* **proponere**) to propose; *see* **porre**

†226. **prorompere** to burst out; *see* **rompere**

227. **proscrivere** to proscribe; *see* **scrivere**

228. **protɛggere** to protect

P. Abs.	protɛssi, proteggesti, *etc.*
P. Part.	protɛtto

†229. **provenire** to proceed from; *see* **venire**

230. **provvedere** to provide; *see* **vedere**

231. **pungere** to sting, prick

P. Abs.	punsi, pungesti, *etc.*
P. Part.	punto

232. **racchiudere** to include; *see* **chiudere**
233. **raccogliere** to gather; *see* **cogliere**
234. **radere** to shave

P. Abs.	rasi, radesti, *etc.*
P. Part.	raso

235. **raggiungere** to overtake; *see* **giungere**
236. **rapprendere** to congeal; *see* **prendere**
237. **rattenere** to restrain; *see* **tenere**
238. **rattorcere** to twist, wring; *see* **torcere**
†239. **rattrarsi** (*contracted from* **rattraersi**) to shrink; *see* **trarre**
†240. **ravvedersi** to repent; *see* **vedere**
241. **ravvolgere** to wrap up; *see* **volgere**
242. **recidere** to cut off; *see* **decidere**
243. **redigere** to draw up, edit; *see* **esigere**
244. **redimere** to redeem

P. Abs.	redensi, redimesti, *etc.*
P. Part.	redento

245. **reggere** to support

P. Abs.	ressi, reggesti, *etc.*
P. Part.	retto

246. **rendere** to render

P. Abs.	resi, rendesti, *etc.*
P. Part.	reso

247. **reprimere** to repress; *see* **comprimere**
248. **resistere** to resist; *see* **assistere**
249. **respingere** to push back; *see* **spingere**
†250. **retrocedere** to retrocede; *see* **concedere**
†251. **ricadere** to fall again; *see* **cadere**
252. **richiedere** to request; *see* **chiedere**
253. **riconoscere** to recognize; *see* **conoscere**
254. **ricoprire** to cover again; *see* **aprire**
†255. **ricorrere** to run again, have recourse; *see* **correre**
256. **ridare** to give back; *see* **dare**
257. **ridere** to laugh

P. Abs.	risi, ridesti, *etc.*
P. Part.	riso

258. **ridire** (*contracted from* **ridicere**) to say again; *see* **dire**

259. **ridurre** (*contracted from* **riducere**) to reduce; *see* **addurre**

260. **rifare** (*contracted from* **rifacere**) to do again, make again; *see* **fare**

261. **riflɛttere** to reflect

> *P. Part.*   riflɛsso *or* riflettuto

†262. **rimanere** to remain

> *Pres. Ind.*   rimango, rimani, rimane, rimaniamo, rimanete,
>   rimangono
> *P. Abs.*   rimasi, rimanesti, *etc.*
> *Fut.*   rimarrɔ̀, *etc.*
> *P. Part.*   rimasto

263. **rimettere** to replace, put again; *see* **mettere**

264. **rimɔrdere** to bite again, feel remorse; *see* **mɔrdere**

265. **rimpiangere** to regret; *see* **piangere**

266. **rimuɔvere** to remove; *see* **muɔvere**

†267. **rinascere** to be born again; *see* **nascere**

268. **rinchiudere** to shut in, enclose; *see* **chiudere**

†269. **rincrescere** to regret (*impersonal*); *see* **crescere**

270. **rinvenire** to find again; *see* **venire**

271. **ripercuɔtere** to reverberate, strike back; *see* **scuɔtere**

272. **riporre** (*contracted from* **riponere**) to put again; *see* **porre**

273. **riprɛndere** to retake, recover; *see* **prɛndere**

274. **riprodurre** (*contracted from* **riproducere**) to reproduce; *see* **addurre**

275. **riscuɔtere** to collect; *see* **scuɔtere**

276. **risɔlvere** to resolve; *see* **assɔlvere**

†277. **risorgere** to rise up again; *see* **sorgere**

278. **rispondere** to answer, reply

> *P. Abs.*   risposi, rispondesti, *etc.*
> *P. Part.*   risposto

279. **ristringere** to tighten again; *reflexive*, shrink; *see* **stringere**

280. **ritenere** to retain; *see* **tenere**

281. **ritrarre** (*contracted from* **ritraere**) to draw; *see* **trarre**

†282. **riuscire** to succeed, go out again; *see* **uscire**

283. **rivedere** to see again; *see* **vedere**

°284. **rivivere** to live again; *see* **vivere**

285. **rivɔlgere** to turn, turn again; *see* **vɔlgere**

286. **rodere** to gnaw

    P. Abs.   rosi, rodesti, *etc.*
    P. Part.   roso

287. **rompere** to break

    P. Abs.   ruppi, rompesti, *etc.*
    P. Part.   rotto

°288. **salire** to ascend, climb, go up, get on

    Pres. Ind.   salgo, sali, sale, saliamo, salite, salgono

289. **sapere** to know, know how

    Pres. Ind.   sɔ, sai, sa, sappiamo, sapete, sanno
    P. Abs.   sɛppi, sapesti, *etc.*
    Fut.   saprɔ̀, *etc.*
    Pres. Subj. sappia, sappiamo, sappiate, sappiano
    Impve.   sappi, sappiamo, sappiate

†290. **scadere** to fall due; *see* **cadere**

291. **scegliere** to select

    Pres. Ind.   scelgo, scegli, sceglie, scegliamo, scegliete, scelgono
    P. Abs.   scelsi, scegliesti, *etc.*
    P. Part.   scelto

°292. **scendere** to descend, go down, get down

    P. Abs.   scesi, scendesti, *etc.*
    P. Part.   sceso

293. **schiudere** to open; *see* **chiudere**

294. **scindere** to separate

    P. Abs.   scissi, scindesti, *etc.*
    P. Part.   scisso

295. **sciogliere** to untie, dissolve

    Pres. Ind.   sciɔlgo, sciɔgli, sciɔglie, sciogliamo, sciogliete, sciɔlgono
    P. Abs.   sciɔlsi, sciogliesti, *etc.*
    P. Part.   sciɔlto

296. **scommettere** to bet; *see* **mettere**

†297. **scomparire** to disappear; *see* **apparire**

298. **scomporre** (*contracted from* **scomponere**) to undo; *see* **porre**

299. **sconfiggere** to defeat; *see* **figgere**
300. **sconnettere** to disconnect; *see* **annettere**
301. **sconoscere** to repay with ingratitude; *see* **conoscere**
302. **scontorcere** to contort, twist; *see* **torcere**
303. **sconvolgere** to overturn, upset; *see* **volgere**
304. **scoprire** to discover; *see* **aprire**
305. **scorgere** to perceive

P. Abs.	scorsi, scorgesti, *etc.*
P. Part.	scorto

†306. **scorrere** to flow; *see* **correre**
307. **scrivere** to write

P. Abs.	scrissi, scrivesti, *etc.*
P. Part.	scritto

308. **scuotere** to shake

Pres. Ind.	scuoto, scuoti, scuote, scotiamo, scotete, scuotono
P. Abs.	scossi, scotesti, *etc.*
Fut.	scoterò, *etc.*
P. Part.	scosso

309. **sedere** to sit

Pres. Ind.	siedo *or* seggo, siedi, siede, sediamo, sedete, siedono *or* seggono

310. **sedurre** (*contracted from* **seducere**) to seduce; *see* **addurre**
311. **seppellire** to bury

P. Part.	sepolto *or* seppellito

312. **smettere** to cease; *see* **mettere**
313. **smuovere** to move, displace; *see* **muovere**
314. **socchiudere** to half shut; *see* **chiudere**
315. **soccorrere** to assist; *see* **correre**
316. **soddisfare** (*contracted from* **soddisfacere**) to satisfy; *see* **fare**
317. **soffrire** to suffer; *see* **offrire**
318. **soggiungere** to add; *see* **giungere**
†319. **solere** to be accustomed

Pres. Ind.	soglio, suoli, suole, sogliamo, solete, sogliono
Pres. Subj.	soglia, sogliamo, sogliate, sogliano
P. Part.	solito

320. **sommεrgere** to submerge; *see* **emεrgere**
321. **sopprimere** to suppress; *see* **comprimere**
322. **sopraffare** (*contracted from* **sopraffacere**) to overcome; *see* **fare**
†323. **sorgere** to arise

P. Abs.	sorsi, sorgesti, *etc.*
P. Part.	sorto

324. **sorprεndere** to surprise; *see* **prεndere**
325. **sorrεggere** to support; *see* **rεggere**
326. **sorridere** to smile; *see* **ridere**
327. **sospεndere** to suspend; *see* **appεndere**
328. **sostenere** to support; *see* **tenere**
329. **sottintεndere** to imply; *see* **tεndere**
330. **sottomettere** to subdue; *see* **mettere**
331. **sottrarre** (*contracted from* **sottraere**) to subtract; *see* **trarro**
332. **spandere** to spread, spill

P. Part.	spanto

333. **spargere** to spread, scatter

P. Abs.	sparsi, spargesti, *etc.*
P. Part.	sparso

†334. **sparire** to disappear

P. Abs.	sparii *or* sparvi, sparisti, *etc.*

335. **spεgnere** *or* **spεngere** to extinguish

P. Abs.	spεnsi, spengesti, *etc.*
P. Part.	spεnto

336. **spεndere** to spend

P. Abs.	spesi, spendesti, *etc.*
P. Part.	speso

†337. **spεrdersi** to disappear; *see* **pεrdere**
338. **spingere** to push

P. Abs.	spinsi, spingesti, *etc.*
P. Part.	spinto

339. **sporgere** to hold out, project; *see* **porgere**

†340. **stare** to stay, stand, be

Pres. Ind.	stɔ, stai, sta, stiamo, state, stanno
P. Abs.	stɛtti, stesti, stɛtte, stemmo, steste, stɛttero
Fut.	starɔ̀, *etc.*
Pres. Subj.	stia, stiamo, stiate, st*iano*
Past Subj.	stessi, *etc.*
Impve.	sta', stiamo, state
P. Part.	stato

341. **stɛndere** to stretch out; *see* **tɛndere**
342. **stɔrcere** to wrest, twist; *see* **tɔrcere**
343. **stringere** to bind fast

P. Abs.	strinsi, stringesti, *etc.*
P. Part.	stretto

344. **struggere** to melt, pine away

P. Abs.	strussi, struggesti, *etc.*
P. Part.	strutto

†345. **succɛdere** to succeed, happen; *see* **concɛdere**
346. **supporre** (*contracted from* **supponere**) to suppose; *see* **porre**
347. **svɛllere** to uproot

Pres. Ind.	svɛllo *or* svɛlgo, svɛlli *or* svɛlgi, svɛlle *or* svɛlge, svelliamo *or* svelgiamo, svellete *or* svelgete, svɛllono *or* svɛlgono
P. Abs.	svɛlsi, svelgesti, *etc.*
Pres. Subj.	svɛlga, svelliamo, svelliate, svɛlgano
P. Part.	svɛlto

†348. **svenire** to faint away; *see* **venire**
349. **svɔlgere** to unfold; *see* **vɔlgere**
350. **tacere** to be silent

Pres. Ind.	taccio, taci, tace, taciamo, tacete, tacciono
P. Abs.	tacqui, tacesti, *etc.*

351. **tɛndere** to tend

P. Abs.	tesi, tendesti, *etc.*
P. Part.	teso

352. **tenere** to hold, have

Pres. Ind.	tɛngo, tiɛni, tiɛne, teniamo, tenete, tɛngono
P. Abs.	tenni, tenesti, *etc.*
Fut.	terrɔ̀, *etc.*

353. **tɛrgere** to wipe, dry

    P. Abs.   tɛrsi, tergesti, *etc.*

    P. Part.   tɛrso

354. **tingere** to dye

    P. Abs.   tinsi, tingesti, *etc.*

    P. Part.   tinto

355. **tɔgliere** *or* **tɔrre** to take from

    Pres. Ind.   tɔlgo, tɔgli, tɔglie, togliamo, togliete, tɔlgono

    P. Abs.   tɔlsi, togliesti, *etc.*

    Fut.   togliɛrɔ *or* torrɔ, *etc.*

    P. Part.   tɔlto

356. **tɔrcere** to twist, writhe

    P. Abs.   tɔrsi, torcesti, *etc.*

    P. Part.   tɔrto

357. **tradurre** (*contracted from* **traducere**) to translate; *see* **addurre**

358. **trafiggere** to transfix, pierce through; *see* **figgere**

359. **transigere** to come to terms; *see* **esigere**

360. **trarre** (*contracted from* **traere**) to draw, pull

    Pres. Ind.   traggo, trai, trae, traiamo, traete, traggono

    P. Abs.   trassi, traesti, *etc.*

    Fut.   trarrɔ, *etc.*

    Pres. Subj.   tragga, traiamo, traiate, traggano

    P. Part.   tratto

361. **trascorrere** to pass over; *see* **correre**

362. **trascrivere** to transcribe; *see* **scrivere**

363. **trasmettere** to transmit, send; *see* **mettere**

†364. **trasparire** to appear through; *see* **apparire**

365. **trattenere** to detain, refrain; *see* **tenere**

366. **travɔlgere** to overpower; *see* **vɔlgere**

367. **uccidere** to kill

    P. Abs.   uccisi, uccidesti, *etc.*

    P. Part.   ucciso

368. **udire** to hear

    Pres. Ind.   ɔdo, ɔdi, ɔde, udiamo, udite, ɔdono

    Pres. Subj.   ɔda, udiamo, udiate, ɔdano

369. **ungere** to grease

| P. Abs. | unsi, ungesti, *etc.* |
| P. Part. | unto |

†370. **uscire** to go out

| Pres. Ind. | ɛsco, ɛsci, ɛsce, usciamo, uscite, ɛscono |
| Pres. Subj. | ɛsca, usciamo, usciate, ɛscano |

†371. **valere** to be worth

Pres. Ind.	valgo, vali, vale, valiamo, valete, valgono
P. Abs.	valsi, valesti, *etc.*
Fut.	varrɔ̀, *etc.*
Pres. Subj.	valga, valiamo, valiate, valgano
P. Part.	valso

372. **vedere** to see

P. Abs.	vidi, vedesti, *etc.*
Fut.	vedrɔ̀, *etc.*
P. Part.	visto *or* veduto

†373. **venire** to come

Pres. Ind.	vɛngo, viɛni, viɛne, veniamo, venite, vɛngono
P. Abs.	venni, venisti, *etc.*
Fut.	verrɔ̀, *etc.*
P. Part.	venuto

374. **vincere** to win

| P. Abs. | vinsi, vincesti, *etc.* |
| P. Part. | vinto |

°375. **vivere** to live

P. Abs.	vissi, vivesti, *etc.*
Fut.	vivrɔ̀, *etc.*
P. Part.	vissuto

°376. **volere** to will, wish, want

Pres. Ind.	vɔglio, vuɔi, vuɔle, vogliamo, volete, vɔgliono
P. Abs.	vɔlli, volesti, *etc.*
Fut.	vorrɔ̀, *etc.*
Pres. Subj.	vɔglia, vogliamo, vogliate, vɔgliano
Impve.	vɔgli, vogliamo, vogliate

377. **vɔlgere** to turn, revolve

    P. Abs.   vɔlsi, volgesti, *etc.*

    P. Part.   vɔlto

IV. PERSONAL PRONOUNS

SUBJECT		OBJECT			
		CONJUNCTIVE			DISJUNCTIVE
	Persons	*Direct Obj.*	*Indirect Obj.*	*Reflexive*	
Singular 1.	io	mi	mi[1]	mi	me
2.	tu	ti	ti	ti	te
3.	egli, ella / esso, essa	lo, la	gli, le[2]	si	lui, lɛi, sè
	Ella, Lɛi	La	Le		Lɛi, sè
Plural 1.	noi	ci	ci	ci	noi
2.	voi	vi	vi	vi	voi
3.	essi, esse	li, le	loro	si	loro, sè
	Loro	Li, Le	Loro		Loro, sè
		ne (*of it, of them, some, any, some of it, some of them, any of it, any of them*)			

[1] **mi, ti, si, ci, vi** become **me, te, se, ce, ve** before **lo, la, li, le,** or **ne**.
[2] **gli** or **le** (indifferently which) contract with **lo, la, li, le,** or **ne**, and become **glielo, gliela, glieli, gliele,** or **gliene**.

ABBREVIATIONS

abs.	absolute	*irr.*	irregular
adj.	adjective	*m.*	masculine
adv.	adverb	*n.*	noun
art.	article	*neg.*	negative
cond.	conditional	*obs.*	obsolete
conj.	conjunction	*p.*	past
def.	definite	*part.*	participle
dem.	demonstrative	*pl.*	plural
des.	descriptive	*poet.*	poetic
f.	feminine	*poss.*	possessive
fut.	future	*prep.*	preposition
imp.	impersonal	*pres.*	present
impve.	imperative	*pron.*	pronoun
ind.	indicative	*rel.*	relative
inter.	interrogative	*subj.*	subjunctive
interj.	interjection	*superl.*	superlative
intr.	intransitive	*tr.*	transitive
inv.	invariable	*v.*	verb

* Words studied in the lessons: active vocabulary.

† Verbs conjugated with ɛssere.

° Verbs conjugated sometimes with ɛssere, sometimes with avere.

(*In order not to confuse the student, this last sign has been omitted in the English-Italian Vocabulary.*)

Nouns ending in –o are masculine, and those ending in –a are feminine, unless otherwise indicated.

In the Italian-English Vocabulary, verb forms are given in parentheses after the infinitive in the following cases: the present indicative 1st person sing. if the stress rests on the third-from-the-last vowel, or if the stressed vowel is e or o, or if the verb belongs to the 3rd conjugation; the past absolute 1st person sing. and the past participle, if the stressed vowel is e or o, or if the form contains an intervocalic s.

In the English-Italian Vocabulary, only the present indicative 1st person sing. is given after an infinitive, and then only if the stress rests on the third-from-the-last *syllable*, or if the verb belongs to the 3rd conjugation.

The preposition commonly used with a verb or an adjective before a dependent infinitive is shown in parentheses after the word.

Italian-English Vocabulary

A

*a, ad to, at, for, in, on, until, with
*abbaiare [abbaio] to bark
*abbastanza enough, quite
*abbracciare [abbraccio] to embrace
*abitante m. inhabitant
*abitare [abito] to dwell, live
*abito suit (of clothes) pl. clothes
abusare to abuse
*abuso abuse
acacia acacia
*accademia academy
*accento accent
*accettare (di) [accetto] to accept
acciaio steel
†accomodarsi [m'accomodo] to make oneself comfortable
accomodatevi please be seated
*accompagnare to accompany
accordare (di) [accordo] to grant
†accorgersi (di) irr. v. [m'accorgo, m'accorsi, accorto] to notice
†*accorrere (a) irr. v. [accorro, accorsi, accorso] to run up, flock together
accorto, p. part. of accorgersi
*accumulare [accumulo] to accumulate, gather
acido acid
*acqua water
acquisto acquisition, purchase
*acre sour
acuto sharp
*ad, see a
*addio farewell, good-bye; dare un —, to say farewell
*adesso now
affare m. affair, business
*affascinante fascinating
*affascinare [affascino] to fascinate
affermativo affirmative

affettuoso affectionate
affianco on the side
affidare to entrust, give
*affinchè (followed by the subj.) in order that, so that
affittare to rent
*affresco fresco
†*affrettarsi (a) [m'affretto] to hasten
*Africa Africa
agente m. agent
agganciare [aggancio] to clasp
aggettivale adjectival
aggettivo adjective
aggio agio, premium
*aggiungere irr. v. to add
aggravio burden
agio leisure
agire [agisco] to act
*agitare [agito] to wave, stir, shake
aglio garlic
*agnello lamb
ago needle
*agosto August
*Agrigento f., a very ancient and famous city of Greek origin on the southern shore of Sicily (population 35,000)
ah! ah! oh!
*ahimè! alas!
Aida Aïda, probably the most famous of Verdi's operas
*aiutare (a) to help, aid
*ala (pl. le ali) wing
*albergo hotel
*albero tree
*albicocca apricot; albicocco apricot tree
*alcuno some, any (pl. few)
*Alfieri, Vittorio (1749–1803), of Asti, Piedmont, one of the noblest Italian poets, supreme as a tragedian

*Alighieri, Dante (1265–1321), *of Florence, author of "The Divine Comedy" — the loftiest of all poems — and of some of the best prose and finest lyrics in Italian literature*

allacciato laced

*allegramente gaily, cheerfully

*allegria cheerfulness

*allegro gay, cheerful, jolly

*allietare [allieto] to rejoice

*alloggiare [alloggio] to lodge, stay

*allora then, at that time; fino —, until then

*Alpi f. pl. Alps

*alto high, tall, lofty; ad alta voce aloud

altrettanto just as much. just the same, same

*altro other, else, any other, anything else; dell' —, some more; l'un l'—, each other, one another; — che! I should say so!

*alunno, alunna pupil

†*alzarsi to rise, get up

*Amalfi f., a charming little town on the bay of Salerno, south of Naples

*Amalia Amelia

*amare to love

*amaro bitter

*America America

*americano American

*amico, amica friend

ammazzare to kill

*ammirare to admire

†ammogliarsi [m'ammoglio] to marry, get married

ammontare n. m. amount

amore m. love; un — di bimba an adorable baby

analisi f. (inv.) analysis

*anche also, too, even

*ancora still, yet, even, again

*andarci or andarvi to go there

†*andare (a) irr. v. [vado or vo] to go, walk, ride

*Andrea Andrew

'anello ring

*anfiteatro amphitheater

*angioino Angevin

*angolo corner; all' —, on the corner

anguilla eel

angusto narrow

*animale m. animal

*anitra duck

*Anna Ann

*annata year (in its duration, or referring to weather or work)

*anno year; l'— venturo next year; l'— scorso last year; di tre anni three years old

†*annottare imp. v. [annotta] to get dark

annunziare (di) [annunzio] to announce

*annunzio announcement, advertisement

*antico ancient, old

*antipasto appetizers

*Antonio Anthony

anzi much more, moreover

*anzichè rather than

*aperto (p. part. of aprire) opened, open; all' —, in the open, outdoors

apocope f. apocopation

*apparecchiare [apparecchio] to prepare, set (a table)

†*apparire irr. v. [apparisco or appaio] to appear, look, seem

apparizione f. apparition

appassionato passionate, fiery

*appena as soon as, scarcely

*appendere irr. v. [appendo, appesi, appeso] to hang, hang up

*Appennini m. pl. Apennines, mountains that run from north to south through Italy

*appetito appetite; aver —, to be hungry

*appiè di at the foot of

*applauso applause, cheers

applicare [applico] to apply

*appuntamento appointment

appunto or per l'appunto exactly, precisely

*aprile *m.* April
*aprire *irr. v.* [apro, apɛrsi, apɛrto]
  to open
ara altar
*arancio orange, orange tree
*arco arch
*argenteria silverware
argɛnto silver
*aria air, aria
*armadio closet, wardrobe
*Arno, *a river in Tuscany on the
  banks of which Florence and Pisa
  are situated*
arra token
†*arrivare (a) to arrive; bɛn arrivato! welcome!
*arrivederci! till we meet again!
  good-bye! so long!
*arrivo arrival
arrostire [arrostisco] to roast;
  — sulla gratɛlla to broil
*arrɔsto roast; pollo —, roast
  chicken
*arte *f.* art
articolato, *see* preposizione
articolo article
artigiano artisan
*artista *m. or f.* artist; fare l'—,
  to be an artist
*artisticamente artistically
*artistico artistic
*ascensore *m.* elevator, lift
asciugare to wipe, wipe dry
*ascoltare [ascolto] to listen,
  listen to
*asino ass, donkey
*aspettare [aspɛtto] to wait, wait
  for; †aspettarsi (di) to expect
*aspɛtto aspect, appearance; *see*
  sala
aspirina aspirin
*assai very, quite, very much, a
  great deal
assegno check
*assɛnte absent
*assicurare (di) to assure, insure
*Assisi *f., a town in Umbria, the
  birthplace of St. Francis* (1182–
  1226)

assolutamente absolutely
assoluto absolute
asterisco asterisk
*atrio lobby, entrance hall
*attɛndere (di) *irr. v.* [attɛndo,
  attesi, atteso] to wait, wait for
*attentamente attentively
*attɛnto attentive
attenzione *f.* attention
attesa waiting, expectation
*attirare to attract
atto act
*attraɛnte attractive
*attraversare [attravɛrso] to cross,
  go through
*attrazione *f.* attraction
augurio wish, season's greeting;
  fare auguri to give one's best
  wishes
*aula classroom
aumentativo augmentative
ausiliare auxiliary
*autista *m.* chauffeur, driver
*autobus *m.* (*inv.*) autobus
*automɔbile *f.* automobile
autorimessa garage
*autunno autumn, fall
*avanti forward, before, ahead,
  first; — che (*followed by the
  subj.*) before
*avere *irr. v.* [hɔ, ɛbbi] to have, receive (*Idioms in which avere
  appears are registered only under
  the other words concerned.*)
avo grandfather; gli avi the
  forefathers
avverbiale adverbial
avvɛrbio adverb
†*avviarsi (a) to start on one's way
*avvocato lawyer; fare l'—, to be
  a lawyer
*Azzorre *f. pl.* Azores, *islands in
  the Atlantic Ocean*
*azzurro blue

B

*babbo dad, daddy
Bacco Bacchus, *god of wine*

*baciare [bacio] to kiss
bacio kiss
baco silkworm
badare (a) to pay attention
*bagaglio baggage (*used in the plural when more than one piece of baggage is meant*)
bagnaiolo bath attendant
†bagnarsi to get wet
*bagno bath, bathing; **costume** (*m.*) **da —**, bathing suit; **fare un —**, to take a bath, go in bathing; **stanza da —**, bathroom; **stabilimento di bagni** bathhouse
*balcone *m.* balcony
*ballare to dance
*ballo ball, dance
*bambina baby, little girl
*bambino baby, little boy
*bambola doll
*bambù *m.* (*inv.*) bamboo
*banca bank
*banchina pier
*banco (*pl.* **banchi**) student's desk, counter
*bandiera flag
bandito bandit
*barba beard; **— e capelli?** shave and haircut? **sapone per la —**, shaving soap; **far la —**, to shave
barbiere *m.* barber
*barca boat; **— a motore** motorboat
bargello constable, police chief; **Palazzo del Bargello** Bargello Palace
Bari *f., the second largest city in Southern Italy* (*population 200,000*)
*barzelletta joke
*basilica basilica
*basso low, short
*basta! enough!
†*bastare (a) to be enough
battaglia battle
*battistero baptistry
*baule *m.* trunk

*Beatrice Beatrice
belare [belo] to bleat
*Belgio Belgium
*bellezza beauty
Bellini, Vincenzo (1802–1835), *born in Catania, Sicily, was one of the foremost opera composers of Italy. "Norma" and "Sonnambula" are his masterpieces.*
bellino pretty
*bellissimo very beautiful
*bello beautiful, fine, handsome; **questa è bella!** that's a good one!
*benchè (*followed by the subj.*) although
*bene well, good; **sta — or va —**, all right, it's all right, very well
*Benedetto Benedict
benedire *irr. v.* [**benedico,** *p. part.* **benedetto**] to bless
*Benevento *f., a very interesting town in Southern Italy* (*population 40,000*)
*benissimo very well
benzina gasoline
*bere *irr. v.* [**bevo, bevvi**] to drink
*Bernini, Giovanni Lorenzo (1598–1680), *famous Italian painter, sculptor, and architect; a native of Naples*
*Bianca Blanche
*bianco white; **vestire di —**, to dress in white
*biblioteca library
*bicchiere *m.* glass
*bicchierino small glass
*biglietto ticket, card; **— da visita** visiting card
bimbo, bimba baby; **un amore di bimba** an adorable baby
*biondo blond
†*bisognare *imp. v.* [**bisogna**] to be necessary, have to, must, ought; **bisognerà** it will be necessary
*bisogno need; **aver — di** to need
bocca mouth
Boccaccio, Giovanni (1313–1375).

one of the greatest writers of all time, born in Paris of a Florentine father and a French mother. The most important of his works is "Il Decameron," a collection of a hundred stories widely imitated in all literatures.

Boito, Arrigo (1842–1918), of Padua, excellent composer and poet, author of "Mefistofele" and "Nerone"

bollire [bollo] to boil

Bologna, a very important Italian city (population 280,000). Its university is not only the oldest, but one of the most famous in the world.

Bordighera, one of the most enchanting towns on the Western Riviera

*bordo board; a —, on board

*borgo hamlet, village

*bosco woods

bottiglia bottle

bottone m. button; bottoni da polsini cuff links

braccialetto bracelet

*braccio (pl. le braccia) arm

*bravo! fine!

*breve brief, short

brezza breeze

*brindisi m. (inv.) toast; fare un —, to give a toast

*bronzo bronze

*bruno brunet, dark

bruto brute

*brutto ugly

buca hole; — per le lettere mailbox

buco hole

*bue m. (pl. i buoi) ox

bufare to snow with a strong wind

*buffo funny, droll, comic

*buio dark; al —, in the dark

*Buonarroti, Michelangelo (1475–1564), the greatest genius in the fields of painting, sculpture, and architecture; a Florentine

*buono good

*burro butter

busta envelope

buttare to throw, cast

C

*cabina cabin, stateroom, booth

caccia hunt

cacciare [caccio] to go hunting

cacio cheese

*caddi, p. abs. of cadere

cadente falling

†*cadere irr. v. to fall, fall down

*caffè m. (inv.) coffee, coffee shop, café

cagione f. cause

cagna female dog

*calamaio inkwell

*calcagno (pl. le calcagna) heel

*caldo adj. warm; n. heat; fa —, it's warm; fa molto —, it's hot

calmare to calm

*calmo calm

*calza stocking

*calzino sock

calzolaio shoemaker

cambiamento change

cambiare [cambio] to change; — idea to change one's mind

cambio change, exchange, rate of exchange

*camera bedroom, room

*cameriera maid, stewardess

*cameriere m. waiter, butler, steward

*camicia shirt

camino fireplace

*camminare to walk

camminatore m. walker

*campagna country, land, farmland; in —, in or to the country

*campana bell

*campanello (small) bell

*campanile m. bell tower, campanile

*Campidoglio Capitol

*campo field

*canale m. canal, channel

*cancellare [cancello] to erase

candela candle
*cane *m.* dog
canino canine
cannɛllo stick
*cantare to sing
*cantico canticle, song
*canto song, singing
*canzone *f.* (*popular*) song, canzone, ballad
*capello (*one*) hair; capelli hair; barba e capelli? shave and haircut?
*capire [capisco] to understand
*capo head, cape
*capolavoro masterpiece
*cappɛlla chapel; Cappɛlla Sistina the Sistine Chapel (*in the Vatican Palace, Rome*)
*cappɛllo hat; — da mattina street hat; — da pomeriggio dressy hat
*cappɔtto overcoat
capra goat
*Capri *f.*, *a beautiful little island facing the bay of Naples; m. an excellent wine*
Caracalla (188–217), *Roman emperor*
carato carat
carattɛri *m. pl.* handwriting
*caratteristico characteristic
*carciɔfo artichoke
cardinale cardinal
caretto rather expensive
carezza caress
cariato carious, decayed
*caricare [carico] to load
*carico *adj.* loaded; *n.* load
carino pretty, cute
*Carlo Charles; il San Carlo the San Carlo Opera House (*in Naples*)
*carne *f.* meat, flesh
*caro dear, expensive
carro wagon, van
*carrɔzza carriage, coach; — a lɛtti sleeping car; — ristorante dining car
*carta paper, card, playing card;

— da visita visiting card; — geografica map; — sugante blotter; — topografica topographical map; giocare a carte to play cards
cartolaio stationer
*cartolina post card; — illustrata picture card
*casa house, home; a — *or* in —, at home, in the house
*Casɛrta, *a town near Naples* (*population* 45,000)
caso case; — mai (*followed by the subj.*) in case
cassa chest, box, cashier's office *or* window
cassetta (*small*) box
cassetto drawer
*cassettone *m.* chest of drawers
cassiɛre *m.* cashier
*castɛllo castle
*casuɛccia hovel, hut
*catacomba catacomb
catalogo catalogue
*Catania, *the second largest city in Sicily* (*population* 246,000)
catena chain
*Caterina Catherine
*cattedrale *f.* cathedral
*cattivo bad, mean
*cattɔlico Catholic
*cauccíù *m.* (*inv.*) rubber
causa cause, (*legal*) case
*cavallo horse
cavità (*inv.*) cavity
*cavolo cabbage
*ce = ci
*c'ɛ there is
*cɛlebre celebrated, famous
*cena supper
cenare [ceno] to eat supper
*cenere *f.* ash
ceneriera ash tray
censimento census
*centɛsimo *adj.* hundredth; *n.* the hundredth part of a lira
centimetro centimeter
*centinaio about a hundred; *pl.* centinaia (*f.*) hundreds

*cɛnto hundred, a hundred, one hundred

centrale central, main

*cɛntro center; al — di in the center of

cera wax

ceralacca sealing wax

*cercare (di) [cerco] to look for, seek, try

cerino wax match

*certamente certainly, of course

*cɛrto *adj.* certain, sure; *adv.* certainly

cestino basket

*che *conj.* that, than; non + *verb* + che only; sia ... che both ... and; altro — ! sure enough ! I should say so !

*che *pron.* who, whom, that, which, what, what a; — cɔsa what; non c'ɛ di —, you are welcome (*said after receiving thanks*); quel —, *or* quello —, *or* ciɔ —, what

*checchè (*followed by the subj.*) whatever

*chi who, whom, whoever, he who, him who, one who, a person who

*chiamare to call, call on; †chiamarsi to be called; come vi chiamate? what is your name? mi chiamo Carlo my name is Charles

*chiaramente clearly

*chiaro clear, light *or* bright (*in color*)

*chiɛdere (di) *irr. v.* [chiɛdo, chiɛsi, chiɛsto] to ask, ask for

*chiɛsa church

*chimica chemistry

chino bent

chiɔdo nail, spike

*chiudere *irr. v.* [chiusi, chiuso] to close, shut, lock

*chiunque (*followed by the subj.*) whoever

*chiuso closed

chiusura closing

*ci *adv.* here, there, in it, on it; c'ɛ there is; ci sono there are;

non c'ɛ di che you are welcome (*said after receiving thanks*)

*ci *pron.* us, to us, ourselves, to ourselves, each other, to each other

Ciaicovski (Tschaikowsky), Peter Ilich (1840–1893), *great Russian composer*

ciancia gossip

ciarla cackle, tattle

*ciascuno each, each one, everyone

*cibo food

*ciɛlo sky, heaven

cifra figure

*ciglio (*pl.* le ciglia) eyelash

*ciliɛgia cherry; ciliɛgio cherry tree

*cima top, summit; in — (a) on *or* to the top (of)

*cimitɛro cemetery

*cinematografico: macchina cinematografica movie camera

*cinematɔgrafo cinema, movie, movie theater

*cinquanta fifty

*cinque five

*cinquecɛnto five hundred; il Cinquecɛnto the sixteenth century

*ciɔ this, that, that fact; — che what

cioccolata chocolate

*cioɛ that is (to say), namely

*cipolla onion

*circa about, almost, nearly, regarding

*circondare [circondo] to surround

circostanza circumstance

*città (*inv.*) city; in —, in *or* to the city, downtown; al cɛntro della —, downtown

*cittadina small town

ciuco ass

ciurma crew

*civiltà (*inv.*) civilization

*Clara Clara

*classe *f.* class

*clima *m.* climate

*codesto *or* cotesto that, that one

*cɔgliere *irr. v.* [cɔlgo, cɔlsi, cɔlto]
to pick
*cognata sister-in-law
*cognato brother-in-law
cognome *m.* family name
colà there
*colazione *f.* lunch, breakfast; far
—, to have lunch, breakfast
*colɛi that woman, the former
*collana necklace
*collezione *f.* collection
*collina hill
colmo filled up
*Colombo, Cristɔforo Christopher
Columbus (1446 ?–1506), *of
Genoa, the discoverer of America*
*colonnato colonnade
*colore *m.* color
*coloro those, those men, those
women, the former
colossale colossal
*Colossɛo Colosseum, *the huge, mag-
nificent amphitheater built by Ves-
pasian and Titus about* A.D. 80,
southeast of the Forum, in Rome
*coltɛllo knife
*coltivare to cultivate, grow
*coltivazione *f.* cultivation
*colui that man, the former
*come how, as, like, such as; così
... come as ... as, so ... as;
— mai ...? how does it happen
that ...?
cɔmico comic
*cominciare (a) [comincio] to
begin, start
*comitiva party
*commɛdia comedy
commerciale commercial
*commɛrcio commerce, business,
trade
*Cɔmo *f., a city of 60,000 inhabitants
at the southern end of Lake Como*
*cɔmodo comfortable
*compagnia company
comparativo comparative
comparazione *f.* comparison
*competɛnte competent
*compleanno birthday

complemento phrase; — oggɛtto
direct object
*completare [complɛto] to com-
plete
complɛto complete
*complimento compliment; far
complimenti to stand on ceremony
*comporre *irr. v.* [compongo,
composi, composto] to compose, make up
composto compound
*comprare [compro] to buy
comprɛssa tablet; — sonnifera
sleeping tablet
*con with
*conca shell
concɛdere (di) *irr. v.* [concɛdo,
concɛssi, concɛsso] to grant
*concertare (di) [concɛrto] to
arrange, plan, concert
concɛrto concert, concerto
concordanza agreement
concorrɛnza competition
condizionale *adj. and n. m.* conditional
condizione *f.* condition, situation;
pl. circumstances
*condurre (a) *irr. v.* [*p. part.* con-
dotto] to conduct, lead, take,
bring along
conduttore *m.* conductor
congiuntivo conjunctive, subjunctive
congiunto joined
congratulazione *f.* congratulation
*coniglio rabbit
coniugare [cɔniugo] to conjugate
coniugazione *f.* conjugation
*conoscɛnza acquaintance, knowl-
edge; fare la — di to become
acquainted with, meet
*conoscere *irr. v.* [conosco, co-
nobbi] to know, be acquainted
with, meet, make the acquaintance of
*consegnare [consegno] to hand,
give, deliver
*conservare [consɛrvo] to keep,

preserve; †conservarsi to remain

*consigliare (di) [consiglio] to advise

consiglio advice

console m. consul

consonante f. consonant

consultare to consult

*contadino farm laborer

contare [conto] to count, reckon; — di to count on, depend, rely

conteggiare [conteggio] to compute, figure

*contenere irr. v. [contengo, contenni] to contain

*contentare [contento] to content, please, satisfy

contentezza contentment, joy

*contento glad, satisfied, happy

*contessa countess

*continuare (a) [continuo] to continue

*continuo continuous

conto account; — corrente checking account

contralto contralto

contrario contrary, opposite

contro, contro di against

*convento convent, monastery

*conversare [converso] to chat, converse, talk

*conversazione f. conversation

*coperta cover, deck

*coperto (di) covered (with)

copia copy

*corallo coral

*cordiale cordial

*cordialmente cordially

†*coricarsi [mi corico] to lie down, go to bed

*corr. (abbreviated from corrente) inst.

*correggere irr. v. [correggo, corressi, corretto] to correct

corrente running, instant; conto —, checking account

°*correre (a) irr. v. [corro, corsi, corso] to run, speed

*correttamente correctly

*corretto correct, proper

*corridoio corridor, passage

corrispondente adj. corresponding; n. m. correspondent

corrispondenza correspondence

*corsa race; — di cavalli horse race

*Corsica, a large island west of the Italian peninsula (population 300,000)

corsivo italics

*corso avenue, course

*cortese courteous, kind

cortesia courtesy, kindness

corto short

*cosa thing, matter; che —? what? qualche —, something; qualche — di buono something good; qualunque —, whatever

*cosetta little thing

*così so, thus, like this, like that; così . . . come as . . . as, so . . . as; per — dire so to say, so to speak

*cosmetico cosmetic

*costa coast, shore

*costà there

*Costantino Constantine, the Great (272–337), the first Roman emperor to become a Christian

†*costare [costo] to cost; quanto costa (or costano)? what's the price?

*costei this woman, the latter

*costì there

costoletta cutlet

*costoro these men, these women, the latter

*costruire irr. v. [costruisco] to build

costruzione f. construction

*costui this man, this fellow, the latter

*costume m. custom, habit, costume; — da bagno bathing suit

*cravatta necktie, cravat

*creare [creo] to create

*creatura creature

*credɛnza buffet, sideboard
*credere (di) [credo] to believe, think
crɛma custard, cream
*crisi f. (inv.) crisis
*cristiano Christian
*Cristɔforo Christopher
croce f. cross; Santa Croce, do not translate
crocicchio crossroad
*crogiɔlo melting pot
crudo raw, crude
*cucchiaino teaspoon
*cucchiaio spoon
cuccia kennel
*cucina kitchen, cooking
*cugino, cugina cousin
*cui whom, which; def. art. + cui whose, of which
*cultura culture, civilization, education, cultivation
cuna cradle
*Cunegonda Cunegonda
*cuɔre m. heart
*cupola dome
cura care, treatment

D

*da conj. to, as to, good enough to
*da prep. from, by, of, at, to, for, at or to the house (shop, office, place, etc.) of; — noi in or to our country, home, place, etc.; — maɛstro as (or like) a teacher
*dà (pres. ind. of dare) gives
dado die
*danaro money
dannare to damn
*Dante, see Alighiɛri
*dare irr. v. [dɔ, diɛdi or dɛtti] to give; — da mangiare a to feed; — su to face; — un addio to say farewell
*darɛi (cond. of dare) I should give
*darɔ (fut. of dare) I shall give
*darvele (= dare + vi + le) to give them to you
*data date

*datemi (impve. of dare + mi) give me; datemene = datemi + ne
*dato che (followed by the subj.) granted that
*davanti (a) before (referring to place), in front (of)
davvero indeed, really
decɛnza decency
*decidere (di), †decidersi (a) irr. v. [decisi, deciso] to decide
*dɛcimo tenth
*deciso (p. part. of decidere) decided
*dedicare [dɛdico] to dedicate, devote
definito definite
degno worthy
delicato delicate
*delizioso delightful, delicious
dɛnte m. tooth
*dentista m. or f. dentist
*depositare [depɔsito] to deposit, check (baggage, a parcel, etc.)
derivare to derive
descrittivo descriptive
*descrivere (di) irr. v. to describe
*desiderare (di) [desidero] to wish, desire
desto awake
*dɛstro right; a dɛstra at or to the right
*dettare [detto] to dictate
*dettato dictation
*dɛvo (pres. ind. of dovere) I must, have to
devoto devoted, devout
*di conj. than, to
*di prep. of, by, from, to; di + def. art. some, any
diagnosi f. (inv.) diagnosis
diagramma m. diagram
*dialogo dialogue
*diamo (impve. of dare) let us give
*diario diary
*dice (pres. ind. of dire) says
*dicɛmbre m. December
*diciannɔve nineteen
*diciassɛtte seventeen
*diciɔtto eighteen

*dicono (*pres. ind. of* dire) they say
*dièci ten
*dièresi *f.* (*inv.*) dieresis
*diètro (a) behind; — richièsta upon request
difesa defense
difettoso faulty
*differènte different
*difficile difficult, hard
digiuno empty (*said with reference to the stomach*)
*dimenticare (di) [dimentico] to forget
diminutivo diminutive
dimostrativo demonstrative
*dintorni *m. pl.* surroundings
*Dio (*pl.* gli dèi) God
dipendènte dependent
†dipèndere *irr. v.* [dipèndo, dipesi, dipeso] to depend; — da to depend on
*diplòma *m.* diploma, degree
†diplomarsi [mi diplòmo] to graduate
*dire (di) *irr. v.* [dico, *p. part.* detto] to say, tell; — di sì to say yes, permit; per così —, so to say, so to speak; voler —, to mean
*direttamente directly
*dirètto *adj.* direct; *n.* express train
direttore *m.* director, manager
*direzione *f.* direction
*dirigere *irr. v.* [dirèssi, dirètto] to direct; †dirigersi to direct one's steps
*dirimpètto (a) opposite
diritto *adj.* straight; *adv.* straight ahead; *n.* right
*dirmi (= dire + mi) to tell me
disco disc; — fonografico phonograph record
discussione *f.* discussion
discutere *irr. v.* to discuss, argue
†*disgiuntivo disjunctive
dispiacere *irr. v.* [dispiaccio] to be displeasing; mi dispiace (di) I am sorry
*disporre (di) *irr. v.* [dispongo,

disposi, disposto] to dispose, arrange
disposto willing
*distanza distance
distintamente distinctly; salutandovi —, with sincere wishes
*distinto distinguished, fine, refined
disturbare to trouble, bother
*disturbo trouble, bother, annoyance; dare — a una persona to trouble a person; niènte —, no bother at all
*dite (*pres. ind. or impve. of* dire) say; — pure please say
*dito (*pl.* le dita) finger
ditta firm
dittòngo diphthong
†*diventare [diventò] to become
divèrso different; *pl.* different, several
*divertire [divèrto] to amuse; †divertirsi (a) to amuse oneself, have a good time
*dividere *irr. v.* [divisi, diviso] to divide
*divino divine
*dizionario dictionary
doccia shower
*dodici twelve
*dogana customs, custom house
*Dòge *m.* Doge, *the chief magistrate in the former republics of Venice and Genoa*
*dolce *adj.* sweet; *n. m.* dessert
*dolcino cookie, French pastry
dòllaro dollar
*dolore *m.* sorrow, pain, ache
*domanda question, application; fare una —, to ask a question
*domandare (di) to ask, ask for
*domani tomorrow
domattina tomorrow morning
*domenica Sunday; la — *or* di —, on Sundays
*domèstico domestic
*dominare [dòmino] to rule, dominate
donare [dono] to give (*as a gift*)

*dɔnna woman
dono gift
*dopo (di), dopo che after, afterward; — un pɔco after a while; pɔco —, soon after
dopodomani day after tomorrow
doppio double, thick
*dormire [dɔrmo] to sleep
Dott. (*abbreviated from* dottore) Dr.
dottore *m.* doctor
*dove where
°*dovere *irr. v.* [dɛvo *or* dɛbbo] to have to, be obliged, must, owe, be supposed
*dovunque everywhere, wherever
dozzina dozen; la —, a dozen
drago dragon
dramma *m.* drama
drammatico dramatic
drɔga drug
*dubbio doubt
dubitare (di) [dubito] to doubt
duca *m.* duke
*due two
*duecɛnto two hundred; il Duecɛnto the 13th century
*duɔmo cathedral
*durante during
†*durare to last
*durata duration

E

*e, ed and
*ɛ̀ (*pres. ind. of* ɛssere) is
*ɛbbe (*p. abs. of* avere) had
Ɛbe Hebe, *Greek goddess*
ecc. etc.
*ɛcco here is, here are, there is, there are, see, look; — ! here ! there !
*ɛco *f.* (*pl.* gli ɛchi) echo
*ed, *see* e
*edifizio building
editore *m.*, editrice *f.* publisher; casa editrice publishing house
*egli he
egrɛgio egregious, esteemed
ɛh! ah ! oh !
*elegante elegant, stylish, smart

eleganza elegance, style
*elementare elementary
*Ɛlena Helen
*elɛttrico electric
*Ella you
*ella she
*Emanuɛle Emmanuel
Emilia Emily
enɛrgico energetic
ɛnfasi *f.* (*inv.*) emphasis
*enorme enormous, huge
†*entrare (a) [entro] to enter; — in una stanza to enter a room
*entrata entrance, entry
*entusiasmo enthusiasm
*ɛpoca epoch, time
*eppure and yet
equivalɛnte *m.* equivalent
*ɛrba grass, herb
*eruzione *f.* eruption
esagerato exaggerated, excessive
*esclamare to exclaim
*escursione *f.* excursion; fare un'—, to take an excursion
*esɛmpio example
*esercizio exercise
*esilio exile
esportazione *f.* export
esposto (*p. part. of* esporre) exposed, on display
*espressione *f.* expression
esprimere *irr. v.* [esprɛssi, esprɛsso] to express
*essa she, it, her
*esse they, them
essenziale essential
†*ɛssere *irr. v.* [sono] to be; — in ritardo to be late
*essi they, them
*esso he, it, him
*ɛst *m.* east
*estate *f.* summer; d'—, in summer
estɛrno outside; all'—, on the outside
ɛstero *adj.* foreign; *n.* foreign countries
*estremamente extremely
*età (*inv.*) age
*etɛrno eternal

*Ɛtna: l'— m. Mt. Etna, a volcano in Sicily
*Eurɔpa Europe
*europɛo European

F

*fa (after an expression of time) ago; pɔco —, a short time ago
*fa' (impve. of fare) do, make
*fabbrica factory
*facchino porter
faccia face
*facciata front (of a building), façade
face f. torch
*facile easy
*facilmente easily
*fagiolino string bean
*fagiɔlo bean
*famiglia family
*famoso famous
*fantino jockey
*fare irr. v. [faccio or fɔ, feci] to do, make, build, let, have; — l'avvocato, il mɛdico, etc. to be a lawyer, a physician, etc.; fare + infinitive, see §151, p. 261. (Other idioms in which fare appears are listed only under the other words concerned.)
*farɛi, faresti, etc. (cond. of fare) I should or would do (or make), etc.
*farfalla butterfly
*farmacia pharmacy, drugstore
*farmacista m. or f. druggist
*farɔ (fut. of fare) I shall or will do (or make)
*farti (= fare + ti) to do (or make) you
*farvi (= fare + vi) to do (or make) you
fascia band, cover; sotto —, under separate cover
fascino fascination
fascio bundle
*fatemi (= fate + mi) do (or make) me

fato fate
*fatto n. fact
*fatto (p. part. of fare) done, made
*favore m. favor; per —, please
favorire [favorisco] to do the favor to, please come, please give
*fazzoletto handkerchief
*febbraio February
fɛbbre f. fever
fede f. faith
*felice happy
felicità (inv.) happiness
feltro felt, felt hat
*fermare [fermo] to stop (somebody or something); †fermarsi (a) to stop (oneself), stay
*fermata stop
*ferrovia railroad; in —, by railroad
*fɛrtile fertile
*fɛsta feast, festivity, festival, holiday, party
*festeggiare [festeggio] to celebrate
fɛudo fief
fiammifero match
FIAT (letters that stand for Fabbrica Italiana Automɔbili Torino), the name of a famous automobile factory in Turin
fico fig, fig tree
*Fiɛsole f., beautiful little town on a high hill near Florence
*figlia daughter, child
*figlio son, child
*fila line, row
filo thread
*filosofia philosophy
*finalmente finally, at last
*finchè, finchè non (followed by the subj.) until
*fine f. end
*finɛstra window
*finestrino small window
°*finire (di) [finisco] to finish, end
*fino a until, as far as, up to; fino allora until then
*fioraio florist
*fiore m. flower

*Firenze f. Florence, *one of the most beautiful and important cities of Italy (population 350,000)*

firma signature

*firmare to sign

*fisica physics

*fissato fixed

*fiume m. river

Flora Flora, *Roman goddess of flowers*

Florio, *a brand of Marsala wine*

*foglia leaf

foglietto small sheet of paper; foglietti e buste paper and envelopes

*fondare [fondo] to found

*fontana fountain

forare [foro] to bore, pierce

forbicette f. pl. small scissors

*forchetta fork

forcina hairpin

*forestiero, forestiera foreigner

forma form, shape

*formaggio cheese

formare [formo] to form

formato size

formazione f. formation

fornire [fornisco] to furnish

*foro forum

*forse perhaps

forte strong

*fortuna fortune, good luck

*fortunatamente fortunately

*fortunato fortunate, lucky

forza force

*fossi (*p. subj. of* essere) were

fotografia photography, photograph

*fotografico photographic; macchina fotografica camera

fotografo photographer

*fra between, among, within

fragile fragile, breakable

fragola strawberry

francamente frankly

*Francesco Francis

*francese French

*Francia France

*Franco Frank

*francobollo stamp

frangia fringe

*frase f. sentence

*fratello brother

fraternità (*inv.*) fraternity

frazione f. fraction

*freddamente coldly

*freddo *adj.* cold; *n.* cold, chill; avere —, to be cold; fa —, it's cold

*freschissimo very fresh

*fresco fresh, cool; al —, in the cool air; fa —, it's cool

*fretta haste, hurry; aver —, to be in a hurry; in —, in a hurry

*fritto *adj.* fried; *n.* fried dish; — misto fried fish of many kinds

*frutta *or* frutto (*pl.* le frutta *or* i frutti, *see footnote* 6, p. 219) fruit, result

*fumare to smoke; sala da —, smoking room

*fumerò (*fut. of* fumare) I shall smoke

*fummo (*p. abs. of* essere) we were

fumo smoke

fuoco fire, focus

*fuori (di) out, out of, outside

futuro future

G

*gabbia cage

gaio gay

gala gala

*galleria gallery, arcade, tunnel

*gallina hen

*gallo rooster

gamba leg

gancio hook

gara contest, match

garantire (di) [garantisco] to guarantee

Garibaldi, Giuseppe (1807–1882), *a very famous Italian patriot, one of the founders of Italian independence and unity. He was born in Nice, and lived for some time in the United States.*

*gatto cat

gelato ice

gemεllo twin

*generale general

*generalmente generally, usually

genere *m.* gender

genero son-in-law

*genesi *f.* (*inv.*) genesis

*genitore *m.* parent

*gennaio January

*Genova, Genoa, *one of the most important Italian cities (population 650,000), the birthplace of Christopher Columbus*

*gente *f.* people

*gentile kind, courteous, gentle

*gentilmente kindly

*geografia geography

*geografico geographic; **carta geografica** map

*Germania Germany

germanico Germanic

*gesso chalk

*Gesù Jesus

*ghiaccio ice

Ghibεrti, Lorεnzo (1378–1455), *famous Florentine sculptor, painter, and architect*

ghiro dormouse

*già already, yes, of course

*giacca coat, jacket; **in —,** in street clothes

†giacere *irr. v.* [giaccio] to lie, rest

*giacinto hyacinth

*Giacomo James

Di Giacomo, Salvatore (1860–1934), *Neapolitan poet and novelist*

*giallo yellow

giara jar

*giardino garden

*Gibiltεrra Gibraltar

giglio lily

ginεstra broom plant

*ginɔcchio (*pl.* le ginɔcchia) knee

*giocare [giɔco] to play; **— a carte**

to play cards; **— a scacchi** to play chess

giocattolo toy

*giɔia joy

*gioielleria jewelry, jewelry store

*gioiellieεre *m.* jeweler

Giorgio George

*giornale *m.* newspaper

giornalista *m. or f.* journalist

*giornata day (*in its duration, or referring to weather or work*)

*giorno day; buɔn **—,** good day, good morning

Giɔtto (di Bondone) (1276–1336), *great Florentine painter and architect*

*giovane *adj.* young; *n. m. or f.* young man, young woman

giovanile youthful

*Giovanni John

*giovanɔtto young man

°giovare [giovo] to help, be of use

*giovedì *m.* Thursday; **il —,** on Thursdays

*girare to turn, go (*or* move) around

*giro tour; **in —,** around; **fare un —,** to take a tour

*gita trip

*giù down; **su per —,** more or less, about

Giuba *m.* Juba, *a large river in Africa*

giubba jacket

*giugno June

Giulio Julius

°*giungere (a) *irr. v.* to arrive, join (*one's hands*)

giurare (di) to swear, vow

Gius., *an abbreviation of* Giusεppe

Giusεppe Joseph

Giusti, Giusεppe (1809–1850), *a great patriot and satirical poet from Tuscany*

*giustizia justice

giusto just, right

*gli *art.* (*pl. of* lo) the

*gli *pron.* to him, to it

*gliela = gli *or* le + la

*gliele = gli *or* le + le

*glieli = gli *or* le + li
*glielo = gli *or* le + lo
*gliene = gli *or* le + ne
gloria glory
*godere *irr. v.* (di) [gɔdo] to enjoy, be happy
gola throat
Goldoni, Carlo (1707–1793), *famous Venetian playwright, the father of modern Italian comedy*
*golfo gulf, bay
*gomma rubber, (rubber) eraser, tire; mi s'ɛ sgonfiata una —, I have a flat tire
*gondola gondola
*gondoliɛre *m.* gondolier
*gɔng *m.* (*inv.*) gong
*gɔtico Gothic
governante *f.* housekeeper
*govɛrno government
gradire [gradisco] to accept with pleasure, appreciate
*grammɑtica grammar
grammaticale grammatical
grammɔfono phonograph
*grande large, big, great
*grandezza greatness, size
*grandioso grand, grandiose
*grano wheat
gratɛlla gridiron; arrostire sulla —, to broil
grato (di) grateful (for)
*grattaciɛlo skyscraper
grave heavy, grave, serious
*grazia grace
*grazie thanks
*grazioso graceful, pretty
*grɛco Greek
*gridare to shout, cry
*grido (*pl.* le grida) shout, cry
*grigio gray
*grɔsso big, heavy
*grɔtta grotto
*gru *f.* (*inv.*) crane
*gruppo group
*guadagnare to earn, gain
*guanto glove
*guardare to look, look at
†guastarsi to spoil

guasto *adj.* spoiled, decayed; *n.* derangement, trouble; che — c'ɛ? what's wrong with it?
guɛlfo Guelph
guɛrra war
*guglia spire
*guida guide, guidance, guidebook
*guidare to guide, lead, drive
Guido Guy, Guido
*gustare to taste, relish, enjoy
*gusto taste; di mio —, to my taste

H

*ha (*pres. ind. of* avere) has; che —? what's the matter with him (her, it)?
havvi *poet.* (= ha + vi) there is

I

*i (*pl. of* il) the
Ida Ida
*idɛa idea; cambiare —, to change one's mind
idɛntico identical, same
idiomɑtico idiomatic
idiɔta *m. or f.* idiot
*iɛri yesterday; — l'altro day before yesterday; — sera last night
*il the
ilarità (*inv.*) hilarity
*illuminare [illumino] to light
illustrato illustrated; cartolina illustrata picture card
†*imbarcarsi to embark
*imbarco embarking
*immaginare (di) [immɑgino] to imagine
immediatamente immediately
*immensamente immensely
*immɛnso immense, great
*imparare (a) to learn; — a memɔria to memorize
*impegnare (a) [impegno] to engage, hire
imperativo imperative

impermeabile *m.* raincoat
impersonale impersonal
*impiegato, impiegata clerk
impiego employment, job
impiombare [impiombo] to fill (*dentistry*)
*imponente imposing
*importante important
°importare [importo] to import, matter; che importa? what's the difference?
importazione *f.* importation
impossibile impossible
*impressione *f.* impression
imputato offender
*in in, into, within
inane inane, useless
*incantevole enchanting, charming
*incanto charm
*incarico task, errand
*inchiostro ink
incisivo incisor
*includere *irr. v.* [inclusi, incluso] to include
*incontrare [incontro] to meet
indefinito indefinite
*indicare [indico] to point at
indicativo indicative
indietro back, backward, behind
indifferente indifferent
*indimenticabile unforgettable
*indipendente independent
indiretto indirect
*indirizzo address
indivia endive
indovinare to guess, guess right
*industria industry
*infatti in fact, indeed
*inferiore lower, inferior
*infimo lowest, very low
infinito *adj.* infinite; grazie infinite many thanks; *n.* infinite, infinitive
informare [informo] to inform
*informazione *f.* information (*used in the plural when more than one item of information is meant*)
*Inghilterra England

*inglese English
ingrandimento enlargement
ingrandire [ingrandisco] to enlarge
†innamorarsi [m'innamoro] to fall in love
*insalata salad
*insegnante *m. or f.* instructor
*insegnare (a) [insegno] to teach
*insieme together
*intanto meantime, meanwhile
*integro righteous
*intendere *irr. v.* (di) [intendo, intesi, inteso] to intend, understand, hear
intenzione *f.* intention
*interessante interesting
interessare [interesso] to interest
*interesse *m.* interest
interrogativo interrogative
*interrotto (*p. part. of* interrompere) interrupted
*intimo intimate, familiar
*intorno (a) around
intreccio plot
intuizione *f.* intuition
*inutile useless
invariabile invariable
*invece (di) instead, on the contrary, on the other hand
*inverno winter
inviare to send
*invitare (a) to invite
*invito invitation
*io I
*ipotesi *f.* (*inv.*) hypothesis
*Irene Irene
irregolare irregular
*Ischia, *a beautiful island near the bay of Naples*
*isola island
isolato block
*isoletta small island
istantanea snapshot
istitutrice *f.* governess, tutor
*Italia Italy
*italiano Italian
*italo-americano Italo-American

L

*la *art.* the
*la *pron.* her, it
*là *adv.* there
*labbro (*pl.* le labbra) lip
laboratorio laboratory
*laggiù down there, over there
*lago lake
laguna lagoon
laico layman
†*lampeggiare *imp. v.* [lampeggia] to lighten
lampo lightning
lana wool
*lapis *m.* (*inv.*) pencil
lapislazzuli *m.* lapis lazuli
*largo broad, wide
*lasciare [lascio] to leave, let
*lassù up there, over there
*Laterano, Lateran, *the church of St. John Lateran, the cathedral church of Rome, and the highest in rank of all Catholic churches*
*latino Latin
*lato side; da un —, on one side; di —, to the side
latore *m.*, latrice *f.* bearer
*latte *m.* milk
*lattuga lettuce
*Laura Laura
lauro laurel
lavabo washbasin
*lavagna blackboard
lavandaia washerwoman
*lavare to wash
*lavorare [lavoro] to work
*lavoro work
*Lazio Latium, *a region in central Italy, the principal city of which is Rome*
*le *art.* (*pl.* of la) the
*le *pron.* them, to her, to it, to you
*legge *f.* law
*leggere *irr. v.* [leggo, lessi, letto] to read
leggero light (*not heavy*)
*legno wood

*Lei you; di —, your
*lei her; di —, her
*lentamente slowly
*lento slow
*lenzuolo (*pl.* le lenzuola) sheet
*Leonardo da Vinci (1452–1519). *History tells of no other man whose genius revealed itself to such a high degree in so many different fields. Equally versed in arts and sciences, he was painter, sculptor, architect, musician, brilliant writer, mathematician, engineer, mechanician, anatomist, and natural philosopher, — a great master in each of his activities. To him we owe the first idea of a submarine and the first studies on aërial navigation.*
*leone *m.* lion
*leonessa lioness
*leopardo leopard
*lettera letter; — raccomandata registered letter
*letteratura literature
*letto bed; a —, in bed; a due letti with two beds; carrozza a letti sleeping car
*lettura reading; libro di —, reader
*levante *m.* east
*levare [levo] to take off, remove
*lezione *f.* lesson
*li *pron.* them
*lì *adv.* there
liberale liberal
*libero free
*libertà (*inv.*) liberty, freedom
*libretto small book, libretto
*libro book; — di lettura reader
*Lido Lido
lieto glad, happy
Liguria, *a beautiful region in Northern Italy the principal city of which is Genoa*
*limitare [limito] to limit
limite *m.* limit
limonata lemonade
*limone *m.* lemon, lemon tree

*limpido limpid, clear
lineetta dash
*lingua tongue, language
lino linen
*lira lira, *the monetary unit of Italy*
liscio smooth
livido livid
livornese from Leghorn; alla —, Leghorn style
*lo *art.* the
*lo *pron.* him, it
*Locarno, *a pretty little town on the northern shore of Lake Maggiore*
locomotiva locomotive
*loggia balcony, open gallery, loggia
*lontano *adj. and adv.* far, far away, distant
*Lorenzo Lawrence
*Loro you
*loro *personal pron.* them, they, to them
*loro *poss. adj. or pron.* their, theirs, your, yours
lozione *f.* lotion; — tonica pei capelli hair tonic
*luce *f.* light
*Lucia Lucy
lucidare [lucido] to polish
lucido glossy
*Lugano, *a little Italian city belonging to Switzerland; the name of a lake partly in Italian and partly in Swiss territory*
*luglio July
*lui him; di —, his
*Luisa Louise
*luna moon
*lunedì *m.* Monday; il —, on Mondays
*lungo *adj.* long; a —, long time, for a long time, at length
*lungo *prep.* along
*luogo place; aver —, to take place
*lupo wolf
lusso luxury; di —, de luxe, fancy
lustrascarpe *m.* bootblack

M

*ma but
*maccherone *m.* macaroni
*macchina machine; — cinematografica movie camera; — fotografica camera
*macchinetta small machine, (*in a barber shop*) clipper
Madama Butterfly, *a well-known opera by Puccini*
*madre *f.* mother
*maestoso majestic
*maestro, maestra teacher, maestro
*maggio May
*maggiore major, greater, older; il —, the greater, the greatest; Lago Maggiore Lake Maggiore; Santa Maria Maggiore, *do not translate*
*magnifico magnificent
*mai ever, never; caso — *or* se — (*followed by the subj.*) in case
*maiale *m.* pig, swine, pork
malato ill, sick
*male *adv.* badly, bad; mi sta —, it isn't good on me
*male *n. m.* ache, pain, evil, wrong; mal di mare seasickness; far — a to hurt; non c'è —, quite well, so so; nulla di —, nothing wrong; meno —! thank Heavens!
*Malta, *a group of little islands south of Sicily; the principal town is La Valletta*
*mamma *or* mammà mamma, mother
*mancare (di) to be lacking, be missing, be without, fail
*mancherò (*fut. of* mancare) I shall fail
mancia tip
*mandare (a) to send, send out
*mangiare [mangio] to eat; dare da — a to feed
mania mania, craze
*manica sleeve

*manico handle

maniera manner

*mano *f.* hand; stringere la — a to shake hands with

Manzoni, Alessandro (1785–1873), *of Milan, famous poet and novelist whose masterpiece is "I Promessi Sposi"*

marca mark, sign, make

Marche *f. pl.* Marches, *a region in Central Italy the principal city of which is Ancona*

*Marco Mark

marconigramma *m.* radiogram

*mare *m.* sea; mal (*m.*) di —, seasickness

Marechiare *m.*, *a Neapolitan dialect form for* Mare chiaro, *denoting a beautiful spot on the Bay of Naples*

*Margherita Margaret

*margherita daisy

*Maria Mary

*Mario Marius

marionetta puppet; teatrino di marionette puppet show

*marito husband

*marittimo maritime

*marmellata marmalade, jam

*marmo marble

*marrone (*inv.*) brown; vestito di —, dressed in brown

Marsala, *a town in Sicily, famous for being the place where Garibaldi landed in 1860 to free Sicily and Southern Italy*

marsala *m.* Marsala, *the name of a well-known Sicilian wine*

*martedì *m.* Tuesday; il —, on Tuesdays

martello hammer

*martirio martyrdom

*marzo March

maschietto young fellow

maschile masculine

massaggio massage; fare un —, to give a massage

*massimo greatest, very great, maximum; al —, at the most

masticare [mastico] to chew

*matita pencil

matrimonio marriage

*mattina morning

*mattinata morning (*in its duration, or referring to weather or work*), morning song

matto crazy; matt, dull *referring to photographic paper*

*maturo mature, ripe

Mazzini, Giuseppe (1805–1872), *one of the great founders of Italian independence and unity. He organized " Young Italy," a society for the education of the youth in patriotic feelings; his many books had a powerful influence on the destinies of Italy. He was born in Genoa.*

*me me, myself

Medici the Medici, *a Florentine family that acquired immense wealth in business and obtained unlimited political power in Florence in the fourteenth, fifteenth, and sixteenth centuries*

*medicina medicine, remedy

*medico physician; fare il —, to be a physician

medio medium, middle

*medioevale medieval

*Medio Evo Middle Ages

*Mediterraneo Mediterranean

*Mefistofele Mephistopheles, *a very beautiful opera by Boito, based on Goethe's "Faust"*

*meglio better; il —, the better, the best

*mela apple; melo apple tree

*melanzana eggplant

*membro (*pl.* le membra) limb; (*pl.* i membri) member

*memoria memory; imparare a —, to memorize

*Menaggio, *a charming little town on Lake Como*

*menare (a) [meno] to lead, take

*meno less, except; a — — che ... non (*followed by the subj.*) unless; **fare a — di** to do without; **— male!** thank Heavens!

mente *f.* mind

***mentre** while

***menzionare (di) [menziono]** to mention

***meraviglia** marvel

***meraviglioso** marvelous, wonderful

***mercato** market; **a buɔn —,** cheap, cheaply

***mercoledì** *m.* Wednesday; **il —,** on Wednesdays

***meridionale** southern

***meritare (di) [merito]** to merit, deserve

***mese** *m.* month; **il—venturo** next month; **il — scorso** last month

***messa** Mass

meta goal

***metà** (*inv.*) half

metallo metal

metro meter

***metrɔpoli** *f.* (*inv.*) metropolis

***mettendo** (*pres. part. of* **mettere**) putting

***mettere** *irr. v.* [**metto, misi, messo**] to put, put on, place

***mezzanotte** *f.* midnight

***mezzo** *adj.* half; *n.* middle, means; **per — di** by means of

***mezzogiorno** noon, south

***mi** me, to me, for me, myself, to myself, for myself

Michelangelo, *see* **Buonarrɔti**

***migliaio** about a thousand; *pl.* **migliaia** (*f.*) thousands

***miglio** (*pl.* **le miglia**) mile

***migliore** better; **il —,** the better, the best

***mila** (*pl. of* **mille**) thousand

***Milano** *f.* Milan, *one of the most important Italian cities* (*population* 1,130,000)

***milione** *m.* million

***mille** (*pl.* **mila**) thousand; **i Mille,** *the one thousand patriots whom Garibaldi led in* 1860 *on his expedition to Sicily*

***minacciare (di) [minaccio]** to menace, threaten

minestrone *m.* vegetable soup

***minimo** least, minimum, very small

***minore** less, smaller, minor, lower, younger

***minuta** bill of fare

***minuto** minute

***mio** (*pl.* **miei**) my, mine

miracolo miracle

***misero** wretched, miserable

***mistero** mystery

misto mixed; **fritto —,** fried fish of many kinds

misura measure, measurement

***mite** mild

mnemɔnico mnemonic; **esercizio —,** memory exercise

***mɔbile** *m.* piece of furniture; **i mɔbili** the furniture

***mɔda** fashion, style

modello model

***moderno** modern

modesto modest

***modista** milliner

***mɔdo** manner, way, mood

mɔdulo blank

***moglie** *f.* (*pl.* **mogli**) wife

molare *m.* molar

mɔlla spring

***molto** *adj.* much, many; *adv.* very, quite, a great deal, a lot

***momento** moment; **da un — all'altro** any moment

***mondo** world

monopɔlio monopoly

***Monreale** *f. a little town near Palermo, famous for its magnificent cathedral_ and for its wonderful location*

***monte** *m.* mountain

***monumento** monument

†***morire** *irr. v.* [**muɔio, mɔrto**] to die

***mɔrto** dead

mosca fly

***Mosè** Moses

***mostrare (di) [mostro]** to show; **mostratemi** show me

*motore *m.* motor; barca a —, motorboat
mughetto lily of the valley
*mulo mule
*municipio city hall, city administration
*muovere *irr. v.* [muovo, mossi, mosso] to move (*somebody or something*); †muoversi to move (*oneself*), get started
*muro (*pl.* i muri *or* le mura) wall
*museo museum
*musica music; fare un po' di —, to play (*or* have) a little music
*musicista *m. or f.* musician
mutandine *f. pl.* drawers, trunks
mutare to change

N

n/, *an abbreviation of* nostro, nostra, nostri, *or* nostre, *used in business letters*
nano dwarf
*napoletano Neapolitan
*Napoli *f.* Naples, *one of the most important Italian cities* (*population* 1,000,000)
†*nascere *irr. v.* to be born
nascita birth
naso nose
Natale *m.* Christmas; buon —! Merry Christmas!
*nativo native
*nato (*p. part. of* nascere) born
*natura nature
*naturale natural
*naturalmente naturally, of course
*nave *f.* ship
*navigare [navigo] to navigate, sail
*nazionale national
nazione *f.* nation
*ne *adv.* from there, thence, of there
*ne *pron.* of it (him, her, them), some of it (them), any of it (them)
*nè *conj.* nor, and not; nè . . . nè neither . . . nor
*neanche not even

necessario necessary
negativa (*photographic*) negative
negativo negative
negazione *f.* negation
*negozio store, shop
*nemico enemy
*nemmeno not even
neolatino Romance
*neppure not even
*nero black
*nessuno *adj.* no, not any; *pron.* no one, nobody, none
*Nettuno Neptune, *Roman god of the sea*
neutro neuter, neutral
*neve *f.* snow
†*nevicare *imp. v.* [nevica] to snow
*niente nothing; — affatto not at all; — di speciale nothing special; — disturbo no trouble at all
*nipote *m. or f.* nephew, niece, grandson, granddaughter, grandchild
Nizza Nice, *the beautiful city on the Western Riviera where Garibaldi was born* (*population* 190,000)
*no no; dire di —, to say no
*noce *f.* walnut; *m.* walnut tree
*noi we, us; da —, in *or* to our country (home, place, etc.)
*nome *m.* name, noun
nominale nominal; proposizione (*f.*) —, noun clause
*non not; non + *verb* + che only
*nonna grandmother
*nonno grandfather
*nono ninth
*nord *m.* north
*normanno Norman
*nostro our, ours
nota note
notaio notary
notizia piece of news, news
*noto known, well-known
*nottata night (*in its duration, or referring to weather or work*)
*notte *f.* night; a —, or di —, *or*

la —, at night; **prima di** —, before nightfall
*novanta ninety
*nɔve nine
*novecɛnto nine hundred; **il Novecɛnto** the twentieth century
novɛllo new
*novɛmbre m. November
nɔvo new
nuca nape, neck
*nulla nothing; **— di male** nothing wrong; **di —,** you are welcome (*said after receiving thanks*)
numerale m. numeral
*numero number
*numeroso numerous, large
nuɔcere *irr. v.* [nɔccio, nɔcqui] to do harm, hurt
*nuotare [nuɔto] to swim
*nuɔvo new; **di —,** again, anew

O

*o or; **o . . . o** either . . . or
obbligato obliged
*ɔca goose
*occasione f. occasion, opportunity
*ɔcchio eye
occorrɛnte m. what is needed
†*occorrere *irr. v.* [occorro, occorsi, occorso] to be necessary
*occupare [ɔccupo] to occupy
*occupato busy, employed
*ocɛano ocean
ɔde f. ode
*odorare [odoro] to smell, smell good
*offrire (di) *irr. v.* [ɔffro, offɛrsi, offɛrto] to offer
*offrirvi (= offrire + vi) to offer you
oggettivo objective
*oggɛtto object; **complemento —,** direct object; **oggɛtti di valore** valuables
*ɔggi today
*ɔgni (*inv.*) every, each
*ognuno every one, everybody, each one

ɔh! oh!
*Olanda Holland
*olandese Dutch
*Ɔlga Olga
ɔlio oil, olive oil
*oliva olive; **olivo** olive tree
oltre (a) beyond, after; **più —,** farther, longer
ombrellaio umbrella maker *or* seller
*ombrɛllo umbrella
omissione f. omission
onomastico Saint's day
ɔpera work, opera, literary work, artistic production
*ora *adv.* now; **or —,** just now
*ora *n.* hour, time; **a che —?** at what time? **che — ɛ?** *or* **che ore sono?** what time is it? **di buɔn'—,** early
orario timetable, schedule
*orchɛstra orchestra
ordinale ordinal
ordinare (di) [ordino] to order
*ordine m. order
orecchino earring
*originale original
*origine f. origin, extraction
*ɔro gold
*orologetto small watch; **— da polso** wrist watch
orologiaio watchmaker
*orolɔgio clock, watch
*orso bear
*ɔrto vegetable garden
ortografico orthographic
*osare (di) [ɔso] to dare
oscurità (*inv.*) darkness, obscurity
*osservare [ossɛrvo] to observe, remark
osservazione f. observation, remark
*ɔsso (*pl.* le ɔssa) bone
ostinato obstinate, stubborn
*ottanta eighty
*ottavo eighth
*ottenere (di) *irr. v.* (ottɛngo, ottenni) to obtain
*ottimamente very well

*ottimo very good, excellent
*otto eight
*ottobre m. October
*ottocento eight hundred; l'Otto-
cento the nineteenth century
*ovest m. west

P

*pacchetto little parcel, package
*pacco parcel, package
pace f. peace
*Padova Padua, *important Italian
city near Venice; famous university (population 150,000)*
*padre m. father
*paese m. country, town
paga pay
Paganini, Niccolò (1784-1840), *a
native of Genoa, the greatest
violinist of all time and a most
original composer of violin music*
*pagare to pay, pay for
*pagina page
paglia straw
*paio (pl. le paia) pair, couple
pala shovel
*palazzo palace, building
*Palermo, *one of the most important
Italian cities (population 425,000)*
Palestrina, Giovanni Pierluigi
(da) (1524-1594), *born in the
small town of Palestrina, near
Rome, shares with Bach the
glory of having been one of the
most profound geniuses among
composers of music*
palla ball
*palma palm, palm tree
*panciotto vest
*pane m. bread; — tostato toast
*panino roll
panna cream
*panorama m. panorama
*pantaloni m. pl. trousers
*Pantheon m., *ancient Roman
temple, now a church containing
the tombs of the kings of Italy*
pantofola slipper

*Paolo Paul
*papa m. pope
papà m. (inv.) daddy
papale papal
pappa pap
parabrezza m. (inv.) windshield
paralisi f. (inv.) paralysis
*parco park
*parecchio quite, quite a, a lot; pl.
several
*parente m. or f. relative
parentela relationship
*parentesi f. (inv.) parenthesis
†*parere irr. v. [paio] to seem, look
like
*parete f. wall (of a room)
*pari m. or f. (inv.) equal
Parigi f. Paris
*parlare to speak, talk, say
*parmigiano Parmesan; alla par-
migiana Parmesan style
*parola word
*parte f. part, share, rôle; da —,
aside
*partenza departure
participio participle
†*partire [parto] to depart, leave,
go away, sail
partitivo partitive
pasciuto (p. part. of pascere)
pastured
*pascolare [pascolo] to graze
pascolo pasture
Pasqua Easter; buona —! Happy
Easter!
*passaporto passport
°*passare to pass, spend (time)
passato past
*passeggiare [passeggio] to take
a walk, stroll, walk up and down
*passeggiata walk, ride, drive;
fare una —, to take a walk or
a ride
*passeggiero, passeggiera passen-
ger
passivo passive
*passo step; fare due passi to take
a little stroll
*pasto meal

*patata potato
patente *f.* licence
paternità (*inv.*) paternity
*patria fatherland, native country,
native city
patriarca *m.* patriarch
pausa pause
*pavimento floor, pavement
*peccato sin, pity; peccato! too
bad! che —! what a pity!
*pecora sheep
*peggio worse; il —, the worse,
the worst
*peggiore worse; il —, the worse,
the worst
*pellegrino pilgrim
*pelliccia fur, fur coat
*pellicola film
pelo hair
pena pain, penalty; non ne vale
la —, it isn't worth the trouble
*pendente leaning
*penisola peninsula
*penna pen; — stilografica foun-
tain pen
pennello brush; — per la barba
shaving brush
*pensare (a) [penso] to think,
think of; — di make up one's
mind, resolve (on)
pensiero thought
pensione *f.* room and board
pepe *m.* pepper
peperone *m.* chili, pepper
*Peppino Joe
*per *conj.* to, in order to
*per *prep.* for, because of, by, on,
through
*pera pear; pero pear tree
*perbacco! by Jove!
*perchè why, because; (*followed
by the subj.*) in order to, so that
perciò therefore
*perdere *irr. v.* [perdo, persi,
perso] to lose, waste
perfetto perfect
†perfezionarsi [mi perfeziono] to
perfect oneself
perla pearl

*permesso permission; con — *or
just* permesso! with your permission!
*permettere *irr. v.* (di) [permetto,
permisi, permesso] to permit,
allow
*pero pear tree
*però however
*persona person; a —, per person
personale personal
*Perù *m.* Peru
*Perugia, *a lovely city in Central
Italy* (*population* 88,000)
Perugino (Pietro Vannucci), *famous painter, Raphael's teacher*
(1446–1524)
pesante heavy
*pesca peach; pesco peach tree
*pescatore *m.* fisherman
*pesce *m.* fish
*pessimamente very badly
*pessimo very bad
*Pesto Paestum, *ancient Greek city
south of Salerno*
*pezzo piece
*piacciono (*pres. ind. of* piacere);
vi —, you like
*piacere *m.* pleasure; per —,
please; piacere! pleased to
meet you!
†*piacere *irr. v.* (piaccio, piacqui)
to be pleasing, please; mi piace,
mi piacciono I like; vi piace,
vi piacciono you like
*piacevole pleasant, agreeable
pianeta *m.* planet
*piangere *irr. v.* to weep, cry
*pianista *m. or f.* pianist
*piano *adj.* slow, soft, quiet; *adv.*
slowly, softly, quietly
*piano *n.* floor; al pian terreno
on the ground floor, downstairs;
al — superiore on the upper
floor, upstairs; all'ultimo —,
on the top floor; al secondo —,
on the third floor
*pianoforte *m.* piano
*pianta plant
*piantare to plant

pianto weeping
*pianura plain
*piatto dish, plate
*piazza square; in —, on the square
*piccolo little, small
*piɛde m. foot; a piɛdi on foot; †andare a piɛdi to walk; in —, standing
*pienamente fully
*piɛno full
*piɛtra stone
*Piɛtro Peter
pigliare [piglio] to take, catch
pilɔta m. pilot
pinacotɛca picture gallery
pino pine tree
*piɔggia rain
piombo lead
piɔppo poplar
†*piɔvere imp. irr. v. [piɔve, piɔvve] to rain
pipa pipe
Pirandɛllo, Luigi (1863–1936), famous playwright and novelist, one of the most original writers of the present century. He was born in Agrigento, Sicily.
*pirɔscafo steamer, liner
*Pisa, important city in Tuscany, on the banks of the river Arno (population 78,000)
*piscina swimming pool
*pisɛllo pea
Pitti, very wealthy Florentine family of the Renaissance; Palazzo —, the Pitti Palace, containing one of the finest art galleries in the world
*pittore m. painter
*più more, any more, any longer, plus; tanto — che all the more (all the better) because
*piuttɔsto rather
platɛa pit, orchestra (as a part of a theater)
platino platinum
plurale m. plural
*Po Po, the largest river in Italy,

passing through Turin, Piacenza, and Cremona
*po', apocopation of pɔco; un — di some, a little, a bit of
*pochino: un —, a little bit
*pɔco little, not much; pl. few; — dopo soon after; — fa a short time ago; fra or tra —, soon, before long
*podere m. farm
poɛma m. poem
*poɛta m. poet
*pɔi then, after, afterward
*pollaio poultry yard
*pollo chicken; — arrɔsto roast chicken
polsino cuff; bottoni (m. pl.) da polsini cuff links
polso wrist, pulse; orologetto da —, wrist watch
*poltrona armchair, best seat in the orchestra of a theater
*pomeriggio afternoon
*pomodɔro tomato; al —, with tomato sauce
*Pompɛi f. Pompeii, a city near Naples, famous for its ruins; it was completely buried under a rain of ashes from Mt. Vesuvius A.D. 79
*ponɛnte m. west
*ponte m. bridge
*pɔpolo people, populace
popoloso populous
*poppa stern; a —, at the stern
*pɔrco pig
*porre irr. v. [pongo, posi, posto] to put, place
*pɔrta door, gate
portafɔglio pocketbook
*portare (a) [pɔrto] to bring, carry, bear, take, wear (clothes)
pɔrtico portico
*pɔrto port, harbor
*Portogallo Portugal
*Posillipo, a cape in the Bay of Naples, green with luxuriant vegetation and rich in beautiful villas

posizione *f.* position

*posporre (di) *irr. v.* [pospongo, posposi, posposto] to post-pone

possessivo possessive

possesso possession

*possibile possible

*posso (*pres. ind. of* potere) I can *or* may

*posta post, post office, mail

postale postal

*posto place, seat, position

**potere *irr. v.* [posso] to be able, can, may

*potrei (*cond. of* potere) I could

*potremo (*fut. of* potere) we shall be able

*povero poor

*pranzare to dine

*pranzo dinner; sala da —, dining room

pratico practical

*prato lawn, meadow

*precipizio precipice

preciso precise, exact

preferenza preference

preferibilmente preferably

*preferire [preferisco] to prefer

*preferirei (*cond. of* preferire) I should prefer

*pregare (di) [prego] to pray, beg; prego please, *or* pardon, *or* you are welcome

pregiato prized, esteemed; la pregiata v/ del your favor of

premere [premo] to press; pre-mendo if you press

premolare *m.* premolar

*prendere *irr. v.* [prendo, presi, preso] to take, take up, get

preoccupazione *f.* worry

*preparare to prepare, get ready

preposizione *f.* preposition; — articolata contraction of def. art. and prep.

presa exposure (*referred to photography*)

*presentare [presento] to present, introduce (*a person*)

*presentarvi (= presentare + vi) to introduce you

*presentazione *f.* introduction

*presente *adj.* present; la —, this letter; *n. m.* gift, present tense

*presso near, c/o; acquistare — di voi to acquire from you

*presto soon, early, quickly; al più —, as soon as possible

*pretendere (di) *irr. v.* [pretendo, pretesi, preteso] to pretend

prezioso precious

*prezzo price; che — fa . . .? what's the price of . . .?

*prima *adv.* first, before (*in time*); — di *prep.* before; — che (*followed by the subj.*) before

*primavera spring

*primo first

*principale principal, main

*principalmente mainly

privato private

problema *m.* problem

*prodigare [prodigo] to lavish

*professione *f.* profession

*professore *m.* professor

profeta *m.* prophet

*profondo deep, profound

profumiere *m.* perfumer

profumo perfume, scent

progettare (di) [progetto] to plan

*programma *m.* program

progressivo progressive

*promettere (di) *irr. v.* [prometto, promisi, promesso] to prom-ise

pronome *m.* pronoun

*pronto ready, prompt; pronto! hello! yes! (*used in telephoning*)

pronunzia pronunciation

*pronunziare [pronunzio] to pro-nounce

*proporre (di) *irr. v.* [propongo, proposi, proposto] to propose

proposizione *f.* clause

*proprietario owner

*proprio *adj.* own, his (her, its) own; *adv.* just, really, right

prossimo next

proteggere *irr. v.* [**protEggo,** **protEssi, protEtto**] to protect

prov., *abbreviation for* **provincia** province

provare (a) [**prɔvo**] to prove, try, try on

*****proverbio** proverb

provetto competent

pubblicazione *f.* publication

*****pubblico** public

*****Puccini, Giacomo** (1858–1924), *great Italian composer, born at Lucca, Tuscany, author of the operas "Manon Lescaut," "La Bohème," "La Tosca," "Madama Butterfly," etc.*

pugno fist, punch

*****pulire** [**pulisco**] to clean; **fare** —, to have cleaned

pulita (*quick*) cleaning

pulitura polishing, cleaning

*****punto** point, dot, period

puntura puncture

*****purchè** (*followed by the subj.*) provided that

*****pure** also; **dite** —, please say; **fate** —, please do

*****puro** pure, real

*****purtrɔppo** unfortunately

Q

*****qua** here

*****quadErno** notebook

*****quadro** picture, painting

*****qualche** some, any, a few; — **cɔsa** something; — **cɔsa di buɔno** something good

*****qualcuno, qualcuna** somebody, someone, some

*****quale** *inter. adj. or pron.* what, which, which one; **il** — (**la quale, i quali, le quali**) *rel. pron.* who, whom, that, which

*****qualità** (*inv.*) quality

*****qualunque** whatever, whichever, any; — **cɔsa** whatever

*****quando** when

quantità (*inv.*) quantity

*****quanto** how much, how many; — **cɔsta?** *or* — **cɔstano?** what's the price? **tanto . . . quanto** as . . . as, so . . . as

*****quantunque** (*followed by the subj.*) although

*****quaranta** forty

*****quartiEre** *m.* ward, section

Quarto, *the place, near Genoa, from which Garibaldi sailed, in 1860, with 1000 patriots, to liberate Sicily and Southern Italy*

*****quarto** *adj.* fourth; *n.* quarter

*****quasi** almost

*****quattordici** fourteen

*****quattro** four

*****quattrocEnto** four hundred; **il QuattrocEnto** the fifteenth century

*****quegli** that man, the former

*****quello** *dem. adj.* that, those; *dem. pron.* he, him, that one, the one, the former; — **che** what; **di quel che** than; **quella** that woman, that one, the former

quErcia oak

*****questi** this man, the latter

questione *f.* question

*****questo** *dem. adj.* this, these; *dem. pron.* this, this one, the latter; **questa** this woman, this one, the latter

*****qui** here, this way

*****quindici** fifteen

*****quinto** fifth

R

*****raccomandare** (**di**) to recommend, register (*at the post office*)

raccomandazione *f.* recommendation, reference

*****raccomandErsi** (*cond. of* **raccomandare**) I should recommend

racconto story

radice *f.* root

*****radio** *f.* (*inv.*) radio

*****RaffaEllo** Raphael; *see* **Sanzio**

raffreddore *m.* cold

*****ragazza** girl, child

*ragazzo boy, child
*raggio ray
raggiungere irr. v. to reach, join, overtake
*ragione f. reason; aver —, to be right
ragno spider
ramo branch
*ramoscello twig
*rapidamente rapidly
*rapido adj. rapid; n. flyer
*rappresentare [rappresento] to represent, perform
rarità (inv.) rarity
raro rare
rasoio razor; — di sicurezza safety razor
*ravanello radish
*Ravello f., one of the most attractive spots on the Sorrento peninsula
*razza race
*re m. (inv.) king
*reale real, royal
*recente recent
*recentemente recently
referenza reference
reggia royal palace
regio royal
*regione f. region
registro register
*regola rule; fare le cose in —, to do things right
*relativo relative
*rendere irr. v. [rendo, resi, reso] to render, make
Reni, Guido (1575–1642), one of the best painters of the seventeenth century
*repubblica republic
†*restare [resto] to remain, be left
reuma m. rheumatism
reumatico rheumatic
*Riccardo Richard
*ricco rich
ricetta prescription
*ricevere [ricevo] to receive
ricevuta receipt
richiedere (di) irr. v. [richiedo, richiesi, richiesto] to require

richiesta request
richiesto (p. part. of richiedere) required, asked for
*riconoscere (di) irr. v. [riconosco, riconobbi] to recognize, admit
*ricordare (di) [ricordo] to remember, recall, remind
*ricordo remembrance, souvenir
ridda reel, brawl
*ridere irr. v. [risi, riso] to laugh; †scoppiare a —, to burst out laughing
*ridire (di) irr. v. [ridico, p. part. ridetto] to say again
riduzione f. reduction
*riempire [riempisco] to fill
*rifare irr. v. [rifaccio or rifò, rifeci] to do (or make) again
riflessivo reflexive
*riflettere irr. v. [rifletto] to reflect
rifugio refuge
*riga ruler, line (of writing)
rigo line (of writing)
rigore m. rigor
riguardo regard, care
†*rimanere irr. v. [p. abs. rimasi] to remain, be left
*rimpianto regret
*Rinascimento Renaissance
*rinfresco refreshment
*ringraziare (di) [ringrazio] to thank
riparare to repair, fix, mend
†*ripartire [riparto] to depart again
*riportare (a) [riporto] to bring back
*riservare [riservo] to reserve
*riso (pl. le risa) laughter
rispettoso respectful
*rispondere (di) irr. v. [rispondo, risposi, risposto] to answer, reply
risposta answer
rissa affray, brawl
*ristorante m. restaurant; carrozza —, dining car

*ritardo delay; in —, late; essere in —, to be late

†*ritirarsi to retire

°*ritornare (a) [ritorno] to return

*ritorno return; viaggio di —, return trip

ritratto portrait

*riunire [riunisco] to assemble (*people or things*); †riunirsi to assemble (*in a reflexive meaning*)

riuscire (a) *irr. v.* [riɛsco] to succeed (in), turn out

*riva shore, bank

*rivedere *irr. v.* [rivedo] to see again

*rivedervi (= rivedere + vi) to see you again

*Riviɛra Riviera; in —, on the Riviera; — di Levante Eastern Riviera; — di Ponɛnte Western Riviera

*rivista review, magazine

†rivɔlgersi (a) *irr. v.* [mi rivɔlgo, mi rivɔlsi, rivɔlto] to turn, apply

rɔba thing, things, clothes

*Robɛrto Robert

*robusto robust, sturdy

*rocca rock

*Roma Rome, *Italy's capital, the seat of the Church, and the center of three civilizations* (*population* 1,250,000)

*romano Roman

*romanzo romance, novel

*rompere *irr. v.* [rompo, rotto] to break

*Rɔsa Rose

Rɔsa, Salvator (1615–1673), *famous painter and satiric poet, a native of Naples*

*rɔsa rose

*Rosetta Rosie

*rosso red

rotto (*p. part. of* rompere) broken

*ruderi *m. pl.* ruins

rupe *f.* cliff

ruppe (*p. abs. of* rompere) broke

russo Russian

S

*sabato Saturday; il —, on Saturdays

*sagrestano sexton

*sala hall, room; — d'aspɛtto waiting room; — da fumare smoking room; — da pranzo dining room

*sale *m.* salt

°*salire (a) *irr. v.* [salgo] to go up, climb, get on

*salɔtto living room, parlor

°*saltare to jump, hop, leap

*salubre healthful

*salutare to greet, salute

*salute *f.* health

*saluto greeting

*san, *apocopation of* santo

San Rɛmo, *one of the most beautiful towns on the Western Riviera*

*santo saint, saintly, holy

Sanzio, Raffaɛllo Raphael (1483–1520), *of Urbino, probably the world's most famous painter*

sapè, *Neapolitan dialect form for* sapere

*sapere *irr. v.* [sɔ, sɛppi] to know (*a thing or a fact*), know how, be able to

sapone *m.* soap; — per la barba shaving soap

sapore *m.* taste

*sarà (*fut. of* ɛssere) will be

*Sardegna Sardinia, *a large Italian island in the Mediterranean* (*population* 1,075,000)

*sarɛi, sarɛbbe, saremmo (*cond. of* ɛssere) I should *or* would be, etc.

*sarete (*fut. of* ɛssere) you will be

*sarta dressmaker; sarto tailor

*sbagliare (a) [sbaglio] to be mistaken, make a mistake, miss

*sbaglio mistake

°*sbarcare to land

*sbarco landing

*scacchi *m. pl.* chess; giocare a —, to play chess

*scaffale *m.* bookshelf

*scala stairs, stairway; **Teatro della Scala** Scala Theater (*in Milan*)

*scambiare [scambio] to exchange

*scarpa shoe

scatola box

scatoletta small box

*scavo excavation

*scegliere (di) *irr. v.* [scelgo, scelsi, scelto] to choose, select

*scelto (*p. part. of* scegliere) chosen

scɛna scene

°*scendere (a) *irr. v.* [scendo, scesi, sceso] to descend, go (*or* get) down, get off

schɛda card, form

scherzo joke, jest

*schiacciare [schiaccio] to crush, squeeze; — **un sonnellino** to take a nap

schiarimento information

*schiavitù *f.* (*inv.*) slavery

schifo loathing, disgust

sciarpa scarf, sash

*sciɛnza science

scimmia monkey

sciɔlto (*p. part. of* sciɔgliere) loosened

sciɔpero strike

sciupare to spoil

*scommettere (di) *irr. v.* [scommetto, scommisi, scommesso] to bet

*scompartimento compartment

*scontentare [scontɛnto] to displease, dissatisfy

*scontɛnto dissatisfied

sconto discount

scɔpo purpose

†*scoppiare [scɔppio] to burst; — **a ridere** to burst out laughing

scoprire *irr. v.* [scɔpro, scopɛrsi, scoperto] to discover

*scorso past, last; **l'anno —,** last year

*scritto (*p. part. of* scrivere) written

*scrittore *m.* writer

*scrivania desk

*scrivere (di) *irr. v.* to write

scudo shield

*scultore *m.* sculptor

scultura sculpture

*scuɔla school

*scuro dark

*scusare (di) [scuso] to excuse

*se *conj.* if, whether; — **mai** (*followed by the subj.*) in case

*se *pron.* = si

*se (stesso) *pron.* himself, herself, itself, themselves, yourself, yourselves, oneself

*sebbɛne (*followed by the subj.*) although

secchia pail

*secchietto little pail

*sɛcolo century

*secondo *adj.* second

*secondo *prep.* according to

*sɛdano celery

*sɛde *f.* seat (*residence*)

*sedere *irr. v.* [siɛdo *or* sɛggo] to sit; †sedersi to sit down

*sɛdia chair

*sedici sixteen

sega saw

segno sign

*seguɛnte following

*seguire [seguo] to follow

*sɛi six

*seicɛnto six hundred; **il Seicɛnto** the seventeenth century

†*sembrare [sembro] to seem, look like

semilucido semi-glossy

*Sempione: il —, Mt. Simplon

*semplice simple

*sɛmpre always, ever

senatore *m.* senator

senso sense, meaning

*sentiɛro path

*sentire (di) [sɛnto] to feel, hear, listen to, smell, taste

*senza, senza di without; — **che** (*followed by the subj.*) without

*seppellire *irr. v.* [seppellisco] to bury

sequεla sequel

*sera evening; a — or di —, in the evening

*serata evening (in its duration, or referring to weather or work)

serbatoio gasoline tank

*sεrie f. (inv.) series

*servire (a) [sεrvo] to serve

*sessanta sixty

*sεsto sixth

*seta silk

*sete f. thirst; aver —, to be thirsty

*settanta seventy

*settantacinque seventy-five

*sεtte seven

*settecεnto seven hundred; il Settecεnto the eighteenth century

*settεmbre m. September

*settentrionale northern

*settimana week; la — ventura next week; la — scorsa last week

*sεttimo seventh

severità (inv.) severity

sevεro severe

sezione f. section

*sforzesco of the (extinct) Sfɔrza family; Castεllo Sforzesco Sfɔrza Castle

sgonfiare [sgonfio] to lower a swelling, let out the air; una gomma sgonfiata a flat tire

*si himself, herself, itself, oneself, themselves, to himself (herself, itself, oneself, themselves), each other, one another, one, people

*sì yes; dire di —, to say yes, permit

*sia . . . che or sia . . . sia both . . . and

*siamo (pres. ind. of εssere) we are

*siccome as, since

*Sicília Sicily, the largest island in the Mediterranean and one of Italy's most important regions (population 4,500,000)

*siciliano Sicilian; alla siciliana Sicilian style

sicuramente surely

sicurezza certainty, safety; rasoio di —, safety razor

sicuro sure

*Siεna, a very attractive city in Tuscany (population 52,000)

sienese of Siεna

sigaretta cigarette

sigaro cigar

sigillare to seal

sigillo seal

significare [significo] to mean

significato meaning

*signora lady, madam, Mrs., wife

*signore m. gentleman, sir, Mr.

*signorina young lady, Miss

*silεnzio silence; in —, silently

sillaba syllable

*simbolo symbol

simile similar

sincεro sincere

singolare singular

*sinistro left; a sinistra at or to the left

sintesi f. (inv.) synthesis

*Sistina: Cappεlla —, the Sistine Chapel, the Pope's private chapel in the Vatican Palace

*situato situated, located

*sɔ (pres. ind. of sapere) I know

socialista m. or f. socialist

*sɔdo solid; (referring to eggs) hardboiled

*soffrire irr. v. [sɔffro, soffεrsi, soffεrto] to suffer

soggettivo subjective

soggεtto subject

*sognare (di) [sogno] to dream

*sogno dream

*solamente only

soldatino little soldier

*sɔldo penny

*sole m. sun, sunlight

sɔlido solid, strong

*sɔlito usual; come al —, as usual; di —, usually

*solo adj. alone, only; adv. only

soltanto only

*sonnellino nap; schiacciare un —, to take a nap
sonnifero somniferous; compressa sonnifera sleeping tablet
*sonno sleep; aver —, to be sleepy
sopra over, above, on, upon
*sopracciglio (pl. le sopracciglia) eyebrow
soprano soprano
*soprascarpa overshoe, rubber
*soprattutto above all
*sorella sister
†*sorgere irr. v. [sorgo, sorsi, sorto] to arise
*sormontare [sormonto] to surmount
*sorpresa surprise; fare una —, to give a surprise
*Sorrento, a lovely little town on the Bay of Naples
*sorridere irr. v. [sorrisi, sorriso] to smile
*sorriso smile
sostituire [sostituisco] to substitute
*sotterraneo underground
*sotto under
*sovranità (inv.) sovereignty
*spaghetti m. pl. spaghetti
*Spagna Spain
*spagnolo Spanish
spazio space
spazzolino small brush; — pei denti toothbrush
*specchietto little mirror
*specchio mirror
*speciale special; niente di —, nothing special
specialista m. or f. specialist
†*specializzarsi to specialize, major
*specialmente especially
*specie f. (inv.) kind, sort, species
spedire [spedisco] to send
*spendere irr. v. [spendo, spesi, speso] to spend
*sperare (di) [spero] to hope
*spesa expense; fare delle spese to shop
*spesso often

spett., an abbreviation of spettabile, respectable, esteemed, used in addressing business firms
*spettacolo show
spia spy
*spiaggia beach
*spiegare (di) [spiego] to explain, unfold
*spilla pin
*spinaci m. pl. spinach
*splendere [splendo] to shine, sparkle
splendido splendid
*sport m. (inv.) sport
*sportello window (of an office), door (of a car)
stabilimento establishment; — di bagni bathhouse
*stagione f. season
stagno tin
*stalla stable
*stamane or stamani this morning
stampa press
stampare to print
stancare to tire
*stanco tired
stanga bar, shaft
*stanotte, if said before noon, last night; if said after noon, tonight
*stanza room; — da bagno bathroom
†*stare irr. v. [sto, stetti] to be, stay, stand; — per to be about to; mi sta male it isn't good on me; sta bene all right, it's all right, very well; come state? how are you?
*stasera this evening, tonight
*stato state, condition; gli Stati Uniti the United States
*stato (p. part. of essere or stare) been
*statua statue
*stavi (p. des. of stare) you were
stavvi poet. or obs. (= sta + vi) there is
*stazione f. station
*Stefano Stephen

*stella star; Stelle d'Oro, *a brand of Italian cigarettes*

*stɛndere *irr. v.* [stɛndo, stesi, steso] to spread, stretch out, hold out, lay

*stesso same, self; fa lo —, it's just as well; lui —, he himself

*stile *m.* style

*stilografico: penna stilografica fountain pen

*stirare to press, iron

stivale *m.* boot

*stɔmaco stomach; a—digiuno on an empty stomach

*stɔria history, story

*stɔrico historic

*strada road, way

*straniɛro *adj.* foreign; *n.* foreigner

*strano strange, odd

stratɛga *m.* strategist

Stravinski (Stravinsky), Igor, *a modern Russian composer* (1882–)

Strɛsa, *a beautiful little town on Lake Maggiore*

*stretto *adj.* narrow, tight; *n.* strait

*stringere *irr. v.* [*p. part.* stretto] to tie, press, clasp; — la mano a to shake hands with

*studɛnte *m.* student

*studentessa *(girl)* student

*studiare [studio] to study

*studio study

stupɛndo stupendous

*stuzzicare [stuzzico] to tease

*su on, upon, up, upstairs; — per giù more or less, about

*subito at once, immediately

*sud *m.* south

*sudicio dirty, filthy

suffisso suffix

*sugante: carta —, blotter

*suo *(pl.* suɔi) his, her, its, your, yours, of his (hers, yours), his own, her own, *etc.*

suɔla sole

ᵃ*suonare [suɔno] to sound, play *(an instrument),* ring

suɔno sound

*supɛrbo superb, proud, haughty

*superiore superior, upper, higher; al piano —, on the upper floor, upstairs

superlativo superlative

*supporre *irr. v.* (di) [suppongo, supposi, supposto] to suppose

*supposto *(p. part. of* supporre) supposed

*suprɛmo supreme, highest

susina plum; susino plum tree

*svago amusement

sviluppare to develop

*Svizzera Switzerland

*svizzero Swiss

T

tabaccaio tobacco dealer, tobacconist

tabacco tobacco

*tacchino turkey

tacco heel

tacere *irr. v.* [taccio, tacqui] to be silent

*tacito silent

tagliare [taglio] to cut

*talɛnto talent

*tanto so much, so many, so, so great; tanto . . . quanto as . . . as, so . . . as; — più che all the more *(or* all the better) because; di — in —, once in a while; una vɔlta —, once in a great while

*Taormina, *the finest spot in Sicily*

*tappeto rug, carpet

*tarantɛlla tarantella, *the characteristic dance of Sorrento*

*tardi *adv.* late

*tardo *adj.* late

targhetta tag

tariffa rate

tartaruga tortoise, tortoise shell

tasca pocket

*tassì *m. (inv.)* taxicab

Tasso, Torquato (1544–1595), *a native of Sorrento, one of the* greatest Italian poets, the author of "Gerusalemme Liberata" and "Aminta"

tatto tact

*tavola table

†tavolino little table, stand

*tazza cup

*te thee, thyself, you, yourself

*tè m. (inv.) tea

*teatrino small theater; — di marionette puppet show

*teatro theater; Teatro della Scala Scala Theater; Teatro di San Carlo San Carlo Theater

*tedesco German

tegolo roof tile

*telefonare (di) [telefono] to telephone

telefonata telephone call

*telefonerò (fut. of telefonare) I shall telephone

*telefono telephone

telegrafare (di) [telegrafo] to telegraph

*telegramma m. telegram

temere (di) [temo] to fear

*tempio temple

*tempo time, weather, tense; che — fa? what kind of weather is it? fa bel —, it is fine weather; fa cattivo —, it is bad weather

tenda tent

*tendere (a) irr. v. [tendo, tesi, teso] to tend, stretch out, hold out

*tenere irr. v. [tengo, tenni] to hold, have, keep, take

tentare (di) [tento] to try

teorema m. theorem

*terme f. pl. thermae, thermal baths

*terra earth, land, ground

*terreno ground, soil; al pian —, on the ground floor, downstairs

*territorio territory

*terzo third

*tesi f. (inv.) thesis

*tesoro treasure

*tetto roof

*Tevere m. Tiber, the river on the banks of which Rome is situated

*ti thee, to thee, thyself, you, to you, yourself

tifo typhus

*tigre f. tiger

*timido timid, bashful

tipo type, kind

tirare to draw, pull; tira vento the wind blows, it's windy

titolo title

toccare [tocco] to touch

*togliere irr. v. [tolgo, tolsi, tolto] to take, take away, take off, carry off

*tomba tomb

tonico tonic

tonno tuna fish

topografico topographic; carta topografica topographic map

*Torino f. Turin, one of the most important Italian cities (population 655,000)

*torre f. tower

*torta cake

*torto wrong; aver —, to be wrong

Tosca, a very beautiful opera by Giacomo Puccini

*Toscana Tuscany, a region in Central Italy the principal city of which is Florence

*tostato toasted; pane —, toast

Tosti, Francesco Paolo (1846–1916), of Ortona, Abruzzi, composer of very beautiful songs

*tovaglia tablecloth

*tovagliolo napkin

*tra between, among, within; — poco soon, before long

Trabucos, a brand of Italian cigars

tradurre irr. v. [p. part. tradotto] to translate

*Traiano Trajan (52–117), great Roman emperor

traino sledge

trama plot

tramontare [tramonto] to set

*tramonto sunset, setting

tranquillo tranquil, calm

*tranvai *m.* (*inv.*) tramway, street-car
*trattato treaty
*traversata crossing
traverso: di —, across
*tre three
*trecento three hundred; il Tre-cento the fourteenth century
*tredici thirteen
*treno train; —diretto express train
*trenta thirty
*trentuno thirty-one
trina lace
trino group of three
*triste sad
*troppo *adj.* too much, too many; *adv.* too, too much
*trovare [trovo] to find, visit, see, experience; †trovarsi to be, find oneself
*tu thou, you
tubercolosi *f.* (*inv.*) tuberculosis
tubetto small tube
tuffo plunge, dive
tufo tufa, *a stone of volcanic origin*
*tuo (*pl.* tuoi) thy, thine, your, yours, of thine, of yours
†*tuonare *imp. v.* [tuona] to thunder
turchese *m.* turquoise
*turista *m. or f.* tourist
tutela guardianship
tutore *m.* guardian
*tutto *adj.* all, entire, whole; — il libro the whole book; tutti i libri all books; tutti noi all of us; tutt'e due both; tutti e tre all three; *pron.* everything, all, everyone; del —, entirely

U

*uccello bird
*udire *irr. v.* [odo] to hear
ufficiale *m.* officer
ufficio *or* uffizio office; Palazzo degli Uffizi Uffizi Palace
*ultimo last, latest, final; all'—piano on the top floor

umano human
*Umberto Humbert
*Umbria, *a region in Central Italy the most important city of which is Perugia*
*un, uno, una, un' a, an, one; l'un l'altro each other, one another
*undicesimo eleventh
*undici eleven
unghia nail, fingernail; forbicette per le unghie manicure scissors
*unificazione *f.* unification
*unire [unisco] to unite, combine
*università (*inv.*) university
*uno, un a, an, one; l'un l'altro each other, one another
*uomo (*pl.* uomini) man
*uovo (*pl.* le uova) egg
usanza custom
usare [uso] to use
uscio door
†*uscire (a) *irr. v.* [esco] to go out, come out, get out
*uso use, usage, custom
*utile useful; in che cosa posso esservi —? what can I do for you?
*utilmente usefully

V

v/, *an abbreviation of* vostro, vostra, vostri, *or* vostre, *used in business letters*
*va (*pres. ind. of* andare) goes
*vacca cow
*vado (*pres. ind. of* andare) I go *or* am going
*vaglia *m.* (*inv.*) money order
†valere *irr. v.* to be worth; non ne vale la pena it isn't worth the trouble
valgono (*pres. ind. of* valere) are worth
*valigetta little valise, bag
*valigia valise, suitcase
*valle *f.* valley

valore *m.* valor, value, worth; **i valori** the valuables
*__vanitoso__ vain, conceited
*__Vanni__ Johnny
*__vantaggio__ advantage
*__vapore__ *m.* steam, steamboat
*__vaporetto__ small steamboat
*__vario__ various, different
*__vaso__ vase
*__vasto__ vast
*__Vaticano__ Vatican (Palace), *the residence of the Pope in the independent little state of Vatican City, in Rome*
*__ve = vi__
*__vεcchio__ old; **Palazzo Vεcchio,** *do not translate*
*__vedere__ *irr. v.* [vedo] to see; **far —,** to show
vela sail
veletta veil
*__velocità__ (*inv.*) speed
*__vendere__ [vendo] to sell
*__vendita__ sale
*__venerdì__ *m.* Friday; **il —,** on Fridays
*__Venεzia__ Venice, *the wonderful City of the Lagoons, for many centuries the mistress of the seas* (*population* 274,000)
†*__venire (a)__ *irr. v.* [vεngo, venni] to come
*__venti__ twenty; **alle —,** at 8 P.M.
ventina: una —, about twenty
*__vεnto__ wind; **tira —,** the wind blows, it's windy
*__venturo__ next, coming
*__venuto__ (*p. part. of* venire) come
*__veramente__ truly, really
*__veranda__ veranda
verbale verbal
vεrbo verb
*__verde__ green
Verdi, Giusεppe (1813–1901), *the greatest of all operatic composers, born near Busseto (Emilia), the author of "Rigoletto," "Il Trovatore," "La Traviata," "Aïda," "Otello," Falstaff," etc.*

*__verdura__ vegetable
verità (*inv.*) truth
*__vero__ true, real; **non è —?** isn't it so? don't you? won't you? hasn't he? won't he? *etc.*
*__Verona,__ *a city in Northern Italy, on the banks of the river Adige* (*population* 170,000)
*__verrεbbe__ (*cond. of* venire) would come
*__verrò, verrai, verrà__ (*fut. of* venire) I shall come, *etc.*
*__versare__ [vεrso] to pour
*__vεrso__ toward; **— le venti** at about 8 P.M.
vescovo bishop
Vespucci, Amerigo (1451–1512), *a great Florentine navigator who in several voyages explored the New World, and for the first time advanced the theory that the newly discovered lands were not a part of Asia but a separate continent. America was named after him.*
*__vεste__ *f.* dress
*__vestire__ [vεsto] to dress; †vestirsi to dress (*oneself*), get dressed
†*__Vesuvio:__ **il —,** Mt. Vesuvius
*__vetrina__ show window, showcase
*__vetro__ glass; **— della finεstra** windowpane
*__vettura__ carriage, car
*__vi__ *adv.* here, there, in it
*__vi__ *pron.* you, yourself, yourselves, to you (yourself, yourselves)
*__via__ *adv.* away
*__via__ *n.* street, way, route
*__viaggiare__ [viaggio] to travel
viaggiatore *m.* traveler, passenger
*__viaggio__ trip, journey, voyage; **— di ritorno** return trip; **fare un —,** to take a trip
*__viale__ *m.* boulevard, (*in a park*) lane
*__viavai__ *m.* (*inv.*) going and coming
vicinanza vicinity
*__vicino__ *adj.* near, next, neighboring, near-by; *adv.* near
*__vicino, vicina__ *n.* neighbor

*vicino a *prep.* near, next
*vigna vineyard
 villa villa, park
*villaggio village
 vimine *m.* wicker twig
 Vinci, *see* Leonardo
 vincolo bond, fetter; San Pietro in Vincoli, *do not translate*
*vino wine
*violetta violet
 violinista *m. or f.* violinist
 violino violin
*virtù *f.* (*inv.*) virtue
*visita visit; biglietto da — *or* carta da —, visiting card; farvi una —, to call on you
*visitare [visito] to visit, call on
*vista sight, view
*visto (*p. part. of* vedere) seen
*vita life
 vitello calf, veal
*Vittorio Victor
°*vivere *irr. v.* to live
*vividamente vividly
 vo', *Neapolitan dialect* = vuole
*voce *f.* voice; ad alta —, aloud
 voglia desire, craving
*voi you
†*volare [volo] to fly
*volentieri gladly, willingly

°*volere *irr. v.* [voglio, volli] to want; — bene a to be fond of; — dire to mean; ci vuole is needed; quando volete whenever you like
†*volgersi (a) *irr. v.* [mi volgo, mi volsi, volto] to turn
 volo flight
*volta time (*turn*); uno alla —, one at a time; una — tanto once in a great while
*vorrei, vorresti, vorrebbe (*cond. of* volere) I should *or* would want, *or* I should *or* would like, *etc.*
*vostro your, yours
*vulcano volcano
 vuoto empty

Z

 zanzara mosquito
 zebra zebra
 zelo zeal
*zia aunt
*zietta dear little aunt
*zio uncle; gli zii uncle and aunt
 zitto silent, quiet
*zoologia zoology
*zoologico zoological
*zucchero sugar

English-Italian Vocabulary

A

a, an un, uno, una, un'; *after a neg. verb,* nessun, nessuno, nessuna, nessun

able: to be —, potere *irr. v.*

about circa; (= *of*) di; (= *almost*) quasi; **to be** — **to** staret per

above sopra; — **all** soprattutto

absent assente

abuse abuso

academy accademia

accent accento

accept accettare (di)

accompany accompagnare

according to secondo

account: on — **of** a causa di

accumulate accumulare [accumulo]

ache dolore *m.*

acquaintance conoscenza

acquainted: be — **with** conoscere *irr. v.*

add aggiungere *irr. v.*

address indirizzo

admire ammirare

advantage vantaggio

advertisement annunzio

advise consigliare (di)

afraid: to be — (**of**) temere (di)

Africa Africa

after dopo; *before an inflected verb,* dopo che; **soon** —, poco dopo

afternoon pomeriggio

afterward poi, dopo; **one hour** —, un'ora dopo

again di nuovo; *after a neg. verb,* più; **till we meet** —! arrivederci!

age età (*inv.*)

ago fa; **a short time** —, poco fa

agreeable piacevole

ah! ah!

aid aiutare (a)

air aria

alas! ahimè!

all tutto; — **alone** solo solo, sola sola; — **books** tutti i libri; — **of us** tutti noi; — **right!** sta bene! — **the more** (— **the better**) because tanto più che; — **three** tutti e tre

allow permettere *irr. v.* (di)

almost quasi; (= *about*) circa

alone solo; **all** —, solo solo, sola sola

along lungo

aloud ad alta voce

Alps Alpi *f. pl.*

already già

also anche, pure (*they usually precede the word to which they refer*)

although benchè, quantunque, sebbene (*each of them followed by the subjunctive*)

always sempre

Amalfi Amalfi *f.*

Amelia Amalia

America America

American americano

among fra, tra

amphitheater anfiteatro

amuse divertire [diverto]

amusement svago

an, *see* a

ancient antico

and e, ed (*used only before a word beginning with* e); **both . . . and** sia . . . che *or* sia . . . sia

Andrew Andrea

anew di nuovo

angel angelo

Angevin angioino

animal animale *m.*

Ann Anna

announcement annunzio

annoyance disturbo

another un altro, un'altra; **one** —, ci, vi, si, l'un l'altro

answer *n.* risposta; *v.* rispondere *irr.* (di)

Anthony Antonio

any di + *def. art.*, (= *a few*) alcuno, qualche (*always singular*), (= *a little*) un po' di; — **more** più; — **of it,** — **of them** ne; — **one who** chi; — **whatever** qualunque; *after a neg. verb: if* any *modifies a* sing. noun, nessun, nessuno, nessuna, nessun'; *if* any *modifies a pl.* noun, do not translate

anybody qualcuno; — **who** chi; *after a neg. verb,* nessuno

anything qualche cosa; *after a neg. verb,* niente, nulla

Apennines Appennini *m. pl.*

appear apparire [apparisco *or* appaio] *irr. v.*†

appearance aspetto

appetite appetito

appetizers antipasto

applause applauso

apple mela; — **tree** melo

appointment appuntamento

apricot albicocca; — **tree** albicocco

April aprile *m.*

Apulia Puglia

arch arco

arise sorgere *irr. v.*†

arm braccio (*irr. f. pl.* le braccia)

armchair poltrona

Arno Arno

around *adv.* attorno, intorno, in giro; *prep.* intorno a; **to go** (*or* **move**) —, girare

arrange concertare (di), disporre *irr. v.* (di)

arrival arrivo

arrive arrivare† (a), giungere *irr. v.*† (a)

art arte *f.*

artichoke carciofo

artist artista *m. or f.*; **to be an** —, fare l'artista

artistic artistico

as così, come, (= *since*) siccome; **as ... as** (*or* **so ... as**) così ... come, tanto ... quanto; **as soon as** appena

ash cenere *f.*

ask, ask for domandare (di), chiedere *irr. v.* (di)

aspect aspetto

ass asino

assemble *tr.* riunire [riunisco]; *intr.* riunirsi†

Assisi Assisi *f.*

assure assicurare (di)

Asti Asti *f.*; (*a wine*) Asti *m.*

at a, ad (*used only before a word beginning with* a); — **last** finalmente; — **once** subito

attention attenzione *f.*; **to pay** —, fare attenzione

attentively attentamente

attract attirare

attraction attrazione *f.*

attractive attraente

August agosto

aunt zia

autobus autobus *m.* (*inv.*)

automobile automobile *f.*

autumn autunno

avenue corso

away via; **far** —, lontano; **right** —, subito; **to take** —, portare via

Azores Azzorre *f. pl.*

B

baby bambino, bambina

back (**of**) dietro (a); **to bring** —, riportare (a); **to come** —, ritornare† (a)

bad cattivo; **too** —! peccato! **very** —, pessimo

badly male; **very** —, pessimamente, malissimo

bag valigetta

baggage bagaglio; (*more than one piece*) bagagli *m. pl.*

balcony balcone *m.*

ball ballo

bank banca; (*of a river*) riva

baptistry battistero

bark abbaiare

bashful timido

basilica basilica

bath bagno; **to take a** —, fare un bagno
bathhouse stabilimento di bagni
bathing suit costume (*m.*) da bagno
bathroom stanza da bagno
bay golfo
be essere *irr. v.*†, stare *irr. v.*†; — **able** potere *irr. v.*; — **about to** stare† per; — **right** aver ragione; — **wrong** aver torto; **how is he?** come sta? (*Other idioms in which to be appears are registered only under the other words concerned.*)
beach spiaggia
bean fagiolo; **string** —, fagiolino
bear orso
beard barba
Beatrice Beatrice
beautiful bello (*see* § **80**, p. 117); **how** — **it is!** com'è bello!
beauty bellezza
because perchè; **all the more** —, **all the better** —, tanto più che; — **of** a causa di
become diventare†
bed letto; **to go to** —, coricarsi† [mi corico], andare† a letto
bedroom camera
before *adv. of place* davanti; *prep. of place* davanti a; *adv. of time* prima, avanti; *prep. of time* prima di; *conj.* prima che *or* avanti che (*followed by the subjunctive*); — **long** fra poco
beg pregare (di)
begin cominciare (a)
behind dietro a
Belgium Belgio
believe credere (di); **to** — **a person** credere a una persona
bell campana; (*small*) campanello
bell tower campanile *m.*
beneath sotto
Benedict Benedetto
best *adj.* il migliore; *adv.* il meglio
bet scommettere *irr. v.* (di)
better *adj.* migliore; *adv.* meglio; **all the** — **because** tanto più che
between fra, tra

big grande (*see* § **80**, p. 117), (*big and heavy*) grosso
bill of fare minuta
bind legare
bird uccello
birthday compleanno
bitter amaro
black nero
blackboard lavagna
Blanche Bianca
bless benedire *irr. v.* [benedico]
blond biondo
blossom fiore *m.*
blotter carta sugante
blow soffiare; **the wind is blowing** tira vento
blue azzurro
board bordo; **on** — a bordo; (= *blackboard*) lavagna
boat barca, (= *ship*) nave *f.*
boiled bollito; **hard-** — (*referring to eggs*) sodo
Bologna Bologna
bone osso (*irr. pl.* le ossa)
book libro
bookshelf scaffale *m.*
born nato; **to be** —, nascere *irr. v.*†
both tutti (tutte) e due; **both . . . and** sia . . . che *or* sia . . . sia
boulevard viale *m.*
boy ragazzo, (*above fifteen years*) giovanotto
bracelet braccialetto
bread pane *m.*
breakfast colazione *f.* (*more specifically*) prima colazione; **to have** *or* **eat** —, fare la prima colazione
bridge ponte *m.*
brief breve
bring portare (a); — **back** riportare (a)
broad largo
bronze bronzo
broth brodo
brother fratello
brother-in-law cognato
brown marrone (*inv.*); **in** —, di marrone
brunet bruno

buffet credenza
build costruire *irr. v.* [costruisco]
building edifizio, (*monumental*) palazzo
burst, burst out scoppiare†; **burst out laughing** scoppiare† a ridere
bury seppellire *irr. v.* [seppellisco]
busy occupato
but ma
butler cameriere *m.*
butter burro
butterfly farfalla
buy comprare
by da, (*indicating authorship*) di; — **now** oramai

C

cab carrozza, vettura
cabbage cavolo
cabin cabina
café caffè *m.* (*inv.*)
cage gabbia
cake torta
California California
call, call on chiamare; **to be called** chiamarsi†
calm calmo
camera macchina fotografica; **movie** —, macchina cinematografica
can (= *to be able*) potere *irr. v.*; (= *to know how*) sapere *irr. v.*
canal canale *m.*; **Grand Canal** Canal Grande *m.*
canticle cantico
cape capo
capital capitale *f.*
Capitol Campidoglio
Capri Capri *f.*; (*a wine*) Capri *m.*
car carro, vagone *m.*; (= *automobile*) automobile *f.*; (= *coach of a train*) carrozza; **dining** —, carrozza ristorante; **sleeping** —, carrozza a letti
card carta; **to play cards** giocare a carte; (*post card*) cartolina
careful prudente
carnation garofano
carpet tappeto

carriage vettura, carrozza
carry portare (a); — **off** togliere *irr. v.*
case caso; **in** —, se mai *or* caso mai (*followed by the subjunctive*)
cast buttare
castle castello; **Sforza Castle,** Castello Sforzesco
cat gatto
catacomb catacomba
Catania Catania
cathedral duomo, cattedrale *f.*
Catherine Caterina
catholic cattolico
celebrate festeggiare
celebrated celebre; **very** —, celeberrimo
celery sedano
cemetery cimitero
center centro
century secolo (*see* § 162, p. 290)
ceremony complimenti *m. pl.*; **to stand on** —, far complimenti
certain certo
certainly certamente
chair sedia
chalk gesso
change cambiare
chapel cappella; **Sistine Chapel,** Cappella Sistina
characteristic caratteristico
Charles Carlo
charm incanto
charming incantevole
chat conversare
chauffeur autista *m.*
cheap, cheaply a buon mercato
check (*a parcel, a suitcase, etc.*) depositare [deposito]
cheerful allegro
cheerfulness allegria
cheers applausi *m. pl.*
cheese formaggio
chemistry chimica
cherry ciliegia; — **tree** ciliegio
chess scacchi *m. pl.*; **to play** —, giocare a scacchi
chest of drawers cassettone *m.*
Chicago Chicago *f.*

chicken pollo; **roast** —, pollo arrosto

child ragazzo, ragazza; (*in the sense of son or daughter*) figlio, figlia

choose scegliere *irr. v.* (di)

Christian cristiano

Christopher Cristoforo

church chiesa

cinema cinematografo

city città (*inv.*); in *or* to the —, in città; **native** —, città nativa, patria

city hall municipio

civilization civiltà (*inv.*)

Clara Clara

class classe *f.*

classroom aula

clean *adj.* pulito

clean *v.* pulire [pulisco]

clear limpido, chiaro

clearly chiaramente

clerk impiegato, impiegata

climate clima *m.*

climb salire *irr. v.*† (a) [salgo]

clock orologio; **o'clock,** *do not translate*

close chiudere *irr. v.*

closed chiuso

closet armadio

clothes abiti *m. pl.*, vestiti *m. pl.*

coach carrozza

coast costa

coat giacca; (= *overcoat*) cappotto; (= *fur coat*) pelliccia

coffee caffè *m.* (*inv.*)

cold freddo; **it's** —, fa freddo

collection collezione *f.*

colonnade colonnato

color colore *m.*

Colosseum Colosseo

Columbus Colombo

combine unire [unisco]

come venire *irr. v.*† (a) [vengo] (*p. part.* venuto); — **back** ritornare† (a); — **down** scendere *irr. v.*† (a); — **in** entrare† (a); — **out** uscire *irr. v.*† (a) [esco]; — **up** salire *irr. v.*† (a) [salgo]; **going and coming** viavai *m.* (*inv.*)

comedy commedia

comely elegante

comfortable comodo

comfortably comodamente

comic buffo

coming venturo; **going and** —, viavai *m.* (*inv.*)

commerce commercio

company compagnia

compartment scompartimento

competent competente

complete completare

compliment complimento

compose comporre *irr. v.*

conceited vano

concert concerto

condition condizione *f.*, stato

conduct condurre *irr. v.* (a)

Constantine Costantino

contain contenere *irr. v.*

contest gara

continue continuare (a) [continuo]

continuous continuo

contrary contrario; **on the** —, invece

convent convento

conversation conversazione *f.*

cooking cucina

cool fresco; **it's** —, fa fresco

coral corallo

cordially cordialmente

corner angolo; **on the** —, all'angolo

correct correggere *irr. v.*

corridor corridoio

Corsica Corsica

cosmetic cosmetico

cost costare†

costume abito

countess contessa

country campagna; in *or* to the —, in campagna; (= *fatherland*) paese *m.*, patria

couple paio (*irr. pl.* le paia)

course corso; **of** —, naturalmente

courteous gentile, cortese

cousin cugino, cugina

cover coperta

covered (**with**) coperto (di)

cow vacca
crane gru *f.* (*inv.*)
create creare
creature creatura
cross attraversare
crossing traversata
cry *n.* grido (*irr. pl.* le grida); *v.*
  (= *shout*) gridare; (= *weep*) piangere *irr. v.*
cultivate coltivare
cultivation coltivazione *f.*
culture cultura
cup tazza
custom uso, costume *m.*
customs, custom house dogana

D

dad, daddy babbo
daisy margherita
dance *n.* ballo; *v.* ballare
Dante Dante
dare osare (di)
dark scuro, (*in complexion*) bruno;
  in the —, al buio; to get —, annottare *imp. v.*†
darling tesoro
date data
daughter figlia
day giorno; (*in its duration*) giornata; — before yesterday ieri
  l'altro; good —! buon giorno!
dead morto
deal: a great — (of) molto, assai
dear caro
December dicembre *m.*
decide decidersi *irr. v.*† (a)
deck coperta
dedicate dedicare [dedico]
deep profondo
degree diploma *m.*
delay ritardo
delicious delizioso
delightful delizioso
de luxe di lusso
dentist dentista *m. or f.*
depart partire† [parto]; — again
  ripartire† [riparto]
departure partenza

deposit depositare [deposito]
descend scendere *irr. v.*† (a)
describe descrivere *irr. v.* (di)
deserve meritare (di) [merito]
desire desiderare (di) [desidero]
desirous desideroso
desk scrivania, (*student's desk*)
  banco (*pl.* banchi)
diary diario
dictate dettare
dictionary dizionario
die morire *irr. v.*† [muoio]
different differente, vario
difficult difficile
dine pranzare
dining room sala da pranzo
dinner pranzo
diploma diploma *m.*
direct dirigere *irr. v.*
direction direzione *f.*
dirty sudicio
dish piatto
displease scontentare; to be dis_
  pleasing dispiacere *irr. v.*†
dispose disporre *irr. v.* (di)
dissatisfied scontento
dissatisfy scontentare
distance distanza
distant distante, lontano
divide dividere *irr. v.*
divine divino
do fare *irr. v.*
dog cane *m.*
Doge Doge *m.*
doll bambola
dome cupola
domestic domestico
donkey asino
door porta; (*of a car*) sportello
double doppio
doubt dubbio
down giù; — there laggiù; —town
  in città; to go — or come — or
  get —, scendere *irr. v.*† (a); to
  sit —, sedersi *irr. v.*†
downstairs al pian terreno
downtown in città
dream sogno
dress *n.* veste *f.*; *v. tr.* vestire

[vɛsto]; *v. intr.* vestirsi†; **to get dressed** vestirsi†
dressmaker sarta
drink bere *irr. v.*
drive *n.* passeggiata; *v.* guidare
driver autista *m. or f.*
droll buffo
druggist farmacista *m. or f.*
drugstore farmacia
duck anitra
duration durata
during durante
Dutch olandese

E

each ciascun, ciascuno, ciascuna, ciascun'; **— one** ciascuno, ognuno; **— other** ci, vi, si, l'un l'altro
ear orecchio
early presto, di buon'ora
earn guadagnare
earring orecchino
earth terra
east est *m.*, levante *m.*, oriente *m.*
eastern di levante; **Eastern Riviera** Riviera di Levante
easy facile
eat mangiare; **— breakfast** *or* **— lunch** far colazione
echo eco *f.* (*pl.* echi *m.*)
education cultura
egg uovo (*irr. pl.* le uova)
eggplant melanzana
eight otto
eighteen diciotto
eighth ottavo
eighty ottanta
either o; **either . . . or** o . . . o, (*after a neg. verb*) nè . . . nè
electric elettrico
elegant elegante
elementary elementare
elevator ascensore *m.*
eleven undici
else altro
embark imbarcarsi†
embarking imbarco
embrace abbracciare

Emmanuel Emanuele
empty libero, vuoto
enchanting incantevole
end *n.* fine *f.*; *v.* finire († *if used intransitively*) (di) [finisco]
enemy nemico
engage impegnare (a)
England Inghilterra
English inglese
enjoy godere *irr. v.* (di), gustare
enormous enorme
enough abbastanza; **to be —,** bastare† (a)
enter entrare (*intr. in Italian*)† (a); **I — a room** entro in una stanza
enthusiasm entusiasmo
entirely del tutto
entrance entrata; **— hall** atrio
epoch epoca
equal pari *m. or f.* (*inv.*)
erase cancellare
eraser gomma
eruption eruzione *f.*
especially specialmente
eternal eterno
Etna: Mt. —, l'Etna *m.*
Europe Europa
European europeo
even anche; (*after a neg. verb*) neanche, nemmeno, neppure; **— though,** *see* **although; not —,** neanche, nemmeno, neppure
evening sera; (*in its duration*) serata; **in the —,** a sera; **this —,** stasera
event evento
ever sempre; (*after a neg. verb*) mai; **more than —,** più che mai
every ogni (*inv.*); **—one** ognuno
everybody, everyone ognuno
everything ogni cosa, tutto
everywhere dovunque
example esempio
excavation scavo
excellent ottimo
exchange scambiare
exclaim esclamare
excursion escursione *f.*; **to take an —,** fare un'escursione

excuse scusare (di)
exile esilio
expensive caro
explain spiegare
express train treno diretto
expression espressione *f.*
extremely estremamente
eye occhio
eyebrow sopracciglio (*irr. pl.* le sopracciglia)
eyelash ciglio (*irr. pl.* le ciglia)

F

façade facciata
face (= *to overlook*) dare su
fact fatto; in —, infatti
factory fabbrica
fail mancare (di)
fall *n.* autunno; *v.* cadere *irr.*†
familiar intimo
family famiglia
famous famoso, celebre
far, far away lontano; as — as fino a
farewell addio; to say —, dare un addio
farm podere *m.*; — laborer contadino, contadina
fascinate affascinare [affascino]
fascinating affascinante
fashion moda
fast rapido
father padre *m.*, babbo
fatherland patria
favor favore *m.*
feast festa
February febbraio
feed dare da mangiare a
feel sentire (di) [sento]
fellow uomo (*irr. pl.* uomini); *expressions of contempt:* this —, costui; these fellows costoro; *without contempt:* this — *or* these fellows questi; that —, colui; those fellows coloro
fertile fertile
festival festa
few pochi; a —, alcuni

field campo
fifteen quindici
fifth quinto
fifty cinquanta
film pellicola
filthy sudicio
final ultimo
finally finalmente
find trovare; — out sapere *irr. v.*
fine bello; (*see* § 80, p. 117); fine! bravo!
finger dito (*irr. pl.* le dita)
finish finire († *if used intransitively*) (di) [finisco]
first *adj.* primo; *adv.* (*place*) avanti, (*time*) prima
fish pesce *m.*
fisherman pescatore *m.*
fixed fissato
flag bandiera
flesh carne *f.*
flock (together) accorrere *irr. v.*† (a)
floor pavimento, (= *story*) piano; on (*or* to) the ground —, al pian terreno; on (*or* to) the upper —, al piano superiore
Florence Firenze *f.*
florist fioraio
flower fiore *m.*
fly volare†
flyer (*a train*) rapido
follow seguire [seguo]
following seguente
food cibo
foot piede *m.*; at the — of appiè di; on —, a piedi
for *prep.* per; *conj.* (= *because*) perchè
foreign straniero
foreigner forestiero, straniero
forest bosco
forget dimenticare (di) [dimentico]
fork forchetta
former: the —, quello, quella, quegli, colui, colei, coloro
fortunate fortunato
fortunately fortunatamente
fortune fortuna
forty quaranta

forum foro
forward avanti
found fondare
fountain fontana; — pen penna
    stilografica
four quattro
fourteen quattordici
fourth quarto
France Francia
Francis Francesco
Frank Franco
free libero
French francese
frequent frequentare
fresco affresco
fresh fresco
Friday venerdì *m.*; on Fridays il
    venerdì
fried fritto
friend amico, amica
from da
front (*of a building*) facciata; in —
    of davanti a
fruit (*as food*) frutto *or* frutta (*pl.
    in both cases* le frutta); (*as pro-
    duce or fruit on a tree*) frutto (*pl.* i
    frutti); *see footnote* 6, p. 219.
full pieno
funny buffo
fur, fur coat pelliccia
furniture mobili *m. pl.*; piece of
    —. mobile *m.*

G

gallery galleria; picture —, pina-
    coteca; Uffizi Gallery Galleria
    degli Uffizi
garden giardino; vegetable —,
    orto; Valentino Gardens Giar-
    dini del Valentino
gate porta
gather accumulare [accumulo]
gay allegro
general generale
Genoa Genova
gentle gentile
gentleman signore *m.*
gently dolcemente
geography geografia

German tedesco
Germany Germania
get prendere *irr. v.*; — down scen-
    dere *irr. v.*† (a); — dressed ve-
    stirsi† [mi vesto]; — on salire
    irr. v.† (a) [salgo]; — out uscire
    irr. v.† (a) [esco]; — up alzarsi†
Gibraltar Gibilterra
gift dono
Giotto Giotto
girl ragazza; — student studentessa
give dare *irr. v.*
gives dà
glad contento, felice
gladly volentieri
glass (*drinking glass*) bicchiere *m.*
glove guanto
go andare *irr. v.*† (a); — around
    girare; — down scendere *irr. v.*†
    (a); — shopping andare† a far
    delle spese; — out uscire *irr. v.*†
    (a) [esco]; — through attraver-
    sare; — to bed andare† a letto *or*
    coricarsi†; — up salire *irr. v.*† (a)
    [salgo]; going and coming
    viavai *m.* (*inv.*); to be going to,
    see § 56, 3, p. 82.
God Dio (*irr. pl.* gli dei)
goes va
going and coming viavai *m.* (*inv.*)
gold oro
Golden Shell Conca d'Oro
gondola gondola
gondolier gondoliere *m.*
gong gong *m.* (*inv.*)
good *adj.* buono (*see* § 80, p. 117);
    — day! *or* — morning! buon
    giorno! very —, ottimo; *adv.* bene
good-bye! arrivederci!
goose oca
gorgeous magnifico
Gothic gotico
government governo
grace grazia
graceful grazioso
grammar grammatica
grand grande (*see* § 80, p. 117) gran-
    dioso; Grand Canal Canal
    Grande *m.*

granddaughter nipote *f.*, nipotina
grandfather nonno
grandiose grandioso
grandmother nonna
grandson nipote *m.*
granted that dato che (*followed by the subjunctive*)
grass erba
gratitude gratitudine *f.*
gray grigio
graze pascolare
great grande (*see* § 80, p. 117); **greater** più grande *or* maggiore; **very —**, grandissimo *or* massimo; **a — deal (of)** molto
greatness grandezza
Greek greco
green verde
greet salutare
greeting saluto
grotto grotta
ground terra; **on** *or* **to the — floor** al pian terreno
group gruppo
grow coltivare
guidance guida
guide *n.* guida; *v.* guidare
guidebook guida
Guido Guido
gulf golfo

H

hair (*a single hair*) capello; (*collectively*) capelli *m. pl.*
half, a half, half a *adj.* mezzo; *n.* metà (*inv.*)
hall sala; **city —**, municipio; **entrance —**, atrio
hamlet borgo
hand *n.* mano *f.*; **on the other —**, invece *or* d'altra parte; **to shake hands with** stringere la mano a
hand, hand in *v.* consegnare
handkerchief fazzoletto
handle manico
handsome bello (*see* § 80, p. 117)
hang, hang up appendere *irr. v.*
happy felice

harbor porto
hard (= *difficult*) difficile; **—-boiled** (*referring to eggs*) sodo
hardly appena
harmony armonia
has ha
haste fretta
hasten affrettarsi† (a)
hat cappello
haughty superbo
have avere *irr. v.*; **— a good time** divertirsi† (a) [mi diverto]; **— breakfast** (*or* **lunch**) far colazione; **— to** (= *must*) dovere *irr. v.*; **— somebody do,** *see* § 151, p. 261
he egli, esso, lui; **— himself** lui stesso; **— who** *or* **— whom** chi
head capo
health salute *f.*
healthful salubre; **very —**, saluberrimo
hear sentire [sento], udire *irr. v.* [odo]
heart cuore *m.*
heat calore *m.*, caldo
heaven cielo
heel calcagno (*irr. pl.* le calcagna)
Helen Elena
help *n.* aiuto; *v.* aiutare (a)
hen gallina
her *personal pron.* la, lei, essa; **to —**, le; **of —**, ne; *poss. adj. or pron.* suo (*m. pl.* suoi)
herb erba
here qua, qui, ci, vi; **— is, — are** ecco; **— he is** eccolo
hers suo (*m. pl.* suoi)
herself si, sè, se stessa, lei stessa
hidden nascosto
high alto; **higher** più alto *or* superiore; **very —**, altissimo *or* supremo
hill collina
him lo, lui, esso; **to —**, gli; **of —**, ne
himself si, sè, se stesso, lui stesso
hire impegnare (a)
his suo (*m. pl.* suoi)
historic storico

history storia
hold tenere *irr. v.*
Holland Olanda
holy santo
home casa; **to go** —, andare a
casa; **at** *or* **to the** — **of** da
honor onore *m.*
hop saltare († *if used intransitively*)
hope sperare (di)
horse cavallo
hot molto caldo; **it's** —, fa molto
caldo
hotel albergo
hour ora
house casa; **at** *or* **to the** — **of** da
how come; — **much** quanto; —
many quanti; — **are you?** come
sta? come state?
however però
Hudson (*river*) Hudson *m.*
huge enorme
Humbert Umberto
hundred, **a hundred, one hun-**
dred cento; **about a** —, un
centinaio; **hundreds** centinaia
f. pl.
hungry: **to be** —, aver appetito
hurry *n.* fretta; **in a** —, in fretta;
to be in a —, aver fretta; *v.* af-
frettarsi† (a)
husband marito
hyacinth giacinto

I

I io; (*after* than) me
ice (*frozen water*) ghiaccio; (*food*)
gelato
idea idea
if se
ill malato
imagine immaginare (di)
immediately subito
immensely immensamente
important importante
imposing imponente
impression impressione *f.*
in in; (*after a superl.*) di; (*before*
the name of a city) a

inclined disposto
include includere *irr. v.*
indeed infatti
independent indipendente
indicate indicare [indico]
industry industria
information informazione *f.* (*used*
in the pl. when more than one
item of information is meant)
inhabitant abitante *m.*
ink inchiostro
inkwell calamaio
inside dentro
instead (**of**) invece (di)
instructor insegnante *m. or f.*
insure assicurare
intend intendere *irr. v.* (di)
interest interesse *m.*
interesting interessante
interrupted interrotto
intimate intimo
into in
introduce (*a person*) presentare
introduction presentazione *f.*
invitation invito
invite invitare (a)
Irene Irene
iron *n.* ferro; *v.* stirare
is è
Ischia Ischia
island isola
it esso, essa, lo, la (*not translated if*
subject of an impersonal verb); **to** —,
gli, le; **of** —, **about** —, **some**
of —, ne
Italian italiano
Italo-American italo-americano
Italy Italia
its suo (*m. pl.* suoi)
itself si, sè, se stesso, se stessa

J

jacket giacca
jam marmellata
James Giacomo
January gennaio
Jesus Gesù
jeweler gioielliere *m.*

jewelry gioielleria
jockey fantino
Joe Peppino
John Giovanni
joke *n.* barzelletta; *v.* scherzare
jolly allegro
journey vi*a*ggio
Jove: by —! perbacco!
joy gi*o*ia
Julius Gi*u*lio
July l*u*glio
jump saltare († *if used intransitively*)
June gi*u*gno
just pr*o*prio
justice giust*i*zia

K

keep conservare, tenere *irr. v.*
kind *adj.* gentile; *n.* sp*e*cie *f.* (*inv.*)
king re *m.* (*inv.*)
kiss *n.* b*a*cio; *v.* baciare
kitchen cucina
knee gin*o*cchio (*irr. pl.* le gin*o*cchia)
knife colt*e*llo
know con*o*scere *irr. v.*, sapere *irr. v.*
(*see* § **122,** p. 199); — **how** sapere
known n*o*to

L

laborer oper*a*io; **farm** —, contadino, contadina
lack, be lacking manc*a*re†
lady signora; **young** —, signorina
lake lago; **Lake Como** il Lago di C*o*mo; **Lake Lugano** il Lago di Lugano; **Lake Maggiore** il Lago Maggiore
lamb agn*e*llo
lamp l*a*mpada
land *n.* t*e*rra; *v.* sbarcare († *if used intransitively*)
landing sbarco
lane viale *m.*
language l*i*ngua
large grande (*see* § **80,** p. 117), (*large and heavy*) gr*o*sso
last *adj.* (*final*) *u*ltimo, (*past*) scorso;

— **year** l'anno scorso; — **night** i*e*ri n*o*tte, la n*o*tte scorsa, (*night* = *evening*) i*e*ri sera; **at** —, finalmente
last *v.* dur*a*re†
late *adj.* tardo; *adv.* tardi, in ritardo (*see footnote*, p. 146); **to be** —, *e*sser†e in ritardo
Lateran Laterano
Latin latino
Latium Lazio
latter: the —, questo, questi, costui, cost*e*i, costoro
laugh r*i*dere *irr. v.*; **to burst out laughing** scoppiare† a r*i*dere
laughter riso (*irr. pl.* le risa)
Laura L*a*ura
lavish prodigare [pr*o*digo]
law legge *f.*
lawn prato
Lawrence Lor*e*nzo
lawyer avvocato; **to be a** —, fare l'avvocato
lay st*e*nd*e*re *irr. v.*
lead menare (a), condurre *irr. v.* (a)
leaf f*o*glia
leaning pend*e*nte
learn imparare (a), (= *to find out*) sapere *irr. v.*
leave lasciare, (= *to go away*) and*a*re† via, (= *to depart, start on a trip*) part*i*re† [parto]; *to be left* re-st*a*re†
lecture confer*e*nza
left sinistro; **at** *or* **to the** —, a sinistra
leisurely senza fretta
lemon, lemon tree limone *m.*
leopard leopardo
less *adj.* minore; *adv.* meno
lesson lezione *f.*
let lasciare, fare *irr. v.* (*see* § **151,** p. 261)
letter l*e*ttera; **registered** —, l*e*ttera raccomandata
lettuce lattuga
liberty libertà (*inv.*)
library bibliot*e*ca
Lido Lido

lie down coricarsi† [mi corico]
life vita
lift n. ascensore m.; v. alzare
light adj. (= not heavy) leggero,
(= not dark) chiaro; n. luce f.; v.
illuminare [illumino]
lighten imp. v. lampeggiare†
lighthouse faro
like conj. come; — **a** (= in the manner of, in the character of) da;
look —, sembrare†, parere irr. v.†
like v. piacere irr. v.† (see § 148, p.
255); **I** —, mi piace; **he likes**
gli piace; **she likes** le piace
limb membro (irr. pl. le membra)
limit limitare [limito]
limpid limpido
line fila
linen biancheria
liner piroscafo
lion leone m.
lioness leonessa
lip labbro (irr. pl. le labbra)
listen, listen to ascoltare
literature letteratura
little (= small) piccolo; (= not
much) poco; **a — of** un po' di
live (= to be alive) vivere irr. v.†;
(= to dwell) abitare [abito]
living room salotto
load n. carico; v. caricare [carico]
loaded carico
lobby atrio
located situato
lodge alloggiare
lofty alto
loggia loggia
long adj. lungo; adv. a lungo, lunga-
mente; **before** —, tra poco; **so**
—! arrivederci!
look, look at guardare; — **for** cercare; — **like** sembrare†, parere
irr. v.†
lose perdere irr. v.
lot: a —, **a — of** molto, parecchio
loud forte; **to talk** —, parlare ad
alta voce
Louise Luisa
love v. amare

lovely delizioso, bello
low basso; **lower** più basso or inferiore; **very** —, bassissimo or
infimo
luck, good luck fortuna
lucky fortunato; **to be** —, aver
fortuna or essere† fortunato
Lucy Lucia
Lugano Lugano f.
lump pezzo
lunch colazione f.; **to have** (or
eat) —, far colazione
luxe: de —, di lusso

M

macaroni maccherone m. (usually
used in the pl.)
machine macchina
madam signora
magazine rivista
magnificent magnifico
maid cameriera
mail posta
main principale
majestic maestoso
major adj. maggiore; v. specia-
lizzarsi†
make fare irr. v.; — **a mistake**
sbagliare (a); — **up** comporre
irr. v.
Malta Malta
mamma mamma
man uomo (irr. pl. uomini); **old** —,
vecchio; **young** —, giovane m.,
giovanotto; **a — who** chi; **this**
—, questi, (with contempt) costui;
these men questi, (with contempt)
costoro; **that** —, quegli, colui;
those men quelli, coloro
manner modo
many molti, molte; **how** —, quanti,
quante; **so** —, tanti, tante; **too**
—, troppi, troppe
map carta geografica
marble marmo
March marzo
Margaret Margherita
maritime marittimo

Marius Mario
Mark Marco
marmalade marmellata
martyrdom martirio
marvel meraviglia
marvelous meraviglioso
Mary Maria
Mass messa
masterpiece capolavoro
match gara
mature maturo
May maggio
may potere *irr. v.*
me mi, me; **to —,** mi
meadow prato
meal pasto
means mezzo; **by — of** per mezzo di
meantime intanto
meanwhile intanto
meat carne *f.*
medicine medicina
medieval medioevale
Mediterranean Mediterraneo
meet incontrare; (= *to make the acquaintance of*) fare la conoscenza di; **till we — again!** arrivederci!
melting pot crogiolo
member (*of a party, a club, etc.*) membro; (*of the body*) membro (*irr. pl.* le membra)
memory ricordo
mention menzionare (di)
Mephistopheles Mefistofele
merit meritare (di) [merito]
metropolis metropoli *f.* (*inv.*)
Michelangelo Michelangelo
Middle Ages Medio Evo
midnight mezzanotte *f.*
Milan Milano *f.*
mild mite
mile miglio (*irr. pl.* le miglia)
milk latte *m.*
milliner modista
million milione *m.*; **two — dollars** due milioni di dollari
mine mio (*m. pl.* miei)
minute minuto
mirror specchio; **little —,** specchietto

Miss signorina
missing: to be —, mancare†
mistake sbaglio; **to make a —,** sbagliare (a)
mistaken: to be —, sbagliare (a)
modern moderno
moment momento; **any —,** da un momento all'altro
monastery convento
Monday lunedì *m.*; **on Mondays** il lunedì
money danaro
money order vaglia *m.* (*inv.*)
Monreale Monreale *f.*
month mese *m.*; **a whole —,** tutto un mese
monument monumento
moon luna
more più; **all the — because** tanto più che; **any —** (*after a neg. verb*) più
moreover anzi
morning mattina; (*in its duration*) mattinata; **— song** mattinata; **in the —,** di mattina; **this —,** stamane *or* stamani; **the following —,** la mattina dopo *or* la mattina seguente; **good —!** buon giorno!
Moses Mosè
most: the —, il (la, i, le) più
mother madre *f.*, mamma
motor motore *m.*
motorboat barca a motore
mountain monte *m.*
move (*somebody or something*) muovere *irr. v.*; (*oneself*) muoversi†; **— around** girare
movie cinematografo; **— camera** macchina cinematografica
Mr. signor *m.*
Mrs. signora
Mt. Etna l'Etna *m.*
Mt. Simplon il Sempione *m.*
Mt. Vesuvius il Vesuvio
much *adj.* molto; **how —,** quanto: **so —,** tanto; **too —,** troppo; *adv.* molto, assai; **too —,** troppo
mule mulo

museum museo
music musica; **to play** (*or* **have**) **a**
little —, fare un po' di musica
musical comedy operetta
musician musicista *m. or f.*
must dovere *irr. v.*
my mio (*m. pl.* miei)
myself mi, me stesso, me stessa;
I —, io stesso, io stessa
mystery mistero

N

name nome *m.*; **my — is Robert**
mi chiamo Roberto
nap sonnellino; **to take a —,** schiacciare un sonnellino
napkin tovagliolo
Naples Napoli *f.*
narrow stretto
nation nazione *f.*
national nazionale
native nativo; **— city** città nativa
or patria
natural naturale
naturally naturalmente
nature natura
navigate navigare [navigo]
near *adj.* vicino; *adv.* vicino; *prep.*
vicino a, presso
near-by vicino
nearly circa
necessary necessario; **to be —,**
bisognare *imp. v.*†; occorrere *irr.*
v.†; **it's —,** bisogna *or* occorre
(*both followed by the subjunctive*)
necklace collana
necktie cravatta
need *n.* bisogno; *v.* aver bisogno di;
I — it ne ho bisogno
neighbor vicino, vicina
neighboring vicino
neither nè; **neither ... nor** nè ...
nè
Neopolitan napoletano
nephew nipote *m.*
nest nido
never mai
new nuovo

New Jersey New Jersey *m.*
New York New York *f.*
news notizia (*used in the pl. if more*
than one item of news is meant)
newspaper giornale *m.*
next (*in place*) vicino; (*in time*)
venturo; **— year** l'anno venturo;
— to vicino a
nice gentile
niece nipote *f.*; **little —,** nipotina
night notte *f.*, (*in its duration*)
nottata; **at —,** di notte; **last —**
la notte scorsa, (*night = evening*)
ieri sera
nine nove
nineteen diciannove
ninety novanta
ninth nono
no no, (*before a noun*) nessun, nessuno, nessuna, nessun' *and the*
following noun always in the sin-
gular, even if it is plural in English:
no students are here nessuno
studente è qui
nobody, no one nessuno
none nessuno
noon mezzogiorno
nor nè; **neither ... nor** nè ... nè
Norman normanno
north nord *m.*
northern settentrionale
not non; **— one, — any** nessuno
notebook quaderno
nothing niente, nulla
noun nome *m.*
novel *adj.* nuovo; *n.* romanzo
November novembre *m.*
now ora, adesso; **in a month**
from —, fra un mese
number numero
numerous numeroso
nut noce *f.*; **— tree** noce *m.*

O

object oggetto
obliged: **to be —,** dovere *irr. v.*
observe osservare
obtain ottenere *irr. v.* (di)

occasion occasione *f.*
occupy occupare [occupo]
ocean oceano
October ottobre *m.*
odd strano
of di
offer offrire *irr. v.* (di) [offro]
office ufficio; at *or* to the — of da
often spesso
oh! oh!
old vecchio, (= *ancient*) antico;
  older (*referring to persons*) maggiore
  (d'età); how — is he? quanti
  anni ha? he is eight years —,
  ha otto anni
Olga Olga
olive oliva; — tree olivo
on su; *before dates, do not translate*
once una volta; — in a while di
  tanto in tanto; at —, subito
one (*used as an adj.*) un, uno, una,
  un'; (*used as a pron.*) uno, una;
  (*used impersonally*) si (*see* § 115,
  p. 180); — another ci, vi, si,
  l'un l'altro; — at a time uno
  alla volta; — who chi; every—,
  ognuno; no —, not —, nessuno;
  this —, questo, questi, costui,
  costei, costoro (*the last three implying contempt*); the — *or* that —,
  quello, quegli, colui, colei, coloro
oneself si
onion cipolla
only *adj.* solo; *adv.* solo, solamente,
  soltanto, non + *verb* + che
open *adj.* aperto; in the —, all'a-
  perto; *v.* aprire *irr. v.* [apro]
opera opera
opinion opinione *f.*
opportunity occasione *f.*
opposite dirimpetto (a)
or o; either ... or, o ... o, (*after
  a neg. verb*) nè ... nè
orange, orange tree arancio
orchestra orchestra
order *n.* ordine *m.*; in — to per;
  in — that affinchè *or* perchè
  (*followed by the subjunctive*);
  money —, vaglia *m.* (*inv.*)

order *v.* ordinare (di) [ordino]
Orient Oriente *m.*
origin origine *f.*
original originale
other altro; each —, ci, vi, si, l'un
  l'altro
ought *cond. of* dovere *irr. v.*
our, ours nostro
ourselves ci, noi stessi
out, outside *adv.* fuori; *prep.* fuori
  di; to go out uscire *irr. v.*† (a)
  [esco]
outdoor, outdoors all'aperto
outside, *see* out
over su; — there lassù, laggiù
overcoat cappotto
overshoe soprascarpa
owe dovere *irr. v.*
own proprio
owner proprietario
ox bue *m.* (*irr. pl.* buoi)

P

package pacco
Padua Padova
page pagina
pail: little —, secchietto
pain dolore *m.*
painter pittore *m.*
painting quadro
pair paio (*irr. pl.* le paia)
palace palazzo; Bargello Palace
  Palazzo del Bargello; Pitti Palace
  Palazzo Pitti
Palermo Palermo *f.*
palm, palm tree palma
panorama panorama *m.*
Pantheon Pantheon *m.*
papal papale
paper carta
parcel pacco
parent genitore *m.*
parenthesis parentesi *f.* (*inv.*)
park parco
parlor salotto
Parmesan parmigiano; — style alla
  parmigiana
part parte *f.*

party (*group of people*) comitiva, (= *festivity*, *reception*) festa

pass passare†

passage corridoio

passenger passeggiero, passeggiera

passport passaporto

past passato; **a quarter — two** le due e un quarto

path sentiero

Paul Paolo

pay, pay for pagare; **— attention** fare attenzione

pea pisello

pear pera; **— tree** pero

pen penna; **fountain —**, penna stilografica

pencil matita, lapis *m.* (*inv.*)

peninsula penisola

penny soldo

people (*many persons*) gente *f.*, *generally used in the singular;* (= *population*) popolo; (*used impersonally*) si (*see* § 115, p. *180*)

perhaps forse

permission permesso; **with your —!** con permesso!

permit permettere *irr. v.* (di)

person persona; **a — who** chi

Perugia Perugia

Peter Pietro; **St. Peter's** (*church*) San Pietro

pharmacy farmacia

philosophy filosofia

phone, *see* **telephone**

photograph fotografia

physician medico; **to be a —**, fare il medico

physics fisica

pianist pianista *m. or f.*

piano pianoforte *m.*

pick cogliere *irr. v.*

picture (*framed*) quadro, (*photograph*) fotografia; **— gallery** pinacoteca

piece pezzo; **— of furniture** mobile *m.*

pier banchina

pig maiale *m.*

pilgrim pellegrino

pilot pilota *m.*

pin spilla

Pisa Pisa

pity pietà; (*in phrases like* **what a —! it was a —!**, *etc.*) peccato!

place *n.* posto, (= *site*, *location*) luogo; **at** *or* **to the — of** da; **to take —**, aver luogo

place *v.* mettere *irr.*, porre *irr.*

plain pianura

plant *n.* pianta; *v.* piantare

plate piatto

play (*an instrument or a piece of music*) suonare; (*a game*) giocare; **to — a little music** fare un po' di musica; **to — cards** giocare a carte; **to — chess** giocare a scacchi

pleasant piacevole

please contentare; **please!** per favore! *or* per piacere! **pleased to meet you!** piacere!

pleasing piacevole; **to be —**, piacere *irr. v.*† (*see* § 148, p. 255)

pleasure piacere *m.*; **with —**, con piacere, volentieri

plentiful molti, molte; **so —**, tanti, tante

Po Po

poem poesia

poet poeta *m.*

point *n.* punto; *v.* indicare [indico]; **— at** *or* **— out** indicare

Pompeii Pompei *f.*

pool: swimming —, piscina

poor povero; (= *bad*) cattivo

pope papa *m.*

populace popolo

pork maiale *m.*

port porto

porter facchino

Portugal Portogallo

possible possibile; **as soon as —**, al più presto

post card cartolina

post office posta

postpone posporre *irr. v.* (di)

potato patata

poultry yard pollaio

pour versare
pray pregare (di)
preceding precedente
precipice precip*i*zio
prefer preferire [preferisco]
prepare preparare, apparecchiare
present *adj.* presente; *n.* dono
present *v.* presentare
press str*i*ngere *irr. v.*; (= *iron*) stirare
pretend pret*e*ndere *irr. v.* (di)
pretty grazioso, bello
price pr*e*zzo; **at a low —,** a buon mercato; **what's the —?** quanto c*o*sta (c*o*stano)?
principal principale
probably probabilmente (*see Future of Probability,* § **58,** 2, p. 83)
profession professione *f.*
professor professore *m.*
profound profondo
program programma *m.*
progress progr*e*sso
promise prom*e*ttere *irr. v.* (di)
prompt pronto
promptly prontamente
pronounce pronunziare
propose proporre *irr. v.* (di)
proud superbo
provided (**that**) purchè (*followed by the subjunctive*)
public pubblico
pupil alunno, alunna
pure puro
put m*e*ttere *irr. v.*, porre *irr. v.*

Q

quality qualità (*inv.*)
quarter quarto
question domanda
quickly presto
quiet, quietly piano
quite parecchio

R

rabbit con*i*glio
race (*contest of speed*) corsa; (*na-*

tion, breed) razza; **horse —,** corsa di cavalli
radio radio *f.* (*inv.*)
radish ravanello
railroad ferrovia
rain *n.* pi*o*ggia; *v.* pi*o*vere *imp. irr.†*
Raphael Raffaello
rapid rapido
rapidly rapidamente
rather piutt*o*sto; **— than** anzichè
Ravello Ravello *f.*
ray raggio
read l*e*ggere *irr. v.*
reader libro di lettura
reading lettura; **— room** sala di lettura
ready pronto
real reale, vero
really pr*o*prio, veramente
reason ragione *f.*
recall ricordare (di)
receive ric*e*vere
recent recente
recently recentemente
recognize ricon*o*scere *irr. v.* (di)
recommend raccomandare (di)
red rosso
reflect rifl*e*ttere *irr. v.*
refreshment rinfresco
region regione *f.*
register (*at the post office*) raccomandare; **registered letter** lettera raccomandata
regret rimpianto
rejoice allietare
relative parente *m. or f.*
relish gustare
remain restare†, rimanere *irr. v.†*
remark osservare
remember ricordare (di)
remembrance ric*o*rdo
remind ricordare (di)
remove levare
Renaissance Rinascimento
render r*e*ndere *irr. v.*
renowned c*e*lebre; **very —,** cele·berrimo
reply risp*o*ndere *irr. v.* (di)

represent rappresentare
republic repubblica
reserve riservare
restaurant ristorante *m.*
retire ritirarsi†
return *n.* ritorno; — trip viaggio
di ritorno; *v.* ritornare† (a)
review rivista
rich ricco
Richard Riccardo
ride *n.* passeggiata; to take a —,
fare una passeggiata; *v.* andare
irr.†, fare una passeggiata
right (= *just*) giusto; (*opposed to
left*) destro; all —! sta bene! at
or to the —, a destra; to be —,
aver ragione; — away subito
righteous integro; very —, in-
tegerrimo
ring *n.* anello; *v.* suonare († *if used
intransitively*)
ripe maturo
rise sorgere *irr. v.*†
risotto risotto
river fiume *m.*
Riviera Riviera; on the —, in
Riviera; Eastern —, Riviera di
Levante; Western —, Riviera di
Ponente
road strada
roast arrosto; — chicken pollo
arrosto
Robert Roberto
robust robusto
rock rocca
Roman romano
romance romanzo
Rome Roma
roof tetto
room stanza; (= *bedroom*) camera;
(= *hall*) sala; bath—, stanza da
bagno; dining —, sala da pranzo;
living —, salotto; reading —, sala
di lettura; smoking —, sala da fumare; waiting —, sala d'aspetto
rooster gallo
Rose Rosa
rose rosa
Rosie Rosetta

row fila
royal reale
rubber (= *overshoe*) soprascarpa
rug tappeto
ruins ruderi *m. pl.*
rule *n.* regola; *v.* dominare [domino]
ruler riga
run correre *irr. v.* († *if used intransitively*) (a); — up accorrere *irr.
v.*† (a)

S

sad triste
sail navigare [navigo]
sailboat barca a vela
saint, saintly santo (*see* § 80, p.
117)
salad insalata
sale vendita
Salerno Salerno *f.*
salt sale *m.*
same stesso
Sardinia Sardegna
satisfied (with) contento (di)
satisfy contentare
Saturday sabato; on Saturdays
il sabato
sauce salsa; with tomato —, al
pomodoro
Saul Saul
say dire *irr. v.* (di) [dico, *p. part.*
detto]; to — farewell dare un
addio; so to —, per così dire;
to — yes dire di sì; to — no dire
di no
scarcely appena
schedule programma *m.*
school scuola
science scienza
sculptor scultore *m.*
sea mare *m.*
seasickness mal (*m.*) di mare
season stagione *f.*
seat posto; (= *residence*) sede *f.*
seated seduto; to be —, sedere
irr. v. or stare† seduto
second secondo
section (*of a city*) quartiere *m.*

see vedere *irr. v.*; — again rivedere *irr. v.*

seek cercare (di)

seem sembrare†, parere *irr. v.*†

select scegliere *irr. v.* (di)

sell vendere

send mandare (a)

sentence frase *f.*

September settembre *m.*

serve servire (a) [servo]

set (*referring to the sun, moon, etc.*) tramontare†; (*the table*) apparecchiare

seven sette

seventeen diciassette

seventh settimo

seventy settanta

several parecchi, parecchie

Sforza Castle Castello Sforzesco

shake agitare [agito]; to — hands with stringere la mano a

share parte *f.*

she ella, essa, lei; — herself lei stessa

sheep pecora

sheet lenzuolo (*irr. pl.* le lenzuola)

shelf scaffale *m.*

shell conca; the Golden Shell la Conca d'Oro

shine splendere

ship nave *f.*

shirt camicia

shoe scarpa

shoemaker calzolaio

shop *n.* negozio; *v.* fare delle spese; to go shopping andare† a fare delle spese

shore (*of the sea*) costa; (*of a river or a lake*) riva

short (*in size*) corto; (*in time*) breve; a — time ago poco fa

shout *n.* grido (*irr. pl.* le grida); *v.* gridare

show *n.* spettacolo; *v.* mostrare (di); — me mi mostri, mostratemi

showcase vetrina

show window vetrina

Sicilian siciliano; — style alla siciliana

Sicily Sicilia

side lato; on one —, da un lato; on the other —, dall'altro lato

sideboard credenza

Siena Siena

sight vista

sign firmare

silence silenzio

silent tacito

silently in silenzio

silk seta

silver argento

silverware argenteria

simple semplice

Simplon: Mt. —, il Sempione

simply semplicemente

sin peccato

since siccome

sing cantare

sir signore *m.*

sister sorella; little —, sorellina

sister-in-law cognata

Sistine Chapel Cappella Sistina

sit sedere *irr. v.*; — down sedersi†

situated situato

six sei

sixteen sedici

sixth sesto

sixty sessanta

size grandezza

sky cielo

skyscraper grattacielo

sleep *n.* sonno; *v.* dormire [dormo]

sleeping car carrozza a letti

sleepy: to be —, aver sonno

sleeve manica

slow piano, lento

slowly piano, lentamente

small piccolo; smaller più piccolo *or* minore; very —, piccolissimo *or* minimo

smart elegante

smell, smell good odorare

smile sorridere *irr. v.*

smoke fumare

smoking room sala da fumare

snow *n.* neve *f.*; *v.* nevicare *imp. v.*† [nevica]

so così; (= *therefore*) perciò; — to

speak per così dire; — **much**
tanto; — **many** tanti, tante; **so**
...as così... come *or* tanto...
quanto
sock calzino
soft, softly piano
solid sodo
some di + *def. art.*, (= *a few*) alcuno, qualche (*always singular*),
(= *a little*) un po' di; — **of it**
(*or* — **of them**) ne
somebody, someone qualcuno,
qualcuna
something qualche cosa
sometimes qualche volta
son figlio
song canto; (*popular*) canzone *f.*
soon presto, fra (*or* tra) poco; —
after poco dopo; **as** — **as** appena;
as — **as possible** al più presto
Sorrento Sorrento *f.*
sorrow dolore *m.*
sorry: I am —, mi dispiace (di);
I was —, m'è dispiaciuto (*see*
§ 149, p. 256)
sound suonare († *if used intransitively*)
soup minestra
sour acre; **very** —, acerrimo
south sud *m.*
southern meridionale
souvenir ricordo
sovereignty sovranità (*inv.*)
spaghetti spaghetti *m. pl.*
Spain Spagna
Spanish spagnolo
sparkle splendere
speak parlare; **so to** —, per così
dire
special speciale
specialize specializzarsi†
speed *n.* velocità (*inv.*); *v.* correre
irr.† (a)
spend (*money*) spendere *irr. v.*;
(*time*) passare
spinach spinaci *m. pl.*
spire guglia
spoon cucchiaio
sport sport *m.* (*inv.*), gioco

spread stendere *irr. v.*
spring primavera
square piazza; **on the** —, in piazza
stable stalla
stairs scala
stamp francobollo
stand *n.* tavolino; *v.* stare *irr.*†,
stare† in piedi
standing in piedi
star stella
start cominciare (a); (= *move*)
muoversi *irr. v.*†; — **on one's way**
avviarsi† (a)
state stato; **the United States** gli
Stati Uniti
stateroom cabina
station stazione *f.*
statue statua
stay stare *irr. v.*†, restare†; (= *lodge*)
alloggiare
steamboat vapore *m.*; **small** —,
vaporetto
steamer piroscafo
steel acciaio
step passo
Stephen Stefano
steward cameriere *m.*
stewardess cameriera
still ancora
stocking calza
stone pietra
stop *n.* fermata; *v.* (*somebody or
something*) fermare, (*oneself*) fer-
marsi† (a)
store negozio
strait stretto
strange strano; **nothing** —, nulla
di strano
street via
streetcar tranvai *m.* (*inv.*)
Stresa Stresa
stretch (out) tendere *irr. v.*
string bean fagiolino
stroll *n.* passeggiata; *v.* passeggiare;
to take a little —, fare due passi
strong forte, robusto
student studente *m.*, studentessa
study *n.* studio; *v.* studiare
sturdy robusto

style stile *m.*, (*referring to clothes*) eleganza; **Parmesan** —, alla parmigiana; **Sicilian** —, alla siciliana
stylish elegante
suddenly all'improvviso
suffer soffrire *irr. v.* [soffro]
sugar zucchero
suit (*of clothes*) abito; **bathing** —, costume (*m.*) da bagno
suitcase valigia
summer estate *f.*; **in** —, d'estate; **next** —, l'estate ventura
sun sole *m.*
Sunday domenica; **on Sundays** la domenica
sunlight sole *m.*
sunset tramonto
superb superbo
supper cena
suppose supporre *irr. v.* (di)
supreme supremo
sure certo
surmount sormontare
surprise sorpresa
surround circondare
surroundings dintorni *m. pl.*
sweet dolce
sweetly dolcemente
swim nuotare
swimming pool piscina
Swiss svizzero
Switzerland Svizzera
symbol simbolo
Syracuse Siracusa

T

table tavola; **little** —, tavolino
tablecloth tovaglia
take, take up prendere *irr. v.*; (= *carry*) portare (a); (= *lead*) menare (a), condurre *irr. v.* (a); — **a bath** fare un bagno; — **an excursion** fare un'escursione; — **a nap** schiacciare un sonnellino; — **a ride** (*or* **a walk**) fare una passeggiata; — **a trip** fare un viaggio; — **a tour** fare un giro; — **away** (*or* **off**) levare *or* togliere *irr. v.*; — **place** aver luogo
talent talento
talk parlare, conversare
tall alto
Taormina Taormina
tarantella tarantella
task incarico
taste *n.* gusto; **to my** —, di mio gusto; *v.* gustare
taxicab tassì *m.* (*inv.*)
tea tè *m.* (*inv.*)
teach insegnare (a)
teacher maestro, maestra
tease stuzzicare [stuzzico]
teaspoon cucchiaino
telegram telegramma *m.*
telephone *n.* telefono; *v.* telefonare (di) [telefono]
tell dire *irr. v.* (di) [dico, *p. part.* detto]; **tells** dice
temple tempio
ten dieci
tend tendere *irr. v.* (a)
tenth decimo
territory territorio
than di, che, che non (*followed by the subjunctive*), di quel che (*see* §§ 97, 2, p. 143 *and* 136, p. 225)
thank ringraziare (di)
thanks grazie
that *conj.* che
that *dem. adj.* quello, codesto; *dem. pron.* quello, codesto, ciò; — **man** quegli, colui; — **woman** colei; **those men** *or* **those women** *or* **those people** coloro; — **is** ecco
that *rel. pron.* che, cui, il quale, la quale, i quali, le quali; **those who** chi
that is (**to say**) cioè
the il, lo, la; *pl.* i, gli, le
theater teatro
their, theirs il loro
them li, le, essi, esse, loro; **to** —, loro; **of** —, ne
themselves si, sè, se stessi, se stesse, essi stessi, esse stesse, loro stessi, loro stesse

then (= *afterward*) poi; (= *at that time* or *in conclusion*) allora; **until** —, fino allora
there là, lì, costà, costì, ci, vi; — **is** c'è *or* v'è, (*pointing*) ecco; — **are** ci sono *or* vi sono, (*pointing*) ecco; **from** —, ne; **up** — *or* **over** —, lassù; **down** — *or* **over** —, laggiù
thermae, thermal baths terme *f. pl.*
thesis tesi *f.* (*inv.*)
they essi, esse, loro; (*used impersonally*) si (*see* § 115, p. 180)
thing cosa
think (**of**) pensare (a), credere (di)
third terzo
thirst sete *f.*
thirsty: to be —, aver sete
thirteen tredici
thirty trenta
this *adj.* questo; *pron.* questo, ciò; — **man** questi, (*with contempt*) costui; — **woman** questa, (*with contempt*) costei; **these men** *or* **these people** questi, (*with contempt*) costoro; **these women** queste, (*with contempt*) costoro
though, even though benchè, quantunque, sebbene (*each of them followed by the subjunctive*)
thousand mille (*pl.* mila); **about a** —, un migliaio; **thousands** migliaia *f. pl.*
three tre
through per, attraverso; **to go** —, attraversare
throw buttare
thunder tuonare *imp. v.*†
Thursday giovedì *m.*; **on Thursdays** il giovedì
thus così
Tiber Tevere *m.*
ticket biglietto
tie cravatta
tiger tigre *f.*
till we meet again! arrivederci!
time (*duration*) tempo; (*succession, turn*) volta; (= *epoch*) epoca; (= *hour*) ora; **a short** — **ago**

poco fa; **at that** —, allora; **at the same** —, allo stesso tempo; **at what** —? a che ora? **one at a** —, uno alla volta; **this** —, questa volta; **to have a good** —, divertirsi† [mi diverto]; **what** — **is it?** che ora è? *or* che ore sono?
timid timido
tin latta
tired stanco
to a, ad (*used only before a word beginning with* a); (= *in order to*) per; **to go** — **Italy** andare† in Italia; **to go** — **Rome** andare† a Roma
toast (= *toasted bread*) pane tostato; (*in drinking*) brindisi *m.* (*inv.*); **to give a** —, fare un brindisi
today oggi
together insieme
tomato pomodoro; **with** — **sauce** al pomodoro
tomb tomba
tomorrow domani
tongue lingua
tonight stanotte, (= *this evening*) stasera
too troppo; (= *also*) anche, pure; — **much** troppo; — **many** troppi, troppe; — **bad!** peccato!
top cima; **on** *or* **to the** — (**of**) in cima (a)
tour giro; **to take a** —, fare un giro
tourist turista *m. or f.*
toward verso
tower torre *f.*; **bell** —, campanile *m.*
town città (*inv.*); **down**—, in città; **small** —, cittadina
trace traccia
trade commercio
train treno; **express** —, treno diretto
Trajan Traiano
tramway tranvai *m.* (*inv.*)
travel viaggiare
treasure tesoro
treaty trattato
tree albero

trip viaggio; **return** —, viaggio di ritorno; **to take a** —, fare un viaggio; **have a good** —! buon viaggio!

trouble n. disturbo; v. dare disturbo (a)

trousers pantaloni m. pl.

true vero

truly veramente

trunk baule m.

try cercare (di)

Tuesday martedì m.; **on Tuesdays** il martedì

tunnel galleria

Turin Torino f.

turkey tacchino

turn (somebody or something) girare; (oneself) volgersi irr. v.† (a)

Tuscany Toscana

twelve dodici

twenty venti

twice due volte

twig ramoscello

two due

type tipo

U

ugly brutto

umbrella ombrello

Umbria Umbria

uncle zio

under sotto

underground sotterraneo

understand capire [capisco]

undertake intraprendere irr. v.

unfold spiegare

unforgettable indimenticabile

unfortunately purtroppo

unification unificazione f.

unite unire [unisco]

United States Stati Uniti m. pl.; **the** — **is my country** gli Stati Uniti sono la mia patria

university università (inv.)

unless a meno che ... non (followed by the subjunctive)

until fino a, finchè (followed by the subjunctive); — **now** finora; — **then** fino allora

up, upon su; — **there** lassù; — **to** fino a; **to go** (or **come**) —, salire irr. v. († if used intransitively) (a)

upper, see floor

upstairs al piano superiore

us ci, noi; **all of** —, tutti noi; **to** —, ci

use n. uso; v. usare

useful utile

useless inutile

usual solito

usually di solito

V

vain vanitoso

Valentino Gardens i Giardini del Valentino

valise valigia

valley valle f.

value valore m.

various vario

vase vaso

vast vasto

Vatican Vaticano

veal vitello

vegetable verdura; — **garden** orto

Venice Venezia

veranda veranda

Verona Verona

very molto, assai

vest panciotto

Vesuvius: Mt. —, il Vesuvio

Victor Vittorio

view vista

village borgo, villaggio

vineyard vigna

violet violetta

virtue virtù f. (inv.)

visit n. visita; v. visitare [visito]

vividly vividamente

voice voce f.

volcano vulcano

voyage viaggio

W

wait, wait for aspettare

waiter cameriere m

waiting room sala d'aspetto
walk *n.* passeggiata; *v.* camminare;
to take a —, fare una passeggiata
or passeggiare
wall (*of a room*) parete *f.*; (*of a
house*) muro, *pl.* i muri; (*of a city*)
muro, *irr. pl.* le mura
walnut noce *f.*; — **tree** noce *m.*
want volere *irr. v.*
ward (*of a city*) quartiere *m.*
wardrobe armadio
warm caldo; **it's** —, fa caldo
wash lavare
waste perdere *irr. v.*
watch orologio; **wrist** —, orologio
da polso
water acqua
wave agitare [agito]
way via; (= *manner*) modo; **to
start on one's** —, avviarsi† (a)
we noi; (*used impersonally*) si (*see
§ 115, p. 180*)
weak debole
wear portare (a)
weather tempo; **what kind of** —
is it? che tempo fa? **it's fine** —,
fa bel tempo; **it's bad** —, fa
cattivo tempo
Wednesday mercoledì *m.*; **on Wednesdays** il mercoledì
week settimana; **a** — **from now**
fra una settimana
weep piangere *irr. v.*
welcome! ben arrivato!
well bene; **very** —, benissimo *or*
ottimamente; **very** —! sta bene!
west ovest *m.*, ponente *m.*
western di ponente
what che, che cosa, quale; (= *that
which*) quel che *or* quello che *or*
ciò che; — **a joy!** che gioia!
whatever checchè *or* qualunque cosa
(*followed by the subjunctive*)
wheat grano
when quando
where dove
whether se
which *inter. adj. or pron.* quale; *rel.
pron.* che (*subject or direct object*),

cui (*object of a preposition*), il quale,
la quale, i quali, le quali (*in all
cases*); **of** — (= *whose*) il cui, la
cui, i cui, le cui
whichever qualunque (*followed by
the subjunctive*)
while mentre; **once in a** —, di tanto
in tanto
white bianco; **to dress in** —, vestire
di bianco
who *inter. pron.* chi; *rel. pron.* che
or il quale, la quale, i quali, le
quali; **he** — (*or* **one** —, **a man**
—, *etc.*) chi
whoever chiunque (*followed by the
subjunctive*)
whole tutto; **the** — **book** tutto
il libro; **a** — **book** tutto un
libro
whom *inter. pron.* chi; *rel. pron.* che
(*direct object*), cui (*object of a
preposition*), il quale, la quale, i
quali, le quali (*in all cases*); **he** —
(*or* **one** —, **a man** —, *etc.*) chi
whose *inter. adj. or pron.* di chi;
rel. pron. il cui, la cui, i cui, le
cui
why perchè
wide largo
wife moglie *f.* (*pl.* mogli)
willing disposto
willingly volentieri
wind vento; **the** — **is blowing** tira
vento
window finestra; **small** —, finestrino; (*of an office*) sportello;
(*show window*) vetrina
windy: **it's** —, tira vento
wine vino
wing ala (*irr. pl.* le ali)
winter inverno; **in** —, d'inverno
Wisconsin Wisconsin *m.*
wish *n.* desiderio; *v.* desiderare
(di) [desidero]
with con, (*in describing*) da
within fra, tra, in, dentro
without senza, senza che (*followed by
the subjunctive*); **to do** —, fare a
meno di

wolf lupo
woman dɔnna; **this** —, questa, (*with contempt*) costɛi; **these women** queste, (*with contempt*) costoro; **that** —, quella, colɛi; **those women** quelle, coloro
wonderful meraviglioso
wood legno, (= *forest*) bɔsco
woods bɔsco
word parɔla
work *n.* lavoro, ɔpera; *v.* lavorare
workman operaio
world mondo
worse *adj.* peggiore; *adv.* pɛggio the —, il peggiore, il pɛggio
worst *adj.* il peggiore; *adv.* il pɛggio
wretched misero; **very** —, misɛrrimo
wrist watch orolɔgio da polso
write scrivere *irr. v.* (di)
writer scrittore *m.*
wrong tɔrto; **to be** —, aver tɔrto

Y

year anno, (*in its duration*) annata; **last** —, l'anno scorso; **next** —, l'anno venturo
yellow giallo
yes sì; **to say** —, dire di sì
yesterday iɛri; **day before** —, iɛri l'altro
yet ancora; **and** —, eppure
you tu, voi, Lɛi, Loro, ti, te, vi, ve, La, Li, Le; **to** —, ti, vi, Le, Loro
young giovane; **younger** più giovane *or* minore (d'età); — **lady** signorina; — **man** giovanɔtto
your, yours tuo (*m. pl.* tuɔi), vɔstro, suo (*m. pl.* suɔi)
yourself ti, vi, si, tu stesso, tu stessa, voi stesso, voi stessa, Lɛi stesso, Lɛi stessa

Z

zoological zoolɔgico
zoology zoologia

Index

Numbers refer to pages; numbers in parentheses refer to sections.